THE SOCIAL WORLD

Edited by

IAN ROBERTSON

WORTH PUBLISHERS, INC.

THE SOCIAL WORLD

The Social World

Copyright © 1981 by Worth Publishers, Inc.

All rights reserved

Printed in the United States of America

Library of Congress Catalog Card Number: 81-52912

ISBN: 0-87901-168-8

First printing, September 1981

Cover: *La Place, Clichy* (detail), Louis Anquetin

Wadsworth Atheneum, Hartford, Connecticut

The Ella Gallup Sumner and Mary Catlin Sumner Collection

Worth Publishers, Inc.

444 Park Avenue South

New York, New York 10016

Preface

*Because of limitations of space and time, introductory
sociology textbooks and lectures generally focus on
the basic principles of the discipline, with appropriate
examples included where practicable. A book of readings, on the other hand, can serve a different and sup-
plementary purpose: to acquaint students at first hand
with a more detailed and leisurely mode of sociological analysis. My main goal in compiling this book of
readings has therefore been to provide examples of
good sociological writing which, in the main, illustrate
the applications of sociological ideas, rather than repeat the exposition of principles found in texts and
lectures.*

*This book contains sixty-two articles drawn from
a variety of sources, ranging from book excerpts and
popular-press articles to material from professional
journals. I selected the articles according to three basic criteria: that they be readable and interesting to
today's students; that they reflect the diversity of concerns and viewpoints in the contemporary discipline;
and that they provide the necessary practical illustra-
tions of sociological theories and principles. Each
reading is preceded by an introductory note and is followed by questions designed to promote reflection and
provoke classroom discussion.*

*Although this book may be used independently or
in conjunction with any text, it provides a particularly
appropriate supplement to my* Sociology, Second Edition *(Worth, 1981), since the sequence of topics parallels that in the text, with at least two readings provided for every text chapter.*

*For their assistance and encouragement in the prep-
aration of this reader, I am grateful to Linda Baron
Davis, researcher, and Peter Deane, editor.*

August 1981   IAN ROBERTSON

Contents

UNIT 1 *Introduction to Sociology*

C. WRIGHT MILLS

The Promise

The sociologist looks at the social world in a special way, with a distinctive perspective that is quite unlike that of the lay person. C. Wright Mills referred to this particular mode of examining our social surroundings as "the sociological imagination." The promise of sociology to the novice, he claimed, is that it ignites that particular imagination, and its possessor never sees society in quite the same way again.

Essentially, the sociological imagination enables us, as it were, to step outside our immediate confines—to see ourselves not just as isolated individuals but rather as beings who exist within, and who are largely shaped by, the broader context of time and place, history and society. As an example, Mills offers his classic distinction between "private troubles" and "public issues"—the former, a problem whose solution lies within range of the individual, the latter, one that is of societal concern. For instance, if only one man in a community is unemployed, the personal characteristics of that individual are probably at issue; but if 15 million workers out of a labor force of 50 million are jobless, then we must look to social forces for an explanation. The point seems obvious enough, but in countless more subtle situations it is habitually overlooked.

In this article, Mills outlines the essence of the "sociological imagination" and its promise to those who take up sociology.

Nowadays men often feel that their private lives are a series of traps. They sense that within their everyday worlds, they cannot overcome their troubles, and in this feeling, they are often quite correct: What ordinary men are directly aware of and what they try to do are bounded by the private orbits in which they live; their visions and their powers are limited to the close-up scenes of job, family, neighborhood; in other milieux, they move vicariously and remain spectators. And the more aware they become, however vaguely, of ambitions and of threats which transcend their immediate locales, the more trapped they seem to feel.

Underlying this sense of being trapped are seemingly impersonal changes in the very structure of continent-wide societies. The facts of contemporary history are also facts about the success and the failure of individual men and women. When a society is industrialized, a peasant becomes a worker; a feudal lord is liquidated or becomes a businessman. When classes rise or fall, a man is employed or unemployed; when the rate of investment goes up or down, a man takes new heart or goes broke. When wars happen, an insurance salesman becomes a rocket launcher; a store clerk, a radar man; a wife lives alone; a child grows up without a father. Neither the life of an individual nor the history of a society can be understood without understanding both.

Yet men do not usually define the troubles they endure in terms of historical change and institutional contradiction. The well-being they enjoy, they do not usually impute to the big ups and downs of the societies in which they live. Seldom aware of the intricate connection between the patterns of their own lives and the course of world history, ordinary men do not usually know what this connection means for the kinds of men they are becoming and for the kinds of history-making in which they might take part. They do not possess the quality of mind essential to grasp the interplay of man and society, of biography and history, of self and world. They cannot cope with their personal troubles in such ways as to control the structural transformations that usually lie behind them.

Surely it is no wonder. In what period have so many men been so totally exposed at so fast a pace to such earthquakes of change? That Americans have not known such catastrophic changes as have the men and women of other societies is due to historical facts that are now quickly becoming "merely history." The history that now affects every man is world history. Within this scene and this period, in the course of a single generation, one sixth of mankind is transformed from all that is feudal and backward into all that is modern, advanced, and fearful. Political colonies are freed; new and less visible forms of imperialism installed. Revolutions occur; men feel the intimate grip of new kinds of authority. Totalitarian societies rise, and are smashed to bits—or succeed fabulously. After two centuries of ascendancy, capitalism is shown up as only one way to make society into an industrial apparatus. After two centuries of hope, even formal democracy is restricted to a quite small portion of mankind. Everywhere in the underdeveloped world, ancient ways of life are broken up and vague expectations become urgent demands. Everywhere in the overdeveloped world, the means of authority and of violence become total in scope and bureaucratic in form. Humanity itself now lies before us, the super-nation at either pole concentrating its most co-ordinated and massive efforts upon the preparation of World War Three.

The very shaping of history now outpaces the ability of men to orient themselves in accordance with cherished values. And which values? Even when they do not panic, men often sense that older ways of feeling and thinking have collapsed and that newer beginnings are ambiguous to the point of moral stasis. Is it any wonder that ordinary men feel they cannot cope with the larger worlds with which they are so suddenly confronted? That they cannot understand the meaning of their epoch for their own lives? That—in defense of selfhood—they become morally insensible, trying to remain altogether private men? Is it any wonder that they come to be possessed by a sense of the trap?

It is not only information that they need—in this Age of Fact, information often dominates their attention and overwhelms their capacities to assimilate it. It is not only the skills of reason that they need—although their struggles to acquire these often exhaust their limited moral energy.

What they need, and what they feel they need, is a quality of mind that will help them to use information and to develop reason in order to achieve lucid summations of what is going on in the world and of what may be happening within themselves. It is this quality, I am going to contend, that journalists and scholars, artists and publics, scientists and editors are coming to expect of what may be called the sociological imagination.

I

The sociological imagination enables its possessor to understand the larger historical scene in terms of its meaning for the inner life and the external career of a variety of individuals. It enables him to take into account how individuals, in the welter of their daily experience, often become falsely conscious of their social positions. Within that welter, the framework of modern society is sought, and within that framework the psychologies of a variety of men and women are formulated. By such means the personal uneasiness of individuals is focused upon explicit troubles and the indifference of publics is transformed into involvement with public issues.

The first fruit of this imagination—and the first lesson of the social science that embodies it—is the idea that the individual can understand his own experience and gauge his own fate only by locating himself within his period, that he can know his own chances in life only by becoming aware of those of all individuals in his circumstances. In many ways it is a terrible lesson; in many ways a magnificent one. We do not know the limits of man's capacities for supreme effort or willing degradation, for agony or glee, for pleasurable brutality or the sweetness of reason. But in our time we have come to know that the limits of "human nature" are frighteningly broad. We have come to know that every individual lives, from one generation to the next, in some society; that he lives out a biography, and that he lives it out within some historical sequence. By the fact of his living he contributes, however minutely, to the shaping of this society and to the course of its history, even as he is made by society and by its historical push and shove.

The sociological imagination enables us to grasp history and biography and the relations between the two within society. That is its task and its promise. To recognize this task and this promise is the mark of the classic social analyst. It is characteristic of Herbert Spencer—turgid, polysyllabic, comprehensive; of E. A. Ross—graceful, muckraking, upright; of Auguste Comte and Emile Durkheim; of the intricate and subtle Karl Mannheim. It is the quality of all that is intellectually excellent in Karl Marx; it is the clue to Thorstein Veblen's brilliant and ironic insight, to Joseph Schumpeter's many-sided constructions of reality; it is the basis of the psychological sweep of W. E. H. Lecky no less than of the profundity and clarity of Max Weber. And it is the signal of what is best in contemporary studies of man and society.

No social study that does not come back to the problems of biography, of history, and of their intersections within a society has completed its intellectual journey. Whatever the specific problems of the classic social analysts, however limited or however broad the features of social reality they have examined, those who have been imaginatively aware of the promise of their work have consistently asked three sorts of questions:

1. What is the structure of this particular society as a whole? What are its essential components, and how are they related to one another? How does it differ from other varieties of social order? Within it, what is the meaning of any particular feature for its continuance and for its change?

2. Where does this society stand in human history? What are the mechanics by which it is changing? What is its place within and its meaning for the development of humanity as a whole? How does any particular feature we are examining affect, and how is it affected by, the historical period in which it moves? And this period—what are its essential features? How does it differ from other periods? What are its characteristic ways of history-making?

3. What varieties of men and women now prevail in this society and in this period? And what varieties are coming to prevail? In what ways are they selected and formed, liberated and repressed, made sensitive and blunted? What kinds of "human nature" are revealed in the conduct and character we observe in this society in this period? And what is the meaning for "human nature" of each and every feature of the society we are examining?

Whether the point of interest is a great power state or a minor literary mood, a family, a prison, a creed—these are the kinds of questions the best social analysts have asked. They are the intellectual pivots of classic studies of man in society—and they are the questions inevitably raised by any mind possessing the sociological imagination. For that imagination is the capacity to shift from one perspective to another—from the political to the psychological; from examination of a single family to comparative assessment of the national budgets of the world; from the theological school to the military establishment; from considerations of an oil industry to studies of contemporary poetry. It is the capacity to range from the most impersonal and remote transformations to the most intimate features of the human self—and to see the relations between the two. Back of its use there is always the urge to know the social and historical meaning of the individual in the society and in the period in which he has his quality and his being.

That, in brief, is why it is by means of the sociological imagination that men now hope to grasp what is going on in the world, and to understand what is happening in themselves as minute points of the intersections of biography and history within society. In large part, contemporary man's self-conscious view of himself as at least an outsider, if not a permanent stranger, rests upon an ab-

sorbed realization of social relativity and of the transformative power of history. The sociological imagination is the most fruitful form of this self-consciousness. By its use men whose mentalities have swept only a series of limited orbits often come to feel as if suddenly awakened in a house with which they had only supposed themselves to be familiar. Correctly or incorrectly, they often come to feel that they can now provide themselves with adequate summations, cohesive assessments, comprehensive orientations. Older decisions that once appeared sound now seem to them products of a mind unaccountably dense. Their capacity for astonishment is made lively again. They acquire a new way of thinking, they experience a transvaluation of values: in a word, by their reflection and by their sensibility, they realize the cultural meaning of the social sciences.

II

Perhaps the most fruitful distinction with which the sociological imagination works is between "the personal troubles of milieu" and "the public issues of social structure." This distinction is an essential tool of the sociological imagination and a feature of all classic work in social science.

Troubles occur within the character of the individual and within the range of his immediate relations with others; they have to do with his self and with those limited areas of social life of which he is directly and personally aware. Accordingly, the statement and the resolution of troubles properly lie within the individual as a biographical entity and within the scope of his immediate milieu—the social setting that is directly open to his personal experience and to some extent his willful activity. A trouble is a private matter: values cherished by an individual are felt by him to be threatened.

Issues have to do with matters that transcend these local environments of the individual and the range of his inner life. They have to do with the organization of many such milieux into the institutions of an historical society as a whole, with the ways in which various milieux overlap and interpenetrate to form the larger structure of social and historical life. An issue is a public matter: some value cherished by publics is felt to be threatened. Often there is a debate about what that value is and about what it is that really threatens it. This debate is often without focus if only because it is the very nature of an issue, unlike even widespread trouble, that it cannot very well be defined in terms of the immediate and everyday environments of ordinary men. An issue, in fact, often involves a crisis in institutional arrangements, and often too it involves what Marxists call "contradictions" or "antagonisms."

In these terms, consider unemployment. When, in a city of 100,000, only one man is unemployed, that is his personal trouble, and for its relief we properly look to the character of the man, his skills, and his immediate opportunities. But when in a nation of 50 million employees, 15 million men are unemployed, that is an issue, and we may not hope to find its solution within the range of opportunities open to any one individual. The very structure of opportunities has collapsed. Both the correct statement of the problem and the range of possible solutions require us to consider the economic and political institutions of the society, and not merely the personal situation and character of a scatter of individuals.

Consider war. The personal problem of war, when it occurs, may be how to survive it or how to die in it with honor; how to make money out of it; how to climb into the higher safety of the military apparatus; or how to contribute to the war's termination. In short, according to one's values, to find a set of milieux and within it to survive the war or make one's death in it meaningful. But the structural issues of war have to do with its causes; with what types of men it throws up into command; with its effects upon economic and political, family and religious institutions, with the unorganized irresponsibility of a world of nation-states.

Consider marriage. Inside a marriage a man and a woman may experience personal troubles, but when the divorce rate during the first four years of marriage is 250 out of every 1,000 attempts, this is an indication of a structural issue having to do with the institutions of marriage and the family and other institutions that bear upon them.

Or consider the metropolis—the horrible, beautiful, ugly, magnificent sprawl of the great city. For many upper-class people, the personal solution to "the problem of the city" is to have an apartment with private garage under it in the heart of the city, and forty miles out, a house by Henry Hill, garden by Garrett Eckbo, on a hundred acres of private land. In these two controlled environments—with a small staff at each end and a private helicopter connection—most people could solve many of the problems of personal milieux caused by the facts of the city. But all this, however splendid, does not solve the public issues that the structural fact of the city poses. What should be done with this wonderful monstrosity? Break it all up into scattered units, combining residence and work? Refurbish it as it stands? Or, after evacuation, dynamite it and build new cities according to new plans in new places? What should those plans be? And who is to decide and to accomplish whatever choice is made? These are structural issues; to confront them and to solve them requires us to consider political and economic issues that affect innumerable milieux.

In so far as an economy is so arranged that slumps occur, the problem of unemployment becomes incapable of personal solution. In so far as war is inherent in the nation-state system and in the uneven industrialization of the world, the ordinary individual in his restricted milieu will be powerless—with or without psychiatric aid—to solve the troubles this system or lack of system imposes upon him. In so far as the family as an institution turns women into darling little slaves and men into their chief providers and unweaned dependents, the problem of a satisfactory marriage remains incapable of purely private solution. In so far as the overdeveloped megalopolis and the overdeveloped automobile are built-in features of the overdeveloped society, the issues of urban living will not be solved by personal ingenuity and private wealth.

What we experience in various and specific milieux, I have noted, is often caused by structural changes. Accordingly, to understand the changes of many personal milieux we are required to look beyond them. And the number and variety of such structural changes increase as the institutions within which we live become more embracing and more intricately connected with one another. To be aware of the idea of social structure and to use it with sensibility is to be capable of tracing such linkages among a great variety of milieux. To be able to do that is to possess the sociological imagination.

III

What are the major issues for publics and the key troubles of private individuals in our time? To formulate issues and troubles, we must ask what values are cherished yet threatened, and what values are cherished and supported, by the characterizing trends of our period. In the case both of threat and of support we must ask what salient contradictions of structure may be involved.

When people cherish some set of values and do not feel any threat to them, they experience *well-being*. When they cherish values but *do* feel them to be threatened, they experience a crisis—either as a personal trouble or as a public issue. And if all their values seem involved, they feel the total threat of panic.

But suppose people are neither aware of any cherished values nor experience any threat? That is the experience of *indifference*, which, if it seems to involve all their values, becomes apathy. Suppose, finally, they are unaware of any cherished values, but still are very much aware of a threat? That is the experience of *uneasiness*, of anxiety, which, if it is total enough, becomes a deadly unspecified malaise.

Ours is a time of uneasiness and indifference—not yet formulated in such ways as to permit the work of reason and the play of sensibility. Instead of troubles—defined in terms of values and threats—there is often the misery of vague uneasiness; instead of explicit issues there is often merely the beat feeling that all is somehow not right. Neither the values threatened nor whatever threatens them has been stated; in short, they have not been carried to the point of decision. Much less have they been formulated as problems of social science.

In the thirties there was little doubt—except among certain deluded business circles—that there was an economic issue which was also a pack of personal troubles. In these arguments about "the crisis of capitalism," the formulations of Marx and the many unacknowledged reformulations of his work probably set the leading terms of the issue, and some men came to understand their personal troubles in these terms. The values threatened were plain to see and cherished by all; the structural contradictions that threatened them also seemed plain. Both were widely and deeply experienced. It was a political age.

But the values threatened in the era after World War Two are often neither widely acknowledged as values nor widely felt to be threatened. Much private uneasiness goes unformulated; much public malaise and many decisions of enormous structural relevance never become public issues. For those who accept such inherited values as reason and freedom, it is the uneasiness itself that is the trouble; it is the indifference itself that is the issue. And it is this condition, of uneasiness and indifference, that is the signal feature of our period.

All this is so striking that it is often interpreted by observers as a shift in the very kinds of problems that need now to be formulated. We are frequently told that the problems of our decade, or even the crisis of our period, have shifted from the external realm of economics and now have to do with the quality of individual life—in fact with the question of whether there is soon going to be anything that can properly be called individual life. Not child labor but comic books, not poverty but mass leisure, are at the center of concern. Many great public issues as well as many private troubles are described in terms of "the psychiatric"—often, it seems, in a pathetic attempt to avoid the large issues and problems of modern society. Often this statement seems to rest upon a provincial narrowing of interest to the Western societies, or even to the United States—thus ignoring two-thirds of mankind; often, too, it arbitrarily divorces the individual life from the larger institutions within which that life is enacted, and which on occasion bear upon it more grievously than do the intimate environments of childhood.

Problems of leisure, for example, cannot even be stated without considering problems of work. Family troubles over comic books cannot be formulated as problems without considering the plight of the contemporary family in its new relations with the newer institutions of the social structure. Neither leisure nor its debilitating uses can be understood as problems without recognition of the extent to which malaise and indifference now form the social and personal climate of contemporary American society. In this climate, no problems of "the private life" can be stated and solved without recognition of the crisis of ambition that is part of the very career of men at work in the incorporated economy.

It is true, as psychoanalysts continually point out, that people do often have "the increasing sense of being moved by obscure forces within themselves which they are unable to define." But it is *not* true, as Ernest Jones asserted, that "man's chief enemy and danger is his own unruly nature and the dark forces pent up within him." On the contrary: "Man's chief danger" today lies in the unruly forces of contemporary society itself, with its alienating methods of production, its enveloping techniques of political domination, its international anarchy—in a word, its pervasive transformations of the very "nature" of man and the conditions and aims of his life.

It is now the social scientist's foremost political and intellectual task—for here the two coincide—to make clear the elements of contemporary uneasiness and indifference. It is the central demand made upon him by other cultural workmen—by physical scientists and artists, by the intellectual community in general. It is because of this task and these demands, I believe, that the social sciences are becoming the common denominator of our cultural period, and the sociological imagination our most needed quality of mind. . . .

QUESTIONS

1. Explain, with examples, what Mills means by the "sociological imagination."

2. How does sociology differ from psychology?

3. Children from middle-class families are more likely to attend college than children from working-class families. Why do you think this is so?

PETER L. BERGER

BRIGITTE BERGER

Why Sociology?

Many newcomers to sociology—possibly most—are not entirely certain about why they are taking the course. The single-minded few, perhaps, are determined to become sociologists, but the motives of others vary a great deal, ranging from a keen interest in the subject to the hope of finding a soft option for a social science course requirement. In time, the inherent fascination of the study of social behavior should make enthusiasts of nearly everyone: but in the meanwhile, why sociology?

In this article, Peter and Brigitte Berger consider some reasons for undertaking the scientific study of society. One set of reasons, they suggest, is more immediately practical: making a living through sociology as part of the "knowledge industry," in education or in the various professional fields where the skills of sociologists are sought. The second set of reasons, which they consider at least equally important, has to do with personal and intellectual development: in ways that become apparent only over time, they claim, a sociological understanding of the world contributes to a greater awareness of self and others, to a deepened appreciation of human liberty and the human potential.

There are, of course, different reasons why students take an introductory course or read an introductory book on sociology. These range all the way from earnest career plans to the tactical requirements of seduction, not to mention the campus reputation and grading habits of sociology instructors. We have no objections to the less than earnest motives. But, optimists by inclination, we assume that having finished the course . . . at least some students will be more rather than less interested in sociology. In that case the question, "Why sociology?" will also be more interesting to them than it was at the outset.

The question can be asked with two different senses: "What can one actually do with sociology?" And, more searchingly: "Is sociology worthwhile?"

Making a Living in the "Knowledge Industry"

One thing that one can obviously do with sociology is to become a sociologist. Only a very small fraction of those who take sociology courses as undergraduates take this direction. For those considering this awesome option, a few words on its practical implications are in order here.

The discipline of sociology is today a well-established and well-organized profession in America. As of late 1969, the membership of the American Sociological Association, the major professional organization of the discipline, was 12,903 if one includes student members and 8,461 if one only counts the fully certified brethren—in either case, a number not to be sneezed at. The association has an impressive headquarters in Washington and holds conventions in enormous hotels.

The visible output of American sociologists is impressive, too. Large numbers of books are published in sociology every year. There are dozens of journals in the field, more than anyone can possibly read and do anything else besides, so that there is now (as in other disciplines) a journal *about* journals, *Sociological Abstracts,* which classifies and summarizes this vast and rapidly growing body of professional lore.

Sociology constitutes a significant division of what Fritz Machlup, an economist, has called the American "knowledge industry." What is probably more important, sociology occupies, and has occupied for a considerable period of time, a respected place on the American intellectual scene. Naturally, there are also detractors, like the sardonic commentator who said some years ago that a sociologist is a man who will spend ten thousand dollars to discover the local house of ill repute. By and large, though, statements about society by sociologists exercising their professional judgment widely command authority or at least gain a serious hearing. This is true in the mass media, in political debate over current issues, among decision-makers in government and business, and in broad segments of the general public. We would not be sociologists if we did not agree that, much of the time, this intellectual status of the discipline is merited. To mention only some of the problems currently troubling American society, sociologists have contributed both important information and clarifying insights to the public discussion of urbanism, of the racial situation, of education, of government measures against crime and against poverty.

American sociology continues to hold a pre-eminent position in the discipline, comparable, say, to the position held by German philosophy and German historical scholarship in the nineteenth century. Sociology in no other country compares with American sociology in terms of academic and intellectual status, the variety and sophistication of theoretical approaches and research technology, both the quantity and quality of output, and the sheer size of the professional establishment. American books and journals throughout the field are necessary reading for foreign sociologists, while the reverse is only true for limited aspects of sociology (as, for example, for sociological theory). Foreign sociology students, if at all possible practically, seek to spend at least some portion of their studies in an American university's sociology department. Not surprisingly, English (one is tempted to add, especially if one looks at the writings of British sociologists, *American* English) has become the lingua franca of sociologists everywhere.

All the same, there has been quite a remarkable upsurge of sociology abroad over the last two decades. Sizable sociological establishments have grown up in Western Europe, particularly in Germany, France, Britain, Holland and the Scandinavian countries. Although the attitude toward sociology by Communist regimes has vacillated between condemning it as a "bourgeois ideology" and gingerly accepting it as a useful instrument in social planning, sociology is now a going concern in the Soviet Union and in the socialist countries of Eastern Europe. The holding of the 1970 World Congress of Sociology in Bulgaria symbolized this new acceptability of the discipline in the "socialist camp" (at least the part of it that is within the Soviet orbit). In the countries of the Third World, sociology is very widely regarded as an important aid for development planning and policy.

What are American sociologists actually doing? The very great majority are engaged in teaching at colleges and universities. This means, quite simply, that anyone planning to become a professional sociologist should reckon with the fact that most jobs in the field are teaching jobs, and that teaching is very probably what he will be doing at least much of the time. The most important other activity of sociologists is research, though for many this is not a source of continuous employment but rather something that they do besides teaching or on occasional leaves from teaching jobs. All the same, there are a good number of full-time research jobs, some connected with university research programs, others in agencies or research institutes of the government, business, labor or other organizations (such as churches) with an interest in discerning societal trends. Thirdly, there is a scattering of sociologists in jobs of the most different sorts, ranging from advertising and personnel management to community action in this country or abroad. Whether interested in teaching or one of the other options, the aspiring sociologist should realize that graduate study, increasingly up to and including the doctorate, is a prerequisite for jobs that carry professional status (not to mention the pay that one associates with such status). Different graduate programs emphasize different aspects of the field and some thought ought to be given to the choice of school, especially since the American academic system does not encourage easy transfers from one school to another.

"Establishment" and "Radical" Sociology

There has recently been much debate within the profession about its present condition, the directions it has been taking and the directions that it should take in the future. There are strong differences of opinion among American sociologists both as to diagnosis and prescription. Political radicals in the field have attacked what they consider to be "establishment sociology" as an ideological tool of the status quo and have demanded a new conception of sociology as a discipline standing in the service of radical or even revolutionary politics. Black sociologists have called for sociological work designed to serve the interests of the black community, sometimes meaning by this nothing more than work that would be more sensitive to the black experience in America than that of (or so they claim) the work of many white sociologists, sometimes going much further by demanding a distinctively black sociology that would be part of and ideologically attuned to "black consciousness." Various movements concerned with "liberation," most recently (and very audibly so) the Women's Liberation movement, have sought to enroll sociologists and sociology in their ranks. Whatever one may think of these critiques and redefinitions of the field, they have greatly enlivened sociological discourse in recent years. All of this has taken place against the background of a much broader feeling that intellectuals and their disciplines should be involved in the agonies of our time and concerned with the solutions of our most agonizing problems. It is understandable that this feeling has been particularly strong among sociologists, proponents of a discipline that explicitly takes society as its object of inquiry.

Since only a small minority of those who take undergraduate courses in sociology goes on to professional work in the field, a rationale for these courses as nothing but pre-professional education (comparable, say, to a pre-medical curriculum) is hardly persuasive. There ought to be other things that one can do with sociology.

Dealing with Men Directly: The Human Sciences and the Humanities

Information and perspectives provided by sociology have wide applicability to other fields. This is obvious in a variety of practical fields that, in one way or another, must take cognizance of social structures. These range all the way from social work to the law. Sociology, by its very nature, has relevance for most other sciences dealing with man (those that the French, very aptly, call "human sciences"). In many places . . . we have seen the relation of sociology to other social sciences—political science, economics, cultural anthropology and social psychology, to name the major ones. But even in the humanities, where there has been a strongly ingrained animus against sociologists and their "barbarian" incursions into territory where they have no business, the recognition of the usefulness of sociological insights has grown. This is especially true among historians, but it may also be found today among scholars of religion and literature.

But what about the individual who has none of these professional or scholarly ambitions? Is sociology worthwhile for him? We think so. Anyone who wants to live with his eyes open will profit from a better understanding of his society and his own situation in it. But perhaps even more important is the ability to understand the situations and the social worlds of others. Contemporary society needs this ability more than ever.

A Pluralistic Society: Is Love Really All You Need?

Good will is not enough. Let us take just one example out of many possible ones. A few years ago a group of white upper-middle-class young people from the New York suburban area decided that, in order to show their concern for the "ghetto" and its people, they would go into some of the black neighborhoods of the city and help in fixing them up. They did so, on one fine weekend, the first and the last of the experiment. They came in full of enthusiasm and started to paint houses, sweep the streets, clean up piles of garbage and engage in other "obviously"

desirable activities. Before long they were surrounded by angry black teenagers, and a good many angry black adults, who yelled obscenities at them, threw disagreeable objects and generally interfered with the progress of operation uplift. There is no reason to impugn the good will of the young whites. At worst, they were guilty of naïveté, slightly spiced with self-righteousness. Even a whiff of sociological insight on their part, however, would have avoided the entire debacle. It hardly needs emphasizing that better insight into the social situation, and therefore the motives and meanings, of others can be very useful for blacks as well.

Contemporary society . . . is becoming increasingly complex and variegated. This is what is commonly called "pluralism." What is more, contemporary society, or any conceivable variation of its present structure, will break down into howling chaos unless a plurality of social groups and social worlds succeeds in existing together with a measure of mutual understanding. Under these circumstances, the insights of sociology are anything but an intellectual luxury. This is especially so if there is a future for democracy in this society. Sociology, as the application of critical intelligence to society, has a particular affinity to democracy, that political form that is based on the assumption that social conflicts can be resolved and social problems alleviated by means of rational persuasion and without recourse to violence. Non-democratic regimes, whether of the "right" or "left," have an instinctive aversion to sociology. Conversely, sociology has developed best in situations where the political structure had some real relationship to democratic ideas.

Awareness Expansion: A Sense of One's Possibilities

If sociology has a particular affinity for democratic types of government, it has another, more personal relation to liberty. Anyone who seriously immerses himself in the perspective of sociology will find that his awareness of society, and thus his awareness of himself, will have changed considerably. This changed awareness is not always or one-sidedly "liberating," in the sense of expanding the individual's sense of being free and being himself. Sociological insight may lead to a recognition of limitations that one was previously unaware of, and it may further lead to the sad conclusion that courses of action that one had previously regarded as capable of realization are, in fact, illusions and fantasies. Working hard in one's vocation is *not* the sure way to wealth and fame. Participating in a campus riot is *not* a step toward the revolutionary overthrow of the capitalist system. And so on and so forth. Also, sociological insight may lead to an understanding of the great fragility of all the things one holds dear, including one's notions as to who one is, because sociology shows their ongoing dependence on social processes of definition and redefinition. This understanding, more than any other provided by sociology, can be deeply upsetting, as it seems to shake the very ground on which one is standing.

Thus the relation of sociology to the individual's sense of his own liberty is not a simple or easy matter. Still, when all is said and done, the perspective of sociology, correctly understood, leads to a deepening of the sense of liberty. Long ago the Stoics declared that wisdom consists in knowing what I can and what I cannot do, and that freedom is only possible on the basis of such wisdom. There is something of this wisdom in sociologically formed awareness. Precisely because sociology teaches the limitations and the fragility of what the individual can do and be in society, it also gives him a better sense of his possibilities. And, leaving aside philosophical sophistication, perhaps this is as good an operational definition of liberty as any—having a sense of one's possibilities. Politics has been described as the art of the possible. If so, in all modesty, sociology might be described as *a science of the possible.*

It is for these reasons, we think, that sociology has a place in a "liberal arts" curriculum. Whatever may be its uses for professional training or scholarly enterprises, sociology has a bearing on the growth of personal awareness of the world, of others and of self. There is much controversy today over the future of college and university education. Whatever this future may turn out to be, we hope that it will have a place for this "liberal" conception of education, and thus for the peculiarly "liberal" discipline of sociology.

QUESTIONS

1. Why did you and other members of the class decide to study sociology? Do the members have much the same motivation and anticipation, or is there a good deal of diversity?

2. How good a case do you think the authors make for the study of sociology?

3. How might sociology enhance an appreciation of human liberty and the human potential? Is it particularly different from other disciplines in this respect?

JAMES T. RICHARDSON
MARY W. STEWART
ROBERT B. SIMMONDS

Researching a Fundamentalist Commune [1]

One of the most fruitful methods of sociological investigation is the case study—a detailed record of some episode of social behavior, such as a riot, a political campaign, or the daily life of a high school. Although the particular case under consideration may have unique features, information gained from studying it can sometimes offer useful insights into other apparently similar cases.

Sociologists need not necessarily take part in the activities of the groups they study, but many researchers prefer to play the role of participant observer. Sometimes these researchers conceal their true identity from the group, usually because they fear that the subjects would not knowingly allow themselves to be studied by sociologists. This practice, however, raises the ethical problem that information is being obtained through the use of deceit. In other cases, the researchers make their identity clear from the outset, although their honesty can sometimes jeopardize their chances of gaining access to the group.

This article discusses some of the problems faced by sociologists who wanted to study a small religious sect, and who preferred to declare their identities and intentions at the beginning of the project. Their approach raised one recurrent problem: group members were determined to convert the visiting sociologists to the sect, but, as it happened, the research ultimately benefited as a result.

We have been involved for almost seven years with research on a large youth, communal, evangelical, fundamentalist organization that originated in the late 1960s as a part of the so-called Jesus Movement (JM).[2] This research, which has resulted in some of the first published reports on the Jesus Movement [2,3], continues even now, and has furnished considerable information to scholars involved in studies of such movements and groups.[3] During the course of the study a number of different methods have been used to gather data, including survey questionnaires, personality assessment instruments, content analysis of organization documents and publications, structured and unstructured interviews with selected members and leaders, participant observation of many different activities of group members, and considerable interpersonal contact with key informants.

One question that arises quite often when we present results of our research to professional and lay groups concerns how we have managed to maintain rapport with the group for such a long period of time, and gain the sorts of information that we have. This question often derives from simple curiosity about how research is "really done." However, the question is fair and important, especially in light of a rather general feeling that long-term research on evangelical groups is difficult to accomplish unless one converts or does covert research (neither of which was done in the present case). This general belief in the difficulty of researching evangelical groups has gained support through the reporting in the scholarly literature of the apparently problematic research experience involving another JM groups . . . [22].

. . .

I

The study of evangelical groups presents a difficult problem that affects both the method of investigation and the content of interpretations. The problem that concerns us here is the proselytizing behavior of members of the evangelical group that is directed toward members of the research team. Pressure to convert, which has taken both overt and covert forms, has been brought to bear on us throughout our study, although such pressure, which was also reported by Robbins, Anthony, and Curtis [22], has lessened somewhat in recent years. In many ways, the overt pressure was easiest to handle. In nearly every interview, early in the research, attempts were made to convert the interviewer. We warned interviewers about this, but even so, some were rather unprepared for the intensity of proselytization attempts. All of us were asked repeatedly what we believed and why we did not "believe in Christ." Open disdain was shown by a few members for the value of what we were doing. They simply defined our presence there as being sent to them by God for conversion. The "subject" often tried to reverse the usual respondent-interviewer relationship, making the interviewer the "subject" of an intense witnessing and conversion effort. Most interviewers were successful in handling such attempts, but problems arose as a result of this overt pressure. Some interviewers got caught up in the situation and wanted to argue with some particularly forceful respondents. We continually counseled against argument *per se,* but it was a problem, particularly for some of the more politically conscious and articulate of the interviewers, some of whom had very strong negative feelings about the apparent "dropout" type of existence being lived by members of the group. A few other interviewers had a different type of problem. They were influenced by the situation to consider converting, and staying in the group. One person in the 1972 interview team, in particular, was hard-pressed when it came time to decide whether or not to return home after interviewing was complete.

The last comment illustrates the more subtle pressures of such research situations. We, being somewhat aware of the possible problems, had chosen carefully among selected mature undergraduates for our interview teams. We talked with them about what to expect and tried to prepare them mentally for the interviewing. The fact that one considered staying with the group, and that a few others found themselves responding so strongly in a negative way only illustrates the problems caused by dropping people literally into a "new and different world."

This "new world" was one where life "outside" was viewed as worthless. The fundamentalist-oriented world view had everything defined and ordered in a way considerably different from the experience of most interviewers. The most compelling aspect of this new world was its total permeation with genuine peace and love. It was obvious to all of us that the people being studied enjoyed being where they were, and that they loved one another. *And*, they "loved" us as well, and treated us as "prodigal sons and daughters." We were welcomed with open arms (not withstanding some concern by a few group leaders), fed, and furnished with a place to sleep. They constantly expressed great concern that we should come to share their "peace that passeth understanding." One has to be hard-hearted indeed not to be moved when his or her

name is mentioned in earnest prayer before meals and during Bible studies. This loving and caring atmosphere was hard to ignore, and different people responded differently to it. Lofland has also reported the use of "love" by a new religious group [14].

As a group, we made serious and systematic attempts to maintain what Berger called the "thin thread of conversation" [15], so that our view of reality would be reinforced. In the June 1972 visit, the research team of seven met every evening and during breaks during the day in a large pickup camper, which was brought to serve as a "headquarters," and which was generally off limits to members of the group being researched (except by special invitation). In these essential meetings in the camper, we talked about the experiences of the day (and also drank a little wine and smoked a little, just for good measure). If we had not had the camper along, we would have been forced to seek refuge by withdrawing, and going to a nearby town, as the smaller interview team of summer, 1971, did. As it was, we had a "retreat" at the research site which allowed us to withdraw quickly if desired, but, at the same time, we were continually around to observe activities and record information.

Our basic approach to research such as this is to be open about our objectives. This does not mean that we explain every detail of our research plans, but it does indicate a basic posture of lack of deception. This contrasts sharply with the work of some past and present researchers who have seen fit to use overtly deceptive tactics [16,17,18]. We think that generally such deception is unnecessary, impractical, and unethical. A more open approach *appears* (and may well be) more humane, more ethical, and it certainly is a demonstration that the researcher *probably* takes the beliefs of the other seriously. From a practical point of view, such an approach seems more honest, and will usually bear the "fruits of honesty" in human interaction.[5] Also, much information may be directly gained in such discussions. In our own research, we discouraged interviewers from engaging in serious discussions (because we feared what Robbins, Anthony, and Curtis had feared, namely, that such might terminate the research project), but we did *not* totally rule them out. Some interviewers and all three of the authors took part in such exchanges on occasion, especially with some group leaders. It was obvious that we did not fear being questioned and entering into serious discussions, and this openness was appreciated by those on whom we were doing research. Thus, instead of being seriously hindered by group beliefs and practices, we think we actually gained considerable information from the willingness of respondents to share their beliefs.

We are aware that this apparently more honest approach is subject to misuse, which raises potential ethical problems. Someone could be "planted," because of his or her personal beliefs, in a group more open to such a person. This is neither what we suggest nor what we did. No member of the interview teams we have used was a "believer" in the tenets of the group studied, although the background of some of us made it easier to understand the jargon of the group and its practices. We simply felt that we wanted to be as open as possible in our research, and that it was possible to do sound research of this type under such conditions. This decision was made mainly out of respect for the people being studied, and it was implemented with some qualms. We were a bit surprised at the "success" of the decision when it became translated into a strategy of research. We found out through personal experience that, at least with the group being studied, a decision to be more open was a "tactical success," although this was not the reason for deciding to operate as we did.

Because of our experience (along with other successful, more open research experiences, such as that of Liebow [19]), we are now convinced that being open with certain kinds of groups is an extremely successful research tactic. And, although we do not recommend it, if one is willing to carefully select interviewers to "match" the characteristics of the group being studied, then researchers of "deviant groups" truly do have a "secret weapon" against which many such will have little defense. Thus, certain groups, such as sectarian religious organizations that have heretofore been studied "successfully" using deceptive practices [16,17,18], may now be studied easier and "better" using "true converts" (or reasonable facsimiles). The question is whether or not to use this technique, and the reason the question is asked derives from ethical considerations, *not* tactical ones. From a tactical point of view, such an approach may be actually easier, and possibly promises more "inside information."

We have suggested several times that group beliefs and practices actually aided (rather than hindered) our research. The following section will discuss this idea more systematically.

A usually unnoticed, or at least uncredited, item, sometimes of great importance to a research project, involves the openness of the "culture" of a group (or the "personality" of a specific subject) to the research and the researcher. It is obvious that normal rules of courtesy generally aid any researcher who asks permission to interview a potential subject. Chances are usually quite good that the potential subject will treat the researcher with courtesy, unless there is some special problem (such as using non-Black interviewers with Black respondents in a time of racial confrontation). This "rule of common courtesy" plainly gives an initial advantage to any researcher willing to intrude her or himself into another's life. Further, Milgram's research on obedience to authority [20] . . . has demonstrated that many people will obey some requests that go far beyond the realm of nor-

mal courtesy, if such requests are couched in certain terms. Also, it is just as obvious that sometimes research is allowed because it is thought to be advantageous by the one (or the group or group leaders) being researched . . . [6]

However, when we talk of the value of group culture and/or personal attributes to our research, we mean something more overt—but in some ways more subtle—than the kinds of things just mentioned (all of which admittedly have operated in our favor). The group studied has an authoritarian structure of organization, a factor that may be based on necessity, but which is usually justified by the group reference to ideology through the medium of quoting certain Bible verses that support such an approach to group life. Because of this definite authority-structure, we were not faced with having to justify our existence to every subject, in an attempt to convince them to grant us an interview. Instead, we had only to persuade the leaders (and only a few of them) that our project was worthy, and that it should be done. When they decided that our work was acceptable, they told the members to allow us to interview them. We had very high response rates (95–100 percent) because of this, and it is worth admitting that the response rate would probably have been virtually zero if we had not cleared the project with those in charge. This is plainly a place where some knowledge of the group ideology (gained through previous experience of one author and through the initial contacts with the group) helped a great deal. If we had not known or found out that the group was authoritarian in nature, we might have just tried to start interviewing selected subjects, a tactic that would have virtually guaranteed the failure of the project, since members would not have cooperated without the express permission of their leaders. So, in a sense, the group was easier to study than a group in which each individual could decide whether or not to be interviewed. This latter situation is, of course, analogous to just about any survey research where interviewers go from house to house, trying to interview as many members of a sample as possible. And the low response rates of some such studies evidences our point.

The actual interview situation . . . was also helped considerably because of group beliefs and practices. Because the subjects really believed that their past life had been "washed clean" by virtue of their conversion, they were very willing to talk about their personal histories. It seemed as if this past life could no longer harm them in any way, and they could treat it in a very objective fashion (the problem of sometimes making it sound worse than it really was notwithstanding).[7] Also, their new beliefs contained a strong emphasis on honesty in personal relations, and, especially since we were "approved" by the leaders of the group, the respondents were quite open to us . . .

It is interesting to examine in more depth the decision

of group leaders that we were to be welcomed, and to look at group beliefs in an effort to understand how and why the decision to be open to us was made. We, of course, do not have secret tape recordings of deliberations of the group leaders as they were trying to decide what to do with us. However, we do have enough knowledge of how the group functions *and* of its belief system to construct fairly well, we think, key elements of the probable scenario. And, here especially, we see the importance of group beliefs to be the success of our research.

Jesus Movement groups, including the one we are researching, generally adopted the traditional dualism of fundamentalist Christianity. This system of thought is one of few categories, and can be described as simplistic in nature [22]. Things are good or bad, black or white, the "work of Satan" or the "work of the Lord." We think that this lack of differentiation served us very well, especially when taken *in conjunction with* some other important group beliefs and practices.

The group is very evangelical, and defines as a (possibly *the*) major goal, the conversion of "sinners" (which, simply defined, means those who do not accept the basic tenets of the group). Also, the ideology of the group is very "God-centered" in that they believe that their God is omniscient and omnipotent, and takes an active role in the affairs of the world, including their personal and group life. According to group beliefs, God *at least* "permits" *all* that happens. These elements of belief combine to force an interpretation of every contact with a "nonbeliever" (including us) as being an opportunity, even responsibility, sent by God to them, so that the nonbeliever might be witnessed to by members of the group.

The dualism of fundamentalist Christianity does, of course, include the concept of an "anti-God" (Satan) who also can move in human history, but we were fortunate enough not to be categorized as being a part of this evil contingent. Instead, partially because of our real and honest interest in what was taking place in the group, and because the group members were sincerely concerned about us, we got classified in just about the only other possible category in this simplistic system of thought, with its inherent lack of differentiation. We were classified as potential converts—converts who obviously were to be "won to Christ" by members of this group. This situation was similar to that reported by Robbins, Anthony, and Curtis [22]; there were, however, important differences.[8] Members and leaders of the group were led by their own beliefs to assume that God had sent or directed us (potentially even against our own wills and without our knowledge) to this group. The least they thought was that God had *permitted* us to come there, and had thereby given us over to this group as a part of their Christian responsibility. It is possible, of course, that we could have been considered a "test" sent from God in a manner akin to the boils visited upon Job, but if some seriously enter-

tained this thought we were unaware of it. And even if some had this thought, *that interpretation would still have probably resulted in our getting to stay with the group,* simply because we desired to do this and intended to stay until asked to leave.

In short, the beliefs of the group rendered members somewhat *passive* in the face of a concerted effort to study them. We, the active agents in all this, were apparently assumed somehow to be tied up with the will of God. Which group member or leader was going to try to thwart that? At least partially because of such ideological considerations, we were welcomed with sincere concern, even relish, and feted (to the extent that group resources allowed). Their usual practices of making potential converts welcome (at least for a time) seemed to be carried to the extreme.

It seemed that there was an implicit contest going on among group members to see who could convert one of us first. As stated, for the first few years of our research, nearly every interview was a contest of wills (and patience—on both sides). We regularly heard our names mentioned in prayers in their public gatherings, and some members made continual efforts to "win us to Christ." The importance of this issue to the group members was graphically illustrated when rumors of the impending conversion of a member of the June 1972 interview team swept the camp. There was much premature rejoicing among group members, who plainly assumed that the only "real purpose" of our being there was to "get converted."[9] Apparently what had happened was that an interviewer had expressed to a respondent an interest in finding out more about the group ideas, and he had started to read the Bible during his spare time. Just the sight of him reading the Bible seemed to be enough to set the rumor mill in motion. In some of our later visits, people still asked about the interviewer, desiring to know if he finally decided to convert. The tenacity of such ideas demonstrates their importance to the group (just as the continued interest of this interviewer in the group evidences the effect the research experience had on him).

II

As has been stated, we are continuing our research, and have been studying the group since early 1971. That is a long time for the group to labor without converting us, and this suggests that there has been some redefining, by the group members, of us and our role *vis-à-vis* the group. We agree that such has occurred, but would suggest that the new definition, while being more elaborate, still is congruent with the basic beliefs of the group. First, we believe that we are still looked at as potential converts and may even be potential converts of special "worth," since we are people of relatively high status *vis-à-vis* the group members. But the days of the "hard sell" seem to be over, and now the approach is much more subtle. We are being witnessed to "by example" instead of using forceful argumentation. Second, the worldview of the group members appears to have gotten more complex in that the basic two-category world (saved and unsaved) has become more differentiated. Perhaps our presence has even hastened the predictable differentiation process. Whatever the cause, there now seem to be several categories of nonmembers, some of whom are viewed much more positively than others. For instance, some of the group view us as people with a special relationship to the group. They apparently think our being associated with the group has some "higher purpose," which will be revealed in due course. The fact that some converts have been gained through our publication of results serves to support such a view. It is entirely possible that the group is coming to think that we have been sent to chronicle their history for the larger public. Group leaders have indicated that they realize someone will eventually write their history, but so far they think it should be done by a member. However, their generally positive (even if somewhat unexpected) reaction to the first publication from our research [2] has caused us to think that perhaps they are reevaluating their view of us and their position on who will "write their history." Thus, our relationship with the group continues, but for reasons that we think are largely "out of control." We give a great deal of credit to the "positive" (from our point of view) features of group culture that have helped us continue our research. . . .

There are, of course, other reasons (some of which may not be known to us) why our research has been allowed to continue. Plainly, some members of the group like the attention we have paid to them, and they like the "anonymous fame" that our publications have brought to them. We have developed some rather strong affective ties with some members over the years of our research, and this means that there is more trust shared by all of us. And the mere passage of time has had another effect, in that the group as a whole may be growing more *tolerant* of outsiders as it gains strength and self-confidence. We have also *invested hard work to maintain contact and rapport* with the group and some key members. We have had our share of good luck, as well. And, one key thing has been the totally unexpected fact that the *group has actually gained some members as a result of our research.* Our first publication of material on the group [2] resulted in well over fifty letters being sent to us by people who wanted to join the group.[10] After some discussion, we sent these queries to the group, since we were bound by our pledge of anonymity and thus could not respond ourselves with the requested information. The next time we visited the group, there were a few people there who had first heard of the group through our publication! This situation demonstrates that no matter how hard one may try

to avoid influencing a group being studied, it is virtually impossible to stop all influences. The gaining of a few members through our publication seemed to demonstrate to some group leaders that somehow we were "agents of God."

QUESTIONS

1. What are the advantages and drawbacks of the participant-observer method of sociological research?

2. Are there any situations in which a researcher is justified in hiding his or her identity from the subjects of the research?

3. Using the article as a case study, identify and discuss some of the difficulties, expected and unexpected, that might be faced in sociological research.

Notes

1. This is an expansion of part of a paper presented at the 1975 annual American Sociological Association meeting, which was derived from the research appendix of a forthcoming monograph, *Organized Miracles* (1978), by the same authors.

2. The organization we have been studying is fully described in our forthcoming book, *Organized Miracles* [I]. The group described desires to remain anonymous, thus we cannot report their name or location, as per our original agreement with them when the research started.

3. Our research is a relatively large study which has resulted in a dozen or so papers being read at professional meetings, along with numerous talks given by the three of us to other professional and lay groups, in the United States, Western Europe, and Scandinavia. Also, about ten papers have been published [2,3,4,5,6,7,8,9,10,11]. Two dissertations have resulted as well [12,13].

4. We, of course, are not claiming that our own research experience is necessarily any more generalizable, but we think that discussing both experiences together may result in some general conclusions of value.

5. We say "usually" because it is plain that certain kinds of research cannot be done without deception. The questions are whether or not such research should be done, and whether or not some professional body should perhaps be charged with allowing such endeavors (in a manner similar to the recent decision of some biologists to organize a review group, and, in the meantime, to refrain from certain kinds of research).

6. We are all aware of the problems brought about by the desire of some to be "studied," with the resulting tendency to volunteer for studies, or the so-called "Hawthorne effect" that can cause workers to continue to put together complex devices in near darkness. Such tendencies "compensate" some for the features of a group or person that make most research "easier" than might first be thought, and must be taken into account in any research.

7. This problem of "negative bragging sessions" seems a classic illustration of the "reconstruction of biography" mentioned by Berger [21]. While we do not think many subjects made deliberate attempts to mislead us, we were aware, because of previous knowledge of the fundamentalist subculture, of the tendency to claim a "more sinful" past than was really the case. In ways that are discussed at more length in the appendix to *Organized Miracles,* there seemed to be an assumption on the part of some respondents that the best Christians were the ones who had sinned the most in their "previous

existence." Because of this possibility, we tried to double-check information that seemed especially prone to this "sinful reconstruction of biography."

8. This definition of researchers as potential converts seems an ultimate example of the benefits of the "outsider role," as discussed by Trice [23]. The problem, of course, is to maintain this privileged status for a long enough time to do the research (and resolve ethical problems inherent in the situation).

9. We should add that this incident led to much discussion among the interview team members so that none of us would do anything to encourage such interpretations of our activities.

10. Our first publication was in *Psychology Today* [2], which, we understand, printed 450,000 copies of that issue. Perhaps we should have expected such a reaction from some in such a large readership, but nonetheless we were a bit taken aback by what happened, and had to make a decision about what to do with the letters. Some will disagree with what we did, but we are still satisfied with the decision.

References

1. James T. Richardson, Mary White Stewart, and Robert B. Simmonds. *Organized Miracles*. Transaction Books, forthcoming.

2. Mary White Harder, James T. Richardson, and Robert B. Simmonds. "Jesus People." *Psychology Today,* 6 December 1972, pp.45-50, 110-113.

3. James T. Richardson, Robert B. Simmonds, and Mary White Harder. "Thought Reform and the Jesus Movement." *Youth and Society* 4 (1972):185-200.

4. Mary White Harder. "Sex Roles in the Jesus Movement." *Social Compass* 21 (1974):345-353.

5. Mary White Harder, James T. Richardson, and Robert B. Simmonds. "Life Style: Sex Roles, Courtship, Marriage, and Family in a Changing Jesus Movement Organization." *International Review of Modern Sociology* 6 (1975):155-172.

6. James T. Richardson. "The Jesus Movement: An Assessment." *Listening: Journal of Religion and Culture* 9 (1974):20-42.

7. James T. Richardson and Robert Simmonds. "Personality Assessment in New Religious Groups: Problems of Interpretation." In preparation, 1977.

8. James T. Richardson, Robert B. Simmonds, and Mary White Harder. "Evolving Structures of a Jesus Movement Organization." *Journal of Voluntary Social Action Research,* in press.

9. James T. Richardson and Mary White Stewart. "Conversion Process Models and the Jesus Movement." *American Behavioral Scientist* 20 (1977):819-838.

10. Robert B. Simmonds, James T. Richardson, and Mary White Harder. "Organization and Structure of a Jesus Movement Community." *Social Compass* 21 (1974):269-281.

11. Robert B. Simmonds, James T. Richardson, and Mary White Harder. "A Jesus Movement Group: An Adjective Check List Assessment." *Journal for the Scientific Study of Religion* 15 (1976):323-337.

12. Mary White Harder. *The Children of Christ Commune: A Study of a Fundamentalist Communal Sect*. Ph.D. thesis, University of Nevada, Reno, 1972.

13. Robert B. Simmonds. *The People of the Jesus Movement: A Personality Assessment of a Fundamentalist Religious Community*. Ph.D. thesis, University of Nevada, Reno, 1977.

14. John Lofland. "Becoming a World-Saver Revisited." *American Behavioral Scientist* 20 (1977):805-818.

15. Peter Berger. *The Sacred Canopy*. Doubleday, 1967.

16. Leon Festinger, H. W. Reicker, and Stanley Schachter. *When Prophecy Fails*. University of Minnesota Press, 1956.

17. John Lofland. *Doomsday Cult*. Prentice-Hall, 1965.

18. Hiley Ward. *The Far-Out Saints of the Jesus Communes*. Association Press, N.Y. 1972.

19. Elliot Liebow. *Tally's Corner*. Little, Brown, 1967.

20. Stanley Milgram. *Obedience to Authority*. Harper & Row, 1973.

21. Peter Berger. *Invitation to Sociology*. Doubleday, 1963.

22. Thomas Robbins, Dick Anthony, and Thomas E. Curtis. "The Limits of Symbolic Realism: Problems of Empathetic Field Observation in a Sectarian Context." *Journal for the Scientific Study of Religion* 12 (1973):259-272.

23. H. M. Trice. "The 'Outsiders' ' Role in Field Study." *In Qualitative Methodology*, pp.77-82. Edited by W. J. Filstead, Markham, Chicago, 1970.

STANLEY MILGRAM
JOHN SABINI

Candid Camera

*The popular television show "Candid Camera" creates
situations in which unsuspecting subjects are placed in
awkward or puzzling predicaments—for example, a
voice comes out of the mailbox as a subject tries to
mail a letter—and then records their attempts to make
sense of the situation. The often comic reactions are of
great interest to the mass TV audience—and perhaps
even more so to sociologists and social psychologists,
who have, additionally, a professional interest in the
process.*

*The method used by the "Candid Camera" produc-
ers is familiar to social scientists: it is, of course, an
experiment, although of a rather crude kind. Like
sociologists, the "Candid Camera" producers carefully arrange an experimental situation, introduce the
subjects to it, record what happens, and draw conclusions; and like sociological experiments, the "Candid
Camera" findings add to our knowledge of human behavior. (Indeed, one school of sociology, called
ethnomethodology, also used disruptive situations to
evoke reactions from the subjects, although the intent
is different—to expose rules of social behavior by violating them.)*

*But despite these similarities, there are also impor-
tant differences. As Stanley Milgram and John Sabini
point out in this article, "Candid Camera" is not
science, and its conclusions cannot be generalized or
relied upon as can those from a truly scientific experiment. Their examination of these differences sharpens
our understanding of the character and merits of the
scientific method.*

Published by permission of Transaction, Inc. from *Society*, Vol. 16, No.
6. Copyright © 1979 by Transaction, Inc.

Since 1947 millions of television viewers have watched
the program *Candid Camera*, created by Allen Funt. The
program consists of filmed records of people spontaneously responding to unusual and sometimes bizarre situations set up by the producer. In a representative episode,
a naive person approaches a mailbox in order to deposit a
letter, and is startled to find a voice from within the mailbox addressing him. The camera focuses on the responses
of the person to this anomaly, and typically the reactions
of a sequence of individuals confronting this situation are
shown. Each episode ends by informing the person that
the experience he has undergone is part of a *Candid
Camera* episode. In the course of a single program, four
or five different situations are shown.

The *Candid Camera* program merits examination for
several reasons. First, the very fact of a program built on
the exposure of spontaneous human behavior is itself
symptomatic of broader cultural currents which we need
to examine. Second, the *Candid Camera* episodes constitute a repository of documented behavior of potential interest to social scientists. We are not the first to recognize
this value. James Maas and his associates at Cornell University have classified and annotated more than 1,500
such episodes. But we need to assess both the utility and
the limits of such an archive. The value of such material
will depend in part on their methods of collection. Here
we note an interesting feature of the *Candid Camera* program: it participates, at least fractionally, in the methodology of the social sciences.

For social science, *Candid Camera* possesses a number
of attractive features. First, each episode begins with a
question about human behavior, for which we do not fully
know the answer. The question is examined in concrete
circumstances somewhat the way an experimental social
psychologist might proceed in his laboratory. An illustra-
tive question might be: "How would a customer in a
clothing store react if the salesman took out a tongue
depressor and started to examine the customer with it?"
One senses that a question such as this touches on a larger sociological issue centering on role theory. We might
tend to think that in the case of the above episode, because the clothing salesman's act is so bizarre, none of the
clients will go along with it. The filmed records show,

however, that at least some clients do cooperate with the salesman; thus, the procedures seem capable of yielding surprises, perhaps even making discoveries.

At least one group of social scientists, experimental social psychologists, shares with *Candid Camera* the idea that one ought to create synthetic situations as a means of revealing human behavior. For social psychologists, the synthesized situation is called the experiment. For *Candid Camera*, it is a typical program episode. Both experimentalists and Funt construct situations into which the participants are brought, but which are unfinished, the completion of the scene being accomplished by the performance of the person. The exact character of the performance is seldom entirely known by those who set up the situation. Indeed, behavior which deviates from what is expected, that is, surprises, are particularly valued by those who organize such occasions.

An obvious merit of *Candid Camera* is that it presents us with behavior, not just hearsay. Through the visual and auditory document, we are able to see how certain situations are set up and exactly how people respond to them. It is not merely a statement of how people think they *would* act or feel they *ought* to act in a given situation; it is a record of how they do in fact act. We are presented with a richly textured, though unanalyzed, record which is precise at the level of the individual case. Such firsthand data would seem to be of considerable value in any science of human behavior.

Because the behavior has been recorded on film, it can continually be reexamined by social scientists, a task now facilitated by the availability of an annotated archives of *Candid Camera* episodes. Generally, in social science, we must be content with an account of an event provided by the investigator. But this account, whether in quantitative or verbal descriptive form, is an abstraction taken from a more complex behavioral situation which is no longer accessible to us. While experiments, and often sociological observations, are in principle replicable, there are many practical limitations to such replication. How much more satisfactory it is to have access to the actual behavior, or at least filmed records of such behavior. We may find in such iconic material features which would never be mentioned in a skeletal verbal account, and we are better informed of the exact tone or expressive character of the event.

Moreover, the events depicted in *Candid Camera* are embedded in the stream of everyday life. Funt creates his episodes in a variety of familiar environments: hotel rooms, banks, on the street, in parks, in bars and canteens, in zoos, elevators, bowling alleys, and numerous other settings that individuals encounter in their daily rounds. Those who serve as confederates play a variety of real life roles: bartenders, salesmen, bank clerks, etc. Insofar as sociological theory has as its goal the explanation of real life behavior, Funt's ecological imagination would

seem to be a considerable advance over the more sterile methods which remove subjects from the natural contexts of life.

Candid Camera shares another feature with certain social science strategies. It gives us a new vision through the disruption of the habitual. It frequently makes evident what we take for granted by altering some of the normal assumptions of daily life. Thus, when a client enters a clothing store, and the salesman begins to examine the client with a tongue depressor, the audience laughs because of the discrepancy between normal expectancies as to the appropriate behavior of the salesman, and the behavior actually engaged in. It has often been observed that harmoniously functioning systems may be more difficult to analyze than those that show some degree of dysfunction. Freud believed that by using neurosis as a point of departure, he could better understand how the normal processes of personality work. Enthnomethodologists such as Harold Garfinkel attain an understanding of the normal rules of everyday life by deliberately violating them. Funt frequently relies on a similar disruption of the usual in order to generate insights.

A further merit of *Candid Camera's* materials is embodied in the very name of the enterprise: the behavior is observed without the awareness of the participant. Ethically, this aspect of *Candid Camera* is problematical; scientifically it is indispensable to a full understanding of human behavior. The essence of a social situation is not merely that there are two people present, but that each of the parties has a representation of the other in his field of awareness. When a person is aware that he is being photographed or filmed or merely observed, he reflexively calls into play a range of self-presentational mechanisms. These include both censorship mechanisms (he suppresses certain behaviors, such as picking his nose) and positive acts (he smiles, straightens his shoulders). When a person is not aware that he is being photographed or observed, he has no chance to make the adjustments needed for a social encounter. Thus *Candid Camera* presents us with behavior uncontaminated with the reactivity of an observer. (Sometimes, however, Funt will use a confederate to create a needed social scene, or to provoke the behavior of the target.)

Funt states that *Candid Camera* catches the person "in the act of being himself." More precisely, the camera catches the person acting under the belief that he is unobserved, or at least that his behavior is not being recorded for the later scrutiny of others.

A final point which social scientists may admire in *Candid Camera* is the sheer creativity evidenced over the years in the construction of *Candid Camera* episodes: taxis that split in half; drivers that land their automobiles in trees; waitresses in an ordinary diner who break into a Broadway chorus as they serve apple pie; bystanders who suddenly find themselves on stage in the midst of a theatrical performance; walls that vanish, mailboxes that talk, etc. The sheer variety and inventiveness of the incidents are undeniable. Funt is not interested in sociological theory per se, but his incidents are informed by a keen, though unarticulated, intuition about the forces that shape behavior in a social context.

But *Candid Camera* is not social science, nor are its materials free of problems for use by scientists. Before examining such deficiencies, let us start by pointing to the most obvious difference between *Candid Camera* and scientific research. This concerns the institutional framework within which each is conducted. Above all, *Candid Camera* is a commercial activity. The overriding goal of the producer is to create materials that can be sold to a network or a sponsor. Such materials are saleable insofar as they are able to attract and hold a large television audience. Thus, within this framework the entertainment value of an episode is the ultimate test of its worth. Funt treats his incursions into the study of human behavior as a marketable commodity, and each episode has a dollar and cents value. The scientific deficiencies of the *Candid Camera* material stem from its origin as commercial entertainment.

The most obvious scientific deficiency of *Candid Camera* is the lack of adequate sampling. There is no guarantee that the behavior depicted is typical behavior. Indeed, we have every reason to feel that the selections actually used in *Candid Camera* are chosen for their maximum value as entertainment. Funt indicates that he often shoots at a film ratio of 100/1; thus, even when a sequence of respondents is shown, we cannot assume the persons depicted represent anything other than a highly uncharacteristic set of responses.

Consider the situation in which a delivery boy finds Funt bound and gagged, asks whether the victim ordered a hamburger, then leaves nonchalantly when Funt indicates no. Clearly, the laughter promoted by this response indicates that it is entertaining. But is the behavior typical? We are not told how many delivery boys needed to be filmed before this particular boy left the incident. It seems that the more appropriate response of untying the victim, and offering him assistance, would be less amusing to an audience and thus less likely to appear in the *Candid Camera* archives. We have no systematic record of the range and centrality of responses to any given situation. We are thus presented with behavior which is shown to be possible (and of no small value for this reason) but with no idea of its probability.

Moreover, we are only shown those segments of the subject's behavior which produce a maximally humorous impact. We are not shown sequelae which may be critical to establishing the meaning of the behavior as experienced by the subject. In the episode cited above, we are not informed whether this particular delivery boy left the scene of his victim permanently, or whether, upon leaving

what he perceived to be a dangerous situation, he immediately called the police. This latter possibility would give an entirely different interpretation to the delivery boy's behavior.

Candid Camera differs from scientific experiments in another important way. Experiments take account of and proceed beyond work that has already been done. Thus an experiment can be evaluated by the degree to which it contributes to the cumulative growth of a discipline. Funt does not evaluate his episodes by this criterion. All that is required is that each episode differs in some way from what has gone before, and that it be entertaining. Thus, while the *Candid Camera* episodes grow in number, they do not accumulate in any specifiable direction. *Candid Camera* is thus an enterprise that offers novelty, but not progress.

Candid Camera shares with experimental social psychology the observation of behavior within constructed situations, but social psychologists make use of experimental variation, in which one systematically alters the situation to find the causes of behavior. Moreover, an experiment must have a certain degree of precision and control. Each subject must confront the same stimulus; there must be a specifiable and metrical aspect to both the stimulus and the response. Some would argue that the quantification of experimental social psychology has led to an impoverished picture of human behavior. But merely to record behavior, for all its surface vitality, gives us no clue as to its significance in some larger framework of understanding. We are left with raw material which may amuse us, but which in itself explains nothing.

In sum, the *Candid Camera* record is probably more important in raising than answering questions, since it is a haphazard rather than a disciplined approach to the study of human behavior. The questions the *Candid Camera* sequences ask are often of the "what would happen if . . . " variety, selected to produce interesting and amusing effects rather than to elaborate a system of causal explanations. This lack of conceptual discipline at the outset of its inquiries finds its parallel in a lack of rigor in the documentation of results; the responses to the situations one sees may not be representative, since entertainment value rather than adequate sampling is the criterion for selection. Further, the film record falls short as a report of empirical results since it does not select, from all that a subject does, the scientifically interesting component. Since the sequences do not flow from some larger body of conceptual issues, there are no criteria for selecting important questions from less-significant possibilities or from abstracting the most important response dimensions. These scientific criticisms are quite irrelevant, of course, to the producer of *Candid Camera,* since his aim is to entertain rather than to inform.

Let us consider further how *Candid Camera* entertains. One important determinant of the viewer's response is his relative superiority to the subject on the screen. The audience is in on the joke; acting from this privileged perspective of full information, viewers laugh at the target's confusion or dilemma rather than share in it.

Instructions in how to respond begin with the show's opening moments, which create an unserious tone. As the show progresses, the viewer is instructed by the narrator about exactly what to look for; his comments reinforce the notion that what we are about to see will be funny. Studio laughter accompanies each episode as a way of continually defining the actions as funny, prompting the home viewer to experience the scene as amusing, rather than feeling sympathy or compassion for the victim's plight, or searching to understand it.

The audience is also offered an opportunity to see things to which it usually has little access. The situations involve circumstances which might not occur without intervention in a lifetime of observation. Although these situations may be somewhat bizarre, they are not beyond the audience's understanding. In order to understand the subject's response, the audience must be given some inkling of the perception of the situation from the subject's point of view. The *Candid Camera* technique invites the viewers to put themselves in place of the subject; they know what he is thinking; they laugh because they can see that his mode of thought will lead to ineffectual or inappropriate behavior. The behavior is funny rather than inexplicable or weird, precisely because the viewer can enter the phenomenology of the subject and understand that it is the unreasonableness of the circumstances rather than irrationality on the part of the subject which produces the maladaptive behavior.

The ability of *Candid Camera*-like techniques to expose the usually covert processes of an actor's phenomenology has made them an attractive tool for theorists of a phenomenological bent. It is apparent that the Garfinkel-type demonstrations, so intimately linked to ethnomethodology, are precisely in the mold of *Candid Camera* episodes. Like *Candid Camera* writers, ethnomethodologists deal with human action from the standpoint of the actor's perception of the situation, the likelihood of his constructing meaning out of novel and even bizarre circumstances, and the belief that he will respond to situations in terms of the meanings he can impute to them. Indeed, we may speculate that *Candid Camera*, a cultural phenomenon of 30 years' standing, has exerted an intellectual influence in stimulating ethnomethodological thought. In *Candid Camera,* we see repeated demonstrations of the ethnomethodological arguments that people continuously construct meanings out of the flux of daily life, even out of incongruity. We laugh at the person's struggle to extract meaning out of a situation so constructed as to frustrate this effort.

Much of the impact of *Candid Camera* results from

the impression that people have been trapped into showing themselves as they "really are." The target's self-presentational mechanisms are thwarted by his incomplete understanding of the real situation. The audience sees him vainly attempting to maintain his proper self in the absence of proper understanding. The attempt to maintain an adequate self fails for a variety of reasons. One aspect of an adequate self-presentation is giving an appropriate response to one's environment, but what is an adequate response to a talking mailbox? In other cases, the subject attempts to conceal a deficiency he believes is personal, while the audience knows that it is the environment which is impossible. (In one sequence, subjects conceal the fact that they cannot open a packet of sugar, while the audience knows that the packet cannot be opened.)

People may appear foolish if they unnecessarily lose their cool when the situation is quite normal, but they can be made to appear just as foolish when they attempt to maintain their cool in an abnormal situation. In stable, everyday experience, self-presentation can be maintained by enacting habituated patterns of behavior; in the extraordinary circumstances of the *Candid Camera* films, the audience sees people actively structuring a self out of the stacked opportunities the situation provides. *Candid Camera* repeatedly shows us that people operate with a certain amount of good faith and trust and that they have certain habitualized or routine ways of dealing with situations that may sometimes by misplaced in the face of bizarre circumstances.

There are several senses in which we may examine *Candid Camera* as a cultural phenomenon. First, we may ask in what way *Candid Camera* is an expression of the larger culture. What continuities does it have with other cultural forms? Is it a completely new form of activity or does it emerge from precedents?

The spirit of *Candid Camera* is largely the spirit of the prank or the practical joke. Consider the archetypic prank. A person walks along the street, sees a wallet lying on the pavement and attempts to pick it up. The wallet is attached to a string which is then pulled out of the reach of the person just as he stoops to pick it up. The person is initially startled, then realizes he has been the butt of a joke. If the prank is performed on April 1, its perpetrators will normally jog the person into a realization of its significance by announcing, "April Fool!" thus giving a cultural legitimacy to their activity and undercutting hostile reaction from the victim by admonishing him to be a "good sport."

Funt has extended April Fool's Day to a year-round activity. Moreover, the program has achieved a certain cultural penetration. Instead of announcing "April Fool," each episode typically ends when Funt says, "Smile, you're on *Candid Camera*." Upon hearing these words, subjects are almost always taken aback. Before responding to this interpretation, they search out the camera to confirm the interpretation. Indeed, pointing to the presence of a concealed camera to support the assertion that the person has been filmed has become part of the ritual of *Candid Camera*. Suddenly, all of the confusing and even bizarre events that preceded these words fall into place. The subject is thus grateful that the strain placed on his coping with the environment was nothing but an extended practical joke. Confusion suddenly crystallizes into a meaningful interpretation. *Candid Camera* has acquired a genuine cultural standing insofar as the words "Smile, you're on *Candid Camera*" give meaning and legitimacy to the events that preceded them.

At an aesthetic level, the *Candid Camera* program elevates the practical joke to the limits that a large budget, technological sophistication, and admirable ingenuity allow. Whatever else one may say about it, asking a cab driver to follow a car which splits in half is a masterful practical joke. *Candid Camera* is funny in part because it is an extension of a preexisting form of humor.

. . .

There is another sense in which *Candid Camera* is closely tied to culture. Many episodes rely on a precise knowledge of the prevailing cultural practice, and derive their humor from a violation of cultural expectancies. Much *Candid Camera* humor, therefore, is effective only within the particular culture in which it was constructed. For example, in one episode, male workers enter a physician's office for a physical examination. The physician turns out to be an attractive woman. The workers feel awkward when they're asked to undress before her. The audience titters at this embarrassing situation. It is clear that such a response can occur only in a society in which women physicians do not typically examine men. Even within other parts of modern society, say in Scandinavia or the Soviet Union, the embarrassed and awkward response of the workers would be less likely. Some *Candid Camera* episodes which prove successful in America do not travel well.

In their willingness to tinker with social reality for the purpose of observing behavior, both social science and *Candid Camera* display a fundamental irreverence toward the existing social order, and thus—some would say—participate in the analytic, disintegrative tendencies of modern life. But for *Candid Camera*, at least, there are clear boundaries to irreverence. Funt carefully avoids incidents or the use of persons that would be regarded as offensive by segments of the population. ". . . we lean over backward not to use a weak or poor sample of a black person . . . if a guy looked as if he was too rough or too ignorant, or too Uncle Tom, I left him out of the picture." Moreover, while Funt does not regard the everyday operation of the social order as sacred, he treats certain social activities as immune from *Candid Camera's* intrusions. For example, *Candid Camera* does not create episodes intruding upon real funerals; nor does it carry out a prank on a person's wedding night, however rich the possibilities for humor. This would be considered too deep a violation of the couple's privileged moments. *Candid Camera* maps for us the domain of the sacred by leaving such activities alone. Like the prankster, it tweaks at the culture, without doing serious violence to it.

Finally, as its very name implies, *Candid Camera* is utterly dependent upon the technical culture of Western society, and specifically on the availability of instruments for audio-visual recording. Thus, it was not possible to undertake an enterprise such as *Candid Camera* until the present century. At best, it was possible, through the use of actors, to re-create a scene that the participants thought was covert (as in Hamlet's re-creation of the poisoning of his father). But this is a far cry from the detailed filmic documentation of behavior enacted under the illusion of being ephemeral and unobserved.

QUESTIONS

1. Why do you think "Candid Camera" has proved such a popular TV show?

2. What are the similarities between "Candid Camera" and sociological experiment? What are the differences?

3. Why is "Candid Camera" not science?

UNIT 2   *The Individual,*
         Culture, and Society

CLYDE KLUCKHOHN

The Meaning of Culture

One of the most significant of all human characteristics is culture. By "culture" sociologists mean the entire way of life of a society, consisting of everything, material and nonmaterial, that human beings create— houses, arrows, coins, spacecraft, and clothing; laws, language, music, democracy, and myths.

No other animal has anything comparable to culture. All species have at least some capacity to learn, and this ability is quite highly developed among mammals. But in all other species, even other primates, most behavior is innate, programmed into the animal by its genes. In human beings, on the other hand, nearly all behavior, other than a few simple reflexes and drives, is learned. And what is learned is supplied by the culture into which we are born. It is this learning ability that makes our species so remarkable, for it frees us from rigid responses to the environment and enables us to create and develop an infinite variety of adaptations to the challenges and opportunities posed by our natural and social surroundings.

In this article, the late anthropologist Clyde Kluckhohn offers a classic analysis of culture and its overriding importance for human society, and thus for our survival.

Why do the Chinese dislike milk and milk products? Why would the Japanese die willingly in a Banzai charge that seemed senseless to Americans? Why do some nations trace descent through the father, others through the mother, still others through both parents? Not because different peoples have different instincts, not because they were destined by God or Fate to different habits, not because the weather is different in China and Japan and the United States. Sometimes shrewd common sense has an answer that is close to that of the anthropologist: "because they were brought up that way." By "culture" anthropology means the total life way of a people, the social legacy the individual acquires from his group. Or culture can be regarded as that part of the environment that is the creation of man.

This technical term has a wider meaning than the "culture" of history and literature. A humble cooking pot is as much a culture product as is a Beethoven sonata. In ordinary speech a man of culture is a man who can speak languages other than his own, who is familiar with history, literature, philosophy, or the fine arts. In some cliques that definition is still narrower. The cultured person is one who can talk about James Joyce, Scarlatti, and Picasso. To the anthropologist, however, to be human is to be cultured. There is culture in general, and then there are the specific cultures such as Russian, American, British, Hottentot, Inca. The general abstract notion serves to remind us that we cannot explain acts solely in terms of the biological properties of the people concerned, their individual past experience, and the immediate situation. The past experience of other men in the form of culture enters into almost every event. Each specific culture constitutes a kind of blueprint for all of life's activities.

One of the interesting things about human beings is that they try to understand themselves and their own behavior. While this has been particularly true of Europeans in recent times, there is no group which has not developed a scheme or schemes to explain man's actions. To the insistent human query "why?" the most exciting illumination anthropology has to offer is that of the concept of culture. Its explanatory importance is comparable to categories such as evolution in biology, gravity in physics, disease in medicine. A good deal of human behavior can be understood, and indeed predicted, if we know a people's design for living. Many acts are neither accidental nor due to personal peculiarities nor caused by supernatural forces nor simply mysterious. Even those of us who pride ourselves on our individualism follow most of the time a pattern not of our own making. We brush our teeth on arising. We put on pants—not a loincloth or a grass skirt. We eat three meals a day—not four or five or two. We sleep in a bed—not in a hammock or on a sheep pelt. I do not have to know the individual and his life history to be able to predict these and countless other regularities, including many in the thinking process, of all Americans who are not incarcerated in jails or hospitals for the insane.

To the American woman a system of plural wives seems "instinctively" abhorrent. She cannot understand how any woman can fail to be jealous and uncomfortable if she must share her husband with other women. She feels it "unnatural" to accept such a situation. On the other hand, a Koryak woman of Siberia, for example, would find it hard to understand how a woman could be so selfish and so undesirous of feminine companionship in the home as to wish to restrict her husband to one mate.

Some years ago I met in New York City a young man who did not speak a word of English and was obviously bewildered by American ways. By "blood" he was as American as you or I, for his parents had gone from Indiana to China as missionaries. Orphaned in infancy, he was reared by a Chinese family in a remote village. All who met him found him more Chinese than American. The facts of his blue eyes and light hair were less impressive than a Chinese style of gait, Chinese arm and hand movements, Chinese facial expression, and Chinese modes of thought. The biological heritage was American, but the cultural training had been Chinese. He returned to China.

Another example of another kind: I once knew a trader's wife in Arizona who took a somewhat devilish interest in producing a cultural reaction. Guests who came her way were often served delicious sandwiches filled with a meat that seemed to be neither chicken nor tuna fish yet was reminiscent of both. To queries she gave no reply until each had eaten his fill. She then explained that what they had eaten was not chicken, not tuna fish, but the rich, white flesh of freshly killed rattlesnakes. The response was instantaneous—vomiting, often violent vomiting. A biological process is caught in a cultural web.

A highly intelligent teacher with long and successful experience in the public schools of Chicago was finishing her first year in an Indian school. When asked how her Navaho pupils compared in intelligence with Chicago youngsters, she replied, "Well, I just don't know. Sometimes the Indians seem just as bright. At other times they just act like dumb animals. The other night we had a dance in the high school. I saw a boy who is one of the best students in my English class standing off by himself. So I took him over to a pretty girl and told them to dance. But they just stood there with their heads down. They wouldn't even say anything." I inquired if she knew whether or not they were members of the same clan. "What difference would that make?"

"How would you feel about getting into bed with your brother?" The teacher walked off in a huff, but, actually, the two cases were quite comparable in principle. To the Indian the type of bodily contact involved in our social dancing has a directly sexual connotation. The incest taboos between members of the same clan are as severe as between true brothers and sisters. The shame of the Indians at the suggestion that a clan brother and sister should dance and the indignation of the white teacher at the idea that she should share a bed with an adult brother represent equally nonrational responses, culturally standarized unreason.

All this does not mean that there is no such thing as raw human nature. The very fact that certain of the same institutions are found in all known societies indicates that at bottom all human beings are very much alike. The files of the Cross-Cultural Survey at Yale University are organized according to categories such as "marriage ceremonies," "life crisis rites," "incest taboos." At least seventy-five of these categories are represented in every single one of the hundreds of cultures analyzed. This is hardly surprising. The members of all human groups have about the same biological equipment. All men undergo the same poignant life experiences such as birth, helplessness, illness, old age, and death. The biological potentialities of the species are the blocks with which cultures are built. Some patterns of every culture crystallize around focuses provided by the inevitables of biology: the difference between the sexes, the presence of persons of different ages, the varying physical strength and skill of individuals. The facts of nature also limit culture forms. No culture provides patterns for jumping over trees or for eating iron ore.

There is thus "either-or" between nature and that special form of nurture called culture. Culture determinism is as onesided as biological determinism. The two factors are interdependent. Culture arises out of human nature, and its forms are restricted both by man's biology and by natural laws. It is equally true that culture channels biological processes—vomiting, weeping, fainting, sneezing, the daily habits of food intake and waste elimination. When a man eats, he is reacting to an internal "drive," namely, hunger contractions consequent upon the lowering of blood sugar, but his precise reaction to these internal stimuli cannot be predicted by physiological knowledge alone. Whether a healthy adult feels hungry twice, three times, or four times a day and the hours at which this feeling recurs is a question of culture. *What* he eats is of course limited by availability, but is also partly regulated by culture. It is a biological fact that some types of berries are poisonous; it is a cultural fact that, a few generations ago, most Americans considered tomatoes to be poisonous and refused to eat them. Such selective, discriminative use of the environment is characteristically cultural. In a still more general sense, too, the process of eating is channeled by culture. Whether a man eats to live, lives to eat, or merely eats and lives is only in part an individual matter, for there are also cultural trends. Emotions are physiological events. Certain situations will evoke fear in people from any culture. But sensations of pleasure, anger, and lust may be stimulated by cultural cues that would leave unmoved someone who has been reared in a different social tradition.

Except in the case of newborn babies and of individuals born with clear-cut structural or functional abnormalities we can observe innate endowments only as modified by cultural training. In a hospital in New Mexico where Zuñi Indian, Navaho Indian, and white American babies are born, it is possible to classify the newly arrived infants as unusually active, average, and quiet. Some babies from each "racial" group will fall into each category, though a higher proportion of the white babies will fall into the unusually active class. But if a Navaho baby, a Zuñi baby, and a white baby—all classified as unusually active at birth—are again observed at the age of two years, the Zuñi baby will no longer seem given to quick and restless activity—*as compared with the white child*—though he may seem so as compared with the other Zuñis of the same age. The Navaho child is likely to fall in between as contrasted with the Zuñi and the white, though he will probably still seem more active than the average Navaho youngster.

It was remarked by many observers in the Japanese relocation centers that Japanese who were born and brought up in this country, especially those who were reared apart from any large colony of Japanese, resemble in behavior their white neighbors much more closely than they do their own parents who were educated in Japan.

I have said "culture channels biological processes." It is more accurate to say "the biological functioning of individuals is modified if they have been trained in certain ways and not in others." Culture is not a disembodied force. It is created and transmitted by people. However, culture, like well-known concepts of the physical sciences, is a convenient abstraction. One never sees gravity. One sees bodies falling in regular ways. One never sees an electromagnetic field. Yet certain happenings that can be seen may be given a neat abstract formulation by assuming that the electromagnetic field exists. Similarly, one never sees culture as such. What is seen are the regularities in the behavior or artifacts of a group that has adhered to a common tradition. The regularities in style and technique of ancient Inca tapestries or stone axes from

Melanesian islands are due to the existence of mental blueprints for the group.

Culture is a *way* of thinking, feeling, believing. It is the group's knowledge stored up (in memories of men; in books and objects) for future use. We study the products of this "mental" activity: the overt behavior, the speech and gestures and activities of people, and the tangible results of these things such as tools, houses, cornfields, and what not. It has been customary in lists of "culture traits" to include such things as watches or lawbooks. This is a convenient way of thinking about them, but in the solution of any important problem we must remember that they, in themselves, are nothing but metals, paper, and ink. What is important is that some men know how to make them, others set a value on them, are unhappy without them, direct their activities in relation to them, or disregard them.

· · ·

Since culture is an abstraction, it is important not to confuse culture with society. A "society" refers to a group of people who interact more with each other than they do with other individuals—who cooperate with each other for the attainment of certain ends. You can see and indeed count the individuals who make up a society. A "culture" refers to the distinctive ways of life of such a group of people. Not all social events are culturally patterned. New types of circumstances arise for which no cultural solutions have as yet been devised.

A culture constitutes a storehouse of the pooled learning of the group. A rabbit starts life with some innate responses. He can learn from his own experience and perhaps from observing other rabbits. A human infant is born with fewer instincts and greater plasticity. His main task is to learn the answers that persons he will never see, persons long dead, have worked out. Once he has learned the formulas supplied by the culture of his group, most of his behavior becomes almost as automatic and unthinking as if it were instinctive. There is a tremendous amount of intelligence behind the making of a radio, but not much is required to learn to turn it on.

The members of all human societies face some of the same unavoidable dilemmas, posed by biology and other facts of the human situation. This is why the basic categories of all cultures are so similar. Human culture without language is unthinkable. No culture fails to provide for aesthetic expression and aesthetic delight. Every culture supplies standardized orientations toward the deeper problems, such as death. Every culture is designed to perpetuate the group and its solidarity, to meet the demands of individuals for an orderly way of life and for satisfaction of biological needs.

However, the variations on these basic themes are numberless. Some languages are built up out of twenty basic sounds, others out of forty. Nose plugs were considered beautiful by the predynastic Egyptians but are not by the modern French. Puberty is a biological fact. But one culture ignores it, another prescribes informal instructions about sex but no ceremony, a third has impressive rites for girls only, a fourth for boys and girls. In this culture, the first menstruation is welcomed as a happy, natural event; in that culture the atmosphere is full of dread and supernatural threat. Each culture dissects nature according to its own system of categories. The Navaho Indians apply the same word to the color of a robin's egg and to that of grass. A psychologist once assumed that this meant a difference in the sense organs, that Navahos didn't have the physiological equipment to distinguish "green" from "blue." However, when he showed them objects of the two colors and asked them if they were exactly the same colors, they looked at him with astonishment. His dream of discovering a new type of color blindness was shattered.

Every culture must deal with the sexual instinct. Some, however, seek to deny all sexual expression before marriage, whereas a Polynesian adolescent who was not promiscuous would be distinctly abnormal. Some cultures enforce lifelong monogamy, others, like our own, tolerate serial monogamy; in still other cultures, two or more women may be joined to one man or several men to a single woman. Homosexuality has been a permitted pattern in the Greco-Roman world, in parts of Islam, and in various primitive tribes. Large portions of the population of Tibet, and of Christendom at some places and periods, have practiced complete celibacy. To us marriage is first and foremost an arrangement between two individuals. In many more societies marriage is merely one facet of a complicated set of reciprocities, economic and otherwise, between two families or two clans.

The essence of the cultural process is selectivity. The selection is only exceptionally conscious and rational. Cultures are like Topsy. They just grew. Once, however, a way of handling a situation becomes institutionalized, there is ordinarily great resistance to change or deviation. When we speak of "our sacred beliefs," we mean of course that they are beyond criticism and that the person who suggests modification or abandonment must be punished. No person is emotionally indifferent to his culture. Certain cultural premises may become totally out of accord with a new factual situation. Leaders may recognize this and reject the old ways in theory. Yet their emotional loyalty continues in the face of reason because of the intimate conditionings of early childhood.

A culture is learned by individuals as the result of belonging to some particular group, and it constitutes that part of learned behavior which is shared with others. It is our social legacy, as contrasted with our organic heredity. It is one of the important factors which permits us to live together in an organized society, giving us ready-made solutions to our problems, helping us to predict the behavior of others, and permitting others to know what to expect of us.

Culture regulates our lives at every turn. From the moment we are born until we die there is, whether we are conscious of it or not, constant pressure upon us to follow certain types of behavior that other men have created for us. Some paths we follow willingly, others we follow because we know no other way, still others we deviate from or go back to most unwillingly. Mothers of small children know how unnaturally most of this comes to us—how little regard we have, until we are "culturalized," for the "proper" place, time, and manner for certain acts such as eating, excreting, sleeping, getting dirty, and making loud noises. But by more or less adhering to a system of related designs for carrying out all the acts of living, a group of men and women feel themselves linked together by a powerful chain of sentiments. Ruth Benedict gave an almost complete definition of the concept when she said, "Culture is that which binds men together."

It is true any culture is a set of techniques for adjusting both to the external environment and to other men. However, cultures create problems as well as solve them. If the lore of a people states that frogs are dangerous creatures, or that it is not safe to go about at night because of witches or ghosts, threats are posed which do not arise out of the inexorable facts of the external world. Cultures produce needs as well as provide a means of fulfilling them. There exists for every group culturally defined, acquired drives that may be more powerful in ordinary daily life than the biologically inborn drives. Many Americans, for example, will work harder for "success" than they will for sexual satisfaction.

Most groups elaborate certain aspects of their culture far beyond maximum utility or survival value. In other words, not all culture promotes physical survival. At times, indeed, it does exactly the opposite. Aspects of culture which once were adaptive may persist long after they have ceased to be useful. An analysis of any culture will disclose many features which cannot possibly be construed as adaptations to the total environment in which the group now finds itself. However, it is altogether likely that these apparently useless features represent survivals, with modifications through time, of cultural forms which were adaptive in one or another previous situation.

Any cultural practice must be functional or it will disappear before long. That is, it must somehow contribute to the survival of the society or to the adjustment of the individual. However, many cultural functions are not manifest but latent. A cowboy will walk three miles to catch a horse which he then rides one mile to the store. From the point of view of manifest function this is positively irrational. But the act has the latent function of maintaining the cowboy's prestige in the terms of his own subculture. One can instance the buttons on the sleeve of a man's coat, our absurd English spelling, the use of capital letters, and a host of other apparently nonfunctional customs. They serve mainly the latent function of assisting individuals to maintain their security by preserving continuity with the past and by making certain sectors of life familiar and predictable.

Every culture is a precipitate of history. In more than one sense history is a sieve. Each culture embraces those aspects of the past which, usually in altered form and with altered meanings, live on in the present. Discoveries and inventions, both material and ideological, are constantly being made available to a group through its historical contacts with other peoples or being created by its own members. However, only those that fit the total immediate situation in meeting the group's needs for survival or in promoting the psychological adjustment of individuals will become part of the culture. The process of culture building may be regarded as an addition to man's innate biological capacities, an addition providing instruments which enlarge, or may even substitute for, biological functions, and to a degree, compensating for biological limitations—as in ensuring that death does not always result in the loss to humanity of what the deceased has learned.

Culture is like a map. Just as a map isn't the territory but an abstract representation of a particular area, so also a culture is an abstract description of trends toward uniformity in the words, deeds, and artifacts of a human group. If a map is accurate and you can read it, you won't get lost; if you know a culture, you will know your way around in the life of a society.

Many educated people have the notion that culture applies only to exotic ways of life or to societies where relative simplicity and relative homogeneity prevail. Some sophisticated missionaries, for example, will use the anthropological conception in discussing the special modes of living of South Sea Islanders, but seem amazed at the idea that it could be applied equally to inhabitants of New York City. And social workers in Boston will talk about the culture of a colorful and well-knit immigrant group but boggle at applying it to the behavior of staff members in the social-service agency itself.

In the primitive society the correspondence between the habits of individuals and the customs of the community is ordinarily greater. There is probably some truth in what an old Indian once said, "In the old days there was no law; everybody did what was right." The primitive tends to find happiness in the fulfillment of intricately involuted cultural patterns; the modern more often tends to feel the pattern as repressive to his individuality. It is also true that in a complex stratified society there are numerous exceptions to generalizations made about the culture as a whole. It is necessary to study regional, class, and occupational subcultures. Primitive cultures have greater stability than modern cultures; they change—but less rapidly.

However, modern men also are creators and carriers of culture. Only in some respects are they influenced differently from primitives by culture. Moreover, there are such wide variations in primitive cultures that any black-and-white contrast between the primitive and the civilized is altogether fictitious. The distinction which is most generally true lies in the field of conscious philosophy.

The publication of Paul Radin's *Primitive Man as a Philosopher* did much toward destroying the myth that an abstract analysis of experience was a peculiarity of literate societies. Speculation and reflection upon the nature of the universe and of man's place in the total scheme of things have been carried out in every known culture. Every people has its characteristic set of "primitive postulates." It remains true that critical examination of basic premises and fully explicit systematization of philosophical concepts are seldom found at the nonliterate level. The written word is an almost essential condition for free and extended discussion of fundamental philosophic issues. Where dependence on memory exists, there seems to be an inevitable tendency to emphasize the correct perpetuation of the precious oral tradition. Similarly, while it is all too easy to underestimate the extent to which ideas spread without books, it is in general true that tribal or folk societies do not possess competing philosophical systems. The major exception to this statement is, of course, the case where part of the tribe becomes converted to one of the great proselytizing religions such as Christianity or Mohammedanism. Before contact with rich and powerful civilizations, primitive peoples seem to have absorbed new ideas piecemeal, slowly integrating them with the previously existing ideology. The abstract thought of nonliterate societies is ordinarily less self-critical, less systematic, nor so intricately elaborated in purely logical dimensions. Primitive thinking is more concrete, more implicit—perhaps more completely coherent than the philosophy of most individuals in large societies which have been influenced over long periods by disparate intellectual currents.

No participant in any culture knows all the details of the cultural map. The statement frequently heard that St. Thomas Aquinas was the last man to master all the knowledge of his society is intrinsically absurd. St. Thomas would have been hard put to make a pane of cathedral glass or to act as a midwife. In every culture there are what Ralph Linton has called "universals, alternatives, and specialties." Every Christian in the thirteenth century knew that it was necessary to attend mass, to go to confession, to ask the Mother of God to intercede with her Son. There were many other universals in the Christian culture of Western Europe. However, there were also alternative cultural patterns even in the realm of religion. Each individual had his own patron saint, and different towns developed the cults of different saints. The thirteenth-century anthropologist could have discovered the rudiments of Christian practice by questioning and observing whomever he happened to meet in Germany, France, Italy, or England. But to find out the details of the ceremonials honoring St. Hubert or St. Bridget he would have had to seek out certain individuals or special localities where these alternative patterns were practiced. Similarly, he could not learn about weaving from a professonal soldier or about canon law from a farmer. Such cultural knowledge belongs in the realm of the specialties, voluntarily chosen by the individual or ascribed to him by birth. Thus, part of a culture must be learned by everyone, part may be selected from alternative patterns, part applies only to those who perform the roles in the society for which these patterns are designed.

. . .

Cultures do not manifest themselves solely in observable customs and artifacts. No amount of questioning of any save the most articulate in the most self-conscious cultures will bring out some of the basic attitudes common to the members of the group. This is because these basic assumptions are taken so for granted that they normally do not enter into consciousness. This part of the cultural map must be inferred by the observer on the basis of consistencies in thought and action. Missionaries in various societies are often disturbed or puzzled because the natives do not regard "morals" and "sex code" as almost synonymous. The natives seem to feel that morals are concerned with sex just about as much as with eating—no less and no more. No society fails to have some restrictions on sexual behavior, but sex activity outside of marriage need not necessarily be furtive or attended with guilt. The Christian tradition has tended to assume that sex is inherently nasty as well as dangerous. Other cultures assume that sex in itself is not only natural but one of the good things of life, even though sex acts with certain persons under certain circumstances are forbidden. This is implicit culture, for the natives do not announce their premises. The missionaries would get further if they said, in effect, "Look, our morality starts from different assumptions. Let's talk about those assumptions," rather than ranting about "immorality."

A factor implicit in a variety of diverse phenomena may be generalized as an underlying cultural principle. For example, the Navaho Indians always leave part of the design in a pot, a basket, or a blanket unfinished. When a medicine man instructs an apprentice he always leaves a little bit of the story untold. This "fear of closure" is a recurrent theme in Navaho culture. Its influence may be detected in many contexts that have no explicit connection.

If the observed cultural behavior is to be correctly understood, the categories and presuppositions constituting the implicit culture must be worked out. The "strain toward consistency" which Sumner noted in the folkways and mores of all groups cannot be accounted for unless one grants a set of systematically interrelated implicit themes. For example, in American culture the themes of "effort and optimism," "the common man," "technology," and "virtuous materialism" have a functional interdependence, the origin of which is historically known.

The relationship between themes may be that of conflict. One may instance the competition between Jefferson's theory of democracy and Hamilton's "government by the rich, the wellborn, and the able." In other cases most themes may be integrated under a single dominant theme. In Negro cultures of West Africa the mainspring of social life is religion; in East Africa almost all cultural behavior seems to be oriented toward certain premises and categories centered on the cattle economy. If there be one master principle in the implicit culture, this is often called the "ethos" or Zeitgeist.

Every culture has organization as well as content. There is nothing mystical about this statement. One may compare ordinary experience. If I know that Smith, working alone, can shovel 10 cubic yards of dirt a day, Jones 12, and Brown 14, I would be foolish to predict that the three working together would move 36. The total might well be considerably more; it might be less. A whole is different from the sum of its parts. The same principle is familiar in athletic teams. A brilliant pitcher added to a nine may mean a pennant or may mean the cellar; it depends on how he fits in.

And so it is with cultures. A mere list of the behavioral and regulatory patterns of the implicit themes and categories would be like a map on which all mountains, lakes, and rivers were included—but not in their actual relationship to one another. Two cultures could have almost identical inventories and still be extremely different. The full significance of any single element in a culture design will be seen only when the element is viewed in the total matrix of its relationship to other elements. Naturally, this includes accent or emphasis, as well as position. Accent is manifested sometimes through frequency, sometimes through intensity. The indispensable importance of these questions of arrangement and emphasis may be driven home by an analogy. Consider a musical sequence made up of three notes. If we are told that the three notes in question are A, B, and G, we receive information which is fundamental. But it will not enable us to predict the type of sensation which the playing of this sequence is likely to evoke. We need many different sorts of relationship data. Are the notes to be played in that or some other order? What duration will each receive? How will the emphasis, if any, be distributed? We also need, of course, to know whether the instrument used is to be a piano or an accordion.

Cultures vary greatly in their degree of integration. Synthesis is achieved partly through the overt statement of the dominant conceptions, assumptions, and aspirations of the group in its religious lore, secular thought, and ethical code; partly through habitual but unconscious ways of looking at the stream of events, ways of begging certain questions. To the naïve participant in the culture these modes of categorizing, of dissecting experience along these planes and not others, are as much "given" as the regular sequence of daylight and darkness or the necessity of air, water, and food for life. Had Americans not thought in terms of money and the market system during the depression they would have distributed unsalable goods rather than destroyed them.

Every group's way of life, then, is a structure—not a haphazard collection of all the different physically possible and functionally effective patterns of belief and action. A culture is an interdependent system based upon linked premises and categories whose influence is greater, rather than less, because they are seldom put in words. Some degree of internal coherence which is felt rather than rationally constructed seems to be demanded by most of the participants in any culture. As Whitehead has remarked, "Human life is driven forward by its dim apprehension of notions too general for its existing language."

In sum, the distinctive way of life that is handed down as the social heritage of a people does more than supply a set of skills for making a living and a set of blueprints for human relations. Each different way of life makes its own assumptions about the ends and purposes of human existence, about what human beings have a right to expect from each other and the gods, about what constitutes a fulfillment or frustration. Some of these assumptions are made explicit in the lore of the folk; others are tacit premises which the observer must infer by finding consistent trends in word and deed.

QUESTIONS

1. What do sociologists mean by culture? Why is the concept of such importance in social science?

2. Why is culture superior to instinct as a response to the challenges of survival?

3. Can you identify some cultural differences between regions or groups within the United States?

HORACE MINER

Body Ritual Among the Nacirema

The anthropologist Ralph Linton once remarked that a fish would be aware of water only if it found itself on dry land. His point as it applies to human culture is that we are so used to our own particular social environment that we take it for granted, remaining almost oblivious even to some of the most distinctive features of our way of life.

One of the advantages of a sociological perspective on the world is that it trains us to become, as it were, outsiders in our own society and culture: we are enabled, at least to some extent, to see ourselves as others might, and to focus on aspects of our cultural reality that we might otherwise have overlooked. We would see ourselves most clearly, in fact, if we could step apart from our culture and view it with the same detachment and curiosity that a visiting anthropologist might apply to an unfamiliar and even exotic culture.

Horace Miner tries to achieve that kind of viewpoint in this whimsical article. The subject of his study is the Nacirema—"American" spelled backward—and his particular focus is the importance of the bathroom and personal hygiene in American society. (It is easy for us to overlook the fact that our concern with cleanliness is, from an historical or cross-cultural view, almost obsessive—such luxuries as bathrooms and deodorants have been unavailable to most people throughout history, and they remain so for much if not most of the world's population today.) Miner thus describes the Nacirema with the kind of mild surprise that we ourselves might reserve for a distant tribe.

Reproduced by permission of the American Anthropological Association from the *American Anthropologist*, 58:503–507, 1956.

The anthropologist has become so familiar with the diversity of ways in which different peoples behave in similar situations that he is not apt to be surprised by even the most exotic customs. In fact, if all of the logically possible combinations of behavior have not been found somewhere in the world, he is apt to suspect that they must be present in some yet undescribed tribe. This point has, in fact, been expressed with respect to clan organization by Murdock (1949:71). In this light, the magical beliefs and practices of the Nacirema present such unusual aspects that it seems desirable to describe them as an example of the extremes to which human behavior can go.

Professor Linton first brought the ritual of the Nacirema to the attention of anthropologists twenty years ago (1936:326), but the culture of this people is still very poorly understood. They are a North American group living in the territory between the Canadian Cree, the Yaqui and Tarahumare of Mexico, and the Carib and Arawak of the Antilles. Little is known of their origin, although tradition states that they came from the east. According to Nacirema mythology, their nation was originated by a culture hero, Notgnihsaw, who is otherwise known for two great feats of strength—the throwing of a piece of wampum across the river Pa-To-Mac and the chopping down of a cherry tree in which the Spirit of Truth resided.

Nacirema culture is characterized by a highly developed market economy which has evolved in a rich natural habitat. While much of the people's time is devoted to economic pursuits, a large part of the fruits of these labors and a considerable portion of the day are spent in ritual activity. The focus of this activity is the human body, the appearance and health of which loom as a dominant concern in the ethos of the people. While such a concern is certainly not unusual, its ceremonial aspects and associated philosophy are unique.

The fundamental belief underlying the whole system appears to be that the human body is ugly and that its natural tendency is to debility and disease. Incarcerated in such a body, man's only hope is to avert these characteristics through the use of the powerful influences of ritual and ceremony. Every household has one or more shrines devoted to this purpose. The more powerful individuals in the society have several shrines in their houses and, in fact, the opulence of a house is often referred to in terms of the number of such ritual centers it possesses. Most houses are of wattle and daub construction, but the shrine rooms of the more wealthy are walled with stone. Poorer families imitate the rich by applying pottery plaques to their shrine walls.

While each family has at least one such shrine, the rituals associated with it are not family ceremonies but are private and secret. The rites are normally only discussed with children, and then only during the period when they are being initiated into these mysteries. I was able, however, to establish sufficient rapport with the natives to examine these shrines and to have the rituals described to me.

The focal point of the shrine is a box or chest which is built into the wall. In this chest are kept the many charms and magical potions without which no native believes he could live. These preparations are secured from a variety of specialized practitioners. The most powerful of these are the medicine men, whose assistance must be rewarded with substantial gifts. However, the medicine men do not provide the curative potions for their clients, but decide what the ingredients should be and then write them down in an ancient and secret language. This writing is understood only by the medicine men and by the herbalists who, for another gift, provide the required charm.

The charm is not disposed of after it has served its purpose, but is placed in the charm-box of the household shrine. As these magical materials are specific for certain ills, and the real or imagined maladies of the people are many, the charm-box is usually full to overflowing. The magical packets are so numerous that people forget what their purposes were and fear to use them again. While the natives are very vague on this point, we can only assume that the idea in retaining all the old magical materials is that their presence in the charm-box, before which the body rituals are conducted, will in some way protect the worshipper.

Beneath the charm-box is a small font. Each day every member of the family, in succession, enters the shrine room, bows his head before the charm-box, mingles different sorts of holy water in the font, and proceeds with a brief rite of ablution. The holy waters are secured from the Water Temple of the community, where the priests conduct elaborate ceremonies to make the liquid ritually pure.

In the hierarchy of magical practitioners, and below the medicine men in prestige, are specialists whose designation is best translated "holy-mouth-men." The Nacirema have an almost pathological horror of and fascination with the mouth, the condition of which is believed to have a supernatural influence on all social relationships. Were it not for the rituals of the mouth, they believe that their teeth would fall out, their gums bleed, their jaws shrink, their friends desert them, and their lovers reject them. They also believe that a strong relationship exists between oral and moral characteristics. For example, there is a ritual ablution of the mouth for children which is supposed to improve their moral fiber.

The daily body ritual performed by everyone includes a mouth-rite. Despite the fact that these people are so punctilious about care of the mouth, this rite involves a practice which strikes the uninitiated stranger as revolting. It was reported to me that the ritual consists of inserting a small bundle of hog hairs into the mouth, along with certain magical powders, and then moving the bundle in a highly formalized series of gestures.

In addition to the private mouth-rite, the people seek out a holy-mouth-man once or twice a year. These practitioners have an impressive set of paraphernalia, consisting of a variety of augers, awls, probes, and prods. The use of these objects in the exorcism of the evils of the mouth involves almost unbelievable ritual torture of the client. The holy-mouth-man opens the client's mouth and, using the above mentioned tools, enlarges any holes which decay may have created in the teeth. Magical materials are put into these holes. If there are no naturally occurring holes in the teeth, large sections of one or more teeth are gouged out so that the supernatural substance can be applied. In the client's view, the purpose of these ministrations is to arrest decay and to draw friends. The extremely sacred and traditional character of the rite is evident in the fact that the natives return to the holy-mouth-men year after year, despite the fact that their teeth continue to decay.

It is to be hoped that, when a thorough study of the Nacirema is made, there will be careful inquiry into the personality structure of these people. One has but to watch the gleam in the eye of a holy-mouth-man, as he jabs an awl into an exposed nerve, to suspect that a certain amount of sadism is involved. If this can be established, a very interesting pattern emerges, for most of the population shows definite masochistic tendencies. It was to these that Professor Linton referred in discussing a distinctive part of the daily body ritual which is performed only by men. The part of the rite involves scraping and lacerating the surface of the face with a sharp instrument. Special women's rites are performed only four times during each lunar month, but what they lack in frequency is made up in barbarity. As part of this ceremony, women bake their heads in small ovens for about an hour. The theoretically interesting point is that what seems to be a preponderantly masochistic people have developed sadistic specialists.

The medicine men have an imposing temple, or *latipso*, in every community of any size. The more elaborate ceremonies required to treat very sick patients can only be performed at this temple. These ceremonies involve not only the thaumaturge but a permanent group of vestal maidens who move sedately about the temple chambers in distinctive costume and headdress.

The *latipso* ceremonies are so harsh that it is phenomenal that a fair proportion of the really sick natives who enter the temple ever recover. Small children whose indoctrination is still incomplete have been known to resist attempts to take them to the temple because "that is where you go to die." Despite this fact, sick adults are not only willing but eager to undergo the protracted ritual purification, if they can afford to do so. No matter how ill the supplicant or how grave the emergency, the guardians of many temples will not admit a client if he cannot give a rich gift to the custodian. Even after one has gained admission and survived the ceremonies, the guardians will not permit the neophyte to leave until he makes still another gift.

The supplicant entering the temple is first stripped of all his or her clothes. In everyday life the Nacirema avoids exposure of his body and its natural functions. Bathing and excretory acts are performed only in the secrecy of the household shrine, where they are ritualized as part of the body-rites. Psychological shock results from the fact that body secrecy is suddenly lost upon entry into the *latipso*. A man, whose own wife has never seen him in an excretory act, suddenly finds himself naked and assisted by a vestal maiden while he performs his natural functions into a sacred vessel. This sort of ceremonial treatment is necessitated by the fact that the excreta are used by a diviner to ascertain the course and nature of the client's sickness. Female clients, on the other hand, find their naked bodies are subjected to the scrutiny, manipulation, and prodding of the medicine men.

Few supplicants in the temple are well enough to do anything but lie on their hard beds. The daily ceremonies, like the rites of the holy-mouth-men, involve discomfort and torture. With ritual precision, the vestals awaken their miserable charges each dawn and roll them about on their beds of pain while performing ablutions, in the formal movements of which the maidens are highly trained. At other times they insert magic wands into the supplicant's mouth or force him to eat substances which are supposed to be healing. From time to time the medicine men come to their clients and jab magically treated needles into their flesh. The fact that these temple ceremonies may not cure, and may even kill the neophyte, in no way decreases the people's faith in the medicine men.

There remains one other kind of practitioner, known as a "listener." This witch-doctor has the power to exorcise the devils that lodge in the heads of people who have been bewitched. The Nacirema believe that parents bewitch their own children. Mothers are particularly suspected of putting a curse on children while teaching them the secret body rituals. The counter-magic of the witch-doctor is unusual in its lack of ritual. The patient simply tells the "listener" all his troubles and fears, beginning with the earliest difficulties he can remember. The memory displayed by the Nacirema in these exorcism sessions is truly remarkable. It is not uncommon for the patient to bemoan the rejection he felt upon being weaned as a babe, and a few individuals even see their troubles going back to the traumatic effects of their own birth.

. . .

Our review of the ritual life of the Nacirema has certainly shown them to be a magic-ridden people. It is hard to understand how they have managed to exist so long under the burdens which they have imposed upon themselves. But even such exotic customs as these take on real meaning when they are viewed with the insight provided by Malinowski when he wrote (1948:70):

> Looking from far and above, from our high places of safety in the developed civilization, it is easy to see all the crudity and irrelevance of magic. But without its power and guidance early man could not have mastered his practical difficulties as he has done, nor could man have advanced to the higher stages of civilization.

QUESTIONS

1. Why is Miner's presentation more effective than if he had simply written a matter-of-fact account?

2. We take our bathrooms, dentists, and hospitals for granted, although they would be matters of great curiosity to the millions of people elsewhere in the world who are unfamiliar with them. Can you think of any particularly distinctive American cultural traits that would surprise outsiders?

3. Using Miner's approach, prepare a short account of some other Nacirema traits.

References

Linton, Ralph. 1936. *The Study of Man.* New York, D. Appleton-Century Co.

Malinowski, Bronislaw. 1948. *Magic, Science, and Religion.* Glencoe, The Free Press.

Murdock, George P. 1949. *Social Structure.* New York, The Macmillan Co.

MARVIN HARRIS

India's Sacred Cow

The cultural practices of other people often seem strange, irrational, and even inexplicable to outsiders. In fact, the very members of the culture in question may be unable to give a rationally satisfying explanation of why they behave as they do: they may respond, perhaps, that the gods wish it so, or that "it is always done that way." Yet it is a fundamental assumption of social science that all human behavior, no matter how peculiar or even bizarre it may appear, can be explained.

One of the more apparently perplexing cultural traits in the modern world is the attitude of most people in India toward cows: Hindus regard the animals as sacred, and will not kill or eat them. In a nation where the vast majority of the people are hungry and malnourished, an exploding population of cows wanders freely through both rural areas and city streets, undisturbed by the millions of hungry—even starving—humans who surround them. Why?

In this article, Marvin Harris suggests a plausible answer. He maintains that Hindu cow-worship and a multitude of other cultural practices around the world can be understood through an ecological analysis: in other words, the practices must be explained in terms of the total environment—social, technological, and natural—in which they exist.

Reprinted with permission from *Human Nature* Magazine, copyright © 1978 by Human Nature, Inc.

News photographs that came out of India during the famine of the late 1960s showed starving people stretching out bony hands to beg for food while sacred cattle strolled behind them undisturbed. The Hindu, it seems, would rather starve to death than eat his cow or even deprive it of food. The cattle appear to browse unhindered through urban markets eating an orange here, a mango there, competing with people for meager supplies of food.

By Western standards, spiritual values seem more important to Indians than life itself. Specialists in food habits around the world like Fred Simoons at the University of California at Davis consider Hinduism an irrational ideology that compels people to overlook abundant, nutritious foods for scarcer, less healthful foods.

What seems to be an absurd devotion to the mother cow pervades Indian life. Indian wall calendars portray beautiful young women with bodies of fat white cows, often with milk jetting from their teats into sacred shrines.

Cow worship even carries over into politics. In 1966, a crowd of 120,000 people, led by holy men, demonstrated in front of the Indian House of Parliament in support of the All-Party Cow Protection Campaign Committee. In Nepal, the only contemporary Hindu kingdom, cow slaughter is severely punished. As one story goes, the car driven by an official of a United States agency struck and killed a cow. In order to avoid the international incident that would have occurred when the official was arrested for murder, the Nepalese magistrate concluded that the cow had committed suicide.

Many Indians agree with Western assessments of the Hindu reverence for their cattle, the zebu, or *Bos indicus*, a large-humped species prevalent in Asia and Africa. M. N. Srinivas, an Indian anthropologist states: "Orthodox Hindu opinion regards the killing of cattle with abhorrence, even though the refusal to kill the vast number of useless cattle which exists in India today is detrimental to the nation." Even the Indian Ministry of Information formerly maintained that "the large animal population is more a liability than an asset in view of our land resources." Accounts from many different sources point to the same conclusion: India, one of the world's great civilizations, is being strangled by its love for the cow.

The easy explanation for India's devotion to the cow, the one most Westerners and Indians would offer, is that cow worship is an integral part of Hinduism. Religion is somehow good for the soul, even if it sometimes fails the body. Religion orders the cosmos and explains our place in the universe. Religious beliefs, many would claim, have existed for thousands of years and have a life of their own. They are not understandable in scientific terms.

But all this ignores history. There is more to be said for cow worship than is immediately apparent. The earliest Vedas, the Hindu sacred texts from the Second Millennium B.C., do not prohibit the slaughter of cattle. Instead, they ordain it as a part of sacrificial rites. The early Hindus did not avoid the flesh of cows and bulls; they ate it at ceremonial feasts presided over by Brahman priests. Cow worship is a relatively recent development in India; it evolved as the Hindu religion developed and changed.

This evolution is recorded in royal edicts and religious texts written during the last 3,000 years of Indian history. The Vedas from the First Millennium B.C. contain contradictory passages, some referring to ritual slaughter and others to a strict taboo on beef consumption. A. N. Bose, in *Social and Rural Economy of Northern India 600, BC.–200 A.D.,* concludes that many of the sacred-cow passages were incorporated into the texts by priests in a later period.

By 200 A.D. the status of Indian cattle had undergone a spiritual transformation. The Brahman priesthood exhorted the population to venerate the cow and forbade them to abuse it or to feed on it. Religious feasts involving the ritual slaughter and consumption of livestock were eliminated and meat eating was restricted to the nobility.

By 1000 A.D., all Hindus were forbidden to eat beef. Ahimsa, the Hindu belief in the unity of all life, was the spiritual justification for this restriction. But it is difficult to ascertain exactly when this change occurred. An important event that helped to shape the modern complex was the Islamic invasion, which took place in the Eighth Century A.D. Hindus may have found it politically expedient to set themselves off from the invaders, who were beefeaters, by emphasizing the need to prevent the slaughter of their sacred animals. Thereafter, the cow taboo assumed its modern form and began to function much as it does today.

The place of the cow in modern India is every place— on posters, in the movies, in brass figures, in stone and wood carvings, on the streets, in the fields. The cow is a symbol of health and abundance. It provides the milk that Indians consume in the form of yogurt and ghee (clarified butter), which contribute subtle flavors to much spicy Indian food.

This, perhaps, is the practical role of the cow, but cows provide less than half the milk produced in India. Most cows in India are not dairy breeds. In most regions, when an Indian farmer wants a steady, high-quality source of milk he usually invests in a female water buffalo. In India the water buffalo is the specialized dairy breed because its milk has a higher butterfat content than zebu milk. Although the farmer milks his zebu cows, the milk is merely a by-product.

More vital than zebu milk to South Asian farmers are zebu calves. Male calves are especially valued because from bulls come oxen which are the mainstay of the Indian agricultural system.

Small, fast oxen drag wooden plows through late-spring fields when monsoons have dampened the dry, cracked earth. After harvest, the oxen break the grain from the stalk by stomping through mounds of cut wheat and rice. For rice cultivation in irrigated fields, the male water buffalo is preferred (it pulls better in deep mud), but for most other crops, including rainfall rice, wheat, sorghum, and millet, and for transporting goods and people to and from town, a team of oxen is preferred. The ox is the Indian peasant's tractor, thresher and family car combined; the cow is the factory that produces the ox.

If draft animals instead of cows are counted, India appears to have too few domesticated ruminants, not too many. Since each of the 70 million farms in India requires a draft team, it follows that Indian peasants should use 140 million animals in the fields. But there are only 83 million oxen and male water buffalo on the subcontinent, a shortage of 30 million draft teams.

In other regions of the world, joint ownership of draft animals might overcome a shortage, but Indian agriculture is closely tied to the monsoon rains of late spring and summer. Field preparation and planting must coincide with the rain, and a farmer must have his animals ready to plow when the weather is right. When the farmer without a draft team needs bullocks most, his neighbors are all using theirs. Any delay in turning the soil drastically lowers production.

Because of this dependence on draft animals, loss of the family oxen is devastating. If a beast dies, the farmer must borrow money to buy or rent an ox at interest rates so high that he ultimately loses his land. Every year foreclosures force thousands of poverty-stricken peasants to abandon the countryside for the overcrowded cities.

If a family is fortunate enough to own a fertile cow, it will be able to rear replacements for a lost team and thus survive until life returns to normal. If, as sometimes happens, famine leads a family to sell its cow and ox team, all ties to agriculture are cut. Even if the family survives, it has no way to farm the land, no oxen to work the land, and no cows to produce oxen.

The prohibition against eating meat applies to the flesh of cows, bulls, and oxen, but the cow is the most sacred because it can produce the other two. The peasant whose cow dies is not only crying over a spiritual loss but over the loss of his farm as well.

Religious laws that forbid the slaughter of cattle promote the recovery of the agricultural system from the dry Indian winter and from periods of drought. The monsoon, on which all agriculture depends, is erratic. Sometimes it arrives early, sometimes late, sometimes not at all. Drought has struck large portions of India time and again in this century, and Indian farmers and the zebus are accustomed to these natural disasters. Zebus can pass weeks on end with little or no food and water. Like camels, they store both in their humps and recuperate quickly with only a little nourishment.

During droughts the cows often stop lactating and become barren. In some cases the condition is permanent but often it is only temporary. If barren animals were summarily eliminated, as Western experts in animal husbandry have suggested, cows capable of recovery would be lost along with those entirely debilitated. By keeping alive the cows that can later produce oxen, religious laws against cow slaughter assure the recovery of the agricultural system from the greatest challenge it faces—the failure of the monsoon.

The local Indian governments aid the process of recovery by maintaining homes for barren cows. Farmers reclaim any animal that calves or begins to lactate. One police station in Madras collects strays and pastures them in a field adjacent to the station. After a small fine is paid, a cow is returned to its rightful owner when the owner thinks the cow shows signs of being able to reproduce.

During the hot, dry spring months most of India is like a desert. Indian farmers often complain they cannot feed their livestock during this period. They maintain cattle by letting them scavenge on the sparse grass along the roads. In the cities cattle are encouraged to scavenge near food stalls to supplement their scant diet. These are the wandering cattle tourists report seeing throughout India.

Westerners expect shopkeepers to respond to these intrusions with the deference due a sacred animal; instead, their response is a string of curses and the crack of a long bamboo pole across the beast's back or a poke at its genitals. Mahatma Gandhi was well aware of the treatment sacred cows (and bulls and oxen) received in India. "How we bleed her to take the last drop of milk from her. How we starve her to emaciation, how we ill-treat the calves, how we deprive them of their portion of milk, how cruelly we treat the oxen, how we castrate them, how we beat them, how we overload them."

Oxen generally receive better treatment than cows. When food is in short supply, thrifty Indian peasants feed their working bullocks and ignore their cows, but rarely do they abandon the cows to die. When cows are sick, farmers worry over them as they would over members of the family and nurse them as if they were children. When the rains return and when the fields are harvested, the farmers again feed their cows regularly and reclaim their

abandoned animals. The prohibition against beef consumption is a form of disaster insurance for all India.

Western agronomists and economists are quick to protest that all the functions of the zebu cattle can be improved with organized breeding programs, cultivated pastures, and silage. Because stronger oxen would pull the plow faster, they could work multiple plots of land, allowing farmers to share their animals. Fewer healthy, well-fed cows could provide Indians with more milk. But pastures and silage require arable land, land needed to produce wheat and rice.

A look at Western cattle farming makes plain the cost of adopting advanced technology in Indian agriculture. In a study of livestock production in the United States, David Pimentel of the College of Agriculture and Life Sciences at Cornell University found that 91 percent of the cereal, legume, and vegetable protein suitable for human consumption is consumed by livestock. Approximately three quarters of the arable land in the United States is devoted to growing food for livestock. In the production of meat and milk, American ranchers use enough fossil fuel to equal more than 82 million barrels of oil annually.

Indian cattle do not drain the system in the same way. In a 1971 study of livestock in West Bengal, Stewart Odend'hal of the University of Missouri found that Bengalese cattle ate only the inedible remains of subsistence crops—rice straw, rice hulls, the tops of sugar cane, and mustard-oil cake. Cattle graze in the fields after harvest and eat the remains of crops left on the ground; they forage for grass and weeds on the roadsides. The food for zebu cattle costs the human population virtually nothing. "Basically," Odend'hal says, "the cattle convert items of little direct human value into products of immediate utility."

In addition to plowing the fields and producing milk, the zebus produce dung, which fires the hearths and fertilizes the fields of India. Much of the estimated 800 million tons of manure produced annually is collected by the farmers' children as they follow the family cows and bullocks from place to place. And when the children see the droppings of another farmer's cattle along the road, they pick those up also. Odend'hal reports that the system operates with such high efficiency that the children of West Bengal recover nearly 100 percent of the dung produced by their livestock.

From 40 to 70 percent of all manure produced by Indian cattle is used as fuel for cooking; the rest is returned to the fields as fertilizer. Dried dung burns slowly, cleanly, and with low heat—characteristics that satisfy the household needs of Indian women. Staples like curry and rice can simmer for hours. While the meal slowly cooks over an unattended fire, the women of the household can do other chores. Cow chips, unlike firewood, do not scorch as they burn.

It is estimated that the dung used for cooking fuel provides the energy-equivalent of 43 million tons of coal. At current prices, it would cost India an extra 1.5 billion dollars in foreign exchange to replace the dung with coal. And if the 350 million tons of manure that are being used as fertilizer were replaced with commercial fertilizers, the expense would be even greater. Roger Revelle of the University of California at San Diego has calculated that 89 percent of the energy used in Indian agriculture (the equivalent of about 140 million tons of coal) is provided by local sources. Even if foreign loans were to provide the money, the capital outlay necessary to replace the Indian cow with tractors and fertilizers for the fields, coal for the fires, and transportation for the family would probably warp international financial institutions for years.

Instead of asking the Indians to learn from the American model of industrial agriculture, American farmers might learn energy conservation from the Indians. Every step in an energy cycle results in a loss of energy to the system. Like a pendulum that slows a bit with each swing, each transfer of energy from sun to plants, plants to animals, and animals to human beings involves energy losses. Some systems are more efficient than others; they provide a higher percentage of the energy inputs in a final, useful form. Seventeen percent of all energy zebus consume is returned in the form of milk, traction and dung. American cattle raised on Western range land return only 4 percent of the energy they consume.

But the American system is improving. Based on techniques pioneered by Indian scientists, at least one commercial firm in the United States is reported to be building plants that will turn manure from cattle feedlots into combustible gas. When organic matter is broken down by anaerobic bacteria, methane gas and carbon dioxide are produced. After the methane is cleansed of the carbon dioxide, it is available for the same purposes as natural gas—cooking, heating, electricity generation. The company constructing the biogasification plant plans to sell its product to a gas-supply company, to be piped through the existing distribution system. Schemes similar to this one could make cattle ranches almost independent of utility and gasoline companies, for methane can be used to run trucks, tractors, and cars as well as to supply heat and electricity. The relative energy self-sufficiency that the Indian peasant has achieved is a goal American farmers and industry are now striving for.

Studies like Odend'hal's understate the efficiency of the Indian cow, because dead cows are used for purposes that Hindus prefer not to acknowledge. When a cow dies, an Untouchable, a member of one of the lowest ranking castes in India, is summoned to haul away the carcass. Higher castes consider the body of the dead cow polluting; if they do handle it, they must go through a rite of purification.

Untouchables first skin the dead animal and either tan the skin themselves or sell it to a leather factory. In the privacy of their homes, contrary to the teachings of Hinduism, untouchable castes cook the meat and eat it. Indians of all castes rarely acknowledge the existence of these practices to non-Hindus, but most are aware that beefeating takes place. The prohibition against beefeating restricts consumption by the higher castes and helps distribute animal protein to the poorest sectors of the population that otherwise would have no source of these vital nutrients.

Untouchables are not the only Indians who consume beef. Indian Muslims and Christians are under no restriction that forbids them beef, and its consumption is legal in many places. The Indian ban on cow slaughter is state, not national, law and not all states restrict it. In many cities, such as New Delhi, Calcutta, and Bombay, legal slaughterhouses sell beef to retail customers and to the restaurants that serve steak.

If the caloric value of beef and the energy costs involved in the manufacture of synthetic leather were included in the estimates of energy, the calculated efficiency of Indian livestock would rise considerably.

As well as the system works, experts often claim that its efficiency can be further improved. Alan Heston, an economist at the University of Pennsylvania, believes that Indians suffer from an overabundance of cows simply because they refuse to slaughter the excess cattle. India could produce at least the same number of oxen and the same quantities of milk and manure with 30 million fewer cows. Heston calculates that only 40 cows are necessary to maintain a population of 100 bulls and oxen. Since India averages 70 cows for every 100 bullocks, the difference, 30 million cows, is expendable.

What Heston fails to note is that sex ratios among cattle in different regions of India vary tremendously, indicating that adjustments in the cow population do take place. Along the Ganges River, one of the holiest shrines of Hinduism, the ratio drops to 47 cows for every 100 male animals. This ratio reflects the preference for dairy buffalo in the irrigated sectors of the Gangetic Plains. In nearby Pakistan, in contrast, where cow slaughter is permitted, the sex ratio is 60 cows to 100 oxen.

Since the sex ratios among cattle differ greatly from region to region and do not even approximate the balance that would be expected if no females were killed, we can assume that some culling of herds does take place; Indians do adjust their religious restrictions to accommodate ecological realities.

They cannot kill a cow but they can tether an old or unhealthy animal until it has starved to death. They cannot slaughter a calf but they can yoke it with a large wooden triangle so that when it nurses it irritates the mother's udder and gets kicked to death. They cannot ship their animals to the slaughterhouse but they can sell them to Muslims, closing their eyes to the fact that the Muslims will take the cattle to the slaughterhouse.

These violations of the prohibition against cattle slaughter strengthen the premise that cow worship is a vital part of Indian culture. The practice arose to prevent the population from consuming the animal on which Indian agriculture depends. During the First Millennium B.C., the Ganges Valley became one of the most densely populated regions of the world.

Where previously there had been only scattered villages, many towns and cities arose and peasants farmed every available acre of land. Kingsley Davis, a population expert at the University of California at Berkeley, estimates that by 300 B.C. between 50 million and 100 million people were living in India. The forested Ganges Valley became a windswept semidesert and signs of ecological collapse appeared; droughts and floods became commonplace, erosion took away the rich topsoil, farms shrank as population increased, and domesticated animals became harder and harder to maintain.

It is probable that the elimination of meat eating came about in a slow, practical manner. The farmers who decided not to eat their cows, who saved them for procreation to produce oxen, were the ones who survived the natural disasters. Those who ate beef lost the tools with which to farm. Over a period of centuries, more and more farmers probably avoided beef until an unwritten taboo came into existence.

Only later was the practice codified by the priesthood. While Indian peasants were probably aware of the role of cattle in their society, strong sanctions were necessary to protect zebus from a population faced with starvation. To remove temptation, the flesh of cattle became taboo and the cow became sacred.

The sacredness of the cow is not just an ignorant belief that stands in the way of progress. Like all concepts of the sacred and the profane, this one affects the physical world; it defines the relationships that are important for the maintenance of Indian society.

Indians have the sacred cow; we have the "sacred" car and the "sacred" dog. It would not occur to us to propose the elimination of automobiles and dogs from our society without carefully considering the consequences, and we should not propose the elimination of zebu cattle without first understanding their place in the social order of India.

Human society is neither random nor capricious. The regularities of thought and behavior called culture are the principal mechanisms by which we human beings adapt to the world around us. Practices and beliefs can be rational or irrational, but a society that fails to adapt to its environment is doomed to extinction. Only those societies that draw the necessities of life from their surroundings without destroying those surroundings, inherit the earth. The West has much to learn from the great antiquity of Indian civilization, and the sacred cow is an important part of that lesson.

QUESTIONS

1. Why did American Indians not worship their buffalo, and Asian Indians not slaughter their cows?

2. Make a list of American cultural practices that might seem strange to outsiders (or even, on reflection, to yourself). Then try to find explanations (not necessarily ecological) for them.

3. Various practices that directly or indirectly limit population growth—such as birth control, abortion, and homosexuality—are far more socially acceptable in the modern United States than they were in the past. Provide an ecological explanation. Does this explanation seem adequate, or might other factors be involved?

HERBERT J. GANS

Values in the News

Innumerable events happen every second of the day, yet only a tiny fraction of these become "news." The content of the news is, in fact, determined by a complex process of selection, in which the mass media—particularly TV, radio, and newspapers—accept some items and reject others in accordance with social conceptions about what is newsworthy and what is not.

Social values—those generally shared ideas about what is good, right, and desirable—strongly influence not only the content of the news but also the way it is interpreted and presented. Herbert Gans gives some examples of this phenomenon: welfare programs are typically described as subject to "waste," whereas military expenditures are said to face "cost overruns"; the president "arrives" in one place, whereas a black militant may be described as "turning up" somewhere else.

In his article, Gans identifies some of the values that appear to underlie the selection and presentation of the news in the United States—values that, in turn, tell us a great deal about American culture itself.

Journalists try hard to be objective, but neither they nor anyone else can in the end proceed without values. Furthermore, reality judgments are never altogether divorced from values. The judgment that the president and leading public officials represent the nation, for example, carries with it an acceptance of, if not a preference for, this state of affairs; otherwise, stories which investigate whether the president does, in fact, represent the nation would be more numerous.

The values in the news are rarely explicit and must be found between the lines—in what actors and activities are reported or ignored, and in how they are described. If a news story deals with activities which are generally considered undesirable and whose descriptions contain negative connotations, then the story implicitly expresses a value about what is desirable. In the process, the news also assumes a consensus about values that may not exist, for it reminds the audience of values that are being violated and assumes that the audience shares these values. When a story reports that a politician has been charged with corruption, it suggests, *sotto voce*, that corruption is bad and that politicians should be honest. Much news is about the violation of values; crime and disasters are not reported because these phenomena are desirable, which is why journalists and audiences alike speak of bad news.

. . .

The list that follows is limited to the enduring values I have found in the news over the last two decades, although all are probably of far more venerable vintage; obviously, it includes those which this inferrer, bringing his own values to the task, has found most visible and important. The list does not claim to be complete; and since I undertook no quantitative analyses, it does not suggest which values appear most frequently.

The methods by which I identified the values were impressionistic; the values really emerged from continual scrutiny of the news over a long time. Some became apparent from . . . the ways actors and activities are described, the tones in which stories are written, told, or filmed, and the connotations that accrue to commonly used nouns and adjectives, especially if neutral terms are available but not used. When years ago the news reported that Stokely Carmichael had "turned up" somewhere, while the president had, on the same day, "arrived" somewhere else; or when another story pointed out that a city was "plagued by labor problems," the appropriate values were not difficult to discern, if only because neutral terms were available but were not used. However, sometimes neutral terms are simply not available. The news could have called the young men who refused to serve in the Vietnam War draft evaders, dodgers, or resisters, but it rarely used the last term. . . .

Enduring Values in the News

The enduring values I want to discuss can be grouped into eight clusters: ethnocentrism, altruistic democracy, responsible capitalism, small-town pastoralism, individualism, moderatism, social order, and national leadership. These last two are more striking than the rest and will therefore be described in greater detail. There are many others, of course, which I shall leave out either for reasons of space or because they are taken for granted, even though they are values. Among these, for example, are the desirability of economic prosperity; the undesirability of war . . . the virtues of family, love, and friendship; and the ugliness of hate and prejudice. The news often supports the kinds of values sometimes unfairly belittled as "motherhood values."

Ethnocentrism

Like the news of other countries, American news values its own nation above all, even though it sometimes disparages blatant patriotism. This ethnocentrism comes through most explicitly in foreign news, which judges other countries by the extent to which they live up to or imitate American practices and values, but it also underlies domestic news. Obviously, the news contains many stories that are critical of domestic conditions, but these conditions are almost always treated as deviant cases, with the implication that American ideals, at least, remain viable. The Watergate scandals were usually ascribed to a small group of power-hungry politicians, and beyond that, to the "Imperial Presidency"—but with the afterthought, particularly following Richard Nixon's resignation, that nothing was fundamentally wrong with American democracy even if reforms were needed.

The clearest expression of ethnocentrism, in all countries, appears in war news. While reporting the Vietnam War, the news media described the North Vietnamese and the National Liberation Front as "the enemy," as if they were the enemy of the news media. Similarly, weekly casualty stories reported the number of Americans killed, wounded, or missing, and the number of South Vietnamese killed; but the casualties on the other side were impersonally described as "the Communist death toll" or the "body count."

Again, as in war reporting everywhere, the committing of atrocities, in this case by Americans, did not get into the news very often, and then only toward the end of the war. Seymour Hersh, the reporter credited with exposing the Mylai massacre, had considerable difficulty selling the story until the evidence was incontrovertible. The end of the war in Vietnam was typically headlined as "the Fall of South Vietnam," with scarcely a recognition that by other values, it could also be considered a liberation, or in neutral terminology, a change in governments.

Altruistic Democracy

While foreign news suggests quite explicitly that democracy is superior to dictatorship, and the more so if it follows American forms, domestic news is more specific, indicating how American democracy should perform by its frequent attention to deviations from an unstated ideal, evident in stories about corruption, conflict, protest, and bureaucratic malfunctioning. That ideal may be labeled altruistic democracy because, above all, the news implies that politics should follow a course based on the public interest and public service.

The news tends to treat politics per se as a contest, identifying winners and losers more than heroes and villains. Although the news has little patience for losers, it insists that both winners and losers should be scrupulously honest, efficient, and dedicated to acting in the public interest. Financial corruption is always news, as is nepotism, patronage appointments, logrolling, and "deals" in general. Decisions based, or thought to be based, on either self-interest or partisan concerns thus continue to be news whenever they occur, even though they long ago ceased to be novel events.

Politicians, politics, and democracy are also expected to be meritocratic; the regular activities of political machines are regularly exposed, and "machine" itself is a pejorative term. Although the news therefore regards civil-service officials more highly than "political appointees," the former are held to a very high standard of efficiency and performance; as a result, any deviant bureaucratic behavior becomes newsworthy. "Waste" is always an evil, whatever the amount; the mass of paperwork entailed by bureaucracy is a frequent story, and the additional paperwork generated by attempts to reduce the amount of paperwork is a humorous item that has appeared in the news with regularity over the years. Officials, whether elected or appointed, are also expected to be spartan in their tastes; consequently, in 1977, Secretary of H. E. W. Joseph Califano got into the news when he hired a chef for his official dining room. The story lasted longer than a concurrent report that he had hired a combination bodyguard-office manager, at almost four times the cook's salary.

The same high standards apply to citizens, however.

Citizens should participate; and "grassroots activity" is one of the most complimentary terms in the vocabulary of the news, particularly when it takes place to foil politicians or bureaucrats, or to eliminate the need for government action. Ideally, citizens should help themselves without having to resort to government aid, and occasionally stories of such an occurrence suggest a revival of a past and now extinct tradition. As a result, the news seems to imply that the democratic ideal against which it measures reality is that of the rural town meeting—or rather, of a romanticized version of it. Citizen participation should also be as unselfish as that of politicians. Organized lobbying and the formation of pressure groups in behalf of citizens' self-interest is still reported in suspect tones, though not as suspect as when corporate lobbyists are covered.

The support for altruism correlates with an emphasis on what one might call the official norms of the American polity, which are derived largely from the Constitution. Consequently, the news endorses, or sets up as a standard, the formal norms of democracy and the formal structures of democratic institutions as established by the Founding Fathers. Concurrently, it treats as suspect the informal norms and structures that have developed in the polity to allocate power and resources; in effect, the news defends democratic theory against an almost inevitably inferior democratic practice.

In the process, the news keeps track of the violations of official norms, but it does so selectively. Over the years, the news has been perhaps most concerned with freedom of the press and related civil liberties; even recurring local violations, by school boards which censor library shelves, have often become national news. Violations of the civil liberties of radicals, of due process, habeas corpus, and other constitutional protections, particularly for criminals, are less newsworthy. . . .

While—and perhaps because—the news consistently reports political and legal failures to achieve altruistic and official democracy, it concerns itself much less with the economic barriers that obstruct the realization of the ideal. Of course, the news is aware of candidates who are millionaires or who obtain substantial amounts of corporate or union campaign money, but it is less conscious of the relationship between poverty and powerlessness, or even of the difficulty that Americans of median income have in obtaining political access. . . .

The relative inattention to economic obstacles to democracy stems from the assumption that the polity and the economy are separate and independent of each other. Under ideal conditions, one is not supposed to affect or interfere with the other, although typically, government intervention in the economy is more newsworthy and serious than private industry's intervention in government. Accordingly, the news rarely notes the extent of public subsidy of private industry, and it continues to describe firms and institutions which are completely or partly subsidized by government funds as private—for example, Lockheed, many charitable organizations, and most privately run universities.

Responsible Capitalism

The underlying posture of the news toward the economy resembles that taken toward the polity: an optimistic faith that in the good society, businessmen and women will compete with each other in order to create increased prosperity for all, but that they will refrain from unreasonable profits and gross exploitation of workers or customers. Bigness is no more a virtue in business or union organization than in government, so that the small and family-owned firm is still sometimes presented as the ideal. While monopoly is clearly evil, there is little explicit or implicit criticism of the oligopolistic nature of much of today's economy. Unions and consumer organizations are accepted as countervailing pressures on business (although the former much less so than the latter), and strikes are frequently judged negatively, especially if they inconvenience "the public," contribute to inflation, or involve violence.

Economic growth is always a positive phenomenon, unless it brings about inflation or environmental pollution, leads to the destruction of a historic landmark, or puts craftsmen or craftswomen out of work. In the past, when anchormen gave the stock market report, even the most detached ones looked cheerful when the market had had a good day, assuming this to be of universal benefit to the nation and the economy.

Like politicians, business officials are expected to be honest and efficient; but while corruption and bureaucratic misbehavior are as undesirable in business as in government, they are nevertheless tolerated to a somewhat greater extent in the former. For example, the January 2, 1978, issue of *Time* included a three-page critique of government bureaucracy, entitled "Rage Over Rising Regulation: To Autocratic Bureaucrats, Nothing Succeeds Like Excess"; but a business-section story reporting that General Motors had sent refunds to the purchasers of Oldsmobiles equipped with Chevrolet engines was only one column long and was headed "End of the Great Engine Flap." Actually, the news often fails to notice that corporations and other large private agencies are also bureaucracies given to red tape.

. . .

Domestic news has by now acknowledged the necessity for the welfare state; even in the good society, the market cannot do everything. The term "welfare state" itself is reserved largely for foreign countries, however, and attitudes toward it are more clearly evident in foreign than in domestic stories. These tend to dwell more on its problems and failures than on its successes, most recently in

England and Sweden, where the welfare state is particularly seen as a threat, from high tax rates and public control over investment, to the ability of the economy to provide sufficient incentives for economic growth. In America, the welfare state is expected to aid people who cannot participate in the market or who are hard-pressed by inflation; that government can provide useful services, or that it can sometimes do so more effectively than private enterprise, is not often acknowledged.

It is now accepted that the government must help the poor, but only the deserving poor, for "welfare cheaters" are a continuing menace and are more newsworthy than people, other than the very rich, who cheat on their taxes. Public welfare agencies are kept under closer scrutiny than others, so that although the news reported on the "welfare mess" in the 1960s, it did not describe equivalent situations in other government agencies in the same way. There was, for example, no "defense mess," and what is "waste" in H.E.W. programs is "cost overruns" in Pentagon programs.

American news is, of course, consistently critical of Communist and democratic-socialist economies. In fact, foreign news is more worried about the political and cultural shortcomings of socialism or communism. To be sure, both are suspect because public ownership and other socialist programs will do away with private property and impair productivity and growth; but descriptions of existing income distributions, in America and elsewhere, now regularly imply that economic inequality is undesirable, even if income redistribution is not the right solution. Still, the primary dangers of socialism are cultural homogeneity, the erosion of political liberties, and the burgeoning of bureaucracy.

Although domestic politicians who criticize governmental welfare measures as socialistic or communistic no longer get the attention they once did, domestic news also remains critical of American socialism. More correctly, the news ignores it, for socialist critiques of the American economy, as well as the activities of America's socialist parties and informal groups, are not newsworthy. The socialist factions in the protest movements of the 1960s, and in the feminist and other movements of the 1970s, have also been ignored. At the same time, however, libertarian groups, which advocate a return to complete market competition, get equally little play in the news.

Small-Town Pastoralism

The rural and anti-industrial values which Thomas Jefferson is usually thought to have invented can also be found in the news, which favors small towns (agricultural or market) over other types of settlements. At one time, this preference was complemented by a celebration of the large city and of the vitality of its business and entertainment districts; but the end of this period can be dated almost exactly by *Life*'s special issue on the cities, which appeared in December 1965.

Although the belief that cities should be fun places and that large, central business-district renewal projects should "revitalize" them still continues to be held, for the last ten years cities have been in the news almost entirely as problematic, with the major emphasis on racial conflict, crime, and fiscal insolvency. Suburbs are not often newsworthy, despite the fact that a near majority of Americans now live in them, and they, too, have generally received a bad press. During the 1950s and 1960s, suburbs were viewed as breeding grounds of homogeneity, boredom, adultery, and other evils; since then, they have come into the news because they are suffering increasingly from "urban" problems, particularly crime, or because they keep out racial minorities and stand in the way of racial integration.

During the 1960s, new towns (like Columbia, Maryland) were welcomed precisely because they were expected to overcome the faults of both city and suburb, restoring the more intimate social relationships and sense of community ascribed to small towns; but that hope was lost when they also encountered fiscal problems and manifested racial conflict and other "urban" ills as well. As a result, the small town continues to reign supreme, not only in Kuralt's "On the Road" but also in television and magazine stories about "the good life" in America. Stories about city neighborhoods judge them by their ability to retain the cohesiveness, friendliness, and slow pace ascribed to small towns, and during the period of journalistic interest in ethnicity, to the ethnic enclaves of the past.

Needless to say, the pastoral values underlying the news are romantic; they visualize rural and market towns as they were imagined to have existed in the past. Today's small towns are reported nostalgically; and their deaths, or their being swallowed up by the expanding suburbs, is a frequent and sentimental story. During the 1960s, the youthful exodus into the hinterlands of Vermont and California was first welcomed as a small-town revival. In recent years, the growth of small towns, especially in the South, has also been reported as a revival; but generally, economic growth is viewed as a danger to "community," even if it is valued in the abstract.

. . .

The virtue of smallness comes through most clearly in stories that deal with the faults of bigness, for in the news, Big Government, Big Labor, and Big Business rarely have virtues. Bigness is feared, among other things, as impersonal and inhuman. In the news as well as in architecture, the ideal social organization should reflect a "human scale." The fear of bigness also reflects a fear of control, of privacy and individual freedom being ground under by organizations too large to notice, much less to value, the individual. As such, bigness is a major threat to individualism, an enduring value in the news, to be discussed below. Consequently, the news often contains stories about new technology that endangers the individual—notably the computer, which is viewed anthropomorphically, either as a robot that will deprive human beings of control over their own lives or as a machine endowed with human failings, which is therefore less of a threat. In any case, there is always room for a gleeful story about computers that break down. The news has, however, always paid attention to the dangers of new technology: when television sets were first mass-produced, they were viewed as dehumanizing because they robbed people of the art of conversation; related fears were expressed at the time of the institution of digit-dialing in telephones.

Conversely, the news celebrates old technology and mourns its passing, partly because it is tied to an era when life was thought to have been simpler, partly because it is viewed as being under more individual control. Sentimental features about the closing of a business based on craftsmanship and about the razing of architectural landmarks, including the industrial mills that were once hated symbols of an exploitative industrialism, are commonplace. Even more attention is paid to the berthing of an ocean liner or the elimination of an old railroad train. The Cunard flagship is in the news about as often as the Queen of England; and the captain of an ocean liner is a far more admired figure than the pilot of a jumbo jet, even if both now use radar to steer their vehicles, and the vehicles themselves are both owned by large corporations.

Small-town pastoralism and old technology may in the end be surrogates for a more general value: an underlying respect for tradition of any kind, save perhaps discrimination against racial, sexual, and other minorities. Tradition is valued because it is known, predictable, and therefore orderly, and order is a major enduring news value. Novel phenomena are, despite their being the basic raw material of news, potential threats to order. Thus, California, which is, from the Eastern perspective of the news, still a new land, is viewed as the fountainhead of bizarre new ideas.

Individualism

It is no accident that many of the characters in Kuralt's pastoral features are "rugged individualists," for one of the most important enduring news values is the preservation of the freedom of the individual against the encroachments of nation and society. The good society of the news is populated by individuals who participate in it, but on their own terms, acting in the public interest, but as they define it.

The ideal individual struggles successfully against adversity and overcomes more powerful forces. The news looks for people who act heroically during disasters, and it pays attention to people who conquer nature without hurting it: explorers, mountain climbers, astronauts, and scientists. "Self-made" men and women remain attractive, as do people who overcome poverty or bureaucracy. Still, the most pervasive way in which the news pays homage to the individual is by its focus on people rather than on groups.

Conversely, the news also continually deals with forces that may rob people of their initiative as individuals. The fear of new technology is, on one level, a fear of its ability to emasculate the individual; computers and data banks invade the privacy that enables people to act as individuals. Communism and socialism are viewed similarly, and capitalism is valued less for itself than for the freedom it offers to at least some individuals. During the 1950s, the suburbs were thought to induce conformity, which would stifle individuality; in recent years, various youth cultures and community developments in the Sunbelt have been criticized in the same fashion. In writing her farewell to California, Kellogg prefers "New York's chaos to ennui," and worries that the easy life of the West would result in "letting the spark die." Her spark is the struggle not only against conformity but against laziness. Individualism is also a source of economic, social, and cultural productivity. The news values hard and task-oriented work, and is upset about the decline of the "work ethic."

Individualism is, in addition, a means of achieving cultural variety, and variety is in turn another weapon against the dangers both of bigness and conformity. The small town is a last hiding place of the stubborn eccentric, and ethnic enclaves consist of people who try to stave off complete Americanization. The news is fearful of mass society, although it neither uses that term nor worries that the masses will overwhelm high culture.

Moderatism

The idealization of the individual could result in praise for the rebel and the deviant, but this possibility is neutralized by an enduring value that discourages excess or extremism. Individualism which violates the law, the dominant mores, and enduring values is suspect; equally important, what is valued in individuals is discouraged in groups. Thus, groups which exhibit what is seen as extreme behavior are criticized in the news through pejorative adjectives or a satirical tone; in many spheres of human activity, polar opposites are questioned and moderate solutions are upheld.

For example, the news treats atheists as extremists and uses the same approach, if more gingerly, with religious fanatics. People who consume conspicuously are criticized, but so are people such as hippies, who turn their backs entirely on consumer goods. The news is scornful both of the overly academic scholar and the oversimplifying popularizer: it is kind neither to highbrows nor to lowbrows, to users of jargon or users of slang. College students who play when they should study receive disapproval, but so do "grinds." Lack of moderation is wrong, whether it involves excess or abstention.

The same value applies to politics. Political ideologists are suspect, but so are completely unprincipled politicians. The totally self-seeking are thought to be consumed by excessive ambition, but the complete do-gooders are not to be believed. Political candidates who talk only about issues may be described as dull; those who avoid issues entirely evoke doubts about their fitness for office. Poor speakers are thought to be unelectable, while demagogues are taken to be dangerous. Those who regularly follow party lines are viewed as hacks, and those who never do are called mavericks or loners—although these terms are pejorative only for the politically unsuccessful; the effective loner becomes a hero.

. . .

Social Order and National Leadership

If one looks at the actors and activities which have dominated the news over the years, it is possible to divide much of what appears on television and in the magazines, particularly as hard news, into two types of stories. One type can be called disorder news, which reports threats to various kinds of order, as well as measures taken to restore order. The second type deals with the routine activities of leading public officials: the day-to-day decisions, policy proposals, and recurring political arguments, as well as the periodic selection of new officials, both through election and appointment. These story types in turn suggest two additional values: the desirability of social order (but as will be seen, of a certain type) and the need for national leadership in maintaining that order.

Disorder and Order

Disorder stories fall into four major categories: natural, technological, social, and moral. Natural disorder news deals with natural disasters, such as floods and earthquakes, as well as industrial accidents which can be ascribed to natural forces, such as many but not all plane crashes or mine cave-ins. Technological disorder concerns accidents which cannot be ascribed to nature. Social disorder news deals with activities which disturb the public peace and may involve violence or the threat of violence against life or physical property; it also includes the deterioration of valued institutions, such as the nuclear two-parent family. Moral disorder news reports transgressions of laws and mores which do not necessarily endanger the social order.

These categories are not used by journalists, nor are they hard and fast. A major fire may first be reported as a natural or technological disaster, but if there is evidence of human failure or arson, it soon becomes a moral disor-

der story. Similarly, once social disorder ends, the news looks for the responsible parties and identifies agents of moral disorder. Conversely, when high officials are guilty of moral disorder, the news may raise the possibility of resulting social disorder. If people lose faith in their leaders, there is fear that the social fabric may unravel.

Social Disorder News

. . .

During the 1960s, domestic social disorder news was dominated by the ghetto disturbances and by anti-war marches, demonstrations, and "trashings." Marches and demonstrations are, from one point of view, protest activities, but the news almost always treated them as potential or actual dangers to the social order. In the beginning, the television cameras focused mainly on bearded and other unusual-looking participants who were, in those days, assumed to threaten the social order by their very appearance. Later, when demonstrations became a conventional strategy, they became particularly newsworthy when reporters noticed trouble.

At first, "trouble" was defined as stone throwing and other physical or verbal violence against the police, or fights between demonstrators and hecklers, often from the American Nazi party. Marches, especially those involving large numbers, were deemed potential threats to the social order because so many people were involved; consequently, trouble was almost inevitable, and if it did not take place, that fact was also newsworthy. "Violence," as well as trouble, was perceived as action against constituted legal authority; and until the 1968 Chicago Democratic Convention, police violence against the demonstrators was viewed as action taken to restore order and was rarely called violence. What the demonstrators described as police brutality was at best shown in passing on television, while day-to-day police brutality in the ghettos was not normally news, perhaps because it was routine.

The turning point in the treatment of anti-war demonstrators came in Chicago when the behavior of the police was reported almost universally as a "police riot." Still, earlier events, and news about them, contributed to the change, for after the ghetto disturbances, police brutality against its residents began to be newsworthy. More important, perhaps, earlier in 1968, most national news media had been persuaded by the Tet offensive that the Vietnam War could or should not be continued. From then on, the news started to see the demonstrators more as protesters, and to pay closer attention to the middle-class, middle-aged, and conventionally dressed young marchers. Eventually, some demonstrations even began to be seen as responses to the moral disorder on the part of the president and his hawkish policy makers.

. . .

Another illustration of the value placed on order restoration can be found in the news about events that do not, on the surface, deal with disorder. A television report covering a demonstration outside the White House moments after Richard Nixon made his resignation speech emphasized that the demonstration was quiet and that there were no signs of incipient panic or violence. Likewise, in the hours after John Kennedy's assassination, network anchorpersons and reporters frequently pointed out that the country was not panicking. Later, I learned that they were, in fact, worried about possible panics and immediately looked for stories which would indicate that none were taking place. They also sought to allay panic by reporting that the transition of Lyndon Johnson to the presidency was taking place quickly and in an orderly fashion. For the same reason, the anchorpersons also took pains to dispel a rumor that the Russians were about to take advantage of the president's death to launch a war.

. . .

Moral Disorder News

The moral disorder story is a hallowed tradition in modern American journalism, prototypically taking the form of exposés based on investigative reporting. Such exposés reveal instances of legal or moral transgression, particularly by public officials and other prestigious individuals who, by reason or virtue of their power and prestige, are not expected to misbehave.

The prime exposé of the 1970s was Watergate. Although defenders of the Nixon Administration have accused the news media of exaggerating the transgressions involved in the events and of blowing up the story in order to drive a president disliked by many journalists out of office, the story was a prototypical exposé, which would have been dealt with in much the same manner had the scandals been committed by a more popular president. Later investigations of CIA and FBI scandals, which implicated Presidents Kennedy and Johnson, were carried out just as energetically. . . .

Nevertheless, the vast majority of moral disorder stories do not involve investigative reporting; often they deal with routine phenomena, such as violent or nonviolent crime or political acts, which are treated as violations of altruistic democracy. Such common practices as logrolling, deals, patronage appointments, or the failure of election candidates to abide by campaign promises are reported in such a way as to indicate that these practices are immoral.

In most moral disorder stories, the values being violated are never made explicit, and that they are being violated is not discussed. Still, the participants in a moral disorder story know they are being identified as transgressors and react accordingly. After an election in New Jersey, supporters of the losing candidate, who was then on trial for bribery and had been accused of conducting a racist campaign, smashed television cameras and attacked reporters. The values in the news, against corruption and for racial integration, had led to campaign stories which the candidate and his supporters felt were responsible for his defeat.

News stories which are announced, or in Erving Goffman's terminology, "framed," as exposés make the search for moral disorder explicit, forcing those identified as transgressors into the difficult position of defending their practices, while at the same time reaffirming the moral values on which the exposé is based. Few people can do so without being defensive, particularly on television documentaries, which are television's primary genre for exposés. Among recent examples are "Migrant," in which fruit-company executives had to react against the documented exploitation of migrant workers; and "The Selling of the Pentagon," in which Defense Department officials had to respond to what the documentary makers considered deviant public-relations practices. If the transgressors refuse to be interviewed, their refusal is also reported and becomes a virtual admission of guilt.

In such instances, the news media become guardians of a moral order; as a result, reporters are generally viewed as representatives of that order, even if they are not looking for moral disorder news. Consequently, when they, and especially television camera crews, arrive on a scene, people begin to perform not only physically for the camera but also morally, denying or eliminating behavior that could be judged as moral disorder. Beatings or tortures of prisoners did not take place in South Vietnam or the American South when cameras were present. . . .

The Nature of Order in the News

The frequent appearance of disorder stories suggests that order is an important value in the news, but order is a meaningless term unless one specifies what order and whose order is being valued. For one thing, there are different types of order; a society can have violence in the streets and a stable family life at home, or public peace and a high rate of family instability. Also, what order is will be judged differently by different people. To the affluent, the slums will appear orderly as long as there are no disturbances and crime does not spill over into wealthy districts; but for slum dwellers, order cannot exist until exploitation, as well as crime, is eliminated. For the parent generation, adolescent order exists when adolescents abide by parental rules; for the young people, order is also freedom of interference from adults.

What Order in the News?

. . .

Social disorder is generally defined as disorder in the public areas of the society. A protest march in which three people die would be headline national news, whereas a family murder that claimed three victims would be a local story. Disorders in affluent areas or elite institutions are more likely to be reported than their occurrence elsewhere. In the 1960s, the looting of a handful of stores on New York's Fifth Avenue received as much attention as a much larger looting spree taking place in a ghetto area that same day. Peaceful demonstrations on college campuses, especially elite ones, are usually more newsworthy than those in factories or prisons. But the major public area is the seat of government; thus, a trouble-free demonstration in front of a city hall or a police station is news, whereas that in front of a store is not.

. . .

Moral disorder stories are, in the end, cued to . . . concern for social cohesion, particularly those stories which report violations of the mores rather than the laws. Such stories are based on the premise that the activities of public officials, public agencies, and corporations should derive from the same moral and ethical values that are supposed to apply to personal, familial, and friendship relations. Even if every political reporter knows that politicians cannot operate with the same ideal of honesty as friends, the failure of politicians to do so continues to be news. In fact, insofar as the news conceives of nation and society anthropomorphically, as having a will and as being held together by moral fibers, the social order persists because it is based on moral values, and the violation of these values is thus an invitation to political and social disintegration. In the last analysis, the values underlying social and moral disorder news are the same, although the two types of news differ in subject and object: social disorder news monitors the respect of citizens for authority, while moral disorder stories evaluate whether authority figures respect the rules of the citizenry.

Whose Order in the News?

National news is ostensibly about and for the entire nation; therefore its values pertain to national order. Since one person's or group's order may be another's disorder, however, and since the news does not report equally about all parts of nation or society, it cannot possibly value everyone's order. Thus, it is relevant to ask whose order is being valued.

Much of the answer has already been suggested. Most of the routine—and thus, by presumption, orderly—activities which appear in the news are carried on by elected and appointed public officials, whereas social and moral disorder news involves, by and large, ordinary people, many of them poor, black, and/or young. Moral disorder stories, however, also identify public officials who have violated the laws or the enduring values. In other words, the news supports those public officials who abide by the enduring values against misbehaving peers and deviant ordinary people.

. . .

In social and economic class terms, then, the news especially values the order of the upper-class and upper-middle-class sectors of society, though it may make fun of some of their very rich members. Although it does not often concern itself with either the social order or the values of the middle and working classes and the poor, it supports the classes when they respect the enduring values; but it can be critical of their popular culture, and among whites, their prejudice toward blacks. The defense of the upper middle-class is stronger in the newsmagazines than on television, but it is common to both.

The news also tends to value the social order of the middle-aged and old against the young. Most public officials, business leaders, and professionals do not act in newsworthy ways until they are in their fifties and sixties, so that the news cannot help but be dominated by this age group; even so, it is rarely reported that old leaders sometimes become senile in office. Similarly, the young are inevitably in the news because criminals or protesters are almost always youthful; even so, juvenile delinquency against adults is commonplace news, whereas adult delinquency against juveniles—other than child abuse—is much less so.

Furthermore, the news reflects a white male social order, although it sides with blacks and women who try to enter it and succeed. Nevertheless, its conception of both racial integration and sexual equality is basically assimilatory; the news prefers women and blacks who move into the existing social order to separatists who want to alter it.

. . .

In short, when all other things are equal, the news pays most attention to and upholds the actions of elite individuals and elite institutions. It would be incorrect to say that the news is about elites per se or a single elite; rather, the news deals mostly with those who hold the power within various national or societal strata; with the most powerful officials in the most powerful agencies; with the coalition of upper-class and upper-middle-class people which dominates the socioeconomic hierarchy; and with the late-middle-aged cohort that has the most power among age groups.

. . .

Leadership

If the news values moral and social order, it also suggests how to maintain them, primarily through the availability of morally and otherwise competent leadership. The news focuses on leaders; and with some exceptions, public agencies and private organizations are represented by their leaders. In the past, magazine cover stories often reported national topics or issues in relation to an individual who played an instrumental or symbolic leadership role in them. When necessary, the news even helps to create leaders; in the 1960s, radical and black organizations functioning on the basis of participatory democracy sometimes complained that journalists would pick out one spokesperson on whom they would lavish most of their attention, thereby making a leader out of him or her.

. . .

Unlike sociology, which sees leadership as a role found in most groups and assumes that someone will inevitably take it, the news focuses instead on the personal qualities and psychological traits of the person taking it. Also, while sociology suggests that group members, in other than totalitarian situations, use formal and/or informal mechanisms for choosing leaders, thereafter influencing their actions, the news tends to treat group members as followers. . . . Whether sociologists or journalists are more correct is not at issue here, for both may be observing different aspects of the same phenomenon. Still, the news divides nation and society into leaders and followers, with the former not only initiating but also being given credit for the activities of the latter. Washington stories routinely tell of the statements or actions of official leaders, while equally routinely ignoring the fact that these are often the work of subordinates. In fact, although the news objectively reports the orders that leaders give, it looks askance at the government bureaucrats who carry them out.

The foremost leader in America is the president, who is viewed as the ultimate protector of order. He is the final backstop for domestic tranquility and the principal guardian of national security, his absence from the White House due to resignation or death evoking, as I indicated earlier, fears of an enemy attack or possible panic by a now leaderless populace. Through his own behavior and the concern he shows for the behavior of others, the president also becomes the nation's moral leader. He sets an example that might be followed by others: should he permit or condone corruption among his associates or appointees, he is suspected of moral disorder. Finally, he is the person who states and represents the national values and he is the agent of the national will.

The news describes the president as the person who actually performs, or who is expected to perform, these functions. Stories which indicate that decisions are actually being made by others, sometimes even without the president's knowledge, are written to suggest that such delegation of power is a departure from the norm and a potential cause for alarm. When a president takes a vacation, the news questions his control over the government during his absence; a presidential illness is always a major story; and his death is the biggest story of all.

. . .

QUESTIONS

1. Whose values do you think the news reflects—those of the whole society, or just part of it?
2. Is it possible to present news objectively?
3. List some important American values (not limited to those mentioned by Gans). Do Americans, on the whole, live up to these values? Do some of them contradict others?

NAPOLEON A. CHAGNON

Yanomamö: The Fierce People

The Yanomamö of the South American jungle inhabit a social world utterly unlike our own. They are an essentially horticultural people, tending gardens that they carve from the forest and then abandon after a few years when the soil is exhausted. Their subsistence strategy has important implications for their society, the primary ones being that their settlements are necessarily small and their social structure is a relatively simple one.

It must also be admitted that the Yanomamö are, if judged by the ethnocentric standards of our own culture, one of the most singularly unappealing peoples in the world: dirty, smelly, cruel, aggressive, dishonest, and "primitive." Yet we must try to suspend such judgments in reading about the Yanomamö. Their society is only one in an immense and diverse range of societal types, each adapted, for better or worse, to the demands and opportunities of its own unique environment. Within the context of their own society, their behaviors, norms, and values form an intricate system that "works."

This article was written by Napoleon Chagnon, an anthropologist who lived among the Yanomamö and studied them in great detail. His findings, summarized here, provide an excellent example of the kind of resources that sociologists can call on in making the cross-cultural comparisons that can highlight aspects not only of other societies but also of our own.

The Yanomamö Indians are a tribe in Venezuela and Brazil who practice a slash-and-burn way of horticultural life. Traditionally, they have been an inland "foot" tribe, avoiding larger rivers and settling deep in the tropical jungle. Until about 1950 they had no sustained contact with other peoples except, to a minor extent, with another tribe, the Carib-speaking Makiritaris to the northeast.

I recently lived with the Yanomamö for more than a year, doing research sponsored by the U.S. Public Health Service, with the cooperation of the Venezuela Institute for Scientific Research. My purpose was to study Yanomamö social organization, language, sex practices, and forms of violence, ranging from treacherous raids to chest-pounding duels.

Those Yanomamö who have been encouraged to live on the larger rivers (Orinoco, Mavaca, Ocamo, and Padamo) are slowly beginning to realize that they are not the only people in the world; there is also a place called Caraca-tedi (Caracas), from whence come foreigners of an entirely new order. These foreigners speak an incomprehensible language, probably a degenerate form of Yanomamö. They bring malaria pills, machetes, axes, cooking pots, and *copetas* ("guns"), have curious ideas about indecency, and speak of a new "spirit."

However, the Yanomamö remain a people relatively unadulterated by outside contacts. They are also fairly numerous. Their population is roughly 10,000, the larger portion of them distributed throughout southern Venezuela. Here, in basins of the upper Orinoco and all its tributaries, they dwell in some 75 scattered villages, each of which contains from 40 to 300 individuals.

The largest, most all-embracing human reality to these people is humanity itself; Yanomamö means true human beings. Their conception of themselves as the only true "domestic" beings (those that dwell in houses) is demonstrated by the contempt with which they treat non-Yanomamö, who, in their language, are "wild." For instance, when referring to themselves, they use an honorific pronoun otherwise reserved for important spirits and headmen; when discussing *nabäs* ("non-Yanomamö"), an ordinary pronoun is enough. Again, in one of the myths about their origin, the first people to be created were the Yanomamö. All others developed by a process of degeneration and are, therefore, not quite on a par with the Yanomamö.

In addition to meaning "people," Yanomamö also refers to the language. Their tribal name does not designate a politically organized entity but is more or less equivalent to our concept of humanity. (This, of course, makes their most outstanding characteristic—chronic warfare, of which I shall speak in detail—seem rather an anomaly.) Sub-Yanomamö groupings are based on language differences, historical separation, and geographical location.

For instance, two distinguishable groups, Waika (from *waikaö*—"to kill off") and Shamatari, speak nearly identical dialects; they are differentiated mostly on the basis of a specific event that led to their separation. The Shamatari, the group I know best, occupy the area south of the Orinoco to, and including portions of, northern Brazil. Their differentiation from the Waika probably occurred in the past 75 years.

According to the Indians, there was a large village on a northern tributary of the upper Orinoco River, close to its headwaters. The village had several factions, one of which was led by a man called Kayabawä (big tree). A notably corpulent man, he also had the name Shamatari, derived from *shama*, the "tapir," a robust ungulate found throughout tropical South America. As the story goes, Shamatari's faction got into a fight with the rest of the village over the possession of a woman, and the community split into two warring halves. Gradually the fighting involved more villages, and Shamatari led his faction south, crossed the Orinoco, and settled there. He was followed by members of other villages that had taken his part in the fight.

Those who moved to the south side of the Orinoco came to be called Shamataris by those living on the north side, and the term is now applied to any village in this area, whether or not it can trace its origin to the first supporters of Shamatari.

For the Yanomamö, the village is the maximum political unit and the maximum sovereign body, and it is linked to other villages by ephemeral alliances, visiting and trade relationships, and intermarriages. In essence, the village is a building—a continuous, open-roofed lean-to built on a circular plan and surrounded by a protective palisade of split palm logs. The roof starts at or near ground level, ascends at an angle of about 45 degrees, and reaches a height of some 20 to 25 feet. Individual segments under the continuous roof are not partitioned; from a hammock hung anywhere beneath it one can see (and hear, thanks to the band shell nature of the structure) all that goes on within the village.

The palisade, about three to six feet behind the base of the roof, is some ten feet high and is usually in various stages of disrepair, depending on the current warfare sit-

uation. The limited number of entrances are covered with dry palm leaves in the evening; if these are moved even slightly, the sound precipitates the barking of a horde of ill-tempered, underfed dogs, whose bad manners preadapt the stranger to what lies beyond the entrance.

A typical "house" (a segment under the continuous roof) shelters a man, his wife, or wives, their children, perhaps one or both of the man's parents, and, farther down, the man's brothers and their families. The roof is alive with cockroaches, scorpions, and spiders, and the ground is littered with the debris of numerous repasts—bird, fish, and animal bones; bits of fur; skulls of monkeys and other animals; banana and plantain peelings; feathers; and the seeds of palm fruits. Bows and arrows stand against housepoles all over the village, baskets hang from roof rafters, and firewood is stacked under the lower part of the roof where it slopes to the ground. Some men will be whittling arrow points with agouti-tooth knives or tying feathers to arrow shafts. Some women will be spinning cotton, weaving baskets, or making hammocks or cotton waistbands. The children, gathered in the center of the village clearing, frequently tie a string to a lizard and entertain themselves by shooting the animal full of tiny arrows. And, of course, many people will be outside the compound, working in their gardens, fishing, or collecting palm fruits in the jungle.

If it is a typical late afternoon, most of the older men are gathered in one part of the village, blowing one of their hallucinatory drugs (*ebene*) up each other's nostrils by means of a hollow tube and chanting to the forest demons (*hekuras*) as the drug takes effect. Other men may be curing a sick person by sucking, massaging, and exhorting the evil spirit from him. Everybody in the village is swatting vigorously at the voracious biting gnats, and here and there groups of people delouse each other's heads and eat the vermin.

In composition, the village consists of one or more groups of patrilineally related kinsmen (*mashis*), but it also contains other categories, including people who have come from other villages seeking spouses. All villages try to increase their size and consider it desirable for both the young men and young women to remain at home after marriage. Since one must marry out of his *mashi*, villages with only one patrilineage frequently lose their young men to other villages; they must go to another village to *siohamou* (to "son-in-law") if they want wives. The parents of the bride-to-be, of course, want the young man to remain in their village to help support them in their old age, particularly if they have few or no sons. They will frequently promise a young man one or more of the sisters of his wife in order to make his stay more attractive.

He, on the other hand, would rather return to his home village to be with his own kinsmen, and the tendency is for postmarital residence to be patrilocal (with the father of the groom). If a village is rich in axes and machetes, it can and does coerce its poorer trading partners into permitting their young women to live permanently with the richer village. The latter thus obtains more women, while the poorer village gains some security in the trading network. The poor village then coerces other villages even poorer, or they raid them and steal their women.

The patrilineages that maintain the composition of the villages, rich or poor, include a man and his brothers and sisters, his children and his brothers' children, and the children of his sons and brothers' sons. The ideal marriage pattern is for a group of brothers to exchange sisters with another group of brothers. Furthermore, it is both permissible and desirable for a man to marry his mother's brother's daughter (his matrilateral cross-cousin) and/or his father's sister's daughter (his patrilateral cross-cousin) and, as we have seen earlier, to remain in his parents' village. Hence, the "ideal" village would have at least two patrilineages that exchanged marriageable people.

There is a considerable amount of adherence to these rules, and both brother-sister exchange and cross-cousin marriage are common. However, there are also a substantial number of people in each village who are not related in these ways. For the most part they are women and their children who have been stolen from other villages, segments of lineages that have fled from their own village because of fights, and individuals—mostly young men—who have moved in and attached themselves to the household of one of the lineage (*mashi*) leaders.

Even if the sex ratio is balanced, there is a chronic shortage of women. A pregnant woman or one who is still nursing her children must not have sexual relationships. This means that for as many as three years, even allowing for violations of the taboos, a woman is asexual as far as the men are concerned. Hence, men with pregnant wives, and bachelors too, are potentially disruptive in every village because they constantly seek liaisons with the wives of other men. Eventually such relationships are discovered and violence ensues.

The woman, even if merely suspected of having affairs with other men, is beaten with a club; burned with a glowing brand; shot with a barbed arrow in a non-vital area, such as the buttocks, so that removal of the barb is both difficult and painful; or chopped on the arms or legs with a machete or ax. Most women over thirty carry numerous scars inflicted on them by their enraged husbands. My study of genealogies also indicates that not a few women have been killed outright by their husbands. The woman's punishment for infidelity depends on the number of brothers she has in the village, for if her husband is too brutal, her brothers may club him or take her away and give her to someone else.

The guilty man, on the other hand, is challenged to a fight with clubs. This duel is rarely confined to the two parties involved, for their brothers and supporters join the battle. If nobody is seriously injured, the matter may be forgotten. But if the incidents are frequent, the two patrilineages may decide to split while they are still on relatively "peaceable" terms with each other and form two independent villages. They will still be able to reunite when threatened by raid from a larger village.

This is only one aspect of the chronic warfare of the Yanomamö—warfare that has a basic effect on settlement pattern and demography, intervillage political relationships, leadership, and social organization. The collective aggressive behavior is caused by the desire to accent "sovereignty"—the capacity to initiate fighting and to demonstrate this capacity to others.

Although the Yanomamö are habitually armed with lethal bows and arrows, they have a graded system of violence within which they can express their *waiteri*, or "fierceness." The form of violence is determined by the nature of the affront or wrong to be challenged. The most benign form is a duel between two groups, in which an individual from each group stands (or kneels) with his chest stuck out, head up in the air, and arms held back and receives a hard blow to the chest. His opponent literally winds up and delivers a close-fist blow from the ground, striking the man on the left pectoral muscle just above the heart. The impact frequently drops the man to his knees, and participants may cough up blood for several days after such a contest. After receiving several such blows, the man then has his turn to strike his opponent, while the respective supporters of each antagonist gather around and frenziedly urge their champion on.

All men in the two villages are obliged to participate as village representatives, and on one occasion I saw some individuals take as many as three or four turns of four blows each. Duels of this type usually result from minor wrongs, such as a village being guilty of spreading bad rumors about another village, questioning its generosity or fierceness, or accusing it of gluttony at a feast. A variant of this form of duel is side slapping, in which an open-handed blow is delivered across the flank just above the pelvis.

More serious are the club fights. Although these almost invariably result from cases in which a wife has been caught in an affair with another man, some fights follow the theft of food within the village. The usual procedure calls for a representative from each belligerent group. One man holds a ten-foot club upright, braces himself by leaning on the club and spreading his feet, then holds his head out for his opponent to strike. Following this comes his turn to do likewise to his adversary. These duels, more often than not, end in a free-for-all in which everybody clubs everybody else on whatever spot he can hit. Such brawls occasionally result in fatalities. However, since headmen of the respective groups stand by with bows drawn, no one dares deliver an intentionally killing blow, for if he does, he will be shot. The scalps of the older men are almost incredible to behold, covered as they are by as many as a dozen ugly welts. Yet, most of them proudly shave the top of their heads to display their scars.

Also precipitated by feuds over women are spear fights, which are even more serious than club fights. Members of a village will warn those of the offending village that they are coming to fight with spears. They specify that they are not planning to shoot arrows unless the others shoot first. On the day of the fight, the attackers enter the other village, armed with five or six sharpened clubs or slender shafts some eight feet long and attempt to drive the defenders out. If successful, the invaders steal all the valuable possessions—hammocks, cooking pots, and machetes—and retreat. In the spear fight that occurred while I was studying the tribe, the attackers were successful, but they wounded several individuals so badly that one of them died. The fighting then escalated to a raid, the penultimate form of violence.

Such raids may be precipitated by woman stealing or the killing of a visitor (visitors are sometimes slain because they are suspected of having practiced harmful magic that has led to a death in the host's village). Raids also occur if a man kills his wife in a fit of anger; her natal village is then obliged to avenge the death. Most raids, however, are in revenge for deaths that occurred in previous raids, and once the vendetta gets started, it is not likely to end for a long time. Something else may trigger a raid. Occasionally an ambitious headman wearies of peaceful times—a rarity, certainly—and deliberately creates a situation that will demonstrate his leadership.

A revenge raid is preceded by a feast in which the ground bones of the person to be avenged are mixed in a soup of boiled, ripe plantains (the mainstay of Yanomamö diet) and swallowed. Yanomamö are endocannibals, which means they consume the remains of members of their own group. This ceremony puts the raiders in the appropriate state of frenzy for the business of warfare. A mock raid—rather like a dress rehearsal—is conducted in their own village on the afternoon before the day of the raid, and a life-size effigy of an enemy, constructed of leaves or a log, is slain. That evening all the participants march, one at a time, to the center of the village clearing, while clacking their bows and arrows and screaming their versions of the calls of carnivorous birds, mammals, and even insects.

When all have lined up facing the direction of the enemy village, they sing their war song, "I am a meat-hungry buzzard," and shout several times in unison until they hear the echo return from the jungle. They then disperse to their individual sections of the village to vomit the symbolic rotten flesh of the enemy that they, as symbolic carnivorous vultures and wasps, partook of in the lineup.

The same thing, with the exception of the song, is repeated at dawn the following morning. Then the raiders, covered with black paint made of chewed charcoal, march out of the village in single file and collect the hammocks and plantains that their women have previously set outside the village for them. On each night they spend en route to the enemy they fire arrows at a dummy in a mock raid. They approach the enemy village itself under cover of darkness, ambush the first person they catch, and retreat as rapidly as possible. If they catch a man and his family, they will shoot the man and steal the woman and her children. At a safe distance from her village, each of the raiders rapes the woman, and when they reach their own village, every man in the village may, if he wishes, do likewise before she is given to one of the men as a wife. Ordinarily she attempts to escape, but if caught, she may be killed. So constant is the threat of raids that every woman leaves her village in the knowledge that she may be stolen.

The supreme form of violence is the *nomohoni*—the "trick." During the dry season, the Yanomamö do a great deal of visiting. An entire village will go to another village for a ceremony that involves feasting, dancing, chanting, curing, trading, and just plain gossiping. Shortly after arrival, the visitors are invited to recline in the hammocks of the hosts. By custom they lie motionless to display their fine decorations while the hosts prepare food for them. But now suppose that a village has a grudge to settle with another, such as deaths to avenge. It enlists the support of a third village to act as accomplice. This third village, which must be on friendly terms with the intended victims, will invite them to a feast. While the guests recline defenseless in the hammocks, the hosts descend on them with axes and sharpened poles, treacherously killing as many as they can. Those that manage to escape the slaughter inside the village are shot outside the palisade by the village that instigated the *nomohoni*. The women and children will be shared between the two accomplices.

Throughout all this ferocity there are two organizational aspects of violence. One concerns leadership: A man must be able to demonstrate his fierceness if he is to be a true leader. It is equally important, however, that he have a large natural following—that is, he must have many male kinsmen to support his position and a quantity of daughters and sisters to distribute to other men. Lineage leaders cannot accurately be described as unilateral initiators of activities; rather, they are the vehicles through which the group's will is expressed. For example, when a certain palm fruit is ripe and is particularly abundant in an area some distance from the village, everybody knows that the whole village will pack its belongings and erect a temporary camp at that spot to collect the fruit. The headman does little more than set the date. When his kinsmen see him packing, they know that the time has come to leave for the collecting trip. True, the headman does have some initiative in raiding, but not even this is completely independent of the attitudes of his followers, which dictate that a death must be avenged. However, when the purpose of a raid is to steal women, the headman does have some freedom to act on his own initiative.

As a general rule, the smaller his natural following, the more he is obliged to demonstrate his personal qualities of fierceness and leadership. Padudiwä, the headman of one of the lineages in Bisaasi-tedi, took pains to demonstrate his personal qualities whenever he could; he had only two living brothers and four living sisters in his group. Most of his demonstrations of ferocity were cruel beatings he administered to his four wives, none of whom had brothers in the village to take their part. Several young men who attached themselves to his household admired him for this.

Padudiwä was also responsible for organizing several raids while I lived with the villagers of Bisaasi-tedi, a village that was being raided regularly by some seven or eight other villages, so that the danger of being raided in return was correspondingly reduced. On one occasion, when three young men from Patanowä-tedi arrived as emissaries of peace, Padudiwä wanted to kill them, although he had lived with them at one time and they were fairly close relatives. The murder was prevented by the headman of the other—and larger—lineage in the village, who warned that if an attempt were made on the lives of the visitors he himself would kill Padudiwä.

Obviously, then, Padudiwä's reputation was built largely on calculated acts of fierceness, which carefully reduced the possibility of personal danger to himself and his followers, and on cunning and cruelty. To some extent he was obliged by the smallness of his gathering to behave in such a way, but he was certainly a man to treat with caution.

Despite their extreme aggressiveness, the Yanomamö have at least two qualities I admired. They are kind and indulgent with children and can quickly forget personal angers. (A few even treated me almost as an equal—in their culture this was a considerable concession.) But to portray them as "noble savages" would be misleading. Many of them are delightful and charming people when confronted alone and on a personal basis, but the greater number of them are much like Padudiwä—or strive to be that way. As they frequently told me, *Yanomamö täbä waiteri!*—"Yanomamö are fierce!"

QUESTIONS

1. Discuss the concepts of ethnocentrism and cultural relativism with reference to the Yanomamö.
2. Could American society be so thoroughly described in so short a space as Chagnon describes the Yanomamö? Justify your answer.
3. Are we really all that different from the Yanomamö?

ERNESTINE FRIEDL

Society and Sex Roles

The various societies that exist, and have existed in the past, can be roughly categorized according to the basic strategy used to meet economic needs: hunting and gathering, pastoralism, horticulture, agriculture, or industrialism. Each of these subsistence strategies offers certain opportunities and imposes certain constraints: for example, hunters and gatherers could never form large, concentrated populations, for they could not collect enough food to support themselves; industrial societies can support huge cities, for most of their members work at jobs other than food production. A society's subsistence strategy has far-reaching implications for a variety of other aspects of social and cultural life as well.

As Ernestine Friedl shows in her article, a people's subsistence strategy also affects the relative status of men and women. In hunting and gathering societies, the sexes are virtually equal; in pastoral and horticultural societies, distinct inequalities emerge; in agricultural and early industrial societies, the inequalities are great; while in advanced industrial societies, women again begin to achieve equality with men. In each case, the crucial factor affecting the status of the sexes is an economic one: the greater the female contribution to the group, the higher the status of women becomes.

"Women must respond quickly to the demands of their husbands," says anthropologist Napoleon Chagnon describing the horticultural Yanomamo Indians of Venezuela. When a man returns from a hunting trip, "the woman, no matter what she is doing, hurries home and quietly but rapidly prepares a meal for her husband. Should the wife be slow in doing this, the husband is within his rights to beat her. Most reprimands . . . take the form of blows with the hand or with a piece of firewood. . . . Some of them chop their wives with the sharp edge of a machete or axe, or shoot them with a barbed arrow in some nonvital area, such as the buttocks or leg."

Among the Semai agriculturalists of central Malaya, when one person refuses the request of another, the offended party suffers *punan*, a mixture of emotional pain and frustration. "Enduring *punan* is commonest when a girl has refused the victim her sexual favors," reports Robert Dentan. "The jilted man's 'heart becomes sad.' He loses his energy and his appetite. Much of the time he sleeps, dreaming of his lost love. In this state he is in fact very likely to injure himself 'accidentally.' " The Semai are afraid of violence; a man would never strike a woman.

The social relationship between men and women has emerged as one of the principal disputes occupying the attention of scholars and the public in recent years. Although the discord is sharpest in the United States, the controversy has spread throughout the world. Numerous national and international conferences, including one in Mexico sponsored by the United Nations, have drawn together delegates from all walks of life to discuss such questions as the social and political rights of each sex, and even the basic nature of males and females.

Whatever their position, partisans often invoke examples from other cultures to support their ideas about the proper role of each sex. Because women are clearly subservient to men in many societies, like the Yanomamo, some experts conclude that the natural pattern is for men to dominate. But among the Semai no one has the right to command others, and in West Africa women are often chiefs. The place of women in these societies supports the argument of those who believe that sex roles are not fixed, that if there is a natural order, it allows for many different arrangements.

The argument will never be settled as long as the opposing sides toss examples from the world's cultures at each other like intellectual stones. But the effect of biological differences on male and female behavior can be clarified by looking at known examples of the earliest forms of human society and examining the relationship between technology, social organization, environment, and sex roles. The problem is to determine the conditions in which different degrees of male dominance are found, to try to discover the social and cultural arrangements that give rise to equality or inequality between the sexes, and to attempt to apply this knowledge to our understanding of the changes taking place in modern industrial society.

As Western history and the anthropological record have told us, equality between the sexes is rare; in most known societies females are subordinate. Male dominance is so widespread that it is virtually a human universal; societies in which women are consistently dominant do not exist and have never existed.

Evidence of a society in which women control all strategic resources like food and water, and in which women's activities are the most prestigious has never been found. The Iroquois of North America and the Lovedu of Africa came closest. Among the Iroquois, women raised food, controlled its distribution, and helped to choose male political leaders. Lovedu women ruled as queens, exchanged valuable cattle, led ceremonies, and controlled their own sex lives. But among both the Iroquois and the Lovedu, men owned the land and held other positions of power and prestige. Women were equal to men; they did not have ultimate authority over them. Neither culture was a true matriarchy.

Patriarchies are prevalent, and they appear to be strongest in societies in which men control significant goods that are exchanged with people outside the family. Regardless of who produces food, the person who gives it to others creates the obligations and alliances that are at the center of all political relations. The greater the male monopoly on the distribution of scarce items, the stronger their control of women seems to be. This is most obvious in relatively simple hunter-gatherer societies.

Hunter-gatherers, or foragers, subsist on wild plants, small land animals, and small river or sea creatures gathered by hand; large land animals and sea mammals hunted with spears, bows and arrows, and blow guns; and fish caught with hooks and nets. The 300,000 hunter-gatherers alive in the world today include the Eskimos, the Australian aborigines, and the Pygmies of Central Africa.

Foraging has endured for two million years and was replaced by farming and animal husbandry only 10,000 years ago; it covers more than 99 percent of human history. Our foraging ancestry is not far behind us and provides a clue to our understanding of the human condition.

Hunter-gatherers are people whose ways of life are technologically simple and socially and politically egalitarian. They live in small groups of 50 to 200 and have neither kings, nor priests, nor social classes. These conditions permit anthropologists to observe the essential bases for inequalities between the sexes without the distortions induced by the complexities of contemporary industrial society.

The source of male power among hunter-gatherers lies in their control of a scarce, hard to acquire, but necessary nutrient—animal protein. When men in a hunter-gatherer society return to camp with game, they divide the meat in some customary way. Among the !Kung San of Africa, certain parts of the animal are given to the owner of the arrow that killed the beast, to the first hunter to sight the game, to the one who threw the first spear, and to all men in the hunting party. After the meat has been divided, each hunter distributes his share to his blood relatives and his in-laws, who in turn share it with others. If an animal is large enough, every member of the band will receive some meat.

Vegetable foods, in contrast, are not distributed beyond the immediate household. Women give food to their children, to their husbands, to other members of the household, and rarely, to the occasional visitor. No one outside the family regularly eats any of the wild fruits and vegetables that are gathered by the women.

The meat distributed by the men is a public gift. Its source is widely known, and the donor expects a reciprocal gift when other men return from a successful hunt. He gains honor as a supplier of a scarce item and simultaneously obligates others to him.

These obligations constitute a form of power or control over others, both men and women. The opinions of hunters play an important part in decisions to move the village; good hunters attract the most desirable women; people in other groups join camps with good hunters; and hunters, because they already participate in an internal system of exchange, control exchange with other groups for flint, salt, and steel axes. The male monopoly on hunting unites men in a system of exchange and gives them power; gathering vegetable food does not give women equal power even among foragers who live in the tropics, where the food collected by women provides more than half the hunter-gatherer diet.

If dominance arises from a monopoly on big-game hunting, why has the male monopoly remained unchallenged? Some women are strong enough to participate in the hunt and their endurance is certainly equal to that of men. Dobe San women of the Kalahari Desert in Africa walk an average of 10 miles a day carrying from 15 to 33 pounds of food plus a baby.

Women do not hunt, I believe, because of four inter-related factors: variability in the supply of game; the different skills required for hunting and gathering; the incompatibility between carrying burdens and hunting; and the small size of seminomadic foraging populations.

Because the meat supply is unstable, foragers must make frequent expeditions to provide the band with gathered food. Environmental factors such as seasonal and annual variation in rainful often affect the size of the wildlife population. Hunters cannot always find game, and when they do encounter animals, they are not always successful in killing their prey. In northern latitudes, where meat is the primary food, periods of starvation are known in every generation. The irregularity of the game supply leads hunter-gatherers in areas where plant foods are available to depend on these predictable foods a good part of the time. Someone must gather the fruits, nuts, and roots and carry them back to camp to feed unsuccessful hunters, children, the elderly, and anyone who might not have gone foraging that day.

Foraging falls to the women because hunting and gathering cannot be combined on the same expedition. Although gatherers sometimes notice signs of game as they work, the skills required to track game are not the same as those required to find edible roots or plants. Hunters scan the horizon and the land for traces of large game; gatherers keep their eyes to the ground, studying the distribution of plants and the texture of the soil for hidden roots and animal holes. Even if a woman who was collecting plants came across the track of an antelope, she could not follow it; it is impossible to carry a load and hunt at the same time. Running with a heavy load is difficult, and should the animal be sighted, the hunter would be off balance and could neither shoot an arrow nor throw a spear accurately.

Pregnancy and child care would also present difficulties for a hunter. An unborn child affects a woman's body balance, as does a child in her arms, on her back, or slung at her side. Until they are two years old, many hunter-gatherer children are carried at all times, and until they are four, they are carried some of the time.

An observer might wonder why young women do not hunt until they become pregnant, or why mature women and men do not hunt and gather on alternate days, with some women staying in camp to act as wet nurses for the young. Apart from the effects hunting might have on a mother's milk production, there are two reasons. First, young girls begin to bear children as soon as they are physically mature and strong enough to hunt, and second, hunter-gatherer bands are so small that there are unlikely to be enough lactating women to serve as wet nurses. No hunter-gatherer group could afford to maintain a specialized female hunting force.

Because game is not always available, because hunting and gathering are specialized skills, because women carrying heavy loads cannot hunt, and because women in hunter-gatherer societies are usually either pregnant or caring for young children, for most of the last two million years of human history men have hunted and women have gathered.

If male dominance depends on controlling the supply of meat, then the degree of male dominance in a society should vary with the amount of meat available and the amount supplied by the men. Some regions, like the East African grasslands and the North American woodlands, abounded with species of large mammals; other zones, like tropical forests and semideserts, are thinly populated with prey. Many elements affect the supply of game, but theoretically, the less meat provided exclusively by the men, the more egalitarian the society.

All known hunter-gatherer societies fit into four basic types: those in which men and women work together in communal hunts and as teams gathering edible plants, as did the Washo Indians of North America; those in which men and women each collect their own plant foods although the men supply some meat to the group, as do the Hadza of Tanzania; those in which male hunters and female gatherers work apart but return to camp each evening to share their acquisitions, as do the Tiwi of North Australia; and those in which the men provide all the food by hunting large game, as do the Eskimo. In each case the extent of male dominance increases directly with the proportion of meat supplied by individual men and small hunting parties.

Among the most egalitarian of hunter-gatherer societies are the Washo Indians, who inhabited the valleys of the Sierra Nevada in what is now southern California and Nevada. In the spring they moved north to Lake Tahoe for the large fish runs of sucker and native trout. Everyone—men, women, and children—participated in the fishing. Women spent the summer gathering edible berries and seeds while the men continued to fish. In the fall some men hunted deer but the most important source of animal protein was the jack rabbit, which was captured in communal hunts. Men and women together drove the rabbits into nets tied end to end. To provide food for the winter, husbands and wives worked as teams in the late fall to collect pine nuts.

Since everyone participated in most food-gathering activities, there were no individual distributors of food and relatively little difference in male and female rights. Men and women were not segregated from each other in daily activities; both were free to take lovers after marriage; both had the right to separate whenever they chose; menstruating women were not isolated from the rest of the group; and one of the two major Washo rituals celebrated hunting while the other celebrated gathering. Men were accorded more prestige if they had killed a deer, and men directed decisions about the seasonal movement of the group. But if no male leader stepped forward, women were permitted to lead. The distinctive feature of groups such as the Washo is the relative equality of the sexes.

The sexes are also relatively equal among the Hadza of Tanzania but this near-equality arises because men and women tend to work alone to feed themselves. They exchange little food. The Hadza lead a leisurely life in the seemingly barren environment of the East African Rift Gorge that is, in fact, rich in edible berries, roots, and small game. As a result of this abundance, from the time they are 10 years old, Hadza men and women gather much of their own food. Women take their young children with them into the bush, eating as they forage, and collect only enough food for a light family meal in the evening. The men eat berries and roots as they hunt for small game, and should they bring down a rabbit or a hyrax, they eat the meat on the spot. Meat is carried back to the camp and shared with the rest of the group only on those rare occasions when a poisoned arrow brings down a large animal—an impala, a zebra, an eland, or a giraffe.

Because Hadza men distribute little meat, their status is only slightly higher than that of the women. People flock to the camp of a good hunter and the camp might take on his name because of his popularity, but he is in no sense a leader of the group. A Hadza man and a woman have an equal right to divorce and each can repudiate a marriage simply by living apart for a few weeks. Couples tend to live in the same camp as the wife's mother but they sometimes make long visits to the camp of the husband's mother. Although a man may take more than one wife, most Hadza males cannot afford to indulge in this luxury. In order to maintain a marriage, a man must supply both his wife and his mother-in-law with some meat and trade goods, such as beads and cloth, and the Hadza economy gives few men the wealth to provide for more than one wife and mother-in-law. Washo equality is based on cooperation; Hadza equality is based on independence.

In contrast to both these groups, among the Tiwi of Melville and Bathurst Islands off the northern coast of Australia, male hunters dominate female gatherers. The Tiwi are representative of the most common form of foraging society, in which the men supply large quantities of meat, although less than half the food consumed by the group. Each morning Tiwi women, most with babies on their backs, scatter in different directions in search of vegetables, grubs, worms, and small game such as bandicoots, lizards, and opossums. To track the game, they use hunting dogs. On most days women return to camp with some meat and with baskets full of *korka*, the nut of a native palm, which is soaked and mashed to make a porridge-like dish. The Tiwi men do not hunt small game and do not hunt every day, but when they do they often return with kangaroo, large lizards, fish, and game birds.

The porridge is cooked separately by each household and rarely shared outside the family, but the meat is prepared by a volunteer cook, who can be male or female. After the cook takes one of the parts of the animal traditionally reserved for him or her, the animal's "boss," the one who caught it, distributes the rest to all near kin and then to all others residing with the band. Although the small game supplied by the women is distributed in the same way as the big game supplied by the men, Tiwi men are dominant because the game they kill provides most of the meat.

The power of Tiwi men is clearest in their betrothal practices. Among the Tiwi, a woman must always be married. To ensure this, female infants are betrothed at birth and widows are remarried at the gravesides of their late husbands. Men form alliances by exchanging daughters, sisters, and mothers in marriage and some collect as many as 25 wives. Tiwi men value the quantity and quality of the food many wives can collect and the many children they can produce.

The dominance of the men is offset somewhat by the influence of adult women in selecting their next husbands. Many women are active strategists in the political careers of their male relatives, but to the exasperation of some sons attempting to promote their own futures, widowed mothers sometimes insist on selecting their own partners. Women also influence the marriages of their daughters and granddaughters, especially when the selected husband dies before the bestowed child moves to his camp.

Among the Eskimo, representative of the rarest type of forager society, inequality between the sexes is matched by inequality in supplying the group with food. Inland Eskimo men hunt caribou throughout the year to provision the entire society, and maritime Eskimo men depend on whaling, fishing, and some hunting to feed their extended families. The women process the carcasses, cut and sew skins to make clothing, cook, and care for the young; but they collect no food of their own and depend on the men to supply all the raw materials for their work. Since men provide all the meat, they also control the trade in hides, whale oil, seal oil, and other items that move between the maritime and inland Eskimos.

Eskimo women are treated almost exclusively as objects to be used, abused, and traded by men. After puberty all Eskimo girls are fair game for any interested male. A man shows his intentions by grabbing the belt of a woman and if she protests, he cuts off her trousers and forces himself upon her. These encounters are considered unimportant by the rest of the group. Men offer their wives' sexual services to establish alliances with trading partners and members of hunting and whaling parties.

Despite the consistent pattern of some degree of male dominance among foragers, most of these societies are egalitarian compared with agricultural and industrial societies. No forager has any significant opportunity for political leadership. Foragers, as a rule, do not like to give or take orders, and assume leadership only with reluctance. Shamans (those who are thought to be possessed by spirits) may be either male or female. Public rituals conducted by women in order to celebrate the first menstruation of girls are common, and the symbolism in these rituals is similar to that in the ceremonies that follow a boy's first kill.

In any society, status goes to those who control the distribution of valued goods and services outside the family. Equality arises when both sexes work side by side in food production, as do the Washo, and the products are simply distributed among the workers. In such circumstances, no person or sex has greater access to valued items than do others. But when women make no contribution to the food supply, as in the case of the Eskimo, they are completely subordinate.

When we attempt to apply these generalizations to contemporary industrial society, we can predict that as long as women spend their discretionary income from jobs on domestic needs, they will gain little social recognition and power. To be an effective source of power, money must be exchanged in ways that require returns and create obligations. In other words, it must be invested.

Jobs that do not give women control over valued resources will do little to advance their general status. Only as managers, executives, and professionals are women in a position to trade goods and services, to do others favors, and therefore to obligate others to them. Only as controllers of valued resources can women achieve prestige, power, and equality.

Within the household, women who bring in income from jobs are able to function on a more nearly equal basis with their husbands. Women who contribute services to their husbands and children without pay, as do some middle-class Western housewives, are especially vulnerable to dominance. Like Eskimo women, as long as their services are limited to domestic distribution they have little power relative to their husbands and none with respect to the outside world.

As for the limits imposed on women by their procreative functions in hunter-gatherer societies, childbearing and child care are organized around work as much as work is organized around reproduction. Some foraging groups space their children three to four years apart and have an average of only four to six children, far fewer than many women in other cultures. Hunter-gatherers nurse their infants for extended periods, sometimes for as long as four years. This custom suppresses ovulation and limits the size of their families. Sometimes, although rarely, they practice infanticide. By limiting reproduction, a woman who is gathering food has only one child to carry.

Different societies can and do adjust the frequency of birth and the care of children to accommodate whatever productive activities women customarily engage in. In horticultural societies, where women work long hours in gardens that may be far from home, infants get food to supplement their mothers' milk, older children take care of younger children, and pregnancies are widely spaced. Throughout the world, if a society requires a woman's labor, it finds ways to care for her children.

In the United States, as in some other industrial societies, the accelerated entry of women with preschool children into the labor force has resulted in the development of a variety of child-care arrangements. Individual women have called on friends, relatives, and neighbors. Public and private child-care centers are growing. We should realize that the declining birth rate, the increasing acceptance of childless or single-child families, and a de-emphasis on motherhood are adaptations to a sexual division of labor reminiscent of the system of production found in hunter-gatherer societies.

In many countries where women no longer devote most of their productive years to childbearing, they are beginning to demand a change in the social relationship of the sexes. As women gain access to positions that control the exchange of resources, male dominance may become archaic, and industrial societies may one day become as egalitarian as the Washo.

QUESTIONS

1. How can such apparently unrelated matters as a society's subsistence strategy and the relative status of the sexes be connected?

2. Marx maintained that the economic base of a society was of paramount importance in shaping the society's social and cultural forms. Cite any evidence (not necessarily restricted to this article) that throws light on this view.

3. What are the implications of Friedl's analysis for the future roles and statuses of the sexes?

D. STANLEY EITZEN

The Structure of Sport and Society

Sport is a subject of considerable and growing interest to sociologists. It is, after all, an important institution in American society: the great majority of people discuss sport regularly, and most are either participants in, or spectators of, some game or another. And like any other institution, sport is an integral part of the society, with its characteristics reflecting those of the surrounding social order.

The kinds of sport that are played can tell us a great deal about the society. American sport, for example, tends to be competitive, specialized, professionalized, profit-oriented, and diversified—all characteristic features of the society as a whole, and particularly of its economy. The values of sport and of the society at large are often identical: discipline, hard work, success, conformity, team spirit. Even social changes, such as increased participation by women and blacks in other areas, are faithfully reflected in sport.

In this article, Stanley Eitzen explores the relationship between American sport and the American social structure, placing particular emphasis on the implications of two sports that lay equal claim to being the great American pastime—baseball and football.

An important indicator of the essence of a society is the type of sport it glorifies. The examination of the structure of a society's dominant sport provides important clues about that society and its culture. For example, answers to the following questions will greatly inform the observer about that society: Is the sport oriented toward a group (team) or the individual? Does the outcome depend essentially on strength, speed, strategy, deception, or the mastery of intricate moves? Is the activity cerebral or physical? Is the primary goal to win or to enjoy the activity?

Let us begin by looking at what Americans consider the essence of sport—winning—to show how other societies have a different view more consonant with their culture. Sport, as played in America, is an expression of Social Darwinism—a survival-of-the-fittest approach where everyone competes to be alone at the top. Players are cut from teams even in our schools if they are not considered good enough. Tournaments are organized so that only one team or individual is the ultimate winner. Corporations sponsor contests for youngsters such as "Punt, Pass, and Kick," where winners are selected at the local level and proceed through a number of district and regional contests until a winner is declared in each category. In 1974, for instance, there were 1,112,702 entrants in the Punt, Pass, and Kick contest, and only six youngsters ended as winners.[1]

In cooperative, group-centered societies, such sporting activities would seem cruel, even barbaric, because success is achieved only at the cost of the failure of others. These societies, rather, would have sports where the object is something other than winning. For instance:

> The Tangu people of New Guinea play a popular game known as *taketak*, which involves throwing a spinning top into massed lots of stakes driven into the ground. There are two teams. Players of each team try to touch as many stakes with their tops as possible. In the end, however, the participants play not to win but to draw. The game must go on until an exact draw is reached. This requires great skill, since players sometimes must throw their tops into the massed stakes without touching a single one. *Taketak* expresses a prime value in Tangu culture, that is, the concept of moral equivalence, which is reflected in the precise sharing of foodstuffs among the people.[2]

This example demonstrates that a society's sports

mirror that society. Cooperative societies have sports that minimize competition, while aggressive societies have highly competitive sports. This raises a question about the nature of the most popular American sports. What do they tell us about ourselves and our society? Let us concentrate on the two most popular team sports—football and baseball—as they are played at the professional level.[3]

The Differing Natures of Football and Baseball

Although there are some similarities between football and baseball, e.g., cheating is the norm in both,[4] these two sports are basically different. In many ways they are opposites, and these incongruities provide insightful clues about Americans and American society.

Two fundamentally different orientations toward time exist in these two sports. Baseball is not bounded by time while football must adhere to a rigid time schedule. "Baseball is oblivious to time. There is no clock, no two-minute drill. The game flows in a timeless stream with a rhythm of its own."[5] In this way baseball reflects life in rural America as it existed in the not-too-distant past compared to football's emulation of contemporary urban society, where persons have rigid schedules, appointments, and time clocks to punch.

The innings of baseball have no time limit, and if the game is tied at the end of regulation innings, the teams play as many extra innings as it takes to determine a winner. Football, on the other hand, is played for sixty minutes, and if tied at the end, the game goes into "sudden death," i.e., the first team to score wins. Thus, even the nomenclature of the two sports—"extra innings" compared to "sudden death"—illustrates a basic difference between them. There are other semantic differences. A baseball player makes an "error," but a football team is "penalized." The object of baseball is to get "home" while the goal of football is to penetrate deep into the opponent's "territory." In baseball there is no home territory to defend; the playing field is shared by both teams. There is no analogue in baseball for the militaristic terms of football, e.g., "blitz," "bomb," "trap," "trenches," "field general," "aerial attack," and "ground attack."

Such linguistic differences imply a basic discrepancy between baseball and football. Baseball is essentially a calm and leisurely activity while football is intense, aggressive, and violent. Football is foremost a form of physical combat, whereas baseball is one of technique. A baseball player cannot get to first base because of his strength, aggression, or ability to intimidate. His only way to get there is through skill. In football, however, survival (success) belongs to the most aggressive. Former football player George Sauer has suggested that aggression on the football field leads to success just as it gets one ahead in American society.

> How does football justify teaching a man to be aggressive against another man? And how does it justify using that aggression for the ends that it has? I think the values of football as it is now played reflect a segment of thought, a particular kind of thought that is pretty prevalent in our society. The way to do anything in the world, the way to get ahead, is to aggress against somebody, compete against somebody, try to dominate, try to overcome, work your way up the ladder, and in doing so, you have to judge yourself and be judged as what you want to be in relation to somebody else all the time. Given the influence football has on young children, the immense influence it has as a socializing force in society, its impact should be rigorously examined. People learn certain values from watching football, from watching aggression, from watching it performed violently and knowing that these guys are going to get a big chunk of money if they do it well often enough.[6]

The two sports require different mentalities of their athletes. Football players must be aggressive while that is not a necessary ingredient for the baseball player. Also, baseball is a game of repetition and predictable action that is played over a 162-game schedule. The players must stay relaxed and not get too excited because to do so for every game would be too physically and emotionally draining over the six months of the season. Moreover, because the season is so long, players must pace themselves and not let a loss or even a succession of losses get them down. In football, though, losing is intolerable because of the short season (sixteen games). Thus, football players must play each game with extreme intensity. As a result the incidence of taking amphetamines ("uppers") has been much greater among football players than among baseball players. The intensity that characterizes football resembles the tensions and pressures of modern society, contrasted with the more relaxed pace of agrarian life and baseball.

One of the more interesting contrasts between these two sports is the equality of opportunity each offers. Baseball promotes equality while football is essentially unequal. This difference occurs in several ways. First, football originated among college elites and even today requires attending college to play at the professional level. Baseball has never been closely identified with college. Essentially, the way to make it in baseball is to work one's way through the minor leagues rather than by attending college (although that is one route).

A second way that baseball is more egalitarian than football is that it can be played by people of all sizes. There have been small All Star players such as Phil Rizzuto, Bobby Shantz, Pee Wee Reese, Joe Morgan, and Freddie Patek. Football, however, is a big man's game. In football the good, big team defeats the good, small team, whereas in baseball, the good, small team has an equal chance of beating the good, big team.

Baseball is also more equal than football because everyone has the opportunity to be a star. Each position has its stars. Pay is divided about equally by position. Except for designated hitters, all players must play both offense and defense. Thus, each player has the chance to make an outstanding defensive play or to bat in the winning run. Stardom in football is essentially reserved for those who play at certain positions. Only backs, receivers, and kickers score points while others labor in relative obscurity, making it possible for the "glamor boys" to score. This is similar, by the way, to American society, where the richest "players" score all the points, call the plays, and get the glory at the expense of the commoners. There is also a wide variance in pay by position in football. In 1977 the average NFL quarterback received $89,354 while the average defensive back received $47,403.

A final contrast on this equality dimension has to do with the availability of each of the sports to the masses. The average ticket price for major league baseball in 1978 was $3.98 compared to $9.67 for professional football.[7] The cheaper tickets for baseball allow families to attend and provide live entertainment for members of all social classes. Football, however, excludes families (except for the rich) and members of the lower classes because of the high prices and the necessity of purchasing season tickets.

Another major dimension on which these two sports differ is individualism. Baseball is highly individualistic. Elaborate teamwork is not required except for double plays and defensing sacrifice bunts. Each player struggles to succeed on his own. As Cavanaugh has characterized it:

> Although there are teams in baseball, there is little teamwork. The essence of the game is the individual with or against the ball: pitcher controlling, batter hitting, fielder handling, runner racing the ball. All players are on their own, struggling (like the farmer) to overcome not another human being but nature (the ball). This individualism is demonstrated when the shortstop, cleanly fielding the ball, receives credit for a "chance" even if the first baseman drops the thrown ball. It is demonstrated when a last-place team includes a Cy Young Award-winning pitcher or a league-leading hitter. It is perhaps most clearly manifest in the pitcher-batter duel, the heart of the game, when two men face each other. Baseball is each man doing the best he can for himself and against nature within a loose confederation of fellow individualists he may or may not admire and respect. This reflects a society in which individual effort, drive, and success are esteemed and in which, conversely, failure is deemed the individual's responsibility.[8]

Football, in sharp contrast, is the quintessence of team sports. Every move is planned and practiced in advance. The players in each of the eleven positions have a specific task to perform on every play. Every player is a specialist who must coordinate his actions with the other specialists on the team. So important is each person's play to the whole, that games are filmed and reviewed, with each play then broken down into its components and each player graded. Each player must subordinate his personality for the sake of the team. The coach is typically a stern taskmaster demanding submission of self to the team. The similarity of the football player to the organization man is obvious. So, too, is the parallel between football and the factory or corporation, where intricate and precise movements of all members doing different tasks are required for the attainment of the organization's objective.

Conclusion

Sociologist David Riesman in his classic book, *The Lonely Crowd*, noted a shift in American character since World War II.[9] Prior to that war Americans were what Riesman called "inner directed," which fit the demands of an essentially agrarian society. The farmer and the small entrepreneur succeeded on their own merits and efforts. "Rugged individualsim" was the necessary ingredient for success. There was the firm belief that everyone was a potential success.

But since the war the United States and Americans have changed. Rural life is replaced by living in cities and suburbs. Individuals now typically are dominated by large bureaucracies, whether they be governments, schools, churches, or factories. In these settings Riesman noted that Americans have become "other directed." Rather than an "automatic pilot" homing the inner-directed person toward his individual goal, the other-directed person has an "antenna" tuned to the values and opinions of others. In short he is a team player and conformist.

Baseball, then, represents what we were—an inner-directed, rural-individualistic society. It continues to be popular because of our longing for the peaceful past. Football, on the other hand, is popular now because it symbolizes what we now are—an other-directed, urban-technical-corporate-bureaucratic society. Thus these two sports represent cultural contrasts (country vs. city, stability vs. change, harmony vs. conflict, calm vs. intensity, and equality vs. inequality). Each sport contains a fundamental myth that it elaborates for its fans. Baseball represents an island of stability in a confused and confusing world. As such, it provides an antidote for a world of too much action, struggle, pressure, and change. Baseball provides this antidote by being individualistic, unbounded by time, nonviolent, leisurely in pace, and by perpetuating the American myths of equal opportunity, egalitarianism, and potential championship for everyone.

Football represents what we are. Our society is violent. It is highly technical. It is highly bureaucratized, and we are all caught in its impersonal clutches. Football fits contemporary urban-corporate society because it is team-oriented, dominated by the clock, aggressive, characterized by bursts of energy, highly technical, and because it disproportionately rewards individuals at certain positions.

The uniquely American sports of football and baseball, although they represent opposites, provide us with insight about ourselves and our society. What will become of these sports as society changes? Will we continue to find football and baseball so intriguing as society becomes more structured? We know that in the future American society will be short of resources. We know that its citizenry will be older and more educated than at present. We also know that society will become more urban. What will these and other trends mean for society and for sport? One thing is certain—as society changes so, too, will its sports. Does this mean that baseball and football will change? Will another sport emerge that is more attuned with the culture and structure of society? Or will baseball become even more popular as we become more nostalgic for the peaceful, pastoral past?

QUESTIONS

1. In what ways are the values of sport—such as competition, winning, perseverance—reflected in other institutions, such as politics, education, or the economy?

2. Can you identify some respects, in addition to those listed in the article, in which American sport reflects characteristics of the society?

3. Can you think of any characteristic differences between American sport and the sports of any other society? Are these differences sociologically significant?

Notes

1. D. Stanley Eitzen and George H. Sage, *Sociology of American Sport* (Dubuque, Iowa: Wm. C. Brown, 1978), pp. 68–69.

2. George B. Leonard, "Winning Isn't Everything: It's Nothing." *Intellectual Digest*, 4 (October, 1973), p. 45.

3. Several sources are especially important for the material that follows: Gerald J. Cavanaugh, "Baseball, Football, Images," *New York Times* (October 3, 1976), p. 28; George Carlin, "Baseball-Football," *An Evening with Wally Londo* (Los Angeles: Little David Records, 1975); Leonard Koppett, "Differing Creeds in Baseball, Football," *Sporting News* (September 6, 1975), pp.4 and 6; Murray Ross, "Football Red and Baseball Green," *Chicago Review* (January/February 1971), pp. 30–40; Richard Conway, "Baseball: A Discipline that Measures America's Way of Life," *Rocky Mountain News Trend* (October 19, 1975), p. 1; "Behind Baseball's Comeback: It's An Island of Stability," *U.S. News & World Report* (September 19, 1977), pp. 56–57; William Arens, "The Great American Football Ritual," *Natural History*, 84 (October, 1975), pp. 72–80; Susan P. Montague and Robert Morais, "Football Games and Rock Concerts: The Ritual Enactment of American Success Models," *The American Dimension: Cultural Myths and Realities*, William Arens (ed.) (Port Washington, New York: Alfred, 1976), pp. 33–52; and R. C. Crepeau, "Punt or Bunt: A Note in American Culture," *Journal of Sport History*, 3 (Winter 1976), pp. 205–212.

4. Cf., D. Stanley Eitzen, "Sport and Deviance."

5. Crepeau, "Punt or Bunt," p. 211.

6. Quoted in Jack Scott, "The Souring of George Sauer," *Intellectual Digest*, 2 (December 1971), pp. 52–55.

7. Tim Fedele, *Left Field*, 1 (April 1978), p. 1.

8. Cavanaugh, "Baseball, Football, Images," p. 25S.

9. David Riesman, *The Lonely Crowd* (New Haven: Yale University Press, 1950). The analysis that follows is largely dependent on Crepeau, "Punt or Bunt," pp. 205–212.

HARRY L. GRACEY

Learning the Student Role: Kindergarten as Academic Boot Camp

Socialization is the lifelong process by which people develop personality and learn the way of life of their society. Since virtually all human behavior is learned rather than inborn, the process is essential for both individual and society; neither could survive without it. The most important agency of socialization is, of course, the family; it is in this context that the child learns such basic skills as language and begins to acquire the norms and values of the culture. But in all modern industrial societies, the child soon experiences another vital agency of socialization, the school.

On the whole, children learn a great deal in school, although what they learn is by no means restricted to the formal curriculum. Equally important is the "hidden curriculum," for children also quickly learn how to fit in with a social system, how to follow rules, how to be punctual, how to respect authority, how to follow orders, how to compete, how to achieve success.

In this article, Harry Gracey compares kindergarten to a military boot camp. He first describes and then analyzes a typical day in a kindergarten classroom, showing that what the children are really learning is the student role—a role which, with various elaborations, they will play for many more years of their lives.

Introduction

. . . Education has been defined by sociologists, classical and contemporary, as an institution which serves society by socializing people into it through a formalized, standardized procedure. At the beginning of this century, Emile Durkheim told student teachers at the University of Paris that education "consists of a methodical socialization of the younger generation." He went on to add:

> It is the influence exercised by adult generations on those that are not ready for social life. Its object is to arouse and to develop in the child a certain number of physical, intellectual, and moral states that are demanded of him by the special milieu for which he is specifically destined. . . . To the egotistic and asocial being that has just been born, [society] must, as rapidly as possible, add another, capable of leading a moral and social life. Such is the work of education.

The educational process, Durkheim said, "is above all the means by which society perpetually re-creates the conditions of its very existence.". . .

. . .

Kindergarten is generally conceived by educators as a year of preparation for school. It is thought of as a year in which small children, five or six years old, are prepared socially and emotionally for the academic learning which will take place over the next twelve years. It is expected that a foundation of behavior and attitudes will be laid in kindergarten on which the children can acquire the skills and knowledge they will be taught in the grades. A booklet prepared for parents by the staff of a suburban New York school system says that the kindergarten experience will stimulate the child's desire to learn and cultivate the skills he will need for learning in the rest of his school career. It claims that the child will find opportunities for physical growth, for satisfying his "need for self-expression," acquire some knowledge, and provide opportunities for creative activity. It concludes, "The most important benefit that your five-year-old will receive from kindergarten is the opportunity to live and grow happily and purposefully with others in a small society." The kindergarten teachers in one of the elementary schools in this community, one we shall call the Wilbur Wright School, said their goals were to see that the children "grew" in all

63

ways: physically, of course, emotionally, socially, and academically. They said they wanted children to like school as a result of their kindergarten experiences and that they wanted them to learn to get along with others.

None of these goals, however, is unique to kindergarten: each of them is held to some extent by teachers in the other six grades at the Wright School. And growth would occur, but differently, even if the child did not attend school. The children already know how to get along with others in their families and their play groups. The unique job of the kindergarten in the educational division of labor seems rather to be teaching children the student role. The student role is the repertoire of behavior and attitudes regarded by educators as appropriate to children in school. Observation in the kindergartens of the Wilbur Wright School revealed a great variety of activities through which children are shown and then drilled in the behavior and attitudes defined as appropriate for school and thereby induced to learn the role of student. Observations of the kindergartens and interviews with the teachers both pointed to the teaching and learning of classroom routines as the main element of the student role. The teachers expended most of their efforts, for the first half of the year at least, in training the children to follow the routines which teachers created. The children were, in a very real sense, *drilled* in tasks and activities created by the teachers for their own purposes and beginning and ending quite arbitrarily (from the child's point of view) at the command of the teacher. One teacher remarked that she hated September, because during the first month "everything has to be done rigidly, and repeatedly, until they know exactly what they're supposed to do." However, "by January," she said, "they know exactly what to do [during the day] and I don't have to be after them all the time." Classroom routines were introduced gradually from the beginning of the year in all the kindergartens, and children were drilled in them as long as was necessary to achieve regular compliance. By the end of the school year, the successful kindergarten teacher has a well-organized group of children. They follow classroom routines automatically, having learned all the command signals and the expected responses to them. They have, in our terms, learned the student role. The following observation shows one such classroom operating at optimum organization on an afternoon late in May. It is the class of an experienced and respected kindergarten teacher.

An Afternoon in Kindergarten

At about 12:20 in the afternoon on a day in the last week of May, Edith Kerr leaves the teachers' room where she has been having lunch and walks to her classroom at the far end of the primary wing of Wright School. A group of five- and six-year-olds peer at her through the glass doors leading from the hall cloakroom to the play area outside. Entering her room, she straightens some material in the "book corner" of the room, arranges music on the piano, takes colored paper from her closet, and places it on one of the shelves under the window. Her room is divided into a number of activity areas through the arrangement of furniture and play equipment. Two easels and a paint table near the door create a kind of passageway inside the room. A wedge-shaped area just inside the front door is made into a teacher's area by the placing of "her" things there: her desk, file, and piano. To the left is the book corner, marked off from the rest of the room by a puppet stage and a movable chalkboard. In it are a display rack of picture books, a record player, and a stack of children's records. To the right of the entrance are the sink and cleanup area. Four large round tables with six chairs at each for the children are placed near the walls about halfway down the length of the room, two on each side, leaving a large open area in the center for group games, block building, and toy-truck driving. Windows stretch down the length of both walls, starting about three feet from the floor and extending almost to the high ceilings. Under the windows are long shelves on which are kept all the toys, games, blocks, paper, paints, and other equipment of the kindergarten. The left rear corner of the room is a play store with shelves, merchandise, and cash register; the right rear corner is a play kitchen with stove, sink, ironing board, and bassinette with baby dolls in it. This area is partly shielded from the rest of the room by a large standing display rack for posters and children's artwork. A sandbox is found against the back wall between these two areas. The room is light, brightly colored, and filled with things adults feel five- and six-year-olds will find interesting and pleasing.

At 12:25 Edith opens the outside door and admits the waiting children. They hang their sweaters on hooks outside the door and then go to the center of the room and arrange themselves in a semicircle on the floor, facing the teacher's chair which she has placed in the center of the floor. Edith follows them in and sits in her chair checking attendance while waiting for the bell to ring. When she has finished attendance, which she takes by sight, she asks the children what the date is, what day and month it is, how many children are enrolled in the class, how many are present, and how many are absent.

The bell rings at 12:30 and the teacher puts away her attendance book. She introduces a visitor, who is sitting against the right wall taking notes, as someone who wants to learn about schools and children. She then goes to the back of the room and takes down a large chart labeled "Helping Hands." Bringing it to the center of the room, she tells the children it is time to change jobs. Each child is assigned some task on the chart by placing his name, lettered on a paper "hand," next to a picture signifying the task—e.g., a broom, a blackboard, a milk bottle, a flag, and a Bible. She asks the children who wants each of the jobs and rearranges their "hands" accordingly. Returning to her chair, Edith announces, "One person should tell us what happened to Mark." A girl raises her hand and when called on says, "Mark fell and hit his head and had to go to the hospital." The teacher adds that Mark's mother had written saying he was in the hospital.

During this time the children have been interacting among themselves, in their semicircle. Children have whispered to their neighbors, poked one another, made general comments to the group, waved to friends on the other side of the circle. None of this has been disruptive, and the teacher has ignored it for the most part. The children seem to know just how much of each kind of interaction is permitted—they may greet in a soft voice someone who sits next to them, for example, but may not shout greetings to a friend who sits across the circle, so they confine themselves to waving and remain well within understood limits.

At 12:35 two children arrive. Edith asks them why they are late and then sends them to join the circle on the floor. The other children vie with each other to tell the newcomers what happened to Mark. When this leads to a general disorder Edith asks, "Who has serious time?" The children become quiet, and a girl raises her hand. Edith nods and the child gets a Bible and hands it to Edith. She reads the Twenty-third Psalm while the children sit quietly. Edith helps the child in charge begin reciting the Lord's Prayer, while the other children follow along for the first unit of sounds and then trail off as Edith finishes for them. Everyone stands and faces the American flag hung to the right of the door. Edith leads the pledge to the flag, with the children again following the familiar sounds as far as they remember them. Edith then asks the girl in charge what song she wants and the child replies, "My Country." Edith goes to the piano and plays "America," singing as the children follow her words.

Edith returns to her chair in the center of the room, and the children sit again in the semicircle on the floor. It is 12:40 when she tells the children, "Let's have boys' sharing time first." She calls the name of the first boy sitting on the end of the circle, and he comes up to her with a toy helicopter. He turns and holds it up for the other children to see. He says, "It's a helicopter." Edith asks, "What is it used for?" and he replies, "For the army. Carry men. For the war." Other children join in, "For shooting submarines." "To bring back men from space when they are in the ocean." Edith sends the boy back to the circle and asks the next boy if he has something. He replies "No" and she passes on to the next. He says "Yes" and brings a bird's nest to her. He holds it for the class to see, and the teacher asks, "What kind of bird made the nest?" The boy replies, "My friend says a rain bird made it." Edith asks what the nest is made of and

different children reply, "mud," "leaves," and "sticks." There is also a bit of moss woven into the nest and Edith tries to describe it to the children. They, however, are more interested in seeing if anything is inside it, and Edith lets the boy carry it around the semicircle showing the children its insides. Edith tells the children of some baby robins in a nest in her yard, and some of the children tell about baby birds they have seen. Some children are asking about a small object in the nest which they say looks like an egg, but all have seen the nest now, and Edith calls on the next boy. A number of children say, "I know what Michael has, but I'm not telling." Michael brings a book to the teacher and then goes back to his place in the circle of children. Edith reads the last page of the book to the class. Some children tell of books which they have at home. Edith calls the next boy, and three children call out, "I know what David has." "He always has the same thing." "It's a bang-bang." David goes to his table and gets a box which he brings to Edith. He opens it and shows the teacher a scale-model of an old-fashioned dueling pistol. When David does not turn around to the class, Edith tells him, "Show it to the children," and he does. One child says, "Mr. Johnson [the principal] said no guns." Edith replies, "Yes, how many of you know that?" Most of the children in the circle raise their hands. She continues, "That you aren't supposed to bring guns to school?" She calls the next boy on the circle and he brings two large toy soldiers to her which the children enthusiastically identify as being from "Babes in Toyland." The next boy brings an American flag to Edith and shows it to the class. She asks him what the stars and stripes stand for and admonishes him to treat it carefully. "Why should you treat it carefully?" she asks the boy. "Because it's our flag," he replies. She congratulates him, saying, "That's right."

"Show and Tell" lasted twenty minutes, and during the last ten, one girl in particular announced that she knew what each child called upon had to show. Edith asked her to be quiet each time she spoke out, but she was not content, continuing to offer her comment at each "show." Four children from other classes had come into the room to bring something from another teacher or to ask for something from Edith. Those with requests were asked to return later if the item wasn't readily available.

Edith now asks if any of the children told their mothers about their trip to the local zoo the previous day. Many children raise their hands. As Edith calls on them, they tell what they liked in the zoo. Some children cannot wait to be called on, and they call out things to the teacher who asks them to be quiet. After a few of the animals are mentioned, one child says, "I liked the spooky house," and the others chime in to agree with him, some pantomiming fear and horror. Edith is puzzled, and asks what this was. When half the children try to tell her at once, she raises her hand for quiet, then calls on individual children. One says, "The house with nobody in it"; another, "The dark little house." Edith asks where it was in the zoo, but the children cannot describe its location in any way which she can understand. Edith makes some jokes, but they involve adult abstractions which the children cannot grasp. The children have become quite noisy now, speaking out to make both relevant and irrelevant comments, and three little girls have become particularly assertive.

Edith gets up from her seat at 1:10 and goes to the book corner, where she puts a record on the player. As it begins a story about the trip to the zoo, she returns to the circle and asks the children to go sit at the tables. She divides them among the tables in such a way as to indicate that they don't have regular seats. When the children are all seated at the four tables, five or six to a table, the teacher asks, "Who wants to be the first one?" One of the noisy girls comes to the center of the room. The voice on the record is giving directions for imitating an ostrich and the girl follows them, walking around the center of the room holding her ankles with her hands. Edith replays the record, and all the children, table by table, imitate ostriches down the center of the room and back. Edith removes her shoes and shows that she can be an ostrich, too. This is apparently a familiar game, for a number of children are calling out, "Can we have the crab?" Edith asks one of the children to do a crab "so we can all remember how" and then plays the part of the record with music for imitating crabs by. The children from the first table line up across the room, hands and feet on the floor and face pointing toward the ceiling. After they have "walked" down the room and back in this posture, they sit at their table and the children of the next table play "crab." The children love this; they run from their tables, dance about on the floor waiting for their turns and are generally exuberant. Children ask for the "inch worm," and the game is played again with the children squirming down the floor. As a conclusion Edith shows them a new animal imitation, the "lame dog." The children all hobble down the floor on three "legs," table by table, to the accompaniment of the record.

At 1:30 Edith has the children line up in the center of the room; she says, "Table one, line up in front of me," and children ask, "What are we going to do?" Then she moves a few steps to the side and says, "Table two over here, line up next to table one," and more children ask, "What for?" She does this for table three and table four and each time the children ask, "Why, what are we going to do?" When the children are lined up in four lines of five each, spaced so that they are not touching one another, Edith puts on a new record and leads the class in calisthenics, to the accompaniment of the record. The children just jump around every which way in their places instead of doing the exercises, and by the time the record

is finished, Edith, the only one following it, seems exhausted. She is apparently adopting the president's new "Physical Fitness" program in her classroom.

At 1:35 Edith pulls her chair to the easels and calls the children to sit on the floor in front of her, table by table. When they are all seated she asks, "What are you going to do for worktime today?" Different children raise their hands and tell Edith what they are going to draw. Most are going to make pictures of animals they saw in the zoo. Edith asks if they want to make pictures to send to Mark in the hospital, and the children agree to this. Edith gives drawing paper to the children, calling them to her one by one. After getting a piece of paper, the children go to the crayon box on the right-hand shelves, select a number of colors, and go to the tables, where they begin drawing. Edith is again trying to quiet the perpetually talking girls. She keeps two of them standing by her so they won't disrupt the others. She asks them, "Why do you feel you have to talk all the time?" and then scolds them for not listening to her. Then she sends them to their tables to draw.

Most of the children are drawing at their tables, sitting or kneeling in their chairs. They are all working very industriously and, engrossed in their work, very quietly. Three girls have chosen to paint at the easels, and having donned their smocks, they are busily mixing colors and intently applying them to their pictures. If the children at the tables are primitives and neorealists in their animal depictions, these girls at the easels are the class abstract-expressionists, with their broad-stroked, colorful paintings.

Edith asks of the children generally, "What color should I make the cover of Mark's book?" Brown and green are suggested by some children "because Mark likes them." The other children are puzzled as to just what is going on and ask, "What book?" or "What does she mean?" Edith explains what she thought was clear to them already, that they are all going to put their pictures together in a "book" to be sent to Mark. She goes to a small table in the play kitchen corner and tells the children to bring her their pictures when they are finished and she will write their message for Mark on them.

By 1:50 most children have finished their pictures and given them to Edith. She talks with some of them as she ties the bundle of pictures together—answering questions, listening, carrying on conversations. The children are playing in various parts of the room with toys, games and blocks which they have taken off the shelves. They also move from table to table examining each other's pictures, offering compliments and suggestions. Three girls at a table are cutting up colored paper for a collage. Another girl is walking about the room in a pair of high heels with a woman's purse over her arm. Three boys are playing in the center of the room with the large block set, with which they are building walkways and walking on them. Edith is very much concerned about their safety and comes over a number of times to fuss over them. Two or three other boys are pushing trucks around the center of the room, and mild altercations occur when they drive through the block constructions. Some boys and a girl are playing at the toy store, two girls are serving "tea" in the play kitchen and one is washing a doll baby. Two boys have elected to clean the room, and with large sponges they wash the movable blackboard, the puppet stage, and then begin on the tables. They run into resistance from the children who are working with construction toys on the tables and do not want to dismantle their structures. The class is like a room full of bees, each intent on pursuing some activity, occasionally bumping into one another, but just veering off in another direction without serious altercation. At 2:05 the custodian arrives pushing a cart loaded with half-pint milk containers. He places a tray of cartons on the counter next to the sink, then leaves. His coming and going is unnoticed in the room (as, incidentally, is the presence of the observer, who is completely ignored by the children for the entire afternoon).

At 2:15 Edith walks to the entrance of the room, switches off the lights, and sits at the piano and plays. The children begin spontaneously singing the song, which is "Clean up, clean up. Everybody clean up." Edith walks around the room supervising the cleanup. Some children put their toys, the blocks, puzzles, games, and so on back on their shelves under the windows. The children making a collage keep right on working. A child from another class comes in to borrow the 45-rpm adaptor for the record player. At more urging from Edith the rest of the children shelve their toys and work. The children are sitting around their tables now, and Edith asks, "What record would you like to hear while you have your milk?" There is some confusion and no general consensus, so Edith drops the subject and begins to call the children, table by table, to come get their milk. "Table one," she says, and the five children come to the sink, wash their hands and dry them, pick up a carton of milk and a straw, and take it back to their table. Two talking girls wander about the room interfering with the children getting their milk and Edith calls out to them to "settle down." As the children sit, many of them call out to Edith the name of the record they want to hear. When all the children are seated at tables with milk, Edith plays one of these records called "Bozo and the Birds" and shows the children pictures in a book which go with the record. The record recites, and the book shows the adventures of the clown, Bozo, as he walks through a woods meeting many different kinds of birds who, of course, display the characteristics of many kinds of people or, more accurately, different stereotypes. As children finish their milk they take blankets or pads from the shelves under the windows and lie on them in the center of the room where Edith sits on her chair showing the pictures. By 2:30 half the class is lying

on the floor on their blankets, the record is still playing, and the teacher is turning the pages of the book. The child who came in previously returns the 45-rpm adaptor, and one of the kindergartners tells Edith what the boy's name is and where he lives.

The record ends at 2:40. Edith says, "Children, down on your blankets." All the class is lying on blankets now. Edith refuses to answer the various questions individual children put to her because, she tells them, "it's rest time now." Instead she talks very softly about what they will do tomorrow. They are going to work with clay, she says. The children lie quietly and listen. One of the boys raises his hand and when called on tells Edith, "The animals in the zoo looked so hungry yesterday." Edith asks the children what they think about this and a number try to volunteer opinions, but Edith accepts only those offered in a "rest-time tone," that is, softly and quietly. After a brief discussion of animal feeding, Edith calls the names of the two children on milk detail and has them collect empty milk cartons from the tables and return them to the tray. She asks the two children on cleanup detail to clean up the room. Then she gets up from her chair and goes to the door to turn on the lights. At this signal the children get up from the floor and return their blankets and pads to the shelf. It is raining (the reason for no outside play this afternoon), and cars driven by mothers clog the school drive and line up along the street. One of the talkative little girls comes over to Edith and pointing out the window says, "Mrs. Kerr, see my mother in the new Cadillac?"

At 2:50 Edith sits at the piano and plays. The children sit on the floor in the center of the room and sing. They have a repertoire of songs about animals, including one in which each child sings a refrain alone. They know these by heart and sing along through the ringing of the 2:55 bell. When the song is finished Edith gets up and coming to the group says, "Okay, rhyming words to get your coats today." The children raise their hands and as Edith calls on them, they tell her two rhyming words, after which they are allowed to go into the hall to get their coats and sweaters. They return to the room with these and sit at their tables. At 2:59 Edith says, "When you have your coats on, you may line up at the door." Half of the children go to the door and stand in a long line. When the three o'clock bell rings, Edith returns to the piano and plays. The children sing a song called "Goodbye," after which Edith sends them out.

Training for Learning and Life

The day in kindergarten at Wright School illustrates both the content of the student role as it has been learned by these children and the processes by which the teacher has brought about this learning or "taught" them the student role. The children have learned to go through routines and to follow orders with unquestioning obedience, even when these make no sense to them. They have been disciplined to do as they are told by an authoritative person without significant protest. Edith has developed this discipline in the children by creating and enforcing a rigid social structure in the classroom through which she effectively controls the behavior of most of the children for most of the school day. The "living with others in a small society" which the school pamphlet tells parents is the most important thing the children will learn in kindergarten can be seen now in its operational meaning, which is learning to live by the routines imposed by the school. This learning appears to be the principal content of the student role.

Children who submit to school-imposed discipline and come to identify with it, so that being a "good student" comes to be an important part of their developing identities, *become* the good students by the school's definitions. Those who submit to the routines of the school but do not come to identify with them will be adequate students who find the more important part of their identities elsewhere, such as in the play group outside school. Children who refuse to submit to the school routines are rebels, who become known as "bad students" and often "problem children" in the school, for they do not learn the academic curriculum and their behavior is often disruptive in the classroom. Today, schools engage clinical psychologists in part to help teachers deal with such children.

In looking at Edith's kindergarten at Wright School, it is interesting to ask how the children learn this role of student—come to accept school-imposed routines—and what, exactly, it involves in terms of behavior and attitudes. The most prominent features of the classroom are its physical and social structures. The room is carefully furnished and arranged in ways adults feel will interest children. The play store and play kitchen in the back of the room, for example, imply that children are interested in mimicking these activities of the adult world. The only space left for the children to create something of their own is the empty center of the room, and the materials at their disposal are the blocks, whose use causes anxiety on the part of the teacher. The room, being carefully organized physically by the adults, leaves little room for the creation of physical organization on the part of the children.

The social structure created by Edith is a far more powerful and subtle force for fitting the children to the student role. This structure is established by the very rigid and tightly controlled set of rituals and routines through which the children are put during the day. There is first the rigid "locating procedure" in which the children are asked to find themselves in terms of the month, date, day of the week, and the number of the class who are present and absent. This puts them solidly in the real world as defined by adults. The day is then divided into

six periods whose activities are for the most part determined by the teacher. In Edith's kindergarten the children went through serious time, which opens the school day, sharing time, play time (which in clear weather would be spent outside), work time, cleanup time, after which they have their milk, and rest time, after which they go home. The teacher has programmed activities for each of these times.

Occasionally the class is allowed limited discretion to choose between proffered activities such as stories or records, but original ideas for activities are never solicited from them. Opportunity for free individual action is open only once in the day, during the part of the work time left after the general class assignment has been completed (on the day reported, the class assignment was drawing animal pictures for the absent Mark). Spontaneous interests or observations from the children are never developed by the teacher. It seems that her schedule just does not allow room for developing such unplanned events. During sharing time, for example, the child who brought a bird's nest told Edith, in reply to her question of what kind of bird made it, "My friend says it's a rain bird." Edith does not think to ask about this bird, probably because the answer is "childish," that is, not given in accepted adult categories of birds. The children then express great interest in an object in the nest, but the teacher ignores this interest, probably because the object is uninteresting to her. The soldiers from "Babes in Toyland" strike a responsive note in the children, but this is not used for a discussion of any kind. The soldiers are treated in the same way as objects which bring little interest from the children. Finally, at the end of sharing time, the child world of perception literally erupts in the class with the recollection of "the spooky house" at the zoo. Apparently, this made more of an impression on the children than did any of the animals, but Edith is unable to make any sense of it for herself. The tightly imposed order of the class begins to break down as the children discover a universe of discourse of their own and begin talking excitedly with one another. The teacher is effectively excluded from this child's world of perception, and for a moment she fails to dominate the classroom situation. She reasserts control, however, by taking the children to the next activity she has planned for the day. It seems never to have occurred to Edith that there might be a meaningful learning experience for the children in re-creating the "spooky house" in the classroom. It seems fair to say that this would have offered an exercise in spontaneous self-expression and an opportunity for real creativity on the part of the children. Instead, they are taken through a canned animal-imitation procedure, an activity which they apparently enjoy but which is also imposed upon them rather than created by them.

While children's perceptions of the world and opportunities for genuine spontaneity and creativity are being systematically eliminated from the kindergarten, unquestioned obedience to authority and rote learning of meaningless material are being encouraged. When the children are called to line up in the center of the room they ask "Why?" and "What for?" as they are in the very process of complying. They have learned to go smoothly through a programmed day, regardless of whether parts of the program make any sense to them or not. Here the student role involves what might be called "doing what you're told and never mind why." Activities which might "make sense" to the children are effectively ruled out, and they are forced or induced to participate in activities which may be "senseless," such as the calisthenics.

At the same time the children are being taught by rote meaningless sounds in the ritual oaths and songs, such as the Lord's Prayer, the Pledge to the Flag, and "America." As they go through the grades children learn more and more of the sounds of these ritual oaths, but the fact that they have often learned meaningless sounds rather than meaningful statements is shown when they are asked to write these out in the sixth grade; they write them as groups of sounds rather than as a series of words, according to the sixth-grade teachers at Wright School. Probably much learning in the elementary grades is of this character, that is, having no intrinsic meaning to the children but rather being tasks inexplicably required of them by authoritative adults. Listening to sixth-grade children read social-studies reports, for example, in which they have copied material from encyclopedias about a particular country, an observer often gets the feeling that he is watching an activity which has no intrinsic meaning for the child. The child who reads, "Switzerland grows wheat and cows and grass and makes a lot of cheese" knows the dictionary meaning of each of these words but may very well have no conception at all of this "thing" called Switzerland. He is simply carrying out a task assigned by the teacher *because* it is assigned, and this may be its only "meaning" for him.

Another type of learning which takes place in kindergarten is seen in children who take advantage of the "holes" in the adult social structure to create activities of their own, during work time or out-of-doors during play time. Here the children are learning to carve out a small world of their own within the world created by adults. They very quickly learn that if they keep within permissible limits of noise and action, they can play much as they please. Small groups of children formed during the year in Edith's kindergarten who played together at these times, developing semi-independent little groups in which they created their own worlds in the interstices of the adult-imposed physical and social world. These groups remind the sociological observer very much of the so-called informal groups which adults develop in factories and offices of large bureaucracies. Here too, within authoritatively imposed social organizations people find "holes" to create little subworlds which support informal, friendly, nonofficial behavior. Forming and participating in such groups seems to be as much part of the student role as it is of the role of bureaucrat.

The kindergarten has been conceived of here as the year in which children are prepared for their schooling by learning the role of student. In the classrooms of the rest of the school grades the children will be asked to submit to systems and routines imposed by the teachers and the curriculum. The days will be much like those of kindergarten, except that academic subjects will be substituted for the activities of the kindergarten. Once out of the school system, young adults will more than likely find themselves working in large-scale bureaucratic organizations, perhaps on the assembly line in the factory, perhaps in the paper routines of the white collar occupations, where they will be required to submit to rigid routines imposed by "the company" which may make little sense to them. Those who can operate well in this situation will be successful bureaucratic functionaries. Kindergarten, therefore, can be seen as preparing children not only for participation in the bureaucratic organization of large modern school systems, but also for the large-scale occupational bureaucracies of modern society.

QUESTIONS

1. Is Gracey's comparison of kindergarten with a boot camp justified?

2. What are the similarities between the student role in the kindergarten and the student role in college? What are the differences?

3. What is distinctively sociological about Gracey's view of the kindergarten classroom? How would his understanding of what was taking place differ from that of the teacher and the children?

EDGAR H. SCHEIN

The Chinese Indoctrination
Program for Prisoners of War

*A relatively unusual but often dramatic type of social-
ization is the process sociologists call resocialization—
the kind of learning that involves a sharp break with
the past and the adoption of radically different norms
and values. Typically, resocialization takes places in a
situation where the individual has been isolated from
his or her previous social environment. The most effective resocialization often occurs in total institutions—
places of residence where the inmates are confined for
a period of their lives under the almost absolute control of a hierarchy of officials. Total institutions include, for example, prisons, concentration camps, military boot camps, traditional boarding schools, mental
asylums, and religious sects that require their members to live apart from the rest of society.*

*Perhaps the most radical form of resocialization is
so-called brainwashing, which aims at radically changing the individual's personality and attitudes. The
term "brainwashing" came into common usage in the
1950s, at the time of the Korean war. During that conflict, the communist Chinese subjected captured American soldiers to a deliberate resocialization that was
intended to change their political views by turning
them into communist sympathizers. The prisoner-of-
war camp is, of course, a total institution in its own
right, and the Chinese used this context for a systematic attempt to change the personality and political
orientation of their captives. In this article Edgar
Schein, a psychiatrist who studied released American
prisoners at the end of the war, describes the methods
that were used—with varying degrees of success—to
resocialize the captives.*

In this article I shall try to present an account of the
"typical" experiences of U.N. prisoners of war in Chinese
Communist hands and to interpret these experiences in a
social-psychological framework. Before the return of
U.N. prisoners, the "confessions" of such prominent men
as Cardinal Mindszenty and William Oatis had already
aroused considerable interest in so-called brainwashing.
This interest was heightened by the widespread rumors of
collaboration among U.N. prisoners of war in Korea. Following their repatriation in August, 1953, a rash of testi-
monial articles appeared in the weekly magazines, some
attempting to show that the Chinese Communist techniques were so terrifying that no one could withstand
them, others roundly condemning the collaborative activities of the so-called progressives as having been selfishly
motivated under conditions in which resistance was possible. These various accounts fall short because they are too
emotionally charged to be objective, and because they fail
to have any generality, since they are usually based on the
personal experiences of only one man.

The data upon which this article is based were gathered in an attempt to form a generalized picture of what
happened to the average man from the time he was captured until the time he was repatriated. The data were
collected during August, 1953, at Inchon, Korea, where
the repatriates were being processed, and on board the
U.S.N.S. *General Black* in transit to the United States
from September 1 to September 16. The method of collecting the data was, in the main, by intensive interviews
conducted in Inchon, where the author was a member of
one of the processing teams.

    . . .

The picture presented is not to be viewed as the experience of any single person, nor as the experience of all
men. Rather, it represents a composite or typical account
which, in all its details, may or may not have been true
for any one prisoner.

The Prisoner-of-War Experience
Capture, the March, and Temporary Camps

U.N. soldiers were captured by the Chinese and North
Koreans at all stages of the Korean conflict, although

From *Psychiatry*, 19: 149–172, 1956. Reprinted with permission.

particularly large groups were captured during November and December, 1950. The conditions under which men were captured varied widely. Some men were captured by having their positions overrun or surrounded; others ran into road blocks and were cut off; still others fought for many days on a shifting front before they succumbed. The situation in the front lines was highly fluid, and there was a good deal of confusion on both sides. When a position was overrun, the men often scattered and became disorganized.

While the initial treatment of prisoners by the North Koreans was typically harsh and brutal—they often took the prisoner's clothing, gave him little if any food, and met any resistance with immediate severe punishment or death—the Chinese, in line with their over-all indoctrination policy, often tried to create an atmosphere of friendliness and leniency. Some men reported that their Chinese captors approached them with outstretched hands, saying, "Congratulations! You've been liberated." It was made clear to the man that he could now join forces with other "fighters for peace." Often the Chinese soldiers pointed out to their captives how lucky they were not to have been captured by the North Koreans. Some men reported incidents of Chinese beating off North Koreans who were "trying to hurt" American prisoners, or of punishing their own guards for being too rough or inconsiderate. The men were usually allowed to keep their clothing, and some consideration was given to the sick and wounded. However, the food and medical attention were only slightly better than that provided by the North Koreans.

For the first 6 to 24 hours after capture, a man was usually in a state of dazed shock, unable to take any kind of integrated action and, later, unable to report any kind of feeling he had had during this period. Following this, he expected death or torture at the hands of his captors, for rumors that this would happen had been widely circulated in the front lines, often based on stories of men who had fallen into North Korean hands. These fears were, however, quickly dispelled by the friendly attitude of the Chinese soldiers; and this friendly attitude with the emphasis on "peace" was the first and perhaps most significant step in making the prisoner receptive to the more formal indoctrination which was to come later. . . .

The men were collected behind the lines and were marched north in groups of varying sizes. The men marched only at night, averaging about 20 miles, and were kept under strict cover in the daytime. Conditions on the march were very hard. Most men reported having great difficulty eating strange and badly prepared foods; however, they were often reminded, whether true or not, that they were getting essentially the same rations as the average Chinese foot soldier. Medical care was almost nonexistent, but this too was depicted as being equally true for Chinese soldiers because of supply shortages. Almost all the men had diarrhea, many had dysentery, and

most of them suffered from exposure. Every day would find a few more dead.

. . .

During these one- to two-week marches the men became increasingly disorganized and apathetic. They developed a slow plodding gait, called by one man a "prisoner's shuffle." Lines of authority tended to break down, and the prevailing attitude was "every man for himself." Open competition for food, clothing, and shelter made the maintenance of group ties almost impossible. Everything that happened tended to be frustrating and depriving, yet there was no ready outlet for hostility, and no opportunity for constructive resistance. The only *realistic* goal was to get to prison camp where, it was hoped, conditions would be better.

Uppermost in the men's minds were fantasies of food—memories of all the good meals they had had in the past, or plans for elaborate menus in the future. The only competing fantasies concerned loved ones at home, or cars, which seemed symbolically to represent the return to their homes and to freedom.

Arrival at one of the temporary camps was usually a severe disappointment. Many men reported that the only thing that had kept them going on the march was the hope of improved conditions in the camp; but they found the food as bad as ever, living conditions more crowded than before, and a continued lack of consideration for the sick and wounded. Moreover, there was now nothing to do but sit and wait. The news given the men was mostly false, playing up Communist military victories, and was, of course, particularly demoralizing. Many of the men became extremely apathetic and withdrawn, and according to some reports these apathy states sometimes became so severe as to result in death.

The Chinese continually promised improvements in conditions or early repatriation, and failures of these promises to materialize were blamed on obstructions created by U.N. air activity or lack of "cooperation" among the prisoners. It was always made clear that only certain prisoners could hope to get a break: those who "did well," "cooperated," "learned the truth," and so on. The Chinese distributed propaganda leaflets and required the men to sing Communist songs. Apparently even guards were sensitized to finding potential collaborators among the prisoners by observing their reactions to such activities. Outright indoctrination was not attempted on the marches and in the temporary camps, but those men who finally reached one of the permanent camps were ill-prepared physically and psychologically for the indoctrination pressures they were about to face.

Life in the Permanent Prisoner-of-War Camp

Most of the permanent camps were parts of small Korean villages, often split into several compounds in different parts of the village. The camps were sometimes surrounded by a fence, by barbed wire, or by natural barriers, although sometimes not enclosed at all. While guards were posted at key places, they were not sufficiently plentiful to prevent escapes or excursions to other parts of the village. The camp usually consisted of a series of mud huts in which the men slept on the floor or on straw matting, and a schoolhouse or other permanent building which was used as administrative headquarters, for lectures, and for recreation. The various Chinese officer and enlisted billets were usually scattered through the village. Mess and latrine facilities were very inadequate, and conditions were crowded, but far better than in the temporary camps.

In camp the men were segregated by race, nationality, and rank, and were organized into companies, platoons, and squads. The squads varied in size from 10 to 15 men, who usually shared the same living area. No formal organization was permitted among the prisoners; thus, the Chinese put their own personnel in charge of the platoons and companies, and appointed certain prisoners as squad leaders without consideration of rank.

Although the daily routine in camp varied, the average prisoner arose at dawn, was required to do calisthenics for an hour or more, was assigned to various details—such as gathering wood, carrying water, cooking, repairing roads, burying other prisoners, and general maintenance of the camp—and then was given a breakfast of potato soup or some form of cereal at around 8:00 A.M. The rest of the morning and afternoon was usually spent on indoctrination or details. Whether there was a midday meal depended on the attitude of the prisoner, the supply of food, and the general state of the political situation. The main meal was served around 5:00 P.M. and usually consisted of vegetables, grains, rice, and occasional bits of pork fat or fish. For men on such a meager diet, details involving many miles of walking or very hard work were especially exhausting.

Recreation varied with the camp and with the political situation. During the first year or so, a heavy emphasis was placed on indoctrination, and recreation was restricted to reading Communist literature, seeing propaganda films, and playing such games as checkers and chess. As the truce talks progressed and repatriation became a possibility, conditions in the camps improved generally.

. . .

The Indoctrination Program

All of these conditions in the permanent camp were, in actual practice, interlocked with the indoctrination program. This program cannot be viewed as a collection of specific techniques routinely applied, but rather as the creation of a whole set of social conditions within which certain techniques operated. Whether the Chinese manipulation of the social setting to create certain effects

was intentional can only be conjectured; intentional or not, it was an important factor in such success as the indoctrination program achieved.

The Removal of Supports to Beliefs, Attitudes, and Values

On matters of opinion, people tend to rely primarily on the opinions of others for determination of whether they themselves are "right" or "wrong"—whether these opinions of others are obtained through mass media of communication or through personal interaction. All of the prisoners' accustomed sources of information concerning daily events on a local, national or international level were cut off by the Chinese, who substituted their own, usually heavily biased, newspapers, radio broadcasts, and magazines. *The Daily Worker* from various cities was available in the camp libraries, as were numerous magazines and journals from China, Poland, Russia, and Czechoslovakia. The radio news broadcasts heard usually originated in China. And the camp headquarters had no scruples concerning accuracy in the news announcements made over the camp public-address system.

The delivery of mail from home was systematically manipulated; the evidence indicates that all mail which contained information about the war or the truce talks, or which contained favorable personal news, was withheld, while letters containing no general information, or bad personal news, were usually delivered.

Personal contact with visitors from outside the camps was very limited, mainly restricted to Communist news correspondents. For most prisoners, there was simply no way to find out accurately what was going on in the world.

The Chinese also attempted to weaken the means of consensual validation by undermining personal contacts among the men. First of all, the men were segregated by race, apparently in order to put special indoctrination pressure on members of certain minorities, especially Negroes. The men were also segregated by rank, in what appeared to be a systematic attempt to undermine the internal structure of the group by removing its leaders. . . .

The Chinese emphasized that rank was no longer of any significance; the entire group was now part of a wider "brotherhood"—the earlier mentioned "fighters for peace"—in which, under communism, everyone was to be equal. The Chinese sometimes put particularly young or inept prisoners in command of the squads to remind the men that former bases of organization no longer counted. While such a procedure aroused only resistance and hostility in most of the prisoners, undoubtedly a few malcontents welcomed the opportunity to gain occupancy of the favored positions that had never been available to them before.

There was also persistent emphasis on undermining all friendships, emotional bonds, and group activities. For instance, the Chinese prohibited all forms of religious expression and ruthlessly persecuted the few chaplains or others who tried to organize or conduct religious services. Bonds to loved ones at home were weakened by the withholding of mail, as the Chinese frequently pointed out to the men that the lack of mail meant that their friends and relatives no longer cared for them.

The systematic use of Chinese spies and also informers from prisoner ranks made it possible for the Chinese to obtain detailed information about almost all activities going on in camp. The men reported that the Chinese were forever sneaking around their quarters and listening to conversations or observing activities from hidden posts, and they also knew that some of their number were acting as informers. These circumstances helped to create a feeling of general distrust, and the only fully safe course was to withdraw from all intimate interaction with other prisoners.

When any semblance of effective organization appeared spontaneously among the men, the Chinese would usually immediately remove and segregate the leaders or key figures; and informal groups which might have supported resistance activities were also usually systematically broken up. The few that were not broken up either were not effective or died because of lack of internal support, thus indicating that this system of social control was highly effective. Usually groups were formed for one of three purposes—to plan for and aid in escapes, to prevent men from collaborating, or for social reasons. According to most reports, the groups organized around escape were highly ineffective. Usually such groups were quickly liquidated by being physically broken up. A few poorly planned escapes were attempted, but the marginal diet, the strangeness of the surrounding terrain, and the carefully built-up fear of the North Koreans all served to minimize escapes. When an escape did occur, the Chinese usually recovered the man easily by offering a bag of rice to anyone turning him in. The groups organized to keep men from collaborating, or to retaliate against them if they did, were usually composed of some of the more outspoken and violent resisters.

. . .

Various other groupings of men existed, some, such as the squad, for administrative reasons, others to support various Chinese enterprises. Soon after capture, the Chinese made a concerted effort to recruit men for a number of "peace committees" whose purpose it was to aid in the indoctrination by conducting personal interviews with resistant prisoners and to deter any resistance activity. They also were charged with such propaganda missions as the preparation of leaflets, peace petitions, and scripts for radio broadcasts—all under the guise of running such innocuous camp activities as recreation. An intercamp

peace organization was also formed to draw up peace appeals and petitions to be submitted to the United Nations, carrying, of course, the endorsement of a large number of prisoners.

. . .

One of the most significant facts about the few types of groups that did exist in camp is that they were highly unstable from an internal point of view because of the possible presence of informers and spies. Mutual distrust existed especially in the peace committees and in groups sanctioned by the Chinese, because no member was ever sure whether any other member was really a pro or was just pretending to "go along." If a man was pretending, he had to hide this carefully lest a real pro turn him in to the Chinese. Yet a man who sincerely believed in the Chinese peace effort had to hide this fact from others who might be pretenders, for fear they might harm him directly or blacklist him for the future, at the same time convincing other pros that he really was sincere.

The members of resistance groups and social groups also had to be wary of each other, because they never knew whether the group had been infiltrated by spies and informers. Furthermore, the fact that the group might be broken up at any time tended to keep any member from becoming too dependent on, or close to, another.

From the point of view of this analysis, the most important effect of the social isolation which existed was the consequent emotional isolation which prevented a man from validating any of his beliefs, attitudes, and values through meaningful interaction with other men at a time when these were under heavy attack from many sources, and when no accurate information was available.

Direct Attacks on Beliefs, Attitudes and Values

The chief method of direct indoctrination was a series of lectures that all prisoners had to attend at some time during their imprisonment. These lectures were given daily and lasted from two to three hours. Each camp had one or more political instructors who read the lectures from a prepared text. Often one instructor read while another seemed to follow a second copy of the text, as if to make sure that the right material was being presented. The lectures were direct, simple, black-and-white propaganda. They attacked the United Nations and particularly the United States on various political, social, and economic issues, at the same time glorifying the achievements of the Communist countries, and making strong appeals for "peace."

. . .

The constant hammering at certain points, combined with all the other techniques used—and in a situation where the prisoners had no access to other information—made it likely that many of the Chinese arguments did filter through enough to make many of the men question some of their former points of view. It is also likely that any appeal for "peace," no matter how false, found a receptive audience among combat-weary troops, especially when it was pointed out that they were fighting on foreign soil and were intervening in a civil war which was "none of their business." . . .

Another direct technique was the distribution of propaganda leaflets and the showing of Communist films glorifying the accomplishments of the Communist regime in Russia and China, and pointing out how much more had been done by communism for the peasant and laborer than by the capitalist system. While such films might have been highly ineffectual under ordinary circumstances, they assumed considerable importance because of the sheer lack of any other audiovisual material.

Perhaps the most effective attack on existing values, beliefs, and attitudes was the use of testimonials from prisoners who were ostensibly supporting Communist enterprises. These included peace petitions, radio appeals, speeches, and confessions. The use of such testimonials had a double effect in that it further weakened group ties while presenting pro-Communist arguments. As long as the men unanimously rejected the propaganda, each of them could firmly hold to the position that his beliefs must be right, even if he could not defend them logically. However, *if even one other man became convinced, it was no longer possible to hold this position.* Each man was then required to begin examining his beliefs and was vulnerable to the highly one-sided arguments that were repeatedly presented.

Of particular importance were the germ-warfare confessions which were extracted from a number of Air Force officers and enlisted men. The Chinese made a movie of one or two of the officers giving their testimony to the "international" commission which they had set up to investigate the problem, and showed this movie in all the camps. Furthermore, one or two of the officers personally went from camp to camp and explained how U.N. forces had used these bombs; this made a powerful impression on many men who had, until then, dismissed the whole matter as a Chinese propaganda project. The great detail of the accounts, the sincerity of the officers, the fact that they were freely going from camp to camp and did not look as if they were then or had previously been under any duress made it difficult for some men to believe that the accounts could be anything but true.

Indirect Attacks on Beliefs, Attitudes, and Values

In the direct attacks which I have been discussing, the source of propaganda was external. In the indirect attacks, a set of conditions was created in which each prisoner of war was encouraged to participate in a way that would make it more possible for him to accept some of the new points of view. One attempt to accomplish this was

by means of group discussions following lectures.

Most lectures ended with a series of conclusions—for example, "The South Koreans started the war by invading North Korea," or "The aim of the capitalist nations is world domination." The men were then required to break up into squads, go to their quarters, and discuss the material for periods of two hours or more. At the end of the discussion each squad had to provide written answers to questions handed out during the lecture—the answers, obviously, which had already been provided in the lecture. To "discuss" the lecture thus meant, in effect, to rationalize the predetermined conclusions.

A monitor was assigned to each squad to "aid" the men in the discussion, to make sure that they stayed on the proper topic, and to collect the answers and make sure that they were the "right" ones. Initially, the monitor for most squads was an English-speaking Chinese, but whenever possible the Chinese turned the job over to one of the squad members, usually the one who was most cooperative or sympathetic to the Communist point of view. If one or more members of the squad turned in "wrong" answers—for example, saying that the North Koreans had invaded South Korea—the entire squad had to listen to the lecture again and repeat the group discussion. This procedure might go on for days. The Chinese never tired of repeating the procedure over and over again, apparently believing that group discussion had a better chance of success in converting men to their point of view than individual indoctrination.

. . .

A second means of indirect attack was interrogation. Interrogations were carried on during all stages of internment, but their apparent function and the techniques utilized varied from time to time. Almost all men went through lengthy and repetitive military interrogations, but failure to answer questions seldom led to severe physical punishment. Instead, various psychological pressures were applied. For instance, all information supplied was cross-checked against earlier interrogations and against the information from other men. If an answer did not tally with other information, the respondent had to explain the discrepancy. Continuous pressure to resolve contrary answers often forced a man to tell the truth.

The Chinese tried to create the impression that they could obtain *any* information from *anyone* by the following interrogation technique: If a man continued to refuse to answer a question, despite great fatigue and continued repetition of the question, the interrogator would suddenly pull out a notebook and point out to the man the complete answer to the question, sometimes in astonishingly accurate detail. The interrogation would then move on to a new topic and the same procedure would be repeated, until the man could not assess whether there was indeed *anything* that the Chinese did *not* know. In most cases the man was told that others had already given information or "confessed," so why should he hold back and suffer?

A further technique was to have the man write out the question and then the answer. If he refused to write it voluntarily, he was asked to copy it from the notebooks, which must have seemed like a harmless enough concession. But the information which he had copied could then be shown to another man as evidence that he had given information of his own volition. Furthermore, it could be used to blackmail him, because he would have a hard time proving that he had merely copied the material.

Another type of interrogation to which almost all men were subjected involved primarily nonmilitary information. The Chinese were very curious about all aspects of life in the Western world and asked many questions about it, often in great detail. They also endeavored, by means of printed forms, to obtain a complete personal history from each prisoner, with particular emphasis on his social-cultural background, his class status, his and his parents' occupational histories, and so on. The purpose was apparently to determine which prisoners' histories might predispose them toward the Communist philosophy and thus make them apt subjects for special indoctrination.

Most men did not give accurate information. Usually the prisoner filled out the form in terms of fictitious characters. But later he would be required to repeat the entire procedure and would usually be unable to remember his earlier answers. He would then be confronted with the discrepancies and would be forced into the fatiguing activity of having to invent justification after justification to resolve them.

If and when the Chinese felt that they had obtained a relatively true account, it was used in discussion between the interrogator and the prisoner to undermine the prisoner's beliefs and values. Various points in the life history were used to show a man the "errors" of his past life—for example, that he or his parents had been ruthless capitalists exploiting workers, yet had really received only meager benefits from such exploitation. The Chinese were particularly interested in any inconsistencies in the life histories and would focus discussion on them in order to bring to light the motivations involved. Whenever possible, any setbacks that a man had experienced economically or socially were searchingly analyzed, and the blame was laid on the capitalistic system.

The fact that many men were unclear about why they were fighting in Korea was a good lever for such discussions. The interrogator or instructor could point out the basic injustices of foreign intervention in a civil war, and simultaneously could arouse longings for home and the wish that the United Nations had never taken up the fight in the first place. It was not difficult to convince some men that being in Korea was unfair to the Koreans, to themselves, and to their families who wanted them home.

. . .

Another effective technique for getting the men to question their own beliefs and values was to make them confess publicly to wrongdoings and to "criticize" themselves. Throughout the time that the men were in camp they were required to go through these rituals over and over again, no matter how trivial the offense. These offenses usually were infractions of camp rules. Soon after the men had arrived in permanent camp they were given copies of the camp rules and were required to sign a statement that they would abide by them. Most of the men were far too hungry and cold to read several pages of script covering every aspect of camp life in such minute detail that it was practically impossible not to break one of the rules from time to time. For example, an elaborate set of rules governed where in camp a man was allowed to expectorate.

Sooner or later a minor or major infraction of the rules would occur. The man would be immediately brought up before the camp commander, where his offense would be condemned as a serious crime—one for which he, the commander would point out, could be severely punished, if it were not for the lenient Chinese policy. In line with the great show which the Chinese made of treating the prisoner as a responsible person, the fact that he had agreed in writing to abide by the rules would be emphasized. The prisoner could not now say that he had not read the rules, for this would expose him to further embarrassment. The camp commander would then ask whether the man would admit that he had broken the rule, whether he was sorry that he had done so, and whether he would promise not to behave in such a "criminal" manner in the future. If the offender agreed, which seemed at the time to be harmless enough and an easy way to get off, he would be asked to write out a confession.

Sometimes this ended the matter. But frequently the man was required to read his confession to a group of prisoners and to follow it by "self-criticism," which meant that the description of the wrong deed had to be analyzed in terms of the wrong *idea* that lay behind it, that the self had to be "deeply and sincerely" criticized in terms of a number of reasons why the idea and deed were "wrong," and that an elaborate set of promises about future conduct had to be made, along with apologies for the past. Such public self-effacement was a humiliating and degrading experience, and it set a bad precedent for other men who had been attempting to resist getting caught in this net.

Writing out confessions, reading them, and criticizing oneself for minor misconduct in camp did not seem too great a concession at first when viewed against the possibility of physical punishment, torture, or imprisonment. However, these techniques could become a psychological torture once the initial concession had been made. A man who had broken a rule and had gone through the whole ritual of criticism would shortly afterward break another rule, which would arouse increased hostility on the part of the Chinese and lead to correspondingly greater demands for confession and self-criticism. Men who had confessed at first to trivial offenses soon found themselves having to answer for relatively major ones.

It should be pointed out, however, that the prisoners found numerous ways to obey the letter but not the spirit of the Chinese demands. For example, during public self-criticism sessions they would often emphasize the wrong words in the sentence, thus making the whole ritual ridiculous: "I am sorry I called Comrade Wong *a no-good son-of-a-bitch*." Another favorite device was to promise never to "get caught" committing a certain crime in the future. Such devices were effective because even those Chinese who knew English were not sufficiently acquainted with idiom and slang to detect subtle ridicule.

There is also some evidence that the Chinese used enforced idleness or solitary confinement to encourage prisoners to consider the Communist point of view. One of the few activities available, in such circumstances, was to read Communist literature and books by Western authors who directly or indirectly attacked capitalism. The camp libraries were wholly made up of such literature. Those who did not have the strength or inclination to go on physically taxing details found themselves with no alternative but to spend their time reading pro-Communist material. In addition, some read because they felt so emotionally isolated from other prisoners that they could enjoy only solitary activities.

The Eliciting of Collaboration by Rewards and Punishments

For a number of propaganda purposes the Chinese seemed to want certain men to cooperate in specific ways, without caring whether they accepted communism or not. These men did not seem to enjoy as much status as other pros and were cast off by the Chinese as soon as they had ceased to be useful. Such collaboration was elicited directly by a system of rewards and incentives on the one hand, and threats and punishments on the other. . . .

It was made clear to all prisoners, from the time of their capture on, that cooperation with the Chinese would produce a more comfortable state of affairs, while noncooperation or open resistance would produce a continuing marginal existence. Which rewards were of primary importance to the men varied with their current condition. On the marches and in the temporary camps physical conditions were so bad that more food, any medication, any clothing or fuel, better and less crowded living conditions, and the like constituted a powerful reward. Promises of early repatriation, or at least of marked improvement of conditions in the permanent camps, were powerful incentives which were chronically exploited.

In the permanent camps there was some improvement in the physical conditions, so that basic necessities became less effective incentives. The promise of early repatriation continued to be a great incentive, however, despite the fact that it had been promised many times before without result. Communicating with the outside world now became a major concern. To let those at home know they were alive, some prisoners began to collaborate by making slanted radio broadcasts or filling their letters with propaganda or peace appeals in order to make sure that they were sent.

As conditions continued to improve, some of the luxury items and smaller accessories to living assumed greater significance. Cigarettes, combs, soap, candy, small items of clothing, a cup of hot tea, a drink of liquor, fresh fruit, and other items of this kind were sought avidly by some men. Obtaining such items from the Chinese was inextricably linked with the degree to which the prisoner was willing to "cooperate." Any tendency toward "cooperation" was quickly followed by an increase in material rewards and promises for the future.

In some cases rewards were cleverly linked with participation in the indoctrination. For example, highly valued prizes such as cigarettes or fresh fruit were offered for essays dealing with certain aspects of world politics. The winning entries were published in the camp newspaper or magazine. Usually the winning entry was selected on the basis of its agreement with a Communist point of view. . . . In order to retain these special privileges—and having in any case incurred the hostility or even ostracism of their own group—some of these men continued to collaborate, rationalizing that they were not really harming the U.N. cause. They became self-appointed secret agents and attempted to infiltrate the Chinese hierarchy to gather "intelligence information," in which capacity they felt that they could actually aid the U.N. cause.

Among the most effective rewards used by the Chinese were special privileges and certain symbolic rewards, such as rank and status in the prison hierarchy. Perhaps the most important of the privileges was freedom of movement; the pros had free access to the Chinese headquarters and could go into town or wherever they wished at any time of the day or night. They were given certain preferred jobs, such as writing for the camp newspaper, and were excused from the more unpleasant chores around the camp. They were often consulted by the Chinese in various policy matters. They received as a status symbol a little peace dove to be worn in the lapel or a Mao Tse-tung button which served as an identification badge. And many rewards were promised them for the future; they were told that they were playing a vital role in the world-wide movement for "peace," and that they could enjoy positions of high rank in this movement if they stayed and continued to work for it.

. . .

Just as the probability of collaborative behavior could be increased through the use of rewards, the probability of resistance could be decreased through negative or painful stimulation. Usually threats of punishment were used when prisoners refused to "cooperate," and actual punishment was meted out for more aggressive resistance. Threats of death, nonrepatriation, torture, reprisals against families, reduction in food and medication, and imprisonment were all used. While the only one of these threats which was carried out with any degree of consistency was imprisonment, which sometimes involved long periods of solitary confinement, the other threats were nevertheless very effective and the possibility that they might be carried out seemed very real. Especially frightening was the prospect of nonrepatriation which seemed a likely possibility before the prisoner lists were exchanged at Panmunjom. The threat of death was also effective, for the men knew that they could be killed and listed officially as having died of heart failure or the like. With regard to food and medication, the men could not determine whether they were actually being punished by having these withheld, or whether the meager supply was merely being reserved for "deserving" prisoners.

An effective threat with officers was that of punishing the whole group for which the officer was responsible if he personally did not "cooperate." The incidence of such group punishment was not revealed in the accounts, but it is clear that if an officer did "cooperate" with the Chinese, he was able both to relieve his own fears and to rationalize his cooperation as being the only means of saving the men for whom he was responsible.

Reinforcing all these threats was the vague but powerful fear of the unknown; the men did not know what they were up against in dealing with the Chinese and could not predict the reactions of their captors with any degree of reliability. The only course that led to a consistent reduction in such tension was participation in Chinese enterprises.

Overt punishment varied with the offense, with the political situation, and with the person administering it. Shortly after capture there were numerous incidents of brutality, most of them committed by North Koreans. During early interrogations the Chinese frequently resorted to minor physical punishment such as face-slapping or kicking when answers were not forthcoming, but a prisoner who continued to be silent was usually dismissed without further physical punishment.

Physical punishments in permanent camps had the effect of weakening rather than injuring the men. They varied from severe work details to such ordeals as standing at attention for long periods; being exposed to bright lights or excessive cold; standing on tiptoe with a noose around the neck; being confined in the "cages," a room too small to allow standing, sitting, or lying down; being thrown in the "hole," a particularly uncomfortable form of solitary confinement; or being kept in filthy surroundings and denied certain essentials for keeping clean. Those who were *chronically* uncooperative were permanently segregated from the rest of the group and put into special camps where more severe forms of discipline backed by harsher punishments were in effect. Basically, the "lenient policy" applied only to those men whom the Chinese hoped they could use.

More common forms of punishment for minor infractions were social in character, intended to degrade or embarrass the prisoner in front of his fellows. Public confessions and self-criticisms were the outstanding forms of such punishment, with blackmail being frequently used if a prisoner had once collaborated to any extent. There is *no* evidence that the Chinese used any drugs or hypnotic methods, or offered sexual objects to elicit information, confessions, or collaborative behavior. Some cases of severe physical torture were reported, but their incidence is difficult to estimate.

General Principles in All Techniques

Several general principles underlay the various phases of the Chinese indoctrination, which may be worth summing up at this point. The first of these was *repetition*. One of the chief characteristics of the Chinese was their immense patience in whatever they were doing; whether they were conducting an interrogation, giving a lecture, chiding a prisoner, or trying to obtain a confession, they were always willing to make their demand or assertion over and over again. Many men pointed out that most of the techniques used gained their effectiveness by being used in this repetitive way until the prisoner could no longer sustain his resistance. A second characteristic was the *pacing of demands*. In the various kinds of responses that were demanded of the prisoners, the Chinese always started with trivial, innocuous ones and, as the habit of responding became established, gradually worked up to more important ones. Thus after a prisoner had once been "trained" to speak or write out trivia, statements on more important issues were demanded of him. This was particularly effective in eliciting confessions, self-criticism, and information during interrogation.

Closely connected with the principle of pacing was the principle of constant *participation* from the prisoner. It was never enough for the prisoner to listen and absorb; some kind of verbal or written response was always demanded. Thus if a man would not give original material in question-and-answer sessions, he was asked to copy something. Likewise, group discussions, autobiographical statements, self-criticisms, and public confessions all demanded an active participation by the prisoner.

In their propaganda campaign the Chinese made a

considerable effort *to insert their new ideas into old and meaningful contexts*. In general this was not very successful, but it did work for certain prisoners who were in some way not content with their lot in the United States. The obtaining of autobiographies enabled each interrogator to determine what would be a significant context for the particular person he was dealing with, and any misfortune or setback that the person had suffered served as an ideal starting place for undermining democratic attitudes and instilling communistic ones.

No matter which technique the Chinese were using, they always structured the situation in such a way that the correct response was followed by some form of *reward*, while an incorrect response was immediately followed by *threats or punishment*. The fact that the Chinese had complete control over material resources and had a monopoly of power made it possible for them to manipulate hunger and some other motives at will, thereby giving rewards and punishments their meaning.

Among the various propaganda techniques employed by the Chinese, their use of *prestige suggestion* was outstanding. The average prisoner had no way of disputing the germ-warfare confessions and testimonials of Air Force officers, or the conclusions of an investigation of the germ-warfare charges by ostensibly impartial scientists from many nations.

Among the positive propaganda appeals made, the most effective was probably the *plea for peace*. The Chinese presented an antiwar and laissez-faire ideology which strongly appealed to the war-weary combat soldier.

In addition, the Chinese used a number of *manipulative tricks*, which were usually successful only if the prisoner was not alert because of fatigue or hunger. One such trick was to require signatures, photographs, or personal information for a purpose which sounded legitimate, then using them for another purpose. Some prisoners reported that they were asked to sign "camp rosters" when they first arrived in camp and later found that they had actually signed a peace petition.

In essence, the prisoner-of-war experience in camp can be viewed as a series of problems which each man had to solve in order to remain alive and well integrated. Foremost was the problem of physical privation, which powerfully motivated each man to improve his living conditions. A second problem was to overcome the fears of nonrepatriation, death, torture, or reprisals. A third problem was to maintain some kind of cognitive integration, a consistent outlook on life, under a set of conditions where basic values and beliefs were strongly undermined and where systematic confusion about each man's role in life was created. A fourth problem was to maintain a valid position in a group, to maintain friendship ties and concern for others under conditions of mutual distrust, lack of

leadership, and systematically created social disorganization. The Chinese had created a set of conditions in which collaboration and the acceptance of communism led to a resolution of conflicts in all these areas.

. . .

The Effectiveness of the Indoctrination Techniques

By disrupting social organization and by the systematic use of reward and punishment, the Chinese were able to elicit a considerable amount of collaboration. This is not surprising when one considers the tremendous effort the Chinese made to discover the weak points in individual prisoners, and the unscrupulousness with which they manipulated the environment. Only a few men were able to avoid collaboration altogether—those who adopted a completely negativistic position from the moment of capture without considering the consequences for themselves or their fellow prisoners. At the same time the number of men who collaborated to a sufficient extent to be detrimental to the U.N. cause was also very small. The majority collaborated at one time or another by doing things which seemed to them trivial, but which the Chinese were able to turn to their advantage. Such behavior did not necessarily reflect any defection from democratic values or ideology, nor did it necessarily imply that these men were opportunists or neurotics. Often it merely represented poor judgment in evaluating a situation about which they had little information, and poor foresight regarding the reactions of the Chinese, other prisoners, and people back home.

The extent to which the Chinese succeeded in converting prisoners of war to the Communist ideology is difficult to evaluate because of the previously mentioned hazards in measuring ideological change, and because of the impossibility of determining the *latent* effects of the indoctrination. In terms of *overt* criteria of conversion or ideological change, one can only conclude that, considering the effort devoted to it, the Chinese program was a failure. Only a small number of men decided to refuse repatriation—possibly for reasons other than ideological change—and it was the almost unanimous opinion of the prisoners that most of the pros were opportunists or weaklings. One can only conjecture, of course, the extent to which prisoners who began to believe in communism managed to conceal their sympathies from their fellows and the degree to which repatriates are now, as a result of their experience, predisposed to find fault with a democratic society if they cannot make a go of it.

It is difficult to determine whether to attribute this relative failure of the Chinese program to the inadequacy of their principles of indoctrination, to their technical inefficiency in running the program, or to both these factors. In actual practice the direct techniques used were usually ineffective because many of the Chinese instructors were deficient in their knowledge of Western culture and the English language. Many of their facts about America were false, making it impossible for them to obtain a sympathetic audience, and many of their attempts to teach by means of group discussion failed because they were not sensitive to the subtle ways in which prisoners managed to ridicule them by sarcasm or other language devices. The various intensive pressures brought to bear on single prisoners and the fostering of close personal relationships between prisoner and instructor were far more effective in producing ideological change, but the Chinese did not have nearly enough trained personnel to indoctrinate more than a handful of men in this intensive manner.

The technique of breaking up both formal and spontaneous organization was effective in creating feelings of social and emotional isolation, but it was never sufficiently extended to make the prisoners completely dependent on the Chinese. As long as the men lived and "studied" together, there remained opportunities for consensual validation and thus for resisting indoctrination. However, as a means of social control this technique was highly effective, in that it was virtually impossible for the prisoners to develop any program of organized resistance or to engineer successful communication with the outside by means of escapes or clandestine sending out of information.

The most powerful argument against the intellectual appeal of communism was the low standard of living which the men observed in the Korean villages in which they lived. The repatriates reported that they were unable to believe in a system of values which sounded attractive on paper but which was not practiced, and they were not impressed by the excuse that such conditions were only temporary.

. . .

In summary, it can be said that the Chinese were successful in eliciting and controlling certain kinds of behavior in the prisoner population. They were less successful in changing the beliefs of the prisoners. Yet this lack of success might have been due to the inefficiency of a program of indoctrination which could have been highly effective had it been better supported by adequate information and adequately trained personnel.

Collaboration with the enemy occurs to a greater or lesser extent in any captive population. It occurred in the Japanese and German prisoner-of-war camps during World War II. But never before have captured American soldiers faced a *systematic effort* to make them collaborate and to convert them to an alien political ideology. . . . By means of extreme and degrading physical and psychological torture the Nazis attempted to reduce the prison population to an "infantile" state in which the jailer would be viewed with the same awe as the child

views his father. Under these conditions, the prisoners tended in time to identify with the punitive authority figures and to incorporate many of the values they held, especially with respect to proper behavior in camp. They would curry the favor of the guards, would imitate their style of dress and speech, and would attempt to make other prisoners follow camp rules strictly.

It is possible that such a mechanism also operated in the Chinese prison camps. However, the Nazis attempted, by brutal measures, to reduce their prisoners to docile slave laborers, while the Chinese attempted, by using a "lenient policy" and by treating the prisoners as men in need of "education," to obtain converts who would actively support the Communist point of view. Only those prisoners who showed themselves to be "backward" or "reactionary" by their inability to see the fundamental "truths" of communism were treated punitively.

The essence of this novel approach is to gain complete control over those parts of the physical and social environment which sustain attitudes, beliefs, and values, breaking down interactions and emotional bonds which support the old beliefs and values, and building up new interactions which will increase the probability of the adoption of new beliefs and values. If the only contacts a person is permitted are with persons who *unanimously* have beliefs different from his own, it is very likely that he will find at least some among them with whom, because of growing emotional bonds, he will identify and whose beliefs he will subsequently adopt.

. . .

Taken singly, there is nothing new or terrifying about the specific techniques used by the Chinese; they invented no mysterious devices for dealing with people. Their method of controlling information by controlling the mass media of communication has been a well-known technique of totalitarian governments throughout history. Their system of propagandizing by means of lectures, movies, reading materials, and testimonials has its counterparts in education and in advertising. Group discussions and other methods requiring participation have their counterparts in education and in psychiatry. The possibility that group discussion may be fundamentally superior to lectures in obtaining stable decisions by participants has been the subject of extensive research in American social psychology. The Chinese methods of interrogation have been widely used in other armies, by the police, by newspaper reporters, and by others interested in aggressively eliciting information. Forced confessions and self-criticism have been widely used techniques in religious movements as a basis for conversion or as a device to perpetuate a given faith. The control of behavior by the manipulation of reward and punishment is obviously the least novel of all the techniques, for men have controlled each other in this way since the beginning of history.

Thus the only novelty in the Chinese methods was the attempt to *use a combination of all these techniques and to apply them simultaneously* in order to gain complete control over significant portions of the physical and social environment of a group of people. . . .

QUESTIONS

1. Have any members of the class experienced resocialization attempts, perhaps in a total institution? Analyze and discuss any such experiences.
2. Why do you think the Chinese indoctrination program was only partially successful?
3. Does indoctrination take place in the United States?

THOMAS POWERS

Learning to Die

*Death has been, and to a great extent still is, a taboo
subject in the modern world. Unlike traditional societies, in which death and dying were an integral and accepted part of community life, we have tended to sani-
tize death and to isolate the dying. The topic of death
is avoided, or spoken of in hushed terms as though it
were shameful; the dying are consigned to hospitals
and nursing homes, as though their presence embarrassed the living.*

*Yet attitudes toward death are gradually changing,
in no small measure because of the public discussion
stimulated by media reports of the extensive sociological research into the subject over the past fifteen years
or so. This research has produced a number of findings that at first seemed surprising—for example, that
dying people prefer to be told the truth about their
condition; that impending death is easier for both the
dying and their loved ones if it is openly discussed
among them; that the dying, in the end, usually accept
death peacefully and without fear.*

*In this article, Thomas Powers traces the case his-
tory of a dying woman, interweaving his account with
some of the findings of sociological research on death.*

From *Harper's Magazine,* June 1971. Copyright © 1971 by Thomas
Powers.

On November 8, 1970, Barbara B., a woman in her middle sixties, was admitted to New York Hospital with an
unexplained intestinal blockage. Because it was a Sunday
and her own doctor was unavailable, the doctor of a
friend took over. He had never met Mrs. B. and knew
nothing of her medical history. When he asked what was
wrong she described her symptoms during the preceding
few days but volunteered nothing else. Dr. C. began making arrangements for an exploratory operation in the next
day or two if the situation did not correct itself.

A friend had accompanied Mrs. B. to the hospital.
Later that day her daughter and son-in-law came up to
see her. Mrs. B. was in considerable pain so there was not
much conversation. When they did talk, it was about
matters of little consequence. Not knowing exactly what
Mrs. B.'s condition was they all hoped that an operation
would not be necessary, but they did not speculate as to
what might have caused the blockage. Each of the four
had a pretty good idea of the cause: none of them mentioned it that first day.

On Monday Dr. C. contacted Mrs. B.'s regular doctor
and was told she had had a cancerous breast removed in
the summer of 1968, that malignant skin nodules had
reappeared in the summer of 1970, and that laboratory
tests showed spreading cancer. It was obvious to Dr. C.
that Mrs. B.'s cancer had reached her abdomen and that
she did not have long to live. When he spoke to Mrs. B.'s
family, however, he was somewhat more tentative. He
said he was not sure (which was true; he was not *absolutely certain*) what was causing the blockage, that the
blockage might disappear, that he advised waiting for a
few days to see how things developed. He admitted, in
response to direct questions, that Mrs. B. was suffering
from a serious case of cancer and that serious in her case
probably meant fatal. He muted only the probable (but
not yet *certain*) fact that Mrs. B. had already begun to
die.

During the following few days Mrs. B. was in continual discomfort but nevertheless remained the same person her family had always known: witty, unsentimental,
interested in gossip, a passionate reader, a stern critic of
everything about President Nixon except the good looks
of his daughters, in all things a woman determined to be

strong. When friends or family came to visit she talked about politics, life on Tenth Street, what she was reading, and so on. Everyone asked how she was feeling. She always answered, "Oh, all right," with a look of disgust. Once or twice she said she hoped she would not need an operation. A kind of unspoken agreement was in effect: cancer was not to be mentioned. The reasons for the agreement varied. Mrs. B. felt it was weak to discuss bodily ills, and wanted to spare her daughter. Her daughter wanted to spare her mother. Mrs. B. and her family all knew her cancer had reappeared, but discussion of the possible operation was based on the unstated assumption that the cancer and the intestinal blockage were two entirely separate conditions. In other words, everyone knew the end was coming, but resisted the notion that it was coming *now*.

When the blockage persisted into the middle of the next week, however, it became increasingly difficult to ignore the seriousness of Mrs. B.'s condition. Mrs. B. had nothing but contempt for people who complained and was inclined to think that any mention of her own condition was a kind of complaining. In spite of this, she began to refer to it elliptically.

One evening, as her son-in-law was just leaving, she abruptly mentioned a Kingsley Amis novel she had once read in which a character visits a hospitalized friend who is dying with cancer (Mrs. B. winced at the word) of the stomach. In the novel, the dying friend makes little pretense of interest in the conversation; he is simply trying to hold on until his next pain shot.

"I'm beginning to feel that way myself," Mrs. B. said with a bitter smile, apologizing for her failure to keep up her end of the conversation and ashamed of herself for bringing it up. "When something really hurts, all you live for is that pain shot."

A couple of days later Mrs. B.'s son-in-law arrived just as Mrs. B.'s roommate was coming out of anesthesia following an operation to determine if she had breast cancer. The son-in-law asked what the verdict had been. "She had two tumors but neither was malignant," Mrs. B. said. "Some people have all the luck."

Mrs. B. refrained from talking about her feelings directly on all but one or two occasions. Once she told her daughter, "I've got so little to look forward to," but then regained her composure. "Sometimes I can't help feeling blue," she explained. There were other slips, but generally she refused to talk about what she was going through, or to let anyone else talk about it. Neither she nor anyone else had yet admitted fully what was now the one great fact in her life: she was dying.

Dying is not a subject to which doctors have traditionally paid much attention. Their first purpose is to preserve life, and once life can no longer be decently extended they tend to lose interest. Until fairly recently, the medical profession reacted to death as if the subject were adequately covered by the children's old skip-rope song:

Doctor, doctor, will I die?
Yes, my child, and so will I.

Since death was inevitable, discussion was restricted to secondary matters, centering on three main questions. The first was how to determine when the patient was really dead. Before the twentieth century, people were occasionally buried while still alive, and wills sometimes included a stipulation that the deceased remain above ground until his body actually began to smell. The second question, still much discussed, was whether or not to tell the patient he was dying. The third question, of more interest to doctors of divinity than of medicine, concerned the individual after the process of dying was complete: specifically, did the soul survive, and if so, in what form? All three questions are still open to dispute, and the first has attracted considerable scientific attention since the advent of organ transplants. Laws that require embalming before burial preclude the possibility of being buried alive, but there is still plenty of contention about identifying the precise moment at which a patient becomes sufficiently dead to justify the removal of vital organs.

The question of dying itself has been ignored. In 1912 a Boston doctor, Roswell Park, suggested that nothing was known about the subject and coined a word for its study—thanatology. No one remembered the word or undertook the study. With the exception of books on death as a religious event, almost nothing was published on the subject. The few books that were often had a cultist flavor, like *Death: Its Causes and Phenomena*, also published in 1912, which included a chapter on "Photographing and Weighing the Soul." Medical scientists acted as if Woodrow Wilson had adequately described death and dying in his last words before dropping into unconsciousness: "I am a broken machine. I am ready to go." Scientists were interested in the machine during, not after, its breakdown. They described dying exclusively in terms of the specific diseases or conditions which accompanied it, almost as if dying would not occur if there were no disease.

Since the second world war the subject has begun to receive some attention. In 1956, the American Psychological Association held a major symposium on death at its annual convention. In 1965, Dr. Elisabeth Kübler-Ross began a prolonged study of dying patients at the University of Chicago's Billings Hospital. Other organizations, institutes, and centers, usually with a highly specialized focus, have been established in Cleveland, Boston, Durham, North Carolina, and elsewhere. In 1967, a number of doctors in New York created the Foundation of Thanatology (the coincidental use of Dr. Park's word was not discovered until later) to encourage the study of death and dying from a broad perspective. They chose the word thanatology to make it easier to raise funds, figuring that philanthropists, like others, would find the word death so disturbing they would prefer to have nothing to do with it. La Rochefoucauld, the seventeenth-century French writer, said, "One can no more look steadily at death than at the sun." The Foundation of Thanatology has found that the attention span of those they approach for funds is generally just long enough to say no. Independent researchers have experienced similar difficulties and disappointments, including outright hostility on the part of doctors, nurses, and hospital administrators. Nevertheless, some important work has been done, and dying as a biological and psychological event is beginning to be understood.

The biological aspects of death have received the most attention. In most, but not all, cases an autopsy will reveal exactly how an individual died, by which doctors now usually mean what caused his brain to cease functioning. Since respirators and other machines can keep the heart beating and other organs functioning virtually indefinitely, doctors have begun to accept "brain death" as adequate confirmation that the patient is actually "dead." The brain is considered to be dead when an electroencephalogram (EEG) is flat, which means that it detects no electromagnetic activity within the brain. It is a useful definition, compromised to some degree by the fact that patients have, if only rarely, recovered completely following two or even three days with an absolutely flat EEG. Brain death is generally (but not always) caused by a lack of oxygen, which is generally (but not always) caused by failure of the heart or lungs. The number of exact ways in which a human can die are, however, vast. Medical scientists are successful in describing how the body breaks down, not quite so successful in explaining why it breaks down; they admit that in a significant number of cases death occurs for no apparent medical reason whatever.

Dying as a psychological event, as an experience, is even more elusive. The principal obstacle to its study has been the fear of death on the part of patients, relatives, doctors, nurses, and the dispensers of funds for research. Since no one can say convincingly what death is, it is not easy to say why people fear it. In general, the fear of death has been broken down into the specific fears of pain, loneliness, abandonment, mutilation, and, somewhat more difficult to define, fear of the loss of self. This is not just another way of saying fear of death, but a kind of disassociation of the self as a conscious entity (the sense of *me*-ness one feels) from the self as a particular individual, with his particular history in the everyday world. That individual is one's closest associate and one fears his loss.

The fear of death also has a primitive, nonrational dimension, like fear of the dark and fear of the unknown.

Conscious effort can bring such fear under control but cannot suppress it entirely. One doctor in New York uses complaints about the food in hospitals as a rule of thumb for gauging the fear of death; the more passionate and unreasonable the complaint, he has found, the greater the fear of dying. Everyone apparently experiences the fear of death in some degree, but reacts to it in his own way. People tend to die as they have lived, as suggested in the saying, "Death is terrible to Cicero, desirable to Cato, and indifferent to Socrates."

The experience of death is obviously related to its immediate cause. Heart disease and stroke are the conditions most likely to grant the widespread wish for death to occur in sleep. Heart patients who have been saved by modern techniques report they felt only a sudden pain and the beginning of mingled alarm and surprise. In earlier times, those sensations would have been death (as they presumably still are for those not saved). Patients who have suffered severe heart attacks often regain consciousness in some hospital's intensive care unit with the words, "I'm dying, I'm dying," suggesting that awareness of death can be almost, but not quite, instantaneous. Nurses then find themselves in the awkward position of having to explain that the patient is not dying, without making clear the fact he still might at any moment. Diseases which do not attack vital centers directly and massively, and especially the forms of breakdown associated with old age, allow considerable warning before death actually arrives.

When an individual begins to die, much of what he suffers is the result of the fear of death on his own part and on the part of those around him. He reminds people that they, too, are going to die, which they naturally are not eager to consider. As a result, the first problem faced by the dying individual is to discover the truth about his condition.

In some rare instances doctors make a practice of telling patients the truth immediately, but in most cases the patient has to find out by himself. In their book, *Awareness of Dying*, Barney G. Glaser and Anselm L. Strauss describe a struggle for the truth which is sometimes Byzantine in its complexity, with patients trying to pick up clues while doctors, nurses, and relatives join in a conspiracy to conceal the patient's actual condition. The reason for withholding the truth, doctors say, is that the patient would find it too upsetting, that he needs hope in order to keep on fighting for life, that one can never be absolutely certain of a diagnosis, that patients really do not want to know.

A number of studies have shown, however, that 80 per cent (more or less, depending on the study) of doctors oppose telling dying patients the truth, while 80 per cent of their patients want to be told. Doctors apparently shy from the subject because death represents a defeat and because, like everybody else, they find death upsetting to talk about. The psychological stratagems of medical students confronting death for the first time are notorious. The atmosphere of autopsy rooms is one of macabre humor, a degree or two short of hysteria. Doctors generally end by suppressing awareness of death so thoroughly some researchers speculate that that is why they are drawn to medicine in the first place.

Even while doctors and nurses do everything in their power to withhold the truth, resorting with a smile to outright lies, they customarily believe that the majority of their patients know the truth anyway. Relatives of the dying have the same mixture of feelings, trying to suppress the truth and yet assuming that eventually the patient will realize what is happening. Husbands and wives, each knowing the truth, often tell a third party that *they* know, but not to let the *other* know because he (or she) "couldn't stand it." The pretense naturally grows harder to sustain as the dying patient approaches a final decline. Nevertheless, the pretense is often maintained by sheer will until the end, even when all parties know the truth, and know the others know it too.

In rare instances patients refuse to recognize the truth, ignoring the most obvious clues (such as the visit of a relative who lives thousands of miles away) and insisting up until the end that they will be better in no time. For such patients almost any explanation will suffice. One woman dying of cancer, for example, believed (or pretended to believe) that she was only the victim of a slightly new strain of flu. Dr. Kübler-Ross describes a woman Christian Scientist who insisted until the end that faith in God was sufficient physic for an open cancer which was clearly killing her. As the woman declined she put on ever more garish makeup, until finally she was painting her white and withered cheeks a deep red, suppressing the distinctive smell of cancer with perfume and using false eyelashes and deep green eye shadow to insist she was still alive and even attractive. In most cases, however, patients eventually sense they are not getting better and either ask their doctors directly (by no means always getting an honest answer) or set verbal traps for nurses, relatives, and other patients, checking their responses for every discrepancy. One woman fatally ill with a rare disease discovered her condition when she casually ran across an article in *Newsweek* which described every symptom in exact detail. Nurses believe that "way deep down" patients sense when they are dying, and there is some evidence this is true. Patients who know they are dying will often tell a nurse, "I'm going to die tonight," and then do so. Occasionally, however, patients feel they are going to die when, in fact, they are going to live. Persuading such a patient he's going to recover can be a frustrating experience, particularly when he has watched doctors and nurses deliberately deceive other patients who really were dying.

When patients finally do realize they are dying, a pattern of behavior often follows which was first described in detail by Dr. Kübler-Ross. Based on interviews with hundreds of dying patients over the past five years, she divides the reaction to knowledge of impending death into five distinctive stages.

The first stage is one of denial, even when a patient has suspected the worst and fought to determine the truth. All his life he has casually accepted the fact that "we all have to go." He is stunned to realize that now *he* has to go. After the discovery, patients often retreat into a self-imposed isolation, remaining silent with friends or relatives or even refusing to see them, while they get used to the fact that no mistake has been made, that they are *now* in the process of dying. Dr. Kübler-Ross believes that the dying never completely lose hope that a cure for their disease will be discovered at the last minute or that an outright miracle will occur ("the Scripture says that nothing is impossible with God"). This hope remains a deep-seated thing, and for practical purposes, such as writing wills and settling their affairs, the dying generally accept the fact they are dying once they have been told, directly or indirectly, that it is truly so.

The second stage is one of anger, especially when the dying individual is young. The anger can be released in any direction: at the doctors for doing nothing, at relatives because they are going to live, at other patients for not being quite so ill, at nurses for being young and healthy, at God for being unjust. In 1603, when Queen Elizabeth was told by her physician, Sir Robert Cecil, that she was seriously ill and must go to bed, she flared back, "*Must!* Is *must* a word to be addressed to princes? Little man, little man! Thy father, were he alive, durst not have used that word." Her mood quickly shifted to gloomy self-pity. "Thou art so presumptuous," she said, "because thou knowest that I shall die."

Eventually the anger subsides and the dying patient enters a curious stage in which he tries to bargain for his life. He begins to talk about all the things he has failed to do but will undertake if he recovers. He laments the fact he spent so much time earning a living and so little with his family, promising to alter his priorities if he gets home again. The most explicit bargains, generally proposed to God, are usually kept a secret. They are often legally precise, offering regular church attendance and sincere belief in return for a few more years. The bargains tend to be selfless, for the dying person knows he is about to lose himself altogether. Bargains can be offered for almost anything, for the chance to attend a son's wedding or to see another spring, but they all have one element in common: they are *never* kept. If the dying person actually does live until spring he immediately proposes another bargain.

Religious individuals often insist they submit themselves happily to God's pleasure ("Thy will be done") but are prepared to propose a reasonable compromise. St.

Anselm, the Archbishop of Canterbury, dying in 1109, told fellow clerics gathered about his deathbed, "I shall gladly obey His call. Yet I should also feel grateful if He would grant me a little longer time with you, and if I could be permitted to solve a question—the origin of the soul." God did not accept the offer, and St. Anselm shortly died, but if He had, Dr. Kübler-Ross suggests that St. Anselm would quickly have proposed another bargain.

The fourth stage is one of altogether reasonable depression, part of the process doctors refer to as "anticipatory grief." In effect, the dying patient is grieving for himself before the fact of death, since he is about to lose everything he loves. It is this grieving which is probably most feared by doctors and relatives. It is painful to witness a death, and doubly painful when the dying person reacts in a fearful or hysterical manner. This is exceedingly rare, and yet doctors and relatives, perhaps unsure what their own reactions would be, fear the possibility so greatly that they put off discussion of death as long as possible and sometimes, as mentioned above, deny the truth until the end. In every other circumstance of life, no matter how bleak, some consolation can be genuinely offered; with those who know they are dying, there is nothing to say. Dr. Kübler-Ross has found, however, that the grieving patient will often come out of his depression and face the prospect of death more calmly for having been through it.

The final stage, not always reached, is one of acceptance.

When Mrs. B. woke up one afternoon following a nap, she saw her daughter standing by her bed with tears streaming down her cheeks. "Now, we're not going to have any tears," Mrs. B. said.

Nevertheless, she, too, had recognized the seriousness of her condition. During the first week she was in the hospital she made a point of telling her daily visitors they really didn't have to come so often. Now she admitted to looking forward to every visit. "It's nice to wake up and find somebody there," she confessed. Her last roommate had remained only a day before moving into a single room, so Mrs. B. was entirely alone between visits. The roommate, a woman in her forties who had also had a cancerous breast removed, had been shifted by her husband when he learned of Mrs. B.'s medical history. He said he wanted to protect the feelings of his wife, but she was acutely embarrassed by the move and came to see Mrs. B. every day. When the woman left the hospital she stopped by to say goodbye and suggested that she and Mrs. B. meet in New York for lunch someday. "Or," she said, "we have a place near you in the country. Maybe we can get together next spring." Mrs. B. said that would be fine and then added, "Good luck."

By the second week it was obvious Mrs. B.'s intestinal blockage was not going to clear by itself. Her doctors told her family the cancer had reached her liver and had probably affected her entire abdominal area. The sole remaining question was how long it would take Mrs. B. to die and whether or not she would be able to go home again in the time remaining. The only way she could leave the hospital, the doctors said, would be to undergo an operation in order to remove whatever was obstructing her intestine. They warned that she was in a weakened condition and might die during the operation, or that cancer might have affected so much of her intestine nothing could be done. The alternatives were also presented to Mrs. B., although in less detail and more tentatively. Both she and her family decided it would be better to go ahead.

Mrs. B.'s eldest daughter, living in California, already had made plans to come East for Thanksgiving, knowing it would probably be her last chance to see her mother. When she was told about the operation she asked over the phone, "Shall I wait until next week or should I come now?"

"I think you'd better come now," her brother-in-law said. She arranged for someone to take care of her three children and made a plane reservation for the day after the operation. Mrs. B.'s two brothers were also called, but they decided to wait until after the operation before coming to New York. "If I came now it would scare her to death," said the brother who lived in Washington.

The operation was scheduled for the morning of Thursday, November 19. Her family remained by the phone throughout the day. At 6 P.M. the surgeon finally called and said Mrs. B.'s intestine was blocked by cancer every two or three inches. There was nothing he could do. He was asked how long Mrs. B. might live. "Perhaps a week," he said.

Later that evening Mrs. B.'s family visited her briefly after she came up from the recovery room. She was pale and drawn and barely able to speak. The operation had obviously been an ordeal. "Never again," she whispered. "Never again."

The next day Mrs. B.'s eldest daughter flew to New York and went to see her mother, already beginning to regain her strength after the operation. Before the family went to see her on Saturday they tried to decide what to say if she should ask about her condition. The hard thing was finding out what Mrs. B. already had been told by her doctors. Until they reached Dr. C., they decided, they would tell Mrs. B. everyone was worried but didn't yet know the full results of the operation. They feared she would press them, and they knew that if she asked directly whether or not the cancer had been cut out, the only possible answers would be the truth or an outright lie. They did not want to lie, knowing how much Mrs. B. would hate being lied to, but they dreaded equally talking about the true situation. They could not have explained why.

As things turned out they need not have worried. Mrs. B. had cross-examined her doctors on a number of occasions since Thursday night, when she had found the strength to say, "It was my cancer, wasn't it?" Dr. C. later explained that Mrs. B. kept after him until she had the truth. His practice was to answer all questions truthfully, leaving it up to the patient to decide which questions to ask. Some patients asked nothing. Others stopped as soon as Dr. C. indicated their condition was serious. Mrs. B. had been unusual, he said, in questioning him precisely about her condition.

On Sunday Mrs. B. began to weaken again. When her son-in-law arrived about 11 A.M., she shooed the nurse out of the room. "I want to be alone with my son-in-law," she said. As soon as the door was closed she said, "I'm dying. There's no use kidding ourselves."

She told her son-in-law where all her papers were and what was in her will, asking him to make sure his mother got the red leather box which Mrs. B. had bought for her in Czechoslovakia the previous summer, and then had liked so much she kept it. "I've been feeling guilty about that," she said.

She also asked her son-in-law to get her lawyer on the phone so she could give him "a pep talk." When she reached him she said, "Now listen, you take care of the kids and try and keep the government from getting it all." She gave her best to his wife and said goodbye.

Finally Mrs. B. asked her son-in-law to make sure her eyes went to the eye bank and that her body was given to "science." (Mrs. B.'s surgeon told her son-in-law he wanted to do an autopsy, but that cancer had destroyed her body's usefulness as far as "science" was concerned. Mrs. B.'s second choice had been cremation without any service, and that wish was carried out.)

After Mrs. B. had straightened out her affairs to her own satisfaction, she relaxed and began to chat and even joke about her situation. A few minutes later she suddenly weakened and seemed to doze off. After awhile she started awake, staring intently at the ceiling. "Is there anything up there, right over my bed?" she asked her son-in-law. He said there was not. A look of resigned disgust came over Mrs. B.'s face. "I'm afraid I'm going to have hallucinations," she said.

During the following days her decline was obvious to herself and her family. She spent more time dozing, was coherent for shorter periods which came farther apart. During one such moment she told her daughter, "I hadn't believed it would happen so fast."

In most American hospitals the experience of death is clouded by drugs. When drugs are necessary to relieve pain there is no alternative, but heavy sedatives, tranquilizers, and pain-killing drugs are also used for purposes of "patient management." In the final stages of dying the greatest fear of patients is abandonment, with good reason. When possible, hospitals will try to send patients home to die. Doctors often cut back their visits, overworked nurses save most of their attention for "those who can be helped," and even the families of the dying frequently begin to detach themselves. The belief that life must go on can be carried to brutal limits, with relatives and even husbands or wives acting as if the dying individual were already dead. When dying patients pester the nursing staff for attention, they are often simply trying to alleviate their loneliness; if the pestering becomes irksome there is a tendency to respond with drugs.

The abandonment which dying patients fear can be as much emotional as literal. Nurses say they do not become hardened to death and often dream about the death of their patients. As a result they attempt to distance themselves from the dying by thinking of them as no longer quite there, referring to the care of unconscious patients, for example, as "watering the vegetables." The terrible moment which demands that life-sustaining equipment be turned off is emotionally masked by the phrase, "pulling the plug."

The impulse to abandon the dying can become overwhelming. It is policy in most hospitals to move dying patients into single rooms as death approaches. Doctors, nurses, and even relatives tend to find good reasons to stay out of the dying patient's room. The pretense is that no one wants to "disturb" the dying person while he is "resting," but nurses say they have seen too many clusters of relatives outside hospital rooms at the moment of death to consider it a coincidence.

As death approaches, the world of the dying gradually shrinks. They talk less of their disease and more about their exact symptoms, how they feel, what they plan to do tomorrow, or this afternoon, or in the next hour. Hope generally remains until the final moments, but its focus tends to shift. The Rev. Robert Reeves, Jr., the chaplain of Columbia-Presbyterian Hospital in New York, tells of one middle-aged man who hoped to get back to his business up until five weeks before his death. During the first week after that he talked about getting home for Thanksgiving. During the second week he hoped to be able to get out of bed again. In the third week he hoped to regain the ability to swallow food. At the beginning of his final week of life he hoped for a good night's sleep. A day later he hoped his pain medicine would work. The day before he died he hoped he would die in his sleep. He was denied every hope except the last, and yet each had eased his way toward death.

When the layman speaks of death he is referring to *somatic* death, or the death of the entire organism. The traditional signs of somatic death are *rigor mortis* (the stiffening of certain muscles), *algor mortis* (the cooling of the body) and *liver mortis* (the purplish-red discoloration of the skin caused by the settling of the blood). Somatic death includes the death of all bodily tissues, but an individual is commonly said to be "dead" long before all his tissues have died. The death of the "person," then, is only one stage in what an increasing number of doctors tend to think of as a distinct physiological process.

One doctor likens the process of death to menopause, which has long been known to include profound biological changes in women going far beyond the simple cessation of ovulation. The fact of putrefaction can also be cited as evidence that dying is a coherent biological event, and not simply the exact condition which precipitates death (heart failure, say, or kidney shutdown). When the body dies, organisms escape the gastrointestinal tract and begin the process of general decomposition by which the body is returned to Biblical ashes and dust. Built into the body, in other words, is the biological mechanism of its own dissolution, a fact which hardly can be dismissed as a coincidence. In arguing for an expanded notion of death, doctors also mention the characteristic return of the dying to infancy. Gradually they sleep longer each day, until they wake for only minutes at a time. Emotionally, the dying become increasingly dependent. Waking in the night they may cry if they discover they are alone, or sink back to sleep if someone is there.

Given a choice, the vast majority of people would prefer to die in their sleep. The next best, they say, would be a "peaceful" death, a consummation largely under the control of doctors. "Dear gentlemen," said the eighteenth-century English doctor, Sir Samuel Garth, to physicians whispering together at the foot of his bed, "let me die a natural death." The ability of doctors to extend the process of dying, if not life, is incomparably greater now. Medical "heroics" can keep the heart beating, the lungs breathing, the kidneys functioning, the brain flickering long after death would normally have arrived. The deterioration of the body from disease, and especially from cancer, proceeds further than it would without medical intervention. The result is that patients often lose consciousness long before they die because doctors, or relatives, refuse to give up when the body does. One nurse with years of experience in an intensive-care unit says she finds it increasingly difficult to tell when a patient has died, since machines sustain his vital signs.

Once the process of dying has begun, death can arrive at any time. Some patients die quickly; some linger for months with conditions that ought to have been quickly fatal. Doctors are still exceedingly cautious about predicting when someone will die, since they are so often surprised. Thomas Lupton, a sixteenth-century English writer, made the following attempt to list sure signs of imminent death:

If the forehead of the sick wax red, and his brows fall down, and his nose wax sharp and cold, and his left eye becomes little, and the corner of his eye runs, if he turn to the wall, if his ears be cold, or if he may suffer no brightness, and if his womb fall, if he pulls straws or the clothes of his bed, or if he pick often his nostrils with his fingers, and if he wake much, these are almost certain tokens of death.

Signs which modern nurses look for are dilated nostrils, sagging of the tongue to one side of the mouth, and a tendency for the thumbs to tuck in toward the palms of the dying patient's hands. Just as dying people frequently sense the imminence of their own death and predict it accurately, nurses develop a sense which tells them (but not always correctly) when a patient is going to die.

In the early stages of dying, the patient remains essentially himself, afflicted only by the knowledge of impending death and the effect of that knowledge on himself and those around him. In the final stages, consciousness in the dying sometimes undergoes qualitative changes. This experience is the least well understood of all, since the nearer a patient approaches to death, the less he can describe what he feels. The crisis for the dying patient characteristically arrives when he stops "fighting" to live. Doctors cannot say just how patients "fight," but they are unanimous in saying that patients do so, and that "fighting" can make all the difference in situations which can go either way. A man fighting to stay alive apparently duplicates the experience of a man fighting to stay awake, i.e., alternating flashes of lucidity and delirium. Patients often signal the approach of death by simply saying, "I can't fight any longer." The period that follows is unlike any other experienced in life.

Until the twentieth century, this final period was often called "the dying hour," although it can last considerably longer than an hour. Physicians described it as being a peaceful period in which the dying person, accepting the lost struggle and the inevitable end, is relaxed and ready to depart. The patient may gradually distance himself from life, actually turning away close friends and relatives, literally turning to the wall (as suggested by Lupton) as he prepares himself to die. Accepting the fact of their own death, the dying frequently turn their attention to those who will live, who are sometimes aggrieved by the readiness of the dying to leave them behind. At the end it is often the dying who comfort the living. Even so self-centered a figure as Louis XIV said to those around his deathbed, "Why weep ye? Did you think I should live forever?" After a pause he reflected with equanimity, "I thought dying had been harder."

Dying patients who remain fully conscious, or nearly so, say they are tired, feel a growing calm, are ready to go, are perhaps even happy. When Stephen Crane died of tuberculosis in England in 1900, only twenty-nine years old, he tried to describe the sensation to a friend: "Robert—when you come to the hedge—that we must all go over. It isn't so bad. You feel sleepy—and you don't care. Just a little dreamy anxiety—which world you're really in—that's all."

Dr. Austin Kutscher, one of the creators of the Foundation of Thanatology, has been studying death and related questions since the death of his wife in 1966. He emphasizes that in some ways the living tyrannize over the dying, studying the experience of the latter for the sake of those who remain. An example is the effort of medical scientists to narrow the definition of death in order to allow the organs of the dying to be used for transplants. The decision to accept brain death as death itself may be valid, Kutscher says, but it can hardly be argued that the definition was framed for the benefit of the dying. As a result of this natural bias on the part of the living, the study of death and dying has tended to ignore the nature of the event, and of its experience.

"Isn't there something rather magical about life that defies measurement by a piece of apparatus?" Dr. Kutscher says. "We are begging the issue by trying to define death when we can't even define life."

The scientific study of dying is relatively recent, but there exists a vast literature, amounting to case studies, of the approach of death. The final moments of great men have always been minutely recorded, these accounts ranging from those in the *Lives of the Saints*, which tend to a dull predictability, to the moment-by-moment narratives of death as experienced by generals, poets, and kings. Again and again the last words of the dying concede their readiness to depart; an unfeigned peace seems to ease the final flickering out. History and modern research agree that, for unknown reasons, the dying do not find it hard to die.

The very last moments are, of course, the least accessible. Some doctors have found evidence that the experience of patients still conscious has an element of the mystical. The doctors are quick to say that they are not talking about God and religion and parapsychological cultism; also they admit that such experiences might be the result of anoxia, or oxygen starvation in the brain. Nevertheless, they say, there is reason to believe the dying can experience a sense of surrender which borders on ecstasy. In a secular age, as practitioners of a science which tends toward mechanism, doctors reluctantly speak of "soul" or "spirit." But, in the safety of anonymity, they return again and again to the puzzle of what it is that dies when the body ceases to function. One doctor, attempting to describe the mystery he had sensed in dying patients, quoted the dying words attributed to the ancient philosopher Plotinus: "I am making my last effort to return that which is divine in me to that which is divine in the universe."

During her final five days of life, Mrs. B. was rarely conscious. The hospital left the second bed in her room empty. Her doctors and family decided not to attempt extreme efforts which could only prolong her dying, but Mrs. B. continued to receive intravenous feeding and was regularly turned by the nurses as a precaution against pneumonia.

On two occasions Mrs. B. started violently awake and insisted, "Something is terribly wrong." She did not know her daughters and believed her doctors were conspiring against her. She was given heavy sedation, and her daughters felt that, in effect, she had already died. Nevertheless, on a few last occasions she regained consciousness and knew her family, if only briefly. Two days before she died, as her surgeon was examining her, she suddenly asked. "Why don't I die?"

"Because you're tough," the surgeon said.

"I don't want to be tough that way," Mrs. B. said.

Because one test of a patient's grip on life is the ability to respond, the doctors and nurses would call her name loudly from time to time to ask if she wanted anything. "Mrs. B.?" one of the nurses nearly shouted one night. "Mrs. B.?"

"I'm gone," said Mrs. B. in a faint whisper.

"No, you're still with us," the nurse said.

Mrs. B. grew steadily weaker. Her kidneys began to fail. She began to breathe rapidly and heavily, then stopped altogether, and after a moment began again. A nurse called this "Cheyne-Stokes breathing" and said it was probably a sign that the end was approaching. Some of the nurses thought Mrs. B. was completely unconscious; others felt she had only lost the ability to respond. Not knowing who was right, her family spoke as if she could hear and understand everything said in the room.

When Mrs. B.'s youngest daughter arrived about 11 A.M. the morning of Thanksgiving Day, November 26, she found her mother breathing slowly and regularly. Her body was completely relaxed over onto one side. It was a bright sunlit day. Mrs. B.'s daughter sat down by the large bank of windows overlooking Manhattan to the south and tried to read, but found herself thinking of her mother. After a while she looked up and saw that her mother had stopped breathing. So long expected, death had arrived unnoticed. For eighteen days Mrs. B.'s daughter had restrained her tears. Now, finally, when her mother was no longer there to comfort or be comforted, she began to cry.

QUESTIONS

1. In what ways is death in modern society treated differently from death in preindustrial societies? Why is discussion of death almost taboo in modern society?

2. How is social science research into death and dying changing public attitudes and practices?

3. Do you think about your own death? Do you discuss the subject with others?

ERVING GOFFMAN

Presenting the Self to Others

Sociology has traditionally focused mainly on the larger structures and processes of society—on institutions like politics and religion, for example, or on issues of social order and social change. But sociologists have a continuing and lively interest in even the most minute and apparently routine details of the social interaction that occurs as people go about their daily lives.

One of the foremost sociologists in this field is Erving Goffman, whose work over more than two decades has provided an extraordinarily rich body of insights into the social behavior that we normally take for granted. Goffman's "dramaturgical" approach sees people as though they were actors, playing various roles in order to present themselves in the most favorable or impressive light from one situation to another. His objective is nothing less than to lay bare the unspoken but generally accepted rules of social interaction that smooth the business of social living, and thus make society possible.

This article, drawn from Goffman's early work, shows how his shrewd eye discerns and interprets patterns of social interaction that even the actors themselves are apt to overlook.

When an individual enters the presence of others, they commonly seek to acquire information about him or to bring into play information about him already possessed. They will be interested in his general socio-economic status, his conception of self, his attitude toward them, his competence, his trustworthiness, etc. Although some of this information seems to be sought almost as an end in itself, there are usually quite practical reasons for acquiring it. Information about the individual helps to define the situation, enabling others to know in advance what he will expect of them and what they may expect of him. Informed in these ways, the others will know how best to act in order to call forth a desired response from him.

For those present, many sources of information become accessible and many carriers (or "sign-vehicles") become available for conveying this information. If unacquainted with the individual, observers can glean clues from his conduct and appearance which allow them to apply their previous experience with individuals roughly similar to the one before them or, more important, to apply untested stereotypes to him. They can also assume from past experience that only individuals of a particular kind are likely to be found in a given social setting. They can rely on what the individual says about himself or on documentary evidence he provides as to who and what he is. If they know, or know of, the individual by virtue of experience prior to the interaction, they can rely on assumptions as to the persistence and generality of psychological traits as a means of predicting his present and future behavior.

However, during the period in which the individual is in the immediate presence of the others, few events may occur which directly provide the others with the conclusive information they will need if they are to direct wisely their own activity. Many crucial facts lie beyond the time and place of interaction or lie concealed within it. For example, the "true" or "real" attitudes, beliefs, and emotions of the individual can be ascertained only indirectly, through his avowals or through what appears to be involuntary expressive behavior. Similarly, if the individual offers the others a product or service, they will often find that during the interaction there will be no time and place immediately available for eating the pudding that the proof can be found in. They will be forced to accept some events as conventional or natural signs of something not directly available to the senses. In Ichheiser's terms,[1] the individual will have to act so that he intentionally or unintentionally *expresses* himself, and the others will in turn have to be *impressed* in some way by him.

The expressiveness of the individual (and therefore his capacity to give impressions) appears to involve two radically different kinds of sign activity: the expression that he *gives*, and the expression that he *gives off*. The first involves verbal symbols or their substitutes which he uses admittedly and solely to convey the information that he and the others are known to attach to these symbols. This is communication in the traditional and narrow sense. The second involves a wide range of action that others can treat as symptomatic of the actor, the expectation being that the action was performed for reasons other than the information conveyed in this way. As we shall have to see, this distinction has an only initial validity. The individual does of course intentionally convey misinformation by means of both of these types of communication, the first involving deceit, the second feigning.

Taking communication in both its narrow and broad sense, one finds that when the individual is in the immediate presence of others, his activity will have a promissory character. The others are likely to find that they must accept the individual on faith, offering him a just return while he is present before them in exchange for something whose true value will not be established until after he has left their presence. (Of course, the others also live by inference in their dealings with the physical world, but it is only in the world of social interaction that the objects about which they make inferences will purposely facilitate and hinder this inferential process.) The security that they justifiably feel in making inferences about the individual will vary, of course, depending on such factors as the amount of information they already possess about him, but no amount of such past evidence can entirely obviate the necessity of acting on the basis of inferences. As William I. Thomas suggested:

> It is also highly important for us to realize that we do not as a matter of fact lead our lives, make our decisions, and reach our goals in everyday life either statistically or scientifically. We live by inference. I am, let us say, your guest. You do not know, you cannot determine scientifically, that I will not steal your money or your spoons. But inferentially I will not, and inferentially you have me as a guest.[2]

Let us now turn from the others to the point of view of the individual who presents himself before them. He may wish them to think highly of him, or to think that he thinks highly of them, or to perceive how in fact he feels toward them, or to obtain no clear-cut impression; he may wish to ensure sufficient harmony so that the interaction can be sustained, or to defraud, get rid of, confuse, mislead, antagonize, or insult them. Regardless of the particular objective which the individual has in mind and of his motive for having this objective, it will be in his interests to control the conduct of the others, especially their responsive treatment of him.[3] This control is achieved largely by influencing the definition of the situation which the others come to formulate, and he can influence this definition by expressing himself in such a way as to give them the kind of impression that will lead them to act voluntarily in accordance with his own plan. Thus, when an individual appears in the presence of others, there will usually be some reason for him to mobilize his activity so that it will convey an impression to others which it is in his interests to convey. Since a girl's dormitory mates will glean evidence of her popularity from the calls she receives on the phone, we can suspect that some girls will arrange for calls to be made, and Willard Waller's finding can be anticipated:

> It has been reported by many observers that a girl who is called to the telephone in the dormitories will often allow herself to be called several times, in order to give all the other girls ample opportunity to hear her paged.[4]

Of the two kinds of communication—expressions given and expressions given off—this report will be primarily concerned with the latter, with the more theatrical and contextual kind, the non-verbal, presumably unintentional kind, whether this communication be purposely engineered or not. As an example of what we must try to examine, I would like to cite at length a novelistic incident in which Preedy, a vacationing Englishman, makes his first appearance on the beach of his summer hotel in Spain:

> But in any case he took care to avoid catching anyone's eye. First of all, he had to make it clear to those potential companions of his holiday that they were of no concern to him whatsoever. He stared through them, round them, over them—eyes lost in space. The beach might have been empty. If by chance a ball was thrown his way, he looked surprised; then let a smile of amusement lighten his face (Kindly Preedy), looked round dazed to see that there *were* people on the beach, tossed it back with a smile to himself and not a smile *at* the people, and then resumed carelessly his nonchalant survey of space.
>
> But it was time to institute a little parade, the parade of the Ideal Preedy. By devious handlings he gave any who wanted to look a chance to see the title of his book—a Spanish translation of Homer, classic thus, but not daring, cosmopolitan too—and then gathered together his beachwrap and bag into a neat sand-resistant pile (Methodical and Sensible Preedy), rose slowly to stretch at ease his huge frame (Big-Cat Preedy), and tossed aside his sandals (Carefree Preedy, after all).
>
> The marriage of Preedy and the sea! There were alternative rituals. The first involved the stroll that turns into a run and a dive straight into the water, thereafter smoothing into a strong splashless crawl towards the horizon. But of course

not really to the horizon. Quite suddenly he would turn on to his back and thrash great white splashes with his legs, somehow thus showing that he could have swum further had he wanted to, and then would stand up a quarter out of water for all to see who it was.

The alternative course was simpler, it avoided the cold-water shock and it avoided the risk of appearing too high-spirited. The point was to appear to be so used to the sea, the Mediterranean, and this particular beach, that one might as well be in the sea as out of it. It involved a slow stroll down and into the edge of the water—not even noticing his toes were wet, land and water all the same to *him*!—with his eyes up at the sky gravely surveying portents, invisible to others, of the weather (Local Fisherman Preedy).[5]

The novelist means us to see that Preedy is improperly concerned with the extensive impressions he feels his sheer bodily action is giving off to those around him. We can malign Preedy further by assuming that he has acted merely in order to give a particular impression, that this is a false impression, and that the others present receive either no impression at all, or, worse still, the impression that Preedy is affectedly trying to cause them to receive this particular impression. But the important point for us here is that the kind of impression Preedy thinks he is making is in fact the kind of impression that others correctly and incorrectly glean from someone in their midst.

I have said that when an individual appears before others his actions will influence the definition of the situation which they come to have. Sometimes the individual will act in a thoroughly calculating manner, expressing himself in a given way solely in order to give the kind of impression to others that is likely to evoke from them a specific response he is concerned to obtain. Sometimes the individual will be calculating in his activity but be relatively unaware that this is the case. Sometimes he will intentionally and consciously express himself in a particular way, but chiefly because the tradition of his group or social status requires this kind of expression and not because of any particular response (other than vague acceptance or approval) that is likely to be evoked from those impressed by the expression. Sometimes the traditions of an individual's role will lead him to give a well-designed impression of a particular kind and yet he may be neither consciously nor unconsciously disposed to create such an impression. The others, in their turn, may be suitably impressed by the individual's efforts to convey something, or may misunderstand the situation and come to conclusions that are warranted neither by the individual's intent nor by the facts. In any case, in so far as the others act *as if* the individual had conveyed a particular impression, we may take a functional or pragmatic view and say that the individual has "effectively" projected a given definition of the situation and "effectively" fostered the understanding that a given state of affairs obtains.

There is one aspect of the others' response that bears special comment here. Knowing that the individual is likely to present himself in a light that is favorable to him, the others may divide what they witness into two parts: a part that is relatively easy for the individual to manipulate at will, being chiefly his verbal assertions, and a part in regard to which he seems to have little concern or control, being chiefly derived from the expressions he gives off. The others may then use what are considered to be the ungovernable aspects of his expressive behavior as a check upon the validity of what is conveyed by the governable aspects. In this a fundamental asymmetry is demonstrated in the communication process, the individual presumably being aware of only one stream of his communication, the witnesses of this stream and one other. For example, in Shetland Isle one crofter's wife, in serving native dishes to a visitor from the mainland of Britain, would listen with a polite smile to his polite claims of liking what he was eating; at the same time she would take note of the rapidity with which the visitor lifted his fork or spoon to his mouth, the eagerness with which he passed food into his mouth, and the gusto expressed in chewing the food, using these signs as a check on the stated feelings of the eater. The same woman, in order to discover what one acquaintance (A) "actually" thought of another acquaintance (B), would wait until B was in the presence of A but engaged in conversation with still another person (C). She would then covertly examine the facial expressions of A as he regarded B in conversation with C. Not being in conversation with B, and not being directly observed by him, A would sometimes relax usual constraints and tactful deceptions, and freely express what he was "actually" feeling about B. This Shetlander, in short, would observe the unobserved observer.

Now given the fact that others are likely to check up on the more controllable aspects of behavior by means of the less controllable, one can expect that sometimes the individual will try to exploit this very possibility, guiding the impression he makes through behavior felt to be reliably informing.[6] For example, in gaining admission to a tight social circle, the participant observer may not only wear an accepting look while listening to an informant, but may also be careful to wear the same look when observing the informant talking to others; observers of the observer will then not as easily discover where he actually stands. A specific illustration may be cited from Shetland Isle. When a neighbor dropped in to have a cup of tea, he would ordinarily wear at least a hint of an expectant warm smile as he passed through the door into the cottage. Since lack of physical obstructions outside the cottage and lack of light within it usually made it possible to observe the visitor unobserved as he approached the house, islanders sometimes took pleasure in watching the visitor drop whatever expression he was manifesting and replace it with a sociable one just before reaching the door. However, some visitors, in appreciating that this examination was occurring, would blindly adopt a social face a long distance from the house, thus ensuring the projection of a constant image.

This kind of control upon the part of the individual reinstates the symmetry of the communication process, and sets the stage for a kind of information game—a potentially infinite cycle of concealment, discovery, false revelation, and rediscovery. It should be added that since the others are likely to be relatively unsuspicious of the presumably unguided aspect of the individual's conduct, he can gain much by controlling it. The others of course may sense that the individual is manipulating the presumably spontaneous aspects of his behavior, and seek in this very act of manipulation some shading of conduct that the individual has not managed to control. This again provides a check upon the individual's behavior, this time his presumably uncalculated behavior, thus re-establishing the asymmetry of the communication process. Here I would like only to add the suggestion that the arts of piercing an individual's effort at calculated unintentionality seem better developed than our capacity to manipulate our own behavior, so that regardless of how many steps have occurred in the information game, the witness is likely to have the advantage over the actor, and the initial asymmetry of the communication process is likely to be retained.

When we allow that the individual projects a definition of the situation when he appears before others, we must also see that the others, however passive their role may seem to be, will themselves effectively project a definition of the situation by virtue of their response to the individual and by virtue of any lines of action they initiate to him. Ordinarily the definitions of the situation projected by the several different participants are sufficiently attuned to one another so that open contradiction will not occur. I do not mean that there will be the kind of consensus that arises when each individual present candidly expresses what he really feels and honestly agrees with the expressed feelings of the others present. This kind of harmony is an optimistic ideal and in any case not necessary for the smooth working of society. Rather, each participant is expected to suppress his immediate heart-felt feelings, conveying a view of the situation which he feels the others will be able to find at least temporarily acceptable. The maintenance of this surface of agreement, this veneer of consensus, is facilitated by each participant concealing his own wants behind statements which assert values to which everyone present feels obliged to give lip service. Further, there is usually a kind of division of definitional labor. Each participant is allowed to establish the tentative official ruling regarding matters which are vital to him but not immediately important to others, e.g., the rationalizations and justifications by which he accounts for his past activity. In ex-

change for this courtesy he remains silent or non-committal on matters important to others but not immediately important to him. We have then a kind of interactional *modus vivendi*. Together the participants contribute to a single over-all definition of the situation which involves not so much a real agreement as to what exists but rather a real agreement as to whose claims concerning what issues will be temporarily honored. Real agreement will also exist concerning the desirability of avoiding an open conflict of definitions of the situation.[7] I will refer to this level of agreement as a "working consensus." It is to be understood that the working consensus established in one interaction setting will be quite different in content from the working consensus established in a different type of setting. Thus, between two friends at lunch, a reciprocal show of affection, respect, and concern for the other is maintained. In service occupations, on the other hand, the specialist often maintains an image of disinterested involvement in the problem of the client, while the client responds with a show of respect for the competence and integrity of the specialist. Regardless of such differences in content, however, the general form of these working arrangements is the same.

In noting the tendency for a participant to accept the definitional claims made by the others present, we can appreciate the crucial importance of the information that the individual *initially* possesses or acquires concerning his fellow participants, for it is on the basis of this initial information that the individual starts to define the situation and starts to build up lines of responsive action. The individual's initial projection commits him to what he is proposing to be and requires him to drop all pretenses of being other things. As the interaction among the participants progresses, additions and modifications in this initial informational state will of course occur, but it is essential that these later developments be related without contradiction to, and even built up from, the initial positions taken by the several participants. It would seem that an individual can more easily make a choice as to what line of treatment to demand from and extend to the others present at the beginning of an encounter than he can alter the line of treatment that is being pursued once the interaction is underway.

In everyday life, of course, there is a clear understanding that first impressions are important. Thus, the work adjustment of those in service occupations will often hinge upon a capacity to seize and hold the initiative in the service relation, a capacity that will require subtle aggressiveness on the part of the server when he is of lower socioeconomic status than his client. W.F. Whyte suggests the waitress as an example:

The first point that stands out is that the waitress who bears up under pressure does not simply respond to her customers. She acts with some skill to control their behavior.

The first question to ask when we look at the customer relationship is, "Does the waitress get the jump on the customer, or does the customer get the jump on the waitress?" The skilled waitress realizes the crucial nature of this question. . . .

The skilled waitress tackles the customer with confidence and without hesitation. For example, she may find that a new customer has seated himself before she could clear off the dirty dishes and change the cloth. He is now leaning on the table studying the menu. She greets him, says, "May I change the cover, please?" and without waiting for an answer, takes his menu away from him so that he moves back from the table, and she goes about her work. The relationship is handled politely but firmly, and there is never any question as to who is in charge.[8]

When the interaction that is initiated by "first impressions" is itself merely the initial interaction in an extended series of interactions involving the same participants, we speak of "getting off on the right foot" and feel that it is crucial that we do so. Thus, one learns that some teachers take the following view:

You can't ever let them get the upper hand on you or you're through. So I start out tough. The first day I get a new class in, I let them know who's boss . . . You've got to start off tough, then you can ease up as you go along. If you start out easy-going, when you try to be tough, they'll just look at you and laugh.[9]

Similarly, attendants in mental institutions may feel that if the new patient is sharply put in his place the first day on the ward and made to see who is boss, much future difficulty will be prevented.[10]

Given the fact that the individual effectively projects a definition of the situation when he enters the presence of others, we can assume that events may occur within the interaction which contradict, discredit, or otherwise throw doubt upon this projection. When these disruptive events occur, the interaction itself may come to a confused and embarrassed halt. Some of the assumptions upon which the responses of the participants had been predicated become untenable, and the participants find themselves lodged in an interaction for which the situation has been wrongly defined and is now no longer defined. At such moments the individual whose presentation has been discredited may feel ashamed while the others present may feel hostile, and all the participants may come to feel ill at ease, nonplussed, out of countenance, embarrassed, experiencing the kind of anomie that is generated when the minute social system of face-to-face interaction breaks down.

In stressing the fact that the initial definition of the situation projected by an individual tends to provide a plan for the co-operative activity that follows—in stressing this action point of view—we must not overlook the crucial fact that any projected definition of the situation also has a distinctive moral character. It is this moral character of projections that will chiefly concern us in this report. Society is organized on the principle that any individual who possesses certain social characteristics has a moral right to expect that others will value and treat him in an appropriate way. Connected with this principle is a second, namely that an individual who implicitly or explicitly signifies that he has certain social characteristics ought in fact to be what he claims he is. In consequence, when an individual projects a definition of the situation and thereby makes an implicit or explicit claim to be a person of a particular kind, he automatically exerts a moral demand upon the others, obliging them to value and treat him in the manner that persons of his kind have a right to expect. He also implicitly forgoes all claims to be things he does not appear to be[11] and hence forgoes the treatment that would be appropriate for such individuals. The others find, then, that the individual has informed them as to what is and as to what they *ought* to see as the "is."

One cannot judge the importance of definitional disruptions by the frequency with which they occur, for apparently they would occur more frequently were not constant precautions taken. We find that preventive practices are constantly employed to avoid these embarrassments and that corrective practices are constantly employed to compensate for discrediting occurrences that have not been successfully avoided. When the individual employs these strategies and tactics to protect his own projections, we may refer to them as "defensive practices"; when a participant employs them to save the definition of the situation projected by another, we speak of "protective practices" or "tact." Together, defensive and protective practices comprise the techniques employed to safeguard the impression fostered by an individual during his presence before others. It should be added that while we may be ready to see that no fostered impression would survive if defensive practices were not employed, we are less ready perhaps to see that few impressions could survive if those who received the impression did not exert tact in their reception of it.

In addition to the fact that precautions are taken to prevent disruption of projected definitions, we may also note that an intense interest in these disruptions comes to play a significant role in the social life of the group. Practical jokes and social games are played in which embarrassments which are to be taken unseriously are purposely engineered.[12] Fantasies are created in which devastating exposures occur. Anecdotes from the past—real, embroidered, or fictitious—are told and retold, detailing disruptions which occurred, almost occurred, or occurred and were admirably resolved. There seems to be no grouping which does not have a ready supply of these games, reveries, and cautionary tales, to be used as a source of humor, a catharsis for anxieties, and a sanction for inducing individuals to be modest in their claims and reasonable in their projected expectations. The individual may tell himself through dreams of getting into impossible positions. Families tell of the time a guest got his dates mixed and arrived when neither the house nor anyone in it was ready for him. Journalists tell of times when an all-too-meaningful misprint occurred, and the paper's assumption of objectivity or decorum was humorously discredited. Public servants tell of times a client ridiculously misunderstood form instructions, giving answers which implied an unanticipated and bizarre definition of the situation.[13] Seamen, whose home away from home is rigorously he-man, tell stories of coming back home and inadvertently asking mother to "pass the fucking butter."[14] Diplomats tell of the time a near-sighted queen asked a republican ambassador about the health of his king.[15]

To summarize, then, I assume that when an individual appears before others he will have many motives for trying to control the impression they receive of the situation. . . .

QUESTIONS

1. How does Goffman's work differ from "mainstream" sociology?

2. How valid is Goffman's "dramaturgical" method—can social interaction really be studied in terms of role-playing? Is this approach a cynical one?

3. Can you apply Goffman's approach to any social situations you have observed?

Notes

1. Gustav Ichheiser, "Misunderstandings in Human Relations," Supplement to *The American Journal of Sociology*, LV (September, 1949), pp. 6–7.

2. Quoted in E. H. Volkart, editor, *Social Behavior and Personality*, Contributions of W. I. Thomas to Theory and Social Research (New York: Social Science Research Council, 1951), p. 5.

3. Here I owe much to an unpublished paper by Tom Burns of the University of Edinburgh. He presents the argument that in all interaction a basic underlying theme is the desire of each participant to guide and control the responses made by the others present. A similar argument has been advanced by Jay Haley in a recent unpublished paper, but in regard to a special kind of control, that having to do with defining the nature of the relationship of those involved in the interaction.

4. Willard Waller, "The Rating and Dating Complex," *American Sociological Review*, II, p. 730.

5. William Sansom, *A Contest of Ladies* (London: Hogarth, 1956), pp. 230–32.

6. The widely read and rather sound writings of Stephen Potter are concerned in part with signs that can be engineered to give a shrewd observer the apparently incidental cues he needs to discover concealed virtues the gamesman does not in fact possess.

7. An interaction can be purposely set up as a time and place for voicing differences in opinion, but in such cases participants must be careful to agree not to disagree on the proper tone of voice, vocabulary, and degree of seriousness in which all arguments are to be phrased, and upon the mutual respect which disagreeing participants must carefully continue to express toward one another. This debaters' or academic definition of the situation may also be involved suddenly and judiciously as a way of translating a serious conflict of views into one that can be handled within a framework acceptable to all present.

8. W. F. Whyte, "When Workers and Customers Meet," Chap. VII, *Industry and Society*, ed. W. F. Whyte (New York: McGraw-Hill, 1946), pp. 132–33.

9. Teacher interview quoted by Howard S. Becker, "Social Class Variations in the Teacher-Pupil Relationship," *Journal of Educational Sociology*, XXV, p. 459.

10. Harold Taxels, "Authority Structure in a Mental Hospital Ward" (unpublished Master's thesis, Department of Sociology, University of Chicago, 1953).

11. This role of the witness in limiting what it is the individual can be has been stressed by Existentialists, who see it as a basic threat to individual freedom. See Jean-Paul Sartre, *Being and Nothingness*, trans. by Hazel E. Barnes (New York: Philosophical Library, 1956), p. 365ff.

12. Goffman, op. cit., pp. 319–27.

13. Peter Blau, "Dynamics of Bureaucracy" (Ph.D. dissertation, Department of Sociology, Columbia University, forthcoming, University of Chicago Press), pp. 127–29.

14. Walter M. Beattie, Jr., "The Merchant Seaman" (unpublished M.A. Report, Department of Sociology, University of Chicago, 1950), p. 35.

15. Sir Frederick Ponsonby, *Recollections of Three Reigns* (New York: Dutton, 1952), p. 46.

MICHAEL ARGYLE

The Laws of Looking

The human capacity for communication is without parallel in the animal world. Apart from our remarkable gift of words, we have a rich repertoire of "body language," most of it consisting of messages that are sent and received unconsciously. An encounter between two people, however simple it may appear on the surface, actually includes the mutual transmission and receipt of countless cues and signals.

Although information can be transmitted by virtually any part of the body, none equals the face for its extraordinary versatility and expressiveness. The fleeting arrangement and rearrangement of facial features can provide a wide array of information about thought and emotion; by one estimate, in fact, the face is capable of about 250,000 different expressions, each with its own shade of meaning that observers can interpret.

In this article, Michael Argyle focuses on the single most important feature of the face—of course, the eyes—and recounts some of the recent findings of the sociologists and social psychologists who have studied human gaze.

Residents of big cities quickly learn the laws of looking. Never make eye contact with a panhandler, or you will be pursued for handouts; with a religious fanatic, or you will be caught in a diatribe; with a belligerent loner, or you will become the object of a menacing tirade; with a lost visitor, or you will feel responsible to help. Never stare back at a stranger who stares relentlessly at you, or your life may be in danger.

There are happier laws, of course. Ovid, wise in the ways of sexual seduction, advised the lover to "Let your eyes gaze into hers, let the gazing be a confession: Often the silent glance brings more conviction than words." The woman was to keep her eyes "gentle and mild, soft for entreating of love. . . . If he is looking at you, return his gaze, and smile sweetly." Ovid understood that gaze is a sensual signal of sexual intention.

What poets suspected, researchers have demonstrated. Patterns of gaze are neither arbitrary nor accidental, but follow definite rules—some apparently innate and other specific to culture. We use vision not just as a channel for collecting information about the world around us, but also as a signal that directs conversation, conveys silent messages, and expresses personality. Gaze is closely coordinated with speaking and listening; it provides feedback, for example, that tells a speaker when to be quiet and the listener when to start talking. You will know from your companion's sullen glare that she is peeved, or from her misty gaze that she is smitten.

Gaze emerged as a social signal early in evolutionary time, as soon as vision developed. Eyes and eyelike designs often acted as protective coloration or a warning to predators. Some butterflies have eye designs on their wings, for instance, and if these patterns are experimentally removed, the butterflies are more likely to be attacked by birds. Some fish have eye spots that expand during attack; small eye spots apparently provoke attack and large ones inhibit it. In primates, eye patterns such as eyebrows and eye rings may play a similar role. Many human societies have believed in the power of the eye to inflict harm (the evil eye), and tribal masks with elaborate eye displays are common devices to ward off danger and assert authority.

The most common meaning conveyed by gaze is a

threat signal. Ralph Exline and Absalom Yellin found that if an experimenter stared at a caged monkey, the monkey attacked or threatened to attack on 76 percent of the trials; if the experimenter looked away almost at once, the monkey responded aggressively about half the time. We have much of the monkey in us. Phoebe Ellsworth and her colleagues found that when they got motorcyclists or pedestrians to stare at car drivers stopped at intersections, the drivers moved off more rapidly from stoplights. Peter Marsh found that a mere glance from a member of a rival group of football supporters is enough to start a fight; the recipient of the glance justifies his attack with cries of "He looked at me!"

Conversely, to avoid or break a stare has a shared meaning among many animal species—appeasement. During battle or courtship, gaze cutoffs reduce the opponent's aggression or the urge to flee. I heard of one man who discovered the appeasement meaning of gaze cutoff just in time. He was riding a New York subway one afternoon when he inadvertently caught the eyes of a large, nervous man sitting opposite, reading about the art of self-control. At once they were locked in a deadly staredown. My friend soon capitulated, smiled, broke the gaze and offered the V sign. The nervous giant laughed, strode across the aisle and, magnanimous victor he, embraced my friend warmly.

The further a species travels up the evolutionary ladder, the greater the range of significance of the eye. Reptiles, birds, and mammals use their eyes and eye rings (such as the raccoon's mask) for many social purposes: territoriality, courtship, dominance, withdrawal. At the primate level, however, gaze takes on a unique capacity to indicate attachment. Only primates—monkeys, apes, and human beings—use gaze to attract as well as attack, to make friends as well as enemies, to seduce as well as repel.

Primates *can* use gaze to threaten, but they are just as likely to gaze fondly. Psychologists have found that couples in love and individuals who are mutually attracted gaze longer at each other than couples who are indifferent. This may not be news to songwriters and lovers, but it is a special talent of primates that should be celebrated.

My colleague Mansur Lalljee suggests that the reason primates use gaze for affiliation is that primate infants and mothers are able to look at each other during breastfeeding. Human babies, for example, are able to focus to a distance of 20 to 30 cm, roughly the proximity of the mother's face when she holds the infant to nurse. Primates are the only mammals in which nursing fosters eye-to-eye contact.

Gaze emerges as a social signal early in the life of infants. By the third week of life babies smile at a nodding head, and by the fifth week they can exchange mutual gazes. Further, babies respond positively to eyes and eye patterns—they smile and their pupils dilate, indicating that they are attending to the stimulus. During the infant's first year, parent and child typically play many mutual-gaze games, such as peekaboo, that seem to delight both players and are among the first forms of social communication.

The physiological underpinning of the meaning of gaze has been established mainly by studies with monkeys. We know, for instance, that one effect of staring eyes is arousal. Various measures of physiological arousal—galvanic skin response, EEG, brain-stem activity—show that organisms can tolerate a certain amount of stimulation and find it interesting, but that overstimulation becomes unpleasant. Too much arousal is unsettling and causes the animal—wolf, bird, or human being—to avoid the prying eyes by fleeing, fighting, or threatening. This is true whether the eyes are those of one's natural predator or those of a stranger on a subway.

When two people like each other there is more gaze and more mutual gaze. Too much gaze, however, is uncomfortable. Janet Dean and I postulated that there are tendencies to approach or to avoid other people, to look or not to look, resulting in an equilibrium level of intimacy. This balance is based on a combination of proximity, gaze, smiling, and other affiliative signals. It would follow that if two people moved away from each other, they would maintain their intimacy level by increasing their gaze, and a number of experiments have confirmed this. Mark Patterson has extended the theory, proposing that signals a person interprets favorably lead him to respond in kind; if he finds the same signals unpleasant or disquieting, he will retreat or look away, thereby restoring equilibrium.

Human beings are able to use the additional cues of context and body language to interpret a gaze. Most people find a steady gaze to be pleasant if they like the gazer and want to be liked by him; the same gaze will be irritating if they think the gazer has undue sexual interests or is seething with anger. If the gazer's stare seems meaningless and vacant, and no other cues allow one to interpret his intentions, the gaze will be even more disturbing.

Usually, though, people within a culture show an excellent ability to decode the message sent in a look. They can readily distinguish affectionate gazes that say "I like you," worried gazes that request help, or threatening gazes that say "Lay off." Although the specific meaning of a look may shift across cultures, people everywhere recognize that a gaze means that the other person is attending, and therefore requires a reaction. The experience of being looked at has a special subjective quality—the feeling of being observed, of being an object of interest for another. Mutual gaze also has such a quality—based on the realization that each person is open to signals from another.

Some meanings and rules of gaze seem to be universal, possibly a result of our biological heritage or the nearly universal experience of being held closely while being fed. Generally, people convey positive attitudes and emotions, such as affection and happiness, with more and longer gazes; they convey negative feelings, such as dislike or depression, with less gazing. In all cultures people notice if a look or stare is done incorrectly. Too much or too little gaze creates an unfavorable impression. A person who gazes too much is usually regarded as disrespectful, threatening, insulting, or supercilious; a person who looks too little is regarded as impolite, inattentive, dishonest, or submissive.

But apart from these universal aspects of gaze, each culture tends to have its own specific variations on the main rules. Sometimes the lessons are taught specifically: "Don't stare, it's impolite," or "Don't look back at him, dear, you'll only encourage him." More often the lessons are indirect, acquired in the course of experience; they remain subtle but strong influences on action.

For example, Navaho children learn not to gaze directly at another person during a conversation. Among the Wituto and Bororo Indians of South America, both the speaker and the listener look at irrelevant objects during conversation, and a storyteller turns *away* from his audience to face the back of the hut. Japanese speakers focus on the listener's neck rather than the eye. A Luo man of Kenya must not look at his mother-in-law. The Mende of Sierra Leone believe that the dead reappear in human guise—but that the dead can be recognized because they never look a live person in the face. Naturally, the Mende are suspicious of people who avert their eyes during a conversation; a Mende would think that America and England are nations of zombies.

The language of the eye is, of course, only one part of a culture's communication system. Variations occur depending on the other communication channels a culture has adopted. Among the Tuareg of North Africa, gaze is an especially important way to send and receive messages, partly because the whole body, apart from the eyes, is covered with clothes and veils. Tuaregs stare steadily at each other while they are conversing in order to glean as much information as possible. In contrast, the Japanese make little use of the facial-visual channel, either to send or receive information; much of their communication takes place through nuances of spoken language and body position. (Possibly the Japanese pay less attention to eyes because Japanese infants are carried on their mothers' backs much of the time, and thus have less visual contact with the mother's face.)

An extensive study of cultural variations in the rules of gaze comes from O. Michael Watson, who worked with male foreign students at the University of Colorado. The students participated in the experiment in pairs, talking about anything they wanted to in their native language while the researchers observed them behind a one-way mirror. Each man's visual style was scored on a scale from one (sharp focusing directly on the other person's eyes) to four (no visual contact at all; looking down or gazing into space). Watson found that young men from contact cultures, where people typically stand close together and frequently touch each other, were far more likely to make eye contact and gaze at each other directly than the men from noncontact cultures:

	Number of men	Average score
Contact cultures:		
Arabs	29	2.57
Latin Americans	20	2.47
Southern Europeans	10	2.19
Noncontact cultures:		
Asians	12	3.25
Indians-Pakistanis	12	3.59
Northern Europeans	48	3.51

Watson also found that these cultural differences in gaze held up no matter how much time each student had spent in the United States or in big cities. Apparently styles of gaze, once learned in childhood, are relatively unaffected by later experience.

Roger Ingham observed how 22 pairs of Swedes and 22 pairs of Englishmen conversed with each other. The Swedish speakers looked at their listeners less often than the English did, with longer glances, and the Swedish pairs had a greater amount of mutual gaze. Swedes, Ingham found, dislike being looked at if they can't look back. This custom differs sharply from other traditions. Indeed, Greek friends have told me Greeks traveling in Europe feel rejected and ignored because, they say, people do not look at them enough.

Such cultural clashes can provoke unexpected problems when a person from one society moves to another that has different rules. Anthropologist Judith Herbstein explains that in Latin America it is considered rude and disrespectful to gaze too long at one's superior. When a Puerto Rican child in an American school is admonished by a teacher, the child will lower his eyes as a sign of respect and obedience. But what do American teachers and parents demand of the child they are scolding? "Look at me! Pay attention!"

Researchers have found individual differences within cultures as well as broad differences across them. Everyone knows the hearty salesman who looks you in the eye and the shy violet who can barely raise his head high enough to look at your nose. Some people look directly at their companions and prefer a few long gazes to frequent darting glances; their characteristic style transcends situation. Individual differences are related to personality traits, though a given person will vary his gaze patterns in different situations.

Richard Christie devised a scale some years ago to measure a person's "Machiavellian" qualities—skepticism about human nature, willingness to use deceit to get one's way, belief in manipulation. In an ingenious experiment on the connections between cheating, lying, and gaze, Ralph Exline and his colleagues arranged to get students implicated in cheating on a project. They managed this by having another subject, who was actually a confederate, pretend to cheat. Then Exline questioned them about the cheating. He found that low-Machiavellian students looked away when lying to protect the subject who cheated; the high Machiavellians looked squarely at him, as much when lying as when telling the truth. Other studies show that most people will look down and otherwise avoid eye contact when they feel guilty or embarrassed, but not psychopaths, high Machiavellians, or, we infer, some used-car dealers. One explanation is that these exceptions do not feel as guilty about lying as most people do, and they probably realize that gaze avoidance indicates lying.

Individual styles can be quite distinctive. Gerhard Nielsen observed pairs of students in conversation and found, as is typical, that people look at their partners less when they are speaking than when they are listening. But individuals varied considerably. Some students looked at their partners only 8 percent of the time, others as much as 73 percent. Extroverts gaze more than introverts, women more than men, adults more than adolescents. Some experiments find that the gaze levels of adolescents may reflect the lower self-esteem or uncertain self-image of many teenagers. It should be emphasized again that a person's gaze level is quite different in different situations. For instance, people tend to look most at people they like, when they are some distance away, and when there is nothing else to look at.

People at the atypical extremes—those who stare too much or who avoid eye contact altogether—may have serious psychological problems. Schizophrenics and depressives tend to avert their gaze (at least when interviewed about their problems), as do some neurotics. Autistic children gaze least. In fact, they are so fearful of looking at others that gaze aversion is one criterion of diagnosis. Autistic children peek at others in abrupt glances, only one half second long, often through their fingers. Or they avoid looking at people by turning their backs or pulling hats over their heads. They avoid looking at eyes and faces, but they do not shun all social contact; they will sit on an adult's lap but avert their gaze.

Corinne Hutt theorizes that autistic children have an abnormally high level of cortical arousal, possibly caused by a genetic defect. Because mutual gaze is arousing, they avoid eye contact to keep their high levels of arousal tolerable. Other researchers, however, think that the overarousal is a consequence, not a cause, of the autism.

At the other end of the spectrum, people with certain psychiatric problems may stare inappropriately for extended minutes. One consequence of the research on gaze is that patients can be taught how to look at other people properly without making them feel uncomfortable or threatened. The patient role-plays an encounter with the therapist. The scene is videotaped and played back to the patient, while the therapist comments on what was correct or incorrect about the patient's gaze level. Practice ensures that the patient learns to get the visual information that he or she needs without excessive staring.

So far I have discussed general patterns of gaze, but in fact we have identified gaze rules to a precise degree. The glances exchanged during a conversation are used to send and to collect information; they are central to the encounter. In conversation, the gazes of speaker and listener are closely linked to the spoken words, and aid in the timing and synchronizing of speech.

We look at people primarily to collect information, to open a channel for observing their expressions and other cues. But the act of looking also becomes a signal for others, and the same glance may serve two purposes. For example, the long glance at the end of an utterance collects feedback and also serves as a full-stop signal to the listener.

The earliest studies of gaze required an observer to watch two speakers through a one-way mirror, recording on a stopwatch how many seconds each participant gazed at the other during a three-minute conversation. Technology has relieved the experimenter of this tedious task. Today we can keep a permanent record of the interaction by using two video cameras, one trained on each speaker, that shows us precisely how gaze is synchronized with speech. Pen recorders keep track, on a moving strip of paper, of continuous gaze sequences—how often speaker A looks at speaker B, how many seconds mutual gazes last, who gazes most, and so on. The reliability of these recordings is very high; two observers agree with each other on the timing and length of gaze sequences virtually all the time.

Gaze provides feedback to the speaker when it is most needed—at the ends of long statements, at grammatical breaks. Adam Kendon studied the timing of gaze in relation to speech for 10 people. He found that the speaker gazes at the listener before the end of an utterance, and the listener looks away. The speaker seeks feedback on whether the listener understands, agrees, is paying attention, or daydreaming. If the speaker does not end an utterance with a full-stop gaze, there is likely to be an awkward delay before the listener realizes it is time to reply. The listener's gaze, in turn, indicates interest, acknowledgment, or impatience. Thus, while the speaker is sending verbal signals, the listener is returning nonverbal signals. This balance of communication permits the conversation to continue with a surprising minimum of overlap and interruption.

Other studies show that there are many nonverbal ways a speaker can keep (or yield) his turn. A raconteur who wants to hold the spotlight does not pause at the end of a sentence, gives no terminal gaze, and keeps a hand in mid-gesture. If interrupted he speaks more loudly, drowning out the interrupter.

The speaker uses gaze for purposes other than feedback and full stops. As Walker recently found, speakers may emphasize a point with an eye flash, a sudden widening of the eye. The speaker can even direct which of several listeners should speak next, simply by a steady look at his choice. Conversely, a listener can get the speaker's attention and good will by looking at him supportively, smiling, and nodding.

If gaze is so important in social exchange, what happens when people do not see each other? If negotiators cannot read visual messages between the spoken lines, what difference does it make? Dozens of experiments have compared face-to-face communication with communication by television video and by voice only (telephone). By and large, the loss of visual signals is not as disastrous as people think. People *prefer* to meet face to face; they prefer videophone to telephone; but the phone is not the antisocial creature that many people think it is. With practice, speakers have adapted beautifully to the nonvisual disadvantage. Most of our phone conversations are well synchronized because we have learned to replace visual signals (gaze, head nods, facial expressions) with audible ones (uh-huhs and hmmms). For the exchange of factual information, the telephone is no worse than face-to-face exchange. Its only disadvantage is that one cannot convey spatial material, such as maps, graphs, and spiral staircases.

There are, in fact, some situations in which the telephone is the best medium. John Short, in a series of studies, showed that it is easier to change someone's opinions over the phone than face to face, especially if the opinion is not a personal attitude but based on official policy or factual data. Ian Morley and Geoffrey Stephenson carried out a series of management-union bargaining simulations to see whether face-to-face or telephone encounters were the more effective. They gave one side or the other a clearly stronger case to defend, and indeed the stronger case was much more likely to win—*but only when it was presented on the telephone!* If the negotiators could see each other, the weaker side won quite often, probably because the participants became more concerned about being thought well of by the opposition. Telephone encounters allow a person to ignore the distracting information of gaze and other nonverbal signs

and concentrate on business. This result augurs well for potential negotiators: Keep to the telephone if you are in a strong position, or your strength may be dissipated by the blandishments of an attractive opponent.

· · ·

Such research has produced a wealth of practical applications. The development of the picture-phone, for instance, may be regarded not just as an extravaganza on the part of Bell Telephone, but as an important aid to diplomacy, business relationships, friendships, and love affairs. Telephones will still do nicely for most business dealings, but people want the benefits of nonverbal language for first contacts, for negotiations when they have a weaker case, for the social signals that make routine conversation work smoothly.

Architects, decorators, and designers are becoming more aware of the subtle ways in which the design of a room or building, and the location of chairs and desks, affect how and whether people interact, even how they feel about each other. Care should be taken, for example, to arrange office furniture so that workers are not forced to stare at each other every time they look up. Otherwise, much time will be wasted in provoked but irrelevant conversation, or in unexpected seductions.

Training in gaze rules is not useful simply for psychiatric patients. Teachers, interviewers, social workers, managers, diplomats, and people who move to another culture have all benefited from learning the cultural rules of the people they meet. Englishmen who learn Arabian gaze customs, for example, do better and are better liked by Arabs than Englishmen who unconsciously follow their own customs.

Looks speak as clearly as the voice. Like speech, gaze is part of our biological heritage, yet wears many cultural disguises. For all the emphasis on spoken words, we would do well to pay more attention to the message of gaze. The eyes, as often as not, have it.

QUESTIONS

1. Why is it so hard to maintain a mutual stare?
2. Some professors read lectures directly; others use notes but look straight at the class most of the time; others look above or to the side of the class. Do these styles affect the interest aroused by the lecture, and if so, why? Does the "body language" of class members reflect their interest, also? How?
3. Are there any personal observations about the "laws of looking" or other "body language" that you can add to the material in the article?

ROBERT N. WILSON

Teamwork in the Operating Room

The group, rather than the individual, is the primary focus of sociology, for it is only in the group—even in one as small as two people—that social processes can be observed. In groups we can see cooperation and conflict, conformity and deviance, authority and obedience, and a host of other forms of social interaction.

Much of the sociological study of groups has taken place in experimental settings, in which groups are created, given tasks to perform, and then observed by sociologists. This research has yielded a great deal of information, but it lacks the "real-life" vitality of group processes in less artificial settings. Many sociologists are now convinced that a better understanding of groups can be achieved by observing the normal behavior of already extant groups as they go about their routine activities.

In this article, Robert Wilson records his observations of surgical teams in the operating room of a large hospital. His study details the many practices and rituals of teamwork that help to preserve the group's cohesion and effectiveness in the highly charged atmosphere that can prevail during operations.

Introduction

Like all dramas, a surgical operation has certain important plots and subplots, a cast of characters, and a spatial setting. In narrative form, surgery at a large general hospital often occurs in a sequence such as the following:

"At seven o'clock in the morning, nurses have arrived on the surgical floor. They find maids finishing the cleaning of the operating suites and corridors. Notices of scheduled operations for the day are posted in prominent places, listing the patient's name, type of case, operating surgeon, and appropriate operating room. Orderlies and nurses' aides are wheeling small tables into the rooms, with sterile equipment laid out ready for use. The charge nurse assigns to their respective cases the scrub nurses (who will actually assist the surgeon) and the circulating nurses (who will perform general tasks around the operating room such as fetching water and counting sponges).

"As the hour of surgery, eight o'clock, approaches, the scrub nurses are washing hands and arms in the small scrub rooms next to the operating rooms; when they are thoroughly washed, according to specific procedures and an allotted time, they slip into sterile gowns and gloves. Their scrubbing must precede that of the doctors, since the nurses will be expected to assist the latter in their scrubbing and gowning. The first patients are in the corridor or preparation room where they have been wheeled by an orderly, and they are already in a semiconscious state from drugs of a sedative type.

"With the arrival of M.D.'s on the scene, the tempo of preparation increases. Nurses are now untying the sterile bundles and spreading instruments out for instant use. Usually, orderlies and the charge nurse are checking lights, suction hoses, etc. The anesthetist is setting up his tanks and dials at the head of the operating table. Interns and their more advanced colleagues, the surgical residents, are ordinarily scrubbing before the operating surgeon appears. Much joking and chatter occurs between these younger doctors and the nurses. When the operating surgeon, an older and more dignified M.D., starts to scrub, the tone of levity may decrease markedly. His appearance signals an even more alert and faster level of

Reproduced by permission of the Society for Applied Anthropology from *Human Organization*, 12(4): 9–14.

preparation on the part of other members of the operating team. The nurses assist the doctors in dressing for surgery: they hold gowns ready for the doctors to step into when scrubbed, and when the gowns are on they tie them securely. They hold rubber gloves up so that the doctors can put them on more easily. At this stage, before the incision has even been made, the motif of watchful cooperation has been established between nurses and doctors in the process of gowning.

"Now the patient has been wheeled into the room, and the anesthetist is busily caring for him, making him comfortable, and applying anesthetic. (The anesthetist is the patient's direct 'companion' in this venture, the person who reassuringly sedates him and establishes a close personal connection.) In a difficult case, the surgeon has perhaps previously consulted a colleague about the technique he plans to use and what conditions he expects to find. As the moment of cutting draws nearer, however, he is 'on his own' as the captain of the team; his lonely responsibility is mitigated by the presence of younger doctors and nurses, but he must be the key decision-maker.

"At the signal from the anesthetist that the patient has reached a proper depth of unconsciousness, the surgeon makes his first incision. (The patient has already been draped and painted by the cooperation of house staff and nurses, under the surgeon's direction.) Immediately, by spoken word or conventional hand signals, the surgeon calls on the nurse for sponges and instruments; the young doctors assisting at the operation are brought into play to hold retractors and clamps which staunch the flow of blood and keep visibility good in the operative field. At each stage in events, the surgeon consults the anesthetist to keep check on the patient's condition. Some portions of the operation may actually be performed by the surgeon's assistants, although he is always in close supervision and handles the critical moves himself. It is a mark of status to be allowed to work in the operative field, and actual surgery is done only by well-trained resident doctors. Nevertheless, the familiarity gained by simply holding the wound open for the surgeon is a vital part of the young intern's experience.

"There are two parallel status lines at work in the room. The surgeon passes on commands to the senior resident, who in turn passes them to junior residents and interns. The scrub nurse likewise initiates action for the circulating nurse and any students present. These chains of authority are crisscrossed by orders from the surgeon to the scrub nurse and from any doctor to any of the nurses; however, action is seldom, if ever, initiated in reverse: nurses do not issue orders to any doctors, and the lower echelons rarely direct the activities of the higher.

"The operating surgeon, after finishing his major task, consults the anesthetist again with respect to the patient's general condition and the length of time required to close the wound. As the closing process begins, there is a visible relaxation of tension and vigilance; joking becomes more frequent, and the pace of work more leisurely. Before a stitch can be taken, however, the nurses must count the sponges used in the operation, as a safeguard against leaving foreign objects in the patient's body. Here, at least, the nurses do initiate action, for the surgeon waits for their assurance that the sponge count is correct.

"During the sewing-up phase, the junior members of the surgical team usually take a more prominent role than they have in earlier stages. Often the chief surgeon will remove his gloves and stand around chatting or even leave the room entirely. The resident is left in charge, and he and the interns proceed to apply the finishing touches. After the sutures are all in place, the anesthetist takes charge of dressing the patient and moving him from the table to a cart which will return him to his bed. In this he is assisted by nurses and usually an orderly; sometimes the junior doctors will help out, but the chief surgeon is not engaged in this phase.

"At length the patient, anesthetist, and doctors leave the room. The nurses are last to leave, as they were first to arrive. They pick up the doctors' discarded gowns and gloves and prepare the room for the next case. The whole process, requiring from thirty minutes to six or more hours, has included a large cast of characters exhibiting much communication. Yet they are so familiar with their jobs that the number of spoken words may have been slight."

A marvelous example of teamwork has taken place. Although innumerable orders have been given, most of them have flowed from the dictates of the patient's presence and condition. In a very real sense, few of the directives issued during surgery are arbitrary decisions on the surgeon's part. Rather, in the last analysis, the patient's needs have been the controlling element in the entire situation. Thus, the person who seems to have been least capable of exerting authority—the prone, unconscious "object"—has in fact assumed the star role and has exercised the preponderant influence on the course of the drama.

In the days before modern techniques of asepsis had been developed but after the idea of cleanliness had begun to be accepted in medicine, it was the custom to spray the operating area with an antiseptic solution. A certain noted surgeon, therefore, used to pause before the operation and intone, "Brethren, let us spray." Somehow this irreverent remark typifies an important aspect of life in the surgery: where the job to be done is intrinsically abnormal and fraught with anxieties, the atmosphere is deliberately made as mundane and casual as possible. In this most serious of situations, efforts are directed toward pulling the psychological climate into "normalcy." Like the small boy whistling past the graveyard, the inhabitants of the room make things prosaic; further, there is reason to think that energies must be mobilized for the work itself, not allowed to drain off in unproductive fear and trembling. While operating rooms are not truly places of levity, and *Ars Chirurgica* advises the surgeon to be "fearful in dangerous things," the pattern of joking and small talk is perhaps the most striking feature of surgery to the outsider. There is drama, but only a fraction of total operating time looks anything like the Hollywood stereotype of tight-lipped tenseness and mute solemnity. The self-consciousness which one would expect to characterize a person invading another's body and literally "holding a life in his hands" is for the most part dispelled by technical considerations; a job must be done, a careful exacting task, and this is the focus of energy and intellect. Operating rooms, then, are workmanlike. The first impression dispels any thought of "constant crisis."

Every operating room is:

1. like *all* other operating rooms
2. like *some* other operating rooms
3. like *no* other operating rooms

This logical scheme was originally applied to the field of personality, but it fits the operating room equally well. In fact, it might well be said that the surgery *has* a personality of its own, a distinctive blend of characteristics setting it apart from the rest of the hospital. It is perhaps a misnomer to speak of "the" operating room; rather, there are probably many types which may be classified in several ways.

Every Operating Room Is Like *All* Other Operating Rooms

What do all operating rooms share as identifying marks? At least the following features are proposed:

Drama, Excitement, Intensity: An Air of Importance

Surgery is so obviously worthwhile and effective that it may be trite to comment on its importance. Yet there are many other aspects of medicine, and many aspects of every job, which lack the immediacy and lauded purpose of surgery. In the operating room, there can be no doubt that what is being done is dangerous and vital. Because we all share a belief in the importance of the body, because it is a basic part of the human being's security, and drastic manipulation (such as cutting) is cause for excitement. Further, the power to enter and change the body signifies an immense responsibility on the surgeon's part and insures that the atmosphere shall include a sense of awe. And there is an element of drama, despite the stricture that it does not resemble the movie version. Each operation is a problem, a challenge, whose course can be plotted but not thoroughly predicted. One piano chord in the old-fashioned cinema announced that "something is going to happen." Just so, in an operating room everyone

knows that "something is going to happen."

As one graduate nurse expressed it:

Down here you have the patient at the most critical time of his life and you know by the time he leaves the operating room what his chances are. You feel as if you are really important in his life. You're only with him a little while but still it's the crucial time so far as he is concerned.

We have stressed the mundane aspects of operating room life and pointed out the joking air which often precedes and follows the surgery. One can hear much talk of fishing trips, much mutual kidding, etc. All these contribute to a reduction of tension. But the tension exists; everything is not sweetness and light. A recurrent index of tension is the tendency to quick flare-ups of "temperament," of irritated and antagonistic remarks. Some impression of this index is gained from a record of part of an operation by an observer seated in the gallery.

At this point, we have an interesting piece of interaction between the scrub nurse and Dr. *M*. The nurse hands him one swab, retaining another in her hand. He takes the swab as she hands it to him, and throws it angrily on the floor on the other side of the operating table. He asks, "Is this phenol?" (referring to the swab left in her other hand). The nurse replies (pointing disgustedly to the floor) "That one was phenol. This one is alcohol." Dr. *M*: When I called for phenol twenty minutes ago, I *meant* phenol. I've got to swab that whole end off. Now get me some phenol." The nurse then fills a small cup with phenol and hands it to Dr. *M*. with a swab. This procedure he accepts.

Dr. *M*. is now under great tension. It shows. His remarks become more brusque, irritated, profane. When the nurses have trouble getting a hose fixed up, he says, "Let's get going here. Dammit, it takes twenty minutes to do a thing and there is one way to do it right." The nurses begin to count sponges in a fairly loud voice. *M*. shouts to them, "Stop counting sponges! Don't do *anything* until I stop this bleeder." A moment later he shouts at *Y* (the assistant resident), "Pull back those fingers. Jesus, let's see this thing."

Emphasis on Teamwork and Cooperation

It might be said that every operation is a *co*-operation. In surgery, no one can "go it alone"; each person is dependent on many others, and the patient is of course dependent on all members of the team. So necessary is teamwork, in the nature of the job, that even individuals who are personally antagonistic often act in concert during the course of surgery. (In this, the operating team is like a jazz band or baseball club. Legend has it that the members of the famous double-play combination of Tinkers to Evers to Chance did not speak off the field for many years.) The individuals composing an operating team are so close-knit and understand the task at hand so thoroughly that verbal signals are often unnecessary. A language of gesture has developed whose meanings are crystal clear to persons following the operation intently. Perhaps the outstanding examples of intuitive cooperation occur in these pairs of team members:

surgeon-nurse

surgeon-anesthetist

surgeon-assistant surgeon

To the nurse, the intimate comprehension of the surgeon's technique and his recognition of her competence may become a prime reward of her job. The desirability of a close harmony is recognized as is illustrated by the comments of an operating nurse and a surgeon respectively:

Morale is high in the operating room because there is a team spirit. The finest point in the nurse's life comes when she is finally taken in and fully accepted as a member of the team. On a certain day, everything changes. There is almost a clean break with the past; . . . the surgeon will recognize you and call you by name. A kind of emotional block is broken, and you know you are accepted. Any nurse feels very wonderful about this. The main reward for doing operating-room nursing lies in a special relationship with the surgeon.

Both instruments and nurses have to be worked with for a couple of years before you know them. If she (nodding at nurse) stayed with the same guy for two years she would do everything before he even asked for it. —A senior resident.

It is obvious that the surgeon and anesthetist must work together. The degree of anesthesia to be given a patient depends on the type of operation and the various stages in its progress. Conversely, the surgeon must be kept informed of changes in his patient's condition. One interview note states:

We then got into a discussion of how the anesthetist works. Dr. *D.* described as perhaps the most important point a close cooperation with the operating surgeon. He said it is desirable that the anesthetist know the surgeon well, know his technique, and be able to cooperate with him almost automatically.

Technical Criteria and "The Religion of Competence"

All operating rooms place great stress on efficiency and expertness. In part, this is due to the complicated nature of surgical work—the fact that it rests on an exacting knowledge of multiple factors. The irascible surgeon who is highly skilled, and thereby gains respect, is a familiar figure. Unpleasant personal characteristics may often be overlooked if competence is high enough. The judgment of colleagues and nurses soon enough labels any doctor according to the degree of mastery he is observed to exercise, and the palm goes to the expert.

In part, too, the importance of cleanliness contributes to a desire for efficiency. The rituals connected with ster-

ility promote a precise mode of behavior which infuses the nonsterile portions or technique. Surgical work is, by definition, careful.

The surgical job itself is such a demanding one in terms of exactitude that it draws all related jobs into the orbit of mechanical perfection. Because surgery must be orderly, the tasks which facilitate it are also orderly. "A neat job," then, can describe everything from a virtuoso performance by a heart surgeon to the measured folding of towels by a nurse's aide.

In the surgery, all tasks are "obvious" and can be quickly judged by ideal criteria; nowhere is the American talent for the admiration of "know-how" more clearly expressed. It is plain that the emphasis on technique and precision is necessary to high-level effort in surgery. Yet we may also mention the possibility that some portion of this emphasis serves a subsidiary function: it keeps the hands and mind busy on detail in a setting where excess imagination or sensitivity might interfere with the psychological boldness required. Inspection, not introspection, is the imperative of operating room activity.

The Surgeon's Authority

The surgeon is like the captain of a ship. He is ultimately responsible for everything that happens in the operating room.—Chief of surgery.

Huge responsibilities demand huge grants of power, for responsibility and power must be some way commensurate. The surgeon's authority is unquestioned, it would seem, because of three interrelated factors. First, there is the right relation between authority and responsibility; a person held to account for something must, fairly, be in a position to affect the process by which the thing comes about. Second, the surgeon stands at the very top of a skilled hierarchy. He is not a replaceable part, and ideally, he knows more about the job at hand than anyone else in the room. Therefore, it is natural that he would be vested with the authority to direct the work on grounds of competence. Third, there is an aura of magic and reverence surrounding the figure of the surgeon; this aura has its roots in the ancient connection of priest and healer. When the three factors are combined, one sees a potent basis of authority. Although the authority is mitigated in several ways, it is a "constant" characteristic of the surgery. Relaxation of power may occur when long acquaintance and close work relations, especially those between doctor and nurse, have vitiated the third factor, the priestly aura, or "charisma." Implicit or explicit resistance (or rarely, transgression) to authority often stems from a surgeon's failure to fulfill wholly the standards of competence, so that respect is weakened. At any rate, the overpowering nature of the surgeon's position is almost certain to produce an undercurrent of resentment among lower-status members of the work team. This is illustrated in the exasperated aphorism of an operating-room nurse: "Nurses spend half their lives waiting on doctors, and the other half waiting *for* them."

Physical and Psychological Isolation from the Rest of the Hospital

For reasons of sterility and general work flow considerations, the operating suite is always separated from the hospital as a whole. It has its own floor, or part of a floor, and is for most purposes a "closed system." Although patients must be brought to surgery and taken back to their beds when the operation is over, this task is performed by orderlies, and other hospital personnel rarely visit the surgery. Of course, casual visiting is prohibited, since nonessential onlookers would tend to disrupt the precision of work and might increase the danger of infection.

The isolation of the operating room means that, in the eyes of other employees, this area is strange and forbidding. All nonsurgical people are in a fundamental sense on the "outside" and may be curious about what occurs in the sanctum. They have, further, a definite attitude of awe and admiration for the activities that go on there and the "initiates."

Conversely, the surgical staff, from doctors to maids, develop a strong feeling of camaraderie. They recognize their status and role as a special group. Their world is the surgery, not the hospital. This implies great warmth and cohesion, as well as agreement on a variety of values. They must and do learn to live together as an elite corps.

Every Operating Room Is Like *Some* Other Operating Rooms

There seems to be a number of *types* of operating room, which share certain secondary characteristics. These qualities are like an overlay, supplementing and modifying but not drastically changing the conditions noted above. They include:

The Extent of Teaching Carried On

On this factor, operating rooms may vary from those that include no personnel in training to those that involve students, nurses, interns, and residents. Obviously, in the teaching situation, part of everyone's energy must go into the initiation process. The presence of students keeps people on their toes, keeps an air of questioning and striving alive, which infuses the surgery. Outdated and incompetent elements, be they surgeons, nurses, or surgical techniques, have little chance of survival.

Methods and attitudes undergo constant changes, as the operating room keeps pace with the advance of medical science. And the surgery is "conscious" of its work,

measuring and evaluating it in the light of high criteria of excellence. The stress on *competence* is heightened because every case is in one sense a model for the learners.

Division of labor is pushed further in teaching hospitals. For one thing, more hands are available; for another, there is a constant effort to split off suitable practice tasks which can give a student experience and afford him a gradual introduction into the core of the operation. Both nurses and doctors in training follow a series of stages whereby they approach ever more closely the condition of standard excellence. Nurses move from circulating duties to scrub nurse, from easy to hard cases. Interns and residents progress from holding retractors and stitching incisions to the actual work of the operating surgeon. The accentuated division of labor means that coordination of all the parts is more difficult to achieve, and, therefore planning is essential. Since a very large number of people are involved, interpersonal relations take on added significance; morale and skill must be high to insure smooth functioning.

Differences in prestige are multiplied in the teaching situation. The ladder of status has many extra rungs, within both medical and nursing staffs. Thus we find not only this invariant distinction between surgeon and nurse, but finer distinctions between scrub nurse and circulating nurse, between chief surgeon, assistant surgeon, resident, and intern. These gradations have the advantage of inducting "raw" individuals through manageable stages, so that they are not thrust from student to full professional in a single immense jump. However, they also tend to increase social distance and multiply the opportunities for friction. An amusing account of status-laden behavior, as told by two operating-room nurses, will illustrate the theme:

They asked the question, "Who is the first person to leave the operating room after an operation?" And immediately answered it with, "The surgeon, of course," They said first the surgeon steps back from the table, takes off his gown and gloves, throws them in a heap on the floor and walks out of the room. Then the lesser fry close up the incision and then they leave, also stripping off their gowns and gloves and dropping them in a heap any place on the floor. They described how even the young resident will rip off a towel from the operating table, perhaps with several instruments on it, and just throw it to the floor while preparing the patient to go back downstairs, and then the resident will wait for the nurse to untie his gown and stalk away. After everyone has gone the nurse or nurses and anesthetist are left to clear up the place and get the patient back downstairs. Miss *R.* exclaimed, "After the great big doctors are all finished, who do you think moves the patient back on to the stretcher to take him downstairs? The nurse, of course." At this point Miss *M.* interjected, "Yes, that is what happens. They just walk out after shouting at you for two solid hours."

The fact of teaching means that each stage in surgery itself will be carefully scrutinized and explained. Although not all surgeons converse during the course of an operation, it is usual for the surgeon, his assistant, and/or the senior resident to carry on a running commentary, describing the significance of the work at hand. In recent years there has been a shift away from didactic teaching in medicine—one demonstrator or lecturer confronting a mass of students. The stress now falls on clinical teaching which introduces material to the student through his active participation in a case. Thus, the learners at an operation will be scrubbed up and actually assisting, rather than watching from the gallery. (Few operating rooms are now being constructed with amphitheaters, as a result of this trend.)

Problems are introduced by the teaching emphasis, many of them concerning the amount of participation allowed to the student. In surgery, only one man can operate; in the teaching of medicine, multiple diagnoses of the same individual may be made for practice purposes. There is a story of a young intern which points up the dilemma. After a particularly impressive piece of surgery, the doctors retired to the surgeons' lounge just off the operating room. The chief, who had performed the operation, began discussing it with his team. At length, turning to a very young intern whose duty at the operation had been to hold the distal end of the retractor, the great man asked, "And what did you learn from this operation, my boy?" The intern replied, "I think I have definitely established, sir, that the assistant resident has a terrible case of dandruff." Yet a chief of neurological surgery has commented that in his own experience the gradual progression up the ladder of responsibility was an excellent introduction to his specialty. He noted especially the fact that the slow rise to a central position in the operating team insured that he would not feel too much pressure when he, at length, held full authority, that he would not feel "on the spot" in his first cases as operating surgeon.

Nonteaching hospitals lack the special difficulties involved in this sort of on-the-job education. On the other hand, they also lack the detailed explanations to members of the team and the general air of competence and easy expertness which the presence of distinguished chiefs instills.

It might also be pointed out that nonteaching hospitals have no scapegoats as ready at hand as students. A latent function of student nurses and interns would seem to be found in their position as legitimate targets for the impatience and anxieties of graduate nurses or surgeons. Without disrupting the rapport of key team members, it is possible to vent anger at the circulating nurse who trips over her own feet or the intern who is woolgathering when he should be watching the operation.

The Difficulty of the Case in Progress

The relative seriousness of an operation determines many features of an operating room. For instance, in general terms, more difficult cases imply the involvement of more personnel, greater lengths of time, greater number of instruments, etc. In these important ways, a chest operation in Hospital *X* will be more nearly like a chest operation in Hospital *Y* than like a hemorrhoidectomy in Hospital *X*. While it is true that no two pieces of surgery are ever *exactly* alike, the major varieties show definite similarities.

In a fairly easy case, the atmosphere of the room tends to be rather relaxed, and the requirements of strict attentiveness and speed on the part of all concerned are less rigorous. The tension which introduces friction into casual interactions is largely absent. However, in avoiding the extremes of pressure, the operating team misses the excitement and feeling of importance that accompany a major challenge to skill. Thus there may be complaints that the work is dull or routine, that the challenge is not great enough to hold one's interest at a high, sustained level.

Because fewer people work on a minor operation, the need for precise coordination is also less pronounced. In the teaching hospital, these cases are often used as opportunities for the young student to begin testing his own skills. A surgical resident may be given a vein ligation as his first solo flight, or a student nurse may serve as scrub nurse on the same type of operation. It is not true that these cases are taken "casually," but they do include a greater margin for error and seldom require split-second timing.

Since minor cases are usually short, the factor of fatigue is also less critical. In a long, exacting surgical effort, physical exhaustion may cause outbursts of temper; mistakes may be less well tolerated toward the close of a lengthy job. Often a long case will involve shifts of personnel, especially nurses, thus adding to the need for tight coordination. The more difficult work, sometimes requiring six or even eight consecutive hours, points up the need for physical endurance in surgical personnel. A noted surgeon once remarked the possession of "good legs" as one of the qualities of a competent surgeon, since long hours of standing are so often necessary.

These two characteristics—the extent of teaching and the nature of the operation—may be viewed as scales having various values. Any operation will fall at a certain point on each scale and share the qualities of that point with other operating rooms to form a "type." Thus we might speak of "major surgery in a teaching hospital," or "minor surgery in a small, nonteaching hospital," and find many elements in common within the designated category. There are undoubtedly other characteristics which contribute to a classification of operating rooms (for instance, whether the surgical staff is "open" or "closed"), but these seem to be the most critical.

Every Operating Room Is Like *No* Other Operating Room

Three elements appear to account for the *unique* quality of each operating room—and, for that matter, of each single operation. They are:

1. the personality of the surgeon
2. the personality of the nurse
3. the creative course of surgery itself

Certain facets of the surgeon's and nurse's personalities have already been discussed, those features which seem to be invariant. Such, for example, are the factors associated with tension and fatigue (stereotypes of the "irritable" surgeon or the "snippy" nurse) or connected with formal lines of status and authority (the "authoritarian" surgeon, or "subservient" nurse). But over and above these behaviors which seemed to be determined by "the situation" is a host of actions, attitudes, and traits which make each individual, in surgery or anywhere, unique.

An interview with a clinical instructor, a graduate nurse, provided an interesting illustration of the variations introduced by the surgeon's particular tastes in the matter of talking and joking during an operation:

> "The operating room," Said Miss *D.*, "takes its tone from the personality and attitude of the surgeon. It is not a joking place if the surgeon does not make jokes, and not a talking place if the surgeon does not like to talk while operating." She described several different staff members and their variations in operating room leadership and atmosphere. She said that Dr. *T*'s operating room was always very friendly and filled with witty exchanges, while Dr. *H*'s, although friendly, was strictly business. One distinguished surgeon allows no talking whatever in his room, while another is so jovial that he always remarks during an operation that he considers himself very lucky to have been given the very best nurses available for *his* operation.

Nurses, too, may be impersonal or warmly involved, although they do usually follow the surgeon's lead. When a nurse and surgeon are extremely well-acquainted and have between them the bond of countless shared experiences, their mutual personality adjustment may greatly enhance the technical efficiency of the team.

Surgery takes a different course each time it is performed. This is natural, since the bodies of patients are by no means uniform. But the truly individual character of some few operations stems from the creative element in new types of surgery. Perhaps a maneuver is being performed for the first time; perhaps the operation is exploratory and uncovers an unexpected cancer; perhaps a dramatic turn of events provokes an unanticipated crisis. In any event, something has been added to routine, and the operating room acquires a distinctive aura of excitement and discovery. In surgery, as in any other creative activity, there is room for novel aspects which thwart the attempt at rigid classification. Part of the peculiar charm and attraction of the operating room lies in this creative facet, the fact that routine may always be upset. If there were no possibility for innovation and inspiration, if surgery were really "routine," it is unlikely that it would attract the caliber of persons who *are* attracted to an operating-room team.

QUESTIONS

1. Would you say that the operating team is a primary or a secondary group?
2. Why does Wilson emphasize "teamwork" in his description? Is it a crucial feature of this particular group?
3. What is the function of humor in the operating team?

ROSABETH MOSS KANTER

How the Top Is Different

One of the outstanding features of modern societies is the growth of large formal organizations, mostly in the form of corporations or government departments. Although secondary groups of this kind are virtually unknown in preindustrial societies, they dominate political and economic life in the modern world. Most American workers, in fact, are employed by large formal organizations, and the chances are good that you will spend at least part of your own working life in such an environment.

Every formal organization has a hierarchical authority structure: the official lines of responsibility, from the top of the organization to its lowest reaches, can be diagrammed on a chart. But sociologists are well aware that the theory and the practice of organizational structure often diverge from one another, for the behavior of officials is partly shaped by personal relationships and other circumstances that the organizational chart could never anticipate. For example, power over the day-to-day affairs of an organization often rests with middle-level managers rather than the supposed decision makers at the top, who are often isolated from, and ignorant of, much of what is taking place.

In this article, Rosabeth Moss Kanter draws on her case study of a large corporation to provide insights into that part of an organization whose inner workings are often least accessible to outsiders—the leadership.

Excerpted from *Men and Women of the Corporation,* by Rosabeth Moss Kanter, © 1977 by Rosabeth Moss Kanter, Basic Books, Inc., Publishers, New York. Pp. 34–36, 48–49, 52–54, 68, 75, 118–22, and additions.

Corporate headquarters of the company I have called Indsco, occupied many floors in a glass and steel office building in a large city. The surroundings were luxurious. At ground level was a changing art exhibit in glass cases with displays of awards to Indsco executives for meritorious public service or newspaper clippings about the corporation. There might be piles of company newspapers on a nearby table or special publications like the report by foreign students who spent the summer with Indsco families. Such public displays almost always stressed Indsco's contributions to the welfare of the larger community. Across from gleaming chrome elevators and a watchman's post were doors leading into the employees' dining room. In the morning a long table with coffee, sweet rolls, and bagels for sale was set up outside the dining room; during the day coffee carts were available on each floor. Inside, the dining room was divided into two parts: a large cafeteria for everyone and a small area with already set tables, hostess seating, menus, and waitress service. Those tables were usually occupied by groups of men; the largely female clerical work force tended to eat in the cafeteria. Special luncheon meetings arranged by managers were held in the individual executive dining rooms and conference areas on the top floor; to use these rooms, reservations had to be made well in advance by someone with executive status.

Indsco executives were also likely to go out for lunch, especially if they were entertaining an outside visitor, to any of the numerous posh restaurants in the neighborhood. At these lunches a drink was a must; at one time it was two extra-dry martinis, but more recently it became a few glasses of wine. However, despite the fact that moderate social drinking was common, heavy drinking was frowned upon. A person's career could be ruined by the casual comment that he or she had alcoholic tendencies. Stories told about men who cavorted and caroused in bars, staying up all night, were told with the attitude that "that was really crazy."

The office floors were quietly elegant, dominated by modern design, white walls, and beige tones. At one end, just off the elevators, sat a receptionist who calls on a company telephone line to announce visitors. A secretary would then appear to escort a visitor to his or her appointment. Offices with windows were for higher-status managers, and their secretaries were often proud of having drapes. Corner offices were reserved for the top. They were likely to be larger in size, with room for coffee tables and couches, and reached through a reception area where a private secretary sat. Inside offices went to assistants and other lower-status salaried personnel; conference rooms were also found along the inside rim. Secretaries and other hourly workers occupied rows of desks with banks of cabinets and files in the public spaces between. There were few signs of personal occupancy of space, except around the secretaries' desks. Managers might put up a painting or poster on the wall, and they usually had a small set of photographs of their families somewhere on or near their desk. Rarely would more than a few books or reports be visible, and the overall impression was one of tidiness, order, and uniformity from office to office. In fact, it was often true that the higher the status of an executive, the less cluttered was his desk. Office furnishings themselves reflected status rather than personality. There was a clear system of stratification. As status increased, desks went from a wood top with steel frame through solid wood to the culmination in a marble-top desk. Type of ashtray was also determined by the status system; and a former executive secretary, promoted into a management position herself, reported that her former peers were upset that she took her stainless steel file trays with her because a secretary working for her would not be entitled to such luxurious equipment. The rational distribution of furniture and supplies was thought to make the system more equitable and to avoid competition for symbols of status. . . .

The secretary also contributed in minor ways to the boss's status. Some people have argued that secretaries function as "status symbol" for executives, holding that the traditional secretarial role is developed and preserved because of its impact on managerial egos, not its contribution to organizational efficiency. Robert Townsend, iconoclastic former president of Avis, claimed in *Up the Organization* that the existence of private secretaries was organizationally inefficient, as proven by his experience in gaining half a day's time by giving up what he called "standard executive equipment." One writer was quite explicit about the meaning of a secretary: "In many companies a secretary outside your door is the most visible sign that you have become an executive; a secretary is automatically assigned to each executive, whether or not his work load requires one. . . . When you reach the vice-presidential level, your secretary may have an office of her own, with her name on the door. At the top, the president may have two secretaries. . . ." A woman professional at Indsco agreed with the idea that secretaries were doled out as rewards rather than in response to job needs, as she talked about her own problems in getting enough secretarial help.

At Indsco, the secretary's function as a status symbol increased up the ranks as she became more and more bound to a specific boss. "It's his image, his status, sitting out in front," a personnel administrator said. "She's the sign of how important he is." . . .

Physical height corresponded to social height at Indsco, like other major corporations. Corporate officers resided at the very top on the forty-fifth floor, which was characterized by many people in Indsco as "a hospital ward." The silence was deafening. The offices were huge. According to one young executive who had served as an assistant to an officer, "One or two guys are sitting there; there's not much going on. It's the brain center, but there is no activity. It's like an old folks' home. You can see the cobwebs growing. A secretary every quarter mile. It's very sterile." An executive secretary told the story of her officer boss's first reaction to moving onto the forty-fifth floor. "He was the one human being," she said, "who was uncomfortable with the trappings of status. When he moved up, he had to pick an office." She wouldn't let him take anything but a corner—it was the secretary who had to tell him that. Finally he agreed for the sake of the corporate image, but he was rarely there, and he set up the office so that everything was in one corner and the rest was useless space.

Some people felt that the physical insulation of top executives also had its counterpart in social insulation. Said a former officer's assistant, "There are courtiers around the top guys, telling them what they want to hear, flattering them. For example, there was a luncheon with some board members. The vice-chairman mentioned that he was looking for a car for his daughter. A courtier thought, 'We'll take care of it.' He went down the line, and someone in purchasing had to spend half a day doing this. The guy who had to do it resented it, so he became antagonistic to the top. The vice-chairman had no idea this was going on, and if he had known, he would probably have stopped it; but you can't say anything at the top without having it be seen as an order. Even ambiguous remarks may get translated into action. At the top you have to figure out the impact of all of your words in advance because an innocent expression can have a major effect. A division president says, 'It might be a good idea to ————.' He's just ruminating, but that gets sent down to the organization as an ultimatum, and everyone scrambles around to make sure it gets done. He looks down and says, 'What the hell is happening?' "

At the same time, officers could also be frustrated by their distance from any real action. One remarked, "You get into a position like mine, and you think you can get anything done, but I shout down an order, and I have to wait years for any action. The guy in the plant turns a valve and sees the reaction, or the salesman offers a price, but I may never live to see the impact of my decisions." For this reason, it was known that once in a while officers could be expected to leave their protected environment and try to get involved in routine company activities. Some would go down and try to do something on the shop floor. Once in a while one would make a sales call at a very high level or make an appearance at a customer golf outing. It was also a legend that an early president had his own private laboratory outside of his office—his own tinkering room. As a manager put it, "He would close the door and go play. It was almost as though he was babied. He was given a playroom." . . .

Conformity Pressures at the Top: Uncertainty and the Growth of Inner Circles

Leaders who already have power seek as new recruits those they can rely upon and trust. They demand that the newcomers to top positions be loyal, that they accept authority, and that they conform to a prescribed pattern of behavior.

Unlike a more communal environment, where eccentrics can be lovingly tolerated because trust is based on mutual commitments and deep personal knowledge, those who run the bureaucratic corporation often rely on outward manifestations to determine who is the "right sort of person." Managers tend to carefully guard power and privilege for those who fit in, for those they see as "their kind." Wilbert Moore was commenting on their phenomenon when he used the metaphor of a "bureaucratic kinship system" to describe the corporation—but a kinship system based on homosocial reproduction in which men reproduce themselves in their own image. The metaphor is apt. Because of the *situation* in which managers function, because of the position of managers in the corporate structure, social similarity tends to become extremely important to them. The structure sets in motion forces leading to the replication of managers as the same kind of social individuals. And people at the top reproduce themselves in kind.

Conformity pressures and the development of exclusive management circles closed to "outsiders" stem from the degree of uncertainty surrounding managerial positions. Bureaucracies are social inventions that supposedly reduce the uncertain to the predictable and routine. Yet much uncertainty remains—many situations in which individual people rather than impersonal procedures must be trusted. "Uncertainty," James Thompson wrote in a recent major statement on organizations, "appears as the fundamental problem for complex organizations, and coping with uncertainty as the essence of the administrative process." Thompson identified three sources of uncertainty in even the most perfect of machine-like bureaucracies: a lack of cause-effect understanding in the culture at large (limiting the possibility for advance planning); contingencies caused by the fact that the bureaucracy is not alone, so that outcomes of organizational ac-

tion are in part determined by action of other elements in the environment; and the interdependence of parts, the human interconnections inside the organization itself, which can never fully be reduced to predictable action. The requirements for a perfectly technically "rational" bureaucracy that never has to rely on the personal discretion of a single individual can never be met: complete knowledge of all cause-effect relationships plus control over all of the relevant variables. Thus, sources of uncertainty that are inherent in human institutions mean that some degree of reliance on individual persons must always be present.

It is ironic that in those most impersonal of institutions the essential communal problem of trust remains. For wherever there is uncertainty, *someone* (or some group) must decide, and thus, there must be personal discretion. And discretion raises not technical but human, social, and even communal questions: trust, and its origins in loyalty, commitment, and mutual understanding based on the sharing of values. It is the uncertainty quotient in managerial work, as it has come to be defined in the large modern corporation, that causes management to become so socially restricting: to develop tight inner circles excluding social strangers; to keep control in the hands of socially homogeneous peers; to stress conformity and insist upon a diffuse, unbounded loyalty; and to prefer ease of communication and thus social certainty over the strains of dealing with people who are "different."

If conditions of uncertainty mean that people have to be relied on, then people fall back on social bases for trust. The greater the uncertainty, the greater the pressures for those who have to trust each other to form a homogeneous group. At different times in an organization's history, and at different places in its structure, a higher degree of uncertainty brings with it more drive for social similarity. . . .

Uncertainty can stem from either the time-span of decisions and the amount of information that must be collected, or from the frequency with which non-routine events occur and must be handled. The impossibility of specifying contingencies in advance, operating procedures for all possible events, leaves an organization to rely on personal discretion. (It is also this pressure that partly accounts for the desire to centralize responsibility in a few people who can be held accountable for discretionary decisions.) Commented a sales manager at Indsco, "The need for flexibility is primary in my job. The situation changes from minute to minute. One minute it's a tank truck that collapsed. Another it's a guy whose wife just had a hysterectomy and is going to die. . . . I'm dealing with such different problems all the time."

The importance of discretion increases with closeness to the top of a hierarchical organization. Despite the institutionalization and routinization of much of the work of large organizations and despite the proliferation of management experts, uncertainty remains a generic condition, increasing with rank. Jobs are relatively unstructured, tasks are non-routine, and decisions must be made about a variety of unknown elements. Issues such as "direction" and "purpose" cannot be reduced to rational formulae. Organizational improvement, or even maintenance, is not a simple matter that can be summarized in statements about "the ten functions of managers" or techniques of operation. If the "big picture" can be viewed from the top, it also looks bigger and fuzzier. Computers have not necessarily reduced the uncertainty of decisions at the top; in some cases, they have merely increased the amount of information that decision-makers must take into account. A major executive of Indsco confessed in a meeting that "we don't know how to manage these giant structures; and I suspect no one does. They are like dinosaurs, lumbering on of their own accord, even if they are no longer functional."

Criteria for "good decisions" or good management performance also get less certain closer to the top. The connection between an upper management decision and a factor such as production efficiency several layers below or gross sales is indirect, if it is even apparent. (An Indsco division president said, "In the 1960s we thought we were really terrific. We patted ourselves on the back a lot because every decision was so successful. Business kept on expanding. Then came the recession, and we couldn't do anything to stop it. We had been lucky before. Everything turned to gold in the 1960s. But it became clear that we don't know the first thing about how to make this enterprise work.")

Financial measures of performance are sometimes even artifactual because of the juggling of figures; for example, when and how a loss is recorded. There are also a variety of dilemmas in trying to evaluate the success of managers: qualitative versus quantitative measures, short-run versus long-run outcomes. Decisions that look good in the short-term might be long-term disasters, but by that time the failure can be blamed on other factors, and those responsible for the decisions might be so entrenched in power that they now call the shots anyway. A former public relations manager at DuPont formulated what he called the Law of Inverse Certainty: "The more important the management decision, the less precise the tools to deal with it . . . and the longer it will take before anyone knows it was right." One example was a rigid cost cutter who helped increase profits by eliminating certain functions; by the time the company began to feel the loss of those functions, he had been promoted and was part of the inner power group. Someone else picked up the pieces.

The uncertainty up the ranks, like the uncertainty of beginnings, also puts trust and homogeneity at a premium. The personal loyalty normally demanded of subordinates by officials is most intense at the highest levels of

organizations, as others have also noted. The lack of structure in top jobs makes it very important for decision-makers to work together closely in at least the harmony of shared understanding and a degree of mutual trust. Since for an organization to function at all requires that, to some extent, people will pull together around decisions, the solidarity that can be mustered through common membership in social networks, and the social control this provides, is a helpful supplement for decision-makers. Indeed, homogeneity of class and ethnic background and prior social experiences is one important "commitment mechanism" found to build a feeling of communion among members of viable utopian communities. Situational pressures, then, place a great emphasis on personal relations and social homogeneity as functional elements in the carrying out of managerial tasks. And privilege is also kept within a small circle.

The social homogeneity of big business leaders from the early-to-middle twentieth century has been noted frequently by critics such as C. Wright Mills as well as business historians. Their class background and social characteristics tended to be similar: largely white, Protestant men from elite schools. Much attention has also been paid to the homogeneity of type within any particular company. In one industrial organization, managers who moved ahead needed to be members of the Masonic Order and the local yacht club; not Roman Catholic; Anglo-Saxon or Germanic in origin; and Republican.

At Indsco, until ten years ago, top executives in the corporation were traceable to the founders of the company or its subsidiaries—people who held stock or were married to people who did. There was a difference between who did well in the divisions, where performance tended to account for more, and who got into top positions in the corporation itself. To get ahead in the corporation, social connections were known to be very important. Indeed, corporate staff positions became a place to put people who were nonmovers, whose performance was not outstanding, but were part of the "family." The social homogeneity of corporate executives was duly noted by other managers. One asked a consultant, "Do all companies have an ethnic flavor? Our top men all seem to be Scotch-Irish." (But as management has become more rationalized, and the corporation has involved itself more heavily in divisional operations, there has also been a trend, over the past five years, toward more "objective" criteria for high-level corporate positions.)

We expect a direct correlation, then, between the degree of uncertainty in a position—the extent to which organizations must rely on personal discretion—and a reliance on "trust" through "homosocial reproduction"—selection of incumbents on the basis of social similarity. . . .

Management becomes a closed circle in the absence of better, less exclusionary responses to uncertainty and communication pressures. Forces stemming from organizational situations help foster social homogeneity as a selection criterion for managers and promote social conformity as a standard for conduct. Concerned about giving up control and broadening discretion in the organization, managers choose others that can be "trusted." And thus they reproduce themselves in kind. Women are occasionally included in the inner circle when they are part of an organization's ruling family, but more usually this system leaves women out, along with a range of other people with discrepant social characteristics. Forces insisting that trust means total dedication and non-diffuse loyalty also serve to exclude those, like women, who are seen as incapable of such a single-minded attachment.

There is a self-fulfilling prophecy buried in all of this. The more closed the circle, the more difficult it is for "outsiders" to break in. Their very difficulty in entering may be taken as a sign of incompetence, a sign that the insiders were right to close their ranks. The more closed the circle, the more difficult it is to share power when the time comes, as it inevitably must, that others challenge the control by just one kind. And the greater the tendency for a group of people to try to reproduce themselves, the more constraining becomes the emphasis on conformity. It would seem a shame, indeed, if the only way out of such binds lay in increasing bureaucratization—that is, in a growth in routinization and rationalization of areas of uncertainty and a concomitant decline in personal discretion. But somehow corporations must grapple with the problem of how to reduce pressures for social conformity in their top jobs. . . .

Conformity Reaches Home

It is one of the prevailing ironies of modern corporate life that the closer to the top of the organization, the more traditional and non-"modern" does the system look. As Max Weber noted, at this point more charismatic, symbolic, and "non-rational" elements come into play. At the top—and especially in interaction with its environment—the organization is most likely to show strong elements of a personal, familistic system imbued with ritual, drawing on traditional behavior modes, and overlaid with symbolism. The irony stems from the fact that it is the top level that prescribes routine and impersonality—the absence of particularism and familism—for the rest of the organization. The modern organization formally excludes the family from participation in organizational life and excludes family ties as a basis for organizational position, even to the extent of anti-nepotism rules. Yet, at the top the wife may come into the picture as a visible member of the husband's "team"; she may be given a position and functions (and, in some cases, may even jump over qualified employees in taking on an official, paid, executive position). The wife who is excluded below may be included at the top, as part of the diplomatic apparatus of the corporation. And she has little freedom to refuse participation.

The dilemma that can confront people at this level is the issue of publicness/privateness. Both husband and wife can be made into public figures, with no area of life remaining untinged with responsibilities for the company. Here, as Wilbert Moore said, "The man, and his wife, simply cannot divest themselves of corporate identification. Their every activity with persons outside the immediate family is likely to be tinged with a recognition of the man's position. He represents the company willy-nilly. His area of privacy, and that of his wife, is very narrowly restricted." One rising young Indsco executive felt that the following had to be considered the "modern risks" of corporate vice-presidential and presidential jobs: traveling 80 percent of the time, getting shot at or kidnapped by radicals, prostituting yourself to customers, and opening your private life to scrutiny.

The higher executive's work spills over far beyond the limits of a working day. There may be no distinction between work and leisure. Activities well out of the purview of the organization's goals and defined as pleasure for other people (golf club memberships, symphony attendance, party-giving) are allowable as business expenses on income tax returns because the definition of what is "business" becomes so broad and nonspecific. People entertain one another on yachts or over long, lavish lunches—all in an attempt to mutually obligate, to create personal relations that will give someone an inside track when it comes to more formal negotiations. Whenever "selling" is a part of the organization's relations with its environment and sufficient sums of money rest on each deal, those who sell tend to offer gifts (tickets to a sports event, dinners at fancy restaurants, expensive pen and pencil sets) to those who buy, trying to bind the others beyond the limits of a rational contractual relationship. Entertaining in the home with the wife as hostess is especially binding, since it appears to be a more personal offering not given to all, sets up a social obligation, implicates others, and also calls on ancient and traditional feelings about the need to reward hospitality.

Fusion of business and private life also occurs around longer-term relationships. At the top, all friendships may have business meaning. Business relations can be made because of social connections. (One unlikely merger between two companies in very different fields was officially said to result from one company's need for a stock exchange listing held by the other, but off the record it was known to have been brought about by the friendship of the two presidents and their wives.) Charitable and community service activities, where the wife's role is especially pivotal, may generate useful business and political connections. Wives may meet each other through volunteer work and bring their husbands into contact, with useful business results. Stratification of the volunteer world paralleling class and ethnic differentiation in the society ensures that husbands and wives can pinpoint the population with which they desire connections by an appropriate choice of activity. As one chief executive wife wrote, "Any public relations man worth his salt will recognize the corporate wife as an instrument of communication with the community far more sincere and believable than all the booze poured down the press to gain their favor."

The importance of the wife stems not only from her own skills and activities (which could be, and are, performed by paid employees) but also from the testimony her behavior provides, its clue to the character and personal side of her husband. The usefulness of this testimony, in turn, is derived from unique aspects of top leadership. Image, appearance, background, and likability are all commodities traded at the top of the system, where actors are visible and where they put pressure on one another to demonstrate trustworthiness. . . . Farther down a hierarchy, jobs can be broken down into component skills and decisions about people and jobs made on the basis of ability to demonstrate those skills. At the top, decisions about people are not so easy or mechanical; they rest on personal factors to a degree perhaps much greater than systems themselves officially admit. The situations that a corporation president or a president of a country face are not routine and predictable; indeed, constituents are less interested in their handling of routine matters than in their capacities for the unexpected. So there is no test except a vague one: Is this person trustworthy? Even questions about philosophy and intelligence are proxies for trust.

Furthermore, the capacities of an organization itself are unknown and cannot be reduced precisely either to history or to a set of facts and figures. Thus, the character of its leaders can become a critical guide to making a decision about a future relationship with it: whether to invest, to donate funds, to allow it into the community, to provide some leeway in the regulation of its activities. Indsco was always concerned about character in its managers. Company newspapers from field locations routinely stressed church leadership in articles about individual managers, and "integrity" and "acceptance of accountability" appeared on the list of eleven traits that must be possessed by candidates for officer level jobs. Disclosures of corrupt practices by other companies in the mid-1970s enhanced Indsco's concerns about public respectability. Whereas, at lower levels of the organization, there was a tendency to formalize demands, to create routinized job descriptions, to ensure continuity of functioning by seeing to it that the occupant did not make over the job in his own image, and to exclude as much as possible of the personal and emotional life of the worker, close to the top, opposite pressure prevailed. Those with whom leaders entered into relationships looked for the private person behind the role and for the qualities and capacities that could not be encompassed by a job description but on which they must bet when deciding to trust the leader or the organization. Here's where the wives are important.

One way leaders can offer glimpses of their private beings is by bringing along their wives, by inviting others into their homes, and by making sure that their wives confirm the impression of themselves they are trying to give. By meeting in social circumstances, by throwing open pieces of private life for inspection, leaders try to convey their taste and their humanity. Wives, especially, are the carriers of this humanity and the shapers of the image of the private person. Of course, to the extent that social events and "informal" occasions are known to communicate an image for the purposes of making appropriate relationships, they may come to be as carefully managed and rationally calculated as any production task within the organization. The public relations department might even stage-manage the performance of the leader and his wife; when Dollie Ann Cole, wife of a General Motors president, wrote that p.r. departments no longer tell the wife what to wear and what to say, she made it explicit that they once did: ". . . a new day has dawned. Corporate wives no longer ask the public relations office what charity they should work with or whether they can debate for a cause on a local or national radio or television show—or even who is coming for dinner."

The wife is thus faced with an added task at the boundary of the public and the private: to make an event seem personal that is instead highly ritualized and contrived. She must recognize also the meanings conveyed by small acts (who sits next to whom, how much time she and her husband spend with each person, the taste implied by objects in the home, how much she drinks, who seem to be the family friends) and manage even small gestures with extreme self-consciousness, as one high-level wife at Indsco recalled she did at managers' meetings: "I had to be very careful to be invariably cordial, friendly, to remember everyone's names—and then to stay away. If I was too involved with someone, it would look like I was playing favorites; that would set up waves in highly inappropriate ways. Some of the young wives were terrified, but there was only so much I could do because I had other things to worry about."

Private life thus becomes penetrable and not very private at the top. Wives face the demand to suppress private beliefs and self-knowledge in the interest of public appearance. As an instrument of diplomacy and a critical part of her husband's image, the corporate wife must often hide her own opinions in order to preserve a united front, play down her own abilities to keep him looking like the winner and the star. The women's intelligence and superior education—assets when the men looked for wives—give way to other, more social traits, such as gregariousness, adaptability, attractiveness, discretion, listening ability, and social graces.

Thus, unless serving as a surrogate for the husband, voicing opinions was not easily allowed of corporate wives at Indsco, like those political wives who must beware of outshining their husbands. An aide to Eleanor McGovern spoke of the contradictory pressures on a candidate's wife: to be able to give the speech when he can't make it but to shut her mouth and listen adoringly when he is there. Indeed, Eleanor was told to stop looking so good when she started getting better press notices than George. Abigail McCarthy recalled the anxiety she felt about how words would affect her husband's prospects: "After every interview, I lay awake in a black nightmare of anxiety, fearful that I had said something which would do Gene irreparable harm." Betty Ford became an object of controversy (and of admiration) precisely because she violated these rules of the game and refused to distort her private life. Yet, wives of upper management at Indsco felt they did not have that luxury, even though they characterized the pressure to suppress independent opinions as "nonsense" and "frustrating." Not everyone complained. One wife reported that she was proud of never having unburdened herself, even to a confidante, and never having forgotten her public role throughout her husband's career.

Stresses, choices, and dilemmas in the top leadership phase, then, center around the tension between the public and the private. If men and their wives at the top gained public recognition, they also lost private freedoms. The emotional pressure this entailed was too much for some wives, as literature in the corporate-wives-as-victims tradition made clear; but it should be pointed out, too, that emotional breakdowns and secret deviances could also reflect defiant independence, unobtainable in any other way under constraining role definitions. The wishes expressed by wives in this position were of two kinds. Some women said that if they were going to be used by the company anyway, they would like the opportunity to do a real job, exercise real skills—by which they meant take on official areas of responsibility. Others wanted merely to be able to carve out more areas of privacy and independence in an otherwise public existence.

Power and Its Prices

The top leadership of an organization has all of the privileges of office: the signs of status, the benefits and perquisites, the material advantages their position is seen to warrant. They play ball in a large field, and the scope of their decisions is vast and far-reaching. They have, on occasion, gigantic power which does not even have to be used; a mere wish on their part is translated into action, with full cooperation and without the show of force.

But such power exists in a vise of checks and constraints; it comes out of a system, and the system, in turn, exacts its price. What if a top leader tries to exercise power that violates the expectations of other top leaders and organization members—if he or she steps out of line, out of character, or out of role? Would obedience be so easily forthcoming? Power at the top is contingent on conformity. Pressures to "fit in" also mean restraints on the unbridled exercise of power.

Furthermore, power which in some respects is contingent on trust for its effective exercise also, ironically, breeds suspicion: Can people at the top trust what they hear? Can they trust each other? What beyond social appearance can they use as keys to trust? Sometimes cut off from the "real action," they are seen by the organization's rank and file as remote from the daily events which truly constitute the organization—as once potent actors who now make whimsical decisions with little real understanding of organizational operations. And, as the final price of power, top leaders have to acknowledge the organization's ownership of that ultimate piece of property, their own private lives and beings. Life at the top is life in a goldfish bowl, an existence in which all the boundaries can be rendered transparent at the twitch of the public's curiosity.

The room at the top is all windows.

QUESTIONS

1. What are the differences between the picture of the corporation we might get from its organizational chart and the picture we get from this sociological case study?

2. Despite their formal authority, the leaders of the organization experience restraints on the exercise of their power. What are these restraints?

3. Many college students hope one day to be senior executives of corporations such as that described by Kanter. On the basis of her findings, would you expect to feel comfortable in such an environment?

D. L. ROSENHAN

On Being Sane in Insane Places

According to the labeling theory of deviance, people become deviant through a process in which significant others "label" them—perhaps as addicts, whores, drunks, crooks, nuts, and the like—with the result that they are generally perceived, and come to perceive themselves, in such terms. Their subsequent behavior tends to live up to the expectations aroused by the label, and their deviance eventually becomes a confirmed habit.

One of the most troubling forms of deviance is mental disorder, which involves a violation of social norms concerning sane behavior. Social scientists are convinced that many forms of mental disorder are in fact learned behaviors that are unconsciously adopted by the individual as a means of escaping from intolerable social or psychological pressures. Once a person is labeled "mentally disordered," after all, he or she can take on a "sick role" that offers exemption from the normal obligations and responsibilities of daily life.

In the study described in this article, David Rosenhan tried to find out what would happen if perfectly sane people presented themselves for admission at mental hospitals. The answer, as you will see, is that these "pseudopatients" were quickly classified as schizophrenics and admitted. Although they behaved quite normally inside the hospitals, their conduct was constantly interpreted in the light of the false label, and taken as further evidence of their mental disorder. Rosenhan's study raises disturbing questions not only about the power of labeling but also about the validity of much psychiatric diagnosis.

From *Science*, 179, pp. 250–258, 19 January 1973. © 1973 by the American Association for the Advancement of Science. Reprinted with permission.

If sanity and insanity exist, how shall we know them?

The question is neither capricious nor itself insane. However much we may be personally convinced that we can tell the normal from the abnormal, the evidence is simply not compelling. It is commonplace, for example, to read about murder trials wherein eminent psychiatrists for the defense are contradicted by equally eminent psychiatrists for the prosecution on the matter of the defendant's sanity. More generally, there are a great deal of conflicting data on the reliability, utility, and meaning of such terms as "sanity," "insanity," "mental illness," and "schizophrenia."[1] Finally, as early as 1934, Benedict suggested that normality and abnormality are not universal.[2] What is viewed as normal in one culture may be seen as quite aberrant in another. Thus, notions of normality and abnormality may not be quite as accurate as people believe they are.

To raise questions regarding normality and abnormality is in no way to question the fact that some behaviors are deviant or odd. Murder is deviant. So, too, are hallucinations. Nor does raising such questions deny the existence of the personal anguish that is often associated with "mental illness." Anxiety and depression exist. Psychological suffering exists. But normality and abnormality, sanity and insanity, and the diagnoses that flow from them may be less substantive than many believe them to be.

At its heart, the question of whether the sane can be distinguished from the insane (and whether degrees of insanity can be distinguished from each other) is a simple matter: do the salient characteristics that lead to diagnoses reside in the patients themselves or in the environments and contexts in which observers find them? From Bleuler, through Kretchmer, through the formulators of the recently revised *Diagnostic and Statistical Manual* of the American Psychiatric Association, the belief has been strong that patients present symptoms, that those symptoms can be categorized, and, implicitly, that the sane are distinguishable from the insane. More recently, however, this belief has been questioned. Based in part on theoretical and anthropological considerations, but also on philosophical, legal, and therapeutic ones, the view has grown that psychological categorization of mental illness is useless at best and downright harmful, misleading, and pejorative at worst. Psychiatric diagnoses, in this view, are in the minds of the observers and are not valid summaries of characteristics displayed by the observed.[3,4,5]

Gains can be made in deciding which of these is more nearly accurate by getting normal people (that is, people who do not have, and have never suffered, symptoms or serious psychiatric disorders) admitted to psychiatric hospitals and then determining whether they were discovered to be sane and, if so, how. If the sanity of such pseudopatients were always detected, there would be prima facie evidence that a sane individual can be distinguished from the insane context in which he is found. Normality (and presumably abnormality) is distinct enough that it can be recognized wherever it occurs, for it is carried within the person. If on the other hand, the sanity of the pseudopatients were never discovered, serious difficulties would arise for those who support traditional modes of psychiatric diagnosis. Given that the hospital staff was not incompetent, that the pseudopatient had been behaving as sanely as he had been outside of the hospital, and that it had never been previously suggested that he belonged in a psychiatric hospital, such an unlikely outcome would support the view that psychiatric diagnosis betrays little about the patient but much about the environment in which an observer finds him.

This article describes such an experiment. Eight sane people gained secret admission to 12 different hospitals.[6] Their diagnostic experiences constitute the data of the first part of this article; the remainder is devoted to a description of their experiences in psychiatric institutions. Too few psychiatrists and psychologists, even those who have worked in such hospitals, know what the experience is like. They rarely talk about it with former patients, perhaps because they distrust information coming from the previously insane. Those who have worked in psychiatric hospitals are likely to have adapted so thoroughly to the settings that they are insensitive to the impact of that experience. And while there have been occasional reports of researchers who submitted themselves to psychiatric hospitalization,[7] these researchers have commonly remained in the hospitals for short periods of time, often with the knowledge of the hospital staff. It is difficult to know the extent to which they were treated like patients or like research colleagues. Nevertheless, their reports about the inside of the psychiatric hospital have been valuable. This article extends those efforts.

Pseudopatients and Their Settings

The eight pseudopatients were a varied group. One was a psychology graduate student in his 20's. The remaining seven were older and "established." Among them were three psychologists, a pediatrician, a psychiatrist, a painter, and a housewife. Three pseudopatients were women,

five were men. All of them employed pseudonyms, lest their alleged diagnoses embarrass them later. Those who were in mental health professions alleged another occupation in order to avoid the special attentions that might be accorded by staff, as a matter of courtesy or caution, to ailing colleagues.[8] With the exception of myself (I was the first pseudopatient and my presence was known to the hospital administrator and chief psychologist and, so far as I can tell, to them alone), the presence of pseudopatients and the nature of the research program was not known to the hospital staff.[9]

The settings were similarly varied. In order to generalize the findings, admission into a variety of hospitals was sought. The 12 hospitals in the sample were located in five different states on the East and West coasts. Some were old and shabby, some were quite new. Some were research-oriented, others not. Some had good staff-patient ratios, others were quite understaffed. Only one was a strictly private hospital. All of the others were supported by state or federal funds or, in one instance, by university funds.

After calling the hospital for an appointment, the pseudopatient arrived at the admissions office complaining that he had been hearing voices. Asked what the voices said, he replied that they were often unclear, but as far as he could tell they said "empty," "hollow," and "thud." The voices were unfamiliar and were of the same sex as the pseudopatient. The choice of these symptoms was occasioned by their apparent similarity to existential symptoms. Such symptoms are alleged to arise from painful concerns about the perceived meaninglessness of one's life. It is as if the hallucinating person were saying, "My life is empty and hollow." The choice of these symptoms was also determined by the *absence* of a single report of existential psychoses in the literature.

Beyond alleging the symptoms and falsifying name, vocation, and employment, no further alterations of person, history, or circumstances were made. The significant events of the pseudopatient's life history were presented as they had actually occurred. Relationships with parents and siblings, with spouse and children, with people at work and in school, consistent with the aforementioned exceptions, were described as they were or had been. Frustrations and upsets were described along with joys and satisfactions. These facts are important to remember. If anything, they strongly biased the subsequent results in favor of detecting sanity, since none of their histories or current behaviors were seriously pathological in any way. Immediately upon admission to the psychiatric ward, the pseudopatient ceased simulating *any* symptoms of abnormality. In some cases, there was a brief period of mild nervousness and anxiety, since none of the pseudopatients really believed that they would be admitted so easily. Indeed, their shared fear was that they would be immediately exposed as frauds and greatly embarrassed. Moreover, many of them had never visited a psychiatric ward; even those who had nevertheless had some genuine fears about what might happen to them. Their nervousness, then, was quite appropriate to the novelty of the hospital setting, and it abated rapidly.

Apart from that short-lived nervousness, the pseudopatient behaved on the ward as he "normally" behaved. The pseudopatient spoke to patients and staff as he might ordinarily. Because there is uncommonly little to do on a psychiatric ward, he attempted to engage others in conversation. When asked by staff how he was feeling, he indicated that he was fine, that he no longer experienced symptoms. He responded to instructions from attendants, to calls for medication (which was not swallowed), and to dining-hall instructions. Beyond such activities as were available to him on the admissions ward, he spent his time writing down his observations about the ward, its patients, and the staff. Initially these notes were written "secretly," but as it soon became clear that no one much cared, they were subsequently written on standard tablets of paper in such public places as the dayroom. No secret was made of these activities.

The pseudopatient, very much as a true psychiatric patient, entered a hospital with no foreknowledge of when he would be discharged. Each was told that he would have to get out by his own devices, essentially by convincing the staff that he was sane. The psychological stresses associated with hospitalization were considerable, and all but one of the pseudopatients desired to be discharged almost immediately after being admitted. They were, therefore, motivated not only to behave sanely, but to be paragons of cooperation. That their behavior was in no way disruptive is confirmed by nursing reports, which have been obtained on most of the patients. These reports uniformly indicate that the patients were "friendly," "cooperative," and "exhibited no abnormal indications."

The Normal Are Not Detectably Sane

Despite their public "show" of sanity, the pseudopatients were never detected. Admitted, except in one case, with a diagnosis of schizophrenia,[10] each was discharged with a diagnosis of schizophrenia "in remission." The label "in remission" should in no way be dismissed as a formality, for at no time during any hospitalization had any question been raised about any pseudopatient's simulation. Nor are there any indications in the hospital records that the pseudopatient's status was suspect. Rather, the evidence is strong that, once labeled schizophrenic, the pseudopatient was stuck with that label. If the pseudopatient was to be discharged, he must naturally be "in remission"; but he was not sane, nor, in the institution's view, had he ever been sane.

The uniform failure to recognize sanity cannot be attributed to the quality of the hospitals, for, although there were considerable variations among them, several are considered excellent. Nor can it be alleged that there was simply not enough time to observe the pseudopatients. Length of hospitalization ranged from 7 to 52 days, with an average of 19 days. The pseudopatients were not, in fact, carefully observed, but this failure clearly speaks more to traditions within psychiatric hospitals than to lack of opportunity.

Finally, it cannot be said that the failure to recognize the pseudopatients' sanity was due to the fact that they were not behaving sanely. While there was clearly some tension present in all of them, their daily visitors could detect no serious behavioral consequences—nor, indeed, could other patients. It was quite common for the patients to "detect" the pseudopatients' sanity. During the first three hospitalizations, when accurate counts were kept, 35 of a total of 118 patients on the admissions ward voiced their suspicions, some vigorously. "You're not crazy. You're a journalist, or a professor [referring to the continual note-taking]. You're checking up on the hospital." While most of the patients were reassured by the pseudopatient's insistence that he had been sick before he came in but was fine now, some continued to believe that the pseudopatient was sane throughout his hospitalization.[11] The fact that the patients often recognized normality when staff did not raises important questions.

Failure to detect sanity during the course of hospitalization may be due to the fact that physicians operate with a strong bias toward what statisticians call the type 2 error.[5] This is to say that physicians are more inclined to call a healthy person sick (a false positive, type 2) than a sick person healthy (a false negative, type 1). The reasons for this are not hard to find: it is clearly more dangerous to misdiagnose illness than health. Better to err on the side of caution, to suspect illness even among the healthy.

But what holds for medicine does not hold equally well for psychiatry. Medical illnesses, while unfortunate, are not commonly pejorative. Psychiatric diagnoses, on the contrary, carry with them personal, legal, and social stigmas.[12] It was therefore important to see whether the tendency toward diagnosing the sane insane could be reversed. The following experiment was arranged at a research and teaching hospital whose staff had heard these findings but doubted that such an error could occur in their hospital. The staff was informed that at some time during the following 3 months, one or more pseudopatients would attempt to be admitted into the psychiatric hospital. Each staff member was asked to rate each patient who presented himself at admission or on the ward according to the likelihood that the patient was a pseudopatient. A 10-point scale was used, with a 1 and 2 reflecting high confidence that the patient was a pseudopatient.

Judgments were obtained on 193 patients who were admitted for psychiatric treatment. All staff who had had sustained contact with or primary responsibility for the patient—attendants, nurses, psychiatrists, physicians, and psychologists—were asked to make judgments. Forty-one patients were alleged, with high confidence, to be pseudopatients by at least one member of the staff. Twenty-three were considered suspect by at least one psychiatrist. Nineteen were suspected by one psychiatrist *and* one other staff member. Actually, no genuine pseudopatient (at least from my group) presented himself during this period.

The experiment is instructive. It indicates that the tendency to designate sane people as insane can be reversed when the stakes (in this case, prestige and diagnostic acumen) are high. But what can be said of the 19 people who were suspected of being "sane" by one psychiatrist and another staff member? Were these people truly "sane," or was it rather the case that in the course of avoiding the type 2 error the staff tended to make more errors of the first sort—calling the crazy "sane"? There is no way of knowing. But one thing is certain: any diagnostic process that lends itself so readily to massive errors of this sort cannot be a very reliable one.

The Stickiness of Psychodiagnostic Labels

Beyond the tendency to call the healthy sick—a tendency that accounts better for diagnostic behavior or admission than it does for such behavior after a lengthy period of exposure—the data speak to the massive role of labeling in psychiatric assessment. Having once been labeled schizophrenic, there is nothing the pseudopatient can do to overcome the tag. The tag profoundly colors others' perceptions of him and his behavior.

From one viewpoint, these data are hardly surprising, for it has long been known that elements are given meaning by the context in which they occur. Gestalt psychology made this point vigorously, and Asch[13] demonstrated that there are "central" personality traits (such as "warm" versus "cold") which are so powerful that they markedly color the meaning of other information in forming an impression of a given personality.[14] "Insane," "schizophrenic," "manic-depressive," and "crazy" are probably among the most powerful of such central traits. Once a person is designated abnormal, all of his other behaviors and characteristics are colored by that label. Indeed, that label is so powerful that many of the pseudopatients' normal behaviors were overlooked entirely or profoundly misinterpreted. Some examples may clarify this issue.

Earlier I indicated that there were no changes in the pseudopatient's personal history and current status beyond those of name, employment, and, where necessary, vocation. Otherwise, a veridical description of personal history and circumstances was offered. Those circumstances were not psychotic. How were they made consonant with the diagnosis of psychosis? Or were those diagnoses modified in such a way as to bring them into accord with the circumstances of the pseudopatient's life, as described by him?

As far as I can determine, diagnoses were in no way affected by the relative health of the circumstances of a pseudopatient's life. Rather, the reverse occurred: the perception of his circumstances was shaped entirely by the diagnosis. A clear example of such translation is found in the case of a pseudopatient who had had a close relationship with his mother but was rather remote from his father during his early childhood. During adolescence and beyond, however, his father became a close friend, while his relationship with his mother cooled. His present relationship with his wife was characteristically close and warm. Apart from occasional angry exhanges, friction was minimal. The children had rarely been spanked. Surely there is nothing especially pathological about such a history. Indeed, many readers may see a similar pattern in their own experiences, with no markedly deleterious consequences. Observe, however, how such a history was translated in the psychopathological context, this from the case summary prepared after the patient was discharged.

> This white 39-year-old male . . . manifests a long history of considerable ambivalence in close relationships, which begins in early childhood. A warm relationship with his mother cools during his adolescence. A distant relationship to his father is described as becoming very intense. Affective stability is absent. His attempts to control emotionality with his wife and children are punctuated by angry outbursts and, in the case of the children, spankings. And while he says that he has several good friends, one senses considerable ambivalence embedded in those relationships also. . . .

The facts of the case were unintentionally distorted by the staff to achieve consistency with a popular theory of the dynamics of a schizophrenic reaction.[15] Nothing of an ambivalent nature had been described in relations with parents, spouse, or friends. To the extent that ambivalence could be inferred, it was probably not greater than is found in all human relationships. It is true the pseudopatient's relationships with his parents changed over time, but in the ordinary context that would hardly be remarkable—indeed, it might very well be expected. Clearly, the meaning ascribed to his verbalizations (that is, ambivalence, affective instability) was determined by the diagnosis: schizophrenia. An entirely different meaning would have been ascribed if it were known that the man was "normal."

All pseudopatients took extensive notes publicly. Under ordinary circumstances, such behavior would have raised questions in the minds of observers, as, in fact, it did among patients. Indeed, it seemed so certain that the notes would elicit suspicion that elaborate precautions were taken to remove them from the ward each day. But the precautions proved needless. The closest any staff member came to questioning these notes occurred when one pseudopatient asked his physician what kind of medication he was receiving and began to write down the response. "You needn't write it," he was told gently. "If you have trouble remembering, just ask me again."

If no questions were asked of the pseudopatients, how was their writing interpreted? Nursing records for three patients indicate that the writing was seen as an aspect of their pathological behavior. "Patient engages in writing behavior" was the daily nursing comment on one of the pseudopatients who was never questioned about his writing. Given that the patient is in the hospital, he must be psychologically disturbed. And given that he is disturbed, continuous writing must be a behavioral manifestation of that disturbance, perhaps a subset of the compulsive behaviors that are sometimes correlated with schizophrenia.

One tacit characteristic of psychiatric diagnosis is that it locates the sources of aberration within the individual and only rarely within the complex of stimuli that surrounds him. Consequently, behaviors that are stimulated by the environment are commonly misattributed to the patient's disorder. For example, one kindly nurse found a pseudopatient pacing the long hospital corridors. "Nervous, Mr. X?" she asked. "No, bored," he said.

The notes kept by pseudopatients are full of patient behaviors that were misinterpreted by well-intentioned staff. Often enough, a patient would go "berserk" because he had, wittingly or unwittingly, been mistreated by, say, an attendant. A nurse coming upon the scene would rarely inquire even cursorily into the environmental stimuli of the patient's behavior. Rather, she assumed that his upset derived from his pathology, not from his present interactions with other staff members. Occasionally, the staff might assume that the patient's family (especially when they had recently visited) or other patients had stimulated the outburst. But never were the staff found to assume that one of themselves or the structure of the hospital had anything to do with a patient's behavior. One psychiatrist pointed to a group of patients who were sitting outside the cafeteria entrance half an hour before lunchtime. To a group of young residents he indicated that such behavior was characteristic of the oral-acquisitive nature of the syndrome. It seemed not to occur to him that there were very few things to anticipate in a psychiatric hospital besides eating.

A psychiatric label has a life and an influence of its own. Once the impression has been formed that the patient is schizophrenic, the expectation is that he will continue to be schizophrenic. When a sufficient amount of time has passed, during which the patient has done noth-

ing bizarre, he is considered to be in remission and available for discharge. But the label endures beyond discharge, with the unconfirmed expectation that he will behave as a schizophrenic again. Such labels, conferred by mental health professionals, are as influential on the patient as they are on his relatives and friends, and it should not surprise anyone that the diagnosis acts on all of them as a self-fulfilling prophecy. Eventually, the patient himself accepts the diagnosis, with all of its surplus meanings and expectations, and behaves accordingly.[5]

The inferences to be made from these matters are quite simple. Much as Zigler and Phillips have demonstrated that there is enormous overlap in the symptoms presented by patients who have been variously diagnosed,[16] so there is enormous overlap in the behaviors of the sane and the insane. The sane are not "sane" all of the time. We lose our tempers "for no good reason." We are occasionally depressed or anxious, again for no good reason. And we may find it difficult to get along with one or another person—again for no reason that we can specify. Similarly, the insane are not always insane. Indeed, it was the impression of the pseudopatients while living with them that they were sane for long periods of time—that the bizarre behaviors upon which their diagnoses were allegedly predicated constituted only a small fraction of their total behavior. If it makes no sense to label ourselves permanently depressed on the basis of an occasional depression, then it takes better evidence than is presently available to label all patients insane or schizophrenic on the basis of bizarre behaviors or cognitions. It seems more useful, as Mischel[17] has pointed out, to limit our discussion to behaviors, the stimuli that provoke them, and their correlates.

It is not known why powerful impressions of personality traits, such as "crazy" or "insane," arise. Conceivably, when the origins of and stimuli that give rise to a behavior are remote or unknown, or when the behavior strikes us as immutable, trait labels regarding the behaver arise. When, on the other hand, the origins and stimuli are known and available, discourse is limited to the behavior itself. Thus, I may hallucinate because I am sleeping, or I may hallucinate because I have ingested a peculiar drug. These are termed sleep-induced hallucinations, or dreams, and drug-induced hallucinations, respectively.

But when the stimuli to my hallucinations are unknown, that is called craziness, or schizophrenia—as if that inference were somehow as illuminating as the others.

The Experience of Psychiatric Hospitalization

The term "mental illness" is of recent origin. It was coined by people who were humane in their inclinations and who wanted very much to raise the station of (and the public's sympathies toward) the psychologically disturbed from that of witches and "crazies" to one that was akin to the physically ill. And they were at least partially successful, for the treatment of the mentally ill *has* improved considerably over the years. But while treatment has improved, it is doubtful that people really regard the mentally ill in the same way that they view the physically ill. A broken leg is something one recovers from, but mental illness allegedly endures forever.[18] A broken leg does not threaten the observer, but a crazy schizophrenic? There is by now a host of evidence that attitudes toward the mentally ill are characterized by fear, hostility, aloofness, suspicion, and dread.[19] The mentally ill are society's lepers.

That such attitudes infect the general population is perhaps not surprising, only upsetting. But that they affect the professionals—attendants, nurses, physicians, psychologists, and social workers—who treat and deal with the mentally ill is more disconcerting, both because such attitudes are self-evidently pernicious and because they are unwitting. Most mental health professionals would insist that they are sympathetic toward the mentally ill, that they are neither avoidant nor hostile. But it is more likely that an exquisite ambivalence characterizes their relations with psychiatric patients, such that their avowed impulses are only part of their entire attitude. Negative attitudes are there too and can easily be detected. Such attitudes should not surprise us. They are the natural offspring of the labels patients wear and the places in which they are found.

Consider the structure of the typical psychiatric hospital. Staff and patients are strictly segregated. Staff having their own living space, including their dining facilities, bathrooms, and assembly places. The glassed quarters that contain the professional staff, which the pseudopatients came to call "the cage," sit out on every day-room. The staff emerge primarily for caretaking purposes—to give medication, to conduct a therapy or group meeting, to instruct or reprimand a patient. Otherwise, staff keep to themselves, almost as if the disorder that afflicts their charges is somehow catching.

So much is patient-staff segregation the rule that, for four public hospitals in which an attempt was made to measure the degree to which staff and patients mingle, it was necessary to use "time out of the staff cage" as the operational measure. While it was not the case that all time spent out of the cage was spent mingling with patients (attendants, for example, would occasionally emerge to watch television in the day-room), it was the only way in which one could gather reliable data on time for measuring.

The average amount of time spent by attendants outside of the cage was 11.3 percent (range, 3 to 52 percent).

This figure does not represent only time spent min-

gling with patients, but also includes time spent on such chores as folding laundry, supervising patients while they shave, directing ward cleanup, and sending patients to off-ward activities. It was the relatively rare attendant who spent time talking with patients or playing games with them. It proved impossible to obtain a "percent mingling time" for nurses, since the amount of time they spent out of the cage was too brief. Rather, we counted instances of emergence from the cage. On the average, daytime nurses emerged from the cage 11.5 times per shift, including instances when they left the ward entirely (range, 4 to 39 times). Late afternoon and night nurses were even less available, emerging on the average 9.4 times per shift (range, 4 to 41 times). Data on early morning nurses, who arrived usually after midnight and departed at 8 a.m., are not available because patients were asleep during most of this period.

Physicians, especially psychiatrists, were even less available. They were rarely seen on the wards. Quite commonly, they would be seen only when they arrived and departed, with the remaining time being spent in their offices or in the cage. On the average, physicans emerged on the ward 6.7 times per day (range, 1 to 17 times). It proved difficult to make an accurate estimate in his regard, since physicians often maintained hours that allowed them to come and go at different times.

The hierarchical organization of the psychiatric hospital has been commented on before,[20] but the latent meaning of that kind of organization is worth noting again. Those with the most power have least to do with patients, and those with the least power are most involved with them. Recall, however, that the acquisition of role-appropriate behaviors occurs mainly through the observation of others, with the most powerful having the most influence. Consequently, it is understandable that attendants not only spend more time with patients than do any other members of the staff—that is required by their station in the hierarchy—but also, insofar as they learn from their superiors' behavior, spend as little time with patients as they can. Attendants are seen mainly in the cage, which is where the models, the action, and the power are.

I turn now to a different set of studies, these dealing with staff response to patient-initiated contact. It has long been known that the amount of time a person spends with you can be an index of your significance to him. If he initiates and maintains eye contact, there is reason to believe that he is considering your requests and needs. If he pauses to chat or actually stops and talks, there is added reason to infer that he is individuating you. In four hospitals, the pseudopatient approached the staff member with a request which took the following form: "Pardon me, Mr. [or Dr. or Mrs.] X, could you tell me when I will be eligible for grounds privileges?" (or " . . . when I will be presented at the staff meeting?" or " . . . when I am likely to be discharged?"). While the content of the question varied according to the appropriateness of the target and the pseudopatient's (apparent) current needs the form was always a courteous and relevant request for information. Care was taken never to approach a particular member of the staff more than once a day, lest the staff member become suspicious or irritated. . . . Remember that the behavior of the pseudopatients was neither bizarre nor disruptive. One could indeed engage in good conversation with them.

. . . Minor differences between these four institutions were overwhelmed by the degree to which staff avoided continuing contacts that patients had initiated. By far, their most common response consisted of either a brief response to the question, offered while they were "on the move" and with head averted, or no response at all.

The encounter frequently took the following bizarre form: (pseudopatient) "Pardon me, Dr. X. Could you tell me when I am eligible for grounds privileges?" (physician) "Good morning, Dave. How are you today?" (Moves off without waiting for a response.)

. . .

Powerlessness and Depersonalization

Eye contact and verbal contact reflect concern and individuation; their absence, avoidance and depersonalization. The data I have presented do not do justice to the rich daily encounters that grew up around matters of depersonalization and avoidance. I have records of patients who were beaten by staff for the sin of having initiated verbal contact. During my own experience, for example, one patient was beaten in the presence of other patients for having approached an attendant and told him, "I like you." Occasionally, punishment meted out to patients for misdemeanors seemed so excessive that it could not be justified by the most radical interpretations of psychiatric canon. Nevertheless, they appeared to go unquestioned. Tempers were often short. A patient who had not heard a call for medication would be roundly excoriated, and morning attendants would often wake patients with, "Come on, you m————f————s, out of bed!"

Neither anecdotal nor "hard" data can convey the overwhelming sense of powerlessness which invades the individual as he is continually exposed to the depersonalization of the psychiatric hospital. It hardly matters which psychiatric hospital—the excellent public ones and the very plush private hospital were better than the rural and shabby ones in this regard, but, again, the features that psychiatric hospitals had in common overwhelmed by far their apparent differences.

Powerlessness was evident everywhere. The patient is deprived of many of his legal rights by dint of his psychiatric commitment.[21] He is shorn of credibility by virtue of his psychiatric label. His freedom of movement is restricted. He cannot initiate contact with the staff, but

may only respond to such overtures as they make. Personal privacy is minimal. Patient quarters and possessions can be entered and examined by any staff member, for whatever reason. His personal history and anguish are available to any staff member (often including the "grey lady" and "candy striper" volunteer) who chooses to read his folder, regardless of their therapeutic relationship to him. His personal hygiene and waste evacuation are often monitored. The water closets may have no doors.

At times depersonalization reached such proportions that pseudopatients had the sense that they were invisible, or at least unworthy of account. Upon being admitted, I and other pseudopatients took the initial physical examinations in a semipublic room , where staff members went about their own business as if we were not there.

On the ward, attendants delivered verbal and occasionally serious physical abuse to patients in the presence of other observing patients, some of whom (the pseudopatients) were writing it all down. Abusive behavior, on the other hand, terminated quite abruptly when other staff members were known to be coming. Staff are credible witnesses. Patients are not.

A nurse unbuttoned her uniform to adjust her brassiere in the presence of an entire ward of viewing men. One did not have the sense that she was being seductive. Rather, she didn't notice us. A group of staff persons might point to a patient in the day-room and discuss him animatedly, as if he were not there.

One illuminating instance of depersonalization and invisibility occurred with regard to medications. All told, the pseudopatients were administered nearly 2100 pills, including Elavil, Stelazine, Compazine, and Thorazine, to name but a few. (That such a variety of medications should have been administered to patients presenting identical symptoms is itself worthy of note.) Only two were swallowed. The rest were either pocketed or deposited in the toilet. The pseudopatients were not alone in this. Although I have no precise records on how many patients rejected their medications, the pseudopatients frequently found the medications of other patients in the toilet before they deposited their own. As long as they were cooperative, their behavior and the pseudopatients' own in this matter, as in other important matters, went unnoticed throughout.

Reactions to such depersonalization among pseudopatients were intense. Although they had come to the hospital as participant observers and were fully aware that they did not "belong," they nevertheless found themselves caught up in and fighting the process of depersonalization. Some examples: a graduate student in psychology asked his wife to bring his textbooks to the hospital so he could "catch up on his homework"—this despite the elaborate precautions taken to conceal his professional association. The same student, who had trained for quite some time to get into the hospital, and who had looked forward to the experience, "remembered" some drag races that he had wanted to see on the weekend and insisted that he be discharged by that time. Another pseudopatient attempted a romance with a nurse. Subsequently, he informed the staff that he was applying for admission to graduate school in psychology and was very likely to be admitted, since a graduate professor was one of his regular hospital visitors. The same person began to engage in psychotherapy with other patients—all of this as a way of becoming a person in an impersonal environment.

The Sources of Depersonalization

What are the origins of depersonalization? I have already mentioned two. First are attitudes held by all of us toward the mentally ill—including those who treat them—attitudes characterized by fear, distrust, and horrible expectations on the one hand, and benevolent intentions on the other. Our ambivalence leads, in this instance as in others, to avoidance.

Second, and not entirely separate, the hierarchical structure of the psychiatric hospital facilitates depersonalization. Those who are at the top have least to do with patients, and their behavior inspires the rest of the staff. Average daily contact with psychiatrists, psychologists, residents, and physicans combined ranged from 3.9 to 25.1 minutes, with an overall mean of 6.8 (six pseudopatients over a total of 129 days of hospitalization). Included in this average are time spent in the admissions interview, ward meetings in the presence of a senior staff member, group and individual psychotherapy contacts, case presentation conferences, and discharge meetings. Clearly, patients do not spend much time in interpersonal contact with doctoral staff. And doctoral staff serve as models for nurses and attendants.

Psychiatric installations are presently in serious financial straits. Staff shortages are pervasive, staff time at a premium. Something has to give, and that something is patient contact. Yet, while financial stresses are realities, too much can be made of them. I have the impression that the psychological forces that result in depersonalization are much stronger than the fiscal ones and that the addition of more staff would not correspondingly improve patient care in this regard. The incidence of staff meetings and the enormous amount of record-keeping on patients, for example, have not been as substantially reduced as has patient contact. Priorities exist, even during hard times. Patient contact is not a significant priority in the traditional psychiatric hospital, and fiscal pressures do not account for this. Avoidance and depersonalization may.

Heavy reliance upon psychotropic medication tacitly contributes to depersonalization by convincing staff that treatment is indeed being conducted and that further pa-

tient contact may not be necessary. Even here, however, caution needs to be exercised in understanding the role of psychotropic drugs. If patients were powerful rather than powerless, if they were viewed as interesting individuals rather than diagnostic entities, if they were socially significant rather than social lepers, if their anguish truly and wholly compelled our sympathies and concerns, would we not *seek* contact with them, despite the availability of medications? Perhaps for the pleasure of it all?

The Consequences of Labeling and Depersonalization

Whenever the ratio of what is known to what needs to be known approaches zero, we tend to invent "knowledge" and assume that we understand more than we actually do. We seem unable to acknowledge that we simply don't know. The needs for diagnosis and remediation of behavioral and emotional problems are enormous. But rather than acknowledge that we are just embarking on understanding, we continue to label patients "schizophrenic," "manic-depressive," and "insane," as if in those words we had captured the essence of understanding. The facts of the matter are that we have known for a long time that diagnoses are often not useful or reliable, but we have nevertheless continued to use them. We now know that we cannot distinguish insanity from sanity. It is depressing to consider how that informaton will be used.

Not merely depressing, but frightening. How many people, one wonders, are sane but not recognized as such in our psychiatric institutions? How many have been needlessly stripped of their privileges of citizenship, from the right to vote and drive to that of handling their own accounts? How many have feigned insanity in order to avoid the criminal consequences of their behavior, and, conversely, how many would rather stand trial than live interminably in a psychiatric hospital—but are wrongly thought to be mentally ill? How many have been stigmatized by well-intentioned, but nevertheless erroneous, diagnoses? On the last point, recall again that a "type 2 error" in psychiatric diagnosis does not have the same consequences it does in medical diagnosis. A diagnosis of cancer that has been found to be in error is cause for celebration. But psychiatric diagnoses are rarely found to be in error. The label sticks, a mark of inadequacy forever.

Finally, how many patients might be "sane" outside the psychiatric hosptal but seem insane in it—not because craziness resides in them, as it were, but because they are responding to a bizarre setting, one that may be unique to institutions which harbor nether people? Goffman [4] calls the process of socialization to such institutions "mortification"—an apt metaphor that includes the processes of depersonalization that have been described here. And while it is impossible to know whether the pseudopatients' responses to these processes are characteristic of all inmates—they were, after all, not real patients—it is difficult to believe that these processes of socialization to a psychiatric hospital provide useful attitudes or habits of response for living in the "real world."

Summary and Conclusions

It is clear that we cannot distinguish the sane from the insane in psychiatric hospitals. The hospital itself imposes a special environment in which the meanings of behavior can easily be misunderstood. The consequences to patients hospitalized in such an environment—the powerlessness, depersonalization, segregation, mortification, and self-labeling—seem undoubtedly countertherapeutic.

I do not, even now, understand this problem well enough to perceive solutions. But two matters seem to have some promise. The first concerns the proliferation of community mental health facilities, of crisis intervention centers, of the human potential movement, and of behavior therapies that, for all of their own problems, tend to avoid psychiatric labels, to focus on specific problems and behaviors, and to retain the individual in a relatively nonpejorative environment. Clearly, to the extent that we refrain from sending the distressed to insane places, our impressions of them are less likely to be distorted. (The risk of distorted perceptions, it seems to me, is always present, since we are much more sensitive to an individual's behaviors and verbalizations than we are to the subtle contextual stimuli that often promote them. At issue here is a matter of magnitude. And, as I have shown, the magnitude of distortion is exceedingly high in the exteme context that is a psychiatric hospital.)

The second matter that might prove promising speaks to the need to increase the sensitivity of mental health workers and researchers to the *Catch 22* position of psychiatric patients. Simply reading materials in this area will be of help to some such workers and researchers. For others, directly experiencing the impact of psychiatric hospitalization will be of enormous use. Clearly, further research into the social psychology of such total institutions will both facilitate treatment and deepen understanding.

I and the other pseudopatients in the psychiatric setting had distinctly negative reactions. We do not pretend to describe the subjective experiences of true patients. Theirs may be different from ours, particularly with the passage of time and the necessary process of adaptation to one's environment. But we can and do speak to the relatively more objective indices of treatment within the hospital. It could be a mistake, and a very unfortunate one, to consider that what happened to us derived from malice or stupidity on the part of the staff. Quite the con-

trary, our overwhelming impression of them was of people who really cared, who were committed and who were uncommonly intelligent. Where they failed, as they sometimes did painfully, it would be more accurate to attribute those failures to the environment in which they, too, found themselves than to personal callousness. Their perceptions and behavior were controlled by the situation, rather than being motivated by a malicious disposition. In a more benign environment, one that was less attached to global diagnosis, their behaviors and judgments might have been more benign and effective.

QUESTIONS

1. What are the implications of Rosenhan's study for labeling theory?

2. Many critics have contended that psychiatry is a pseudoscience, in which diagnostic labels and other jargon are used to obscure the fact that psychiatrists really understand very little about mental disorder. How much support does the study give to this view?

3. Was Rosenhan's study a fair one? Could he have reasonably expected the pseudopatients to be detected, given that hospital personnel had no expectation that any sane person would attempt to gain admittance?

References and Notes

1. P. Ash, *J. Abnorm. Soc. Psychol.* **44**, 272 (1949); A. T. Beck, *Amer. J. Psychiat.* **119**, 210 (1962); A. T. Boisen, *Psychiatry* **2**, 233 (1938); N. Kreitman, *J. Ment. Sci.* 107, 876 (1961); N. Kreitman, P. Sainsbury, J. Morrisey, J. Towers, J. Scrivener, *ibid.*, p. 887; H. O. Schmitt and C. P. Fonda, *J. Abnorm. Soc. Psychol.* **52**, 262 (1956); W. Seeman, *J. Nerv. Ment. Dis.* **118**, 541 (1953). For an analysis of these artifacts and summaries of the disputes, see J. Zubin, *Annu. Rev. Psychol.* **18**, 373 (1967); L. Phillips and J. G. Draguns, *ibid.* **22**, 447 (1971).

2. R. Benedict, *J. Gen. Psychol.* **10**, 59 (1934).

3. See in this regard H. Becker, *Outsiders: Studies in the Sociology of Deviance* (Free Press, New York, 1963); B. M. Braginsky, D. D. Braginsky, K. Ring, *Methods of Madness: The Mental Hospital as a Last Resort* (Holt, Rinehart & Winston, New York, 1969); G. M. Crocetti and P. V. Lemkau, *Amer. Sociol. Rev.* **30**, 577 (1965); E. Goffman, *Behavior in Public Places* (Free Press, New York, 1964); R. D. Laing, *The Divided Self: A Study of Sanity and Madness* (Quadrangle, Chicago, 1960); D. L. Phillips, *Amer. Sociol. Rev.* **28**, 963 (1963); T. R. Sarbin, *Psychol. Today* **6**, 18 (1972); E. Schur, *Amer. J. Sociol.* **75**, 309 (1969); T. Szasz, *Law, Liberty and Psychiatry* (Macmillan, New York, 1963); *The Myth of Mental Illness: Foundations of a Theory of Mental Illness* (Hoeber-Harper, New York, 1963). For a critique of some of these views, see W. R. Gove, *Amer. Sociol. Rev.* **35**, 873 (1970).

4. E. Goffman, *Asylums* (Doubleday, Garden City, N.Y., 1961).

5. T. J. Scheff, *Being Mentally Ill: A Sociological Theory* (Aldine, Chicago, 1966).

6. Data from a ninth pseudopatient are not incorporated in this report because, although his sanity went undetected, he falsified aspects of his personal history, including his marital status and parental relationships. His experimental behaviors therefore were not identical to

those of the other pseudopatients.

7. A. Barry, *Bellevue Is a State of Mind* (Harcourt Brace Jovanovich, New York, 1971); I. Belknap, *Human Problems of a State Mental Hospital* (McGraw-Hill, New York, 1956); W. Caudill, F. C. Redlich. H. R. Gilmore, E. B. Brody, *Amer. J. Orthopsychiat.* **22,** 314 (1952); A. R. Goldman, R. H. Bohr, T. A. Steinberg, *Prof Psychol.* **1, 427** (1970); unauthored, *Roche Report* **1** (No. 13), 8 (1971).

8. Beyond the personal difficulties that the pseudopatient is likely to experience in the hospital, there are legal and social ones that, combined, require considerable attention before entry. For example, once admitted to a psychiatric institution, it is difficult, if not impossible, to be discharged on short notice, state law to the contrary notwithstanding. I was not sensitive to these difficulties at the outset of the project, nor to the personal and situational emergencies that can arise, but later a writ of habeas corpus was prepared for each of the entering pseudopatients and an attorney was kept "on call" during every hospitalization. I am grateful to John Kaplan and Robert Bartels for legal advice and assistance in these matters.

9 However distasteful such concealment is, it was a necessary first step to examining these questions. Without concealment, there would have been no way to know how valid these experiences were; nor was there any way of knowing whether whatever detections occurred were a tribute to the diagnostic acumen of the staff or to the hospital's rumor network. Obviously, since my concerns are general ones that cut across individual hospitals and staffs, I have respected their anonymity and have eliminated clues that might lead to their identification.

10. Interestingly, of the 12 admissions, 11 were diagnosed as schizophrenic and one, with the identical symptomatology, as manic-depressive psychosis. This diagnosis has a more favorable prognosis, and it was given by the only private hospital in our sample. On the relations between social class and psychiatric diagnosis, see A. deB. Hollingshead and F. C. Redlich, *Social Class and Mental Illness: A Community Study* (Wiley, New York, 1958).

11. It is possible, of course, that patients have quite broad latitudes in diagnosis and therefore are inclined to call many people sane, even those whose behavior is patently aberrant. However, although we have no hard data on this matter, it was our distinct impression that this was not the case. In many instances, patients not only singled us out for attention, but came to imitate our behaviors and styles.

12. J. Cumming and E. Cumming. *Community Ment. Health* **1,** 135 (1965); A. Farina and K. Ring, *J. Abnorm. Psychol.* **70,** 47 (1965); H. E. Freeman and O. G. Simmons, *The Mental Patient Comes Home* (Wiley, New York, 1963); W. J. Johannsen, *Ment. Hygiene* **53,** 218 (1969); A. S. Linsky, *Soc. Psychiat.* **5,** 166 (1970).

13. S. E. Asch, *J. Abnorm. Soc. Psychol.* **41,** 258 (1946); *Social Psychology* (Prentice-Hall, New York, 1952).

14. See also I. N. Mensh and J. Wishner, *J. Personality* **16,** 188 (1947); J. Wishner, *Psychol. Rev.* **67,** 96 (1960); J. S. Bruner and R. Tagiuri, in *Handbook of Social Psychology.* G. Lindzey, Ed. (Addison-Wesley, Cambridge, Mass., 1954), vol. 2, pp. 634-654; J. S. Bruner, D. Shapiro, R. Tagiuri, in *Person Perception and Interpersonal Behavior,* R. Tagiuri and L. Petrullo, Eds. (Stanford Univ. Press, Stanford, Calif., 1958), pp. 277-288.

15. For an example of a similar self-fulfilling prophecy, in this instance dealing with the "central" trait of intelligence, see R. Rosenthal and L. Jacobson, *Pygmalion in the Classroom* (Holt, Rinehart & Winston, New York, 1968).

16. E. Zigler and L. Phillips, *J. Abnorm. Soc. Psychol.* **63,** 69 (1961). See also R. K. Freudenberg and J. P. Robertson. *A.M.A. Arch. Neurol. Psychiatr.* **76,** 14 (1956).

17. W. Mischel, *Personality and Assessment* (Wiley, New York, 1968).

18. The most recent and unfortunate instance of this tenet is that of Senator Thomas Eagleton.

19. T. R. Sarbin and J. C. Mancuso, *J. Clin. Consult. Psychol.* **35,** 159 (1970); T. R. Sarbin, *ibid.* **31, 447**
    (1967); J. C. Nunnally, Jr., *Popular Conceptions of Mental Health* (Holt, Rinehart & Winston, New York, 1961).

20. A. H. Stanton and M. S. Schwartz, *The Mental Hospital: A Study of Institutional Participation in Psychiatric Illness and Treatment* (Basic, New York, 1954).

21. D. B. Wexler and S. E. Scoville, *Ariz. Law Rev.* **13,** 1 (1971).

22. I thank W. Mischel, E. Orne, and M. S. Rosenhan for comments on an earlier draft of this manuscript.

JOHN Z. DE LOREAN
J. PATRICK WRIGHT

Bottom-Line Fever at General Motors

When people think of deviants, they are apt to have in mind such low-status, stigmatized persons as pickpockets, heroin addicts, vagrants, prostitutes, and skid-row bums. But, as sociologists have long pointed out, some of the most significant criminal deviance occurs among "respectable" people of high status. Such typically white-collar crimes as fraud, tax evasion, and embezzlement undoubtedly involve far greater sums than the more familiar blue-collar property crimes such as burglary, larceny, and auto theft.

Most white-collar crime is committed by business people in the ordinary course of their occupations. Yet deviance among white-collar executives is not usually recognized as a major problem. One reason is that their offenses are harder to detect and punish than other property crimes. Another reason is that it is people of high status, not low, who have the power to define what is deviant; and, in fact, many white-collar criminals have little sense that what they are doing is wrong at all. It often happens that a general climate develops in corporate suites that ignores, tolerates, or even encourages shady ethics or criminal conduct, particularly where the intent of the act is to advance the ends of the corporation rather than the individual directly.

In this article John De Lorean, a former executive at General Motors, recounts some situations in which senior corporate personnel made decisions that were reckless, negligent, deceitful, dishonest, or even criminal, but which, in the prevailing atmosphere of the corporation, seemed simply part of the day's routine.

"We feel that 1972 can be one of Chevrolet's great years. . . . Most of the improvements this year are engine and chassis components aimed at giving a customer a better car for the money. . . . I want to reiterate our pledge, the 1972 Chevrolets will be the best in history. . . ."

The words seemed to fall out of my mouth like stones from an open hand. Effortlessly. Almost meaninglessly. It was August 1971. I was powergliding through the National Press Preview of 1972 Chevrolet cars and trucks at Raleigh House, a mock-Tudor restaurant in suburban Detroit. The audience was filled with reporters from all over the country along with a plentiful sprinkling of Chevrolet managers. The presentation and question-answer session went smoothly. I was stepping down from the podium and receiving the usual handshakes and compliments when a strange feeling hit me:

"My God! I've been through all this before."

Somehow I felt detached from it all, looking down on myself in the banquet hall surrounded by executives, newsmen and glittering Chevrolets and questioning why I was there and what I was doing. The answers were not satisfactory.

"This whole show is nothing but a replay of last year's show, and the year before that and the year before that," I thought. "The speech I just gave was the same speech I gave last year, written by the same guy in public relations about the same superficial product improvements. And the same questions were being asked by the same newsmen. Almost nothing has changed."

I looked around the room for a moment searching for anything that could show me that there was real meaning in the exercises we were going through, that the national press conference and the tens of similar dealer product announcements I conducted across the country were something more than just hypes. But I found nothing.

Instead, I got the empty feeling that what I was doing there might be nothing more than perpetuating a gigantic fraud. A fraud on the American consumer by promising him something new but giving him only surface alterations—"tortured sheet metal" as former chairman Frederic G. Donner used to say—or a couple of extra horsepower and an annual price increase. A fraud on the

American economy, because I always had a vague suspicion that the annual model change might be good for the auto business in the short term but not good for the economy and the country.

And a fraud on our own company. When General Motors began to grow, on the principle of annual model changes and the promotion of something new and different, cars were almost all alike, with the same basic color—black. There was room for cosmetic changes as well as substantial advancement in technology with new and better engines, more sophisticated transmissions, improved performance and comfort characteristics. But by now there was nothing new and revolutionary in car development and there hadn't been for years. As a company, we were kidding ourselves that these slight annual alterations were innovative. They were not. We were living off the gullibility of the consumer combined with the fantastic growth of the American economy in the 1960s—salting away billions of dollars of profits in the process and telling ourselves we were great managers. This bubble was surely going to break, I thought. The consumer is going to get wise to us, and when he does we will have to fight for a long time to get back into his favor.

Those feelings during the preview led me to tell newsmen during lunch that I would probably leave the auto industry when I was age 55 or so, to get involved in helping find answers to America's problems. There was skepticism and disbelief in their voices as we talked.

The Fourteenth Floor, the executive stronghold of GM's world headquarters in midtown Detroit, went through the ceiling when the stories appeared the next day saying I was going to forsake GM in eight or nine years. It looked to them as if I was trying to force their hand by saying: "Make me president by then or I'll quit."

To anyone in the corporation who asked, I explained that my luncheon comments, though not irrevocable, were sincere and that I was having some internal conflicts about my job. My doubts about the worth of the annual model change were just a part of a growing concern I had about the general level of morality practiced in GM in particular and parts of American business in general.

It seemed to me then, and still does now, that the system of American business often produces wrong, immoral, and irresponsible decisions, even though the personal morality of the people running the business is often above reproach. The system has a different morality as a group than the people do as individuals, which permits it willfully to produce ineffective or dangerous products, deal dictatorially and often unfairly with suppliers, pay bribes for business, abrogate the rights of employees by demanding blind loyalty to management, or tamper with the democratic process of government through illegal political contributions.

I am not a psychologist, so I can't offer a professional opinion on what happens to the freedom of individual minds when they are blended into the group management thought-process of business. But my private analysis is this:

Morality has to do with people. If an action is viewed primarily from the perspective of its effect on people, it is put into the moral realm. Business in America, however, is impersonal. This is particularly true of large American multinational corporations. They are viewed by their employees and publics as faceless. The ultimate measure of the success and failure of these businesses is not their effect on people, but their earnings per share of stock. The first question to greet any business proposal is, how will it affect profits? *People* do not enter the equation of a business decision except to the extent that their reaction will hurt or enhance earnings per share.

In such a completely impersonal context, business decisions of questionable personal morality are easily justified. A person who shoots and kills another is sentenced to life in prison. A businessman who makes a defective product which kills people may get a nominal fine or a slap on the hands, if he is ever brought to trial at all.

The impersonal process of business decision-making is reinforced by a sort of mob psychology that results from group management. Watergate certainly proved what can happen when blind devotion to a system or a process of thought moves unchecked. Members of the Nixon administration never raised any real questions about the morality of the break-in and cover-up. Their only concern was to save the system. So too in business. Too often the only questions asked are: What is the expedient thing to do? How can we increase profits per share?

Never once while I was in GM's management did I hear substantial concern raised about the impact of our business on America, its consumers, or the economy. When we should have been planning switches to smaller, more fuel-efficient, lighter cars in the late 1960s, in response to a growing demand in the marketplace, GM refused because "we make more money on big cars." It mattered not that customers wanted the smaller cars, or that a national balance-of-payments deficit was being built, in large part because of the burgeoning sales of foreign cars in the American market.

Refusal to enter the small car market when the profits were better on bigger cars, despite the needs of the public and the national economy, was not an isolated case of corporate insensitivity. It was typical. And what disturbed me is that it was indicative of fundamental problems with the system.

GM certainly was no more irresponsible than many American businesses. But the fact that the "prototype" of the well-run business engaged in questionable practices and delivered decisions which I felt were sometimes illegal, immoral, or irresponsible is an indictment of the

American business system.

Earlier in my career, I accepted these decisions at GM without question. But as I was exposed to more facets of the business, I came to a realization of the responsibilities we had in managing a giant corporation and making a product which substantially affected people and national commerce. It bothered me how cavalierly these responsibilities were often regarded.

Unsafe at Any Profit

The Corvair case is a first-class example of a basically irresponsible and immoral business decision which was made by men of generally high personal moral standards.

The Corvair was unsafe as it was originally designed. It was conceived along the lines of the Porsche. These cars were powered by engines placed in the rear and supported by an independent, swing-axle suspension system. In the Corvair's case, the engine was all-aluminum and air-cooled (compared to the standard water-cooled iron engines). This, plus the rear placement of the engine, made the car new and somewhat different in the American market.

However, there are several bad engineering characteristics inherent in rear-engine cars which use a swing-axle suspension. In turns at high speeds they tend to become directionally unstable and therefore difficult to control. The rear of the car lifts or "jacks," and the rear wheels tend to tuck under the car, which encourages the car to flip over. In the high-performance Corvair, the car conveyed a false sense of control to the driver when in fact he might have been very close to losing control of the vehicle. The result could be fatal.

These problems with the Corvair were well documented inside GM's engineering staff long before the Corvair was offered for sale. Frank Winchell, now vice-president of engineering but then an engineer at Chevy, flipped one of the first prototypes on the GM test track in Milford, Michigan. Others had the same experience.

The questionable safety of the car caused a massive internal fight among GM's engineers over whether the car should be built with another form of suspension. On one side of the argument was Chevrolet's then general manager, Ed Cole, an engineer and product innovator. He and some of his engineering colleagues were enthralled with the idea of building the first modern, rear-engine American car. I am convinced they felt the safety risks of the swing-axle suspension were minimal. On the other side was a wide assortment of top-flight engineers, including Charles Chayne, then vice-president of engineering, Von D. Polhemus, engineer in charge of chassis development, and others.

These men collectively and individually made vigorous attempts inside GM to keep the Corvair, as designed, out

of production or to change the suspension system to make the car safer. One top corporate engineer told me that he showed his test results to Cole but by then, he said, "Cole's mind was made up."

Albert Roller, who worked for me in Pontiac's advanced engineering section, tested the car and pleaded with me not to use it at Pontiac. Roller had been an engineer with Mercedes-Benz before joining GM, and he said that Mercedes had tested similarly designed rear-engine, swing-axle cars and had found them far too unsafe to build.

At the very least, then, within GM in the late 1950s, serious questions were raised about the Corvair's safety. At the very most, there was a mountain of documented evidence that the car should not be built as it was then designed.

But Cole, who later became GM's president, was a strong voice in company affairs. In addition, the car as he proposed it would cost less to build than the same car with a conventional rear suspension. Management not only went along with Cole, it also told the dissenters in effect to "stop these objections. Get on the team, or you can find someplace else to work." The ill-fated Corvair was launched in the fall of 1959.

The results were disastrous. I don't think any one car before or since produced as gruesome a record on the highway as the Corvair. It was designed and promoted to appeal to the spirit and flair of young people, and sold in part as a sports car. Young Corvair owners, therefore, were trying to bend their cars around curves at high speeds and were killing themselves in alarming numbers.

It was only a couple of years or so before GM's legal department was inundated with lawsuits over the car. And the fatal swath that this car cut through the automobile industry ironically touched the lives of many GM executives, employees, and dealers themselves. The son of Cal Werner, general manager of the Cadillac Division, was killed in a Corvair. Werner was absolutely convinced that the design defect in the car was responsible. He said so many times. The son of Cy Osborne, an executive vice-president in the 1960s, was critically injured in a Corvair and suffered irreparable brain damage. Bunkie Knudsen's niece was brutally injured in a Corvair. And the son of an Indianapolis Chevrolet dealer also was killed in the car. Ernie Kovacs, my favorite comedian, was killed in a Corvair.

While the car was being developed at Chevrolet, we at Pontiac were spending 1.3 million on a project to adapt the Corvair to our division. The corporation had given us the go-ahead to work with the car to give it a Pontiac flavor. Our target for introduction was the fall of 1960, a year after Chevy introduced the car.

As we worked on the project, I became absolutely convinced by Chayne, Polhemus and Roller that the car was unsafe. So I conducted a three-month campaign, with Knudsen's support, to keep the car out of the Pontiac lineup. Fortunately, Buick and Oldsmobile at the time were tooling up their own compact cars, the Special and F-85, which featured conventional front-engine designs.

We talked the corporation into letting Pontiac switch from a Corvair derivative to a version of the Buick-Oldsmobile car. We called it the Tempest and introduced it in the fall of 1960 with a four-cylinder engine as standard equipment and a V-8 engine as an option.

When Knudsen took over the reins of Chevrolet in 1961, he insisted that he be given corporate authorization to install a stabilizing bar in the rear to counteract the natural tendency of the Corvair to flip off the road. The cost of the change would be about $15 a car. But his request was refused by The Fourteenth Floor as "too expensive."

Bunkie was livid. As I understand it, he went to the Executive Committee and told the top officers of the corporation that if they didn't give him permission to make the Corvair safe, he was going to resign from GM. The fear of the bad publicity that surely would result from Knudsen's resignation forced management's hand. They relented, and Bunkie put the stabilizing bar on the Corvair in the 1964 models. The next year a completely new and safer independent suspension designed by Frank Winchell was put on the Corvair. It became one of the safest cars on the road.

But the damage done to the car's reputation by then was irreparable. Corvair sales began to decline precipitously after the waves of unfavorable publicity following Ralph Nader's book and the many lawsuits being filed across the country. Production of the Corvair was halted in 1969, four years after it was made a safe and viable car.

There wasn't a man in top GM management who had anything to do with the Corvair who would purposely build a car that he knew would hurt or kill people. But, as part of a management team pushing for increased sales and profits, each gave his approval to decisions which produced the car in the face of the serious doubts that were raised about its safety.

The corporation became almost paranoid about the leaking of inside information on the car. In April 1971, 19 boxes of microfilmed Corvair owner complaints, which had been ordered destroyed by upper management, turned up in the possession of two suburban Detroit junk dealers. When The Fourteenth Floor found this out, it went into panic. We at Chevrolet were ordered to buy the microfilm back and have it destroyed.

I refused, saying that a public company had no right to destroy documents of its business and that GM's furtive purchase would surely surface. Besides, the $20,000 asking price was outright blackmail.

When some consumer groups showed an interest in getting the film, the customer relations department was ordered to buy the film, which it did. To prevent similar slip-ups in the future, the corporation tightened its scrapping procedures.

Poor Recall

Chevrolet products were involved in the largest product recall in automotive history when, in 1971, the corporation called back 6.7 million 1965–69 cars to repair defective motor mounts. The rubber mounts, which anchor the engine to the car, were breaking apart and causing the engine to lunge out of place; this often locked the accelerator open at about 25 miles per hour. Cars were smashing up all across the country when panicky drivers couldn't stop them or jumped out in fright.

The defect need never have been. At Pontiac, when I was chief engineer, we developed a safety-interlock motor mount which we put on our 1965 car line. It was developed because we discovered that the mounts we were using were defective. We made our findings and the design of the new motor mount available to the rest of the car divisions. None of them opted to use it.

However, reports started drifting in from the field in 1966 that the Chevrolet mounts were breaking apart after extensive use. Chevrolet did nothing. Dealers replaced the mounts—and charged the customers for parts and labor.

When I got to Chevrolet in 1969, the reports about motor mount failures were reaching crisis proportions. When a motor mount failure was blamed for a fatal accident involving an elderly woman in Florida, I asked Roger Kyes, my boss, to let me quietly recall the cars with these problems and repair them at GM's expense. He refused, on the grounds that it would cost too much. By 1971, however, the trouble was becoming widely known outside of the corporation because owners were complaining to local newspapers, the National Highway Traffic Safety Administration, and several consumer groups.

The pressure began to build on General Motors to recall the cars. GM started to repair these cars at company expense, but it refused to recall them, preferring to wait until the mounts broke in use before doing anything. Bob Irvin, of the Detroit *News,* who was receiving huge numbers of complaints, wrote stories almost daily about GM's steadfast refusal to recall all the cars.

The fires of discontent were further fanned when Ed Cole, who was opposing the recall internally, was asked by a reporter why GM continued to refuse to recall the cars. He replied that anyone who "can't manage a car at 25 miles per hour shouldn't be driving." It was an unfortunately callous remark, for which I am sure Cole was later sorry. But he became more rigid in his stance against a recall campaign. So I wrote a memo to my immediate boss, Tom Murphy, which said in part:

At this point in time, it seems to me that we have no alternative (but to recall the Chevrolets). Certainly if GM can spend over $200 million a year in advertising, the $30 or $40 million this would cost is not a valid reason for delaying. Certainly, it would be worth the cost to stop the negative publicity, even if management cannot agree to recall these cars on moral grounds.

Murphy received the memo and returned it to me, refusing to accept it.

Finally, about a month or so later, under the weight of government, consumer group and newspaper pressure, GM recalled the 6.7 million cars with defective engine mounts. The price was about $40 million to recall the cars and wire the engines to the car so they wouldn't slip out of place when the mounts broke.

But the cost was much greater in the incredibly bad publicity GM received because of its own unwillingness to admit its reponsibility for the defect and to repair the cars on its own. It was a case of the corporation taking an attitude of "the owners be damned." The motor mount affair reflected GM's corporate attitude toward the consumer movement, an attitude shared in a variety of ways in a wide variety of industries.

Vote for 'Cash'

GM's consumer image also suffered from a dearth of product innovations. This produced an unquenchable thirst at GM for information on what the competition was doing. This led the company into areas which I felt were of questionable legality. So concerned was management with the plans of the competition, especially Ford, that the final okay on product programs was often delayed until we received the latest intelligence report on Ford's product programs.

I was told by Lou Bauer, once Chevrolet's comptroller, that when Bunkie Knudsen took over Chevrolet in 1961, he was shocked to find on the payroll two men who worked for Ford. They worked in Ford's product planning area and passed on new product information to Chevrolet. Knudsen, I was told, fired the spies the day he confirmed their existence. But GM continued to keep Ford under close—and questionable—surveillance.

This habit reached a height of sorts when several of us walked into a meeting of the Administration Committee sometime after 1971, and found the top corporate officers poring over a very confidential "spread sheet." This report gave the definitive breakdown, product-by-product, of what it cost Ford to build and sell its cars. It was the kind of information which, for our products, never got off The Fourteenth Floor. GM top management wouldn't even let its own divisional management in on all the corporate costs. But somehow top management had gotten this information about Ford, and they were studying it with deep concentration. Corporate counsel Ross Malone

was incensed. He snapped, "Goddamnit! You guys shouldn't be doing this."

His voice was angry and pleading. It was obvious to me that Malone thought what was taking place had serious legal overtones.

After he spoke, someone scooped up the Ford cost report and hustled it off to one of the front offices. None of us at the divisional level ever heard about the report again. Now, I am sure that the men studying these confidential cost sheets and giving their approval to a system which procured them would be outraged at the suggestion of similar conduct in their personal lives. Like most Americans, they were probably angered by the disclosures in the wake of Watergate that the CIA, U.S. Army, FBI, and other government agencies spied on unsuspecting citizens. And yet, at GM, they were justifying the very same sort of conduct on the ground that "this is business."

GM also took its place in the line with scores of other American businesses in promoting what I think are, at the very least, improper political campaign contributions from its top executives. The system was complicated and far more secretive than the outright corporate political gifts for which a number of major corporations have paid fines.

The contributions program was operated, as I understood it, by the financial side of the business with assistance from some people on the public relations staff. The finance staff apparently collected the money and a few PR people distributed it with guidance from The Fourteenth Floor.

There were two tiers to the system. Middle level managers were generally allowed to contribute a sum of money to the party of their choice. However, once an executive reached upper management levels it was decided for him how much he would contribute and to whom it would go.

When I was a general manager, the divisional controller once walked into my office with a sheet of paper that apparently had been given to him by the corporate finance staff. On the sheet was written my name and the amount I was to donate to that year's election campaigns—national, state, or local. I was told to make a check out to "cash" for the amount assigned to me and give it to the controller. Once the check was made out, an executive did not know to whom or for whom the political contribution was made, nor the manner in which it was made: whether it was an anonymous cash contribution, one that was made in his name or a corporate gift. All the executive knew was that he wrote a check to "cash" for the predetermined amount.

The sums were big. For a GM vice president, it might be as much as $3,000 in a presidential campaign, less for an off-year congressional election, and so on down to a few hundred dollars for a city election.

I participated in the system several times at Pontiac. I cannot recall whether I made the donations myself or wrote a check to "cash." But finally, I just couldn't accept the practice, and I refused to participate. The thing seemed wholly improper. My franchise to vote and donate as I saw fit was too important to me as a citizen to delegate it to management or some guy on one of the corporate staffs. The corporation has no right to tell any executive how to vote, or to know how he votes.

After I refused to participate in the contribution program at GM on several different occasions, top management hit the roof. As in the past, the chore of trying to bring me into line fell to Kyes. He was ready for battle.

"John, you'd better damn well play this game," he said. "If you don't, you are telling us you aren't on the team. We don't think highly of guys who aren't on the team at GM."

Then he sought to reduce the doubts in my mind to money, the common rationalization in business.

"We take care of you at bonus time. When you make this contribution, you get it back as part of your bonus. And if you don't make the contribution, then you aren't going to get that much bonus."

The meeting ended angrily, as usual, with neither of us giving an inch. I continued to boycott the political contribution system at GM, and instead made personal donations to candidates I thought were worthy. And I must admit I never noticed an inexplicable drop in the bonus I received for my work at GM thereafter.

The Big Greenback Team

While these business practices involved questionable ethics exercised for the good of the business, sometimes upper management executives used their positions of power and knowledge to profit *personally* in corporate business. These were by no means widespread and perhaps confined to a few individuals.

When I was directing Pontiac, several GM dealers were purchasing the troubled National Car Rental Company for almost nothing—less than $4 million. The price, as I remember, was two or three dollars per share.

While they were doing this, they also worked a deal with upper corporate management for GM to provide $22 million in advertising assistance, because National was going to emphasize GM cars in its business and promotion. The confirmation of this arrangement was known only to a few people. But once it became public the stock of the company would surely jump in value. One day one of the participants in the purchase of National came to me and said, "You've got to get some of this stock." I said, "That's an obvious conflict of interest. I can't."

He said, "Hell, I'll buy it for you and keep it in my name. Tell me how much you want." I refused his second offer because it was wrong, and what's more, once you let a guy do something like that, he owns you forever. You're his puppet. He was irritated by my refusal and said, "Hell, we're doing it for————" and he named a high-ranking GM official. It was quite a surprise.

I never personally verified whether the guy this dealer named was in on the deal or not, which is why I am not disclosing the names involved. But I do know that the word was rife through the corporation that officers were making bundles from insider information on National stock. So widespread was this rumor that management conducted an investigation and demanded to examine National's stockholder list to see if any GM executives were on it. There were none. But then there wouldn't be—if the stock were held in someone else's name.

On another occasion when I was at Chevrolet, word got around that company and divisional executives were speculating on land around the Lordstown assembly plant in Ohio. Since these people were privy to our plans for the Lordstown area, they could buy the land and sell when its value rose.

Again the corporation conducted an investigation and apparently fingered several people, including one of our Chevy managers. Word was that the culprits would be fired. One day, the Chevy executive in question walked into my office obviously nervous and excited, and snapped: "If you guys make something out of this, I'm going to blow the lid off this goddamn thing."

"What the hell do you mean?" I asked.

He replied by telling me the name of a real estate man in the Lordstown area who he said was acting as the agent in these land transactions, and who was willing to implicate top corporate managers. Some of the executives were the same ones trying to have him fired in the brewing scandal. I told the guy I knew nothing about the matter and was not part of the firing action. But he must have put the same threat to his prosecutors in the corporation—because it wasn't too long before this executive who was on the verge of being fired was plucked from Chevy management, promoted to a corporate job, and given a $5,000 raise.

QUESTIONS

1. Why is white-collar crime so readily overlooked?

2. What are some of the forms of "corporate" deviance mentioned in this article? From your knowledge, can you think of any other deviance by corporations in recent years?

3. Does the social status of the offender affect the response of the criminal justice system to an offense? If so, how and why?

STEVEN PHILLIPS

Justice for Whom?

It is common knowledge that the U.S. criminal justice system is close to breaking down, particularly in the nation's largest cities. Many crimes are never reported, partly because the victims feel it would be a waste of time. Many reported crimes go uninvestigated through lack of police resources, and a majority of crimes (except for homicide) go unsolved. Yet even so, the number of people arrested each year on criminal charges threatens to clog the court system.

Largely as a response to the pressures of time on the courts, the police, and the public prosecutors, the American courts have developed a curious informal system, virtually unknown in most other countries, called plea bargaining. Under this behind-the-scenes system, the prosecuting and defense attorneys, with the connivance of the judge, privately negotiate the exchange of a guilty plea for a reduced charge. Thus, a person accused of attempted murder and facing a possible fifteen-year prison sentence may, through plea bargaining, end up pleading guilty to a lesser charge of aggravated assault in return for the prosecutor's promise to ask for no more than eighteen months' imprisonment. The actual courtroom proceeding takes a few minutes, rather than the hours, days, or even weeks that a full criminal trial might occupy. The overwhelming majority of cases, in fact, are now settled by plea bargaining.

In this even-handed article, Steven Phillips looks at the merits and demerits of plea bargaining from various perspectives, using as his point of departure an actual case study of a homicide prosecution.

From *Psychology Today*, March 1977. Reprinted by permission of Wallace and Sheil Agency, Inc. Copyright © 1977 by Steven Phillips.

He was on his way home from a schoolyard pickup basketball game, dribbling his ball down Arthur Avenue in the Bronx, when a white teenager walked up and stabbed him once in the abdomen. The black boy was dead before he hit the ground. The assailant turned and fled, leaving his victim sprawled face upward on the sidewalk. From start to finish, the killing took no more than five seconds.

It took the detective almost a month before he broke the case. At first it was a total mystery, with no apparent motive for the killing and no decent leads to work on. In fact, several days passed before the detective even learned the victim's identity.

When they undressed the boy at the morgue, all the detective found were a set of keys and a dollar and a half in change. There was no wallet and no identification cards. He fingerprinted the corpse and ran the prints through the computer, but drew a blank. The dead boy had never been arrested. Finally, the detective took photographs of the victim's face, and distributed copies to the desk officers and detective squads of all the neighboring precincts. He hoped someone reporting a missing person would identify the photo. As it happened, the boy's parents had reported him missing on the day of his death. Four days had passed, however, before anyone remembered to show them a copy of the morgue photo. He was 17 when he was killed, a senior in high school.

For two weeks the detective got nowhere. The boy had no enemies, he had not been robbed, and no clues had been found at the scene of the crime. A canvass of the scene had produced only one eyewitness, a middle-aged black gas-station attendant who had seen the killing from about half a block away. He described the assailant as a white teenager of about average height and weight, with dark hair. He did not remember what the youth was wearing, or anything else about him.

The detective interviewed students at the dead boy's high school, where he had been an honor student. He also questioned members of the local youth gangs. But he made no progress. As the investigation stretched into its third fruitless week, the detective's squad commander began to talk about pulling him off the case. Summer was approaching, the homicide rate was climbing as fast as the temperature, and vacation schedules were cutting into available police manpower. The commander figured it made no sense to waste a good man on what appeared to be a hopeless task. They talked it over and decided to give the case one more week.

A Lead on the Killer

On the final day of that third week a lead finally developed. The gas-station attendant called and told the detective that a kid driving an old souped-up Thunderbird had been around the gas station several times asking what he knew about the homicide. The attendant decided these questions were suspicious. Although the driver did not resemble the killer, he took down the license-plate number and passed it along to the detective.

It took the detective a day and a half to track down the driver of the Thunderbird. He was the kind of street tough who had been in and out of minor trouble since he was 13. The youngster denied all knowledge of the killing. In a whining, plaintive voice he asked why he had been brought in. The detective then took his cigar out of his mouth, put his face close to the boy's and grabbed him by the shirt front with both hands. Like the Marine noncom he had once been, he told the boy the facts of life. "Now you listen to me, you punk. This isn't an auto larceny or a burglary I'm investigating, it's a goddamn murder. And I know that one of your punk friends did it! You're going to tell me who did it, 'cause if you don't I'm gonna lock your ass up for hindering prosecution! And you'd better believe I'm gonna make it stick! I'm gonna send you upstate for sure. You understand?"

The detective left the boy alone in the squadroom to think that over. Within an hour, he told the detective everything he knew. He had not been an eyewitness to the killing, and his knowledge was second-hand. The killer was an 18-year-old who worked as a delivery boy for a local pastry shop. The detective also learned the names of a number of youngsters who had actually witnessed the stabbing.

There was no need to run right out to arrest the suspect. The detective knew from long experience that if the boy had not already vanished after three weeks, he was not about to. Instead, the detective rounded up all the eyewitnesses (an easy task, since they were all attending local high schools), and brought them back to the station house. He kept them separated, and spoke to each one individually. A half hour later he had six signed eyewitness statements identifying the killer. The time had come to make the arrest.

The suspect lived with his aged parents in a two-bedroom apartment over a shoemaker's shop, not four blocks from the scene of the killing. The apartment was immaculate, and had a warm, old-world immigrant flavor the detective knew all too well. He had grown up in such a home himself. In the entrance hallway were framed pictures of Pope John, John Kennedy, and the Virgin Mary.

"I Didn't Mean to Do It"

The boy's father answered the door. He was a frail but intense white-haired man in his 60s, and he spoke with a heavy Italian accent. Asked what he wanted, the detective said he had to speak to the boy about a crime that had been committed. As he stood there, the detective was embarrassed by the old man. He could see that the boy's father did not have the slightest inkling of what this was all about, and the detective had little stomach for what he knew was about to happen. Grimly he pushed on.

"Where is the boy?"

"He's in his bedroom, studying," the father replied. "I'll call him, but first you tell me what crime this is you want to talk to him about."

"It's a murder. A black kid was killed up on Arthur Avenue three weeks ago. I've got to talk to him about it."

"Are you here to arrest my boy?"

"Yes, I am," the detective said softly.

The old man looked hard at the detective, and began to shake. His eyes widened, and he began to look a little wild. But then, just as suddenly, he seemed to regain control of himself. He called out the boy's name.

The boy emerged from his bedroom and walked up to his father and the detective. He was short and slender, almost fragile in build, dressed in blue jeans and a white T-shirt. He was smooth-cheeked, and the detective was struck by the boy's eyes. They were large and dark and liquid, the sort of eyes you would expect to see on a beautiful woman. The boy looked straight at the detective and then lowered his eyes. He knew what this was all about.

The old man spoke first.

"This man says you killed a black kid up on Arthur Avenue three weeks ago."

The boy hung his head and began to cry. "Papa, I did it. I didn't mean to do it, and I wanted to tell you, but I couldn't. It just happened, and I'm sorry." The old man was in a state of shock. The three of them stood silently, and then the old man too began to cry. The detective waited a minute and then put the boy in handcuffs and led him away.

It was almost 24 hours from the time of arrest until the boy was arraigned. They spent it waiting for transportation, waiting for the Correction Department red tape at Central Booking, and finally, waiting for the court. The boy and the detective chatted to kill the time. The detective found that he liked his prisoner, and it bothered him. As he reflected upon what was in store for the boy in prison he felt sick. For the first time in his career he found himself wishing he had not broken a case.

By the time the boy was arraigned, his father had spoken to his neighbors, and a delegation of them went with him to the Bronx Criminal Court Building on Washington Avenue and 161st Street. When his case was called, they all stepped forward to vouch for the boy, his character, and his family. Impressed by this unusual show of neighborhood solidarity, and by the impeccable character of the local merchants who spoke up for the boy, the judge set bail at the modest sum (for a murder) of $15,000. It was raised within the hour. The boy walked out of the court after spending only one night in jail, and the case was referred to the grand jury.

There were over 400 homicides in Bronx County that year. Almost 350 were solved by the police, leading to arrests that were turned over for prosecution to the 12 of us in the Homicide Bureau of the District Attorney's office. The death of the black boy on Arthur Avenue was only one of these homicides.

An Airtight Case

It was bound to be a low-priority case, with the defendant out on bail at a time when we had prisoners who had been languishing in jail for up to two years awaiting trial. This case had to be put on a back burner. Besides, with six eye-witnesses, an oral confession, and a vicious, senseless crime to work with, any trial of the case was bound to result in a murder conviction and a mandatory life sentence.

From the very beginning, when I was first assigned the case, I knew no defense attorney would risk taking it to trial. It was foreordained to result in a plea bargain. The grand-jury presentation took a little less than 15 minutes. Two of the eyewitnesses and the detective testified, and I read from the medical examiner's report. The grand jury deliberated about 30 seconds before handing up a murder indictment.

It was two months or so before I heard from the boy's defense attorney, a man I had dealt with before and respected. Late one afternoon, several days later, we met in my office. Although I was eager to avoid a trial, there wasn't much I could offer the boy as a plea bargain and I said so. I had close to an airtight case, one that was bound to lead to a murder conviction. The crime itself was both shocking and senseless, and the defendant, then 18 years old, would be treated as an adult . . . I saw no reason why I should not take a very hard position.

The defense attorney listened, and then asked me what I would offer the boy. I thought for a minute, and told him I would agree to a plea to manslaughter in the first degree. I added that at the time of sentence I would ask the judge to impose a very lengthy jail term with a fixed minimum to guarantee that substantial time would actually be served.

The defense attorney was candid in his response. He acknowledged right away that his client was guilty and admitted he didn't dare take the case to trial. He had to plead his client guilty, and did not care what particular crime he pleaded to so long as it was not murder, which carried with it a mandatory life sentence. What he did care about was the sentence his client would receive, and in this regard he had two requests. Before discussing the question of sentencing he asked me to read a report on his client prepared at his family's request by a forensic psychiatrist. Then he asked me to meet the boy myself and size him up. I agreed.

Killer on the Couch

The psychiatrist's report read, in part, as follows:

. . . Although I am unable to state that [this young man] was unaware of the nature and consequences of his actions, or that he was unaware of the fact that his conduct was morally wrong, I do believe that there are circumstances that should weigh heavily in determining the disposition of his case.

. . . [he] is the only son of immigrant parents and was born at a time when his parents were already on the brink of middle age. Since early childhood he has been overprotected and overindulged by his mother who had made him the central focus of her life. His father, a stern disciplinarian, has always attempted to instill in [this young man] his own rather rigid set of values. Needless to say, this interparental conflict over the nature and style of his rearing, has left [the boy] with an ambivalent and deeply troubled at-titude toward his parents.

This ambivalence was exacerbated by a phenomenon that is rather common in the first general offspring of newly arrived immigrants. [The boy], whose English is, of course, fluent and unaccented, and who is very much a product of this society, is ashamed of his parents' heavy accents, and what he described as their "foreign ways." He is reluctant to bring friends into the house for fear that his parents might embarrass him, and is equally reluctant to share his "American" school or "street" life with his parents, for fear that they would misunderstand or disapprove of things he has come to cherish as he struggles to find his own identity. On the other hand, [the boy] loves his parents deeply, and has great difficulty coping with this shame over their "old fashionedness."

. . . [He] has also had serious trouble in coping with peer-group pressure which is, of course, a particularly intense force in late adolescence. The young people in [his] neighborhood place great emphasis upon a young man's having "machismo," e.g., on being both sexually and physically powerful. These values directly conflict with the overprotected and unyielding values the

percent of the prison population was black or Hispanic? Once they find out what the boy is in jail for they would probably cut his throat. He said his client would never survive a lengthy jail term.

I did not argue with the defense attorney as he said this. I too had considered this possibility, and frankly, I just did not know whether he was right or wrong. I heard him out, and then excused myself. It was a bad week for me. The case would not leave my mind, and the more I thought about it, the more impossible it seemed to reach a sentencing decision. I would have liked to have had more information about the boy before making a decision. But with our crushing caseloads, neither I nor the detective could possibly devote more time to this particular case.

I turned to my colleagues for advice, but as I expected, they showed no inclination to make the decision for me. This was only one case among many, and only I had any knowledge of its complexity. The advice I got was both wise and useless. "Do the right thing, and don't worry," I was told.

The trouble, of course, was that I did not know what the right thing was, and I could not stop worrying. I wanted to reach a just result, but justice, I quickly came to realize, was a relative thing. It all depended upon your perspective. Justice for an emotionally disturbed boy, gripped by psychological forces partially beyond his control, or for his aged parents, faced with the loss of their only son? Justice for the dead boy, senselessly cut down in his youth, or for his family, grief-stricken and embittered by their loss, and by the seeming indifference of the judicial process? Society needed justice too. But what kind? Stern justice to clearly show that racial violence would not be tolerated? Or a more humane justice that sought to heal and rehabilitate rather than punish?

There was no end to the conflicting values at stake, and the conflicts, such as they were, would not resolve themselves in my mind. I had no difficulty articulating the arguments to justify either harsh or lenient treatment. But in the end, I came to realize that the arguments were pointless. Each one was based upon a different assumption about the purpose of punishment; and in effect, in making the argument, the unspoken assumption would dictate the conclusion reached. For example, if the purpose of punishment was retribution, then the very seriousness of the boy's offense, independent of all other considerations, required harsh punishment. But if the idea was rehabilitation rather than retribution, then I had a boy who most probably could be transformed through sympathetic and therapeutic, i.e., lenient, treatment into a valuable member of society.

If, on the other hand, punishment was designed to be exemplary, if it was to teach and to deter, then harsh treatment was necessary to demonstrate that racial violence would not be tolerated.

Retribution, rehabilitation, and deterrence, they all have a certain validity, and I could not easily choose between them. Besides, I was haunted by the images of the two families, and concerned about the impact of my decision upon all of these decent and innocent people

I tried to take a pragmatic approach and asked myself what was to be gained by sending the boy to prison. It wasn't going to bring the dead boy back, and it wasn't really going to end racial violence or make the streets of the Bronx any safer. In one way or another, prison would probably destroy the boy, and in the final analysis, wasn't it more important to save this life, then to bow to the imagined dictates of abstract social justice? The boy was so young, and in a sense he was the victim of powerful social and psychological forces that were beyond his control. Was it right to make him pay as an individual for a crime that found its origins, at least in part, in peer-group pressure and the collective racial attitudes of society in general? I toyed with all these arguments, but I could not escape the idea that the boy, however young, bore an individual responsibility for his actions, and had to answer for that responsibility.

A decision had to be made, and one week later I made a sentencing recommendation. Later, at the time of sentence, the judge followed it. Whether or not I did the right thing I shall never know. No doubt reasonable people will differ about the rightness of my decision and what ought to have been done.

The boy is currently serving a 15-year term in state prison. He will be eligible for parole in three years. Two months after sentence, the white youth's father suffered a stroke. He is now an invalid. The dead boy's brother is now under indictment, charged with armed robbery. There has been no noticeable decrease in the amount of crime or racial violence in the Bronx.

QUESTIONS

1. What are the advantages of plea bargaining? What are the disadvantages?

2. Would you agree that the right decision was made in the case discussed? Do you think it likely that the same decision would have been made if the races of the offender and victim were reversed?

3. Only a tiny handful of criminals end up in jail. Is this the result of random chance, or is their fate the result of a process of social selection? Explain.

ABE FORTAS

The Case Against
Capital Punishment

The judicial death sentence, applied at one time or another in virtually every country of the world, is now widely obsolete. In the modern world, in fact, it is practiced primarily by three main groups of nations: those of Africa, those of the Middle East, and the communist countries. In much of the rest of the world, and particularly in the Western democracies, capital punishment has either been formally abolished or has fallen into disuse. The exception to this pattern, of course, is the United States, where, after years of uncertainty about the constitutionality of the death penalty, executions recommenced in the late 1970s and are currently continuing to take place.

The question of whether the state has the right to take a person's life raises one of the most controversial of all moral issues. The subject has been fiercely argued for decades, but the debate has usually generated more heat than light. Many important aspects of the problem remain unresolved. Is the death penalty really a deterrent? Is its justification the protection of society, or simply revenge? How can it be fairly applied, given that a criminal's chances of a death sentence are many times greater in one state than another? Is the moral tone of a society enhanced or debased if it practices capital punishment?

In this article, former Supreme Court Justice Abe Fortas presents what is, according to opinion polls, a minority view at present—that capital punishment is ineffective and morally wrong.

I believe that most Americans, even those who feel it necessary, are repelled by capital punishment; the attitude is deeply rooted in our moral reverence for life, the Judeo-Christian belief that man is created in the image of God. Many Americans were pleased when on June 29, 1972, the Supreme Court of the United States set aside death sentences for the first time in its history. On that day the Court handed down its decision in *Furman v. Georgia,* holding that the capital-punishment statutes of three states were unconstitutional because they gave the jury complete discretion to decide whether to impose the death penalty or a lesser punishment in capital cases. For this reason, a bare majority of five Justices agreed that the statutes violated the "cruel and unusual punishment" clause of the Eighth Amendment.

The result of this decision was paradoxical. Thirty-six states proceeded to adopt new death-penalty statutes designed to meet the Supreme Court's objection, and beginning in 1974, the number of persons sentenced to death soared. In 1975 alone, 285 defendants were condemned—more than double the number sentenced to death in any previously reported year. Of those condemned in 1975, 93 percent had been convicted of murder; the balance had been convicted of rape or kidnapping.

The constitutionality of these death sentences and of the new statutes, however, was quickly challenged, and on July 2, 1976, the Supreme Court announced its rulings in five test cases. It rejected "mandatory" statues that automatically imposed death sentences for defined capital offenses, but it approved statutes that set out "standards" to guide the jury in deciding whether to impose the death penalty. These laws, the court ruled, struck a reasonable balance between giving the jury some guidance and allowing it to take into account the background and character of the defendant and the circumstances of the crime.

The decisions may settle the basic constitutional issue until there is a change in the composition of the Court, but many questions remain. Some of these are questions of considerable constitutional importance, such as those relating to appellate review. Others have to do with the sensational issues that accompany capital punishment in our society. Gary Gilmore generated an enormous national debate by insisting on an inalienable right to force the people of Utah to kill him. So did a district judge who ruled that television may present to the American people the spectacle of a man being electrocuted by the state of Texas.

The recent turns of the legislative and judicial process have done nothing to dispose of the matter of conscience and judgment for the individual citizen. The debate over it will not go away; indeed, it has gone on for centuries.

Through the years, the number of offenses for which the state can kill the offender has declined. Once, hundreds of capital crimes, including stealing more than a shilling from a person and such religious misdeeds as blasphemy and witchcraft, were punishable by death. But in the United States today, only two principal categories remain—major assaults upon persons, such as murder, kidnapping, rape, bombing and arson, and the major political crimes of espionage and treason. In addition, there are more than 20 special capital crimes in some of our jurisdictions, including train robbery and aircraft piracy. In fact, however, in recent years murder has accounted for about 90 percent of the death sentences and rape for most of the others, and the number of states prescribing the death penalty for rape is declining.

At least 45 nations, including most of the Western democracies, have abolished or abandoned capital punishment. Ten U.S. states have no provision for the death penalty. In four, the statutes authorizing it have recently been declared unconstitutional under state law. The Federal Criminal Code authorizes capital punishment for various offenses, but there have been no executions under Federal civil law (excluding military jurisdiction) since the early 1960's.

Public-opinion polls in our nation have seesawed, with some indication that they are affected by the relative stability or unrest in our society at the time of polling. In 1966, a public-opinion poll reported that 42 percent of the American public favored capital punishment, 47 percent opposed it and 11 percent were undecided. In 1972–1973, both the Gallup and Harris polls showed that 57 percent to 59 percent of the people favored capital punishment, and a recent Gallup poll asserts that 65 percent favor it.

Practically all scholars and experts agree that capital punishment cannot be justified as a significantly useful instrument of law enforcement or of penology. There is no evidence that it reduces the serious crimes to which it is addressed. Professor William Bowers, for example, concludes in his excellent study, "Executions in America," that statutory or judicial developments that change the risk of execution are not paralleled by variations in homicide rates. He points out that over the last 30 years, homicide rates have remained relatively constant while the number of executions has steadily declined. He concludes that the "death penalty, as we use it, exerts no influence on the extent or rate of capital offenses."

I doubt that fear of the possible penalty affects potential capital offenders. The vast majority of capital offenses are murders committed in the course of armed robbery that result from fear, tension or anger of the moment, and murders that are the result of passion or mental disorder. The only deterrence derived from the criminal process probably results from the fear of apprehension and arrest, and possibly from the fear of significant punishment. There is little, if any, difference between the possible deterrent effect of life imprisonment and that of the death penalty.

In fact, the statistical possibility of execution for a capital offense is extremely slight. We have not exceeded 100 executions a year since 1951, although the number of homicides in death-sentence jurisdictions alone has ranged from 7,500 to 10,000. In 1960, there were only 56 executions in the United States, and the number declined each year thereafter. There have been no executions since 1967. In the peak year of 1933, there were only 199 executions in the United States, while the average number of homicides in all of the states authorizing capital punishment for 1932–1933 was 11,579.

A potential murderer who rationally weighed the possibility of punishment by death (if there is such a person), would figure that he has considerably better than a 98 percent chance of avoiding execution in the average capital-punishment state. In the years from 1960 to 1967, his chances of escaping execution were better than 99.5 percent. The professional or calculating murderer is not apt to be deterred by such odds.

An examination of the reason for the infrequency of execution is illuminating:

(1) Juries are reluctant to condemn a human being to death. The evidence is that they are often prone to bring in a verdict of a lesser offense, or even to acquit, if the alternative is to impose the death penalty. The reluctance is, of course, diminished when powerful emotions come into play—as in the case of a black defendant charged with the rape of a white woman.

(2) Prosecutors do not ask for the death penalty in the case of many, perhaps a majority, of those who are arrested for participation in murder or other capital offenses. In part, this is due to the difficulty of persuading juries to impose death sentences; in part, it is due to plea bargaining. In capital cases involving more than one participant, the prosecutor seldom asks for the death penalty for more than one of them. Frequently, in order to obtain the powerful evidence necessary to win a death sentence, he will make a deal with all participants except one. The defendants who successfully "plea bargain" testify against the defendant chosen for the gallows and in return receive sentences of imprisonment.

This system may be defensible in noncapital cases because of practical exigencies, but it is exceedingly disturbing where the result is to save the witness's life at the hazard of the life of another person. The possibility is obvious that the defendant chosen for death will be selected on a basis that has nothing to do with comparative guilt, and the danger is inescapable that the beneficiary of the plea-bargain, in order to save his life, will lie or give distorted testimony. To borrow a phrase from Justice Byron R. White: "This is a grisly trade . . ." A civilized nation should not kill A on the basis of testimony obtained from B in exchange for B's life.

(3) As a result of our doubts about capital punishment, and our basic aversion to it, we have provided many escape hatches. Every latitude is allowed the defendant and his counsel in the trial; most lawyers representing a capital offender quite properly feel that they must exhaust every possible defense, however technical or unlikely; appeals are generally a matter of right; slight legal errors, which would be disregarded in other types of cases, are grounds for reversal; governors have, and liberally exercise, the power to commute death sentences. Only the rare, unlucky defendant is likely to be executed when the process is all over.

In 1975, 65 prisoners on death row had their death-penalty status changed as a result of appeals, court actions, commutation, resentencing, etc. This was more than 20 percent of the new death-row prisoners admitted during that peak year.

It is clear that American prosecutors, judges and juries are not likely to cause the execution of enough capital offenders to increase the claimed deterrent effect of capital-punishment laws or to reduce the "lottery" effect of freakish selection. People generally may favor capital punishment in the abstract, but pronouncing that a living person shall be killed is quite another matter. Experience shows that juries are reluctant to order that a person be killed. Where juries have been commanded by law to impose the death penalty, they have often chosen to acquit or, in modern times, to convict of a lesser offense rather than to return a verdict that would result in execution.

The law is a human instrument administered by a vast number of different people in different circumstances, and we are inured to its many inequalities. Tweedledee may be imprisoned for five years for a given offense, while Tweedledum, convicted of a similar crime, may be back on the streets in a few months. We accept the inevitability of such discriminations, although we don't approve of them, and we constantly seek to reduce their frequency and severity. But the taking of a life is different from any other punishment. It is final; it is ultimate; if it is erroneous, it is irreversible and beyond correction. It is an act in which the state is presuming to function, so to speak, as the Lord's surrogate.

We have gone a long way toward recognition of the unique character of capital punishment. We insist that it

be imposed for relatively few crimes of the most serious nature and that it be imposed only after elaborate precautions to reduce the possibility of error. We also inflict it in a fashion that avoids the extreme cruelty of such methods as drawing and quartering, though it still involves the barbaric rituals attendant upon electrocution, the gallows or the firing squad.

But fortunately, the death penalty is and will continue to be sought in only a handful of cases and rarely carried out. So long as the death penalty is a highly exceptional punishment, it will serve no deterrent or penological function; it will fulfill no pragmatic purpose of the state; and inevitably, its selective imposition will continue to be influenced by racial and class prejudice.

All of the standards that can be written, all of the word magic and the procedural safeguards that can be devised to compel juries to impose the death penalty on capital offenders without exception or discrimination will be of no avail. In a 1971 capital-punishment case, Justice John Harlan wrote on the subject of standards. "They do no more," he said, "than suggest some subjects for the jury to consider during its deliberations, and [the criteria] bear witness to the intractable nature of the problem of 'standards' which the history of capital punishment has from the beginning reflected."

Form and substance are important to the life of the law, but when the law deals with a fundamental and constitutional issue—the disposition of human life—the use of such formulas is not an acceptable substitute for a correct decision on the substance of the matter.

The discrimination that is inescapable in the selection of the few to be killed under our capital-punishment laws is unfortunately of the most invidious and unacceptable sort. Most of those who are chosen for extinction are black (53.5 percent in the years 1930 to 1975). The wheels of chance and prejudice begin to spin in the police station; they continue through the prosecutor's choice of defendants for whom he will ask the death penalty and those he will choose to spare; they continue through the trial and in the jury room, and finally they appear in the Governor's office. Solemn "presumptions of law" that the selection will be made rationally and uniformly violate human experience and the evidence of the facts. Efforts to bring about equality of sentence by writing "standards" or verbal formulas may comfort the heart of the legislator or jurist, but they can hardly satisfy his intelligence.

If deterrence is not a sufficient reason to justify capital-punishment laws and if their selective application raises such disturbing questions, what possible reason is there for their retention? One other substantive reason, advanced by eminent authorities, is that the execution of criminals is justifiable as "retribution." This is the argument that society should have the right to vent its anger or abhorrence against the offender, that it may justifiably impose a punishment people believe the criminal "deserves." Albert Camus, in a famous essay, says of capital punishment: "Let us call it by the name which, for lack of any other, will at least give the nobility of truth, and let us recognize it for what it is essentially: a revenge."

We may realize that deep-seated emotions underlie our capital-punishment laws, but there is a difference between our understanding of the motivation for capital punishment and our acceptance of it as an instrument of our society. We may appreciate that the *lex talionis,* the law of revenge, has its roots in the deep recesses of the human spirit, but that awareness is not a permissible reason for retaining capital punishment.

It is also argued that capital punishment is an ancient sanction that has been adopted by most of our legislatures after prolonged consideration and reconsideration, and that we should not override this history.

But the argument is not persuasive. If we were to restrict the implementation of our Bill or Rights, by either constitutional decisions or legislative judgments, to those practices that its provisions contemplated in 1791, we would indeed be a retarded society. In 1816, Thomas Jefferson wrote a letter in which he spoke of the need for constitutions as well as other laws and institutions to move forward "hand in hand with the progress of the human mind." He said, "We might as well require a man to wear still the coat which fitted him when a boy, as civilized society to remain ever under the regimen of their barbarous ancestors."

. . .

We have also long recognized that the progressive implementation of the Bill of Rights does not depend upon first obtaining a majority vote or a favorable Gallup or Harris poll. As the Supreme Court stated in the famous 1943 flag-salute case, "The very purpose of a Bill of Rights was to place [certain subjects] beyond the reach of majorities and officials. . . ."

Indeed, despite our polls, public opinion is unfathomable; in the words of Judge Jerome Frank, it is a "slithery shadow"; and if known, no one can predict how profound or shallow it is as of the moment, and how long it will persist. Basically, however, the obligation of legislators and judges who question whether a law or practice is or is not consonant with our Constitution is inescapable; it cannot be delegated to the Gallup poll, or to the ephemeral evidence of public opinion.

We will not eliminate the objections to capital punishment by legal legerdemain, by "standards," by procedures or by word formulas. The issue is fundamental. It is wrong for the state to kill offenders; it is a wrong far exceeding the numbers involved. In exchange for the pointless exercise of killing a few people each year, we expose our society to brutalization; we lower the essential value that is the basis of our civilization: a pervasive, unqualified respect for life. And we subject ourselves and our legal institutions to the gross spectacle of a pageant in which death provides degrading, distorting excitement. Justice Felix Frankfurter once pointed out: "I am strongly against capital punishment. . . . When life is at hazard in a trial, it sensationalizes the whole thing almost unwittingly; the effect on juries, the bar, the public, the judiciary, I regard as very bad. I think scientifically the claim of deterrence is not worth much. Whatever proof there may be in my judgment does not outweigh the social loss due to the inherent sensationalism of a trial for life."

Beyond all of these factors is the fundamental consideration: In the name of all that we believe in and hope for, why must we reserve to ourselves the right to kill 100 or 200 people? Why, when we can point to no tangible benefit; why, when in all honesty we must admit that we are not certain that we are accomplishing anything except serving the cause of "revenge" or retribution? Why, when we have bravely and nobly progressed so far in the recent past to create a decent, humane society, must we perpetuate the senseless barbarism of official murder?

In 1971, speaking of the death penalty, Justice William O. Douglas wrote: "We need not read procedural due process as designed to satisfy man's deep-seated sadistic instincts. We need not in deference to those sadistic instincts say we are bound by history from defining procedural due process so as to deny men fair trials." I hope and believe we will conclude that the time has come for us to join the company of those nations that have repudiated killing as an instrument of criminal law enforcement.

QUESTIONS

1. What are the arguments for capital punishment? What are the arguments against it?

2. Opinion polls show that many of the people who support the antiabortion right-to-life movement are also in favor of capital punishment. Do you think these views can be consistent with one another?

3. Hypothesize as to why the United States is one of the few Western democracies that still has capital punishment.

JOHN C. MESSENGER

Sexuality: The Lack of the Irish

Perhaps more than any other form of social behavior, human sexual conduct seems to be "instinctive." People generally experience their sexual thoughts and feelings as though these were innate, an inevitable product of their biological being. Cross-cultural research by the social scientists has proven, however, that different societies have markedly different sexual norms, and that the sexual behavior of individuals is primarily the product of their socialization experiences in a particular culture.

Like many societies, modern and traditional, the United States is, on the whole, fairly permissive. Ireland, on the other hand, is a sexually restrictive society, and this is especially true of the more remote western parts of that country. In some areas, in fact, sexuality is so clouded with guilt and shame that even some married partners never see one another fully naked. These and similar attitudes, of course, are the product of historical and social forces, which shape the sexuality of the rural Irish no less than that of people in any other culture.

In this article, John Messenger describes the sexual norms that prevail in a small community in an island off the western coast of Ireland. You might bear in mind that, had you been born in that community, these would doubtless be your norms too.

Misconceptions about sex and lack of sexual knowledge among adults make Ireland's Inis Beag one of the most sexually naive of the world's societies, past or present. Sex is never discussed in the home when children are about; almost no mothers advise their daughters. Boys are better advised than girls, but the former learn about sex informally from older boys and men as well as from what they see animals do. Adults rarely give sexual instruction to youths, believing that after marriage nature takes its course, thus negating the need for anxiety-creating and embarrassing personal confrontations between parents and their offspring.

Unlike various other parts of peasant Ireland, Inis Beag has no case of childlessness based on the sexual ignorance of spouses. On the other hand the people of Inis Beag evince no knowledge of such sexual activities as insertion of tongue while kissing, male mouth on female breast, female hand on penis, cunnilingus, fellatio, femoral coitus, anal coitus, extramarital coitus, postmarital coitus, manifest homosexuality, sexual contact with animals, fetishism, or sadomasochistic behavior. Some of these activities may be practiced by particular individuals and couples. They are, however, deviant forms about which information is difficult to come by.

Anxiety

Inis Beag is the name that my wife and I gave to the small island community off the coast of Ireland where, since 1958, we have spent 19 months conducting ethnographic research. Most of our data on sex came from my involvement as a participant-observer in personal and often intimate conversations with men, and from my wife's giving advice to women bothered by such matters as explaining and coping with menstruation, the menopause, mental illness, the sexual curiosity of their children, and the "excessive" sexual demands of their spouses. Our sexual knowledge and sympathy, coupled with their needs and inquisitiveness, gave rise to counselor-client type relationships between us and many of the islanders. They came to speak freely, albeit indirectly at times, with each of us about this sphere of behavior which arouses so much anxiety and fear. I must mention that the relationship arose partly out of our desire to alleviate distress and not simply to collect information.

Menstruation and menopause arouse profound misgivings among women of the island because few of them comprehend their physiological significance. My wife was called on to explain these processes more than any other phenomena related to sex. Most girls on the island, when they reach puberty, are unprepared for the first menstrual flow and find the experience traumatic—especially when their mothers are unable to provide a satisfactory explanation. It is commonly believed that the menopause can induce insanity; in order to ward off this condition some women have retired from life in their mid-40s and in a few cases have confined themselves to bed until death years later. Others have retired as a result of depressive and masochistic states. Yet these harbingers of insanity are simply the physical symptoms . . . of menopause—severe headaches, hot flashes, faintness in crowds and enclosed places, and severe anxiety.

Sin

Sexual misconceptions are myriad in Inis Beag. The islanders share with most Western peoples the belief that men by nature are far more sexually disposed than women. Women are taught by the curate and in the home that sexual relations with their husbands are a duty that must be "endured," for to refuse coitus is a mortal sin. A frequently encountered Inis Beag assertion affixes the guilt for male libidinal strivings on their enormous intake of potatoes. Asked to compare the sexual proclivities of Inis Beag men and women, one woman said, "Men can wait a long time before wanting 'it,' but we can wait a lot longer." There is much evidence to indicate that the female orgasm is unknown—or at least doubted, or considered a deviant response. One middle-aged bachelor, who considers himself wise in the ways of the outside world, has a reputation for making love to willing tourists during the summer. He described to me the violent bodily reactions of a girl to his fondling and asked for an explanation; told the facts of life—about what obviously was an orgasm—he admitted that he had not realized that women could achieve climax, although he was aware that some of them apparently enjoyed lovemaking.

Inis Beag men share the belief, common in many primitive and folk societies, that sexual intercourse is debilitating. They will desist from sex the night before they are to do a job that takes great energy. They do not approach women sexually during menstruation or for months after childbirth; a woman is considered dangerous to the male at these times.

Returned "Yanks" have been denounced from the pulpit for describing American sexual practices to island youths. Such "pornographic" magazines as *Time* and *Life*, mailed by relatives from abroad, have aroused curates to spirited sermon and instruction.

Habit

It is often asserted that the major escape valve of frustration among single persons in Ireland is masturbation; however, frustration-aggression theorists would stress the ubiquity of drinking, alcoholism, pugnacity and factionalism as alternative outlets. Male masturbation seems to be common in Inis Beag, but premarital coitus is unknown and marital copulation limited as to foreplay and the manner of consummation.

My wife and I never witnessed courting—"walking out"—in the island. Elders proudly insist that it does not occur, but male youths admit to it in rumor. The claims of young men focus on petting with tourists and a few local girls; the bolder boys will kiss these girls and fondle them through their clothing. Island girls, it is held by their lovers, do not confess these sins because they do not enjoy the play. Their young men also shun the confessional—more probably because they fear the priest.

Marriage

Inis Beag has a population of approximately 350 persons living in 72 cottages distributed among four settlements, called villages. Although there are 59 nuclear families only 13 surnames exist today. There is much inbreeding, as might be expected, and the Church carefully checks genealogies to ascertain the degree of consanguinity of couples. Most marriages are arranged with little concern for the desires of the young people involved. Late marriage, bachelorhood and spinsterhood are as prevalent in Inis Beag as elsewhere in Ireland. The average marriage age is 36 for men and 25 for women, and 29 per cent of persons eligible for marriage remain celibate. The functions of the family are mainly economic and reproductive, and conjugal love is extremely rare. There is a sharp dichotomy between the sexes; men interact mostly with men and women with women, both before and after marriage. The average family has seven offspring, and many women are unhappy about being forced by the unauthorized decree of local priests to produce as many children as possible.

We were unable to determine the frequency of marital coitus. . . Evidence indicates that there is stress on privacy in the act. Foreplay is limited to kissing and to rough fondling of the lower body, especially the buttocks. The husband invariably initiates sexual activity. Male-superior is the only position; both wear underclothes; the man achieves orgasm quickly—and falls asleep almost immediately. (I must stress the provisional nature of these data, for they are based on a limited sample of respondents and relate to the sexual area of most circumspection.)

Nudity

Many kinds of behavior that other societies disassociate

from sex—nudity, for example, and evacuation of bowel and bladder—are considered sexual in Inis Beag. Islanders abhor nudity. The consequences of this attitude are numerous and significant for health and survival. Only an infant has his entire body sponged on Saturday nights; children, adolescents and adults on the same night wash only their faces, necks, lower arms, hands, lower legs and feet. Several times my wife and I caused intense embarrassment by entering a room in which a man had just finished his weekly wash and was barefooted; once when this occurred the man hurriedly pulled on his stockings, saying with obvious relief, "Sure, it's good to get your clothes on again." Clothing is always changed in private, sometimes under the bedcovers, and islanders ordinarily sleep in their underclothes.

The sexual symbolism of nudity has cost lives. Seamen who never learned to swim because swimming would have involved scant dress have drowned when they might have saved themselves. Sick men who were unwilling to face a nurse because it might mean baring their bodies to her were beyond help when they finally were treated. While my wife and I were on the island the mother of a young man assaulted a nurse for diagnosing his illness in the mother's absence and bathing his chest. (In this case Oedipal attitudes were probably at work with sexual attitudes.)

"Dirty"

Secrecy surrounds elimination. Islanders discourage infants from evacuating before siblings and strangers. They drive out animals that discharge in the house and soon kill and eat chickens that habitually "dirty" their nests while setting.

Although some women drink spirits privately, they seldom do so at parties. In part this is because of the embarrassment of having to make the trip to the outside toilet with men looking on. Other major manifestations of sexual puritanism in Inis Beag are the lack of a dirty-joke tradition (at least as the term is understood by ethnologists and folklorists), and a style of dancing that allows little bodily contact among participants. I have heard men use various verbal devices—innuendos, puns, asides—that they believed bore sexual connotations; relatively speaking they were pallid. In a ballad that I composed, one line refers to an islander who arises late in the day after "dreaming perhaps of a beautiful mate." Islanders regard this as highly suggestive and I have seen it redden cheeks and lower glances in a pub.

Church

When we search for the mainsprings of sexual repression in Inis Beag we must consider the role of the curate, the influence of visiting "missions," enculturation in the home, and what I will term secular social control—the behavioral regulations that adolescents and adults impose on themselves.

Priests of Jansenist persuasion have used subtle means to repress the sex drives of the islanders as supplements to the more extreme behavior-control methods, such as the use of informers, the withholding of the sacraments, and the placing of curses on miscreants. Curates have free use of the pulpit and the national school. Priests often have sought out erring islanders and talked to them privately when their transgressions have become known through gossip, informers, or the confessional. Some curates have roamed the trails and fields at night seeking out young lovers and have halted dances with their threatening presence. Most folks resent overt intrusion into island affairs as they do the more inward intrusion of priestly remonstrances; they ask what right the young, virginal, inexperienced and sexually unknowledgeable curates have to give advice and pass judgment in the sexual sphere.

The Church also exerts its influence through missions that visit Inis Beag every three to five years. On these occasions priests (Redemptorists usually, but Franciscans, Dominicans and Passionists also come) spend a week on the island, where they conduct Mass each morning and preach long sermons in the chapel every afternoon or early evening. A mission usually has a theme and the visiting priests explore its variations with high emotion and eloquence in their exhortations. The most common theme is "controlling one's passions," but two others often recur: abstaining from intoxicating drink and maintaining the faith as an emigrant. Children make collections to support the missions, posting a public list of contributors and their respective donations. The curate also uses this technique of social control at the several yearly offerings.

Function

The seeds of repression are planted early in children through parental instruction, conscious imitation, and unconscious internalization. Although mothers give much attention and affection to their children, especially to their sons, such physical love as fondling and kissing is rare in Inis Beag. Even breast-feeding is rare because of its sexual connotation, and verbal affection comes to replace contact affection by late infancy. Parents and relatives severely punish any direct or indirect sexual expression by children—masturbation, mutual exploration of bodies, use of either standard or slang words relating to sex, and open urination and defecation. Mothers take care to cover the bodies of infants in the presence of their siblings and outsiders, and sex is never discussed before children.

Lad

To the man in his late 20s and 30s who is secure in his home and has established regularized patterns of conduct (and has a mother who acts as a wife-surrogate), the general responsibilities of marriage, specifically its sexual responsibility, militate against his seeking a spouse. Some men who have land, the consent of their parents, and a willing woman will balk at a match because they are too happy "with the lads." If they are persuaded to marry they will try to retain within marriage as much of the bachelor role as possible. (A man is a "lad" until he is 40.) Islanders hinted to my wife and me on several occasions that particular island bachelors and spinsters almost married several times in succession only to find the sexual commitment too difficult to make at the last moment.

Poor

The population of Inis Beag has dropped from a high of 532 in 1861 (up 76 from the pre-famine census of 1841) to 497 in 1881, 483 in 1901, 409 in 1926, 376 in 1956, and approximately 350 four years later.

By far the most important reason why Inis Beag has long had a faltering population is the total cultural impact of sexual puritanism and the secular "excesses" of the clergy. Paul Blanshard writes in *The Irish and Catholic Power:* "When all the reasons for a flight from Ireland have been mentioned, there still remains a suspicion that Irish young people are leaving their nation largely because it is a poor place in which to be happy and free. Have the priests created a civilization in which the chief values of youth and love are subordinate to Catholic discipline?" What "remains a suspicion" to Blanshard is fully confirmed by a wealth of data from Inis Beag.

QUESTIONS

1. How would you characterize the sexual norms prevalent in rural Ireland? What social forces created and maintain those norms?

2. How would you characterize the sexual norms prevalent in the United States? How do these differ from the norms of a generation ago? What social factors have facilitated the emergence of the present norms?

3. "Normal" sexual behavior in one place or time may be "abnormal" in another. Given this fact, is there any universal standard for sexual morality?

DONNA D. SCHRAM

Rape

Rape is one of the most brutal of crimes, for its effects endure long after the physical assault is over: the psychological scars may take years to heal. It is also a common crime—about 280,000 incidents are believed to occur in the United States each year—although the victims are so reluctant to face police and courtroom interrogation that only about a quarter actually report the offense. The fear of rape, too, is a pervasive one, affecting the routine lives of women and restricting when and where they can go out alone.

For many years rape has been severely misunderstood, its reality largely obscured by a series of myths: that women who are raped were "asking for it"; that many secretly enjoy it; that rapists usually act on sudden impulse; that rape is an act of uncontrolled sexual passion. Only recently have these myths been proved false, largely through a dovetailing of two separate social trends: a concerted series of studies by sociologists and psychologists of this hitherto neglected area, and a determination by the women's movement to campaign against rape and to bring out the facts about rape and rapists. The crime is now revealed for what it usually is: an act of violence, not passion, by men whose sexual inadequacy leads them to assert their "masculinity" by humiliating and debasing the opposite sex.

In this article, Donna Schram presents a comprehensive survey of the findings of social science research on the subject.

"Rape," by Donna D. Schram, reprinted from *The Victimization of Women*, Jane Roberts Chapman and Margaret Gates (eds.), © 1978 by Sage Publications, Beverly Hills.

Rape can be the most terrifying event in a woman's life. The sexual act or acts performed are often intended to humiliate and degrade her: bottles, gun barrels, or sticks may be thrust into her vagina or anus; she may be compelled to swallow urine or perform fellatio with such force that she thinks she might strangle or suffocate; her breasts may be bitten or burned with cigarettes. In many instances, her hope is to save her life, not her chastity. Her terror may be so great that she urinates, defecates, or vomits. If she escapes without serious outward signs of injury, she may suffer vaginal tears or infections, contract venereal disease, or be impregnated. For months or years afterward, she may distrust others, change residences frequently, and sleep poorly. Her friends and family may blame or reject her.

If she chooses to report her offense to authorities, she may suffer further trauma. She must relate her account to patrol officers, detectives, medical personnel, counselors, filing prosecutors, and, perhaps, trial prosecutors. She might be *required* to submit to a polygraph or psychiatric examination to determine the veracity of her statement. If a suspect is arrested, she might be subjected to direct and cross-examination at a preliminary hearing and trial. Her testimony may not be protected against inquiries into her previous sexual relationships with other men or with the defendant. Thus, her private life may be exposed in a public and open forum; testimony regarding her prior chastity may be used to discredit her account of the rape.

Given these circumstances, it is not surprising that many women choose not to report rape offenses to the police. Indeed, victimization studies have shown that rape is probably the most underreported of all major crimes. If victimization estimates are accurate, the *actual* number of rapes is approximately four times the reported number, or one quarter of a million rapes per year. Thus, rape is *not* an infrequent offense; it is simply an infrequently reported offense.

Public interest in the crime of rape has been generated primarily by activists in the women's movement. The act of forcible sexual assault and the subsequent treatment of the victim by criminal justice authorities have come to symbolize the most extreme example of the abuse of a woman's body and her integrity. As these abuses have been exposed to public scrutiny, this previously "unmentionable" act has become the subject of media dramatizations, as well as discussions in public schools, churches, and civic organizations. This attention has created an atmosphere conducive to the reform of antiquated rape legislation, the development of more rigorous procedures for rape enforcement (e.g., Still, 1975; Lichtenstein, 1974; Bard and Ellison, 1974; Cottell, 1974), and an insistence on more sensitive treatment of victims by agents of the criminal justice system and the medical profession (e.g., Putnam and Fox, 1976; Hayman, 1970; Burgess and Holmstrom, 1976). In addition to these more institutionalized changes, rape crisis lines, victim advocacy services, and mental health services have been established to assist victims in communities large and small throughout the United States.

Precisely because of this public interest in the crime of rape, research in this area has proliferated during recent years. The first large national study (Brodyaga et al., 1975) resulted in the publication by the Law Enforcement Assistance Administration of a Prescriptive Package intended to provide guidelines for police, prosecutors, medical personnel, and service groups involved with rape victims. A second national study, and the one from which much of the information for this article was drawn, was conducted by the Battelle Institute Law and Justice Center Study under grants from the National Institute of Law Enforcement and Criminal Justice of the Law Enforcement Assistance Administration. Taken together, these and other studies have helped to identify and understand the dynamics of rape, the circumstances under which such offenses usually occur, the social and psychological implications of victimization, needed legislative change, and improvement in the treatment of victims and the enforcement of rape statutes. Thus, we are beginning to understand this crime and the most appropriate response to it.

The Rapist

Despite a rather considerable literature on sex offenders, it is extremely difficult to draw a consistent picture of the rapist, his motives, or his potential for "successful" treatment. For example, rapists have been variously described as antisocial or psychopathic (Henn et al., 1976), autistic and depressive (Takakuwa et al., 1971), less intelligent than other convicted felons (Ruff and Templer, 1976), average or above in intelligence (Cormier and Sickert, 1969; Perdue and Lester, 1972), good treatment prospects (Marshall and McKnight, 1975; Sadoff, 1975), or poor treatment prospects (Pacht, 1976). Still other authors suggest that it is a myth to presume that rapists share common characteristics. According to Pacht and Cowden (1974), the obvious lack of homogeneity among assaultive sex offenders suggests that there are more similarities between rapists and ourselves than there are differences. Thus, readers who search the literature on rapists are likely to emerge from the process more confused and perplexed than before they began.

One cause of this confusion is the sampling bias inherent in research on rapists. Of all the rapes actually reported to the police, only a very small number of suspects are ever arrested, charged, and convicted of rape. Recent research conducted at the Battelle Law and Justice Study Center (1977) suggests that suspect attrition is so great at each stage of the criminal process that less than 3% of rape reports are disposed as rape convictions. The remaining 97% of the offenders are never arrested, never charged, never convicted, and never participate in research intended to explore the psychodynamics of sexual assault. The subjects in such research are usually drawn from that tiny fraction of the rapist population which is actually adjudicated and convicted. Whether this small sample of rapists is representative of the entire population of offenders is subject to serious question.

Despite the methodological limitations of research on sex offenders, Cohen et al. (1971) conducted extensive clinical assessments of convicted rapists. These authors describe three basic types of offenders, differentiated on the basis of the underlying motivation for the sexual assault. In the first type, *aggressive aim*, rape serves to humiliate, degrade, and defile the victim. These offenders often describe their own emotional state as anger. The rape itself is often accompanied by sexual mutilation or insertion of objects into the vagina or anus of the victim. These rapists are often highly skilled, competitive, and physically attractive. Human relationships, however, are usually shallow, friendships are rare. Prognosis for treatment is good. In the second type of offender, rape serves a *sexual aim*. Rapes committed by these offenders usually demonstrate a relative absence of violence and lack characteristics of brutality. Victims are almost always strangers. These rapists are shy, socially inept, and isolated from male peers. School records usually show poor performance and, frequently, withdrawal before graduation. Long-term treatment prognosis is good. In the third type of rapist, *sexual aggression diffusion*, the offenders demonstrate a strong component of sadism which appears to be necessary to achieve sexual arousal. These offenders are often impotent until they are able to provoke resistance from their potential victims. In the extreme, lust, murder, or mutilation may occur. These offenders are often assertive, manipulative, and somewhat hostile in all situations. This type of rapist demonstrates the greatest paranoid features and does not appear to benefit from therapy. This assessment suggests that rapists do not fit any particular stereotype. Furthermore, the sexuality associated with rape may be less important for many offenders than the pain and humiliation they are able to inflict on their victims. Thus, rape might be appropriately viewed as a crime of violence, rather than a crime of passion.

The more recent Battelle study of rape relied on two other methods to examine the characteristics and behaviors of offenders. The first of these methods was an analysis of 1,261 rape victim reports made to the police in Seattle, Detroit, Kansas City (Missouri), New Orleans, and Phoenix. Of particular interest were the age and race of offenders, the circumstances of the initial contact between victims and offenders, the location of the rape offense, and threats or weapons used against the victims. The second research method consisted of interviews with a group of 50 incarcerated offenders who were patients at Atascadero State Hospital in California, a maximum security mental institution for the treatment of sex offenders. Topics explored in the course of the interviews included types of victims selected, the amount and kind of prerape planning undertaken, modus operandi, the effects of victim resistance on offender behavior, and the perceived influence of potentially sexually arousing stimuli, such as victim clothing and pornographic materials. This combination of research methods (police reports and offender interviews) provided the offender information discussed below.

Age of Offenders

Victim estimates indicated that the majority of offenders were between the ages of 18 and 25 years old. In much the same way that women over 30 were not likely to be raped, men over 30 were not likely to be rapists. Men 40 years old or older were almost never involved in forcible sexual assaults; they made up less than 4% of the offender population.

Race of Offenders

According to victim reports, minority males were consistently overrepresented in the offender population. This overrepresentation was true in all jurisdictions examined, whether the minority population was small or large. In the overwhelming majority (80%) of all cases that involved multiple rapists the offenders were minority males.

Number of Offenders

There is a substantial literature which suggests that the psychological and sociological dynamics of pair rape (two offenders) or group rape (three or more offenders) differ significantly from those which underlie rapes committed by single individuals. Group rape, in particular, has been variously explained as the manifestation of frustration/ aggression, where hostility and inadequacy are coupled with a collective need to dominate (MacDonald, 1974),

the eroticized adulation of one boy for another (Blanchard, 1959), or the outcome of social resentment based upon a general pattern of social disorganization (Woods, 1969). Whatever the genesis of paired or group rape, it has been thought to constitute a substantial proportion of all sexual assaults. In Amir's (1971) well-known study of rape in Philadelphia, for example, 43% of the victim reports examined involved more than one offender. From this, one might conclude that multiple offender rapes account for as many as one half of all reported rapes. More recent data, however, do *not* substantiate this conclusion.

Analyses of 1974 and 1975 police reports from Seattle, Detroit, Kansas City, New Orleans, and Phoenix indicate that the overwhelming majority of rapes are committed by a single individual who attacks a lone woman. Paired rapes accounted for 11–17% of the complaints; group rapes accounted for 3–4% of the victimizations. Thus, multiple rapists are rare. When such offenses were observed, they usually involved juvenile males under the age of 18 years.

Location of First Contact Prior to Offense

The traditional view of rape assumes that sex-crazed males lurk in alleys and roam darkened streets in search of unsuspecting prey whom they may assault. Although this type of rape certainly exists, it does not describe the most frequent circumstances under which victims and offenders come into contact. Indeed, in the cases studied, it was not the street that represented the greatest risk of sexual assault to a woman—it was her own home. This location was followed in frequency by street encounters. Of the nine other initial contact locations identified from the police reports, only the automobile of the offender stood out as a consistently high-risk location. Initial contacts established at taverns, social gatherings, and so forth were relatively uncommon.

Location of Offense

The location of the initial contact between the offender and the victim was not always a good indicator of the actual location of the offense. There was a general tendency to move the actual crime scene to an indoor or more private location. Thus, although the victim's residence remained the most likely location of the assault, the offender's residence or his automobile became the next most frequent locations. Relatively few rapes were actually consummated in public places, such as streets or parks.

Threats

Approximately 70% of all rape reports included clear indications that the offender threatened force or used force against the victim. In most instances, these consisted of verbal threats of harm or death to the victim or to someone related to the victim. In other cases, the mere presence of a weapon was defined as a threat; no verbalizations were necessary. Occasionally, threats, physical force, and a weapon were all used. The victim statement in one police report illustrates such a case.

> He hit me in the face and knocked me on the floor. He pulled off my robe and nightgown and I screamed and he threatened to kill me. He stuffed the nightgown in my mouth and tied the rest around my throat and the gown strangled me. He tied my hands behind my back and he pressed my neck so hard I passed out. Then he asked me if I needed air and I nodded and he let it loose a bit but still kept it in my mouth. He tied my legs up to the tie on my hands . . . then he got my butcher knife from the kitchen and ran the point all over my body.

Weapons

The frequency with which weapons were present or used during sexual assaults varied considerably from one police jurisdiction to another. Nearly 60% of all reported rapes in Detroit involved weapons of some kind; in contrast, only 33% of the rapes reported to Seattle authorities involved weapons.

The weapon of choice was usually a handgun, although knives were used almost as frequently. In addition to guns and knives, an incredible variety of other weapons were also used or threatened. Occasionally these "weapons" were everyday items, such as pencils, metal combs, and rolling pins. In other instances, menacing weapons were formed from broken bottles, fire pokers, burning cigarette butts, and rocks. Some type of weapon was identified in approximately one half of all police reports examined.

Type of Victim Selected

Rape is not a crime inflicted on random members of the female population. Many victims share similar characteristics which, it is assumed, influence their selection as victim targets. The first and most obvious of these characteristics is age. In general, rape is a crime committed against young women. Based upon analyses of rapes reported in the five police jurisdictions, more than 50% of all rapes were committed against women who were less than 21 years old. Once a woman reached the age of 30, the likelihood of being raped decreased precipitously.

Perhaps no other myth is more prevalent in rape lore than that which asserts that most sexual assaults occur in dating situations in which the victim provoked her own attack. Although such cases may occur, the frequency of such attacks is inconsequential. In one half or more of all rapes, the offender and the victim are completely unknown to one another. Almost without exception, the of-

fenders interviewed at Atascadero committed this type of rape. Even though the victim targets were strangers to these offenders, most of the subjects professed some reasonably firm concept of the type of woman they preferred to rape and the methods necessary to locate such individuals. When offenders were asked to describe their victim preferences in detail, the picture which emerged was that of the "all American woman"—a nice, friendly, young, pretty, white housewife or college student. These same offenders were asked to indicate those characteristics that would make women undesirable victims. Leading the list were females who were crippled, dirty, children, sick, pregnant, retarded, fat, middle-aged, or prostitutes (Chappell and James, 1976:8–9).

Planning the Rape

Earlier research suggested that a significant proportion of rapes were spontaneous or explosive acts wherein the offender exploited an opportunity to attack a vulnerable target. Thus, a burglar might discover that a dwelling he has entered is occupied by a lone woman. Because of the circumstances, the burglar takes advantage of the situation and woman, and rapes her.

The extent to which a rape of this type is truly spontaneous is a matter of conjecture. A large proportion of the rapists interviewed at Atascadero had prior arrests for both burglary and robbery. While details of these earlier arrests and convictions for offenses other than rape were not obtained during interviews, almost a third of the subjects indicated that their primary objective had been rape in previously committed burglaries and robberies. Further, seemingly spontaneous rapes that resulted in the offenders' present incarceration exhibited a certain degree of premeditation or planning. When questioned generally about the planning engaged in before a rape, 36% of the group said they did none, 52% said some, and 12% said a considerable amount. There was quite a bit of leeway in the definition of planning, as the following three cases illustrate (Chappell and James, 1976:11).

CASE 1

It was spur of the moment. I would fantasize it. My sort of planning was that I would just find a piece of ass and take it because I was only concerned for myself. I wanted some sex. Actually there was no planning but there was planning already about the idea. There was no planning like, I would say, a robbery. You know, at 10 o'clock you're going to do this, at 10:05 you're going to be in there. With mine, there was not that kind of tactic planning. I was in the restaurant and I was pretty well bombed and I thought my friend took me home but evidently he didn't. He took me instead to my girlfriend's house. Then she took me home, that was about an hour and a half. Then I blacked out. Somewhere in there I grabbed this woman and had a piece of ass.

CASE 2

I found a couple of guy friends I knew. We started a party up—a big party and we went down to a place where a hangout is—where a lot of people hang out—and we picked up three chicks and took then over to the party. All the three chicks were jumping from car to car and were pretty wild and we figured it would be easy to put the make on. So we got over there to the party and we had some weed. We were there about an hour and I asked the girl if she wanted to go out in the car and get some fresh air. Like she had been kind of standoffish at the party towards me and so I imagined the whole thing to take her out in the car and rape her. I didn't know for sure but—anyway, we got out in the car and I tried to kiss her and she pushed me away and that got me mad. I grabbed her neck and told her that if she made a sound or made a struggle, I would kill her.

CASE 3

I went to work. There were two girls at work who planned to go to the park—the lake the next day which we did. One girl we dropped off home; the other girl I went to a bar with and she said, "I want to be with you tonight." So I figured I'd have a piece of ass, but I got too drunk and threw up and she went off with somebody else that she picked up at the bar. I went home and woke up angry in the morning and I was determined to get a piece of ass—if I couldn't I would rape. I drove around this area that I knew there were some girls living in these apartments and this one girl that I particularly wanted to rape—I rang her doorbell, this guy answered the door and I made up some excuse about my car being broken down and I wanted some assistance and to use the telephone. I saw this girl walk into her apartment carrying her laundry and I asked her if she had a telephone and she said "yes." And that I could use it and I made a couple of phony phone calls working my courage up and she offered to give me a dime and I grabbed her and pulled her down and I told her I wouldn't hurt her if she cooperated. I was in her apartment and I made sure the door was locked when I went in. I tied her up and took her clothes off and went to the bedroom and raped her. I was feeling angry. Afterwards, I had a cigarette and talked to her abour 45 minutes and I split.

The subject in Case 1 denied any specific planning prior to the rape and distinguished the sex offense from robbery in this regard. Case 2 illustrates apparent premeditation, but only after a potential victim had been observed. Indeed, this offender appeared to be attracted by the standoffish behavior of the least provocative woman. Finally, Case 3 portrays an act of pure premeditation. This offender was determined to rape any vulnerable woman while, at the same time, minimizing the risk of interruption or apprehension.

Release of the Victim

According to the offender interview responses, victims were usually released immediately after the rape event, although a number of offenders subsequently engaged the victim in a conversation or drove her to a less accessible spot before letting her go. Approximately one half of the sample made some effort to convince the woman not to report the offense to police. The most common tactic used to deter such a report was to threaten bodily harm to the victim. Sixteen percent of the offenders also threatened to return again because they knew the identity of the victim and where she lived.

Almost a third of the sample said they would rape the same woman twice. This rather surprising proportion of potentially repeating offenders based their reason for return on the following (in order of importance): victim responded well; they were invited back; a good relationship was established; a desire to further humiliate the woman; the woman agreed not to report the rape to police. The remainder of the offenders expressed no desire to return, usually because of fear of being caught.

In many cases, associated crime was found to be part of the release situation. Approximately three quarters of the offenders indicated that they would commit some additional crime beyond the rape. Robbery was the most common, followed by theft, then assault. After leaving the victim, 18% of the subjects said they would consider committing another rape the same evening (Chappell and James, 1976).

Attitudes Toward Women

Although many men who rape may suffer serious psychological disturbances, there is no reason to assume that their attitudes toward women, sex, and violence are significantly different from those of other males. Even the offenders interviewed at Atascadero, for example, believed that the prevention or avoidance of rape was the responsibility of the female. When asked specifically how such acts could be prevented, the rapists sounded very much like crime prevention officers. Women were advised not to go out alone (32%), not to hitchhike (36%), to learn self-defense (16%), to buy a dog (8%), to carry weapons (6%), to dress conservatively (6%), and not to drink alone (2%).

These findings and this advice will depress or enrage many women, for they represent an impingement on their basic freedoms. However, the findings and advice should come as no surprise, for they reflect, in part, the male attitudes toward women that have been so thoroughly condemned by feminist writers such as Brownmiller (1975) and Russell (1975).

Offenders at Atascadero not only believed that women were responsible for rape avoidance, they also considered many of their offenses the result of provocative or "lead on" situations created by their victims. The following statements by rapists typify these attitudes:

CASE 1

I believe that women who want to be fashionable in some of the styles that are sexually stimulating to men should try to realize some of the consequences of wearing some of these styles before they wear them. Carrying themselves a little better in public when they do wear them—men are going to look, quite naturally, but all men aren't the same. Some of them are going to make more advancements—more aggressive advancements than others in certain situations. If a woman just happens to be weak and not realize what it means, then she's in trouble. That's just the way it is.

CASE 2

Once again, I would say again, by body language—or unconsciously they flirt—sometimes the way that they dress—their minds say one thing—their bodies say another—or some come on with their seduction-type overall tone—that says one thing but could possibly mean something else. Or they put themselves in the position of being alone.

CASE 3

By hitchhiking—being real loose with themselves—maybe not wearing bras or something like this—so you can see through—or where you can tell where they are drooping down or something like that—by wearing short dresses—being alone at night time walking around.

All three statements imply that victim behavior or apparel arouses an overwhelming sexual desire which men are unable to overcome short of ravaging the provocateur. Thus, the responsibility for the rape is shifted from the helpless male to the cunning or careless female. The error of such misplaced responsibility is best expressed by Bromberg and Coyle (1974):

The average rapist . . . rarely admits his aggressive motives, either during or after the offense; he prefers to accept his act as evidence of sexual need which other men will understand. The purely sexual aspect of rape is more congenial to the perpetrator's inner feelings than his basic desire to demean women.

This statement succinctly describes precisely why it is that rape has so often been viewed merely as an unwanted, albeit illegal, act of sexual intercourse. The underlying element of violence and the offender's intent to humiliate and degrade the victim are usually overlooked. Instead, it is the woman's behavior that is judged to determine the extent of her contributory negligence.

The Victim

Most of the information on rape victims comes from those who report offenses to police or to medical personnel. The means by which they report and their reasons for doing so suggest that these victims share much in common. In the course of the Battelle study (1977), for example, victims were asked to specify their main reasons for reporting to police. When victim responses were analyzed, a very interesting pattern of reasons emerged. These victims reported because they wanted the criminal justice system to *do* something to the offender. Anger, revenge, and outrage were common motivations that apparently were so intense that they overcame any concern for personal embarrassment or fear of mistreatment by the criminal justice system. In essence, these women reported because they wanted protection for themselves and for other women.

These same victims were also asked whether, on the basis of their experience, they would advise other women to report a rape to the police. An overwhelming 98% of the victims responded affirmatively; i.e., they would recommend reporting. When victims were asked why women should report, the majority indicated that official complaints might serve to *save* others:

"If a lady lets it go, he might go on to kill another woman."

"Save another woman's life."

"To protect themselves and others from the sickness of people who rape."

or to *punish* others:

"Help get some of these sadists off the street."

"Why let the rapist go fancy free?"

or to assure treatment and emotional support:

"It helps to talk to someone."

"To get medical and counseling help."

Only two victims advised against reporting. In both instances, the victims felt that police treatment was so poor that other women should be discouraged from making official complaints.

In the course of the Battelle research project, 1,261 initial rape complaints were obtained from five large police agencies throughout the United States. On the basis of these reports, it was possible to gather an enormous quantity of data regarding the characteristics of victims, the circumstances prior to and during the sexual assaults, victim resistance, victim injury, and the kinds of forced sexual acts attempted or performed. The information presented below summarizes some of those findings.

Age of Victims

Victim ages obtained from police reports clearly demonstrate that rape is a crime committed against young women. More than 50% of the rapes were committed against women under the age of 21. In much the same way that men over the age of 30 were not likely to be rapists, women over the age of 30 were not likely to be victims. Elderly women were almost never raped.

Race of Victim

In most jurisdictions from which records were obtained, minority women were overrepresented in the victim population. This finding was particularly true in the 61 cases in which there was more than one victim. Fifty-nine percent of all multiple victim cases involved black and Asian-American women.

Relationship Between Victim and Offender

For the purposes of this research, the relationships between the victim and the offender were divided into four categories. The first category consisted of *strangers*; that is, the actors had no acquaintance or knowledge of one another before the sequence of events that terminated in the assault. The second and third categories, *acquainted* or *friends*, were more difficult to distinguish. Victims and offenders were defined as "acquaintances" if they had merely met or were known to one another by reputation prior to the offense. In contrast, the term "friend" was used to define long-standing or previously intimate relationships. The fourth category included all rapes between persons who, either by blood or by marriage, were *related* to one another.

The findings indicated that, among the police jurisdictions studied, approximately one half of all rapes involved strangers. An additional one quarter of all rapes occurred between acquaintances. Rape between friends made up less than 20% of the reported assaults in any jurisdiction. In general, these rapes occurred subsequent to planned dating situations or other social interactions. Finally, rapes involving relatives were extremely rare. When such rapes were reported, they usually involved an offender who was related to the victim by marriage, i.e., stepfather or brother-in-law, for example.

Victim Resistance

Police records indicated the majority of women resisted their sexual assault. Initial resistance was usually verbal and fell into one of three categories. The first category included verbal methods whereby the victim attempted to make herself unattractive to the offender or elicit his sympathy; the woman indicated that she was pregnant, sick, diseased, virginal, or menstruating. Examples of this method drawn from case records include the following:

CASE 1

He just stood there over the kid with his flashlight in my face and told me to take my nightgown off—QUICK! I didn't move at all. I couldn't see his face because he kept the light in my eyes. He reached down and pulled back the covers. I told him, I couldn't have intercourse. I told him I was hemoraging (*sic*) and had just been to the doctor the day before.

He said "Good, you bitch. I can play like you are a virgin."

CASE 2

————and me had just been listening to music. We had drunk a little wine and he started pulling at my sweater. He told me to take my clothes off and lay on the rug or he would break my arm off. I told————that I hadn't ever done it before and I was afraid I would have a baby. ————said what the hell did I come over there for if I didn't want a screw. Girls just didn't come over and drink his wine and think they could leave when they wanted to.

The second category of verbal resistance consisted of *threats* that, if the offender persisted, the victim would prosecute or seek retaliation from her family or friends. Finally, some victims attempted to feign stipulated consent, that is, they indicated a willingness to engage in sexual activity if they could first use the restroom, change clothes, call a friend, or so forth. Although these latter ruses sometimes allowed an occasional victim to escape the situation, verbal resistance was singularly ineffective in thwarting sexual assaults. Victims were seldom able to deter the rapist with "talk" no matter which of the various verbal tactics were used.

A related method of victim resistance consisted of crying, either from fear or as a means to underscore her lack of consent. Again, as in cases of verbal resistance, rapists were seldom deterred by this behavior.

Approximately 20% of all victims reported that they screamed or used some device (a whistle, for example) in an effort to attract attention. Whether or not the victims' actions actually attracted assistance from others, this was the most effective method of terminating a sexual assault. Unfortunately, it was also likely to cause some offenders to become more violent in attempts to silence the screams.

Many victims attempted to physically resist their assailants. In general, this resistance took the form of struggling, hitting, biting, and kicking the offender. Nearly 20% of the victims attempted to run from the scene. Although struggling or fighting with the assailant seldom terminated the assault, victims who were able to run sometimes escaped their attackers. Examples from police records indicated the futility most victims experienced when they attempted physical resistance.

CASE 1

He pulled real hard on my right arm and I fell down on one knee. I bit him hard on the arm but he hit me real hard on my ear with his fist. . . . Then I tried to hit him with my fists but he just laughed . . .

CASE 2

I told————I would poke his m————f————eyes out

if he laid one finger on me. He just sat there for a minute and stared out the windshield. Then he looked back at me and said something like "Ain't six of you could stop me when I get fired up." I tried to hit him but he just grabbed my arms and shoved them over mine [*sic*] head.

Victim Injury

The rape reports indicated that approximately one third of all victims were injured. In most instances, the physical injuries were relatively minor and consisted of bruises and cuts that did not require extensive medical treatment. More serious injuries usually involved severe bruises or cuts, vaginal tears, internal bleeding or bruising, broken bones, broken teeth, or concussions. (Note: No records of rape-homicide were examined in the course of this research. Thus, injuries that caused the death of victims were not included in this analysis.)

Counseling/Advocacy Services

During the course of the present research, many different forms of victim counseling and advocacy services were observed. In many cities, for example, rape crisis lines were operated by community volunteers who had undergone some form of specific training in crisis intervention, rape law, and criminal process. These volunteers were usually available around the clock so that they could respond quickly to the immediate emotional needs of rape victims and provide important medical and legal information. In other cities, services were available through mental health professionals who could provide more traditional, long-term counseling and assure proper medical follow-ups.

Although it was impossible to establish the total number of victims who used such services at each of the sites included in this study, the researchers were able to question victim interview respondents about their experiences. Of the 146 victims who answered this set of inquiries, one third had been in contact with a local rape crisis center or rape crisis line. Although most victims learned of the existence of such services from the media (38%) or family/friends (29%), it was not unusual for referrals to be made by police (15%) or by medical personnel (6%). If victims sought assistance from rape crisis centers/lines, they usually did so within one day of the assault.

When victims were asked their *main* reason for contacting the crisis/line center (multiple answers accepted), the most frequently mentioned answer (71%) was that they "needed to talk to someone." Other reasons for contact included the following: "needed criminal justice information" (46%); "needed someone to go with you to the medical facility" (35%); "needed medical information" (25%); and "wanted to make a third-party (anonymous) report to the police" (10%). In general, victims

seemed very satisfied with the services rendered. For example, *all* victims believed that the information they obtained from rape crisis workers was accurate, and all victims believed that they were treated either with a great deal of understanding (78%) or with understanding (22%). No victim believed she was treated with indifference or with disrespect.

A total of 114 victim respondents received some form of medical treatment. In most instances, the treatment related specifically to the victim's health, including examinations for injuries and tests for the presence of venereal diseases and pregnancy. The majority of victims also underwent vaginal and/or anal examinations to determine the presence of semen or sperm.

A substantial proportion of all rape victims experience some physical problem as a result of forcible sexual assaults. Among the victims interviewed, for example, 49% reported physical complications whether or not they received immediate medical treatment. The most frequent of these complications were bruises, cuts, or other injury (21%); vaginal infections (15%); urinary tract infections (9%); side effects from "morning after treatment" to prevent pregnancy (5%); venereal disease (4%); and pregnancy (2%). Thus, in addition to the psychological trauma of rape, many victims also experienced significant and lingering physical trauma as well.

Victim assessment of the *quality* of medical treatment afforded them was very mixed. For example, nearly one half of the victims had to wait two or more hours at a facility before they received any medical attention. The examinations themselves often required three or more additional hours. In fact, 34% of the victims spent a total of six or more hours at a medical facility between the time they arrived and the completion of their examinations.

In addition, more than one quarter of the victims were not satisfied with the treatment they received. Examining physicians, in particular, were often believed to have treated victims with indifference (19%) or disrespect (12%). Some victims (20%) complained that they were not given sufficient information about the medical tests performed. Finally, more than one third of all examinations (39%) were performed in general purpose emergency rooms which offered no privacy. Although this lack of privacy did not disturb all victims, many felt embarrassed and humiliated by this procedure.

Emotional Impact of Rape

Researchers and medical personnel have interviewed victims of rape immediately after the assault and during the weeks and months that follow. They have observed a common sequential pattern of emotional reactions which has come to be known as the *rape trauma syndrome*. Not all victims follow the identical pattern of response or experience the symptoms with the same intensity. However, virtually all victims experience some of the emotions described; thus the rape trauma syndrome provides a useful way to discuss the general reaction of victims to rape.

The first reaction, or acute phase, can last for several days after the rape and is most commonly characterized as extreme psychological shock. Since the victim may be unable to comprehend her situation or what she should do, she sometimes behaves in ways that appear illogical or irrational. The victim may not, for example, contact the police for several hours after the rape or she may bathe and wash her clothes repeatedly.

Every victim also experiences some degree of fear or terror. The forcible rape itself is most often perceived as a life-threatening event rather than a sexual intrusion. In all likelihood, threats were made on her life. This fear, once aroused, does not always diminish immediately upon termination of the sexual assault. It is this continued sense of apprehension and danger that may determine and explain many victim actions during the hours and days immediately after the rape.

In addition to fear, the victim is likely to experience a variety of other emotions. These can include anger, shame, guilt, anxiety, revenge, powerlessness, and humiliation. It is common for a victim to experience severe and abrupt mood swings immediately after the rape. A counselor or police officer may be talking with a victim when suddenly she demonstrates a surge of anger followed by expressions of guilt and self-blame. Such mood swings can be as surprising and unexpected to the victim as they are to the interviewer. Victims experience these feelings at different times and in different ways depending on the manner in which they normally cope with crisis.

A common style of victim response to an interview situation during this time is a calm, composed "I'm okay" demeanor which is sometimes known as the controlled reaction. Unfortunately, this type of response occasionally causes others to doubt the victim's account because she appears too "flat" and unemotional. Furthermore, this reaction of external calm allows others to form the mistaken belief that the victim will have no emotional consequences from the sexual assault.

During this time of crisis, a victim can revert to a state of dependence or helplessness. Because the sexual assault has disrupted her normal coping abilities, decision-making can become an ordeal. For some victims, it is easier and safer to seek direction and protection from friends, family members, or a person in a position of authority. This factor can be important if, for example, a relative or a friend has a strong opinion that the victim should or should not prosecute the rapist. The victim is also very sensitive to the attitudes and behavior of patrol officers, detectives, and prosecutors involved with her case. Lack of support from criminal justice personnel is likely to render the victim confused and uncooperative.

Victims often report significant disruptions in their daily routines. Some women, for example, are unable to sleep at night and are easily awakened by noises that would not have bothered them previously. Eating habits can also be affected by the stress of the rape. Frequently, women report loss of appetite or inability to eat. Others find that eating causes nausea and vomiting, especially if they were forced to perform oral sex. The victim's ability to concentrate may be greatly diminished and her attention span temporarily shortened. In sum, the victim's normal methods of coping with daily stress work so ineffectively that almost all of her life functions are temporarily disrupted.

Following the victim's intense emotional reaction to the rape, she often gives every appearance that she has learned to cope with the experience. Very often she does this by blocking out all thoughts of the rape and rearranging her daily life so that she is not reminded of the crisis. Although denial is usually only a temporary stage, it can interfere with criminal justice proceedings because the victim may wish to withdraw her complaint or become uncooperative with detectives or prosecutors who want her to relive the incident.

The final stage of dealing with rape trauma occurs over a long period of time and requires the victim to fully integrate the experience into her life as a whole. Because rape so dramatically upsets a woman's normal routines, the crisis can be a time for self-evaluation and new decisions. Many facets of the victim's life may be different after the rape. Some women find it necessary to change residences to feel safer and more secure. This is a particularly common behavior for women who are raped in their own homes or apartments. Other women spend a great deal of time, energy, and money to secure their living quarters with new locks, bolts, and alarm systems.

Victims may perceive themselves as changed by the rape either because they feel differently about themselves or because they believe that others see them as changed. Family support can be crucial at this time. Unfortunately, family members sometimes respond in ways that are not helpful to the woman. Victims describe husbands who doubt their account of what happened and are suspicious and accusatory. Parents sometimes find it difficult to talk about the sexual assault and try to dissuade the victim from thinking or talking about the incident. While they may wish to save the victim from recalling disturbing emotions surrounding the rape, it is not uncommon for the victim to conclude that what has happened to her has brought shame and embarrassment to her family.

Dreams, especially nightmares, are a common experience for women who have been raped. The dreams often consist of vivid pictures in which the victim relives the terror of the rape situation. The paralyzing feeling of doom is re-created with such reality that the victim awakens to the frightening powerlessness, loss of autonomy, and life-threatening fear of the rape itself.

In summary, the emotional impact of rape is often intense and may persist for months or even years. It is clear, however, that these symptoms can be alleviated if victims receive support from friends, family, criminal justice personnel, and the community. Certainly, rapes occur with sufficient frequency and destructiveness that the victims deserve special consideration.

Rape Law

The last half decade has seen unprecedented activity in the area of rape law reform. During the years 1973–1976, for example, new rape legislation was enacted in 36 states and proposed in an additional 13 states. The majority of these legislative changes have taken two forms: adoption of new and wider definitions of rape, and/or relaxation of the proof requirements for the crime. Rape has sometimes been redefined in terms of sex-neutral assault or battery, with several degrees based on the dangerousness of the circumstances of the assault or the kind of assault. One state, Michigan, has entirely abandoned the traditional law of rape and has created a new legal terminology to define a variety of sexual crimes.

Changes in proof requirements have taken a variety of forms. In many states, corroboration requirements have been eliminated or minimized. In addition, many legislatures have moved to restrict the admission of evidence of the victim's prior sexual conduct, and to eliminate both the cautionary instruction to the jury that the testimony of the victim is suspect and the chastity instruction that permits the jury to infer that a woman who has once consented to sexual intercourse is more likely to consent again than one who has not.

Other legal modifications include legislative mandates to provide special training for police and special medical procedures for the examination of rape victims. Some states have begun to provide high school instruction in self-defense. Finally, an earlier trend toward protecting the victim from public exposure (particularly exposure through the media) has been noted, although this movement has largely disappeared as a result of several Supreme Court cases which expanded freedom of the press with respect to criminal proceedings (Battelle Report, 1977:7).

Traditional Rape Law

Traditional rape law evolved through case-by-case judicial determination of what acts constituted the crime. This process of lawmaking, known as the common law system, defined rape as *unlawful carnal knowledge of a woman by force and against her will*. The slightest sexual penetration by the male penis of the female vagina was sufficient to complete the crime if the other elements were present. The common law instituted a resistance standard for the victim as a means to distinguish forcible carnal knowledge (rape) from consensual carnal knowledge (fornication or adultery). Both forms of carnal knowledge were crimes, but if the act were forcible, the victim escaped punishment for fornication or adultery (Battelle Report, 1977:11).

Legal theory has long held that

> a crime exists only when there is concurrence of an unacceptable act and a criminal intent with respect to that act. The unacceptable act is called the *actus reus*; the criminal intent is called the *mens rea*. In traditional definition of rape, the *actus reus* is the unconsented-to sexual intercourse and the *mens rea* is the intention or knowledge of having the intercourse without the consent of the victim. Lack of consent of the victim is ultimately the characteristic that distinguishes rape. The concurrence of the act and the intent requires both that the victim in fact not consent and that the perpetrator know at the time that the victim did not consent. [Battelle Report, 1977:34].

Thus, according to theory and common law tradition, the definition of rape depends upon both the perception of the victim that the intercourse was not consensual, and the perception of the defendant of that lack of consent. This two-pronged legal requirement raises obvious problems of interpretation since there will be no criminal intent in many instances where there is an unacceptable act. The victim may well perceive an intercourse as rape when the perpetrator does not.

Redefinition

As a result of this legal dilemma, several states have redefined rape in terms of the conduct of the rapist (force), rather than the behavior of the victim (resistance) or her state of mind (lack of consent). To date, eight states have eliminated the word "rape" from their statutes and developed a new vocabulary, using terms such as "criminal sexual assault" or "sexual battery," to connote a crime defined by the behavior of the offender. In addition, many states have made the crime of rape sex-neutral, thereby eliminating the presumption of female victims and male offenders (Battelle Report, 1977:17).

Proof Requirements

Although statutes differ from one state to another, there are generally three elements that must be proven in cases of rape: (1) the occurrence of sexual penetration or other forms of sexual contact; (2) the identification of the perpetrator; and (3) the establishment of force or lack of victim consent. Evidentiary rules to establish these elements are generally the same as those that apply to all criminal cases. However, a special set of rules that applies only to cases of rape has been devised.

Traditional common law did *not* require corroborative

evidence of each element of the crime to support a criminal conviction for rape. Courts simply relied upon juries to weigh the evidence, which might consist of nothing more than the victim's testimony, and render a verdict. It was assumed that a false complaint would be exposed in the adversary process, with the presumption of innocence serving to protect the defendant. Some courts departed from this tradition and established special corroboration requirements to confirm the victim's testimony (Battelle Report, 1977:69).

Where all three elements of the crime have required corroboration, very low conviction rates have been obtained. This result was most graphically shown under the strict corroboration requirements of the New York rape statute prior to 1972. In 1969 in New York City, for example, there were 1,085 arrests for rape and only 18 convictions. However, relaxation of the corroboration requirement does not necessarily lead to high rates of conviction.

> Even in states where there is no corroboration requirement, few cases are taken to trial without corroborating evidence. Furthermore, some states without corroboration requirements have erected other barriers to conviction, such as cautionary instructions or psychiatric examination of the victim. Thus, regardless of the formal corroboration requirements, an informal corroboration requirement and other screening devices may operate to exclude uncorroborated charges from the criminal justice system. It is only where corroboration requirements are extensive and narrowly interpreted that there appears to be a significant negative impact on the conviction rate. (Battelle Report, 1977:71).

In lieu of corroboration, such states have utilized an instruction to the jury that warns them to consider the testimony of the victim with caution. In its most common form, the instruction reads as follows:

> A charge such as that made against the defendant in this case, is one which is easily made and, once made, difficult to defend against, even if the person accused is innocent. Therefore, the law requires that you examine the testimony of the female person named in the information with caution.

The cautionary instruction, which arose from the 18th century writings of Sir Mathew Hale, has been eliminated in all but 13 states. The instruction has been attacked by feminists because it symbolizes a contemptuous attitude toward rape victims by the criminal justice system. Prosecutors have also objected to the instruction on the grounds that it creates unjustified doubt in the minds of jurors.

Some states have adopted a provision for the psychiatric examination of victims as an alternative to corroboration requirements. According to Wigmore (1970) and other legal scholars, all rape complainants should be psychiatrically examined as a means to eliminate false rape complaints. This belief is premised on the assumptions that many complaints are false, that false complaints arise from mental disorders, and that psychiatric examinations are able to discriminate between the truthful and the false complaints (Battelle Report, 1977:80).

Both victims and prosecutors have strongly opposed these examinations. The examination may constitute an affront to the victim that her account is inherently untrustworthy and her integrity questionable. She may choose to withdraw her complaint rather than accept this insult (Battelle Report, 1977:82).

Corroboration requirements, cautionary instructions, and psychiatric examinations of victims have all served to limit successful rape prosecutions. Although all of these special exceptions have been introduced to protect innocent defendants, they have done so by assuming that victims are lying. In addition, the attitudes that created these special requirements in rape cases have so infiltrated the criminal justice system that, even without common law or statutory exceptions, prosecution of rape cases often appears extremely timid. It is hoped that the recent legislative activity to remove these exceptions may make the proof for rape similar to the proof for other major crimes and, at the same time, alter attitudes to increase the successful prosecution of this offense.

Conclusion

Interest in rape victimization and its aftermath is not likely to dissipate in the near future. Although this interest may change its focus or form, rape will never again be an "unmentionable" topic to be kept from the ears and eyes of children and teenagers. Rape is a terrible crime that oftens imparts devastating consequences on the lives of victims and their families. Fortunately, society and its institutions seem to be responding in ways which suggest that rape victims will someday be treated with the respect they deserve.

QUESTIONS

1. Place the act of rape in the context of the general cultural norms and values concerning the relationship of the sexes.
2. What are the myths about rape? What are the realities?
3. Why are women afraid to report rape? How do police and courtroom interrogations tend to differ from those applied to the victims of other crimes? How is this phenomenon related to the patterns of sexual interaction in society?

References

Amir, M. (1971). Patterns in forcible rape. Chicago: University of Chicago Press.

Bard, M., and Ellison, K. (1974). "Crisis intervention and investigation of forcible rape." Police Chief, (May):68.

Battelle Law and Justice Study Center Report (1977). Forcible rape: An analysis of legal issues. (Published by the National Institute of Law Enforcement and Criminal Justice.) Washington, D.C.: U.S. Government Printing Office.

Blanchard, W. (1959). "The group process in gang rape." Journal of Social Psychology, 49:259-266.

Brodyaga, L., Gates, M., Singer, S., Tucker, M., and White, R. (1975). Rape and its victims: A report for citizens, health facilities, and criminal justice agencies. Washington, D.C.: U.S. Government Printing Office.

Bromberg, W., and Coyle, E. (1974). "Rape. A compulsion to destroy." Medical Insight, 22:21-25.

Brownmiller, S. (1975). Against our will: Men, women and rape. New York: Simon and Schuster.

Burgess, A., and Holmstrom, L. (1974). "Rape trauma syndrome." American Journal of Psychiatry, 131(September):9.

——— (1976). "Copying behavior of the rape victim." American Journal of Psychiatry, 133(4):413-418.

Chappell, D., and James, J. (1976). "Victim selection and apprehension from the rapist perspective: A preliminary investigation." Paper presented at the Second International Symposium on Victimology, Boston, September.

Cobb, K., and Schauer, N. (1974). "Legislative note: Michigan's criminal sexual assault law." Journal of Law Reforms, 81(1):221.

Cohen, M., Garofalo, R., Boucher, R., and Seghorn, T. (1971). "The psychology of rapists." Seminars in Psychiatry, 3(3):307-327.

Cormier, B., and Sickert, S. (1969). "Forensic psychiatry: The problem of the dangerous sexual offender." Canadian Psychiatric Association Journal, 14(4):329-335.

Cottell, L. (1974). "Rape: The ultimate invasion of privacy." FBI Law Enforcement Bulletin, (May):2-6.

Federal Bureau of Investigation (1976). Uniform crime reports. Washington, D.C.: U.S. Government Printing Office.

Hayman, C. (1970). "Sexual assaults on women and girls." Annals of Internal Medicine, 72(2):447-452.

Henn, F., Herjanic, M., and Vanderpeall, R. (1976). "Forensic psychiatry: Profiles of two types of sex offenders." American Journal of Psychiatry, 133(6):894-896.

Johnson, E.G. (1975). "Evidence—rape—trials—victims' prior sexual history." Baylor Law Review, 27(2):222-237.

Lichtenstein, G. (1974). "Rape squad." New York Times Magazine, March 3, p. 10.

Luginbill, D. (1975). "Repeal of the corroboration requirement: Will it tip the scales of justice?" Drake Law Review, 24(3):669-683.

MacDonald, J. (1974). "Group rape." Medical Aspects of Human Sexuality, 8(2):58-88.

Marshall, W., and McKnight, R. (1975). "An integrated treatment program for sexual offenders." Canadian Psychiatric Association Journal, 20(2):133-138.

McCombie, S. (1976). "Characteristics of rape victims seen in crisis intervention." Smith College Studies in Social Work, 46:137-158.

Minnesota Department of Correction (1964). The sex offender. St. Paul: State of Minnesota.

Notman, M., and Nadelson, C. (1976). "The rape victim: Psychodynamic considerations." American Journal of Psychiatry, 133:408-413.

Pacht, A. (1976). "The rapist in treatment: Professional myths and psychological realities." In M. Walker and S. Brodsky (eds.), Sexual assault. Lexington, Mass.: D.C. Heath.

Pacht, A., and Cowden, J. (1974). "An exploratory study of five hundred sex offenders." Criminal Justice and Behavior, 1:13-20.

Perdue, W., and Lester, D. (1972). "Personality characteristics of rapists." Perceptual and Motor Skills, 35(2):514.

President's Commission on Law Enforcement and Administration of Justice (1967). The challenge of crime in a free society. Washington, D.C.: U.S. Government Printing Office.

Putnam, J., and Fox, D. (1976)."A program to help the victims of crime." Police Chief, 36(March).

Ruff, C., and Templer, D. (1976). "The intelligence of rapists." Archives of Sexual Behavior, 5(4):327-329.

Russell, D. (1975). The politics of rape: The victim's perspective. New York: Stein and Day.

Sadoff, R. (1975). "Treatment and violent sex offenders." International Journal of Offender Therapy and Comparative Criminology, 19(1):75-80.

Schram, D. (1977). Final report: Techniques for improving the effectiveness of the criminal justice response to forcible rape. Washington, D.C.: National Institute of Law Enforcement and Criminal Justice.

State of California, Subcommittee on Sex Crimes of the Assembly Interim Committee on Judicial System and Judicial Process (1950). Preliminary report 26. Sacramento: Author.

Still, A. (1975). "Police enquiries in sexual offenses." Journal of Forensic Social Sciences, 15:183-187.

Sutherland, S., and Schere, D. (1970). "Patterns of response among victims of rape." American Journal of Orthopsychiatry, 40:503-511.

Takakuwa, M., Matsumato, Y., and Sato, T. (1971). "A psychological study of Rape." Bulletin of the Criminological Department, Ministry of Justice, Japan.

Wigmore, J., (1970). Evidence.

Woods, G. (1969). "Some aspects of group rape in Sydney." Australian and New Zealand Journal of Criminology, 2(2):105-119.

UNIT 3 *Social Inequality*

SHEILA K. JOHNSON   *Sociology of Christmas Cards*

As sociologists are well aware, social practices are rarely exactly what they seem to be: there is usually more to them than meets the eye. This tendency is well illustrated by the various rituals surrounding Christmas festivities. Christmas cards, for example, are supposedly greetings exchanged among friends and relatives in joyous celebration of the birth of Jesus many centuries ago. Yet that event is probably far from most people's minds when they send or receive Christmas cards. Rather, this greetings ritual has other functions, although they may be only dimly recognized by the senders and recipients themselves. One useful function of Christmas cards, for example, is that they offer a convenient means of keeping in touch with sundry distant relatives and associates whom we rarely see, cannot be bothered to write a full letter to, but feel we ought to remain in contact with. The ritual exchange of cards thus provides a simple way of annually reasserting kinship with great aunts and second cousins and of reconfirming relationships with former neighbors, casual friends, and other acquaintances.

As Sheila Johnson points out, Christmas cards may do even more. The United States is a society in which different categories of the population have different access to the social rewards of power, wealth, and prestige: in other words, it is a class society. Moreover, it is a society that places special value on upward social mobility, or movement from a lower to a higher social status. Sociologists have always recognized the extraordinary influence that class membership has on almost every aspect of the individual's social and personal life, ranging from life expectancy, choice of spouse, and level of education to tastes in sport, literature, and food. It is hardly surprising, therefore, that the class system—and people's desire for mobility within it—should affect even such an apparently unrelated ritual as the exchange of greetings in a supposedly religious festival.

From *Transaction* 8 (January 1971): 27–29. Reprinted by permission.

Anyone who has ever composed a Christmas card list has pondered the inclusion and exclusion of names on the basis of a variety of fairly explicit considerations. Shall I send so-and-so a card this year, since he didn't send me one last year? Or, I *must* send so-and-so a card this year, even though he probably won't send me one, because I want to be remembered by him. Like the decisions we make about whom to vote for, we like to think of these choices as purely individual, rational matters. Nevertheless, sociologists have demonstrated that, regardless of how and why we choose a candidate, voting behavior can be analyzed as a function of one's socioeconomic status, mobility aspirations, ethnicity, and religious affiliations. Similarly, it seems likely that the patterns in which people send and receive Christmas cards can also be explained in terms of certain social characteristics, especially their social status and mobility aspirations.

This proposition first occurred to me several years ago as I was opening some Christmas cards and noticed that there was a strange disjunction between the cards we were receiving and the ones we had sent out. About half of the cards we received were from people to whom we had also sent cards, but the other half came from people to whom we had not sent cards and to whom we had had no intention of sending cards, and we ourselves had sent half of our cards to people from whom we had not expected to receive (and did not receive) a card in return. When I studied the names that fell into each of these three categories, it dawned on me that the people with whom we had exchanged cards reciprocally were either relatives or people with whom we were on equal social footing—professional friends of my husband or personal friends in different, but nevertheless comparable, occupations. The cards we had sent but to which we had received no reply, I discovered, went invariably to individuals whom *we* wanted to cultivate—people with regard to whom we were, in sociological terms, "upwardly mobile," such as professional acquaintances who might someday prove useful or important or social acquaintances whom we wished we knew better. By the same token, the cards we received and to which we did not reply came from individuals who wanted to cultivate us—some of my husband's graduate students and office employees, the liquor

159

store, the hairdresser, and foreign scholars who obviously expected to visit the United States at some time in the future.

In order to test out my theory, I telephoned several friends shortly after Christmas and asked them to sort the cards they had received into two piles—reciprocals and those to whom they had not sent cards—and also to count up the number of cards they had sent "upward." (Some of the incensed replies to this request would indicate that the nature of Christmas-card sending is a very touchy subject indeed.) Those of my friends who continued to speak to me and who complied with my request corroborated my theory. Several couples in their late thirties or early forties who, although in different professions, were rather similar to ourselves in their mobility aspirations and in the number of people they knew who were upwardly mobile with regard to them found that their Christmas cards could be grouped into equal thirds (one-third sent and not received, one-third sent and received, and one-third received but not sent). However, a young graduate student reported that about 70 percent of his cards were reciprocal, with 30 percent sent upward and none received from people who were trying to curry favor with him. This is clearly the pattern for those with their foot on the bottom rung of the status ladder. At the other end, several retired people reported that 90 percent of their cards were reciprocal, with only 5 percent sent upward and 5 percent received from people who still regarded them as important. A man who had retired but taken a second job, however, reported that 70 percent of his cards were reciprocal but that 10 percent had been sent upward and 20 percent had come from people trying to cultivate him.

While the percentages of cards an individual sends and receives tell us a good deal about his mobility aspirations, the fact that he sends Christmas cards at all places him rather firmly in the middle class. Members of the upper class—particularly a closed upper class to which one gains admission by birth rather than through the acquisition of wealth—have no need to send cards upward, and sending cards to other members of the upper class is a formality that many are dispensing with. In England, for example, it is increasingly common for upper-class families to place an ad in the personal columns of the *London Times* stating that Lord and Lady So-and-So send warm greetings to all their friends for Christmas and the New Year as they will not be sending cards. (Several years ago an upper-class English wit poked fun at these ads by placing one asking *his* friends to send him Christmas cards as he would not be able to read the *Times* columns during December.) In the United States, because the upper class is more fluid than in England and because the country is simply too large for all one's upper class friends to read the same daily newspaper, the custom of sending cards among upper-class individuals has not died out. One

would predict, however, that most of the private card sending of the upper class is reciprocal and that only its business Christmas cards are sent upward, since there is always room for upward mobility in the business world.

Lower-class and working-class individuals also send few or no Christmas cards but for entirely different reasons. Sociologists have demonstrated that lower- and working-class individuals tend to rely upon tightly knit family networks and neighbors for their friendships and that they are less geographically mobile than the middle class. Thus a skilled union man will probably have a large number of relatives living in the same town or same general area as he does, and he will be on friendly terms with many of his neighbors. There is no need to send these people Christmas cards, however, since he sees them nearly every day. He may be upwardly mobile in terms of his job, but this is handled by the union, and a Christmas card to the front office is not likely to do the trick. Only if he is upwardly mobile to the extent of trying to leave his stratum and become a white-collar worker may he take to sending Christmas cards to people who can help him. In that case he may adopt other middle-class behavior patterns, such as joining various clubs and lodges, in which he will make a broader range of friends to whom he will also want to send cards at Christmas.

Senders and Recipients

It is the middle class—particularly the upper middle class, consisting of high managerial and professional people—who are the Christmas card senders par excellence. These are the people who are both geographically and socially mobile—growing up in one place, going to college somewhere else and then moving about as success in one's firm or profession seems to dictate. Kinship ties tend to be far-flung and tenuous, since it would not be advantageous to be tied down to a given area by one's aging parents or embarrassed by the sudden appearance of a lower-class cousin. Friendships are formed among social equals—at school, at work, in professional or social organizations—but these, too, change as one moves up the ladder of success or to a different section of the country. Such are the ideal conditions for the exchange of Christmas cards. Friends and relatives are scattered widely, but one wants to keep "in touch," and there are vast sources of upward mobility to be tapped.

I realize that some people will object strenuously to this analysis of their Christmas-card sending and receiving. While I was attempting to collect data on the subject, several of my friends declined to cooperate on the grounds that they did not fit into the pattern I had just described to them. "Really," one of them said self-righteously, "I keep an up-to-date Christmas list, and the only people I send cards to are people who send me cards. There is no upward sending or downward receiving in our family: it's strictly reciprocal." This is pure propaganda, nurtured by the myth of absolute social equality that exists in this country. Everyone can think of some acquaintances to whom he simply *has* to send cards, regardless of whether he gets one in return. The obligatory nature of the act is the real tip-off to the social pressures at work. As for people who receive cards they were not expecting—that is, cards being sent upwards to them—and who then shamefacedly rush out on Christmas Eve to mail the forgotten sender one of theirs, they are simply insecure in their status position. Imagine the president of Chase Manhattan Bank receiving a Christmas card from the janitor and saying remorsefully, "Oh, My God, and I didn't send *him* one." Yet thousands of people do roughly the same thing when they receive a card from someone who looks up to them. What should they do instead? The answer is nothing, except sit back and enjoy it. Of course, if the upward sender shows other indications of increased social status, it might be wise to send him a Christmas card next year, but that would depend on circumstances ranging far beyond the scope of this article.

In a recent film, "Diary of a Mad Housewife," the husband is shown counting the family's Christmas cards and remarking to his wife "One-hundred-and-fifty-three. That's fine. Three more weeks to go until Christmas and we've already reached the half-way mark . . . We sent out 300." He then goes on to instruct his wife to note carefully who has sent cards to them, since there's "no point" in sending cards the following year to people who have not sent them one this year. Here the authors of the film have missed a bet, however, since the husband is depicted as a social climber of the first order who would clearly insist on sending Christmas cards to certain "important" people—the same people whom he invites to his abysmal party and tries to cultivate in other ways.

In addition to scrutinizing the number of Christmas cards people send and receive for signs of social status and mobility aspirations, one can also tell a good deal about the personality of the sender by the kind of card he chooses. There may still be a few rare individuals who choose every Christmas card individually to suit the *recipient* but for the most part those days went out with the advent of boxed cards. Somewhat more common is the tendency for people with two radically different constituencies—for example, businessmen who keep their business and private acquaintances well compartmentalized—to choose two different sets of cards. However, in such cases it is not at all clear whether the two sets of cards are chosen to suit the different sets of recipients or to reflect the different personality that the businessman wishes to convey to each group—sober and elegant cards for his business acquaintances and mod, swingerish cards for his personal friends. In general one may assume that cards reflect the sender rather than the receiver, and that a Madison Avenue executive would no more receive a

museum card from his Aunt Emma in Vermont than he would send her a Hallmark Santa Claus with a rhymed poem inside.

How can one classify some of the cards that people consciously or subconsciously select to convey not only their Christmas wishes but also their personality? Among university types, whom I know best, there seem to be several distinct patterns. Well established WASP professors tend to send museum cards or rather small studio cards of abstract design. Usually, the more powerful the professor, the smaller the card. (This appears to be a snobbish, willful inversion of the usual business pattern: the more important the executives, the bigger and more lavish the card. An academic friend argues that there are exceptions to this rule and cites Professor Henry Kissinger, from whom last year he received an absolutely gigantic Christmas card portraying both sides of the globe. I would maintain, however, that this Christmas card merely illustrates Professor Kissinger's defection from the academic ranks and his adoption of the big-business ethos of the Nixon administration.) Jewish and youngish, slightly left-of-center professors tend to send UNICEF cards, often choosing a design that reflects their area of academic interest—India specialists send the Indian-designed card, Africa specialists send the African-designed card, and so forth. A similar tendency may be observed among government officials.

From professors who have (or think they have) artistic wives we get hand-screened, hand-blocked, or otherwise handcrafted Christmas cards. From professors who have just had their first child we get (you guessed it) baby photographs, and from professors who are doing research abroad we often get photos of their children in native dress. From professors abroad sans children or from those who've been there before we get interesting Chinese, Japanese, or Thai renderings of the nativity. (The most fascinating Thai card we ever received, from a high-ranking Thai army officer, was a photograph of the gentleman himself posed proudly beside his new Jaguar XKE. *Joyeux Noel* indeed!)

People with strong political convictions tend to remind us of these at Christmas time. Thus we get our share of CORE and CND cards. From less political but equally morally outraged friends we get a strange assortment of messages: cards that say on them "printed by spastics" or "designed by the deaf" and cards depicting felled redwood trees or oil-stained beaches. From our wealthier, nonacademic friends we get cards supporting the Symphony Association and the Junior League.

In addition to all of these types of cards, we get, every year, a couple of photographs of houses. These are never from the academic world—although some professors I know live in very nice houses—because the houses displayed on Christmas cards have a special status significance. Most of the houses that I have seen on Christmas cards belonged to friends who had just retired to Florida or Hawaii, or they were the dream-come-true of people who had finally bought that acre in the country. Whatever the occasion, the house depicted is usually the visible sign of a major change in social status and it is certainly no accident that the president's Christmas card almost always features the White House.

Finally, and perhaps hardest of all to pin down sociologically, there is the category of Christmas card known as the mimeographed Christmas letter. I would like to hold a contest sometime for the most fatuous Christmas letter, but I'm afraid I'd be deluged with entries. It is hard to attribute the Christmas letter to a particular type of person or a particular station in life, because almost everyone who has ever had an eventful year, taken an exciting trip, or accomplished a great deal has felt the urge to compose one. I have received them from internationally famous professors who were attempting to describe their world travels, from graduate students describing their Ph.D. research in the field, and from relatives recounting the latest family gossip. Perhaps mimeographed Christmas letters should be used as a vanity indicator, since they expose those among us who yielded to, rather than resisted, the pervasive temptation to blow one's own horn.

A Matter of Tone

The chief defect of the Christmas letter is its tone—that peculiar half-personal, half-distant note that makes most of them sound as if they were addressed to mentally defective thirteen-year-olds. This tone is the inevitable result of trying to address a single letter to a score or more of different friends. As any letter writer knows, one usually manipulates the tones of a letter to convey a certain personal image to a specific correspondent. If it is often difficult to send the same *card* to business as well as personal acquaintances because of the image to be conveyed to each group, how much more difficult to compose a letter that will ring true to a variety of recipients.

Not only is the tone of Christmas letters muddled by the lack of a clearly defined recipient, but it also often lacks the unifying voice of a single sender. Most Christmas cards can convey the status and life style of a couple or a family as readily as they can those of an individual. But this is because cards deal in visual symbols whereas letters traffic in words. It is always hard to believe that a mimeographed letter from "Betty and Bob" is really a joint verbal product, and so one looks for telltale "I's" and "he's" or "she's" to pin down the author. In a genuine Christmas letter, however, such slips never occur, and one is left to figure out for himself who is being the more sanctimonious from sentences that announce: "While Bob worked like a demon interviewing local politicians and village chiefs, Betty spent her time learning how to cook native dishes and teaching English to some of the wives and children." (For the full effect, one must try substituting "I" for each of the proper nouns in turn.)

There are doubtless still other sociological and psychological facets to the sending and receiving of Christmas cards. However, having said all of this, I would not want readers to conclude that I am trying to denigrate Christmas cards or that I personally am above sending them. Far from it. Having already passed through my family photograph, foreign, and UNICEF phases, I may even succumb to sending a Christmas letter one of these years. . . .

QUESTIONS

1. In your own experience, what criteria influence the selection of guests for weddings, bar mitzvahs, birthdays, and similar ceremonies?

2. The article implies that Americans are much more class-conscious than is commonly realized. Do you agree? To what extent do class considerations enter into your routine activities and attitudes, such as your schooling, dating, political opinions, leisure activities, and career plans?

3. Ceremonies involving such holidays as Christmas, Thanksgiving, the Fourth of July, and Passover all purport to commemorate specific historical events. What other social functions (including latent, or generally unrecognized ones) might they perform?

HERBERT J. GANS

The Uses of Poverty:
The Poor Pay All

The United States is, by many measures, the richest society on earth. It could well afford to eliminate poverty by providing an income "floor" for the poorest members of society, at a cost that would be almost negligible in the context of total governmental expenditures. Moreover, Americans are agreed that poverty is undesirable, that it breeds ignorance, ill health, crime, and many other forms of human misery. Why, then, does poverty persist?

Perhaps a little tongue-in-cheek, Herbert Gans suggests that poverty remains an enduring feature of the society because it is functional: in other words, it is a feature of society—like religion, the family, the courts, the schools, and so on—that helps to maintain the stability of the entire social system. In his provocative article, Gans maintains that poverty is so useful to the society, or at least to that part of society that benefits from it, that its persistence is hardly surprising.

The underlying message of Gans's argument is that an act of political will would be required to redistribute wealth and income from the rich to the poor. And since the rich, not the poor, have political power, poverty will remain a feature of the society, with only token efforts made to redress its effects. If the privileged benefit from the plight of the underprivileged, change is unlikely unless the power relationship between the two groups changes also.

Reprinted from *Social Policy,* July-August 1971, pp. 20–24, published by Social Policy Corporation, New York, New York 10010. Copyright 1971 by Social Policy Corporation.

Some twenty years ago Robert K. Merton applied the notion of functional analysis to explain the continuing though maligned existence of the urban political machine: if it continued to exist, perhaps it fulfilled latent—unintended or unrecognized—positive functions. Clearly it did. Merton pointed out how the political machine provided central authority to get things done when a decentralized local government could not act, humanized the services of the impersonal bureaucracy for fearful citizens, offered concrete help (rather than abstract law or justice) to the poor, and otherwise performed services needed or demanded by many people but considered unconventional or even illegal by formal public agencies.

Today, poverty is more maligned than the political machine ever was; yet it, too, is a persistent social phenomenon. Consequently, there may be some merit in applying functional analysis to poverty, in asking whether it also has positive functions that explain its persistence.

Merton defined functions as "those observed consequences [of a phenomenon] which make for the adaptation or adjustment of a given [social] system." I shall use a slightly different definition; instead of identifying functions for an entire social system, I shall identify them for the interest groups, socioeconomic classes, and other population aggregates with shared values that "inhabit" a social system. I suspect that in a modern heterogeneous society, few phenomena are functional or dysfunctional for the society as a whole, and that most result in benefits to some groups and costs to others. Nor are any phenomena indispensable; in most instances, one can suggest what Merton calls "functional alternatives" or equivalents for them, i.e., other social patterns or policies that achieve the same positive functions but avoid the dysfunctions.

Associating poverty with positive functions seems at first glance to be unimaginable. Of course, the slumlord and the loan shark are commonly known to profit from the existence of poverty, but they are viewed as evil men, so their activities are classified among the dysfunctions of poverty. However, what is less often recognized, at least by the conventional wisdom, is that poverty also makes possible the existence or expansion of respectable professions and occupations, for example, penology, criminology, social work, and public health. More recently, the poor have provided jobs for professional and para-professional "poverty warriors," and for journalists and social scientists, this author included, who have supplied the information demanded by the revival of public interest in poverty.

Clearly, then, poverty and the poor may well satisfy a number of positive functions for many nonpoor groups in American society. I shall describe thirteen such functions—economic, social, and political—that seem to me most significant.

The Functions of Poverty

First, the existence of poverty ensures that society's "dirty work" will be done. Every society has such work: physically dirty or dangerous, temporary, dead-end and underpaid, undignified and menial jobs. Society can fill these jobs by paying higher wages than for "clean" work, or it can force people who have no other choice to do the dirty work—and at low wages. In America, poverty functions to provide a low-wage labor pool that is willing—or, rather, unable to be *un*willing—to perform dirty work at low cost. Indeed, this function of the poor is so important that in some Southern states, welfare payments have been cut off during the summer months when the poor are needed to work in the fields. Moreover, much of the debate about the Negative Income Tax and the Family Assistance Plan has concerned their impact on the work incentive, by which is actually meant the incentive of the poor to do the needed dirty work if the wages therefrom are no larger than the income grant. Many economic activities that involve dirty work depend on the poor for their existence: restaurants, hospitals, parts of the garment industry, and "truck farming," among others, could not persist in their present form without the poor.

Second, because the poor are required to work at low wages, they subsidize a variety of economic activities that benefit the affluent. For example, domestics subsidize the upper middle and upper classes, making life easier for their employers and freeing affluent women for a variety of professional, cultural, civic, and partying activities. Similarly, because the poor pay a higher proportion of their income in property and sales taxes, among others, they subsidize many state and local governmental services that benefit more affluent groups. In addition, the poor support innovation in medical practice as patients in teaching and research hospitals and as guinea pigs in medical experiments.

Third, poverty creates jobs for a number of occupations and professions that serve or "service" the poor, or protect the rest of society from them. As already noted, penology would be minuscule without the poor, as would the police. Other activities and groups that flourish because of the existence of poverty are the numbers game,

the sale of heroin and cheap wines and liquors, pentecostal ministers, faith healers, prostitutes, pawn shops, and the peacetime army, which recruits its enlisted men mainly from among the poor.

Fourth, the poor buy goods others do not want and thus prolong the economic usefulness of such goods—day-old bread, fruit and vegetables that would otherwise have to be thrown out, second-hand clothes, and deteriorating automobiles and buildings. They also provide incomes for doctors, lawyers, teachers, and others who are too old, poorly trained, or incompetent to attract more affluent clients.

In addition to economic functions, the poor perform a number of social functions.

Fifth, the poor can be identified and punished as alleged or real deviants in order to uphold the legitimacy of conventional norms. To justify the desirability of hard work, thrift, honesty, and monogamy, for example, the defenders of these norms must be able to find people who can be accused of being lazy, spendthrift, dishonest, and promiscuous. Although there is some evidence that the poor are about as moral and law-abiding as anyone else, they are more likely than middle-class transgressors to be caught and punished when they participate in deviant acts. Moreover, they lack the political and cultural power to correct the stereotypes that other people hold of them and thus continue to be thought of as lazy, spendthrift, etc., by those who need living proof that moral deviance does not pay.

Sixth, and conversely, the poor offer vicarious participation to the rest of the population in the uninhibited sexual, alcoholic, and narcotic behavior in which they are alleged to participate and which, being freed from the constraints of affluence, they are often thought to enjoy more than the middle classes. Thus many people, some social scientists included, believe that the poor not only are more given to uninhibited behavior (which may be true, although it is often motivated by despair more than by lack of inhibition) but derive more pleasure from it than affluent people (which research by Lee Rainwater, Walter Miller, and others shows to be patently untrue). However, whether the poor actually have more sex and enjoy it more is irrelevant; so long as middle-class people believe this to be true, they can participate in it vicariously when instances are reported in factual or fictional form.

Seventh, the poor also serve a direct cultural function when culture created by or for them is adopted by the more affluent. The rich often collect artifacts from extinct folk cultures of poor people; and almost all Americans listen to the blues, Negro spirituals, and country music, which originated among the Southern poor. Recently they have enjoyed the rock styles that were born, like the Beatles, in the slums; and in the last year, poetry written by ghetto children has become popular in literary circles. The poor also serve as culture heroes, particularly, of course, to the left; but the hobo, the cowboy, the hipster, and the mythical prostitute with a heart of gold have performed this function for a variety of groups.

Eighth, poverty helps to guarantee the status of those who are not poor. In every hierarchical society someone has to be at the bottom; but in American society, in which social mobility is an important goal for many and people need to know where they stand, the poor function as a reliable and relatively permanent measuring rod for status comparisons. This is particularly true for the working class, whose politics is influenced by the need to maintain status distinctions between themselves and the poor, much as the aristocracy must find ways of distinguishing itself from the *nouveaux riches*.

Ninth, the poor also aid the upward mobility of groups just above them in the class hierarchy. Thus a goodly number of Americans have entered the middle class through the profits earned from the provision of goods and services in the slums, including illegal or nonrespectable ones that upper-class and upper-middle-class businessmen shun because of their low prestige. As a result, members of almost every immigrant group have financed their upward mobility by providing slum housing, entertainment, gambling, narcotics, etc., to later arrivals—most recently to Blacks and Puerto Ricans.

Tenth, the poor help to keep the aristocracy busy, thus justifying its continued existence. "Society" uses the poor as clients of settlement houses and beneficiaries of charity affairs; indeed, the aristocracy must have the poor to demonstrate its superiority over other elites who devote themselves to earning money.

Eleventh, the poor, being powerless, can be made to absorb the costs of change and growth in American society. During the nineteenth century, they did the backbreaking work that built the cities; today, they are pushed out of their neighborhoods to make room for "progress." Urban renewal projects to hold middle-class taxpayers in the city and expressways to enable suburbanites to commute downtown have typically been located in poor neighborhoods, since no other group will allow itself to be displaced. For the same reason, universities, hospitals, and civic centers also expand into land occupied by the poor. The major costs of the industrialization of agriculture have been borne by the poor, who are pushed off the land without recompense; and they have paid a large share of the human cost of the growth of American power overseas, for they have provided many of the foot soldiers for Vietnam and other wars.

Twelfth, the poor facilitate and stabilize the American political process. Because they vote and participate in politics less than other groups, the political system is often free to ignore them. Moreover, since they can rarely support Republicans, they often provide the Democrats with a captive constituency that has no other place to go.

As a result, the Democrats can count on their votes, and be more responsive to voters—for example, the white working class—who might otherwise switch to the Republicans.

Thirteen, the role of the poor in upholding conventional norms (see the *fifth* point, above) also has a significant political function. An economy based on the ideology of laissez faire requires a deprived population that is allegedly unwilling to work or that can be considered inferior because it must accept charity or welfare in order to survive. Not only does the alleged moral deviancy of the poor reduce the moral pressure on the present political economy to eliminate poverty but socialist alternatives can be made to look quite unattractive if those who will benefit most from them can be described as lazy, spendthrift, dishonest, and promiscuous.

The Alternatives

I have described thirteen of the more important functions poverty and the poor satisfy in American society, enough to support the functionalist thesis that poverty, like any other social phenomenon, survives in part because it is useful to society or some of its parts. This analysis is not intended to suggest that because it is often functional, poverty *should* exist, or that it *must* exist. For one thing, poverty has many more dysfunctions than functions; for another, it is possible to suggest functional alternatives.

For example, society's dirty work could be done without poverty, either by automation or by paying "dirty workers" decent wages. Nor is it necessary for the poor to subsidize the many activities they support through their low-wage jobs. This would, however, drive up the costs of these activities, which would result in higher prices to their customers and clients. Similarly, many of the professionals who flourish because of the poor could be given other roles. Social workers could provide counseling to the affluent, as they prefer to do anyway; and the police could devote themselves to traffic and organized crime. Other roles would have to be found for badly trained or incompetent professionals now relegated to serving the poor, and someone else would have to pay their salaries. Fewer penologists would be employable, however. And pentecostal religion could probably not survive without the poor—nor would parts of the second- and third-hand-goods market. And in many cities, "used" housing that no one else wants would then have to be torn down at public expense.

Alternatives for the cultural functions of the poor could be found more easily and cheaply. Indeed, entertainers, hippies, and adolescents are already serving as the deviants needed to uphold traditional morality and as devotees of orgies to "staff" the fantasies of vicarious participation.

The status functions of the poor are another matter. In

a hierarchical society, some people must be defined as inferior to everyone else with respect to a variety of attributes, but they need not be poor in the absolute sense. One could conceive of a society in which the "lower class," though last in the pecking order, received 75 percent of the median income, rather than 15–40 percent, as is now the case. Needless to say, this would require considerable income redistribution.

The contribution the poor make to the upward mobility of the groups that provide them with goods and services could also be maintained without the poor's having such low incomes. However, it is true that if the poor were more affluent, they would have access to enough capital to take over the provider role, thus competing with, and perhaps rejecting, the "outsiders." (Indeed, owing in part to antipoverty programs, this is already happening in a number of ghettos, where white storeowners are being replaced by Blacks.) Similarly, if the poor were more affluent, they would make less willing clients for upper-class philanthropy, although some would still use settlement houses to achieve upward mobility, as they do now. Thus "Society" could continue to run its philanthropic activities.

The political functions of the poor would be more difficult to replace. With increased affluence the poor would probably obtain more political power and be more active politically. With higher incomes and more political power, the poor would be likely to resist paying the costs of growth and change. Of course, it is possible to imagine urban renewal and highway projects that properly reimbursed the displaced people, but such projects would then become considerably more expensive, and many might never be built. This, in turn, would reduce the comfort and convenience of those who now benefit from urban renewal and expressways. Finally, hippies could serve also as more deviants to justify the existing political economy—as they already do. Presumably, however, if poverty were eliminated, there would be fewer attacks on that economy.

In sum, then, many of the functions served by the poor could be replaced if poverty were eliminated, but almost always at higher costs to others, particularly more affluent others. Consequently, a functional analysis must conclude that poverty persists not only because it fulfills a number of positive functions but also because many of the functional alternatives to poverty would be quite dysfunctional for the affluent members of society. A functional analysis thus ultimately arrives at much the same conclusion as radical sociology, except that radical thinkers treat as manifest what I describe as latent: that social phenomena that are functional for affluent or powerful groups and dysfunctional for poor or powerless ones persist; that when the elimination of such phenomena through functional alternatives would generate dysfunctions for the affluent or powerful, they will continue to persist; and that phenomena like poverty can be eliminated only when they become dysfunctional for the affluent or powerful, or when the powerless can obtain enough power to change society.

QUESTIONS

1. Gans lists only the functions of poverty. Can you list some dysfunctions that poverty might have for American society?

2. Who do you think Americans would tend to regard more highly: an idle millionaire whose wealth was inherited or an unemployed person on welfare in an inner-city area of high unemployment? Why?

3. Discuss some of the ways in which economic power can be translated into political power.

MAURICE ZEITLIN

Who Owns America?
The Same Old Gang

Like most societies, the United States is a stratified one: in other words, different categories of the population have different access to the socially valued rewards of wealth, power, and prestige. Stratification in the United States takes the form of a class system, in which wealth (which can be readily converted to power or prestige) is the main determinant of social status. This inequality is deeply structured into the society, in that it tends to be transmitted from one generation to the next: the children of the rich are likely to be wealthy; the offspring of the poor will probably be poor also.

"Wealth" actually contains two elements: income (earnings such as wages, salaries, and interest) and assets (property such as real estate, stocks, and gold). The distribution of income and assets in a society tells us a great deal about how unequal it is. In the United States, data on income are fairly easy to get, since income must be reported to the IRS. These data show that the richest fifth of American families receives over 40 percent of the income, while the poorest fifth receives about 5 percent. Information on wealth in the form of assets, however, is much harder to come by. Yet these data would be even more meaningful since ownership of assets (unlike receipt of income) implies control: those who own corporate stock, for example, can control the corporation, and thus indirectly influence its employees, its consumers, the legislators it lobbies, and so on. As Maurice Zeitlin suggests, in a sense those who own the bulk of America's assets own America. In this article, he tries to establish who those owners are.

Do you remember those full-page newspaper ads that showed a little old lady stroking *her* locomotive, supposedly owned by millions of ordinary Americans just like her? Or Standard Oil's gushing claim, "Yes, the people own the tools of production. . . . How odd to find that it is here, in the capitalism [Karl Marx] reviled, that the promise of the tool has been fulfilled." Well, it's happening again.

A current Texaco television commercial has Bob Hope asking us to "take a look at the owners of America's oil companies," and then leads us on a tour of a typical community made up of just plain folks like you and me. A recent book, received with much fanfare in the press, repeats the refrain. Its author, long-time management consultant and publicist Peter Drucker, tells us that an "unseen revolution" has wrought "a more radical shift in ownership than Soviet communism." Even more amazing, "the socialism of Marxist theory has been realized for the first time on American soil."

Not only are the means of production now in everyone's hands, but the U.S. Chamber of Commerce confides that [we are] a "post-industrial society." College textbooks inform us that a "dramatic shift from blue collar to white collar, from brawn to brain [has] occurred," and the best-seller *Future Shock* rhapsodizes that "for the first time in human history," a society—*our* society—has "managed within a few short decades to throw off the yoke of manual labor." A book on "power in America" celebrates the passing of classes and suggests that we organize popular visits to "Newport, and bus tours through Grosse Pointe, for purely educational purposes—like seeing Carlsbad Caverns once." It is time, the author advises us, to shout, "The Working Class is dead. Long live the memory of the Working Class." And, summing it all up, a popular book on how to be a politician announces that "the economic class system is disappearing. . . . Redistribution of wealth and income . . . had ended economic inequality's political significance."

So, what has happened to classes? Who does own America, and how has it all been changing? Has the capitalist class really been "lopped off" at the top, as Harvard's Talcott Parsons once pithily put it? Has the ownership of American corporations become so dispersed that control has shifted to "professional managers" who are merely the "trustees" for all of us—"stockholders, employees, suppliers, consumers, and the public"—as Donald S. McNaughton, the chairman of Prudential Life, announced in a recent speech? Has the yoke of manual labor really been lifted? Is the working class now a mere memory? Or are the claims that prompt these questions really pseudofacts that are as plausible and persuasive as they are deceptive? The answer, I think, is clear: Economic inequality weighs as heavily and cuts as deeply as ever, and neither capitalists nor workers have vanished from American life.

Let's look first at who owns what. It's certainly hard enough to find out, even if, like Government economists, you have access to Internal Revenue Service (IRS) data. No law requires Americans to report their net worth, and besides, wealth is deliberately hidden, whether out of modesty or to avoid taxes. Still, an ingenious method of estimating wealth has been devised, to make the dead disclose what the living conceal. It is called the "estate multiplier technique," and it uses IRS data on estate tax returns. It treats those who die in any year as a "stratified sample" of the living on whose estate tax returns would have to be filed if they died during the year—that is, those with estates worth $60,000 or more. All told, only 4 per cent of the adults in this country have estates as large as $60,000, counting everything they own, including cash in hand or under the mattress, and the mattress itself. But within that group, a minute number of Americans make up the real owners of America.

The Rose Bowl's 104,696 seats would still be half empty if only every adult American who owns $1 million or more in corporate stock came to cheer, and it would be even emptier if only those who have $100,000 in state and local bonds got a seat. If you counted all state, local, and Federal bonds (except U.S. Savings Bonds), and added Treasury bills, certificates, notes, and mortgages—and even foreign bonds—held by Americans in amounts of at least $200,000, you would still find well over a quarter of the Rose Bowl seats not taken. Only 55,400 adults have $1 million or more in corporate stock. A mere 40,000 have $100,000 or more in state and local bonds (all Federal tax exempt), and 73,500 adults have $200,000 or more if we count all bonds and debtholdings.

This tiny owning class at the tip of the top, barely more than one-twentieth of 1 per cent of American adults, has a fifth of all the corporate stock, nearly two-thirds of the worth of all state and local bonds, and two-fifths of all bonds and notes. No wonder it took five years of trying by an outstanding economist, James D. Smith, to get the IRS to allow him to study its information—and by then some of the data had been destroyed.

Contrast what this propertied class owns to what the rest of us have. Nine out of ten adults in the United States could sell everything they own, pay off their debts, and have no more than $30,000 left. Worse, more than half of all Americans would have a total "net worth" of no more than $3,000. The bottom half of all American families combined have only three cents of every dollar's worth of all the wealth in the country.

Back at the top, if we count up what the richest 1 per cent of the population own, we find that they have a seventh of all the real estate in the country, more than half the corporate stock, and almost all the trust assets. They even had a seventh of all the cash in every checking and savings account and pocket and purse in America.

Summed up, that is a quarter of the net worth of the entire population held by the top 1 per cent. If we take a slice as large as the richest 4 per cent—everyone whose total gross assets (not counting debts) are worth at least $60,000—their combined wealth is more than a trillion dollars—enough to buy the entire national product of the United States and have plenty left over to pick up the combined output of a few small European countries, including Switzerland, Norway, Denmark, and Sweden.

So it's clear who owns America—but has this propertied class been slipping in its hold on the nation's wealth? Maybe, but if it slipped at all, it was not because of any egalitarian tendencies in American capitalism. It took the country's worst crash, the Great Depression, when many fortunes (and even a few of the fortune-holders) took the plunge from the pinnacle, to make a dent on what they own. Even the modest shrinkage that supposedly took place then is probably more apparent than real, because just before the crash there was a phenomenal rise in the price of stock, the biggest asset in the portfolios of the rich.

But since the end of World War II, there has been no change in their share of the nation's wealth; it has been constant in every year studied, at roughly five-year intervals, since 1945. The richest 1 per cent own a quarter, and the top half of 1 per cent a fifth, of the combined market worth of everything owned by every American. Remarkably, economic historians who have culled manuscript census reports on the past century report that on the eve of the Civil War the rich had the same cut of the total: The top 1 per cent owned 24 per cent in 1860 and 24.9 per cent in 1969 (the latest year thoroughly studied). Through all the tumultuous changes since then—the Civil War and the emancipation of the slaves, the Populist and Progressive movements, the Great Depression, the New Deal, progressive taxation, the mass organization of industrial workers, and World Wars I and II—this class has held on to everything it had. They owned America then and they own it now.

Any notion that income has been redistributed, even though property is intact, is also illusory: The higher the income bracket, the higher the percentage in it that derives its income from the ownership of property. At the top, almost all income is in dividends, rents, royalties, and interest. Among all American families and unrelated individuals combined, not more than one in eight receives any stock dividends at all. Not one in a hundred receives even a dollar from any "trust or estate." But among those with incomes of $100,000 or more, 97 per cent receive stock dividends and more than half receive inherited income directly from a trust or estate.

The 5 per cent of Americans with the highest incomes take in almost half of all the income from property in the country. They receive sixty-four cents out of every dollar in dividends earned on publicly traded stock and ninety-three cents of the dividends on stock owned in "closely held corporations" (those having just a few owners). Furthermore, they take in thirty cents of every dollar earned in interest, thirty-seven cents in rents and royalties, and sixty-four cents of every dollar in America coming from trusts and estates.

If we divide Americans into five brackets from low to high, and count all known income, the top fifth gets about forty cents of every dollar of personal income. The bottom fifth gets just one nickel. That is a ratio of eight to one, and that ratio has remained almost exactly the same in every year since World War II ended. (Here, in the capitalism celebrated by the Advertising Council and Bob Hope, the gap between the top and bottom fifths is wider than in Britain, Holland, West Germany, or even Japan. Among industrial nations, only France has a wider gap.) And the *real income* gap between the top and bottom has been growing, though the ratio has stayed the same: The average real income difference between the top and bottom fifth, measured in constant 1969 dollars, rose from $11,000 to $19,000 in the twenty years between 1949 and 1969.

All those "redistributive efforts" and wars on poverty we have heard about have not made a dent in income distribution. The overall tax burden has probably become more *regressive* since World War II—taxes are taking an increasing bite of the incomes of people in the lower rather than in the higher brackets. One reason is that state and local taxes, which are typically more regressive than Federal taxes, have grown in comparison to Federal taxes—from forty-two cents to every dollar of Federal taxes collected in 1950 to fifty-one cents in 1961 and fifty-eight cents in 1970.

But even Federal taxes have become more regressive during the same years. Corporate taxes have gone down, from twenty-seven cents of every Federal tax dollar received in 1950 to only sixteen cents in 1970, and at the same time Social Security and payroll taxes have jumped from just nine cents to twenty-six cents of each tax dollar pumped into Washington. So, when the impact of all taxes and all Government spending is taken into account—even though there has been a sizable increase in Government "benefits" to low-income Americans—the level of income inequality ("post-fiscal") has not changed since 1950.

The notion that classes are withering away in America rests not only on the mistaken assumption that the propertied have been lopped off at the top, but on the equally unfounded notion that the working class itself has been vanishing and the "white collar" strata of the so-called middle class have been multiplying. So renowned a pundit as Harvard's John Kenneth Galbraith, among many others, believes the class struggle is a "dwindling phenomenon" because "the number of white-collar workers in the United States almost fifteen years ago overtook the number in the blue-collar working force and is, of course, now greater."

Of course? The sort of counting done here misses and distorts what has really happened; it confuses occupational composition with class lines. Since the 1900s, especially during World War II, and in quickening pace in recent years, women—and increasingly married women—have been moving into the labor force. About four out of ten people in the labor force are now women, and almost half of all women now have paying jobs or are looking for them. It is this influx of women into paying jobs that accounts for the growing number of "white-collar" jobs—mainly in "clerical or sales" work—in the past few decades. Of all working women, not even one in ten was a "clerical or sales" worker in 1900. By 1940, on the eve of World War II, the figure jumped to almost three in ten, and it climbed until it reached more than four in ten in 1970.

At the same time, the proportion of women working in crafts or as operatives and laborers (except on the farm) dropped. It also dropped in so-called "service" occupations which, for women, are typically dirty and menial jobs as domestics or "food service" workers. Some "white-collar" jobs are now almost entirely filled by women—and ten occupations alone, among them waitress, typist, cashier, hairdresser and beautician, nurse and dietician, sales clerk, and teacher, account for more than two out of five employed women. Of all clerical and sales jobs, two out of three, and the same ratio in service jobs, are filled by women. In contrast, of all those working in crafts or as operatives and laborers (off the farm), only one in six is a woman.

Among men, meanwhile, the proportion with clerical and sales jobs has not risen in three decades. Only seven in a hundred men at work had clerical or sales jobs in 1900, and it rose to just twelve in a hundred by 1940. In the three decades since, the ratio has not grown at all: It is still about twelve in a hundred. In the same years, though, there has been a significant rise in the proportion of men classified as "professionals and technicians" by the U.S. Census—from three, to six, to fourteen in a hundred. But many such "professionals" are vocational school products, and about four out of ten in the rapidly growing category of "technicians" are not college graduates. This, of course, is scarcely the image evoked by the terms "professional" or "technician." Many are really highly skilled workers; advanced education or certification is not required to fill their jobs, nor does their work differ much in independence and control from the work done by those classified as "craftsmen."

The plain fact is that the category of "manual workers" has not shrunk at all in this century. Fewer than forty in a hundred men worked in 1900 as a "craftsman, operative, or nonfarm laborer." In 1920, the figure rose to forty-five in a hundred, and it has barely changed since: In 1970, forty-seven out of every hundred men in the labor force were classified as manual workers. But to this figure we must add many if not most of the men who are called "service workers"—a U.S. Census category that hides a host of blue-collar jobs within its semantic recesses: janitors, porters, waiters, garage mechanics, dishwashers, and laundry workers. How many of the seven in a hundred men in such service jobs in 1970 should be identified as "real workers" is anybody's guess—and mine is that it is most. We must also add an uncounted number of jobs that strangely get catalogued in the Census as "white collar"—among them stock clerks, baggagemen, newspaper carriers ("sales"), and even mailmen. Their work is certainly—and often heavily—"manual labor."

A safe estimate, then, is that more than five of every ten men who work in this country are manual workers, maybe as many as six in ten—and this does not count the three out of a hundred who work as agricultural laborers. Perhaps the only real difference in the working class today compared to past decades is that many working men now count on their wives' (or daughters') earnings to make the family's ends meet.

In fact, their wives are typically manual workers themselves, for among employed women, the division is sharp between those whose husbands are workers and those who are married to "professionals" or "managers." Among the latter's working wives, only one in six is in manual (or service) jobs. But among the working wives of craftsmen, two in five have such jobs; among the working wives of operatives, almost one out of two; and among the wives of laborers, about two out of three. They certainly are not smuggling any middle-class values, loyalties, or way of life into the working class based on their own experience at work. For them, on the contrary, as for most men in America, the "yoke of manual labor" is yet to be lifted.

Besides, whatever the social images "manual labor" evokes or whatever pain it involves, in real class terms the distinction between it and "nonmanual" or "white-collar" employment is, at best, misleading. How does wearing a white collar lift you into another class? Perhaps there is more prestige attached, though even this is doubtful, particularly among workers themselves. For some

"white-collar" workers there may be increased security, but how many cashiers, typists, or beauticians get "salaries" rather than hourly wages, or are less subject to layoffs than highly organized manual workers?

Since most "white-collar" employees are women, and don't wear collars, white or otherwise, anyway, the name itself surely fools us about what it represents. The vast majority of the clerical and sales workers of today are, in any event, not the respectable clerks of yesteryear. Their work is not only routinized and standardized, but they often work in offices that are larger than (and even as noisy as) small manufacturing shops—tending steno machines, typewriters, accounting machines, data processors, or keypunch equipment. They work in supermarkets and department stores with hundreds of others who punch in and punch out and wait to be relieved before they take a break. They are as bereft of control over their work and the products of their work as "manual" workers—in fact, they have *less* independence and control than such workers as crane operators and longshoremen. Beneath their nice clean collars (if they wear them at all), they are propertyless workers, entirely dependent for their livelihoods on the sale of their capacity to work. And this is the essence of working-class reality.

So, neither the working class nor the propertied class has yet departed our fair land. But do the propertied really make up a *capitalist* class? Haven't they, because ownership of the large corporations has become so dispersed, lost *control* of these decisive units of production in America? Of all the pseudofacts behind the notion that classes have withered away in America, none is as persistent as the doctrine of the "managerial revolution" or "unseen revolution" implied by these questions.

The claim is that there has been a "separation of ownership and control" in large corporations—that as the corporations have grown immense, as the original founders have died off or their fortunes supposedly dwindled, as their kids have taken to mere coupon-clipping and jetsetting, and as stock ownership has spread out widely, the capitalists have lost control of the means of production. The result, we are told, is that not capital but bureaucracy, not capitalists but "anonymous administrators," now control large corporations and hold decisive power in contemporary America. The "managers" have usurped their capitalist predecessors.

With the capitalists gone and the managers no longer their mere agents, the inherent conflict that used to exist between labor and capital also supposedly becomes a relic of the past. Instead, we now have not a system of class domination but an occupational order based on merit: "rewards" get distributed according to ability ("functional importance"). What's more, with capital dissolved and new managers motivated by other urges and the pride of professionalism in control, pumping out profit is no longer what drives the corporations in the new "postcapitalist society" we are alleged to be living in. Instead, they have become the "trustees," as Prudential's chairman said—and he was just paraphrasing Harvard economist Carl Kaysen's words of twenty years ago—for all of us in the "new industrial state."

The intent of such notions is clear: We are to believe that "labor" and "management" are just parts of the same team, doing different tasks. It is a theoretical shell game that hides the fact of class domination—of the ownership *and* control of the mines, mills, and factories by a class whose lives are certainly made easier if we don't know they're there, right behind the "anonymous bureaucrats." It hides the simple but profound fact that they live on what the rest of us produce.

One reason that the illusion of managerialism persists is that it is incredibly difficult to figure out who does control a large corporation. And the illusion is nurtured, as the late Senator Lee Metcalf put it bluntly and accurately, by a "massive cover-up" of the principal owners. There are several closely related ways that capital really controls the corporations. First, the real owners do not actually have to *manage* the corporation, or hang around the executive suite with its top officers or directors, or even be formally represented on the board, in order to have their objectives realized—that is, to exert *control.* And how much stock it takes to control a corporation is neither fixed nor standard.

The few recent studies that claim to find "management control" in most large corporations simply assume that it always takes at least 10 per cent of the stock in one pair of hands in order to assure control, but it does not work that way. If you own 10 per cent of the stock in a corporation, you are supposed to report it to the Securities and Exchange Commission (SEC), but if the same percentage is split among several of your close associates, without any formal ties between you, or with a few of your relatives, you don't have to report it—and even if you *are* required to report, who is to know if you don't? When Senator Metcalf died, he had been trying for years to get at such information, but his staff so far has had to rely on its own investigations and volunteered data.

How much stock is needed to control a corporation depends on how big the other stockowners are—and who they are, and how they are connected—and how dispersed the rest of the stock is: it also depends on how deeply the firm is indebted to the same few large banks or creditors. What sorts of ties the corporation has to others, and especially to big banks and other "financial institutions" allied with it, is also crucial. The ability to exert control grows with the number of other major firms in which any family, individual, or group of associates has an interest or actual control.

What a particular large holding of stock implies for any attempt at control depends to an unknown extent on who holds it. If it is held, say, by a leading capitalist family like the Mellons—who control at least four firms in the top 500 nonfinancials (Gulf, Alcoa, Koppers Co., Carborundum Co.) as well as the First Boston Corp., the General Reinsurance Corp., and Mellon National Bank and Trust (the fifteenth largest bank in the country, measured by deposits), and perhaps also, through the Mellon Bank's 7 per cent shareholding, Jones and Laughlin Steel—the meaning is just not the same as if some otherwise unconnected shareowner held it.

Even in corporations that a family like Mellon does not control, the presence of its representative among the principal shareowners, or on the board, can be critical. So the late Richard King Mellon as one of the principal shareowners in General Motors carried a rather different clout in its corporate policy than, say, Billy Rose did in AT&T, though he was reputed to be one of its biggest shareowners. Precisely because the number of shareowners is so large and their holdings typically so minute compared to the few biggest shareowners in a large corporation, it may not take more than 1 or 2 per cent of a company's stock to control it.

The critical holdings and connections that make control possible are invisible to the uninformed eye, and often even to the seasoned investigator. Senator Metcalf's staff found, for instance, that Laurance S. Rockefeller owns a controlling block of almost 5 per cent of the voting stock in Eastern Airlines, though his name did not appear on the required listing of its thirty top stockholders for the Civil Aeronautics Board. Neither the SEC nor the CAB nor Eastern itself could find all the accounts in which his shares were held and aggregate them until they asked *him* to do it for them—in response to Metcalf's prodding.

This helps explain why even the "insiders" who work as financial analysts at *Fortune, Forbes,* or *Business Week*, with their immense research resources and excellent files, have to rely heavily on gossip to estimate the holdings of even the leading families in corporations they have long controlled. These holdings are hidden in a welter of accounts held by brokers, dealers, foundations, holding companies, other corporations, associates, intermediaries, and "street names" (as the fictitious firms that just hold stock for someone are called on Wall Street) or other "nominees."

The extent of a leading capitalist family's holdings is also concealed by a finely woven though tangled web of kinship relations. Apparently unrelated persons with entirely different surnames can be part of a single cohesive set of kindred united to control a corporation. In Dow Chemical Company, for instance, there are seventy-eight dependents (plus spouses) of H.W. Dow who own a total of 12.6 per cent of Dow's stock. So, without research aimed at penetrating the web of kinship, any effort to find out who really controls a large corporation is hobbled at the outset.

In an outstanding recent study, Philip Burch Jr. mined the "inside information" presented over the years in the financial press and found that at least 60 per cent of the 500 top industrial corporations are "probably" (236) or "possibly" (64) under the control of an identifiable family or group of associates. Even these estimates are probably short of the mark because, in Ralph Nader's words, "no one really knows who owns the giant corporations that dominate our economic life." My own guess is that behind the thick veil of nominees, there are real controlling owners in most if not all of the large corporations that now appear to be under so-called management control.

Even if some large corporations were not really controlled by *particular* owning interests, this would not mean power had passed to the "new princes" from the old economic royalists. The higher executives would still have only *relative* independence in their activities and would be bound by the *general* interests of capital. The heads of the large corporations are the main formal agents or functionaries of capital. Their personal careers, interests, and commitments are closely tied to the expansion of corporate capital. Some are among the principal shareholders of the companies they run, and most own stock that not only provides much of their income but ranks them among the population's largest stockowners—and puts them in the propertied few.

Typically, the managers also move in the same intimate circles as the very rich. You'll find them together at debutante balls, select clubs, summer resorts and winter retreats, and other assorted watering places; and their kids attend the same private schools and rush the same fraternities and sororities—and then marry each other. Scratch a top executive and the chances are he will prove to be related to a principal shareowner. Intimate social ties and entangling kinship relations, common interests and overriding commitments unify the families of the heads of the largest corporations and their principal owners into the same cohesive, dominant class in America.

Finally, even if "management" alone had full control of the corporations, it would still have to try to pump the highest possible profits out of their workers and make the most of their investments. The conduct of management is shaped above all by the imperatives of capital accumulation—the competitive struggle among the giants (now global rather than national), the types of investments they make and markets they penetrate, and the relations they have with their workers. High managerial income and status depend, directly and indirectly, on high corporate profits. "Stock options" and bonuses and other forms of executive "compensation" aside from salaries are closely tied to corporate profit rates. Whatever their so-called professional motivations or power urges, their technocratic teamwork and bureaucratic mentality, managers' decisions on how to organize production and sales

have to be measured against the bottom line: They dare not imperil corporate profitability.

The recent spate of articles in the financial press on "how to fire a top executive"—you have them "take early retirement"—and the new placement services now catering to them, are rather pointed indicators of what happens to supposed "management control" in times of receding profit margins. In 1974, a year of severe economic crisis around the world, about half of all the chief executives in the nation's top 500 firms were expected to be replaced—in what a weekly newsletter to corporate heads called "a wave of executive ousters" that would "cause the greatest disruption in the business community since the 1929 depression."

Any obvious lowering in profit rates is also reflected in a drop in the price of the corporation's stock; this squeezes its capital base and makes it an attractive—and vulnerable—target for takeover. And this, in turn, leads to executive ousters. In addition, with the marked centralization of huge shareholdings in the trust departments of a few of the biggest banks that administer the investment portfolios of the very rich—typically, they will not take a trust of under $200,000—the tremors would be deep and the impact rather painful for any managers who turned out a below-average rate of return. The banks must unflinchingly act as "trustees" only for the top investors and real owners who control the large corporations.

Any political strategy that ignores or distorts these realities or is blind to the deep class divisions in our country cannot meet the common needs of the majority of Americans. So long as the illusion persists that our economic life has been "democratized" or that a "silent revolution" has already interred capital, emancipated labor, and redistributed wealth and income, we can be sure that a real effort to achieve those aims will be slated for yet another postponement.

QUESTIONS

1. Is there any justification for inequality in the United States?

2. How concentrated is wealth in America? What are the social, economic, and political implications of this concentration?

3. Why is information on the distribution of wealth so difficult to obtain?

DANIEL YANKELOVITCH

Who Gets Ahead in America?

One of the most cherished of all American beliefs is that everyone has the same chance to "make it" up the economic and social ladder—or, to put it in more sociological terms, that there is equality of opportunity for social mobility. The successful maintenance of the class system requires, of course, that such a belief be widespread. So long as the poor believe they have as good a chance as the next person to become rich, and that they have only themselves to blame if they do not, they will tend to accept the system.

But actually the poor, like most Americans, are deceived by the myth. Decades of sociological research have produced overwhelming evidence that many of the factors that influence social mobility are beyond personal control. In general, the offspring of the advantaged accrue more advantages, and the offspring of the disadvantaged remain relatively disadvantaged; but the picture is complicated by a variety of other factors, such as sex, race, and education.

Exactly who, then, is likely to achieve social mobility? Christopher Jencks surveyed the sociological literature to find the answer to this question for his book Who Gets Ahead? *(1979). In this article, Daniel Yankelovitch summarizes some of Jencks's main findings.*

Seven years ago, Christopher Jencks unsettled many believers in traditional American values with his book, *Inequality: A Reassessment of the Effect of Family and Schooling in America.* What Jencks and several colleagues found, by examining the body of research material then available, was that neither family background nor education could account for all the variations in income and status among Americans. Economic success, he concluded, was explained not as much by birth, or striving, or "competence" as by a number of other unmeasured variables, which he described collectively as "luck."

Even though it discounted the importance of family advantage, Jencks's analysis upset liberals by downplaying the value of education and special compensatory programs—which educational reformers and antipoverty warriors believed would eventually narrow the income gap between the rich and the poor. As Jencks saw it, the only real way to achieve economic equality in America was some form of income redistribution that would remove inequities through the tax system or through government subsidies.

Now, Jencks and 11 colleagues at the Harvard Center for Educational Policy Research have published a new report that analyzes a broader range of studies covering a number of new variables. In *Who Gets Ahead?—The Determinants of Economic Success in America*, Jencks abandons the conclusion that "luck" is the most critical factor in economic success. He and his colleagues report a host of other findings that appear, on the surface, to be less controversial, but may turn out to be more so.

The investigators examined five large-scale national surveys of men, covering a 12-year span, along with six special-purpose surveys, four of which had never been previously analyzed. They worked during a five-year period, with research costs estimated at $400,000 (most of it from the U.S. Department of Health, Education, and Welfare and from private foundations).

The portrait drawn by Jencks and his colleagues is of a classridden America in which being born into the "right" family looms large. It is a rigid America, in which a man's academic test scores in the sixth grade shape his own expectations and those of others toward him. The men who were studied (none of the 11 surveys included women, a serious drawback) seem to be divided at an early stage of their lives into two fixed groups: those with promise and those without. Those with promise finish college, the gateway to success.

Who Gets Ahead? also depicts a superficial America, in which surface characteristics, such as college credentials or the color of a man's skin, count so heavily that what he is really worth as a person, his moral character, what he knows, what he can do, how hard he tries, hardly seem to count at all. Finally, although Jencks's group would acknowledge it was concerned with just one important set of values—economic success—their report furthers the impression of a unidimensional America, in which only making money and achieving occupational success seem to count in life. I recognize Jencks's America as one might recognize a friend whose features suddenly appear abstract, contorted, remote. I know the image from my own surveys—yet something is amiss.

Jencks's report contains many important findings, but we cannot draw valid prescriptions for action from them unless we see the work in a broader social context. For several powerful reasons, we must exercise extreme caution in accepting its messages at face value.

Probably to avoid the controversy stimulated by *Inequality*, Jencks's team has gone out of its way to avoid discussing the policy implications of its findings. The conclusions are largely descriptive, leaving the task of drawing inferences to the reader.

. . .

What Really Counts? Possible Interpretations

Inevitably, academic readers, for whom the book is primarily intended, will draw one kind of inference, policy analysts another, and journalists still another. The public itself will draw no direct inferences at all, because not many people will be able to read the book. But the determined journalist, on whom the public ultimately depends, might reasonably uncover the following logical but misleading messages in *Who Gets Ahead?*:

• If you are black and have been persuaded to stay in high school because "finishing high school will help you find a better job later on," forget what you've been told. Even for whites, the economic advantages of finishing high school without going on to college are marginal at best; for blacks, they count for almost nothing.

• If you are black and in college and suspect that finishing college is not going to help you economically, you are wrong. Buckle down, hang in, and finish—at all costs. If it's money and a good job you are after, stay in college and graduate, no matter how you do it. Take gut courses, if necessary. Go to some second- or third-rate college, if you must. Economically, it doesn't matter what you

study, how much you learn, or where you go to college—as long as you finish.

• If you are white, the same holds true. It is the degree that really counts; that credential is worth more than almost anything else—including what you may have learned.

• Be careful to be born into the "right" family. The right family is one in which your father occupies a high-status position in a field like law, medicine, or business. He earns an excellent income. He and your mother received good educations, have used birth control so you are part of a small family, and have had the foresight to be white. If you come from a family that, measured by income and status, is one of the top one-fifth in the country, your earnings are likely to be 150 to 186 percent of the national average. If you come from a family in the bottom one-fifth, your earnings are likely to be only 56 to 67 percent of the national average. Your occupational status will be affected by "family foresight" even more sharply than your income will be.

• If you have not exercised such foresight, do not despair—as long as you had good test scores in the sixth grade. If your academic test scores are high (about 15 points or more above average), you may still get ahead—poor family background notwithstanding. That is because you are likely to be encouraged to go to college. There is, however, some cash value to being academically "test smart." Among those who have the same family background and the same level of educational attainment, the ones that test well earn about 11 to 14 percent more than their less intelligent cohorts. But, lest you rejoice prematurely, it should be pointed out that 11 to 14 percent is not very much, once you realize that the difference between the lowest-paying and the highest-paying jobs in America lies on a 600-percent spectrum!

• If you have not done well on academic tests in the sixth grade, perhaps you should think of giving up. Your test grades are not likely to improve, because people are not going to encourage you much after that point, and you are not likely to motivate yourself to do better. You will probably not go to college.

• If you have high academic test scores but decide to forgo college, the chances are that your superior intelligence will not do you much good economically, unless it enables you to capitalize on unexpected opportunities.

• If you have leadership ability—and clearly exhibit it from the sixth to 10th grades—this gift of personality is worth as much to you as your cognitive skills are (especially if you finish college).

• If you are sociable in high school and date heavily, you are likely to end up in a lower-status position than some of your less sociable friends who are more attentive to their studies. But there is one consolation: apparently your sociability will gain you extra earnings, within the limits of your lower occupational status.

• If you come from the right kind of family and are academically gifted, you may develop highly cultural interests. If so, you are likely to wind up with lots of education, but your refined tastes will be of little extra economic value to you.

• If you are Jewish, WASP, or German Catholic, you have a small economic edge over other ethnic groups; if you are Italian, French Catholic, or Irish Protestant, you are at a small but not decisive disadvantage. If you were born in the South and choose to stay there, you are likely to earn less money than if you chose to leave the South. (The same holds true for being born on a farm and choosing to stay there.)

• If you are determined not to succeed economically, you must be careful to do all of the following: fail to finish college; choose the wrong family background; express low aspirations about your future; undervalue your leadership abilities and under no circumstances display them for others to see. If you follow that prescription, you will not make out very well—statistically—even if you are smarter than the other boys and perform well on academic tests.

All these generalizations could be extracted from the patchwork of 11 surveys analyzed by Jencks and his colleagues that covered men from the ages of 25 to 64 in a period from the early 1960s to the early 1970s. To bring this massive study into sharper focus, it is necessary to take a closer look at the sources of the information and the analysis to which the data was subjected.

Among the national studies were a survey of "productive Americans" conducted by the University of Michigan's Survey Research Center in 1965, and the U.S. Current Population Survey of 1962. The special-purpose surveys included a study of veterans under the age of 35 done in 1964, and another of brothers who were given questionnaires twice, once in 1960, when they were in the 11th and 12th grades, and again [in 1971–1972.]

The two measures of success the researchers used were earned income, determined in several ways, and occupational status, as reflected on the Duncan scale, a well-established measure that ranks occupations according to the number of years of education they require and how much people in them earn.

The Jencks team tried to determine the degree to which four sets of factors studied in the surveys were associated with success. They were: family background; cognitive ability, as reflected in scores on academic tests in primary and secondary school; personality traits and behavior in high school, as described by the subjects themselves and their teachers; and number of years of school completed.

Through statistical analysis, an effort was made to isolate how much of the variation in men's later economic success was attributable to each of those variables when considered independently of the others. Since the four sets of factors interact with one another in complex fashion, pulling them apart to assess the contribution of each was not easy. It involved some deft statistical footwork, especially since complete data for all four sets of factors were not available for any of the respondents.

The breakdown shows that some factors contributed more to occupational status than to earnings. If all other factors were ignored, for example, the years of schooling men completed would have accounted for 45 to 55 percent of the variations in occupational status, but only 15 to 20 percent of variations in earnings. Family background was reckoned to account for 45 to 50 percent of the variation in occupational status, but apparently for only about 15 to 35 percent of variations in men's incomes.

Of the 13 demographic specifics that came under the heading of "family background," not all have equal weight. One of the 13, "father's occupation" by itself accounts for about one-third of the influence attributed to family background; another third is accounted for by a cluster of variables that included father's and mother's education, parental income, family size, and race.

Another group of variables appears to have a weight equal to each of the others. That is the group of "unmeasured variables," which were part of what Jencks in his first study referred to as "luck," and which deserve special attention.

How could the researchers attribute so much weight to variables their sources of data had failed to identify? One ingenious feature of the research design permitted them to do so: an analysis of the occupational parallels between large numbers of pairs of brothers. Suppose, for example, we select a sample of doctors. On the Duncan scale, doctors would stand well above the national average for all occupations. If one looks at the occupational status of their brothers, one finds that *their* occupations are also well above the national average. The similarity between the brothers can be accounted for partly by the occupational status of the father, and partly by various demographic factors, race and size of family, for example. That leaves roughly one-third of the resemblance unexplained. The authors conclude: "The remaining third is presumably due to unmeasured social, psychological, or genetic factors that vary within demographic groups."

One difficulty in discerning relative influences on economic success stems from the fact that everything seems to be related to everything else. If you come from the right family background, you are more likely to finish college, to have high academic test scores, and to have the personality traits associated with economic success. But the correlations are far from perfect. In fact, 52 percent of the variations in occupational status come from factors other than family background.

The most important of those is educational attainment: the number of years of schooling completed. One of the most interesting findings shows how important the last year of college is, relative to other years. What counts is *finishing* college and getting credentials, rather than what one might learn in the last year, or any year. Besides family background, the single most important factor contributing to a man's economic success is finishing college. Of course, academic promise, motivation, and other personality characteristics may help a man graduate. But if you don't translate promising academic ability into college credentials, you gain precious little economic advantage.

For men coming from the same types of homes and having similar test scores, the earnings advantage of completing only high school is not great, especially for nonwhites. Completing college, on the other hand, brings considerable economic advantage. Completing high school gives whites a 15 to 25 percent future earnings advantage over those not completing high school (the figure is smaller for blacks). But completing college gives whites a whopping 49 percent advantage over those who do not—the percentage is even larger for blacks. This income advantage derives primarily from the fact that those who finish college have won the credential needed for entering higher-status occupations. "Unless high school attendance is followed by a college education," the researchers conclude, "its economic value appears quite modest"—especially for blacks.

The results of academic tests in the sixth grade can predict future success, as can scores on tests taken in later years. The ability to predict from early performance is attributed to the presence of stable motivational attitudes in the person being tested. The researchers point out that this pattern has remained fairly constant since the turn of the century. They underscore the point, frequently made, that those with academic ability succeed because they are selectively encouraged to have higher aspirations and to attend school for longer periods. The researchers emphasize that the mere ability to remain in school is more important than the results of academic test scores. "A man's ability in the sixth to 11th grade has important effects on his later occupational status," they say, "but 60 to 80 percent of the effect is explained by *the amount of schooling he gets*" (italics added).

The contribution of personality characteristics to success is more elusive. Indeed, the chapter on personality in *Who Gets Ahead?* is meager, reflecting the paucity of survey data on such characteristics. The material covered by Jencks and his team included only self-descriptions of personality traits by 10th-graders, followed up by a mail questionnaire that large numbers of respondents failed to return; 10th grade teachers' observations of "executive ability" and other characteristics in their pupils, and descriptions by the students themselves, in self-administered questionnaires, of their goals, aspirations, study habits, and participation as leaders in various activities.

The authors admit, "All our conclusions about . . . noncognitive traits have been general and tentative." Among their tentative findings is that "leadership, assessed both by the individual himself or his teacher, or expressed through behavior, has an appreciable positive effect on earnings." However, such personality attributes as being "vigorous, calm, and tidy" produce no economic advantage. Men who rated themselves high in sociability (including such activity as frequent dating) were destined to end up in lower-status jobs than those who claimed to have good study habits.

The data on racial factors in success are more clearcut. Given the same test scores and years of schooling, blacks have fewer opportunities to get ahead than whites do. The researchers state: "A strong prima facie case can be made for assuming . . . that despite affirmative action, nonwhites suffer from discrimination." Discrimination appears to operate less for those who graduate from college than for those who attain lower levels of education, the investigators conclude.

. . .

Some Crucial Reservations

If we are not to be misled by literal interpretations of the analysis—such as those I sketched earlier—we must keep in mind the limited scope of the data. Jencks's report excludes women. Several of the studies it examines focus solely on a man's characteristics when he *first* enters the labor market and how those match up with both initial and subsequent earnings; none takes into account changes in skill, competence, and emotional growth after he is launched on his career, and how those factors affect earnings. (I have no quarrel with the conclusion that traits measured in the sixth and 10th grades may have an important bearing on eventual occupational success or failure. I have more difficulty in believing that changes occurring in those factors during a man's career have *no* bearing on subsequent earnings and status.) And, perhaps most seriously of all, there is virtually no data later than 1973. Jencks and his associates are forthcoming in acknowledging the limitations in the scope of their study, but they do not tell us how to adjust for them.

The time gap is particularly serious. If the six-to-17-year lag between the data and the analysis had occurred in any earlier period, it would pose a difficulty, but not a grave one. However, the period from 1973 to the present has brought changes in the country's economic position and in the public's outlook that substantially affect the interpretation of prior research findings on issues of economic success.

Not only was the nation shaken by the Arab oil embargo in 1973, but since that time we have become familiar with the phenomenon of stagflation—high inflation combined with high unemployment. In the past, our political stability has depended heavily on economic growth, high rates of productivity, and material abundance. In the years since 1973, overall economic growth has slowed down and the rate of increase in productivity has been cut in half. At the same time, women have flooded the work force, filling jobs that policymakers had assumed would go to blacks, and once again widening the gap between white and nonwhite incomes—after a trend toward closing the gap in earlier years. In the period since 1973, we have entered an age of shrinking expectations: we have begun to realize that we must accustom ourselves to limits, shortages, and inflation as disagreeable facts of life. Those changes are of such a magnitude that, while they do not invalidate Jencks's findings, they oblige us to interpret them in a different light.

I worry, too, about the "unmeasured variables" in the study, because I interpret this category more broadly than the Harvard team does. Jencks and his associates assume that most of the unmeasured variables are clustered under the heading of family background. But some of them must surely enter in disguised form in the category they call noncognitive factors. They have gone further in identifying and acknowledging such factors in their models than have many previous researchers. While conceding that that part of their analysis is thin, they are pleased that their study attributes greater importance to individual personality characteristics than previous research does. Nevertheless, the measures of noncognitive factors they are forced to use are quite narrow and insubstantial. Indeed, most of the noncognitive factors discovered to be important by social scientists in the past 150 years have been excluded from consideration.

The researchers have no really sensitive measures of cultural influence beyond those subsumed under family background. Parents, friends, teachers, ministers, and others in the larger culture convey to children the norms, rules, meanings, and behaviors that are critical to their eventual success or failure. But few questions are raised about possible differences in the values, authority, and impact of those adult figures that may contribute to success or failure.

The Harvard researchers take up the question of genetic influences on success, but push it aside like a hot potato; they say the existing data cannot measure the impact of heredity adequately. In addition, there are almost no measures in the study of how attitudes and values may correlate with income and status. Apart from some assessments by young boys of their own qualities, the all-important category of ego strength and characteristics associated with it that seem important to success, such as self-esteem and assertiveness, are absent. Finally, and most important of all, there is virtually no discussion of "character" or "judgment," which blend cognitive and noncognitive skills.

Even if Jencks's model had taken into account all the important variables, I would still have trouble accepting the rather deterministic picture it draws of mobility in America. In the history of humankind, needless suffering has often been rationalized as "fate." Slaves, on occasion, were taught that their condition was dictated by divine providence, which was not to be questioned. For centuries, poverty was assumed to be the inevitable lot of the majority. In the 19th and early 20th centuries, the Social Darwinists saw fate in the evolutionary principle of "survival of the fittest," which enabled the successful to assert their inherent superiority. And Freud saw anatomy as destiny.

The newest and most devious version of this ancient form of tyranny is that of statistical norms. Mere averages are reified into the national norms against which many individuals measure themselves. Properly understood, these averages constitute useful bits of information, but their meaning for any individual calls for exquisite qualification.

It would be tragic, for example, if Jencks's findings were interpreted to mean that blacks should drop out of high school, that people with low scores in the sixth grade should give up trying, that people who don't finish college should assume they cannot achieve the kind of success they seek, that lack of leadership ability in school closes the door to future economic success, and that credentials count more heavily than skill, character, knowledge, or judgment.

It would be tragic and yet, almost inevitably, that is what will happen. Few people will give research studies such as this the kind of attention required to understand the true meaning of the findings. Decades of research and five years of analysis will be mined for the few obvious "messages" that lie closest to the surface.

Another caveat: In the light of some of my recent research, the Harvard group's preoccupation with economic success rings a faintly old-fashioned and archaic note. American values have been changing in far-reaching ways over the past decade. To be sure, economic success and mobility continue to play an important role in our lives. People still want money; they still want to be successful. But, in complex and subtle ways, many Americans also want to give less of themselves to what they've come to regard as a nose-to-the-grindstone way of life. Jencks's analysis presupposes a homogeneity in American values centering on the idea of getting ahead. It fails to take even passing note of the pluralism in values that has developed in recent years.

For millions of Americans, new questions are appearing. Instead of just asking, "Will I be able to make a good living?" "Will I be successful?" "Will I raise happy, healthy, successful children?"—the typical questions of the 1950s and 1960s—Americans today are pondering more introspective matters. "How can I find self-fulfillment?" they are now asking. "What kinds of commitments should I be making?" "What is worth sacrificing for?" "How can I grow?"

Fifty-eight percent of the respondents in one of our recent studies indicated that they no longer believe it is the responsibility of a man with a family to take the job that pays the most, rather than one that may be more satisfying but pays less. Although predictably larger proportions of high- and middle-income Americans who can afford that sentiment subscribe to it, fully half of those in the sample with family incomes under $10,000 agreed that self-fulfillment is an important part of the definition of success—suggesting that the shift in values is not confined to the upper and middle classes.

Science, Intuition, and Policy

Jencks and his colleagues have taken long strides in developing techniques to study the enigma of economic success in America. But even after this excellent and thorough study, we must assume that the present state of the investigative art does not yet tell us why some people achieve success while others do not. We may know more now than we did before, but not enough to allow us to build public policy on the results with any confidence.

Eventually, effective bridges may be built between scientific study and public policy. But they have not yet been built, and, in the end, studies such as this one will always be haunted by philosophical questions that have not yet been resolved: Can we ever understand complex human behavior by preselecting all the relevant variables and measures (thereby excluding other, perhaps more elusive, influences)? Will this approach ever bring us deeper knowledge of human behavior than more direct, insightful approaches? In its present form, social science forces us to choose between, on the one hand, *a priori* statistical models of human behavior and, on the other, understanding based on intuition, experience, insight, judgment, and observation—all of which pose serious difficulties of their own. Until the two paths of study are integrated and understood, as many uneasy questions must be raised about computer-based models as about intuitive judgment. Calling one "science" and the other "intuition" does not prove the superiority or inadequacy of either method.

The effort put forth in *Who Gets Ahead?* is a little like that of someone who has put on blinders to show what a wonderful job he can do finding his way with a cane. The virtuoso performance is impressive, but the practical person cannot resist asking, "Why not open your eyes and look?" When the next large-scale study of success in America is done, I hope it will rely on fewer equations and contain more sensitive interpretation of factors that

may affect success but do not lend themselves to statistical analysis.

Even with all its drawbacks, the Jencks report, properly understood, can be of considerable value. One of the most provocative suggestions in the book, for instance, is that the nature of racial prejudice in America may be changing in significant ways. I believe that it is. In earlier years, racial discrimination was due more to the kinds of gross disenfranchisement that could be combated by legal action and legislative mandate. More recently, it seems to be based mainly on stereotype and "image" factors, some of which operate subliminally.

These sterotypes serve, in much the same way as the presence or absence of academic credentials do, to close the door to minority groups, whose cultural styles and mannerisms are different from those of the white majority. They are quick, mindless methods of communicating information about people, much of which may not be germane to questions of competence or employability.

Many blacks mistrust survey findings that show a lessening of prejudice, believing they are meaningless when evidence shows that the economic situation of blacks has, in fact, grown worse in recent years. This is a complex and distressing situation, and I believe Jencks's findings suggest a number of constructive approaches to the problem.

The psychological aspects of the problem, though intangible, may be even more important for individual blacks. To blacks, there may be little difference between being blocked from advancement by a "real prejudice" and being blocked by a "negative stereotype." Such fine distinctions may seem like hair-splitting—evidence of obtuseness or bad faith. Perhaps the fault lies in our language.

Deeply rooted racial prejudice is difficult to extirpate. To do so requires all the authority, even the coerciveness, of the law. But the kind of stereotypes that appear to exist today may be easier to get around. For example, the Jencks findings show that where a negative black stereotype is upheld (the black-as-high-school-dropout, for instance), blacks fare worse economically than comparable white high school dropouts. But when the black stereotype is broken (the black-as-college-graduate), blacks do *better* than white counterparts when other variables are controlled. The black who finishes college makes two significant breakthroughs: he measurably improves his occupational and employment position, and he breaks the stereotype for himself and for others. If social and economic stereotypes can be broken by education, then they are not totally racial (based on skin color alone), but at least partly a matter of social-class prejudice and mental laziness.

Equal rights leaders, it seems to me, must unceasingly monitor the sources of negative stereotypes in the media. They should be especially careful to avoid the inadvertent effects of some of their own strategies. By stressing the accumulated failures of vocational and educational programs targeted for blacks, they may reinforce negative stereotypes. Television producer Norman Lear's recent withdrawal of a new series that reinforced such existing stereotypes about blacks was an act of statesmanship for which the country should be grateful. Techniques exist in abundance for conveying, both in the media and educational institutions, stereotype-breaking aspects of black experience, black competence, and black success that whites may not encounter in their daily experience.

Also, public policy should probably focus sharply on developing cognitive skills normally associated with high school training through actual work experience. When people who do not intend to go to college realize that a high school degree has lost much of its economic value, some will be reluctant to go through with what they may view as an empty ritual. Under present conditions, they have little choice. But federal (CETA) monies and other programs have just begun to lay the groundwork for job training that combines high school level skills with actual experience in the workplace. Those programs can be upgraded and improved if we give the matter real thought.

If *Who Gets Ahead?* provides clues on how to undermine the social damage done by racism, prejudice, and excessive credentialism, then that alone makes it a major contribution to American society. But if implications for educational, governmental, and familial behavior are plucked prematurely and indelicately from the study's regression equations, the good work done by Jencks and his colleagues will become part of the problem rather than part of the solution.

QUESTIONS

1. Will those who work hard in the United States get ahead? Is there equal opportunity in this country?
2. What social, rather than individual, factors can affect a person's social mobility?
3. To what extent are the poor responsible for their poverty?

HOWELL RAINES

Struggling for Power and Identity

When white settlers and the indigenous inhabitants of North America fought a series of bitter conflicts over possession of land and natural resources, the victory went to the side with superior military technology. The vanquished were banished to reserves, relegated to second-class citizenship and wretched material conditions, and absurdly stereotyped (notably in Western movies) as warlike savages who had cruelly and without provocation gone to war, and thus brought retribution upon themselves.

In recent years, history has been gradually revised, and most Americans are now aware of the injustices visited on Indians in the past. If anything, there is something of a collective guilt among whites on the issue, a sense that some recompense is due the Indians. As it happens, militant Indian organizations have successfully demanded recompense in many ways—for example, by claiming title to lands illegally seized from them, or by asserting their controversial rights over the rivers that flow through their reserves and the rich mineral resources that lie below them.

Inevitably, however, the rising militancy of the Indians threatens to generate new tension between them and the whites, for once again the two groups face the prospect of conflict over access to scarce resources. In this article, Howell Raines examines the changing attitude of the Indians and the potential difficulties that they face as they demand a larger slice of the American pie.

American Indians gave up beads-and-blanket capitalism on Jan. 31, 1975, in Billings, Mont. That day, at a meeting in a small college planted on a frigid escarpment of the Rockies, a group of tribal leaders got a look at the generous contracts under which American energy companies now do business with oil-rich third-world nations. For the Indians, it was an instant education in the real value of their "worthless" reservations. They learned that, unlike the canny oil merchants of the Middle East, their tribes were still being ripped off with Colonial-era prices for the vast mineral wealth that lies under the feet of this nation's most impoverished minority. Prophetically, the meeting in Billings was entitled "Indian Tribes as Emerging Nations."

In the ensuing years, more and more Indians have come to think of their reservations as tiny sovereign nations within the United States. If a new generation of Indian leaders has its way, they are going to be rich little nations, too. For the 50 million acres of despised and for the most part barren lands pawned off on the Indians in the last century contain about one-third of the American West's stripable coal and half of the nation's uranium, not to mention enough oil to bedazzle the eyes of Texas. At today's prices, the 70 billion tons of coal under Indian land is worth over $1,000 billion, or $1 trillion.

Swiftly, the drive for economic power has become the main thrust of Indian activism throughout the nation—in the Rocky Mountain coal fields, along the salmon rivers of the Northwest and on vast Eastern tracts where, after almost 200 years of silence, Indians stunned and infuriated whites by claiming "aboriginal title." "We are trying to prove," said LaDonna Harris, the Comanche activist whose Americans for Indian Opportunity organized the Billings conference, "that you don't have to be poor to be an Indian."

But development-minded Indians face formidable obstacles, including proposals to take over their energy reserves by abolishing the reservations. Indeed, white sympathy and guilt over the treatment of Indians seem to be fading before a new mood of fiscal austerity. The first Americans are facing a white backlash that, spreading east from Seattle in ever-widening circles of outrage, may be felt all the way from oil-company board rooms to the

United States Supreme Court. Last summer's 3,000 mile, cross-country trek to the nation's capital, the Longest Walk, was an attempt to combat this problem, but because of deep and historic divisions in their own ranks, Indians have so far been unable to meet the backlash with an effective, united front.

There is, for instance, the cultural gap between the 650,000 Indians living on or near reservations and the 350,000 urban Indians in the red ghettos of Minneapolis, Chicago, Los Angeles and other cities. Also, the tribal tradition means that many native Americans think of themselves as, say, Kiowas first and Indians second. Within most major tribes, government is so radically democratic that it is virtually impossible to find a native American who expects to see the emergence of a red Martin Luther King Jr. who can speak for Indian America. Beyond that, conservative Indians view with suspicion those tribal leaders who want to rip open Mother Earth. To them, the cancer outbreak among Navajo uranium miners symbolizes the deadly dangers of bringing white commerce to Indian Country.

The term Indian Country first came into the language as a name for the seemingly limitless territories beyond the westernmost white settlements. As used by today's Indians, it refers to both their scattered pockets of land and to a state of mind. What should white Americans think about both the territory and the mentality that is Indian Country? Can even a rough justice be now imposed on the despair-filled history of the nation's oldest social conflict? Does history, in fact, demand a justice that penalizes 220 million people for the good of a minority that has willfully resisted the assimilative process that has brought prosperity to other impoverished minorities? The answers, such as they are, are as diverse as the terrain and people of an Indian Country that stretches from the beige corridors of the Bureau of Indian Affairs in Washington, D.C., to the red grit hills of Arizona and New Mexico.

Coal-Smoke Signal

In her tarpaper shack on a windy hilltop in Fruitland, N.M., Emma Yazzie dreams of an enchanted ancestral past. But she is living, literally and quite unwillingly, on the ramparts of the Indian future. "I want it to be as though I was living a long time ago," said the 72-year-old Navajo sheepherder, speaking carefully in English, her second language. It used to be such a beautiful place. We had all kinds of colored grass."

Today, the grass that feeds Emma Yazzie's 19 sheep is uniformly brown. For this, she blames pollution from the nearby Four Corners Power Plant, the huge, coal-fired electrical generator whose plume of smoke is visible for miles across the desert.

That plant towers over Emma Yazzie's tiny farmstead on the northern rim of the 14-million-acre Navajo Reservation. To the west, where the one-room hogans of her relatives once dotted the mesas, lies the 31,000-acre strip mine leased from her tribe to provide the Four Corners plant with cheap Navajo coal. To the south, along the San Juan River where the Yazzie clan once held idyllic summer encampments, the pumps of the generating plant suck at the stream beside which Miss Yazzie was born.

Emma Yazzie has lost much and gained nothing. Gone are the landscapes and pellucid skies she loved. Yet, the pumps bring her no water, and the humming power lines bypass her lightless shack. So, of course, does the money. Utah International Mining Company, a subsidiary of General Electric, pays a royalty of only 15 cents per ton to the Navajo tribe for the coal used at Four Corners. Yet, on today's market, a white landowner would receive a royalty of $1.50 per ton. Utah International and General Electric owe this windfall to the Bureau of Indian Affairs: For years, the B.I.A. negotiated all reservation coal leases for the Indians to assure that the tribal leaders wouldn't make any naive or stupid deals.

But Emma Yazzie and the other American Indians who own 4 percent of the nation's land want to make their own decisions about how their lands are used. "Self-determination" and "sovereignty" are the Indians' new catchwords. Like the black movement that started in the South in the 50's, the Indian movement gained its momentum from Federal court decisions that have upset many whites. In 1975, for example, the courts upheld tribal claims to the northern two-thirds of Maine, and that case signaled Easterners that the "Indian problem" was not restricted to the Far West. Last October, the Maine case was finally settled when the Passamaquoddy and Penobscot tribes gave up their claim to 12.5 million acres in return for a relatively modest payment of $37 million and the right to expand their reservations by 100,000 acres. But the settlement left standing the ruling that Indians have an aboriginal title to lands occupied by whites who never obtained the Congressional approval required by the long-ignored Indian Non-Intercourse Act of 1790.

Comparisons between the black movement and the Indian movement can be pushed too far. Indians lack the numbers and unity of the black minority, and, while blacks sought assimilation into the American mainstream, Indians face the far more complicated question of whether to preserve separate Indian culture. Morever, the key issue to the blacks was social justice, and, to many Indian leaders, at least, it is economic power. They want to take advantage of the world's new competition for scarce land and dwindling resources. So, Emma Yazzie notwithstanding, the leaders want to use the new leverage gained from the mineral wealth of their reservations as a substitute for the marching feet that carried black demands to national attention.

Emma Yazzie has been educated by history to view all developers, white and Indian alike, with contempt and despair. "They want to stick their noses in the ground like a pig," she says. Clasping rough hands around her chipped turquoise brooch, the old woman gazes toward the plant. "They kill the grass," she continues. "They kill a lot of Navajo, too. That smoke smells bad and it goes into our hearts. The horse is not strong anymore. It's weak. And the sheep come up blind."

Indian OPEC

Eighty miles from Emma Yazzie and her dreams of the past, lives the man who has offered himself as the hope of the Indian future. He drives a Lincoln Continental, favors pin-striped suits and when indicted for embezzlement in 1977 hired F. Lee Bailey to plead his case, which ended in a hung jury. The most important icon in his office in Window Rock, Ariz., is not a tribal artifact, but a softball-sized lump of coal on a brass stand. Peter MacDonald, the 50-year-old chairman of the Navajo Nation, is organizer and chairman of the Council of Energy Resources Tribes (CERT), which he described in a letter to President Carter as "the native American OPEC." Mr. MacDonald intends for CERT to serve much the same function for the Indian tribes, whose reservations he views as "dependent, yet sovereign," nations within the United States.

We used the same trick that John Wayne would use," Mr. MacDonald said of the impulse that led to the founding of CERT. "We circled the wagons. We circled the tribes and said, 'By golly, if you're going to get the coal, you're not going to deal just with the Crow or just with the Navajo or just with the Cheyenne. You've got to deal with the rest of us.'"

The CERT wagons are circled over the richest unexploited fossil fuel and mineral deposits on the continent. Mr. MacDonald created a public-relations crisis for the organization in 1977 when, snubbed in his request for a White House meeting, he announced he had contacted OPEC's Arab oil experts for advice on how to develop the reservations most profitably. Rather quickly, $200,000 and then $2 million in Federal grants showered on CERT—presumably to divert the Indians from striking an alliance with the Arab organization. Despite this Federal largesse, Mr. MacDonald, a Marine veteran of World War II, is still furious about accusations that he was unpatriotic to consult OPEC. "It sounded like I'm a traitor, that CERT tribes are enemies of the United States," he said. "It's all because I'm trying to cling to what little is left to us."

It is simply a matter, noted Mr. MacDonald, an electrical engineer who once worked in missile development for Hughes Aircraft, of Indians learning to play by the white man's rules. After all, the reservation system was structured to confine Indians to land that the Government experts of 100 years ago believed forever worthless. "We have now decided," he said with obvious delight at the irony, "to use the very structure devised by whites for their protection to assert what we describe as Indian self-determination, meaning that this is our reservation, that we have a certain sovereignty and we're going to exercise it."

As defined by CERT, self-determination and sovereignty mean, for one thing, that tribal governments rather than the Bureau of Indian Affairs ought to negotiate energy contracts. The argument heard all over Indian Country is that Indians couldn't possibly do any worse than the B.I.A. The bureau, for instance, neglected to put escalation or termination clauses in leases negotiated when coal was selling for $6 a ton. As a result, the Navajos are saddled with the 15-cents- to 37.5-cents-per-ton royalties even though the retail price of coal has soared to $15 to $20 per ton and standard royalties are up to $1.50 and more. The CERT tribes are, indeed, doing better. For one thing, the tribes are insisting on joint-venture contracts rather than the B.I.A.-approved leases under which the Indians signed over most of their powers as landowners to the mining companies. The Navajo tribal council recently received $6 million in front money in a proposed joint venture with Exxon to develop the uranium deposits on the nation's largest reservation. (Its 14 million acres in Utah, New Mexico and Arizona make the Navajo Nation the equal in size of West Virginia.) Unhappy with the 17.5-cents-per-ton royalty negotiated for them by the B.I.A., the Crow tribe of Montana is suing to overturn strip-mining contracts with Shell and AMAX, and is now shopping for a better deal. Mr. MacDonald and his tribe's Wall Street-trained attorney, George Vlassis of Phoenix, plan to challenge every company that enjoys a cheap lease, including the coal suppliers at the Four Corners Power Plant. "The next one on the hit list," Mr. Vlassis says bluntly, "is Utah International."

Mr. MacDonald's critics question whether his government can, and will, use the increased income to give the reservation the self-sufficient, business economy he envisions. With its $200 million a year in Federal subsidies, the reservation has, by tradition, a welfare-state economy in which the tribal government, with 7,000 workers, is the largest employer. Also, in the past few years, a number of other tribal officials have been charged with embezzlement, sparking demonstrations in which dissidents accused the "Mac-Dollar" government of ripping off tribal income. (Mr. MacDonald said his own indictment, in which he was accused of getting about $7,900 by submitting false travel vouchers to an Arizona utility, was part of a conspiracy to discredit him as an Indian spokesman.) . . .

Such controversies aside, Mr. MacDonald and leaders

of other tribes may face political obstacles to their plans to use mining income for economic development. So far, only a handful of Indians have benefited personally from the coal boom. For example, the 160 Navajos at a Gulf Oil subsidiary's strip mine near Window Rock make $9 to $12 per hour. But per capita income on the reservation remains only about $1,000 per year—one-seventh of the national average. In many cases, grandparents, parents and children live on dirt floors of one-room hogans with no plumbing and no privacy. And there is always the possibility that these impoverished reservation residents might vote against investment programs for their energy income and demand "per caps"—lump-sum, per capita payments that have a disastrous history of winding up in the pockets of a few white merchants and Indian hustlers.

"In a generation, the resource will be played out and you'll have a few native American sheiks and an impoverished mass," predicted John Redhouse, a Navajo activist who has organized traditionalist Indians to fight a coal-gasification plant proposed for Burnham, N.M., in the Four Corners area of the reservation. The Government and energy companies are simply using CERT, he says, to legitimize their plans to turn the Western reservations into "national-sacrifice areas." He called the plans "spiritual and physical genocide." Even Indians sympathetic to Mr. MacDonald's general goal of economic development fear that his tactics will contribute to the backlash. "My notion is that it's harmful to Indians," says Sam Deloria, the Standing Rock Sioux who heads the American Indian Law Center at the University of New Mexico, "to communicate the idea that Indians are going to get rich off other Americans' heating bills."

. . .

The Red and The White

If the prospect of unaccustomed prosperity looms before the Western reservations, a familiar despair still lurks in the bars of the red ghetto along East Franklin Avenue in Minneapolis. "The State Alcohol and Drug Commission says 43 to 45 percent of the Indian population are directly involved in alcoholism," says Dennis Hisgun, a 35-year-old Sioux. "And 80 to 85 percent are indirectly involved; that is, they belong to the family of a drinker. I can't prove those figures, but I think they're pretty accurate. We're now seeing our chronic age dropping to the late 20's and early 30's. It used to be in the 40's. So that means alcoholism is epidemic. We have three counselors. We're hardly making a dent."

Mr. Hisgun is social-services director of the Minneapolis Native American Center, and a former alcoholic who has discovered the Catch-22 of many Government programs for Indians. "Indian alcoholism is getting worse. Traditional treatment modalities don't work. Yet we're forced to use them to get funding. For instance, when I sobered up, I did it by turning to a group of Indian people attempting to stay sober. All we had was a house—a place to help one another get up off the ground. They were very unorthodox and that's not acceptable to funding agencies."

The nation's red ghettos are, like the alcohol therapies described by Mr. Hisgun, showcases for Federal policies and programs that don't work. The Eisenhower Administration's termination policy—so named because it sought to end the Government's legal relationship with the tribes—encouraged the relocation of Indians to the cities. Today, an estimated 8,000 to 15,000 Chippewas, Sioux and Oneidas live in what Mr. Hisgun describes as a chronically frustrated community that combines the worst of the reservation and urban worlds.

"One of the detrimental things of reservation life is it's a welfare state—homes, everything, on a hand-out basis—and they bring a lot of that to the city," Mr. Hisgun says. "But I think everybody who comes to the city has a dream—a dream of making it, a dream about improving their lives. But then prejudice slaps them right in the face and they're worse off. Call it culture shock. When your bubble is burst, there's nothing left but to go back home and start dreaming again. They get into that cycle. There's a high mobility between reservations and cities."

In the cities, Indians are not moving in any substantial way into the middle class, and they suffer disproportionately from the social, economic and health problems that go along with urban poverty. Half the Indian families in Minneapolis are on welfare; in more than half there is only one parent. At the American Indian Health Center, one of several agencies funded in response to the burst of activism that spawned the American Indian Movement (AIM) in 1968, the staff considers a patient over 50 "an old Indian." Infant mortality is three times the rate for whites, and doctors see a disproportionately high rate of mental-health problems.

One response to that panoply of problems has been a rebirth of faith in apocalyptic Indian prophecies about the doom of the white world. Clyde Bellecourt, the militant founder and president of AIM, has turned from confrontation politics to running the Heart of the Earth Survival School. It is one of several "bilingual, bicultural" schools around the country that, according to Mr. Bellecourt, are the only institutions that can save Indians from sharing the white man's fate.

"For our children to survive," he says, "they have to be able to hunt, fish, put up a tepee and go into a sacred sweat to purify themselves." A tall man who wears his hair in long braids, he fiddles with a butane cigarette lighter. "When the energy crisis closes the Safeway store, our children will be able to survive."

Such doomsday prophecies have been a powerful force

in Indian Country since 1889, when the Ghost Dance cult sprang from a medicine man's vision that predicted the disappearance of the white man and the return of the buffalo. Last July's Longest Walk to Washington was inspired by the vision of a Sioux holy man, Eagle Feather. The protest, which was intended to remind Congress to respect Indian treaty rights, had little impact, and perhaps one reason is that many of its participants, including Mr. Bellecourt, now have less faith in the political process than in the Old Prophecy that the end for the white man must be near.

. . .

Taos Tug-of-War

The Taos have never been a craft people. They were an agricultural people. Just in the last five years they've started making crafts. "There's no reason not to accommodate the tourist traffic." As he speaks, the proprietor of Tony Reyna's Indian Shop in Taos, N.M., leans on a showcase full of turquoise jewelry and contemplates the paradox of his "traditionalist" tribe adapting itself to the marketplace. "It's a money age we live in," he concludes rather sadly. "Now we don't have time to raise our own crops. It's a deterioration of our heritage and culture. But let's face it. We're not pure."

The cultural tug-of-war he describes has been going on for almost 500 years, and remains the most heated debate in Indian Country. Even in the cities, Indian leaders give lip service to the slogan of the Red Power activists who proclaimed during the 1969 occupation of Alcatraz Island that "we must keep the old ways." But as the Pueblos of Taos and the Reyna family have learned, keeping the old ways is not so easy.

Mr. Reyna's shop—"Indian-owned since 1950"—is halfway between the Anglo town of Taos, where D.H. Lawrence and Mabel Dodge Luhan established a famed artists' colony, and the Pueblo village of Taos, where 1,700 Indians still live in the adobe high-rises that have stood on this red earth for more than 900 years. With one eye on the past and one on the future, Mr. Reyna built his shop in the old way, shaping the adobe bricks by hand. He stocked only genuine Indian goods made in the traditional patterns. As a member of the tribal council, he worked for return to tribal ownership of the sacred Blue Lake, from which, according to the tribe's religion, the Taos people first emerged. Mr. Reyna supported the ordinance passed by the council that prohibited electric lights and modern plumbing within 50 yards of the village walls.

Thus, every morning, as in centuries past, the Taos women fill water buckets at the clear creek that tumbles down to the village from the Blue Lake in the Sangre de Cristo Mountains. Alas, many mornings bring angry exchanges, too, between the villagers and the camera-toting tourists who are at once the village's curse and its indispensable economic resource. At Mrs. Luhan's suggestion, the Taos tribe long ago began charging admission at the village gate. Today, "photographers fees" and "artists fees" range from $2 for a still camera to $25 for the right to make a finished painting. The daily flow of out-of-state cars into the Taos Pueblo parking lot—at a $1.50 each—aggravates that deep sense of anger that Indians feel at being regarded as tourist attractions for the master race. Yet, as J. Vince Lujan, the tribal secretary explains, "a bulk of the tribal government is financed from tourist fees."

Equally paradoxical, is the village rule against electricity. The ambiance it creates attracts tourists but the inconvenience works against the goal of cultural preservation by creating a village of the elderly. "Most of our young people are giving way to Western culture," says Mr. Lujan. "They're moving out and finding dwellings in the countryside."

The same shift that is taking place in the Taos Pueblo is taking place in Tony Renya's gift shop. Philip Reyna, 19, helps his father in the shop and is extremely knowledgeable about Indian jewelry and art. Philip does not credit the talk that the Indian economic movement will spark a Pan-Indian cultural renaissance among people his age. "It would be nice, but it's not going to happen," he says. "Indians have always been fighting among themselves—the Navajos were always attacking the Pueblos—and it hasn't changed. Then you have urbanized Indians in Los Angeles and elsewhere, and they have a completely different point of view. Their only contact with their culture is the powwows, and that's not real. Look at the costumes—polyester and artificial dyes. No uprising will ever occur because, as times go by, the culture will go down."

Philip himself is studying to become a sound engineer in a rock-and-roll recording studio.

Fishing Rights, Civil Rights

"We've been called the niggers of Washington," says Ramona Bennett, a small woman with a fine-boned face and a fierce manner. Her outrage fairly fills her office in the Puyallup headquarters at Tacoma, Wash., as she speaks of the court's guaranteeing "our rights that we can't get enforced because our skins are the wrong color."

"I was shot at last November when I was seven months pregnant," says Mrs. Bennett, former chairman of the tribal council, to which she still belongs as an elected member. She suspects it was white fishermen who "tried to blow my head off—our fishermen have been facing this harassment for 90 years."

And as so often happened with the black movement in the South, a gritty and lonely Federal judge stands at the epicenter of this controversy. George H. Boldt, now 74 and in frail health, was nearing the end of his career in 1974 when the fishing-rights case came before him. Then, like his fellow Eisenhower appointees to the Federal bench—Judges Frank Johnson and Richard Rives in Montgomery, Ala., and Elbert Tuttle in Atlanta—Judge Boldt found himself compelled by his reading of the law to render a civil-rights decision that made him a social and political outcast in the eyes of many whites who expected conservative rulings from a judge appointed by a conservative President.

In a rare interview, Judge Boldt recalls how he summoned his law clerk to his office in the Tacoma Post Office building and instructed him "to put on that table every single case from the beginning of the country that pertains in any way to the rights of Indians. The two of us went through every single one—an enormous task. We came down on Sundays."

Treaties enacted with Washington's Indians more than 100 years ago guaranteed the Indians the right to fish "at all usual and accustomed grounds . . . in common with all citizens of the territory." After studying 19th-century legal dictionaries, Judge Boldt decided that the term "in common with" meant, at the time the treaties were drafted, that the Indians had a right to the opportunity to take 50 percent of the fish in an annual salmon catch now worth $200 million a year.

White reaction was intense. When state fishery officials refused to enforce the judge's ruling, he took over regulation of the fishery, Washington's fifth-largest industry, in much the same way that other Federal judges have taken over school districts that refused to desegregate. His critics claimed to have raised $100,000 to finance an impeachment campaign. He was accused of having an Indian mistress. The Interstate Congress for Equal Rights and Responsibilities, which was formed to combat the decision and is now a political presence in 23 states, investigated the "background" of the judge and his wife. Bumper stickers read: "Let's Give 50 Percent of Judge Boldt to the Indians." A bomb was exploded in the Federal building at Tacoma. When Judge Boldt had heart surgery in February, he was confined to an isolated, heavily guarded wing of the hospital.

"I was burned in effigy and they still do that," Judge Boldt says. "The [non-Indian] fishermen have a champion and he maligns me continually and steadily, and he's spurred on by the Attorney General here. He's got to be with the fishermen, don't you see? You can't just be honest in this state and get anywhere because of the enormous amount of condemnation heaped on me since I wrote that decision that day."

. . .

Sid Mills, with the music of the Nisqually roaring in his ears, sings the heart song of Indian Country. Two Seattle writers, Roberto Maestas and Bruce Johansen, have discovered that faith in white greed is so deeply ingrained in Indian culture that when the first white miners swept into the Black Hills gold fields, the Lakota didn't even bother to identify the invaders by skin color. They simply called them *Wasi-chu*—a campfire term that means "greedy person" or "he who takes the fat."

Who is to take the fat of the Indians' land is, of course, the issue to be decided. On some reservations, the militant young and old Indians who weep with nostalgia at the sight of a buffalo are banding together to stop the bulldozers. Others like LaDonna Harris, the wife of former Senator Fred Harris of Oklahoma, believe that, in an energy-hungry nation grumpily facing leaner times, development is inevitable. The only choice before the Indians, she said, is whether they get a good price or simply more beads and blankets.

The Indians who are ready to do business believe money from the earth can provide a defense against a threat to Indian survival that could prove as devastating as the Indian wars that ended in 1890 with the slaying of 200 Sioux at Wounded Knee, S.D. This new threat is the toughening mood of an American majority disenchanted with a doctrine of white guilt. As expressed in lawsuits challenging special treatment for minorities and in the spread of organizations such as the Interstate Congress for Equal Rights and Responsibilities, this view holds that there are no due bills to be collected from history. "I get sick and tired of these tribal leaders saying you took our land away," says Howard Gray, the dapper, 72-year-old Seattle public-relations man who founded the I.C.E.R.R. "There's not a soul living today that had anything to do with the injustice done to the Indians. I say discount the past. We're living in the present."

To Indians who cannot so easily forget the past, those words are as frightening as the rattle and thunder of approaching cavalry.

QUESTIONS

1. It has long been federal policy to treat reservation Indians as a separate group, rather than to encourage their integration into society. Comment on this policy.

2. Indians suffer today because of wrongs perpetrated generations ago. But do whites today still have a moral obligation to make amends for past injustices?

3. What was the stereotype of Indians in Western movies until a few years ago? How and why is this stereotype changing? What is the current stereotype, and how accurate do you think it might be?

ALLAN M. BRANDT

Racism and Research: The Case of the Tuskegee Syphilis Study

The Tuskegee study of untreated syphilis was one of the most sordid episodes in American race relations— and American medicine—in this century. For a period of forty years, until 1972, doctors and public officials held a deathwatch over some 400 syphilitic black sharecroppers in Alabama, in a "scientific" experiment that was riddled with invalid methods and in any case could produce no new useful information about syphilis.

The subjects of the study were never told they were participating in an "experiment"; treatment that could easily have cured them was deliberately withheld; and they were systematically deceived about the purpose of this "health program." As a result, scores of people died of the disease; others became permanently blind or insane: and the children of several were born with congenital syphilis.

How could this extraordinary episode, requiring the collaboration of doctors, county and state health departments, draft boards, and the U.S. Public Health Service, ever have occurred? As Allan Brandt suggests, the Tuskegee study can be understood only in terms of racism. It had its roots in pseudoscientific theories about race and about black sexuality. The study's willingness to treat people as less than human merely reflected the deep, irrational prejudice that permeated the rest of American life.

In 1932 the U.S. Public Health Service (USPHS) initiated an experiment in Macon County, Alabama, to determine the natural course of untreated, latent syphilis in black males. The test comprised 400 syphilitic men, as well as 200 uninfected men who served as controls. The first published report of the study appeared in 1936 with subsequent papers issued every four to six years, through the 1960s. When penicillin became widely available by the early 1950s as the preferred treatment for syphilis, the men did not receive therapy. In fact on several occasions, the USPHS actually sought to prevent treatment. Moreover, a committee at the federally operated Center for Disease Control decided in 1969 that the study should be continued. Only in 1972, when accounts of the study first appeared in the national press, did the Department of Health, Education and Welfare halt the experiment. At that time seventy-four of the test subjects were still alive; at least twenty-eight, but perhaps more than 100, had died directly from advanced syphilitic lesions.[1] In August 1972, HEW appointed an investigatory panel which issued a report the following year. The panel found the study to have been "ethically unjustified," and argued that penicillin should have been provided to the men.[2]

This article attempts to place the Tuskegee Study in a historical context and to assess its ethical implications. Despite the media attention which the study received, the HEW *Final Report*, and the criticism expressed by several professional organizations, the experiment has been largely misunderstood. The most basic questions of *how* the study was undertaken in the first place and *why* it continued for forty years were never addressed by the HEW investigation. Moreover, the panel misconstrued the nature of the experiment, failing to consult important documents available at the National Archives which bear significantly on its ethical assessment. Only by examining the specific ways in which values are engaged in scientific research can the study be understood.

Racism and Medical Opinion

A brief review of the prevailing scientific thought regarding race and heredity in the early twentieth century is fundamental for an understanding of the Tuskegee

From *Hastings Center Magazine*, December 1978. Reprinted with permission of The Hastings Center. © Institute of Society, Ethics and the Life Sciences, 360 Broadway, Hastings-on-Hudson, N.Y. 10706.

Study. By the turn of the century, Darwinism had provided a new rationale for American racism.[3] Essentially primitive peoples, it was argued, could not be assimilated into a complex, white civilization. Scientists speculated that in the struggle for survival the Negro in America was doomed. Particularly prone to disease, vice, and crime, black Americans could not be helped by education or philanthropy. Social Darwinists analyzed census data to predict the virtual extinction of the Negro in the twentieth century, for they believed the Negro race in America was in the throes of a degenerative evolutionary process.[4]

The medical profession supported these findings of late nineteenth– and early twentieth-century anthropologists, ethnologists, and biologists. Physicians studying the effects of emancipation on health concluded almost universally that freedom had caused the mental, moral, and physical deterioration of the black population.[5] They substantiated this argument by citing examples in the comparative anatomy of the black and white races. As Dr. W. T. English wrote: "A careful inspection reveals the body of the negro a mass of minor defects and imperfections from the crown of the head to the soles of the feet . . ."[6] Cranial structures, wide nasal apertures, receding chins, projecting jaws, all typed the Negro as the lowest species in the Darwinian hierarchy.[7]

Interest in racial differences centered on the sexual nature of blacks. The Negro, doctors explained, possessed an excessive sexual desire, which threatened the very foundations of white society. As one physician noted in the *Journal of the American Medical Association,* "The negro springs from a southern race, and as such his sexual appetite is strong; all of his environments stimulate this appetite, and as a general rule his emotional type of religion certainly does not decrease it."[8] Doctors reported a complete lack of morality on the part of the blacks.

> Virtue in the negro race is like angels' visits—few and far between. In a practice of sixteen years I have never examined a virgin negro over fourteen years of age.[9]

A particularly ominous feature of this overzealous sexuality, doctors argued, was the black males' desire for white women. "A perversion from which most races are exempt," wrote Dr. English, "prompts the negro's inclination toward white women . . ."[10] Though English estimated the "gray matter of the negro brain" to be at least a thousand years behind that of the white races, his genital organs were overdeveloped. As Dr. William Lee Howard noted:

> The attacks on defenseless white women are evidences of racial instincts that are about as amenable to ethical culture as is the inherent odor of the race. . . . When education will reduce the size of the negro's penis as well as bring about the sensitiveness of the terminal fibers which exist in the Caucasian, then will it also be able to prevent the African's birthright to sexual madness and excess.[11]

One southern medical journal proposed "Castration Instead of Lynching," as retribution for black sexual crimes. "An impressive trial by a ghost-like kuklux klan [sic] and a 'ghost' physician or surgeon to perform the operation would make it an event the 'patient' would never forget," noted the editorial.[12]

According to these physicians, lust and immorality, unstable families, and reversion to barbaric tendencies made blacks especially prone to venereal diseases. One doctor estimated that over 50 percent of all Negroes over the age of twenty-five were syphilitic.[13] Virtually free of disease as slaves, they were now overwhelmed by it, according to informed medical opinion. Moreover, doctors believed that treatment for venereal disease among blacks was impossible, particularly because in its latent stage the symptoms of syphilis become quiescent. As Dr. Thomas W. Murrell wrote:

> They come for treatment at the beginning and at the end. When there are visible manifestations or when harried by pain, they readily come, for as a race they are not averse to physic; but tell them not, though they look well and feel well, that they are still diseased. Here ignorance rates science a fool. . . .[14]

Even the best educated black, according to Murrell, could not be convinced to seek treatment for syphilis.[15] Venereal disease, according to some doctors, threatened the future of the race. The medical profession attributed the low birth rate among blacks to the high prevalence of venereal disease which caused stillbirths and miscarriages. Moreover, the high rates of syphilis were thought to lead to increased insanity and crime. One doctor writing at the turn of the century estimated that the number of insane Negroes had increased thirteen-fold since the end of the Civil War.[16] Dr. Murrell's conclusion echoed the most informed anthropological and ethnological data:

> So the scourge sweeps among them. Those that are treated are only half cured, and the effort to assimilate a complex civilization driving their diseased minds until the results are criminal records. Perhaps here, in conjunction with tuberculosis, will be the end of the negro problem. Disease will accomplish what man cannot do.[17]

This particular configuration of ideas formed the core of medical opinion concerning blacks, sex, and disease in the early twentieth century. Doctors generally discounted socioeconomic explanations of the state of black health, arguing that better medical care could not alter the evolutionary scheme.[18] These assumptions provide the backdrop for examining the Tuskegee Syphilis Study.

The Origins of the Experiment

In 1929, under a grant from the Julius Rosenwald Fund, the USPHS conducted studies in the rural South to determine the prevalence of syphilis among blacks and explore the possibilities for mass treatment. The USPHS found Macon County, Alabama, in which the town of Tuskegee is located, to have the highest syphilis rate of the six counties surveyed. The Rosenwald Study concluded that mass treatment could be successfully implemented among rural blacks.[19] Although it is doubtful that the necessary funds would have been allocated even in the best economic conditions, after the economy collapsed in 1929, the findings were ignored. It is, however, ironic that the Tuskegee Study came to be based on findings of the Rosenwald Study that demonstrated the possibilities of mass treatment.

Three years later, in 1932, Dr. Taliaferro Clark, Chief of the USPHS Venereal Disease Division and author of the Rosenwald Study report, decided that conditions in Macon County merited renewed attention. Clark believed the high prevalence of syphilis offered an "unusual opportunity" for observation. From its inception, the USPHS regarded the Tuskegee Study as a classic "study in nature," rather than an experiment.[20] As long as syphilis was so prevalent in Macon and most of the blacks went untreated throughout life, it seemed only natural to Clark that it would be valuable to observe the consequences. He described it as a "ready-made situation."[21] Surgeon General H.S. Cumming wrote to R.R. Moton, Director of the Tuskegee Institute:

> The recent syphilis control demonstration carried out in Macon County, with the financial assistance of the Julius Rosenwald Fund, revealed the presence of an unusually high rate in this county and, what is more remarkable, the fact that 99 per cent of this group was entirely without previous treatment. This combination, together with the expected cooperation of your hospital, offers an unparalleled opportunity for carrying on this piece of scientific research which probably cannot be duplicated anywhere else in the world.[22]

Although no formal protocol appears to have been written, several letters of Clark and Cumming suggest what the USPHS hoped to find. Clark indicated that it would be important to see how disease affected the daily lives of the men:

> The results of these studies of case records suggest the desirability of making a further study of the effect of untreated syphilis on the human economy among people now living and engaged in their daily pursuits.[23]

It also seems that the USPHS believed the experiment might demonstrate that antisyphilitic treatment was unnecessary. As Cumming noted: "It is expected the results of this study may have a marked bearing on the treatment, or conversely the non-necessity of treatment, of cases of latent syphilis."[24]

The immediate source of Cumming's hypothesis appears to have been the famous Oslo Study of untreated syphilis. Between 1890 and 1910, Professor C. Boeck, the chief of the Oslo Venereal Clinic, withheld treatment from almost two thousand patients infected with syphilis.

He was convinced that therapies then available, primarily mercurial ointment, were of no value. When arsenic therapy became widely available by 1910, after Paul Ehrlich's historic discovery of "606," the study was abandoned. E. Bruusgaard, Boeck's successor, conducted a follow-up study of 473 of the untreated patients from 1925 to 1927. He found that 27.9 percent of these patients had undergone a "spontaneous cure," and now manifested no symptoms of the disease. Moreover, he estimated that as many as 70 percent of all syphilitics went through life without inconvenience from the disease.[25] His study, however, clearly acknowledged the dangers of untreated syphilis for the remaining 30 percent.

Thus every major textbook of syphilis at the time of the Tuskegee Study's inception strongly advocated treating syphilis even in its latent stages, which follow the initial inflammatory reaction. In discussing the Oslo Study, Dr. J. E. Moore, one of the nation's leading venereologists wrote, "This summary of Bruusgaard's study is by no means intended to suggest that syphilis be allowed to pass untreated."[26] If a complete cure could not be effected, at least the most devastating effects of the disease could be avoided. Although the standard therapies of the time, arsenical compounds and bismuth injection, involved certain dangers because of their toxicity, the alternatives were much worse. As the Oslo Study had shown, untreated syphilis could lead to cardiovascular disease, insanity, and premature death.[27] Moore wrote in his 1933 textbook:

> Though it imposes a slight though measurable risk of its own, treatment markedly diminishes the risk from syphilis. In latent syphilis, as I shall show, the probability of progression, relapse, or death is reduced from a probable 25–30 percent without treatment to about 5 percent with it; and the gravity of the relapse if it occurs, is markedly diminished.[28]

"Another compelling reason for treatment," noted Moore, "exists in the fact that every patient with latent syphilis may be, and perhaps is, infectious for others."[29] In 1932, the year in which the Tuskegee Study began, the USPHS sponsored and published a paper by Moore and six other syphilis experts that strongly argued for treating latent syphilis.[30]

The Oslo Study, therefore, could not have provided justification for the USPHS to undertake a study that did not entail treatment. Rather, the suppositions that conditions in Tuskegee existed "naturally" and that men would not be treated anyway provided the experiment's rationale. In turn, these two assumptions rested on the prevailing medical attitudes concerning blacks, sex, and disease. For example, Clark explained the prevalence of venereal disease in Macon County by emphasizing promiscuity among blacks:

> This state of affairs is due to the paucity of doctors, rather low intelligence of the Negro population in this section, de-

pressed economic conditions, and the very common promiscuous sex relations of this population group which not only contribute to the spread of syphilis but also contribute to the prevailing indifference with regard to treatment.[31]

In fact, Moore, who had written so persuasively in favor of treating latent syphilis, suggested that existing knowledge did not apply to Negroes. Although he had called the Oslo Study "a never-to-be-repeated human experiment,"[32] he served as an expert consultant to the Tuskegee Study:

I think that such a study as you have contemplated would be of immense value. It will be necessary of course in the consideration of the results to evaluate the special factors introduced by a selection of the material from negro males. Syphilis in the negro is in many respects almost a different disease from syphilis in the white.[33]

Dr. O. C. Wenger, chief of the federally operated venereal disease clinic at Hot Springs, Arkansas, praised Moore's judgment, adding, "This study will emphasize those differences."[34] On another occasion he advised Clark, "We must remember we are dealing with a group of people who are illiterate, have no conception of time, and whose personal history is always indefinite."[35]

The doctors who devised and directed the Tuskegee Study accepted the mainstream assumptions regarding blacks and venereal disease. The premise that blacks, promiscuous and lustful, would not seek or continue treatment, shaped the study. A test of untreated syphilis seemed "natural" because the USPHS presumed the men would never be treated; the Tuskegee Study made that a self-fulfilling prophecy.

Selecting the Subjects

Clark sent Dr. Raymond Vonderlehr to Tuskegee in September 1932 to assemble a sample of men with latent syphilis for the experiment. The basic design of the study called for the selection of syphilitic black males between the ages of twenty-five and sixty, a thorough physical examination including x-rays, and finally, a spinal tap to determine the incidence of neuro-syphilis.[36] They had no intention of providing any treatment for the infected men.[37] The USPHS originally scheduled the whole experiment to last six months; it seemed to be both a simple and inexpensive project.

The task of collecting the sample, however, proved to be more difficult than the USPHS had supposed. Vonderlehr canvassed the largely illiterate, poverty-stricken population of sharecroppers and tenant farmers in search of test subjects. If his circulars requested only men over twenty-five to attend his clinics, none would appear, suspecting he was conducting draft physicals. Therefore, he was forced to test large numbers of women and men who did not fit the experiment's specifications. This involved considerable expense since the USPHS had promised

Macon County Board of Health that it would treat those who were infected, but not included in the study.[38] Clark wrote to Vonderlehr about the situation: "It never once occurred to me that we would be called upon to treat a large part of the county as return for the privilege of making this study . . . I am anxious to keep the expenditures for treatment down to the lowest possible point because it is the one item of expenditure in connection with the study most difficult to defend despite our knowledge of the need therefor."[39] Vonderlehr responded: "If we could find from 100 to 200 cases . . . we would not have to do another Wassermann on useless individuals . . ."[40]

Significantly, the attempt to develop the sample contradicted the prediction the USPHS had made initially regarding the prevalence of the disease in Macon County. Overall rates of syphilis fell well below expectations; as opposed to the USPHS projection of 35 percent, 20 percent of those tested were actually diseased.[41] Moreover, those who had sought and received previous treatment far exceeded the expectations of the USPHS. Clark noted in a letter to Vonderlehr:

I find your report of March 6th quite interesting but regret the necessity for Wassermanning [sic] . . . such a large number of individuals in order to uncover this relatively limited number of untreated cases.[42]

Further difficulties arose in enlisting the subjects to participate in the experiment, to be "Wassermanned," and to return for a subsequent series of examinations. Vonderlehr found that only the offer of treatment elicited the cooperation of the men. They were told they were ill and were promised free care. Offered therapy, they became willing subjects.[43] The USPHS did not tell the men that they were participants in an experiment; on the contrary, the subjects believed they were being treated for "bad blood"—the rural South's colloquialism for syphilis. They thought they were participating in a public health demonstration similar to the one that had been conducted by the Julius Rosenwald Fund in Tuskegee several years earlier. In the end, the men were so eager for medical care that the number of defaulters in the experiment proved to be insignificant.[44]

To preserve the subjects' interest, Vonderlehr gave most of the men mercurial ointment, a noneffective drug, while some of the younger men apparently received inadequate dosages of neoarsphenamine.[45] This required Vonderlehr to write frequently to Clark requesting supplies. He feared the experiment would fail if the men were not offered treatment.

It is desirable and essential if the study is to be a success to maintain the interest of each of the cases examined by me through to the time when the spinal puncture can be completed. Expenditure of several hundred dollars for drugs for these men would be well worth while if their interest and cooperation would be maintained in so doing. . . . It is my desire to keep the main purpose of the work from the negroes in the county and continue their interest in treatment. That is what the vast majority wants and the examination seems relatively unimportant to them in comparison. It would probably cause the entire experiment to collapse if the clinics were stopped before the work is completed.[46]

On another occasion he explained:

Dozens of patients have been sent away without treatment during the past two weeks and it would have been impossible to continue without the free distribution of drugs because of the unfavorable impression made on the negro.[47]

The readiness of the test subjects to participate of course contradicted the notion that blacks would not seek or continue therapy.

The final procedure of the experiment was to be a spinal tap to test for evidence of neuro-syphilis. The USPHS presented this purely diagnostic exam, which often entails considerable pain and complications, to the men as a "special treatment." Clark explained to Moore:

We have not yet commenced the spinal punctures. This operation will be deferred to the last in order not to unduly disturb our field work by any adverse reports by the patients subjected to spinal puncture because of some disagreeable sensations following this procedure. These negroes are very ignorant and easily influenced by things that would be of minor significance in a more intelligent group.[48]

The letter to the subjects announcing the spinal tap read:

Some time ago you were given a thorough examination and since that time we hope you have gotten a great deal of treatment for bad blood. You will now be given your last chance to get a second examination. This examination is a very special one and after it is finished you will be given a special treatment if it is believed you are in a condition to stand it. . . .

REMEMBER THIS IS YOUR LAST CHANCE FOR SPECIAL FREE TREATMENT. BE SURE TO MEET THE NURSE.[49]

The HEW investigation did not uncover this crucial fact: the men participated in the study under the guise of treatment.

Despite the fact that their assumption regarding prevalence and black attitudes toward treatment had proved wrong, the USPHS decided in the summer of 1933 to continue the study. Once again, it seemed only "natural" to pursue the research since the sample already existed, and with a depressed economy, the cost of treatment appeared prohibitive—although there is no indication it was ever considered. Vonderlehr first suggested extending the study in letters to Clark and Wenger:

At the end of this project we shall have a considerable number of cases presenting various complications of syphilis, who have received only mercury and may still be considered untreated in the modern sense of therapy. Should these cases be followed over a period of from five to ten years many interesting facts could be learned regarding the course and complications of untreated syphilis.[50]

"As I see it," responded Wenger, "we have no further interest in these patients *until they die*."[51] Apparently, the physicians engaged in the experiment believed that only autopsies could scientifically confirm the findings of the study. Surgeon General Cumming explained this in a letter to R. R. Moton, requesting the continued cooperation of the Tuskegee Institute Hospital:

This study which was predominantly clinical in character points to the frequent occurrence of severe complications involving the various vital organs of the body and indicates that syphilis as a disease does a great deal of damage. Since clinical observations are not considered final in the medical world, it is our desire to continue observation on the cases selected for the recent study and if possible to bring a percentage of these cases to autopsy so that pathological confirmation may be made of the disease processes.[52]

Bringing the men to autopsy required the USPHS to devise a further series of deceptions and inducements. Wenger warned Vonderlehr that the men must not realize that they would be autopsied:

There is one danger in the latter plan and that is if the colored population become aware that accepting free hospital care means a post-mortem every darkey will leave Macon County and it will hurt [Dr. Eugene] Dibble's hospital.[53]

"Naturally," responded Vonderlehr, "it is not my intention to let it be generally known that the main object of the present activities is the bringing of the men to necropsy."[54] The subjects' trust in the USPHS made the plan viable. The USPHS gave Dr. Dibble, the Director of the Tuskegee Institute Hospital, an interim appointment to the Public Health Service. As Wenger noted:

One thing is certain. The only way we are going to get post-mortems is to have the demise take place in Dibble's hospital and when these colored folks are told that Doctor Dibble is now a Government doctor too they will have more confidence.[53]

After the USPHS approved the continuation of the experiment in 1933, Vonderlehr decided that it would be necessary to select a group of healthy, uninfected men to serve as controls. Vonderlehr, who had succeeded Clark as Chief of the Venereal Disease Division, sent Dr. J. R. Heller to Tuskegee to gather the control group. Heller distributed drugs (noneffective) to these men, which suggests that they also believed they were undergoing treatment.[56] Control subjects who became syphilitic were simply transferred to the test group—a strikingly inept violation of standard research procedure.[57]

The USPHS offered several inducements to maintain contact and to procure the continued cooperation of the men. Eunice Rivers, a black nurse, was hired to follow their health and to secure approval for autopsies. She gave the men noneffective medicines—"spring tonic" and aspirin—as well as transportation and hot meals on the days of their examinations.[58] More important, Nurse Rivers provided continuity to the project over the entire forty-year period. By supplying "medicinals," the USPHS was able to continue to deceive the participants, who believed that they were receiving therapy from the government doctors. Deceit was integral to the study. When the test subjects complained about spinal taps one doctor wrote:

They simply do not like spinal punctures. A few of those who were tapped are enthusiastic over the results but to most, the suggestion causes violent shaking of the head; others claim they were robbed of their procreative powers (regardless of the fact that I claim it stimulates them).[59]

Letters to the subjects announcing an impending USPHS visit to Tuskegee explained: "[The doctor] wants to make a special examination to find out how you have been feeling and whether the treatment has improved your health."[60] In fact, after the first six months of the study, the USPHS had furnished no treatment whatsoever.

Finally, because it proved difficult to persuade the men to come to the hospital when they became severely ill, the USPHS promised to cover their burial expenses. The Milbank Memorial Fund provided approximately $50 per man for this purpose beginning in 1935. This was a particularly strong inducement as funeral rites constituted an important component of the cultural life of rural blacks.[61] One report of the study concluded, "Without this suasion it would, we believe, have been impossible to secure the cooperation of the group and their families."[62]

Reports of the study's findings, which appeared regularly in the medical press beginning in 1936, consistently cited the ravages of untreated syphilis. The first paper, read at the 1936 American Medical Association annual meeting, found "that syphilis in this period [latency] tends to greatly increase the frequency of manifestations of cardiovascular disease."[63] Only 16 percent of the subjects gave no sign of morbidity as opposed to 61 percent of the controls. Ten years later, a report noted coldly, "The fact that nearly twice as large a proportion of the syphilitic individuals as of the control group has died is a very striking one." Life expectancy, concluded the doctors, is reduced by about 20 percent.[64]

A 1955 article found that slightly more than 30 percent of the test group autopsied had died *directly* from advanced syphilitic lesions of either the cardiovascular or the central nervous system.[65] Another published account stated, "Review of those still living reveals that an appreciable number have late complications of syphilis which probably will result, for some at least, in contributing materially to the ultimate cause of death."[66] In 1950, Dr. Wenger had concluded, "We now know, where we could only surmise before, that we have contributed to their ailments and shortened their lives."[67] As black physician

Vernal Cave, a member of the HEW panel, later wrote, "They proved a point, then proved a point, then proved a point."[68]

During the forty years of the experiment the USPHS had sought on several occasions to ensure that the subjects did not receive treatment from other sources. To this end, Vonderlehr met with groups of local black doctors in 1934, to ask their cooperation in not treating the men. Lists of subjects were distributed to Macon County physicians along with letters requesting them to refer these men back to the USPHS if they sought care.[69] The USPHS warned the Alabama Health Department not to treat the test subjects when they took a mobile VD unit into Tuskegee in the early 1940s.[70] In 1941, the Army drafted several subjects and told them to begin antisyphilitic treatment immediately. The USPHS supplied the draft board with a list of 256 names they desired to have excluded from treatment, and the board complied.[71]

In spite of these efforts, by the early 1950s many of the men had secured some treatment on their own. By 1952, almost 30 percent of the test subjects had received some penicillin, although only 7.5 percent had received what could be considered adequate doses.[72] Vonderlehr wrote to one of the participating physicians, "I hope that the availability of antibiotics has not interfered too much with this project."[73] A report published in 1955 considered whether the treatment that some of the men had obtained had "defeated" the study. The article attempted to explain the relatively low exposure to penicillin in an age of antibiotics, suggesting as a reason: "the stoicism of these men as a group; they still regard hospitals and medicines with suspicion and prefer an occasional dose of time-honored herbs or tonics to modern drugs."[74] The authors failed to note that the men believed they already were under the care of the government doctors and thus saw no need to seek treatment elsewhere. Any treatment which the men might have received, concluded the report, had been insufficient to compromise the experiment.

When the USPHS evaluated the status of the study in the 1960s they continued to rationalize the racial aspects of the experiment. For example, the minutes of a 1965 meeting at the Center for Disease Control recorded:

Racial issue was mentioned briefly. Will not affect the study. Any questions can be handled by saying these people were at the point that therapy would no longer help them. They are getting better medical care than they would under any other circumstances.[75]

A group of physicians met again at the CDC in 1969 to decide whether or not to terminate the study. Although one doctor argued that the study should be stopped and the men treated, the consensus was to continue. Dr. J. Lawton Smith remarked, "You will never have another study like this; take advantage of it."[76] A memo prepared by Dr. James B. Lucas, Assistant Chief of the Venereal Disease Branch, stated: "Nothing learned will prevent, find, or cure a single case of infectious syphilis or bring us closer to our basic mission of controlling venereal disease in the United States."[77] He concluded, however, that the study should be continued "along its present lines." When the first accounts of the experiment appeared in the national press in July 1972, data were still being collected and autopsies performed.[78]

The HEW Final Report

HEW finally formed the Tuskegee Syphilis Study Ad Hoc Advisory Panel on August 28, 1972, in response to criticism that the press descriptions of the experiment had triggered. The panel, composed of nine members, five of them black, concentrated on two issues. First, was the study justified in 1932 and had the men given their informed consent? Second, should penicillin have been provided when it became available in the early 1950s? The panel was also charged with determining if the study should be terminated and assessing current policies regarding experimentation with human subjects.[79] The group issued their report in June 1973.

By focusing on the issues of penicillin therapy and informed consent, the *Final Report* and the investigation betrayed a basic misunderstanding of the experiment's purposes and design. The HEW report implied that the failure to provide penicillin constituted the study's major ethical misjudgment; implicit was the assumption that no adequate therapy existed prior to penicillin. Nonetheless medical authorities firmly believed in the efficacy of arsenotherapy for treating syphilis at the time of the experiment's inception in 1932. The panel further failed to recognize that the entire study had been predicated on nontreatment. Provision of effective medication would have violated the rationale of the experiment—to study the natural course of the disease until death. On several occasions, in fact, the USPHS had prevented the men from receiving proper treatment. Indeed, there is no evidence that the USPHS ever considered providing penicillin.

The other focus of the *Final Report*—informed consent—also served to obscure the historical facts of the experiment. In light of the deceptions and exploitations which the experiment perpetrated, it is an understatement to declare, as the *Report* did, that the experiment was "ethically unjustified," because it failed to obtain informed consent from the subjects. The *Final Report*'s statement, "Submitting voluntarily is not informed consent," indicated that the panel believed that the men had volunteered *for the experiment*.[80] The records in the National Archives make clear that the men did not submit voluntarily to an experiment; they were told and they believed that they were getting free treatment from expert government doctors for a serious disease. The failure of the HEW *Final Report* to expose this critical fact— that the USPHS lied to the subjects—calls into question

the thoroughness and credibility of their investigation.

Failure to place the study in a historical context also made it impossible for the investigation to deal with the essentially racist nature of the experiment. The panel treated the study as an aberration, well-intentioned but misguided.[81] Moreover, concern that the *Final Report* might be viewed as a critique of human experimentation in general seems to have severely limited the scope of the inquiry. The *Final Report* is quick to remind the reader on two occasions: "The position of the Panel must not be construed to be a general repudiation of scientific research with human subjects."[82] The *Report* assures us that a better designed experiment could have been justified:

> It is possible that a scientific study in 1932 of untreated syphilis, properly conceived with a clear protocol and conducted with suitable subjects who fully understood the implications of their involvement, might have been justified in the pre-penicillin era. This is especially true when one considers the uncertain nature of the results of treatment of late latent syphilis and the highly toxic nature of therapeutic agents then available.[83]

This statement is questionable in view of the proven dangers of untreated syphilis known in 1932.

Since the publication of the HEW *Final Report*, a defense of the Tuskegee Study has emerged. These arguments, most clearly articulated by Dr. R. H. Kampmeier in the *Southern Medical Journal*, center on the limited knowledge of effective therapy for latent syphilis when the experiment began. Kampmeier argues that by 1950, penicillin would have been of no value for these men.[84] Others have suggested that the men were fortunate to have been spared the highly toxic treatments of the earlier period.[85] Moreover, even these contemporary defenses assume that the men never would have been treated anyway. As Dr. Charles Barnett of Stanford University wrote in 1974, "The lack of treatment was not contrived by the USPHS but was an established fact of which they proposed to take advantage."[86] Several doctors who participated in the study continued to justify the experiment. Dr. J. R. Heller, who on one occasion had referred to the test subjects as the "Ethiopian population," told reporters in 1972:

> I don't see why they should be shocked or horrified. There was no racial side to this. It just happened to be in a black community. I feel this was a perfectly straightforward study, perfectly ethical, with controls. Part of our mission as physicians is to find out what happens to individuals with disease and without disease.[87]

These apologies, as well as the HEW *Final Report*, ignore many of the essential ethical issues which the study poses. The Tuskegee Study reveals the persistence of beliefs within the medical profession about the nature of blacks, sex, and disease—beliefs that had tragic repercussions long after their alleged "scientific" bases were known to be incorrect. Most strikingly, the entire health of a community was jeopardized by leaving a communicable disease untreated.[88] There can be little doubt that the Tuskegee researchers regarded their subjects as less than human.[89] As a result, the ethical canons of experimenting on human subjects were completely disregarded.

The study also raises significant questions about professional self-regulation and scientific bureaucracy. Once the USPHS decided to extend the experiment in the summer of 1933, it was unlikely that the test would be halted short of the men's deaths. The experiment was widely reported for forty years without evoking any significant protest within the medical community. Nor did any bureaucratic mechanism exist within the government for the periodic reassessment of the Tuskegee experiment's ethics and scientific value. The USPHS sent physicians to Tuskegee every several years to check on the study's progress, but never subjected the morality or usefulness of the experiment to serious scrutiny. Only the press accounts of 1972 finally punctured the continued rationalizations of the USPHS and brought the study to an end. Even the HEW investigation was compromised by fear that it would be considered a threat to future human experimentation.

In retrospect the Tuskegee Study revealed more about the pathology of racism than it did about the pathology of syphilis; more about the nature of scientific inquiry than the nature of the disease process. The injustice committed by the experiment went well beyond the facts outlined in the press and the HEW *Final Report*. The degree of deception and damages have been seriously underestimated. As this history of the study suggests, the notion that science is a value-free discipline must be rejected. The need for greater vigilance in assessing the specific ways in which social values and attitudes affect professional behavior is clearly indicated.

QUESTIONS

1. Give a critique of the methodology of the Tuskegee syphilis study. Why would any results have been scientifically invalid?

2. Is it conceivable that the study could have used white rather than black subjects? Explain your answer.

3. Would you consider that racism is still prevalent in the United States today? Do black and white students in the class have different opinions on this subject? If so, why?

References

1. The best general accounts of the study are "The 40-Year Death Watch," *Medical World News* (August 18, 1972), pp. 15–17; and Dolores Katz, "Why 430 Blacks with Syphilis Went Uncured for 40 Years." Detroit *Free Press* (November 5, 1972). The mortality figure is based on a published report of the study which appeared in 1955. See Jesse J. Peters, James H. Peers, Sidney Olansky, John C. Cutler, and Geraldine Gleeson, "Untreated Syphilis in the Male Negro: Pathologic Findings in Syphilitic and Nonsyphilitic Patients," *Journal of Chronic Diseases* 1 (February 1955), 127–48. The article estimated that 30.4 percent of the untreated men would die from syphilitic lesions.

2. *Final Report* of the Tuskegee Syphilis Study Ad Hoc Advisory Panel, Department of Health, Education, and Welfare (Washington, D.C.: GPO, 1973). (Hereafter, HEW *Final Report*).

3. See George M. Frederickson. *The Black Image in the White Mind* (New York: Harper and Row, 1971), pp. 228–55. Also, John H. Haller, *Outcasts From Evolution* (Urbana, Ill.: University of Illinois Press, 1971), pp. 40–68.

4. Frederickson, pp. 247–49.

5. "Deterioration of the American Negro," *Atlanta Journal-Record of Medicine* 5 (July 1903), 287–88. See also, J. A. Rodgers, "The Effect of Freedom upon the Psychological Development of the Negro," *Proceedings* of the American Medico-Psychological Association 7 (1900), 88–99. "From the most healthy race in the country forty years ago," concluded Dr. Henry McHatton, "he is today the most diseased." "The Sexual Status of the Negro—Past and Present," *American Journal of Dermatology and Genito-Urinary Diseases* 10 (January 1906), 7–9.

6. W. T. English, "The Negro Problem from the Physician's Point of View," *Atlanta Journal-Record of Medicine* 5 (October 1903), 461. See also, "Racial Anatomical Peculiarities," *New York Medical Journal* 63 (April 1896), 500–01.

7. "Racial Anatomical Peculiarities," p. 501. Also, Charles S. Bacon, "The Race Problem," *Medicine* (Detroit) 9 (May 1903), 338–43.

8. H. H. Hazen, "Syphilis in the American Negro," *Journal of the American Medical Association* 63 (August 8, 1914), 463. For deeper background into the historical relationship of racism and sexuality see Winthrop D. Jordan, *White Over Black* (Chapel Hill: University of North Carolina Press, 1968; Pelican Books, 1969), pp. 32–40.

9. Daniel David Quillian, "Racial Peculiarities: A Cause of the Prevalence of Syphilis in Negroes," *American Journal of Dermatology and Genito-Urinary Diseases* 10 (July 1906), p. 277.

10. English, p. 463.

11. William Lee Howard, "The Negro as a Distinct Ethnic Factor in Civilization," *Medicine* (Detroit) 9 (June 1903), 424. See also, Thomas W. Murrell, "Syphilis in the American Negro," *Journal of the American Medical Association* 54 (March 12, 1910), 848.

12. "Castration Instead of Lynching," *Atlanta Journal-Record of Medicine* 8 (October 1906), 457. The editorial added: "The badge of disgrace and emasculation might be branded upon the face or forehead, as a warning, in the form of an 'R,' emblematic of the crime for which this punishment was and will be inflicted."

13. Searle Harris, "The Future of the Negro from the Standpoint of the Southern Physician," *Alabama Medical Journal* 14 (January 1902), 62. Other articles on the prevalence of venereal disease among blacks are: H. L. McNeil, "Syphilis in the Southern Negro," *Journal of the American Medical Association* 67 (September 30, 1916), 1001–04; Ernest Philip Boas, "The Relative Prevalence of Syphilis Among Negroes and Whites," *Social Hygiene* 1 (September 1915), 610–16. Doctors went to considerable trouble to distinguish the morbidity and mortality of various diseases among blacks and whites. See, for example, Marion M. Torchia, "Tuberculosis Among American Negroes: Medical Research on a Racial Disease, 1830–1950," *Journal of the History of Medicine and Allied Sciences* 32 (July 1977), 252–79.

14. Thomas W. Murrell, "Syphilis in the Negro: Its Bearing on the Race Problem," *American Journal of Dermatology and Genito-Urinary Diseases* 10 (August 1906), 307.

15. "Even among the educated, only a very few will carry out the most elementary instructions as to personal hygiene. One thing you cannot do, and that is to convince the negro that he has a disease that he

cannot see or feel. This is due to lack of concentration rather than lack of faith; even if he does believe, he does not care; a child of fancy, the sensations of the passing hour are his only guides to the future." Murrell, "Syphilis in the American Negro," p. 847.

16. "Deterioration of the American Negro," *Atlanta Journal-Record of Medicine* 5 (July 1903), 288.

17. Murrell, "Syphilis in the Negro; Its Bearing on the Race Problem," p. 307.

18. "The anatomical and physiological conditions of the African must be understood, his place in the anthropological scale realized, and his biological basis accepted as being unchangeable by man, before we shall be able to govern his natural uncontrollable sexual passions." See, "As Ye Sow That Shall Ye Also Reap," *Atlanta Journal-Record of Medicine* 1 (June 1899), 266.

19. Taliaferro Clark, *The Control of Syphilis in Southern Rural Areas* (Chicago: Julius Rosenwald Fund, 1932), 53–58. Approximately 35 percent of the inhabitants of Macon County who were examined were found to be syphilitic.

20. See Claude Bernard, *An Introduction to the Study of Experimental Medicine* (New York: Dover, 1865, 1957), pp. 5–26. (In 1865, Claude Bernard, the famous French physiologist, outlined the distinction between a "study in nature" and experimentation. A study in nature required simple observation, an essentially passive act, while experimentation demanded intervention which altered the original condition. The Tuskegee Study was thus clearly not a study in nature. The very act of diagnosis altered the original conditions. "It is on this very possibility of acting or not acting on a body," wrote Bernard, "that the distinction will exclusively rest between sciences called sciences of observation and sciences called experimental.")

21. Taliaferro Clark to M. M. Davis, October 29, 1932. Records of the USPHS Venereal Disease Division, Record Group 90, Box 239, National Archives, Washington National Record Center, Suitland, Maryland. (Hereafter, NA-WNRC). Materials in this collection which relate to the early history of the study were apparently never consulted by the HEW investigation. Included are letters, reports, and memoranda written by the physicians engaged in the study.

22. H. S. Cumming to R. R. Moton, September 20, 1932, NA-WNRC.

23. Clark to Davis, October 29, 1932, NA-WNRC.

24. Cumming to Moton, September 20, 1932, NA-WNRC.

25. Bruusgaard was able to locate 309 living patients, as well as records from 164 who were diseased. His findings were published as *"Ueber das Schicksal der nicht specifizch behandelten Luctiken," Archives of Dermatology and Syphilis* 157 (1929), 309–32. The best discussion of the Boeck-Bruusgaard data is E. Gurney Clark and Niels Danbolt, "The Oslo Study of the Natural History of Untreated Syphilis," *Journal of Chronic Diseases* 2 (September 1955), 311–44.

26. Joseph Earle Moore, *The Modern Treatment of Syphilis* (Baltimore: Charles C. Thomas, 1933), p. 24.

27. Moore, pp. 231–47; see also, John H. Stokes, *Modern Clinical Syphilology* (Philadelphia: W. B. Saunders, 1928), pp. 231–39.

28. Moore, p. 237.

29. Moore, p. 236.

30. J. E. Moore, H.N. Cole, P.A. O'Leary, J. H. Stokes, U. J. Wile, T. Clark, T. Parran, J. H. Usilton, "Cooperative Clinical Studies in the Treatment of Syphilis: Latent Syphilis," *Venereal Disease Information* 13 (September 20, 1932), 351. The authors also concluded that the latently syphilitic were potential carriers of the disease, thus meriting treatment.

31. Clark to Paul A. O'Leary, September 27, 1932, NA-WNRC. O'Leary, of the Mayo Clinic, misunderstood the design of the study, replying: "The investigation which you are planning in Alabama is indeed an intriguing one, particularly because of the opportunity it affords of observing treatment in a previously untreated group. I assure you such a study is of interest to me, and I shall look forward to its report in the future." O'Leary to Clark, October 3, 1932, NA-WNRC.

32. Joseph Earle Moore, "Latent Syphilis," unpublished typescript (n.d.), p. 7. American Social Hygiene Association Papers, Social Welfare History Archives Center, University of Minnesota, Minneapolis, Minnesota.

33. Moore to Clark, September 28, 1932, NA-WNRC. Moore had written in his textbook, "In late syphilis the negro is particularly prone to the development of bone or cardiovascular lesions." See Moore, *The Modern Treatment of Syphilis*, p. 35.

34. O. C. Wenger to Clark, October 3, 1932, NA-WNRC.

35. Wenger to Clark, September 29, 1932. NA-WNRC.

36. Clark Memorandum, September 26, 1932, NA-WNRC. See also, Clark to Davis, October 29, 1932, NA-WNRC.

37. As Clark wrote: "You will observe that our plan has nothing to do with treatment. It is purely a diagnostic procedure carried out to determine what has happened to the syphilitic Negro who has had no treatment." Clark to Paul A. O'Leary, September 27, 1932, NA-WNRC.

38. D. G. Gill to O. C. Wenger, October 10, 1932, NA-WNRC.

39. Clark to Vonderlehr, January 25, 1933, NA-WNRC.

40. Vonderlehr to Clark, February 28, 1933. NA-WNRC.

41. Vonderlehr to Clark, November 2, 1932, NA-WNRC. Also, Vonderlehr to Clark, February 6, 1933, NA-WNRC.

42. Clark to Vonderlehr, March 9, 1933, NA-WNRC.

43. Vonderlehr later explained: "The reason treatment was given to many of these men was twofold: First, when the study was started in the fall of 1932, no plans had been made for its continuation and a few of the patients were treated before we fully realized the need for continuing the project on a permanent basis. Second it was difficult to hold the interest of the group of Negroes in Macon County unless some treatment was given." Vonderlehr to Austin V. Diebert, December 5, 1938, Tuskegee Syphilis Study Ad Hoc Advisory Panel Papers, Box 1, National Library of Medicine, Bethesda, Maryland. (Hereafter, TSS-NLM). This collection contains the materials assembled by the HEW investigation in 1972.

44. Vonderlehr to Clark, February 6, 1933, NA-WNRC.

45. H. S. Cumming to J. N. Baker, August 5, 1933, NA-WNRC.

46. January 22, 1933; January 12, 1933, NA-WNRC.

47. Vonderlehr to Clark, January 28, 1933, NA-WNRC.

48. Clark to Moore, March 25, 1933, NA-WNRC.

49. Macon County Health Department, "Letter to Subjects," n.d., NA-WNRC.

50. Vonderlehr to Clark, April 8, 1933, NA-WNRC. See also, Vonderlehr to Wenger, July 18, 1933, NA-WNRC.

51. Wenger to Vonderlehr, July 21, 1933, NA-WNRC. The italics are Wenger's.

52. Cumming to Moton, July 27, 1933, NA-WNRC.

53. Wenger to Vonderlehr, July 21, 1933, NA-WNRC.

54. Vonderlehr to Murray Smith, July 27, 1933, NA-WNRC.

55. Wenger to Vonderlehr, August 5, 1933, NA-WNRC. (The degree of black cooperation in conducting the study remains unclear and would be impossible to properly assess in an article of this length. It seems certain that some members of the Tuskegee Institute staff such as R. R. Moton and Eugene Dibble understood the nature of the experiment and gave their support to it. There is, however, evidence that some blacks who assisted the USPHS physicians were not aware of the deceptive nature of the experiment. Dr. Joshua Williams, an intern at the John A. Andrew Memorial Hospital [Tuskegee Institute] in 1932, assisted Vonderlehr in taking blood samples of the test subjects. In 1973 he told the HEW panel: "I know we thought it was merely a service group organized to help the people in the area. We didn't know it was a research project at all at the time." [See, "Transcript of Proceedings," Tuskegee Syphilis Study Ad Hoc Advisory Panel, February 23, 1973, Unpublished typescript. National Library of Medicine, Bethesda, Maryland.] It is also apparent that Eunice Rivers, the black nurse who had primary responsibility for maintaining contact with the men over the forty years, did not fully understand the dangers of the experiment. In any event, black involvement in the study in no way mitigates the racial

assumptions of the experiment, but rather demonstrates their power).

56. Vonderlehr to Wenger, October 24, 1933, NA-WNRC. Controls were given salicylates.

57. Austin V. Diebert and Martha C. Bruyere, "Untreated Syphilis in the Male Negro, III," *Venereal Disease Information* 27 (December 1946), 301–14.

58. Eunice Rivers, Stanley Schuman, Lloyd Simpson, Sidney Olansky, "Twenty-Years of Followup Experience In a Long-Range Medical Study," *Public Health Reports* 68 (April 1953), 391–95. In this article Nurse Rivers explains her role in the experiment. She wrote: "Because of the low educational status of the majority of the patients, it was impossible to appeal to them from a purely scientific approach. Therefore, various methods were used to maintain their interest. Free medicines, burial assistance or insurance (the project being referred to as 'Miss Rivers' Lodge'), free hot meals on the days of examination, transportation to and from the hospital, and an opportunity to stop in town on the return trip to shop or visit with their friends on the streets all helped. In spite of these attractions, there were some who refused their examinations because they were not sick and did not see that they were being benefitted." (p. 393).

59. Austin V. Diebert to Raymond Vonderlehr, March 20, 1939, TSS-NLM, Box 1.

60. Murray Smith to Subjects, (1938), TSS-NLM, Box 1. See also, Sidney Olansky to John C. Cutler, November 6, 1951, TSS-NLM, Box 2.

61. The USPHS originally requested that the Julius Rosenwald Fund meet this expense. See Cumming to Davis, October 4, 1934, NA-WNRC. This money was usually divided between the undertaker, pathologist, and hospital. Lloyd Isaacs to Raymond Vonderlehr, April 23, 1940, TSS-NLM, Box 1.

62. Stanley H. Schuman, Sidney Olansky, Eunice Rivers, C. A. Smith, Dorothy S. Rambo, "Untreated Syphilis in the Male Negro: Background and Current Status of Patients in the Tuskegee Study," *Journal of Chronic Diseases* 2 (November 1955), 555.

63. R. A. Vonderlehr and Taliaferro Clark, "Untreated Syphilis in the Male Negro," *Venereal Disease Information* 17 (September 1936), 262.

64. J. R. Heller and P. T. Bruyere, "Untreated Syphilis in the Male Negro: II. Mortality During 12 Years of Observation," *Venereal Disease Information* 27 (February 1946), 34–38.

65. Jesse J. Peters, James H. Peers, Sidney Olansky, John C. Cutler, and Geraldine Gleeson, "Untreated Syphilis in the Male Negro: Pathologic Findings in Syphilitic and Non-Syphilitic Patients," *Journal of Chronic Diseases* 1 (February 1955), 127–48.

66. Sidney Olansky, Stanley H. Schuman, Jesse J. Peters, C. A. Smith, and Dorothy S. Rambo, "Untreated Syphilis in the Male Negro, X. Twenty Years of Clinical Observation of Untreated Syphilitic and Presumably Nonsyphilitic Groups," *Journal of Chronic Diseases* 4 (August 1956), 184.

67. O. C. Wenger, "Untreated Syphilis in Male Negro," unpublished typescript, 1950, p. 3. Tuskegee Files, Center for Disease Control, Atlanta, Georgia. (Hereafter TF-CDC).

68. Vernal G. Cave, "Proper Uses and Abuses of the Health Care Delivery System for Minorities with Special Reference to the Tuskegee Syphilis Study," *Journal of the National Medical Association* 67 (January 1975), 83.

69. See for example, Vonderlehr to B. W. Booth, April 18, 1934; Vonderlehr to E. R. Lett, November 20, 1933, NA-WNRC.

70. "Transcript of Proceedings—Tuskegee Syphilis Ad Hoc Advisory Panel," February 23, 1973, unpublished typescript, TSS-NLM, Box 1.

71. Raymond Vonderlehr to Murray Smith, April 30, 1942; and Smith to Vonderlehr, June 8, 1942, TSS-NLM, Box 1.

72. Stanley H. Schuman, Sidney Olansky, Eunice Rivers, C. A. Smith, and Dorothy S. Rambo, "Untreated Syphilis in the Male Negro: Background and Current Status of Patients in the Tuskegee Study," *Journal of Chronic Diseases* 2 (November 1955), 550–53.

73. Raymond Vonderlehr to Stanley H. Schuman, February 5, 1952, TSS-NLM, Box 2.

74. Schuman et al. p. 550.

75. "Minutes, April 5, 1965," unpublished typescript, TSS-NLM, Box 1.

76. "Tuskegee Ad Hoc Committee Meeting—Minutes, February 6, 1969," TF-CDC.

77. James B. Lucas to William J. Brown, September 10, 1970, TF-CDC.

78. Elizabeth M. Kennebrew to Arnold C. Schroeter, February 24, 1971, TSS-NLM, Box 1.

79. See *Medical Tribune* (September 13, 1972), pp. 1, 20; and Report on HEW's Tuskegee Report," *Medical World News*, (September 14, 1973), pp. 57–58.

80. HEW *Final Report*, p. 7.

81. The notable exception is Jay Katz's eloquent "Reservations About the Panel Report on Charge 1," HEW *Final Report*, pp. 14–15.

82. HEW *Final Report*, pp. 8, 12.

83. HEW *Final Report*, pp. 8, 12.

84. See R. H. Kampmeier, "The Tuskegee Study of Untreated Syphilis," *Southern Medical Journal* 65 (October 1972), 1247–51; and "Final Report on the 'Tuskegee Syphilis Study,'" *Southern Medical Journal* 67 (November 1974), 1349–53.

85. Leonard J. Goldwater, "The Tuskegee Study in Historical Perspective," unpublished typescript, TSS-NLM; see also, "Treponemes and Tuskegee," *Lancet* (June 23, 1973), p. 1438; and Louis Lasagna, *The VD Epidemic* (Philadelphia: Temple University Press, 1975), pp. 64–66.

86. Quoted in "Debate Revives on the PHS Study," *Medical World News* (April 19, 1974), p. 37.

87. Heller to Vonderlehr, November 28, 1933, NA-WNRC; quoted in *Medical Tribune* (August 23, 1972), p. 14.

88. Although it is now known that syphilis is rarely infectious after its early phase, at the time of the study's inception latent syphilis was thought to be communicable. The fact that members of the control group were placed in the test group when they became syphilitic proves that at least some infectious men were denied treatment.

89. When the subjects are drawn from minority groups, especially those with which the researcher cannot identify, basic human rights may be compromised. Hans Jonas has clearly explicated the problem in his "Philosophical Reflections on Experimentation," *Daedalus* 98 (Spring, 1969), 234–37. As Jonas writes: "If the properties we adduced as the particular qualifications of the members of the scientific fraternity itself are taken as general criteria of selection, then one should look for additional subjects where a maximum of identification, understanding, and spontaneity can be expected—that is, among the most highly motivated, the most highly educated, and the least 'captive' members of the community."

JOEL DREYFUSS

Blacks and Hispanics: Coalition or Confrontation?

As the largest (and often the most militant and vocal) racial or ethnic minority in the nation, blacks have long been the primary focus of concern about racial inequality in the society. The many reforms that ultimately resulted from the civil rights movement of the 1960s—particularly in voting, housing, employment, and education—were directed primarily toward helping black Americans. But the position of blacks as the preeminent minority is soon to be challenged, with potential results that remain unpredictable.

The 1980 census confirmed what sociologists had suspected during the late 1970s: that Hispanic-Americans, the second-largest minority, are growing so rapidly in number that they will probably overtake blacks some time during the 1980s. Although the Hispanics have a highly diversified background (they consist primarily of Chicanos and Puerto Ricans, but include a large component of Cubans and others from Central and South America), they are beginning to show signs of political cohesion and an awareness of the immense clout that their numbers will imply.

A fundamental insight of the sociology of race relations is that antagonism among groups stems not from their physical or cultural differences but rather from competition for scarce social resources, such as land, jobs, and other benefits. A crucial question, then, is this: Will black and Hispanic Americans overlook their differences to present a united front in demanding a greater share of the society's resources—or will they compete among themselves for such resources as are available, with resulting antagonisms between the two groups? Joel Dreyfuss discusses this important issue.

They have been called the "Minority for the 1980s." They grace the covers of national news magazines and the front pages of big-city newspapers. . . . They have made their impact on American culture and the first exploitation films about them have appeared in the theaters. "They" are the Hispanics, the Mexican-Americans or Chicanos who—along with Puerto Ricans, Cubans and other Latino immigrants—will soon outnumber blacks and become the largest minority group in the country.

Already, Hispanics have displaced blacks in the media's consciousness. When President Carter visited Los Angeles in May [1979], he stayed with a Chicano family and addressed a political rally in "Georgia" Spanish. California Gov. Jerry Brown, always the political weathervane, is reported to have declared that "blacks are the wrong symbol for the 1970s" when he came into office. Also, Brown has appointed more Chicanos to office than did any of his predecessors in Sacramento.

If blacks are apprehensive about this sudden surge of interest in Hispanics, it is partly because they are aware that their own struggle for liberation is not ended. Quite naturally, many blacks fear they will lose their "most favored status" as a minority with the emergence of Chicanos.

Recently, the National Association of Black Social Workers complained that the term "minority" had hurt black progress.

"Other ethnic and religious groups have piggybacked on our real and conceptual thrusts and like parasites have walked away with resources authorized by Congress and allocated by the president intentionally to benefit black people," said Cenie J. Williams, the association's executive director.

Few blacks can take comfort from the fact that the Hispanic struggle for equality has its roots in the black struggle. For many blacks the question is simple: Will Hispanics become an obstacle to black progress or does their emergence mean a new ally in the increasingly complex struggle for a share of the American dream, for a share of the economic pie?

A coalition of blacks and Hispanics would mean a bloc of 50 million people. Such an alliance would provide these groups with the kind of political clout that would be impossible to ignore. Political leaders are unanimous in their assessment of the value of such a coalition.

"It's the only obvious avenue we have," says Rep. George (Mickey) Leland, a member of the Congressional Black Caucus whose Houston district includes both blacks and Chicanos.

"We have no option but to form an alliance," says Vilma Martinez, president and general counsel of the Mexican-American Legal Defense Fund (MALDEF).

"When you get down to the nitty-gritty, it's the only way to deal," says an aide to Rep. Robert Garcia, the only Puerto Rican congressman.

"It's going to be tough. It's going to take a lot of patience and hard work, but we've got to build a coalition of blacks, Chicanos and Asians, gays and women and senior citizens," says former California lieutenant governor Mervyn Dymally.

At the National Urban League's 1978 convention in Los Angeles, Vernon Jordan called for minority groups to work together on issues of common interest, such as affirmative action, employment, job training, housing, and health care.

But, while everyone seems to agree that coalition would be a good thing, there has been no great push toward serious political alliance. In various parts of the country, black and Hispanic leaders have begun to explore the possibilities. In interviews with the press, however, they agree that a number of political and cultural obstacles must first be resolved.

The major obstacle to political alliance is the mistrust that the two groups have of each other. Other problems include differences on key political issues, competition for federal funds, and a sense of unequal power. While blacks are accustomed to complaining about their lack of influence, many Chicano leaders view with envy the gains that blacks have made.

In economic and political terms, the differences are real. In 1978, the median weekly earning of Hispanics was $174 against $181 for blacks. Both minorities are far behind the $277 median for the total work force. While 18.9 percent of blacks have completed only eight years of school, the figure for Hispanics is 30 percent.

In the 1976 elections, only 31.8 percent of Hispanics voted, against 48.7 percent of blacks and 60.9 percent of whites. There are 17 blacks in the Congress but just five Hispanics. New York City, with nearly one million Puerto Ricans, has just one Puerto Rican congressman.

Many of these disparities are exemplified in California, which provides an interesting case study of relations between blacks and Hispanics. "If the present trends continue," says Mervyn Dymally, "the emerging ethnic groups will constitute more than half the population of California by 1990, and we will become the country's first 'Third World' state." Chicanos are about 16 percent of California's population and blacks about 8 percent.

Yet blacks hold eight seats in the state legislature against six for Hispanics. There are three black members of Congress from California and only one Chicano. . . . Los Angeles Chicanos have outnumbered blacks since 1970, but the mayor and three members of the city council are black, and there is no Hispanic on the city council or on the county board of supervisors. The potential for change in the near future is not good, concedes assemblyman Art Torres, "because the districts have been gerrymandered."

Other Hispanic leaders attribute the lack of representation as much to passivity as to political manipulation. "The Mexican culture focuses on responsibility rather than rights," says Eduardo Sandoval, president of the influential Mexican-American Political Association (MAPA). "Anglo-Saxon culture focuses on rights. When our folks came into the Southwest, they were obsessed with working."

But the last decade has seen an explosion of Mexican-American political and cultural consciousness very much like the black power movement of the 1960s. Chicanos have become more assertive about their rights and culture and have joined their search for power with an examination of "Chicanismo," their equivalent of "Black Is Beautiful." "There is an intimate connection between the black civil rights movement and the Mexican-American civil rights movement," says Sandoval. "Even if only from jealousy, we become involved in national and local issues."

Just as it did for blacks a decade ago, this self-discovery often makes for abrasive relations with other groups. "If Vernon Jordan wants a national coalition," says Sandoval, "then as a precondition we want the National Urban League to support our position on general amnesty [for illegal immigrants]. We've been on the short end for a long time. We're going to be the biggest minority in five years. We'll wait until our bargaining position is stronger."

Hispanic leaders also make it clear that they feel their first task should be the organizing of their own communities before they form alliances. "The only things that a politician understands are votes," says state senator Alex Garcia of Los Angeles. "That's the key and that must be our priority." Door-to-door voter registration is being carried out in East Los Angeles by the United Neighborhoods Organization and in Texas by the Southwest Voter Registration Education Project.

But the ferment in the Hispanic community has not always been welcome among blacks. "They think they're white," says Paul Cobb, head of Oakland Citizens Committee for Urban Renewal (OCCUR), a public interest group. "Chicanos are politically immature. They have not had experience in confrontation politics." Margaret Pryor, a founder of Black Women Organized for Political Action, another East Bay group, says she has found it difficult to form alliances with Hispanics. "The only time Chicanos want to be minorities is when it's convenient," Pryor complains. "They react very strongly to the fact that blacks are in control of an organization. They like to challenge us. But," she adds, "a lot of the conflict has to do with plain and simple trust." Sandoval argues, however, that blacks often approach Hispanics the wrong way. "The black American sees the Hispanic mushroom and he wants to step in and lead us."

One issue that has caused some conflict is immigration. Last year, Vilma Martinez of MALDEF was invited to address the Urban League convention. She made an impassioned plea for understanding of the immigration problem that was well received. But less than an hour later, a high-ranking black labor official was charging that immigrants were taking jobs away from blacks. "The country as a whole doesn't understand the issue," says Martinez, "and the black community doesn't understand the issue either." Chicanos view the flow of immigrants across the border as a historical fact that cannot be stopped by fences or legislation. The movement of workers will stop, they say, when economic conditions in Mexico improve.

There are other differences that have their roots in culture. When blacks in California voted to support homosexual rights last year, the majority of Chicanos voted the other way. While blacks strongly favor the right of public employees to strike, Hispanics oppose such rights. And in the fall of 1978, a poll of voters showed that while blacks favored a second term for Jimmy Carter by a 61–16 margin, Hispanics supported him by only a 39–38 percent vote.

"The Mexican-American culture is basically conservative," says Sandoval, a fact that has not been lost on the Republican Party. "We're planning to meet with both parties. I, for one, am not going to be caught in an ideological corner." Sandoval's group, MAPA, leans toward the right end of the political spectrum and has endorsed Governor Jerry Brown's call for a constitutional convention to act on the balanced budget. Most black and Hispanic politicians, on the contrary, have come out against such a constitutional amendment for balancing the budget.

Recently, California's state legislature passed a ballot proposition to end busing for integration. The eight black legislators voted against the bill but five of the six Chicanos supported the proposal. "We have no permanent friends," said outraged black state senator Diane Watson, who has insisted on busing as an option for blacks. "We're finding all the groups who were in our coalition have gone off in their own directions."

One of the legislators who had originally supported busing said he changed his vote to reflect the sentiment of his constituents. "The poeple in East Los Angeles are not opposed to integration," said state assemblyman Art Torres. But, he said, Chicanos in Los Angeles were being bused 55 minutes a day to schools, often in areas where they were not welcome and which lacked adequate bilingual programs.

The language issue is another potential area of conflict. "Their hustle is the language," says a California black politician. "You don't have to lose your culture but learn the language. A lot of blacks agree with [Sen. S.I.] Hayakawa [a conservative Republican opposed to bilingualism], but they won't say so publicly."

"They're in the same boat as we are," says Paul Cobb of the Oakland Citizens Committee. "We need special care. They want extra-special care. That costs money." In the competition for public funds, many blacks see bilingual programs as an unnecessary expense which often pits them against Chicanos.

"Blacks are Anglos," explains Miguel Chavoya, an Oakland community organizer. "A Chicano needs to isolate himself from black and white. The way money is distributed has divided the Chicano and black communities. We need to bring key leaders together and air our prejudices and differences and realize we have certain things in common."

Fortunately, such steps are being taken at the national level. Early this year, a number of black and Hispanic organizations, including the National Urban Coalition, the National Council of La Raza, and ASPIRA, a Puerto Rican organization, met in Washington. The groups agreed to fight reductions in domestic program funding, cuts in CETA and bilingual programs. The group's resolution said cuts in domestic programs would be "more symbolic than effective in holding down inflation . . . and they will hurt most those least able to protect their own interests."

On the immigration issue, the black members agreed "to issue no further statements of undocumented workers until they conferred with Hispanics to reach a better understanding of Hispanic concerns."

An even more ambitious step toward coalition was taken at the Democratic Party's mid-term convention when a Black and Hispanic Coalition was formed which includes several members of Congress and a cross section of Chicano, Cuban-American and Puerto Rican groups. Members include Reps. Ron Dellums, Shirley Chisholm, John Conyers and Robert Garcia, Texas state representative Ben T. Reyes, Colorado state senator Polly Baragan, Florida State Democratic Party chairman Alfredo Duran and Luis Laurado, president of the Cuban-American Coalition.

Duran cites a common black concern that Hispanics will pass as whites once they have won their political objectives. "It's not only a problem with blacks," says Lauredo, "but it's often a problem within our own community." But Chicano leaders deny that Hispanics will just fade into the mainstream. "We're not whites as such," says Sandoval. "We want to emulate in terms of economics and civil rights, but the emphasis of the Chicano is on his Hispanicness. We are not going to give up the Spanish language or culture. The Spanish were here 100 years before the *Mayflower*."

Of course, there are minority politicians who see the concept of racial identity as a limiting factor. "As a black elected official, I'm not interested in representing only a minority base—I'm interested in getting into the mainstream of government," says Rep. Julian Dixon of Los Angeles.

If California is the political trendsetter many consider it to be, that may be the future for elected officials. Blacks who have won statewide office, Dymally and schools superintendent Wilson Riles, have had to appeal to large numbers of white voters by presenting an essentially liberal Democratic platform. Dymally and Yvonne Burke, who gave up a safe Congressional seat to run for state attorney general, lost to conservative Republicans last year despite their efforts to reach the mainstream.

The most serious obstacle to coalition politics lies in the fact that all these minorities are not just black or brown. There are Afro-Americans, West Indians, Dominicans, Cubans and Puerto Ricans who jealously guard their cultural differences. In an age of shrinking economic opportunities, it is more tempting for one group to see the other as a potential rival than as an ally. Those who have the most to gain from a fragmentation of minority groups will do their best to exploit those differences.

The future depends on the Chicanos—because by sheer number they will become a dominant force—and on blacks—because of their relative political clout. Blacks must understand that in opening opportunities for themselves, they have given hope to others. If the demands of other groups sometimes seem shrill and irritating, the blacks should remember the events of the 1960s. There is no way that emerging groups can be prevented from getting what is rightfully theirs.

"Once blacks and Hispanics realize that they are natural allies, that they have the same basic problems, the same political problems, they will begin to work together," says Laurado. In the continuing pursuit of the American dream, there is no other choice.

QUESTIONS

1. What causes bad race or ethnic relations to develop? Consider specific examples, for example, settlers and Indians, blacks and whites, Chicanos and Anglos.

2. Unlike other non-English-speaking immigrant groups, who were willingly assimilated into American society, Chicanos seem eager to retain their language and customs, even if this means making the United States, or parts of it, bilingual. What would be the best policy to follow on this issue?

3. What obstacles are there to a black-Hispanic coalition? What advantages would there be? Do you think such a coalition is a likely prospect?

CARL GERSHMAN

A Matter of Class

*From the time of their forcible importation to the
United States as slaves, black Americans have occupied a subordinate place in the society. Membership of
a particular racial group has, at least until recently,
been deemed sufficient grounds for denying blacks the
opportunities available to whites. That, after all, is the
substance of racism.*

*Since the civil rights campaigns of the 1960s, how-
ever, significant changes have occurred. Racial segregation and other forms of discrimination have become
illegal. Controversial steps have been taken in the attempt to achieve equality of opportunity in education,
housing, and employment. There has been measurable
progress on many fronts, reflected most notably, perhaps, in the fact that an unprecedented number of
blacks—perhaps a third—have entered the American
middle class.*

*Yet this visible progress has obscured the continuing
failure of American society to incorporate, in any real
sense, a large part of the black minority. Despite the
economic success of some blacks, the gap between the
income of the average black and the average white is
now larger than it was a decade ago. The reality is
that a black "underclass" has been left behind. Living
in impoverished rural areas and decaying inner-city
ghettos, ill-educated, and facing chronic unemployment, this underclass is a powder keg in America's future. But a new controversy has developed over the
predicament of the underclass. Is it the result of continuing racism? Or is it simply a feature of the American class system, in which the inevitable underdogs are
only coincidentally black? Carl Gershman discusses
the issue in this article.*

Of all the grievances voiced by black leaders in the wake
of [the May 1980] racial violence in Miami, the one repeated most frequently was that the country no longer
cares about the problems of blacks. That such a view
should be expressed by black leaders shows how far we
have come since the 1960's, when issues pertaining to
racial equality were at the top of the American political
agenda. Today, according to Benjamin Hooks, executive
director of the National Association for the Advancement of Colored People, "the pendulum is swinging back.
Black folks ain't worth a damn in this country." As
Mayor Richard G. Hatcher, of Gary, Ind., put it, "The
black man has become invisible again."

The concern felt by black leaders that the country has
grown indifferent to black needs comes after a decade in
which blacks made significant political gains. This apparent contradiction was alluded to by Hatcher in his key-
note address to a national black-leadership conference
that met last February in Richmond, Va. Recalling a previous national black conference in Gary in 1972, he noted
that "in just eight years we have more than tripled the
number of blacks serving in the legislatures, the city
halls, the courtrooms and on the school boards of America." Yet, he went on, "as our voice has grown stronger,
our nation's commitment has grown weaker."

Neither Hatcher nor any of the other black leaders
who attended the Richmond conference—including
Hooks; the Rev. Jesse L. Jackson, executive director of
Operation PUSH; former United Nations Ambassador
Andrew Young; Vernon E. Jordan Jr., president of the
National Urban League, and Cardiss Collins, chairman
of the Congressional Black Caucus—was able to account
for this paradoxical situation. One argument advanced at
Richmond attributed the difficulties encountered by
black leaders to the growth of antiblack sentiment in the
country—as seen, for example, in the increased activity
of the Ku Klux Klan. But while it is true that the Klan
now has about 10,000 members, a gain of 50 percent
since 1975, this growth does not reflect the mood in the
country in general or even in the South, where the Klan is
primarily based. All the polls, in fact, show that the
American people are much more favorably disposed toward racial equality now than they were at the height of

The New York Times Magazine, October 5, 1980. © 1980 by the New
York Times Company. Reprinted by permission.

the civil-rights movement in the 1960's.

The apparent "invisibility" of the black poor is also attributed to the growing mood of fiscal conservatism, as symbolized by the passage in 1978 of Proposition 13 in California. But the view that the country is retrenching on its commitment to the black poor is not borne out by the facts. The Federal Government's antipoverty expenditures during the 1970's doubled in real terms and now total $67.5 billion a year, a figure that does not include more than $20 billion in antipoverty spending by state and local governments.

A third explanation, which was stressed repeatedly by the speakers at the Richmond conference, was that black leaders were not being listened to because of the country's preoccupation with national defense in the wake of the Soviet invasion of Afghanistan. But this argument is also unpersuasive, for there is no reason why a commitment by the United States to oppose foreign aggression must necessarily involve a retreat on efforts to eliminate domestic injustices. In fact, the period of the black revolution in America, which began with A. Philip Randolph's March on Washington Movement in 1941 and culminated with the great March on Washington in 1963, coincided with America's entrance onto the world scene as a great power, committed to the defeat of Nazi aggression and then to the containment of Communism.

What, then, accounts for the feeling among black leaders that the country is "abandoning the black cause," as Patricia Roberts Harris, the Secretary of Health and Human Services, said following the Miami riot? Her own analysis was that whites see the progress made by some blacks and assume that "the task is finished." But it is hard to believe that most Americans are unaware of the existence of large black ghettos, such as Liberty City in Miami, which are plagued by high unemployment, crime, drug abuse and other social ills. And if they are unaware of the problem, or not sufficiently concerned about it, one must then ask why the current black leadership cannot arouse the nation's attention. It has much more access to power than the old civil-rights leadership, which was able to dramatize a problem—legalized segregation in the South—that was at least as remote from the consciousness of most Americans. Why, then, does its voice not resonate in the country with the same force?

To understand what has gone wrong, it is necessary to go back a full 15 years to a moment when the black movement faced certain crucial choices regarding its future perspective and program. In early 1965, just as the civil-rights movement was winning its greatest victories in Congress, several important analyses appeared that challenged the prevailing optimism with respect to eliminating racial inequality. The basic point of all these analyses—Kenneth B. Clark's study, "Dark Ghetto," Bayard Rustin's article, "From Protest to Politics," and Daniel

Patrick Moynihan's Labor Department report, "The Negro Family"—was that in spite of the gains of the civil-rights movement, the life of the black poor in the urban ghettos was getting worse, not better, and that much more than just the removal of legal barriers to equal opportunity was needed to save these people. This point of view had far-reaching implications that were never absorbed by the black leadership, a critical failure that may well explain its inability to arouse the nation's attention to the urgent problem of the ghetto poor.

All three analyses agreed that the central problem that now had to be addressed was the existence of a growing black underclass in the urban ghetto. As the Moynihan report pointed out, it was particularly important to focus attention on this group since "the emergence and increasing visibility of a Negro middle class may beguile the nation into supposing that the circumstances of the remainder of the Negro community are equally prosperous, whereas just the opposite is true at present, and is likely to continue so."

As Clark's study made painfully clear, the ghetto poor were trapped in a "self-perpetuating pathology" whose symptoms were "low aspiration, poor education, family instability, illegitimacy, unemployment, crime, drug addiction and alcoholism, frequent illness and early death." This "disease" was the result of centuries of accumulated injustices, starting with slavery and continuing with segregation and poverty. But it had now taken on a life of its own, so that the elimination of discrimination, in and of itself, would not bring about its cure. Moreover, according to Rustin, the disease was spreading as a result of structural changes in the economy—for example, the elimination of unskilled and semiskilled jobs by automation—that were excluding growing numbers of black youth from the modern labor market. There clearly could be no solution to the problem in the absence of a massive, systematic effort by the Federal Government (along the lines of the 10-year "Freedom Budget" proposed by Rustin's mentor, A. Philip Randolph) to rescue the underclass, looking ultimately to its gradual transformation into a stable working-class population and the abolition of the ghetto itself.

This view became the basis for President Johnson's famous civil-rights address delivered at Howard University on June 4, 1965. The address, which Moynihan helped draft, summarized the essential arguments of the "Negro Family" report by way of defining "the next and more profound stage of the battle for civil rights." Declaring that "freedom is not enough," the President dwelt at length upon "the scars of centuries," the "ancient brutality, past injustice and present prejudice" that had buried much of the black population "under a blanket of history and circumstance." For these reasons, the President explained, there were "deep, corrosive, obstinate differences" between black and white poverty, the most important—because its influence radiated "to every part of life"—being "the breakdown of the Negro family structure."

The President announced he would convene a special White House conference in the fall. But before the conference was held, the Watts riot occurred and the White House released the internal Government report on "The Negro Family"—"specifically to assert" as Moynihan later wrote, "that something was known about the otherwise inexplicable events in California."

The report, which called attention to the growing incidence of female-headed black families dependent on welfare, aroused a storm of indignation. Actually, it only reinforced what President Johnson had said in his speech—that legal equity was insufficient in that the damage history and present circumstance had caused in the life of the Negro American had to be repaired if there was to be genuine racial equality. For Moynihan himself, the report was a brief for the Government's adoption of a jobs strategy that would seek to strengthen the role of the father as the family provider. Such a strategy, he also felt, would have to be supplemented by a plan for child allowances as a way of offsetting the subversive effect on family stability of a wage system not geared to family size and need.

But in the bitter post-Watts atmosphere, Moynihan was accused of blaming the black poor for their own plight and offering an excuse for Government inaction. These were really secondary issues, however, because the underlying objection to the report—which was reflected in its critics' argument that the female-headed family was actually a healthy adaptation to harsh conditions—was its contention that history had inflicted debilitating wounds on the black American. What was being denied, in other words, was the idea, implicit in the Moynihan argument, that there was something pathological in the social fabric of the ghetto underclass.

This denial, which was insisted upon ever more strongly as racial tensions and black-nationalist tendencies grew in the late 1960's, expressed itself in a political attitude that dignified the violence and degradation in the culture of the ghetto underclass. The attitude took its most explicit form in the emergence of the Black Panthers, who extolled the revolutionary character of the "*lumpen* proletariat" (a term knowingly misappropriated from Marx, for whom the underclass was not revolutionary but "a recruiting ground for thieves and criminals of all kinds"), and whose politics of nihilism and street violence were countenanced and encouraged by fashionable liberal opinion. It also found subtler expression in the growing acceptance of the idea that the sole obstacle to black advance was white racism. The "disease" that had to be cured—the *problem*, in short—was not the ghetto with its growing underclass, but the racist and repressive character of America itself—a view that was given an

international dimension in the ideology of third-world radicalism that was then rapidly becoming popular.

At the same time, no effort was made to conceal the misery of the ghetto. On the contrary, this condition was brandished as conclusive proof of America's sickness and as the basis of demands for immediate Government relief. And, since it was also denied that there was anything inherently pathological in this condition, it followed that the misery was solely a function of the maldistribution of power, money and jobs, and that relief would come simply from their redistribution. Thus, the idea of abolishing the ghetto gave way to demands for "community control" over its institutions. Welfare came increasingly to be seen not as a debilitating condition from which one should try to escape, but as a right that had to be more adequately fulfilled. And emphasis was placed not on attacking the structural causes of unemployment, such as the discrepancy between the skills and motivation required for productive employment and the lack of these among youth trapped in the ghetto, but on demanding racial quotas—an approach that actually bypassed the underclass since there were ample numbers of middle-class black youths better prepared to fill the available openings.

The sad irony in all of this is that what appeared to be a form of racial militancy was, in reality, a policy of racial accommodation. Though demands for redistribution were frequently couched in such radical-sounding terms as "black power," "reparations" and "self-determination," nothing was being proposed that would, or was intended to, lead to the dissolution of the ghetto underclass. On the contrary, the new approach both rationalized and subsidized the underclass's continued existence. It appealed to many whites by offering them a convenient excuse to evade the whole problem while, at the same time, allowing them to show proper "concern" for the disadvantaged by submitting to "black demands." And it also appealed to a new class of black political leaders and Federally funded antipoverty workers who became, in effect, the power brokers between the Government and the black poor. These workers had a stake in preserving the underclass as a political base from which they could threaten—and extract concessions from—white society.

The nature of the relationship between the underclass and its self-appointed political spokesmen was obscured by the invocation of a "black perspective" according to which both shared a common interest based solely on race. This perspective, by assuming the existence of a monolithic black community set off against an alien and hostile white society, ruled out any serious consideration of the underclass as a distinct social group suffering from unique disabilities and requiring special attention. The underclass became, instead, a symbol of black suffering and white cruelty, a living reminder of past and present injustices and of the continuing debt that American society owed to all blacks, regardless of the position they had achieved in life. Thus, while the problems of the underclass could not be honestly discussed, its condition was made the basis of an ideology of racial victimization that was applied to the entire "black experience" in America.

But even as this ideology was developing and gaining a greater hold on many black leaders, it was becoming increasingly defective both as a description of the actual condition of the black population in America and as an explanation of the present causes of racial inequality. Even before this perspective took root, in fact, the black population was not monolithic—this, of course, being the very reason why President Johnson and others had raised the issue in the first place. Moreover, since 1965 there has been a deepening class schism among blacks, a trend identified a decade ago in a speech at Tuskegee Institute by the black economist Andrew F. Brimmer, then a member of the Board of Governors of the Federal Reserve System.

Between 1965 and 1977, the number of blacks attending college more than quadrupled—from 274,000 to 1.1 million. As their numbers rose, so, too, did their aspirations, as seen in the growing numbers of blacks studying for careers in business, engineering, chemistry, computer science and other highly professionalized fields. Because of these educational advances and the decline in job-market discrimination, the number of blacks in professional and managerial jobs nearly doubled during the 1970's, to 1.9 million, and the income of young college-educated blacks rose to about the same level as that of their white counterparts. (Black males earned slightly less than white males, and black females earned slightly more than white females.)

The earnings ratios for all blacks employed full-time have not been as high, but even here the gains have been impressive: Black males earned 77 percent as much as white males in 1975, up from 63 percent in 1955, while, over the same period, the income of black females rose from 57 percent to 98.6 percent in relation to the earnings of white females.

While the current recession has eroded some of the gains made by middle- and working-class blacks, the progress reflected in these figures has been real and not, as some have maintained, meager and illusory. And because it has been rooted in profound and enduring institutional changes in employment practices, Government policies, education, labor and other areas, there is no reason to believe that it will not continue. But it has benefited, at best, two-thirds of the black population, divided almost equally between middle-class and working-class blacks. The bottom third has not only failed to participate in the progress of the last 15 years, but its social and economic position has deteriorated to an alarming extent.

During the 1970's, for example, the unemployment rate for 16- to 19-year-old blacks rose by more than half—from 24 percent to over 37 percent today. The percentage of all black males over 16 who dropped out of the labor force entirely—who neither worked nor sought work and thus did not even appear in the unemployment statistics—also increased by more than half, from 20 percent in the mid-1960's to nearly 40 percent today. And though the problem of female-headed black families has scarcely been mentioned since the acrimonious controversy over the Moynihan report, it has grown steadily worse—from 23.2 percent of all black families in 1962 to 28 percent in 1969, 37 percent in 1976 and 40.5 percent in 1979.

What has been happening is clear: The black underclass of the ghetto has been expanding at precisely the same time as the black middle class has also been expanding and moving ahead. Moreover, this schism shows every sign of growing still wider in the future. The structural barriers to employment for the underclass are greater now than they were 15 years ago, for during this period thousands of manufacturing plants seeking space for expansion have relocated out of the central cities, leaving potential black workers in the ghetto more cut off than before from the economic mainstream. And the ghetto's "tangle of pathology" is now more deadly. Another layer of damage has thus been added to the legacy of history and circumstance, one that is particularly crushing to the spirit in that it followed upon a moment when there seemed to be hope.

Though the problem of the underclass has grown more intractable and has, in fact, been brought more sharply into focus by the "deepening schism" in the black population, there is no greater readiness now than there was 15 years ago to acknowledge its true character. In an article discussing the underclass, William J. Raspberry, a black columnist for the Washington Post, wrote that "everybody knows" that "there are some blacks for whom it is enough to remove the artificial barriers of race" and others "for whom hardly anything would change if, by some magical stroke, racism disappeared from America. . . . And yet hardly anyone is willing to say it." It's hard enough, Raspberry added, "to rehabilitate those people who have been crippled by the long-term effects of racism . . . and it is made no easier by our refusal to acknowledge the problem for what it is."

In fact, many black intellectuals and political leaders have actively discouraged efforts to raise the issue of the underclass in these terms. A significant case in point is the controversy that has surrounded the 1978 book "The Declining Significance of Race," in which the black sociologist William Julius Wilson argues that the worsening condition of the underclass, not racism, is the problem that requires urgent attention. Wilson, who heads the sociology department at the University of Chicago, said recently that he "had not anticipated the depth of the political-emotional response" the book has elicited. He readily concedes that his arguments are "hardly revolutionary" but just expand on the position adumbrated by Bayard Rustin in the mid-1960's. Clearly, however, many blacks find this position just as objectionable today as they did 15 years ago.

Wilson's basic thesis is that in the modern industrial period, unlike the earlier periods of slavery and industrialization, class plays a more significant role than race in determining a black's position in society. He does not deny that racial antagonisms persist in "social, political and community" areas. He merely contends that blacks with the requisite skills can now advance economically and have done so, while the underclass—a product of the disadvantages accumulated over generations and of modern economic developments—cannot. The net effect, he says, is a growing class division among blacks.

Under these circumstances, Wilson argues, an emphasis on race obscures significant differences of experience and suffering among blacks. Even more importantly, it also leads to faulty analysis and to policies that don't address "the specific needs and concerns of those who are the most disadvantaged."

In the epilogue of the forthcoming paperback edition of his book, Wilson shows, for example, that the recent decline in the composite black-white income ratio from 61 percent in 1969 to 59 percent in 1978—figures stressed by black leaders and intellectuals in arguments for more affirmative-action programs—is misleading in that it obscures the sharply divergent trends "within" the black population. Thus, he notes that the black-white ratio of median family income in male-headed homes *increased* over the same period from 72 percent in 1969 to 80 percent in 1978, while "the exploding number of black female-headed families," with median incomes about one-third those of black male-headed families, brought down the overall income ratio. The emphasis on affirmative action, he adds, has the effect of widening this class division among blacks since it benefits primarily the middle class while not addressing the specific needs of the underclass.

Wilson's thesis was discussed at a symposium convened last year by the University of Pennsylvania's Afro-American Studies Program. Lerone Bennett Jr., the senior editor at Ebony magazine, observed that "it verges on the sacreligious to spend so much time discussing the declining significance of race . . . in the face of the systematic destruction of a whole generation of black people." Kenneth Clark, whom Wilson called "the scholar who first made me conscious of these issues," nonetheless differed strongly with Wilson's main argument, calling it "a dangerous delusion" that "drains energy and diverts attention from the stark fact that racial injustices perpetrated against all blacks—middle-class and underclass blacks—remain the unfinished business of American democracy."

Wilson has countered such criticisms by applying his class analysis of race to the "race politics" of the black intelligentsia. At the University of Pennsylvania symposium, he observed that "the group that would have the most to gain by a shift in emphasis from race to economic dislocation, the black lower class, is not the group that is really defining the issues." Rather, he added, "the issues are being defined by the articulate black intelligentsia—the very group that has benefited the most in recent years from antidiscrimination programs" and which therefore has "a vested interest in keeping race as the single most important issue in developing policies to promote black progress." Taking note of "the increasing class hostilities in the black community," he remarked that if "the little man" ever gains his voice, he might well use it "to beat down the mythology developed by the black intelligentsia: Blacks, regardless of their station in life, have a uniform experience in a racist society."

The issues raised by Wilson have far-reaching political implications because the "mythology" he has sought to expose is ascendant today within the black leadership. The extent to which racial politics has distorted the perspective of the black leadership was made abundantly clear at the Richmond conference last February.

Thus, according to Jesse Jackson, the starting point of any analysis of the black situation had to be the recognition that "race is the most pervasive fact in the Afro-American experience." Richard Hatcher took the view that racism accounted for the worsening condition of blacks. In spite of all the efforts made over the years "to lift the American nightmare," he said, "insensitive" politicians "continue to this day to mistreat us, misrepresent us and to insult us." And now, he added, the country is "falling victim to a ruse of anti-Russian hysteria intended to make us forget about" domestic injustices. As a result, Hatcher concluded, "We are poorer, sicker and hungrier than we were just 10 years ago." Cardiss Collins of the Congressional Black Caucus added that, because none of the Presidential candidates, in her view, had demonstrated any real concern about black problems, there was "no point in arguing who the slave master is going to be."

The only solution for blacks, then, was to look to themselves and to seek "self-reliance" as a unified and independent entity within American society. This independence strategy, as the "black agenda" adopted at the conference made clear, places great emphasis on demands for special Government assistance to black businesses and programs—demands that both Jackson and Hatcher justified as "reparations" owed blacks for past and present injustices. It also stresses the need for blacks to become, as one speaker put it, "intermediaries" in relations between the United States and the third world, a role, he said, that would strengthen the black "negotiation position" in this country and also create new opportunities for black businesses in the field of foreign trade.

While this strategy is based on the concept of racial solidarity—both within the American black population and between it and the third world—the distinguishing feature of this approach is its overwhelming orientation toward the interests of one component of the black population, the middle class, to the exclusion of any meaningful emphasis on the problems of the black underclass.

There were some token references at the conference to the need for full employment, and a resolution was passed that encouraged community leaders "to find ways of organizing the grass-roots, problem-ridden blacks by focusing on specific, concrete issues to which they can relate." But to the extent that the black leaders, themselves, addressed these issues at Richmond, they did so in every case by denying the real problem facing the underclass and recasting the question in terms consistent with their own racial perspective and class interests.

Thus, while violent crime is one of the most destructive symptoms of ghetto pathology, victimizing chiefly the black poor, the Richmond conference focused on the issue of "criminal justice" and its denial to blacks in general. The first priority, according to the resolution adopted at the conference, was the necessity for blacks "to be employed at every level of the criminal-justice system, particularly at the policy-making level"—a proposal more likely to enhance employment opportunities for black professionals than to reduce ghetto crime. The resolution also decried the death penalty, police brutality, new prison construction and the "unequal application of the law at all levels." But nowhere was any serious attention paid to the problem of violent crime in the ghetto.

The question of the black female-headed family was also virtually ignored. It was alluded to only once, in the course of a resolution on the Equal Rights Amendment. And here again, the "problem" was not the alarming disintegration of the family structure of the black poor, but the absence of "quality developmental child care" for "the significant number of black women who head families in the United States."

Nor was the ghetto itself thought to constitute a problem. Fifteen years ago, Kenneth Clark wrote about what happens to people "who are confined to depressed areas and whose access to the normal channels of economic mobility and opportunity is blocked." But today, when far-reaching structural changes in the economy have helped make the ghetto an even more confining, desolate and pathological wasteland, the black leaders gathered at Richmond opposed "policies which encourage spatial deconcentration." Instead, they called for more "direct funding of black community-based organizations" for the purpose of "revitalizing existing black communities."

This preference for keeping the ghetto was not an incidental aspect of the "black agenda" adopted at Richmond but an integral part of the whole strategy for "in-

dependence." One is naturally tempted to draw the parallel between the orientation toward "self-reliance" promoted at the Richmond conference and the traditional tendency of the "black bourgeoisie," as analyzed so brilliantly many years ago by the great black sociologist E. Franklin Frazier, to prefer a segregated situation within which it could "monopolize the Negro market" and "enjoy a sheltered and relatively secure position in relation to the lower economic classes." But the new black-leadership class represented at Richmond is in many important respects an entirely new phenomenon.

For one thing, it speaks—or at least claims to speak—for a considerably enlarged black professional class. Moreover, it is not a conservative, inward-looking group that retreats behind racial myths, as Frazier described the earlier black middle class. Rather, it is a politically dynamic leadership group, with a global "third-world" perspective, that uses racial myths ideologically in the pursuit of real and important interests. In this respect, the myth that all blacks are equally the victims of racism serves a dual purpose, justifying the claims of the most successful blacks to racial entitlements and, by allowing such claims to be made in the name of all blacks, concealing the specific class interest that is served.

To be sure, not all black leaders either consciously or unconsciously use racial myths in this way. Some may emphasize race because they believe it to be the only way to call attention to black problems, and they may also fear that, without this emphasis, black organizations would lose their raison d'être. And some, of course, may simply feel that the country has not changed to an extent that racism is no longer the central problem. Whatever the explanation, racial politics of the kind that dominated the Richmond conference has gone unchallenged within the black leadership.

One result is that much of the black movement has been drawn inexorably into the universe of third-world radicalism, a trend that has reinforced the ideology of racial victimization. In the short run, this trend affects mainly the moderate black leaders, who have been increasingly pressed to take stands—on an issue like supporting the Palestine Liberation Organization, for example—that alienate political allies and isolate the black movement from the American mainstream. In the long run, however, it affects the whole society, since a black leadership given over to such racial politics enormously complicates any effort to deal with the problem of the black underclass—a problem that remains, as it was in 1965, the most formidable and explosive social issue the society faces.

It is hard to see, for example, how the underclass can be brought into the economic mainstream outside the framework of a strategy that looks ultimately toward the dissolution of the ghetto. Yet this is precisely what the Richmond conference opposed and what has been stricken from the civil-rights agenda since the pivotal controversy over the Moynihan report.

The degree to which retaining the ghetto has come to be viewed as an actual advantage for blacks was well illustrated several years ago at a hearing on urban policy conducted by the House Committee on Banking, Currency and Housing. In response to a proposal by Paul R. Porter, an urban specialist, that poor blacks wishing to relocate to areas of industrial growth and job opportunities be assisted in doing so by Government training and other support, Representative Parren J. Mitchell (Democrat of Maryland) asked: "Will not the relocation of blacks—moving them out of cities—destroy the political base that we blacks have begun to develop in this country?" Porter replied, "I think it might, but I don't know of any way we can tell people that they ought to stay in a city where they are unable to find jobs, merely in order to support a candidate for office on the basis of race. I think we have to find a more constructive solution than that."

There may be some who believe that it is unrealistic even to attempt to solve the problem of the underclass. One suspects here an insidious convergence between left and right, the one maintaining that the society is too racist to solve the problem, the other that the underclass is too mired in its own pathology to uplift itself, even if properly assisted. Certainly nothing said here is meant to suggest that there is a magic answer to the problem of the underclass. But to date, the problem has not been seriously discussed, much less acknowledged to be the core question for which an answer must be found. Instead, all attention has been focused on the divisive and diversionary issue of racial entitlements, while the Government has provided for the subsistence of the underclass with antipoverty allowances that have become increasingly expensive yet are inevitably branded as "inadequate."

One cannot escape the conclusion that the crisis within the black movement is related to the failure of this whole approach, which has benefited those least in need and has perpetuated the dependency of the underclass. If the current black leadership has lost credibility in the eyes of many Americans, this is certainly in part the consequence of its failure to address the real issue—the condition of the underclass—in a way that clarifies our understanding of the problem and promotes a common effort to solve it.

Whether society would respond to a different approach—one that looked toward the elimination of the ghetto and the achievement by the black underclass of *genuine* self-reliance—cannot now be known. In any event, it should not be necessary to arouse the conscience of the nation on this issue as the old civil-rights leadership did in the fight against Jim Crow. It should be enough merely to appeal to the self-interest of the country. The existence of a permanent underclass in all of the major American cities is not, after all, just a black issue. It is an issue that affects the future of America as a viable urban civilization.

QUESTIONS

1. Do you think the persistence of poverty in the black community is better explained through class divisions or through racism?

2. To what extent would you say that the United States is still a racist society? Is there a difference of opinion among members of different race groups in the class?

3. Are affirmative-action programs, which in some cases give preference in employment to minority-group members, justified?

SANDRA BEM
DARYL BEM

Homogenizing the American Woman: The Power of an Unconscious Ideology

In many respects, the inequality of the sexes is a form of social stratification, like inequalities of class, caste, or race. As with other forms of structured social inequality, the relationship between the sexes is not maintained primarily by force. Rather, it rests on the usually unquestioned power of tradition, which ensures that all concerned are socialized for their respective roles and provides an ideology, or belief system, that justifies the situation.

The inequality of the sexes is justified by such an ideology, whose content is learned by both men and women in the ordinary course of socialization. According to this set of beliefs, the inequality between men and women is rooted in the facts of nature, and is perhaps even divinely ordained: men are supposedly prepared by biology and even instinct to be more dominant, aggressive, logical; women are supposedly more submissive, nurturant, emotional. From these differences in temperament and aptitude flow, accordingly, the various sex-role distinctions in the family and the economy. For generations, men and women have apparently found this ideology easy to believe, and until recently few have ever questioned whether the differences between the sexes might, in reality, be primarily the result of cultural, not biological, factors—and therefore subject to change.

In this article, Sandra and Daryl Bem examine the ideological roots and real consequences of sexism, showing that women are "trained" to know their place, not born into it.

Originally titled "Case Study of a Nonconscious Ideology: Training the Woman to Know Her Place," by Bem, S. L., and Bem, D. J., in D. J. Bem, *Beliefs, Attitudes and Human Affairs*. Belmont, California: Brooks/Cole, 1970. Reprinted with permission of Sandra L. and Daryl J. Bem.

In the beginning God created the heaven and the earth . . . And God said, Let us make man in our image, after our likeness; and let him have dominion over the fish of the sea, and over the fowl of the air, and over the cattle, and over all the earth . . . And the rib, which the Lord God had taken from man, made he a woman and brought her unto the man . . . And the Lord God said unto the woman, What is this that thou has done? And the woman said, The serpent beguiled me, and I did eat . . . Unto the woman God said, I will greatly multiply thy sorrow and thy conception; in sorrow thou shalt bring forth children; and thy desire shall be to thy husband, and he shall rule over thee. [Gen. 1, 2, 3]

There is a moral to that story. St. Paul spells it out even more clearly.

For a man . . . is the image and glory of God; but the woman is the glory of the man. For the man is not of the woman, but the woman of the man. Neither was the man created for the woman, but the woman for the man. [1 Cor. 11]

Let the woman learn in silence with all subjection. But I suffer not a woman to teach, nor to usurp authority over the man, but to be in silence. For Adam was first formed and then Eve. And Adam was not deceived, but the woman, being deceived, was in the transgression. Notwithstanding, she shall be saved in childbearing, if they continue in faith and charity and holiness with sobriety. [1 Tim. 2]

Now one should not assume that only Christians have this kind of rich heritage of ideology about women. So consider now, the morning prayer of the Orthodox Jew:

Blessed art Thou, oh Lord our God, King of the Universe, that I was not born a gentile.

Blessed art Thou, oh Lord our God, King of the Universe, that I was not born a slave.

Blessed art Thou, oh Lord our God, King of the Universe, that I was not born a woman.

Or, consider the Koran, the sacred text of Islam:

Men are superior to women on account of the qualities in which God has given them preeminence.

Because they think they sense a decline in feminine "faith, charity, and holiness with sobriety," many people today jump to the conclusion that the ideology expressed in these passages is a relic of the past. Not so, of course. It has simply been obscured by an equalitarian veneer, and the same ideology has now become unconscious. That is, we remain unaware of it because alternative beliefs and attitudes about women, until very recently, have gone unimagined. We are very much like the fish who is unaware of the fact that his environment is wet. After all, what else could it be? Such is the nature of all unconscious ideologies in a society. Such, in particular, is the nature of America's ideology about women.

What we should like to do in this paper is to discuss today's version of this same ideology.

When a baby boy is born, it is difficult to predict what he will be doing 25 years later. We can't say whether he will be an artist, a doctor, a lawyer, a college professor, or a bricklayer, because he will be permitted to develop and fulfill his own unique potential—particularly, of course, if he happens to be white and middle class. But if that same newborn child happens to be a girl, we can predict with almost complete confidence how she is likely to be spending her time some 25 years later. Why can we do that? Because her individuality doesn't have to be considered. Her individuality is irrelevant. Time studies have shown that she will spend the equivalent of a full working day, 7.1 hours, in preparing meals, cleaning house, laundering, mending, shopping and doing other household tasks. In other words, 43% of her waking time will be spent in activity that would command an hourly wage on the open market well below the federally set minimum for menial industrial work.

Of course, the point really is not how little she would earn if she did these things in someone else's home. She will be doing them in her own home for free. The point is that this use of time is virtually the same for homemakers with college degrees and for homemakers with less than a grade school education, for women married to professional men and for women married to blue-collar workers. Actually, that's understating it slightly. What the time study really showed was that college-educated women spend slightly *more* time cleaning their houses than their less-educated counterparts!

Of course, it is not simply the full-time homemaker whose unique identity has been rendered largely irrelevant. Of the 31 million women who work outside the home in our society, 78% end up in dead-end jobs as clerical workers, service workers, factory workers, or sales clerks, compared to a comparable figure of 40% for men. Only 15% of all women workers in our society are classified by the Labor Department as professional or technical workers, and even this figure is misleading—for the single, poorly-paid occupation of non-college teacher absorbs half of these women, and the occupation of nurse absorbs an additional quarter. In other words, the two

jobs of teacher and nurse absorb three-quarters of all women classified in our society as technical or professional. . . .

Even an I.Q. in the genius range does not guarantee that a woman's unique potential will find expression. There was a famous study of over 1300 boys and girls whose I.Q.'s averaged 151 (Terman & Oden, 1959). When the study began in the early 1900's, these highly gifted youngsters were only ten years old, and their careers have been followed ever since. Where are they today? Eighty-six percent of the men have now achieved prominence in professional and managerial occupations. In contrast, only a minority of the women were even employed. Of those who were, 37% were nurses, librarians, social workers, and non-college teachers. An additional 26% were secretaries, stenographers, bookkeepers, and office workers! Only 11% entered the higher professions of law, medicine, college teaching, engineering, science, economics, and the like. And even at age 44, well after all their children had gone to school, 61% of these highly gifted women remained full-time homemakers. Talent, education, ability, interests, motivations: all irrelevant. In our society, being female uniquely qualifies an individual for domestic work—either by itself or in conjunction with typing, teaching, nursing, or (most often) unskilled labor. It is this homogenization of America's women which is the major consequence of our society's sex-role ideology.

It is true, of course, that most women have several hours of leisure time every day. And it is here, we are often told, that each woman can express her unique identity. Thus, politically interested women can join the League of Women Voters. Women with humane interests can become part-time Gray Ladies. Women who love music can raise money for the symphony. Protestant women play Canasta; Jewish women play Mah Jongg; brighter women of all denominations and faculty wives play bridge.

But politically interested *men* serve in legislatures. *Men* with humane interests become physicians or clinical psychologists. *Men* who love music play in the symphony. In other words, why should a woman's unique identity determine only the periphery of her life rather than its central core?

Why? Why nurse rather than physician, secretary rather than executive, stewardess rather than pilot? Why faculty wife rather than faculty? Why doctor's mother rather than doctor? There are three basic answers to this question: (1) discrimination; (2) sex-role conditioning; and (3) the presumed incompatibility of family and career.

Discrimination

In 1968, the median income of full-time women workers

was approximately $4500. The comparable figure for men was $3000 higher. Moreover, the gap is widening. Ten years ago, women earned 64% of what men did; the percentage has now shrunk to 58%. Today, a female college graduate working full-time can expect to earn less per year than a male high school dropout.

There are two reasons for this pay differential. First, in every category of occupation, women are employed in the lesser-skilled, lower-paid positions. Even in the clerical field, where 73% of the workers are women, females are relegated to the lowest status positions and hence earn only 65% of what male clerical workers earn. The second reason for this pay differential is discrimination in its purest form: unequal pay for equal work. According to a survey of 206 companies in 1970, female college graduates were offered jobs which paid $43 per month less than those offered to their male counterparts in the same college major.

New laws should begin to correct both of these situations. The Equal Pay Act of 1963 prohibits employers from discriminating on the basis of sex in the payment of wages for equal work. In a landmark ruling on May 18, 1970, the U.S. Supreme Court ordered that $250,000 in back pay be paid to women employed by a single New Jersey glass company. This decision followed a two-year court battle by the Labor Department after it found that the company was paying men selector-packers 21.5 cents more per hour than women doing the same work. In a similar case, the Eighth Circuit Court of Appeals ordered a major can company to pay more than $100,000 in back wages to women doing equal work. According to the Labor Department, an estimated $17-million is owed to women in back pay. Since that estimate was made, a 1972 amendment extended the Act to cover executive, administrative and professional employees as well.

But to enjoy equal pay, women must also have access to equal jobs. Title VII of the 1964 Civil Rights Act prohibits discrimination in employment on the basis of race, color, religion, national origin—and sex. Although the sex provision was treated as a joke at the time (and was originally introduced by a Southern Congressman in an attempt to defeat the bill), the Equal Employment Opportunities Commission discovered in its first year of operation that 40% or more of the complaints warranting investigation charged discrimination on the basis of sex (Bird, 1969).

Title VII has served as one of the most effective instruments in helping to achieve sex equality in the world of work. According to a report by the E.E.O.C., nearly 6,000 charges of sex discrimination were filed with that agency in 1971 alone, a 62% increase over the previous year.

But the most significant legislative breakthrough in the area of sex equality was the passage of the Equal Rights Amendment by both houses of Congress in 1972.

The ERA simply states that "Equality of rights under the law shall not be denied or abridged by the United States or by any state on account of sex." This amendment has been introduced into every session of Congress since 1923, and its passage now is clearly an indication of the changing role of the American woman. All of the various ramifications are hard to predict, but it is clear that it will have profound consequences in private as well as public life.

Many Americans assume that the recent drive for equality between the sexes is primarily for the benefit of the middle-class woman who wants to seek self-fulfillment in a professional career. But in many ways, it is the woman in more modest circumstances, the woman who *must* work for economic reasons, who stands to benefit most from the removal of discriminatory barriers. It is *she* who is hardest hit by unequal pay; it is *she* who so desperately needs adequate day-care facilities; it is *her* job which is often dead-ended while her male colleagues in the factory get trained and promoted into the skilled craft jobs. And if both she and her husband work at unfulfilling jobs eight hours a day just to make an adequate income, it is still *she* who carries the additional burden of domestic chores when they return home.

We think it is important to emphasize these points at the outset, for we have chosen to focus our remarks in this particular paper on those fortunate men and women who can afford the luxury of pursuing self-fulfillment through the world of work and career. But every societal reform advocated by the new feminist movement, whether it be the Equal Rights Amendment, the establishment of child-care centers, or basic changes in America's sex-role ideology, will affect the lives of men and women in every economic circumstance. Nevertheless, it is still economic discrimination which hits hardest at the largest group of women, and it is here that the drive for equality can be most successfully launched with legislative and judicial tools.

Sex-Role Conditioning

But even if all discrimination were to end tomorrow, nothing very drastic would change. For job discrimination is only part of the problem. It does impede women who choose to become lawyers or managers or physicians. But it does not, by itself, help us to understand why so many women "choose" to be secretaries or nurses rather than executives or physicians; why only 3% of 9th grade girls as compared to 25% of the boys "choose" careers in science or engineering; or why 63% of America's married women "choose" not to work at all. It certainly doesn't explain those young women whose vision of the future includes only marriage, children, and living happily ever after; who may, at some point, "choose" to take a job, but who almost never "choose" to pursue a career. Discrimination frustrates choices already made. Something more pernicious perverts the motivation to choose.

That "something" is an unconscious ideology about the nature of the female sex, an ideology which constricts the emerging self-image of the female child and the nature of her aspirations from the very beginning; an ideology which leads even those Americans who agree that a black skin should not uniquely qualify *its* owner for a janitorial or domestic service to act as if the possession of a uterus uniquely qualifies *its* owner for precisely such service.

Consider, for example, the 1968 student rebellion at Columbia University. Students from the radical Left took over some administration buildings in the name of equalitarian ideals which they accused the university of flouting. Here were the most militant spokesmen one could hope to find in the cause of equalitarian ideals. But no sooner had they occupied the buildings than the male militants blandly turned to their sisters-in-arms and assigned them the task of preparing the food, while they— the menfolk—would presumably plan future strategy. The reply these males received was the reply that they deserved—we will leave that to your imagination—and the fact that domestic tasks behind the barricades were desegregated across the sex line that day is an everlasting tribute to the class consciousness of these ladies of the Left. And it was really on that day that the campus women's liberation movement got its start—when radical women finally realized that they were never going to get to make revolution, only coffee.

But these conscious co-eds are not typical, for the unconscious assumptions about a woman's "natural" talents (or lack of them) are at least as prevalent among women as they are among men. A psychologist named Phillip Goldberg (1968) demonstrated this by asking female college students to rate a number of professional articles from each of six fields. The articles were collated into two equal sets of booklets, and the names of the authors were changed so that the identical article was attributed to a male author (e.g., John T. McKay) in one booklet and to a female author (e.g., Joan T. McKay) in the other booklet. Each student was asked to read the articles in her booklet and to rate them for value, competence, persuasiveness, writing style, and so forth.

As he had anticipated, Goldberg found that the identical article received significantly lower ratings when it was attributed to a female author than when it was attributed to a male author. He had predicted this result for articles from professional fields generally considered the province of men, like law or city planning, but to his surprise, these women also downgraded articles from the fields of dietetics and elementary school education when they were attributed to female authors. In other words, these students rated the male authors as better at everything, agreeing with Aristotle that "we should regard the

female nature as afflicted with a natural defectiveness." Such is the nature of America's unconscious ideology about women.

When does this ideology begin to affect the life of a young girl? Research now tells us that from the day a newborn child is dressed in pink, she is given "special" treatment. Perhaps because they are thought to be more fragile, six-month-old infant girls are actually touched, spoken to, and hovered over more by their mothers while they are playing than are infant boys (Goldberg & Lewis, 1969). One study even showed that when mothers and babies are still in the hospital, mothers smile at, talk to, and touch their female infants more than their male infants at two days of age (Thoman, Leiderman, & Olson, 1972). Differential treatment can't begin much earlier than that.

As children begin to read, the storybook characters become the images and the models that little boys and little girls aspire to become. What kind of role does the female play in the world of children's literature? The fact is that there aren't even very many females in that world. One survey (Fisher, 1970) found that five times as many males as females appear in the titles of children's books; the fantasy world of Doctor Seuss is almost entirely male; and even animals and machines are represented as male. When females do appear, they are noteworthy primarily for what they do *not* do. They do not drive cars, and they seldom even ride bicycles. In one story in which a girl does ride a bicycle, it's a two-seater. Guess where the girl is seated! Boys in these stories climb trees and fish and roll in the leaves and skate. Girls watch, fall down, and get dizzy. Girls are never doctors, and although they may be nurses or librarians or teachers, they are never principals. There seemed to be only one children's book about mothers who work, and it concludes that what mothers love "best of all" is "being your very own Mommy and coming home to you." And although this is no doubt true of many daddies as well, no book about working fathers has ever found it necessary to apologize for working in quite the same way.

As children grow older, more explicit sex-role training is introduced. Boys are encouraged to take more of an interest in mathematics and science. Boys, not girls, are usually given chemistry sets and microscopes for Christmas. Moreover, all children quickly learn that mommy is proud to be a moron when it comes to math and science, whereas daddy is a little ashamed if he doesn't know all about such things. When a young boy returns from school all excited about biology, he is almost certain to be encouraged to think of becoming a physician. A girl with similar enthusiasm is usually told that she might want to consider nurse's training later on, so she can have "an interesting job to fall back upon in case—God forbid— she ever needs to support herself." A very different kind of encouragement. And any girl who doggedly persists in her enthusiasm for science is likely to find her parents as horrified by the prospect of a permanent love affair with physics as they would be either by the prospect of an interracial marriage or, horror of horrors, no marriage at all. Indeed, our graduate women report that their families seem convinced that the menopause must come at age 23.

These socialization practices take their toll. When they apply for college, boys and girls are about equal on verbal aptitude tests, but boys score significantly higher on mathematical aptitude tests—about 60 points higher on the College Board Exams, for example (Brown, 1965). Moreover, for those who are convinced that this is due to female hormones, it is relevant to know that girls improve their mathematical performance if the problems are simply reworded so that they deal with cooking and gardening, even though the abstract reasoning required for solution remains exactly the same (Milton, 1958). That's not hormones! Clearly, what has been undermined is not a woman's mathematical ability, but rather her confidence in that ability.

But these effects in mathematics and science are only part of the story. The most conspicuous outcome of all is that the majority of America's women become full-time homemakers. And of those who do work, nearly 80% end up in dead-end jobs as clerical workers, service workers, factory workers or sales clerks. Again, it is this "homogenization" of America's women which is the major consequence of America's sex-role ideology.

The important point is not that the role of homemaker is necessarily inferior, but rather that our society is managing to consign a large segment of its population to the role of homemaker—either with or without a dead-end job—solely on the basis of sex just as inexorably as it has in the past consigned the individual with a black skin to the role of janitor or domestic. The important point is that in spite of their unique identities, the majority of American women end up in virtually the *same* role.

The socialization of the American male has closed off certain options for him, too. Men are discouraged from developing certain desirable traits such as tenderness and sensitivity, just as surely as women are discouraged from being assertive and, alas, "too bright." Young boys are encouraged to be incompetent at cooking and certainly child care, just as surely as young girls are urged to be incompetent at math and science. The elimination of sex-role stereotyping implies that each individual would be encouraged to "do his own thing." Men and women would no longer be stereotyped by society's definitions of masculine and feminine. If sensitivity, emotionality, and warmth are desirable *human* characteristics, then they are desirable for men as well as for women. If independence, assertiveness, and serious intellectual commitment are desirable *human* characteristics, then they are desirable for women as well as for men. Thus, we are not

implying that men have all the goodies and that women can obtain self-fulfillment by acting like men. That is hardly the utopia implied by today's feminist movement. Rather, we envision a society which raises its children so flexibly and with sufficient respect for the integrity of individual uniqueness that some men might emerge with the motivation, the ability, and the opportunity to stay home and raise children without bearing the stigma of being peculiar. Indeed, if homemaking is as glamorous as women's magazines and television commercials would have us believe, then men, too, should have that option. And even if homemaking isn't all that glamorous, it would probably still be more fulfilling for some men than the jobs in which they now find themselves forced because of their role as breadwinner. Thus, it is true that a man's options are also limited by our society's sex-role ideology, but as the "predictability test" reveals, it is still the women in our society whose identity is rendered irrelevant by America's socialization practices.

. . .

. . . Even our concept of mental health has been distorted by America's sex-role stereotypes. Here we must indict our own profession of psychology. A recent survey of seventy-nine clinically-trained psychologists, psychiatrists, and social workers, both male and female, revealed a double standard of mental health (Broverman, Broverman, Clarkson, Rosenkrantz, & Vogel, 1970). That is, even professional clinicians have two different concepts of mental health, one for men and one for women; and these concepts parallel the sex-role stereotypes . . . Thus, according to these clinicians, a woman is to be regarded as healthier and more mature if she is: more submissive, less independent, less adventurous, more easily influenced, less aggressive, less competitive, more excitable in minor crises, more susceptible to hurt feelings, more emotional, more conceited about her appearance, less objective, and more antagonistic toward math and science! But this was the very same description which these clinicians used to characterize an unhealthy, immature man or an unhealthy, immature adult (sex unspecified)! The equation is clear: Mature woman equals immature adult.

Given this concept of a mature woman, is it any wonder that few women ever aspire toward challenging and fulfilling careers? In order to have a career, a woman will probably need to become relatively more dominant, independent, adventurous, aggressive, competitive, and objective, and relatively less excitable, emotional and conceited than our ideal of femininity requires. If she were a man (or an adult, sex unspecified), these would all be considered positive traits. But because she is a woman, these same traits will bring her disapproval. She must then either be strong enough to have her "femininity" questioned; or she must behave in the prescribed feminine manner and accept second-class status, as an adult and as a professional.

And, of course, should a woman faced with this conflict seek professional help, hoping to summon the strength she will need to pursue her career goals, the advice she is likely to receive will be of virtually no use. For, as this study reveals, even professional counselors have been contaminated by the sex-role ideology.

It is frequently argued that a 21-year-old woman is perfectly free to choose a career if she cares to do so. No one is standing in her way. But this argument conveniently overlooks the fact that our society has spent 20 years carefully marking the woman's ballot for her, and so it has nothing to lose in that 21st year by pretending to let her cast it for the alternative of her choice. Society has controlled not her alternatives (although discrimination does do that), but more importantly, it has controlled her motivation to choose any but one of those alternatives. The so-called "freedom-to-choose" is illusory, and it cannot be invoked to justify a society which controls the woman's motivation to choose.

Biological Considerations

Up to this point, we have argued that the differing life patterns of men and women in our society can be chiefly accounted for by cultural conditioning. The most common counter argument to this view, of course, is the biological one. The biological argument suggests that there may really be inborn differences between men and women in, say, independence or mathematical ability. Or that there may be biological factors beyond the fact that women can become pregnant and nurse children which uniquely dictate that they, but not men, should stay home all day and shun serious outside commitment. What this argument suggests is that maybe female hormones really are responsible somehow. One difficulty with this argument, of course, is that female hormones would have to be different in the Soviet Union, where one-third of the engineers and 75% of the physicians are women (Dodge, 1966). In America, by way of contrast, women constitute less than 1% of the engineers and only 7% of the physicians. Female physiology is different, and it may account for some of the psychological differences between the sexes, but America's sex-role ideology still seems primarily responsible for the fact that so few women emerge from childhood with the motivation to seek out any role beyond the one that our society dictates.

But even if there really were biological differences between the sexes along these lines, the biological argument would still be irrelevant. The reason can best be illustrated with an analogy.

Suppose that every black American boy were to be socialized to become a jazz musician on the assumption that he has a "natural" talent in that direction; or suppose that parents and counselors should subtly discourage him from other pursuits because it is considered "inap-

propriate" for black men to become physicians or physicists. Most Americans would disapprove. But suppose that it *could* be demonstrated that black Americans, *on the average*, did possess an inborn better sense of rhythm than white Americans. Would *that* justify ignoring the unique characteristics of a *particular* black youngster from the very beginning and specifically socializing him to become a musician? We don't think so. Similarly, as long as a woman's socialization does not nurture her uniqueness, but treats her only as a member of a group on the basis of some assumed *average* characteristic, she will not be prepared to realize her own potential in the way that the values of individuality and self-fulfillment imply that she should.

The Presumed Incompatibility of Family and Career

If we were to ask the average American woman why she is not pursuing a full-time career, she would probably not say that discrimination has discouraged her; nor would she be likely to recognize the pervasive effects of her own sex-role conditioning. What she probably would say is that a career, no matter how desirable, is simply incompatible with the role of wife and mother.

As recently as the turn of the century, and in less technological societies today, this incompatibility between career and family was, in fact, decisive. Women died in their forties and they were pregnant or nursing during most of their adult lives. Moreover, the work that a less technological society requires places a premium on mobility and physical strength, neither of which a pregnant woman has a great deal of. Thus, the historical division of labor between the sexes—the man away at work and the woman at home with the children—was a biological necessity. Today it is not.

Today, the work that our technological society requires is primarily mental in nature; women have virtually complete control over their reproductive lives; and most important of all, the average American woman now lives to age 74 and has her last child before age 30. This means that by the time a woman is 35 or so, her children all have more important things to do with their daytime hours than to spend them entertaining some adult woman who has nothing fulfilling to do during the entire second half of her life span.

But social forms have a way of outliving the necessities which gave rise to them. And today's female adolescent continues to plan for a 19th century life style in a 20th century world. A Gallup poll has found that young women give no thought whatever to life after forty (Gallup & Hill, 1962). They plan to graduate from high school, perhaps go to college, and then get married. Period!

The Woman as Wife

At some level, of course, this kind of planning is "realistic." Because most women do grow up to be wives and mothers, and because, for many women, this means that they will be leaving the labor force during the child-rearing years, a career is not really feasible. After all, a career involves long-term commitment and perhaps some sacrifice on the part of the family. Furthermore, as every "successful" woman knows, a wife's appropriate role is to encourage her husband in *his* career. The "good" wife puts her husband through school, endures the family's early financial difficulties without a whimper, and, if her husband's career should suddenly dictate a move to another city, she sees to it that the transition is accomplished as painlessly as possible. The good wife is selfless. And to be seriously concerned about one's own career is selfish—if one is female, that is. With these kinds of constraints imposed upon the work life of the married woman, perhaps it would be "unrealistic" for her to seriously aspire toward a career rather than a job.

. . .

Accordingly, the traditional conception of the husband-wife relationship is now being challenged, not so much because of . . . widespread discontent among older, married women, but because it violates two of the most basic values of today's college generation. These values concern personal growth, on the one hand, and interpersonal relationships on the other. The first of these emphasizes the [person's] individuality and self-fulfillment; the second stresses openness, honesty, and equality in all human relationships.

Because they see the traditional male-female relationship as incompatible with these basic values, today's young people are experimenting with alternatives to the traditional marriage pattern. Although a few are testing out ideas like communal living, most seem to be searching for satisfactory modifications of the husband-wife relationship, either in or out of the context of marriage. An increasing number of young people claim to be seeking fully equalitarian relationships and they cite examples like the following:

> Both my wife and I earned college degrees in our respective disciplines. I turned down a superior job offer in Oregon and accepted a slightly less desirable position in New York where my wife would have more opportunities for part-time work in her specialty. Although I would have preferred to live in a suburb, we purchased a home near my wife's job so that she could have an office at home where she would be when the children returned from school. Because my wife earns a good salary, she can easily afford to pay a housekeeper to do her major household chores. My wife and I share all other tasks around the house equally. For example, she cooks the meals, but I do the laundry for her and help her with many of her other household tasks.

Without questioning the basic happiness of such a marriage or its appropriateness for many couples, we can legitimately ask if such a marriage is, in fact, an instance

of interpersonal equality. Have all the hidden assumptions about the woman's "natural" role really been eliminated? Have our visionary students really exorcised the traditional ideology as they claim? There is a very simple test. If the marriage is truly equalitarian, then its description should retain the same flavor and tone even if the roles of the husband and wife were to be reversed:

> Both my husband and I earned college degrees in our respective disciplines. I turned down a superior job offer in Oregon and accepted a slightly less desirable position in New York where my husband would have more opportunities for part-time work in his specialty. Although I would have preferred to live in a suburb, we purchased a home near my husband's job so that he could have an office at home where he would be when the children returned from school. Because my husband earns a good salary, he can easily afford to pay a housekeeper to do his major household chores. My husband and I share all other tasks around the house equally. For example, he cooks the meals, but I do the laundry for him and help him with many of his other household tasks.

Somehow it sounds different, and yet only the pronouns have been changed to protect the powerful! Certainly no one would ever mistake the marriage *just* described as equalitarian or even very desirable, and thus it becomes apparent that the ideology about the woman's "natural" place unconsciously permeates the entire fabric of such "pseudo-equalitarian" marriages. It is true the wife gains some measure of equality when she can have a career rather than have a job and when her career can influence the final place of residence. But why is it the unquestioned assumption that the husband's career solely determines the initial set of alternatives that are to be considered? Why is it the wife who automatically seeks the part-time position? Why is it *her* housekeeper rather than *their* housekeeper? Why *her* household tasks? And so forth throughout the entire relationship.

The important point is not that such marriages are bad or that their basic assumptions of inequality produce unhappy, frustrated women. Quite the contrary. It is the very happiness of the wives in such marriages that reveals society's smashing success in socializing its women. It is a measure of the distance our society must yet traverse toward the goal of full equality that such marriages are widely characterized as utopian and fully equalitarian. It is a mark of how well the woman has been kept in her place that the husband in such a marriage is almost always idolized by women, including his wife. Why? Because he "permits her" to squeeze a career into the interstices of their marriage as long as his own career is not unduly inconvenienced. Thus is the white man blessed for exercising his power benignly while his "natural" right to that power forever remains unquestioned. Such is the subtlety of America's ideology about women.

In fact, however, even these "benign" inequities are now being challenged. More and more young couples really are entering marriages of full equality, marriages in which both partners pursue careers or outside commitments which carry equal weight when all important decisions are to be made, marriages in which both husband and wife accept some compromise in the growth of their respective careers for their mutual partnership. Certainly such marriages have more tactical difficulties than more traditional ones: It is simply more difficult to coordinate two independent lives rather than one-and-a-half. The point is that it is not possible to predict ahead of time, *on the basis of sex*, who will be doing the compromising at any given point of decision.

It should be clear that the man or woman who places career above all else ought not to enter an equalitarian marriage. The man would do better to marry a traditional wife, a wife who will make whatever sacrifices his career necessitates. The woman who places career above all else would do better—in our present society—to remain single. For an equalitarian marriage is not designed for extra efficiency, but for double fulfillment.

The Woman as Mother

In all marriages, whether traditional, pseudo-equalitarian or fully equalitarian, the real question surrounding a mother's career will probably continue to be the well-being of the children. All parents want to be certain that they are doing the very best for their children and that they are not depriving them in any important way, either materially or psychologically. What this has meant recently in most families that could afford it was that mother would devote herself to the children on a full-time basis. Women have been convinced—by their mothers and by the so-called experts—that there is something wrong with them if they even want to do otherwise.

For example, according to Dr. Spock (1963), any woman who finds full-time motherhood unfulfilling is showing "a residue of difficult relationships in her own childhood." If a vacation doesn't solve the problem, then she is probably having emotional problems which can be relieved "through regular counseling in a family social agency, or if severe, through psychiatric treatment . . . Any mother of a pre-school child who is considering a job should discuss the issues with a social worker before making her decision." The message is clear: If you don't feel that your two-year-old is a stimulating, full-time, companion, then you are probably neurotic.

In fact, research does not support the view that children suffer in any way when mother works. Although it came as a surprise to most researchers in the area, maternal employment in and of itself does not seem to have any negative effects on the children; and part-time work actually seems to benefit the children. Children of working mothers are no more likely than children of non-working mothers to be delinquent or nervous or withdrawn or anti-social; they are no more likely to show neurotic symptoms; they are no more likely to perform poorly in school; and they are no more likely to feel deprived of their mother's love. Daughters of working mothers are more likely to want to work themselves, and, when asked to name the one woman in the world that they most admire, daughters of working mothers are more likely to name their own mothers! (Nye & Hoffman, 1963). This is one finding that we wish every working woman in America could hear, because the other thing that is true of almost every working mother is that she *thinks* she is hurting her children and she feels guilty. In fact, research has shown that the worst mothers are those who would like to work, but who stay home out of a sense of duty (Yarrow, Scott, de Leeuw, & Heinig, 1962). The major conclusion from all the research is really this: What matters is the quality of a mother's relationship with her children, not the time of day it happens to be administered. This conclusion should come as no surprise; successful fathers have been demonstrating it for years. Some fathers are great, some fathers stink, and they're all at work at least eight hours a day.

Similarly, it is true that the quality of substitute care that children receive while their parents are at work also matters. Young children do need security, and research has shown that it is not good to have a constant turnover of parent-substitutes, a rapid succession of changing baby-sitters or housekeepers (Maccoby, 1958). Clearly, this is why the establishment of child care centers is vitally important at the moment. This is why virtually every woman's group in the country, no matter how conservative or how radical, is in agreement on this one issue: that child care centers ought to be available to those who need them.

. . .

But even the woman who is educationally and economically in a position to pursue a career must feel free to utilize these alternative arrangements for child care. For once again, America's sex-role ideology intrudes. Many people still assume that if a woman wants a full-time career, then children must be unimportant to her. But of course, no one makes this assumption about her husband. No one assumes that a father's interest in his career necessarily precludes a deep and abiding affection for his children or a vital interest in their development. Once again, America applies a double standard of judgment. Suppose that a father of small children suddenly lost his wife. No matter how much he loved his children, no one would expect him to sacrifice his career in order to stay home with them on a full-time basis—even if he had an independent source of income. No one would charge him with selfishness or lack of parental feeling if he sought professional care for his children during the day.

It is here that full equality between husband and wife

assumes its ultimate importance. The fully equalitarian marriage abolishes this double standard and extends the same freedom to the mother. The equalitarian marriage provides the framework for both husband and wife to pursue careers which are challenging and fulfilling and, at the same time, to participate equally in the pleasures and responsibilities of child-rearing. Indeed, it is the equalitarian marriage which has the potential for giving children the love and concern of two parents rather than one. And it is the equalitarian marriage which has the most potential for giving parents the challenge and fulfillment of two worlds—family and career—rather than one.

In addition to providing this potential for equalized child care, a truly equalitarian marriage embraces a more general division of labor which satisfies what we like to call "the roommate test." That is, the labor is divided just as it is when two men or two women room together in college or set up a bachelor apartment together. Errands and domestic chores are assigned by preference, agreement, flipping a coin, alternated, given to hired help, or—perhaps most often the case—left undone.

It is significant that today's young people, so many of whom live precisely this way prior to marriage, find this kind of arrangement within marriage so foreign to their thinking. Consider an analogy. Suppose that a white male college student decided to room or set up a bachelor apartment with a black male friend. Surely the typical white student would not blithely assume that his black roommate was to handle all the domestic chores. Nor would his conscience allow him to do so even in the unlikely event that his roommate would say: "No, that's okay. I like doing housework. I'd be happy to do it." We suspect that the typical white student would still not be comfortable if he took advantage of this offer because he and America have finally realized that he would be taking advantage of the fact that such a roommate had been socialized by our society to be "happy" with such obvious inequity. But change this hypothetical black roommate to a female marriage partner, and somehow the student's conscience goes to sleep. At most it is quickly tranquilized by the comforting thought that "she is happiest when she is ironing for her loved one." Such is the power of an unconscious ideology.

Of course, it may well be that she *is* happiest when she is ironing for her loved one.

Such, indeed, is the power of an unconscious ideology.

QUESTIONS

1. How great a part do you think cultural learning plays in the content of sex roles?

2. How are men trained to play *their* sex roles?

3. What are the similarities between sexual and other forms of social stratification? Are there any differences?

References

Bird, C. *Born female: the high cost of keeping women down.* New York: Pocket Books, 1969.

Broverman, I.K., Broverman, D.M., Clarkson, F.E., Rosenkrantz, P.S., & Vogel, S.R. Sex-role stereotypes and clinical judgments of mental health. *Journal of Consulting and Clinical Psychology*, 1970, *34*, 1–7.

Brown, R. *Social psychology.* New York: Free Press, 1965.

Dodge, N. D. *Women in the Soviet economy.* Baltimore: Johns Hopkins Press, 1966.

Fisher, E. The second sex, junior division. *The New York Times Book Review*, May, 1970.

Gallup, G., & Hill, E. The American woman. *The Saturday Evening Post*, Dec. 22, 1962, pp. 15–32.

Goldberg, P. Are women prejudiced against women? *Transaction*, April, 1968, *5*, 28–30.

Goldberg, S., & Lewis, M. Play behavior in the year-old infant: early sex differences. *Child Development*, 1969, *40*, 21–31.

Horner, M.S. Fail: bright women. *Psychology Today*, November, 1969.

Maccoby, E.E. Effects upon children of their mothers' outside employment. In *Work in the lives of married women.* New York: Columbia University Press, 1958.

Milton, G.A. Sex differences in problem solving as a function of role appropriateness of the problem content. *Psychological Reports*, 1958, *5*, 705–708.

Nye, F.I., & Hoffman, L.W. *The employed mother in America.* Chicago: Rand McNally, 1963.

Ringo, M. The well-placed wife. Unpublished manuscript, John Paisios & Associates, 332 South Michigan Ave., Chicago, Illinois 60604.

Spock, B. Should mothers work? *Ladies' Home Journal*, February, 1963.

Terman, L.M., & Oden, M.H. *Genetic studies of genius, V. The gifted group at mid-life: Thirty-five years' follow-up of the superior child.* Stanford, California: Stanford University Press, 1959.

Thoman, E.B., Leiderman, P.H., & Olson, J.P. Neonate-mother interaction during breast feeding. *Developmental Psychology*, 1972, *6*, 110–118.

U.S. Department of Labor, Wage and Labor Standards Administration, Women's Bureau. Fact sheet on the earnings gap, February, 1970.

U.S. Department of Labor, Wage and Labor Standards Administration, Women's Bureau. *Handbook on women workers,* 1969. Bulletin 294.

Yarrow, M.R., Scott, P., de Leeuw, L., & Heinig, D. Child-rearing in families of working and non-working mothers. *Sociometry*, 1962, *25*, 122–140.

DAVID KENT

A Man in No-Man's-Land

Patterns of interaction between men and women are deeply influenced by the sex-role expectations that society offers them. In every sphere of life, men are generally expected to be more dominant and aggressive, and women, more submissive and docile.

These expectations are particularly relevant in the various social rituals of sexual flirtation and seduction. It is still widely anticipated that the male will take the initiative in such matters, playing the role of the aggressive pursuer, while the female's role is essentially to react to the pursuit, preferably without displaying too much enthusiasm too soon. Quite often, women complain that men are inclined to treat them as sex objects, valuing them less as persons than as a means of gratification.

In this article, David Kent describes an unusual situation, one that many men might envy: he was one of a handful of males at a women's college. But this experience proved less blissful than he had expected, for he found himself the object of often unwelcome advances by women who seemed to care little for him as a person.

First published in *Esquire*, October 1980. Reprinted by permission of Ellen Levine Literary Agency, Inc. Copyright © 1980 by David Kent.

Two years ago I participated in an academic exchange that included twelve New England colleges. I wanted to spend a year at a university with the resources to extend certain areas of study I'd pursued at Bowdoin, my home-town college in Brunswick, Maine. What I needed was a college that had more writing courses, better theater facilities, a regular faculty in drama and writing, and a place where I could continue to see my own plays produced. Before I knew it, I was one of five men who were going to live among two thousand women for an academic year at Wellesley College. And that in itself seemed like a fantasy come true.

Thirty minutes outside Boston, Wellesley College is one of the few remaining bastions of single-sex higher education. The five-hundred-acre campus sprawls in the middle of the town of Wellesley, a respectable upper-middle-class suburb with a strong sense of its New England heritage. The college was established in 1875, around the time Mt. Holyoke, Vassar, Radcliffe, Bryn Mawr, Barnard, and Smith were founded. These were the first institutions to boast, "The cooks are men and the professors are women." Wellesley attracted an outstanding student body and became famous for its contributions to the arts and sciences and to the women's movement.

The Wellesley campus has been called "eternally beautiful" by Yeats, and Jean Giraudoux described it as "the paradise where the first laughter was heard." With its lake and woodlands, its arboretum, and its footpaths weaving in and out among the stately Gothic buildings, the college is almost too picturesque. It is a world unto itself, like no other, aesthetically perfect and trance-inducing at the same time.

When my roommates in Maine learned of my decision to go to Wellesley, they were astonished. Most people spent their junior year in London or Paris; that was understandable. Word spread like wildfire. My women friends studiedly avoided me. Their expressions said it all: "Can't find a woman here, huh? We're not good enough? Well, you're not such a deal yourself."

When the smoke cleared a bit, the helpful advice began. Nudges. Winks. "You ought to rest up over the summer." But I took it in stride. Heck, I was above all that. I didn't think of women as sexual playthings or as my inferiors. I had rationalized the situation: why shouldn't I take advantage of any college that had what I needed? "We all need *that*," a friend replied, swiveling his pelvis and making an "oomph" sound.

I'll never forget my arrival at Wellesley. Before I had even stepped onto the grassy quadrangle in front of my dorm, my father's station wagon was being unloaded by tanned women in short shorts. They seemed only too eager to get a look at one of the men who would be living in their dorm. The only things I carried up to my room were a lampshade and a Frisbee. I have to admit that "scared to death" is an understatement of how I felt that September day. But attention and pampering from some of the most beautiful women I had ever met smoothed things out pretty quickly. The girls in the dorm mothered and cooed and fought over the five of us. Now, I am merely an average-looking fellow. I've had my luck with women in the past, but under normal circumstances none of this would have happened.

I observed that most of the women at Wellesley had pictures of old boyfriends displayed on their bureaus. They dropped masculine names in conversation to let you know that they had a man in the closet. At all-female schools, social status depends very heavily on the male in your life. To have a man who lives on campus: for many women that is true prestige. At least that's how I saw it.

I never spent a more enjoyable presemester week in my whole college career. I quickly forgot why I had come to Wellesley in the first place. Being one of the only male students gave me distinct social advantages. I could show up at a Saturday-night mixer, with its lines of Harvard and MIT men waiting to pay to get in, and just stroll past them up to the desk. The girl there, recognizing me, would smile and wave me in. I'd turn and wink at the line of would-be studs staring wide-eyed and wondering what fabulous con I had pulled.

I was a kid with a sweet tooth in the biggest candy store in the world. I was walking on air. For the first few months, I was enthralled by the beauty of every woman I saw. I could not say no. Often when I think back on that time, I have to pinch myself to believe that it really happened. I was dating three different women a night, scheduling five to nine, nine to twelve, one to morning, meeting in three different places to avoid disaster. Instead of walking, I strutted. I rarely spent a night in my own room. The ratio of women to men was 400 to 1. Everything was in my favor. I could pick women up in the evening and drop them the next morning. What's more, I didn't always have to do the picking up.

In my twentieth-century English literature class, a blond classmate sitting beside me slipped me a note: "Aren't you an exchange?" I nodded and turned my attention back to D. H. Lawrence. Five minutes later, I felt a hand moving up my thigh. It was stopped only by the bell. As class broke up, she introduced herself. Call her Sima; I have changed the names of all the women mentioned in this story. Sima loved men who liked literature. She said it would be a valuable part of her college experience to love me. I didn't argue.

During a morning jog around the lake, a sweat-suited woman I recognized from my writing class caught up with me and yelled, "I'll race you back!" We raced, ending up at her dorm. She invited me up to rest, perhaps have breakfast with her. "I think it's great that a guy would have the courage to come to a women's college."

"Aw, it's nothing," I said.

"I also think it's crazy." It turned out that she loved crazy men. She thought it would be a valuable part of her college experience to love me. I didn't argue.

While taking a shower one afternoon, I heard the door to the bathroom open. Someone turned on the sink taps. "Hi, David," a female voice called. "It's Laurie." She lived on the floor below me; we had met at dinner a few evenings before. "The showers on the third floor are broken, so I came up to use these. Okay?"

I didn't answer in time. She pulled back the shower curtain and stepped in. "We'll share, okay?" I didn't argue.

You're probably thinking that I've made all this up. I haven't. This sort of thing happened all the time. I could have gone out on regular dates—flowers, dinner, a movie—but I chose that route only on very special occasions. I was overwhelmed by what was happening. I was in love with myself.

Of course, all this bed-hopping changes a person. Suddenly I was careful to keep my hair combed and my socks clean, careful to wear boxer shorts instead of briefs (the latter, I was told, aren't very sexy). But there were more subtle changes. I became incapable of talking to a woman without imagining how much she craved me and what she'd be like in the sack. Well, what would you expect in a situation like this?

One night in November, around 2:30 in the morning, I was up working on the first play I'd written in the two and a half months I had been at Wellesley. It was a play about women, one I eventually saw produced. I had always joked that I couldn't create a believable female character, that going to Wellesley might help me do this. It did. But I wouldn't finish the play that night.

There was a knock at my door. A girl I had often spoken to at the student union entered. I was in bed, writing on a yellow sketch pad, not dressed to receive guests. I explained that I was busy and declined her offer for a late run over to Bagel Nosh. She came in and closed the door; she locked it. I went back to my pad and tried to ignore her. "Write! Write!" I kept saying to myself.

"You know, I was telling some of the girls at the union

that I know you," she remarked, removing her coat. "And they said that any guy who'd have the balls to come here for a year must have great skill to go with those balls." She slipped off her pants and slid in next to me, pushing the yellow pad aside. She smiled. "On behalf of the student body, welcome to Wellesley College!"

The next day at the union I sat down behind a table of four girls, whose faces I didn't see. After a minute I realized that they were all acquaintances of mine, one of them the visitor from the night before. They spoke loudly enough for me to hear. "He's got little love-handles on his hips," the first girl commented. "When I got him, he was pretty drunk, so you can imagine how great that was," the second one blared. "Oh, he was fair, but he shouldn't stay another semester on the basis of overall performance," the third girl put in. My visitor from the night before, meeting my eyes and smiling, said, "He'll do for a good lay whenever I get the urge." They laughed and prodded one another, winking at me, throwing kisses. Eventually, they got up and left.

I felt I would never walk again. Each word stung with accuracy. I went back to my room, deeply humiliated. My ego was so badly slashed by this sudden viciousness that the lesson I should have accepted made me bitter and resentful instead.

Women have always chastised men for the cold, insensitive locker-room talk they claim we enjoy. They picture us comparing notes on this one-nighter and that love affair. But here the tables were turned, and each deliberate blow sounded like "Off with his head!" This was no teenagers' kiss-and-tell.

I had a hard time showing my face during the next few days, and it was weeks before I was able to return to the union. I was sure my story had gotten tremendous play. Feigning illness in order to stay out of classes, eating only when everyone had left the dining room, I went underground. I trusted no one and took a secret vow to give up Wellesley women; they seemed to offer nothing but trouble. I tried a number of escape valves, from playing basketball in Cambridge to starting a romance with a girl who lived in Boston.

As it turned out, two of the other four male exchanges were secretly experiencing the same depression. They were as confused and as inept at dealing with it as I was. It was easy for us to meet and discuss one another's plight, as we all lived together on the fourth floor of one of the dorms. For the first time that year, we became more than acquaintances.

We had come to Wellesley for very different reasons; under normal circumstances it is unlikely that we would have been friends. Preoccupied with our individual social lives, we had rarely gone out as a group. We'd spent only a couple of nights in bull sessions to relieve the tension of heavy dating and to "be with the men." Now, though, we had more than the casual camaraderie enforced by our

living arrangement. Now that our balloons were being simultaneously popped, we were talking survival. We spent inordinate amounts of time analyzing, scheming, and even planning revenge, which we never took. Meanwhile, unable to keep my vow of abstinence, I began to seek more discreet meetings with the women of Wellesley.

As time passed, I understood my attitude toward women better. We live in a man's world, and no matter how liberated we think we are, we always have the feeling that women will bow at our feet. I was surprised to find this attitude in myself. Having been brought up with two sisters, I'd imagined that I had intelligence enough to understand women. (Any man who says he does is as half-cocked as someone who says he understands the nature of the universe.)

The incident in the union shocked me into realizing that Wellesley was a woman's world and I was a visitor. I didn't fit into the Wellesley system, so I was categorized and abused and discriminated against. A number of things I had never noticed before began to take on new significance. I settled into a state of paranoia.

It was always a challenge to find a men's room in the main classroom buildings. Most of the soft-drink machines on campus were stocked only with Tab. On weekends all the outlets in the bathrooms were overloaded with hair dryers and curling machines; a guy could go for days with dirty stubble on his chin before he'd find a free outlet for his electric shaver. The men's locker room at the gym was the size of a small crypt. It was never washed down; purple fungus covered the walls.

I could not miss a class without the professor's noticing that I was absent. In class, I was called on to present the male point of view, which always seemed to get me into deep trouble. Once I was swiftly shot down when I used the word *mankind*. I was told it was antiquated and chauvinistic. "It should be *personkind*," a biology major yelled at me. "Well, *personkind* still has *son* in it," I shot back. "Why not neutralize it to *peroffspringkind*?" Thirty women just stared at me while the professor shook her head, embarrassed on my behalf.

Gossip was intense at Wellesley. I heard the most amazing things about myself. That I had been seen naked atop the one-hundred-eighty-two-foot Galen Stone Tower in the middle of campus. That I had floated out onto the lake with two women in the middle of the night. Even that I had gone in drag for an examination by the campus gynecologist.

A number of times I was picked up by campus police as I walked across campus after dark. The security force was suspicious of any men on campus. I was nearly arrested late one night when I walked up behind a girl who lived across the hall. Not recognizing the tall stranger in a hooded red sweat suit who seemed to know her name, she began to scream.

One of the most striking features of Wellesley College is the elaborate security system that is activated when people call or visit the dorms. Each hall has a front desk called the Bell Desk. All incoming calls go through this desk, which each student in the dorm manages at least once a week. If a man calls someone on the phone, the Bell Desk monitor rings that girl's floor and says she has a "call" at the desk. If it's a female voice on the line, the student is told it's a "phone call." Likewise, a male visitor who shows up at the front desk is described as a "caller." If it's a woman, she is a mere "visitor."

With men living in the dorm, the system suffered some terrible upheavals. Many Bell Desk monitors didn't know whether to reverse the system for us, or what. It was not uncommon to hear over the intercom: "You have a vis— no, a caller—no " (whispering to a friend) "what the hell *is* this, anyway?" I had to cover the phones in my turn, and many protective parents went into shock at hearing a man's voice in their daughter's secure outpost.

Another aspect of the Bell Desk arrangement was a requirement that visitors check in. Strangers to the dorm could not enter it without an escort. At all-female institutions, every man is automatically considered a nonstudent visitor. On one of the first nights of the semester, when my face was still not universally recognized, I returned late from an evening in Boston. I walked past the Bell Desk girl, tired and somewhat stoned. As I circled around behind her and headed up the stairs, she demanded that I identify myself. She was a scared sophomore who suddenly turned into a neo-Nazi. "Halt! Who goes there!" she yelled.

"Me," I said, striding on up the stairs.

"Identify yourself. Who are you going to see?"

"I'm going to see myself," I said, smiling. "I live here."

She figured that was a giveaway that I was deranged and dangerous. "I'm calling security," she screamed.

It would have been an easy matter to turn and show her my ID, but I was feeling outraged at being hassled when I entered my own dorm. The seeds of discrimination were sprouting. The system was not adapting to my needs. A half hour later, lying on my bed in boxer shorts and socks, I was visited by two security officers, who were inclined to search the room for the missing female student I had done in. I showed them my ID, but they figured it for a phony. "Get dressed, son," they ordered. The commotion woke my neighbors, and the girl next door peered in. "Oh, he's all right," she told security. "He's just one of the co-eds."

Co-eds. It was the first time I had heard that word applied to myself, and it was something we men always despised. Women had been called co-eds when they entered predominantly male universities at the turn of the

century. But for us to have to bear the same label was degrading and sexist.

I was stranded in Cambridge one evening because the shuttle bus driver didn't believe my ID was valid and there was no one around to vouch for me. I was pinched on three different occasions: on an elevator, during a wait in line at the student union, and at a Wednesday Tea (one of the many traditions fondly perpetuated at Wellesley). The first time it happened I turned around with fists clenched, ready to punch the culprit. Unfortunately, the sight of three pretty women, their eyes darting innocently back and forth, took the fight out of me. The next two times, I just wanted to crawl into a hole and die.

I tried to explain what was happening to me to friends who went to other schools in the Boston area. They'd laugh and tell me not to look a wonderful gift horse in the mouth. They didn't care about my troubles so long as I set up dates for them every weekend from September to May. I had become a private singles service, supplying women at all hours of the night, posting invitations all over campus to parties throughout the Boston area. My greatest feat was arriving at a Harvard friend's party with close to twenty-five Wellesley freshwomen who had never been to Cambridge before. My friends couldn't have understood my problems.

I guess I was finding out what it means to be a sex object. When you're treated on the basis of what hangs or doesn't hang between your legs, you lose a certain sense of purpose. "There is more to me!" I wanted to cry. "Love me for my mind, my kindness, my soul!"

I became self-conscious and insecure. I developed a deep fear of not measuring up to whatever I was supposed to measure up to; I felt the women were judging me by a set of invisible standards.

There is a Rodin sculpture in front of the arts center at Wellesley, and every male who has ever spent much time on campus can easily feel an identification with it. It is the statue of a man, headless, armless, and apparently castrated. It made me wonder uncomfortably about how the women were sizing me up when I entered a lecture hall.

I thought back to the very first conversation I had ever had about attending Wellesley. A guy named Ted, a swimmer, had been there the year before me. We were talking in the student cafeteria the spring I made my decision to go.

"What's it like?" I asked.

He kept eating. "No one can describe it," he mumbled.

"What does that mean?"

"Come back and talk to me next year."

I got up, feeling dejected. "Hey," he said, reconsidering a bit. "Just this little tip." He pointed to his lunch tray, on which sat the remains of a whole chicken.

"This," he said tapping the tray. I waited. "Hold it right when you walk through the dining rooms . . . I mean, don't drop it." It seemed like half-crazy advice then, but a year later I understood what he meant. We felt a deep fear at Wellesley, which we could not hide. Privacy didn't exist. The last thing you wanted to do was draw more attention to yourself by letting a tray of chicken slip from your hands.

I began to notice that many of the Wellesley women resented my presence on campus and were defensive around me. They wanted to put me in my place, to show me that this was a woman's haven, which no man could take away. I remember a rare occasion when we male exchange students were sitting together. A gorgeous woman, a member of the student senate, sat down with us. She slammed her hand on the table and fired a question at my Dartmouth friend: "And why did you come to Wellesley?"

Eric swallowed his pudding. "My best friend lives in Boston, and I don't get to see him much." (This was in fact his reason.)

She turned to Richard and fired the same question at him. "And why did *you* come to Wellesley?"

"My best friend also lives in Boston," he said, smiling. Her finger pointed at me and it was my turn. *"My* best friend lives in Boston, believe it or not," I said. "Well, fancy that," Axel added. "My best friend's got a flat in Boston, too." Raj finished the survey by confirming that his best friend also lived in Boston.

One March afternoon I slipped and half-fell down the library steps, scattering my books across the yard. Six girls stopped to applaud, and one snapped a picture for the college newspaper. I wasn't feeling very well liked in those days.

Male exchange students at Wellesley are traditionally rotated to a different dormitory each year, to spread the glory or the humiliation, depending on how you look at it. The five men who were there the year I was were all assigned to Pomeroy Hall, one of the older houses, situated in an area of the campus known as the Quad. The dorm housed one hundred thirty-five women of all four classes.

Pomeroy was very significant to us. Living there gave us the chance to take full advantage of what Wellesley had to offer. It was in this dorm that I discovered a number of women who were willing to befriend me after I got off my high horse. We had a unique opportunity in living together; I finally began to enjoy it.

It wasn't until halfway through my year at Wellesley that I started staying up till three in the morning with women dressed in nightgowns, who talked openly and honestly about their romances and heartbreaks. I listened to their comments as they cut out pinups from *Playgirl*.

They talked to me about the depressions and disappointments they were experiencing at Wellesley and in job-hunting. It became clear that the choice of career or marriage and motherhood was a great dilemma for my new friends.

We went to porn films together, discussed machismo, abortion, sexual promiscuity, birth control. We often role-played little sequences. A woman would tell me all about some guy she was going out with, and I would pretend to be he. "Now, what would you do if I told you I loved you?" And I would react, giving my male point of view. It may have been helpful to them in some cases, but mostly it simply brought us all closer.

On my side, I reached out to them. I complained of having been stereotyped on the basis of the mistakes I had made in the first few months. I was struggling for a second chance but was meeting with discrimination because of the many true—and false—allegations against me. How was I to be taken seriously, to express the changes I had undergone? My friends would smile and say, "Now you know what it's like to be a woman in a man's world." They explained that they had come to Wellesley because their needs wouldn't be taken seriously at co-ed schools. I was trying to do among two thousand women what they were trying to do in the world at large. And Wellesley gave them support. "When I walk around campus and see all these great ladies carrying on without men breathing down their necks, telling them what to do or just being damned patronizing, I feel a real sense of group strength," my friend Alice said one night. I didn't argue.

Students at Wellesley are bright, aggressive, and ambitious, and the faculty is strong. The rigorous academic program was an essential part of my life there; I began to talk with my classmates about the books we were reading. I had never considered a certain author lacking because his female characters were weakly constructed, or the theories of a socialist writer incomplete because he had failed to outline the role women would play in a new revolutionary society. I began to think things out from a broader intellectual perspective.

By the time spring rolled around, I was a changed man. I had made some of the closest friendships of my four years in college. My self-confidence with women and my appreciation of them had grown considerably. I had reshaped a confidence in my own sexuality that was far more honest than it had ever been before. I had begun to seek out women who challenged me intellectually and who were looking for a friend. Perhaps it is not too far-fetched to propose that my change in attitude was also related to my falling in love for the first time.

When Henry Fowle Durant founded Wellesley, he wanted it to be a place that would prepare women for "great conflicts" and "vast reforms in social life." Wellesley has affirmed its belief in single-sex education by consistently electing to remain solely a women's college. From my own experiences there, I expect never to see men admitted on a full-time basis; and I hope they aren't.

There are still a great many contradictions in the ideals Wellesley stands for, as well as certain gaps in its curriculum: poor athletic facilities, no education major, no women's studies department. Wellesley women tend also to have a warped view of things. Some graduates are awkward with men socially and professionally. At Wellesley mixers I repeatedly saw women who had moments before talked to me in an intelligent, self-assured manner become coy females, taking all sorts of nonsense from men who were putting the moves on them. But the positive aspects of the Wellesley community definitely outweigh the drawbacks. Wellesley is racially and culturally well-balanced, and its students are united by a deep pride in womanhood.

Since my year there, I have maintained a large network of Wellesley friends all over the country. I have even asked a few of my financially successful friends to "keep" me; but they are too independent, they have too much to do, to let a man into their lives now. (The ironies of modern times.)

I have stayed in contact with my four male associates; we are bound by an everlasting feeling of having been among the few men on earth to live out a male fantasy. I have changed dramatically since the September day when I entered Wellesley, and I am not a bad catch for any liberated woman, if I must say so myself.

QUESTIONS

1. In a sense, the author found himself in a situation where some of the norms of sexual interaction for men and women were reversed. What lessons can be learned from his experience?

2. How great do you think the difference is between the content of sex roles in your generation and that of your parents?

3. Are women still widely regarded as sex objects? Do men and women in the class have the same or different views on the subject?

LILLIAN B. RUBIN

Women of a Certain Age

Much has been written in recent years of the "midlife crisis," a time, usually around the late forties or early fifties, when people are said to anxiously take stock of what they have become and what the future holds for them.

For men, the "crisis" is usually centered around their careers: if a man has not "made it" and achieved his goals at this point, he must face the strong likelihood that he never will, and must make the difficult adjustment to that sobering fact. But for women who reach the midlife period today, its content is very different. These women are caught in forces of social change that they were never socialized to expect or to deal with: nearly all were brought up to be homemakers and child-rearers, and few had any real commitment to a career. By midlife, however, they find themselves with an "empty nest" after their children have become adult and left home, so that source of fulfillment is denied them. Meanwhile, they see other women, mostly younger than they, embarking on significant roles in hitherto "masculine" careers; but they lack the training or confidence to follow suit.

Lillian Rubin conducted many interviews with today's "women of a certain age," and found that for them the midlife period is often one of dismay and confusion. Their plight is worsened by their particular location in time and place, history and society. Their mothers, born before women's liberation, would have expected no more at midlife than the fulfillments of family, and would have suppressed any disquiet they felt; their daughters, on the other hand, will probably have a career and many other interests to occupy their energies at this point in the life cycle; they themselves are caught in the middle. This article summaries some of the findings from Rubin's data.

Most women don't speak about, often don't even think about themselves and their lives without reference to their husbands. Ask a midlife woman about her plans for her future, and she more than likely will speak of her husband's. Some talk about his retirement:

> In another ten, fifteen years at most, my husband will be retiring. Then we'll be able to do all those things we've always wanted to do and never had the time.

Never mind that most can't spell out what "all those things" are, that under questioning they usually say some vague things about traveling or having fun. Never mind that these same women at other points in our discussion speak of their fears of those retirement years—wondering what they will do, how they will feel when their husbands are home all day; worrying about how their husbands will manage. The point here is simply that when I ask them about *their* future, they speak about their husband's. Imagine, if you can, forty-, forty-five- or fifty-year-old men responding in kind.

Some speak of their husband's work plans—a potential transfer, a sabbatical. Not surprising in a world where family life and the needs of other family members are expected to be subordinated to a man's work. What did surprise me, however, is that this is true also among women who have themselves gone back into the work force, even among those who are seeking advanced degrees in order to carve out a career for themselves. Listen, for example, to this forty-five-year-old woman, half way through a doctoral program, who had talked excitedly and at length about how important it is for her to be en route to a professional degree.

> *Now that you're coming close to the end of this program, what do you see in your future?* Oh, there's all kinds of possibilities, I suppose. I don't expect to have too much trouble finding a part-time teaching job. I *will* have to be somewhat careful about what I take on though because my husband is due for a sabbatical in a couple of years. So, of course, we'll be doing that.

Nonchalantly, as if it were the most natural thing in the world—"So, of course, we'll be doing that." Could it really be that with a doctoral degree close at hand, her life still is planned around part-time work, and her husband's sabbatical is looked toward as an option in *her* life? I asked; she replied.

> Yes, of course. He's been planning for some years to go to Kenya to do some research on this sabbatical. Naturally, he expects me to go with him, *And you just as naturally assume that you'll go?* Sure! What else could I do? I can hardly let him go alone.

And, of course, it's equally unthinkable to either one that he might change his plans to suit her needs.

But, some will say, such things are changing. Look at all the stories around about dual-career families, about families where husbands and wives work in different cities, even different regions of the country. Yes, look at them. They're written by, for and about a select few—the academic couple, the wife and husband who are business executives or professionals. How many such marriages are we talking about? A few hundred? A few thousand? And how much will even these small numbers dwindle once there are children? To point to these families as the wave of the future is to delude ourselves about the difficulties of effecting large-scale changes in the culture—difficulties that are the expected consequences of any threat to the existing structure of power and authority in the society. And the entry of masses of women into the labor market on equal terms with men is just such a threat. That's why it is resisted so tenaciously, fought against with every weapon at the society's command—from the differential socialization of girls and boys to the development and elaboration of ideologies of femininity that serve to keep women in their place.

Woman's Choice?

But never mind the future. What about the reality of the present, even among this small and privileged elite? For at least one alternative version of that reality, look in the daily press—not in the new women's sections where such two-career couples sometimes are presented as if they represent a significant shift in family life and values, or in what's probable in the relationship between women and men, but in the news section. There, we read that on December 30, 1977, the director of California's Department of Conservation, a former professor of geothermal energy at the University of California, resigned her job to join her geologist husband who was to be on an expedition in Australia for eight months. "I had a really tough choice to make," she said. "I really love the job but it just seemed too long to be apart." Eight months—a long separation—just as long in Australia as in Sacramento. But she leaves her job, his expedition goes on.

In the same news columns, we read also that the President has had difficulty in finding women to fill high level posts in the federal government because they are loathe to leave their husbands behind in their city of residence. We read this, and we hear the muttering—muttering about how women can't *really* be counted on in such jobs, about how they don't take advantage of opportunity even when it comes looking for them, about how their concerns for family and their need for security transcend all other commitments, even service to their government.

But who reminds the mutterers that a man doesn't have to make those choices, that his wife and children are expected to move with him when such an opportunity comes his way? There are few indeed to make those reminders, fewer still who will be heard and responded to respectfully—who won't be written off as "another one of those libbers." And who is there to say that a husband ought to support a wife's career just as she has supported his? Who is there to suggest that he ought to move to Washington so that she can accept the appointment the President offers and still live inside a family? Who is there to talk to him about the importance of his family and his responsibility for keeping it intact, to give him the kind of advice that women in such situations get? Surely not the same people who criticize, sometimes even vilify, a wife who refuses to give up whatever she's doing so that her husband can accept such a high honor.

An overstatement? Read the daily press. There, on a day in November, 1977, two women wrote to "Dear Abby"—that arbiter of morals and values read daily by many millions in every corner of the land. The first, a thirty-eight-year-old recently-married professional woman, complained that her husband had given her an ultimatum. Either she stopped her overnight business trips or the marriage was finished. Abby's advice? Invite him along on the trips in the hope that he'll feel less threatened. "If that doesn't work, you will have to choose between your husband and your business trips." The second woman wrote to complain that her husband was about to be transferred to a job in a city five hundred miles away from the place where she and her children had lived all their lives, where they had all their friends and family, and where they had just built a lovely home—the dream of her lifetime. "Every time I think of moving," she wrote, "I burst into tears . . . I know I sound selfish, but I can't help it. My husband wants to move. If I need a good lecture, let me have it." And Abby did. A man's "greatest asset is a wife who is always in his corner," she scolded. "You and your children will make new friends. Help your husband climb the ladder of success by being supportive and you will have another lovely home that his 'Jack' built."

Who is there to challenge such advice? Not Abby's readers—or at least not very many. Not a word of protest appeared in the column over the next few months. That is, after all, the way of the world. Two lives devoted to one job—that is, if the job holder is male. If it's a woman, then the advice is: Try to change him; if you can't, do his bidding or prepare to lose the marriage. No word to her husband about his obligation to be supportive, no comment about his unreasonable demands. And just in case this wife and others continue to insist on their rights not to be moved about as if they were pawns on a chess board, the corporate world is preparing its response. In a feature story in May, 1978, the *Wall Street Journal* reports that several of the nation's largest corporations now favor divorced men because they have no wives and children to inhibit their geographic mobility. Indeed, some corporations now either implicitly or explicitly encourage divorce where family considerations stand in the way of a man's transfer.

No wonder it's so hard to write about women without also dealing with their men. While the lives of both are inextricably interwoven, for women, family is at the core of their lives; for men, it's at the periphery. Thus, there are plenty of books about men—about men and their work, for example—that never mention the women in their lives, never consider the fact that most men live in families where their lives are entwined with others, never concern themselves with the way men's work affects women's lives. One could argue, of course, that this is a failing of those books—that in wrenching men's work lives out of the context of the rest of their lives, such books present a distorted view of the world in which both men and women live. One could quarrel, also, with the implicit judgment they carry about what's important and deserving of attention in the lives of men.

While such criticisms are valid, it must also be said that those books reflect quite accurately what the world is like—reflect the fact that work and family are distinct and separate spheres of living for most men. For a man, marriage is what he *does* in addition to what he *is*. First, he's a "doctor, lawyer, merchant, chief." Then, he marries and some small part of him becomes husband and father as well. Work, not family, is a man's most important social task—the task for which he was reared. Work, not family, is the basis of his social identity—his success or failure gauged by what he does on the job, not by whether his house is clean or how his children grow. I asked an engineer who is also the father of four:

When you were small, what did you think you'd be doing when you were grown up? Well, I didn't know what it would be, but I knew I'd work. I always knew I had to be something. *What about getting married and being a father? Did you ever think about that?* No. I never gave any thought to having a family or being a parent. I don't remember having any fantasies about who I'd marry or about having children. I don't know. I guess I just assumed a wife and kids would be in my life one day, but it wasn't anything to dream about.

A crucial, life-shaping difference between boys and girls. For a boy, marriage and parenthood aren't "anything to dream about." For a girl, if it's not the only dream in her life, it's surely the dominant one. In adulthood, it's marriage and motherhood that define a woman, locate her in the world, ground her in a social identity. Therefore, it's how she defines herself. First, she's wife and mother. Work is permitted only in the interest of the family and/or only after all the needs of its members are tended. No matter if she works outside the home as well as in it, no matter how important her work or how successful she may be at it, the tasks by which she is defined, judged and validated are those of the family; therefore, those are the ones by which she measures herself—as novelist Lois Gould reminds us with these wry words in *Final Analysis:*

My real work, writing, has never been fraught with . . . guilt. Nobody ever checks on my real work. I know there are spiteful strangers all over the world whispering about the dust in my apartment, but no one gossips about the fact that I only wrote three pages today instead of fifteen. No one cares if I write no pages. When am I going to dust that apartment, though?

Homemaker or Worker?

Indeed, in the lives of women a distinction that seems simple—the distinction between homemakers and workers—turns out to be complex, impossible, in fact, to distinguish between the two and write about them separately. Homemakers work; workers make homes. Their lives obstinately resist neat labels and clean categories. Ask a woman what her occupation is, and one who works for wages outside the house may say she's a homemaker, while one who does not may say she's a worker. Both speak the truth. The woman who works outside the home also puts in long hours inside. The choice she makes when asked to define herself depends on several things—not least of them her class background, how she feels about the work she does outside the house, how she feels about the label *homemaker*, how she relates to the women's movement and feminist ideology.

The woman who says she's a worker but earns no wages is caught in her own binds. She may speak four languages fluently and travel the world over as her husband's interpreter in his export-import business, but no matter what she calls herself, the world sees her as "just a housewife" because she doesn't earn a paycheck. Worse yet, whatever she calls herself, *she* has her own doubts. Without a salary, does she have a right to the title *worker*?

I hate questions about my occupation. Whatever I say, it's not real. I'm not just a housewife. But the fact is that I don't earn any money for what I do. I'm an interpreter. My husband couldn't run his business—at least he certainly couldn't travel—without me or someone to replace me. But when I say that, people act as if I'm trying to upgrade myself from a housewife. A couple of weeks ago, we met some people and when I told them what I did, they said, "Oh, you help your husband out in your spare time," I was furious. But you know, when you hear if often enough, you begin to wonder if maybe you're not just kidding yourself.

So it is also with the woman who is a serious but unknown artist, an unpublished writer, a talented craftswoman— all activities from which she earns little or no wages, therefore not recognized as work.

> My painting is my life, but it's not really acceptable to say it's my work, is it, if I'm not earning any significant amount of money at it? I'd feel very much better about saying I work if I could earn a reasonable income from it.

As Virginia Woolf knew so well, in a culture where productivity in the world of work is so highly valued, "money dignifies what is frivolous if unpaid for." Thus, only earning what she calls a reasonable income would give this woman the right to be taken seriously, to take herself seriously, to call her art her work. For that income would be the visible, tangible symbol of the worth of her art— the statement that it is valued in the world and, with it, that the person who creates it is valuable also.

Homemakers and workers, workers and homemakers—impossible to disentangle the two cleanly. Homemakers work both inside and outside the house. Some get paid; those are the easy ones to classify. Others don't—the woman who spends two days a week without pay in her husband's office, the volunteer who spends forty hours a week at high-level administrative work, the artist who works twenty hours at her easel, the full-time student in a degree program—these are harder. And what about the woman who invested a small inheritance in real estate twenty-five years ago and now manages her properties which earn $50,000 a year—all done from her home, all in an hour or two each morning? Asked for her occupation, she gestures as if to wave the question away and says, "I'm only a housewife." "And what about the work you do managing your property?" I ask. "Oh hell," she snaps, "that's not work."

Homemakers and workers, workers and homemakers. Perhaps the most we can say is that the balance between them often differs according to a woman's situation, and that it shifts at different times of life as family needs and her responsibilities for them ebb and flow. Today's homemaker may be tomorrow's worker; tomorrow's worker, the homemaker of the days ahead. But whichever the dominant orientation at a particular moment in the history of a life, one generally does not wholly exclude the other.

It's this very flexibility that sometimes is pointed to as the singular advantage of women's role in the family— the fact that, when it works in its ideal form, women do not have to go out to work every day of their lives, that many women, at least, are protected from the harsh and bitter realities that most men face daily in the world of work. Often, especially for women in working-class and poor families, real life is far removed from that ideal, as the soaring proportion of young mothers in the labor force attests. For those women, there's little advantage in the traditional role since it means only that they're stuck with two jobs—one inside the house and the other outside. Among the others—those who can afford to live out the ideal—some do, indeed, use that flexibility in their daily lives well, developing a broad range of interests that enhance growth and enrich life. But the world doesn't give much credit for such activities, doesn't validate them as important, worthy, socially productive. Consequently, women don't either. Thus, while they tick off an impressive list of activities and accomplishments, the women I met often seem at sea—unsure of who they are, what they want, what interests them. "I've never had any *real* interests"—a theme heard surprisingly often, one that was difficult at first to understand.

What does it mean to speak of real interests? These women have plenty of interests—community service, politics, sports, church activities, weaving, ceramics, decorating, sewing, painting, all kinds of cultural and intellectual pursuits. Many have been taking classes at the local college or university for years—classes in literature, art history, music, psychology, child development, and the like. And although they have no credentials to show for these efforts because the work was not undertaken for credit in a degree program, many have become quite expert in one or another of these fields. Yet this expertise usually is diffidently and ambivalently acknowledged, if at all. Interesting, isn't it? Years spent in studying—in deepening interest and knowledge—years of activities that expand intellect and consciousness, tossed off as if they count for nothing. Why? The women agree that they have many things with which they keep busy, many things they enjoy doing, enjoy learning. But, most insist, these are not the kinds of activities that give meaning and direction to life. But what does that mean?

For some, it means that they don't bring in a paycheck, don't provide the resources to permit feeling like an independent adult.

> If you don't earn any money, it's hard to take yourself seriously or to feel like what you're doing is important or worth anything. I try to tell myself that's a very materialistic viewpoint and that I don't really believe it. But what's the difference what I believe? It's what the world believes that counts.

For others, it means that the activities don't have any particular use in the world, that they're not productive of anything but personal satisfaction, that no one cares whether they do them or not.

> It doesn't make a damn bit of difference to the world what I do with my life or whether I do anything. It's as if I don't

count; you know, like outside of my family, the world wouldn't notice if I just stopped existing.

Whatever they say, however they say it, one thing is clear: These activities are labeled as not real interests in part, at least, because they're not recognized and valued in the outer world, therefore suspect in the inner one as well.

> Sure there are things I like to do, but I've always felt rather directionless, as if I were a dilettante because I don't really ever get engaged in anything or committed to anything.

Not "engaged in anything," not "committed"? Words and ideas expressed repeatedly by women who literally have given their lives to their families, women who have committed themselves almost wholly to the well-being of others. To me, it seemed odd indeed, hard to believe that women could say such things about themselves. Yet, as I turned the words over in my mind, there also seemed something true about them. For in the process of making such commitments to others, they generally had abandoned important parts of themselves. Whatever personal ambitions or interests might have stirred in them over the years were systematically stifled as they sought to meet the obligations and responsibilities of wifehood and motherhood. This is the only serious commitment, the only vocation, for which they had been reared, the only one permitted to them without question or censure.

Indeed, husbands and children often want wives and mothers all to themselves, complaining—sometimes quietly and covertly, sometimes noisily and without restraint—if the woman of the household becomes occupied or preoccupied with activities or interests outside the house. One man who claimed to be liberated from such traditional male desires and supportive of his wife's efforts to train herself for a career, nevertheless put it thus:

> I don't mind what she does during the day. But a woman has to be sensitive to how her husband feels when she comes home talking about things he doesn't know anything about. No matter how excited she is about what she's doing, she's better off to tear that page out of the book and come home quietly without saying much about it.

The rule about her interests, then, would seem to be: Limit involvement only to the times when he's not around, and keep it quiet. With such advice, a woman would find it difficult, indeed, to be comfortable with the flowering of sustained and consuming interests. In fact, in such circumstances, the stirrings of interest can be experienced as endangering her primary commitments; therefore also as an aberration, an unwelcome, guilt-producing intrusion that keeps her from devoting all her energy and attention to what she has been trained to regard as the main task of life.

Love or Work?

Thus, although women study, learn, and do many things, these activities are kept at a distance—defined as not *really* central to life, not *really* important to definition of self, not even *really* a serious interest. That way, they threaten no one and nothing. That way, a woman doesn't have to take herself and her interests seriously, nor does her husband. He may think it's cute that she keeps taking courses, a nice way for her to keep busy. Despite her expanding knowledge and skills, she colludes in that definition—denying her accomplishment, dismissing her commitment. All too soon, she isn't just calling herself a dilettante, she's believing it. In so many ways, women's lives—the quality, the character, the choices they are permitted, whether early in life or late—are dominated by their relationships with men. Of course, women play an important role in men's lives as well. But that's precisely the difference: They play a *role*. Men are not dominated by those relationships, almost determined by them, in the same way that women are.

There are, for example, among the women I met, some with professional degrees taken in their youth and never again used after marriage or the birth of the first child. Most were in traditional women's fields—teaching, social work, nursing. But a half dozen were lawyers, research scientists, medical doctors—male dominated professions which, especially in that generation, surely required a high level of interest and an enormous effort of will and determination to enter. Yet, when the time came, these six gave up their work just as their nonprofessional sisters gave up jobs as secretaries, bookkeepers, clerks, and the like. Asked about regrets, a lawyer says:

> It was marriage or a career. It didn't seem like much of a choice. I always knew I wanted to marry and have children, and by the time I was twenty-five and not married, I had no more illusions that I could have both.

A doctor says:

> Of course, I've regretted it some. But it's not a great thing beating at my innards.

They all had reasons for giving up a hard-won profession. Nothing dramatic, nothing big, just the requirements of daily life: Small children who needed care—*their* children, *her* responsibility; a husband's career that kept them moving for the first years of the marriage; or simply conflict between wife and husband about her work. Whatever the reasons, they add up to conflict between his needs and hers, between his career and hers—his needs, his wishes, his career, his interest taking precedence over hers.

Even those few women who went back to their professions when the children were still relatively young made job choices that put husband, children, home first. Faced with two jobs—one higher paying, more stimulating, more desirable in every way than the other except that it is thirty minutes further from home—a woman will almost always choose the one closer to home.

> It never felt like I had a *real* choice. It just seemed like the right thing to do, you know, to take the job that was nearer even if it wasn't as good. That way, I would be more available for stuff around the home—for when the children or Gary needed me, or even just to have fun with them.

Small wonder, then, that women feel a lack in themselves—a lack of engagement, of commitment, of interest. Theirs is a lifetime of muting or denying any strivings that might require a serious commitment to anything outside the family. It is precisely those interests that might have engaged them most profoundly to which they feared making a commitment, those interests that are most deeply related to self that they subdued and suppressed. By midlife, it feels as if they never existed. Too often, however, women are so mystified about the matter of their interests that they believe this is something in which they are inherently deficient, something for which they are blameworthy—a personal failing to be viewed with contempt.

> Gary would never have made the choice to take the less demanding jobs as I've always done. I suppose that says I never made that kind of serious commitment to my work. Disgusting, isn't it, to be so frivolous.

Not "disgusting," not "frivolous," but a way of life to which women are carefully bred; their self-denial and passivity not a cause but a consequence of their gender, of the role assigned them at birth. A lifetime in which they have been taught to believe they need only marry the right man, breed and raise the perfect children to find fulfillment simply does not prepare them for the internal search, for the kind of commitment to self, that the full-blown development of serious interests requires. Consequently, women can be bewildered about how they happen, often speaking as if they expect to find interests somewhere outside themselves.

> I've never had anything come down and strike me like George has had in his life. I've never had that kind of calling.

But George wasn't called any more than she was. He was just born male and complied with the expectations that go with his gender just as she did with hers. Being born male means living in a different world from anything most women know, anything they will ever know. It means not having to define oneself vicariously through the lives of others. It means having work to do, a reason to get up every day, a place in the world that's visible. It means never having to answer questions about one's fu-

ture by talking about someone else's. It's true that even men who do work they love may come suddenly to question its meaning, to realize at midlife that they're stuck in a rut. But at least they know what the job is. It's true that they may have reason to lament the predictability of their lives. But at least they know with some certainty that they'll be doing something. It's not until retirement, at sixty-five, that most men must wonder what they'll be doing in the years to come, or whether they'll be doing anything at all. It's not until then that they'll ask themselves, "What am I going to do with the rest of my life?"

Still, one might argue, men also face problems with the midlife transition. They, too, often hate what they do each day, often feel the world has rejected them, passed them by. Most men also have severely limited options for growth and self-development, so consumed are both their time and energy with the need to support the household. It's true, and it's also beside the point. One indignity doesn't excuse another; one kind of oppression doesn't erase the other. In a society that distorts human life—female and male—we need not measure whose sadness is greater; both have more than they need. Still, there's a particular sharpness to the deprivations a woman experiences at this time of life because of the nature of the choices, the limits to the options that were hers until now.

At forty or forty-five, her job is gone, not out of some failure of her own but because, as one woman said, "Motherhood self-destructs in twenty years." She doesn't know what she'll do tomorrow, still less the day after. She wakes up wondering how to keep busy, whether she can fill up the time, what meaning it has if she does.

> There are all kinds of things I like to do. I work in the garden; I have friends over; I go to the woman's club at church twice a month; I love to make bread and cook and sew. And I read. [*Softly, as if to shield her ears from her own words*] But somehow, that's not enough to fill up a life. It doesn't seem to add up to a whole, real person.

Often a woman anticipates this stage of life, even looks forward to it eagerly. But unless she has also prepared well for it, she usually finds that the years, the demands of family life, have taken their toll—paid in the erosion of self-confidence; in the fears that she is undisciplined, incapable of commitment, without real interests; even in her failure to know whether she "adds up to a whole, real person."

Thus, when it comes to wanting something for themselves outside the home as well as in it—to thinking about their lives and to planning them in some autonomous and independent way—women bear the limitations and restrictions that come with their gender, a fact of birth that settles their future, almost without question, on the day they are born. Not for them the dreams of conquering new worlds, of high adventure, of exciting and stimulating work. Not for them the chance, however slim, of transcending the limitations, whatever they may be. Not for them—not because of class or color, not because of lack of capacity—but because they were born girls. *Because they were born girls*—transcendence, if it comes at all, commonly will come through a good marriage, a good catch. *Because they were born girls*—they'll live vicariously through their men and their children, rarely inside and through themselves.

But that was yesterday, some will say, the world is different today. Is it? A conversation overheard recently in an enlightened and liberated nursery school suggests, at the very least, that the future is not yet here.

> JOHNNY: When I grow up, I'm going to be a sea monster.
> SUSIE: And I'll be your mommy.

No parent, no teacher within earshot thought the conversation was anything but natural. No one suggested to Susie that she, too, might enjoy the excitement and adventure of fantasizing herself a monster. No one told her that, like it or not, she'll be mommy for only a few years. Then, life will require something else if she's to remain vital, healthy, alive in some meaningful way. Then, she'll have to ask herself that agonizing question, that question that dominates the thoughts of midlife women, that question uniquely theirs: "What am I going to do with the rest of my life?"

. . .

QUESTIONS

1. In what ways is the experience of "women of a certain age" different from that of similarly aged men?

2. To C. Wright Mills, the "sociological imagination" implied the ability to perceive ourselves as the product of an intersection of biography and history in society. Explain this view and apply it to the situation of these women.

3. What have sex roles and sexism to do with the situation and attitudes of the women studied by Rubin?

RASA GUSTAITIS

Old vs. Young in Florida: Preview of an Aging America

In many respects, the relationships between different age categories in society are a form of social stratification. In other words, some age categories have more power, wealth, and prestige than others, in much the same way as these differences appear among social classes, race or ethnic groups, and between the sexes.

The particular age category that has the highest social status varies according to social factors. In most traditional societies, the old have the highest status, largely because they own the land (which is the main source of wealth) and have more accumulated knowledge than those younger than themselves. In most modern industrial societies, the middle-aged are dominant: it is they who control the newer means of production (such as factories and corporations), and they are better educated than the old. In these societies the young and the old have relatively low status.

But conditions can alter, and they are gradually changing in the United States. As a result of several demographic factors—increased life expectancy, the post-World War II "baby boom," and remarkably low birth rates over the past two decades—the United States is becoming steadily older. Around the turn of the century, the society will be "top-heavy" with the elderly, and sheer weight of numbers will give them increasing influence. As Rasa Gustaitis points out in this article, Florida offers a preview of this future, for the state has an unusually large population of senior citizens. Unhappily, too, it shows signs of a predictable conflict between age strata.

A 14-year-old who lives in one of the beach-front condominiums in Ft. Lauderdale knows that elderly women clutch their purses as he passes on his bike. So he likes to ride up behind them close and slow, just to tease.

He is a clean-cut, polite youngster, a nice boy by any mother's definition, and he means no harm. Nevertheless, he relishes this private little joke on the aged. It is his way of getting a bit of revenge for the many times he has been made to feel suspect and unwelcome simply because of his youth.

His story is not an unusual one in Broward County, where the old and the young are engaged in what almost amounts to a war of generations. Only newcomers are likely to be surprised by the hostility between the two combatants. A recently arrived New Yorker, for instance, was shocked that the other customers in a restaurant refused to sit next to her and three children. A co-worker at her office explained: "Kids make noise, they throw things—who needs it?" The young can be equally scathing toward the elderly. "The problem with the o.p.s (common term for "old people" here) is not how to take care of them; it's how to keep them from killing the rest of us," remarked a young policeman's wife.

For the moment the U.S. remains largely free of the generational hostility so evident in Broward County. But there is good reason to believe that within decades the attitudes prevalent there will have spread throughout America. For demographically, Florida, and especially Broward, mirrors the future of the nation.

The number of old people in the U.S. has been growing faster than the general population. Between 1970 and 1978, the total population increased by 7 percent, while the elderly population grew 20 percent. In Florida, the growth of the elderly population has been even more dramatic: Their numbers have jumped 50 percent between 1970 and 1978, according to Jacob Siegel, senior demographic statistician at the population division of the Census Bureau. And while it is estimated that 11 percent of the current U.S. population is over 65, in Florida nearly 18 percent is elderly. Within the next 50 years, close to one out of every five Americans will be over 65. In Florida, the traditional population pyramid will be turned upside down: Those over 65 will outnumber those under 14.

The vast social and political consequences of this concentration of the elderly can already be seen in Broward County, located northeast of Miami. Broward has long been a mecca for the retired. Today over one-third of the county's population is over 60, and the number is on the rise. The conflict between the young and the old is possibly the most ominous fallout from this immense migration.

There are many reasons why the two groups have been cast as adversaries—differences of values and lifestyles, for instance. But ultimately the struggle comes down to one major issue: money, particularly government money. Both old and young rely heavily on the government for needed social services. However, the ability of the government to provide these services in an inflationary economy has shrunk, while the elderly continue to expand in number and power. The net result is almost inevitably more for the old, less for the young. There is no way to prove categorically that a direct trade-off favoring the old at the expense of the young is taking place. Yet signs of the trend are unmistakable. The fate of certain public spending programs, the widespread discrimination against children and young people in housing, the increasingly punitive attitude toward youthful offenders in the schools and in the criminal justice system, and the political clout of the old all testify to the pervasiveness of the climate created by the growing elderly population.

The aged in Florida have bought the American promise of work followed by earned leisure. So now they shy away from social concerns with the catchphrase, "We've paid our dues." Thus, when Dade County proposed a drastic budget cut last summer, hoping thereby to avert a tax-cut initiative of disastrous proportions, the biggest slice came out of Headstart, a preschool program. As it turned out, the ballot initiative included a printing error that would have almost completely abolished taxes. It failed, and children's advocates soon succeeded in restoring the Headstart budget to the amount of the previous year. Nevertheless, with inflation taken into account, the net effect was still a cut.

Spending for schools has also shrunk in Florida, although dollar levels have remained relatively stable. In 1978 Florida, one of the richest states, spent the smallest percentage of its wealth on education, according to an in-depth report by the *Miami Herald*. In per pupil expenditures it ranked 32nd of the 50 states. Although Governor Robert Graham has announced that the state will increase spending by 10 percent in 1980, he has simultaneously proposed that the percentage of property taxes going to schools, which has already dropped in the last 10 years, should be still further reduced. According to Scott Rose, school finance expert in Pinellas County, the pro-

posed levels will not permit schools to keep pace with inflation. As the proportion of the elderly in Florida grows, and as inflation keeps shriveling incomes, public support for education can be expected to erode even more—especially since in some areas a growing proportion of the public-school children will come from minority groups. In the words of Hillsborough County School Superintendent Raymond O. Shelton, "It's going to be difficult to keep education in the limelight as a high priority social issue."

Cutbacks have hit other youth-related programs as well. Six years ago, Dr. Georgia Reynolds, a physician who has specialized in community health practices, started a mobile health unit for preschoolers. Not long ago, Broward County failed to find the funds needed to keep the program alive. The failure has had a price. Visiting child-care centers, Dr. Reynolds found "children who had not seen a doctor since they dropped out of the baby clinic before age one. They had problems that could easily have been remedied earlier. But by the time the kids are five or six, not much can be done." She saw cases of amblyopia (lazy eye), children who were neglected and malnourished. "One three-year-old girl was totally deaf and nobody knew it. We had her in a special program within a week." When asked why the mobile health unit had been discontinued, Dr. Reynolds replied, "I think it's the old people, mostly. They say they've already paid their dues." Having struggled to raise their own children and to make sure that they are not a burden to them, many elderly want simply to be left alone to enjoy their "golden years."

A direct consequence of this attitude has been widespread discrimination in housing against young couples and children. (Florida has no law forbidding housing discrimination against children. When a St. Petersburg city councilman proposed that a local antidiscrimination ordinance be extended to cover exclusion of children, other councilmen quickly rebuffed him.) The old and the young probably live more separate existences in Florida than anywhere else in the world. Promised a life of carefree safety in the sun, the elderly settled in droves in developer-built communities that had been designed to keep apart, rather than join, people of different ages, races, and classes. As a result, Broward today is a sprawling county with no focus. Each of its municipalities has a separate government and a separate—sometimes almost nonexistent—system of taxation. The smallest is Lazy Lakes, with 550 people; the largest, Ft. Lauderdale, with 160,000. Across the patchwork of these communities, running roughly along the railroad tracks that parallel the water, live most of the county's blacks, squeezed more tightly together as real estate prices keep rising. The wealthy elderly tend to live along the beach; the poorer, farther inland; and families with children cluster in whatever developments accept them.

Just how difficult it can be to cross the borders is evidenced by the story of the eight-year-old boy who came for an overnight stay with his great-grandparents at one of the many expensive adults-only condominiums. When the child arrived, the doorman handed him a sheet of rules: "Children require the constant supervision of those responsible for them. They must be kept from interfering in any way with the quiet and comfort of residents." The grandparents, nearly 80, were a lively couple fond of dancing and ocean cruises, but they regarded the rules as reasonable. After all, hadn't they chosen to live there precisely to be free from disturbances?

A young woman recounted that when she looked for an apartment with her husband she was asked several times by a rental agent whether she was planning to have children. She assured him that she was not, yet was nevertheless turned away with a suspicious look. For a single woman with more than one child, the options are far slimmer. Carol Fleck, a divorced mother of three, frantically searched for months after her apartment building was turned into a condominium. She had decided she could not afford to buy in, but soon discovered that no place would rent to anyone with three children. "I make more than most of the women in my office—$220 a week before taxes. And my oldest, who is 20, has a job, so we can pay a bit more," she said. "But I've looked everywhere. Occasionally apartments will take a 16-year-old, but my youngest is nine."

What underlies the discrimination against the young in housing is, of course, fear—a fear that also accounts for the harsh penalties meted out to the young lawbreakers in Florida. In the popular view, brutal and drug-crazed young hoods are particularly partial to old people as victims. This image is wrong—the elderly are victimized less than other age groups, and when the perpetrator is a youth, the victim is most often another youth—but it is constantly reinforced by the press. Last year, the media devoted much attention to 85-year-old Ralph Germano, who was attacked in his Miami home by five juveniles. He was taunted, beaten, and left bleeding on the floor, not to be found until 12 hours later. He died 37 days after the assault. One of his attackers, Eve Postell, is now the youngest female serving a life sentence in Florida's adult prison system. She is 13 years old.

The entire Florida prison population has been getting younger, as more and more juveniles like Eve are funneled into it. The view expressed by David Waksman, the assistant state attorney who prosecuted Postell, is all too typical: "These kids have shown they can't be rehabilitated," he told the *St. Petersburg Times.* "There is only one thing left. Warehouse them so they won't mug or kill anybody." He added: "Eve will be out one day and I would hate to see her then. She'll probably be 10 times worse, but that's a lot better than having her on the street. What else can we do?"

Such attitudes have led some to predict that Florida, which has more people on death row than any other state and was the first state to put a prisoner to death against his will in 10 years, may also become the first to execute a juvenile. "I don't see why all that time and money should be spent on people who have no consideration for their victims," commented an elderly woman, secretary in a church in Pinellas County. "We're much better off without them."

This severity toward the young is especially ironic in light of the fact, pointed to by Gary Feinberg, a sociologist at Nova University, that the elderly have much in common with the young. "Both have only one aim: fun. . . ." "What we do as recreation—drinking, smoking, driving," says Feinberg, "they do as a way of life. Both old and young are on the outside of society." Both are aliens.

Perhaps because of this, there is a similarity in the pattern of crimes committed by the old and by juveniles. Elderly shoplifters have become a serious problem in Broward County, and vandalism and assaults by the elderly have also risen. Feinberg talks of "elderly delinquency," which he says has been spawned by the "short-run hedonism" of people who live for today because they do not have a strong grasp on tomorrow and who have no meaningful social role.

In spite of all the elderly population's struggles to mold Florida into their private world, life there is a bitter disappointment to many who worked so hard to afford it. They believed the ads: Harry is lounging by his pool, a cold drink in his hand, and he's phoning the boys back at the plant in drizzle city. Wish you were here. Smiles all around. The ad does not show that the call may be the high point of Harry's week (and how many times can he make such a phone call?). A few days spent next to the pool, and Harry may be feeling the sort of depression children experience at Christmas or on birthdays when the presents have all been opened and there's nothing more to do. "We used to go down to the beach when we first came," said a 55-year-old resident of a condo along the water. He had retired early from a small business he owned and operated in California. "But now we don't go much. Maybe because it's so close. Maybe if we had to drive there we'd go more."

Some people don't have cars or can't drive. For them, Florida is particularly desolate. The streets were designed for cars, not pedestrians, and public transportation is sparse. "We had a guest from Germany," a retired Ft. Lauderdale woman reported, "who kept asking, 'Where are all the people?' "

Where many of them are is at home, sitting in front of the TV, in an air-conditioned room. Others, to be sure, have made a successful adjustment. They enroll in classes, they engage in volunteer work. Some even find romance. One businessman was reunited with his World

War I sweetheart at a writing workshop. Both had raised families and were widowed. They rediscovered each other and now spend part of their year at his home in Ft. Lauderdale, part in hers on Long Island.

But they are the rare exceptions. Too often the elderly merely "hang out," perhaps in the shopping center, one of the few places they can easily get to by public transit. They wander, they watch different kinds of people mingling, they browse in the shops—and sometimes they take something.

"They rarely do it out of economic need," said Peter Vallone, counselor at the county criminal justice division's pretrial intervention program. "Seems that a lot are acting out against the establishment. They're lonely. They've lost a mate. So they strike out against society," he said, echoing a similar wisdom about juveniles. Some shoplift to get attention or to keep from being bored. "A lot are on drugs and they're spacey," said Jacob Messina, a planner in the criminal justice division. "Nothing illegal about the drugs, of course. They are medication." Law enforcement officers are sympathetic to the elderly—far more so than they are to juvenile offenders. A few officers are even embarrassed. Yet stores insist on pressing charges because they "lose millions a year on this problem," according to Vallone. Jail sentences are rare, however. "Our facilities are so bad they would die," said Sandra Hunter, supervisor of the county probation department.

Arrest is often a blessing in disguise for the elderly because it leads to sessions with a counselor who can become a lifeline. "For the first time in a long while someone is paying attention to them," said Hunter. "One man was stealing five wallets a day. He had a quota. He didn't need the wallets, but he did have a need. One of our volunteers got him involved in building doll houses. He doesn't steal anymore." Sometimes arrest means a call to a distant son or daughter who has failed to heed many plaintive invitations to come down to visit. The arrest becomes a reproach: See what you let happen to your father? And to get an extra bit of attention, one of the counselors has noticed, many are arrested on their birthdays.

In the meantime, the juvenile justice system, which was meant to provide just that sort of support for youngsters, is being abandoned as a failure—largely because of pressure from the elderly.

The political arena is the main battleground in the conflict between the generations. Because the elderly can vote—nationally, 15 percent of those who cast ballots are over 65—they have legislative power, and they use it to further their interests. The House Select Committee on Aging, set up only four years ago, is now one of the largest committees and one of the most sought-after assignments in Congress. It was expanded last year from 32 to 45 members after almost a fourth of the House requested a seat.

The committee is chaired by 79-year-old Claude Pepper, a Democrat from Dade County who has proved to be one of the most successful legislators on the Hill. Pepper was responsible for the bill that abolished mandatory retirement from federal employment at 70 and raised the age limit from 65 to 70 in private employment. "We've had good luck with other legislation too," he said in an interview, referring to housing and home health-care bills for the elderly.

By contrast, Pepper said, youth-oriented legislation has had a hard time finding support. Recently he fought against a bill that would have made certain expenditures—child care, shelter, and medical costs—nondeductible from income when determining eligibility for food stamps. If passed as written, the bill would have disqualified many families and elderly people. Pepper was able to protect the elderly from the proposed cuts, but not young families.

. . .

The political power of the elderly is, as one would expect, particularly evident in Florida, where almost a third of the ballots are cast by seniors. In Broward County the figures are even more startling. An aide of Representative Edward Stack, who at 69 is the oldest freshman in the House, estimated that half of the voters who turned out in his district in the fall of 1977 were 65 or over. The state, moreover, has some very determined lobbyists for the elderly. "There are numerous, excellent elderly advocacy groups. They do their homework, and when they address an issue they are well prepared," said Betty Lou Barbieri of the Community Action Agency in Dade County. "Would that I could say that of the advocacy groups for children."

The two most effective lobbying groups are the American Association of Retired Persons, to which nearly half of Florida's retired people belong, and its parent organization, the American Retired Teachers Association, which has put forward proposals that have sometimes sparked the ire of the rest of the population. In one community, residents of a project for the elderly demanded that a traffic light be installed, even though one existed a block away, and the new light would have meant terrible traffic snarls. In Dade County, after a group of senior citizens demanded reduced cab fare for elders, the *Miami Herald* objected in an editorial that such a subsidy "would discriminate against all persons under 65. They could not use the service, regardless of need, yet would have to subsidize the elderly, all of whom would be eligible, also regardless of need."

To be fair, elderly advocacy groups have also been instrumental in passing legislation that benefits society as a whole. Thanks to the elderly lobby, Florida is the first state to require pharmacists to inform customers about less expensive generic alternatives to brand-name prescription drugs. Largely because of the elderly lobbyists, too, the state has revoked a ban on advertising by optometrists, thereby encouraging price competition. It has also outlawed the 99-year recreational lease that forced many condominium buyers to pay gigantic fees for use of pools and gyms.

The best hopes for a happy resolution to the old vs. young conflict lie precisely at the intersection of self-interest and public interest. Advocates of state-subsidized day care, for instance, scored a victory in Florida, although such programs are being cut back in many states. Advocates in the state persuaded legislators that "day care is not a youth issue; it is an economic and labor-related issue," according to Phoebe Carpenter, coordinator of community child care in central Florida. Her group had produced a study which showed that when adequate day care is available, welfare case loads drop by 50 percent and family income rises, thus easing the tax burden for other citizens. By couching the argument in those terms, Carpenter said, "We lost some supporters and won others. We lost do-gooders and won bankers and chambers of commerce. We lost the liberals and won conservatives."

Similar arguments are likely to be made by other advocates for children and youth in the coming years. Instead of talking in terms of children's needs and appealing for sympathy, they will talk of taxpayer benefits. Appeals to a sense of fairness and social justice worked politically in the expansive civil-rights Sixties and ceased to be effective in the "era of limits" decade just ended. But the Eighties could turn out to be a time of snythesis, when self-interest demands the well-being of the entire body social—including both the old and the young.

QUESTIONS

1. In what ways might a markedly older population alter life in the United States, in such fields as politics, economics, education, sport, and so on?

2. In what ways can inequalities between age categories be considered a form of social stratification? Can valid comparisons be made with other forms of stratification?

3. What causes conflict between generations? Is this conflict inevitable?

UNIT 4   *Social Institutions*

LILLIAN B. RUBIN

Changing Expectations:
New Sources of Strain

*If you study the relationship between husband and
wife revealed in such old TV shows as "I Love Lucy,"
you will see how dramatically American sex roles have
changed since the early campaigns of the women's
movement some twenty years ago. But although these
changes have been generally welcomed, they have inevitably caused some disruption to the traditional American family system—a system, after all, which a majority of Americans were socialized to participate in.*

*There is little question that changing sex-role ex-
pectations have been one of the factors that have
placed a new stress on American marriages, particularly among the working class, where allegiance to the
old sex roles is most firmly entrenched. Traditional
roles called for the husband to be the breadwinner, the
rational, emotionally aloof, undisputed family head,
and for the wife to be the homemaker, the source of
emotional support for her husband and children, and
the subservient partner in all matters of consequence.
But today the family these roles were designed for
scarcely exists: most wives work, and most husbands
are no longer the sole breadwinner. Women are taking
on new and challenging roles outside the home, and
are increasingly expecting to be treated as equal partners within the marriage.*

*In this article, Lillian Rubin interweaves quotations
from her studies of working-class husbands and wives
with an analysis of how changing expectations have
placed new strain on working-class marriages.*

I give her a nice home, a nice car, all those fancy appliances.
I don't cheat on her. We got three nice kids—nobody could
ask for better kids. And with all that, she's not happy. I
worry about it, but I can't figure out what's the matter, so
how can I know what to do? I just don't know what she
wants. [*Twenty-nine-year-old truck driver, married nine
years*]

"I just don't know what she wants"—that's the plaintive
and uncomprehending cry of most working-class men, the
cry that bedevils most marriages. Sadly, she often also
doesn't know what she wants. She knows only that the
dream is not being fulfilled—that she's married but feels
lonely:

It sounds silly, I know, but here I am in a house with three
kids and my husband, and lots of time I feel like I might just
as well be living alone.

. . . that life feels curiously empty:

You wake up one day and you say to yourself, "My God, is
this all there is? Is it really possible that this is what life is all
about?"

. . . that she's often filled with an incomprehensible anger:

I feel like I go crazy-angry sometimes. It makes me say and
do things to Randy or the kids that I hate myself for. I keep
wondering what makes me do those things when one part of
me knows I don't really mean it.

. . . and that guilt and anxiety are her steady companions:

I don't know what's the matter with me that I don't appreciate what I've got. I feel guilty all the time, and I worry
about it a lot. Other women, they seem to be happy with
being married and having a house and kids. What's the matter with me?

"What's the matter" with her is that, even apart from
the financial burdens incurred in buying all those goods,
they add little to the emotional satisfactions of life. The
advertisers' promises of instant happiness prove to be a
lie—good for the gross national product but not for the
human soul.

Sure, it's great to show those goodies off to friends and

From *Worlds of Pain* by Lillian Breslow Rubin, Chapter 7. © by Lillian
Breslow Rubin. Published by Basic Books, Inc., New York. Reprinted
by permission.

neighbors. After all those years of poverty, it makes you feel good finally to have something and let people see it. Besides, they make life easier, more comfortable. Now there's time for things other than household drudgery. But what things? Companionship? Intimacy? Sharing? What are those things? And how does one find them?

She has a vague idea. Television shows, the women's magazines—they all talk about something called communication. Marriage partners have to communicate, they say; they have to talk, to tell each other how they feel. So she talks. And he tries to listen. But somehow, it doesn't work. He listens, but he cannot hear. Sometimes sooner, sometimes later, he withdraws in silence, feeling attacked:

> When she comes after me like that, yapping like that, she might as well be hitting me with a bat.

. . . vulnerable:

> It makes me feel like I'm doing something wrong, like I'm not a very good husband or something.

. . . and helpless:

> No matter what I say, it's no good. If I try to tell her she's excited over nothing, that only makes it worse. I try to keep my cool and be logical, but nothing works.

This is the dilemma of modern marriage—experienced at all class levels, but with particular acuteness among the working-class families I met. For once marriage is conceived of as more than an economic arrangement—that is, as one in which the emotional needs of the individual are attended to and met—the role segregation and the consequent widely divergent socialization patterns for women and men become clearly dysfunctional. And it is among the working class that such segregation has been most profound, where there has been least incentive to change.

Thus, they talk *at* each other, *past* each other, or *through* each other—rarely *with* or *to* each other. He blames her: "She's too emotional." She blames him: "He's always so rational." In truth, neither is blameworthy. The problem lies in the fact that they do not have a language with which to communicate, with which to understand each other. They are products of a process that trains them to relate to only one side of themselves—she, to the passive, tender, intuitive, verbal, emotional side; he, to the active, tough, logical, nonverbal, unemotional one. From infancy, each has been programmed to be split off from the other side; by adulthood, it is distant from consciousness, indeed.

They are products of a disjunction between thought and feeling, between emotionality and rationality that lies deep in Western culture. Even though she complains, both honestly believe what the culture has taught them. To be rational is the more desired state; it is good, sane, strong, adult. To be emotional is the less desired state; it

is bad, weak, childlike. She:

> I know I'm too emotional and I can't really be trusted to be sensible a lot of the time. I need him; he's the one in the family you can always count on to think about things right, not mixed up, like me.

He:

> She's like a kid sometimes, so emotional. I'm always having to reason with her, to explain things to her. If it weren't for me, nothing would happen very rational around here.

This equation of emotional with nonrational, this inability to apprehend the logic of emotions lies at the root of much of the discontent between the sexes, and helps to make marriage the most difficult of all relationships.

Her lifetime training prepares her to handle the affective, expressive side in human affairs; his, to handle the nonaffective, instrumental side. Tears, he has been taught, are for sissies; feelings, for women. A *real* man is the strong, silent type of the folklore—a guy who needs nothing from anyone, who ignores feelings and pain, who can take it on the chin without a whimper. For a lifetime, much of his energy has gone into molding himself in that image—into denying his feelings, refusing to admit they exist. Without warning or preparation, he finds himself facing a wife who pleads, "Tell me your feelings." He responds with bewilderment. "What is there to tell?"

When they try to talk, she relies on the only tools she has, the mode with which she is most familiar; she becomes progressively more emotional and expressive. He falls back on the only tools he has; he gets progressively more rational—determinedly reasonable. She cries for him to attend to her feelings, her pain. He tells her it's silly to feel that way; she's just being emotional. That clenched-teeth reasonableness invalidates her feelings, leaving her sometimes frightened:

> I get scared that maybe I'm crazy. He's always so logical and reasonable that I begin to feel, "What's the matter with me that I'm so emotional?"

. . . sometimes angry:

> When he just sits there telling me I'm too emotional, I get so mad, I go up the wall. Sometimes I get so mad I wish I could hit him. I did once, but he hit me back, and he can hurt me more than I can hurt him.

. . . almost always tearful and despairing:

> I wind up crying and feeling terrible. I get so sad because we can't really talk to each other a lot of times. He looks at me like I'm crazy, like he just doesn't understand a word I'm saying.

Repeatedly, the experience is the same, the outcome of the interaction, predictable. Yet, each has such a limited repertoire that they are consigned to playing out the same theme over and over again—he, the rational man;

she, the hysterical woman.

. . .

It hardly need said that such relationships between men and women are not given to the working-class alone. Without doubt, the description I have been rendering represents the most common interactional pattern in American marriage. These are the behavioral consequences of the dominant sex-role socialization patterns in the culture and of the existing structure of family relations within which boys and girls internalize an appropriate identity—patterns which generate the role stereotypes that women and men bring to marriage and which effectively circumscribe their emotional negotiations.

Still, it is also true that the norms of middle-class marriage for much longer have called for more companionate relationships—for more sharing, for more exploration of feelings, and for more exchange of them. Thus, middle-class women and men have more practice and experience in trying to overcome the stereotypes. And, perhaps more important, they have more models around them for how to do so. This is not to suggest that they have done it so well, as a casual glance at the divorce rate will show; only that the demands on the marriage partners for different behaviors have been around for much longer, that there is a language that gives those demands legitimacy, and that there has been more experimentation in modifying the stereotypes.

Among working-class couples, the demand for communication, for sharing, is newer. Earlier descriptions of working-class family life present a portrait of wives and husbands whose lives were distinctly separate, both inside and outside the home—the wife attending to her household role, the husband to his provider role. He came home at night tired and taciturn; she kept herself and the children out of his way. For generations, it was enough that each did their job adequately—he, to bring home the bacon; she, to cook it. Intimacy, companionship, sharing—these were not part of the dream.

But dreams change—sometimes before the people who must live them are ready. Suddenly, new dreams are stirring. *Intimacy, companionship, sharing*—these are now the words working-class women speak to their men, words that turn *both* their worlds upside down. For while it is the women who are the discontented, who are pushing for change, they, no less than their men, are confused about what they are asking:

I'm not sure what I want. I keep talking to him about communication, and he says, "Okay, so we're talking; now what do you want?" And I don't know what to say then, but I know it's not what I mean.

. . . and frightened and unsure about the consequences:

I sometimes get worried because I think maybe I want too much. He's a good husband; he works hard; he takes care of

me and the kids. He could go out and find another woman who would be very happy to have a man like that, and who wouldn't be all the time complaining at him because he doesn't feel things and get close.

The men are even worse off. Since it's not *their* dream, they are less likely still to have any notion of what is being asked of them. They only know that, without notice, the rules of the game have been changed; what worked for their fathers, no longer works for them. They only know that there are a whole new set of expectations—in the kitchen, in the parlor, in the bedroom—that leave them feeling bewildered and threatened. She says:

I keep telling him that the reason people get divorced isn't *only* financial but because they can't communicate. But I can't make him understand.

He says:

I swear, I don't know what she wants. She keeps saying we have to talk, and then when we do, it always turns out I'm saying the wrong thing.

I get scared sometimes. I always thought I had to think things to myself; you know, not tell her about it. Now she says that's not good. But it's hard. You know, I think it comes down to that I like things the way they are, and I'm afraid I'll say or do something that'll really shake things up. So I get worried about it, and I don't say anything.

For both women and men, the fears and uncertainties are compounded by the fact that there are no models in their lives for the newly required and desired behaviors. Television shows them people whose lives seem unreal—outside the realm of personal experience or knowledge. The daytime soap operas, watched almost exclusively by women, *do* picture men who may be more open and more available for intimacy. But the men on the soaps don't work at ordinary jobs, doing ordinary things, for eight, ten, twelve hours a day. They're engaged either in some heroic, life-saving, glamour job to which working-class viewers can't relate or, worse yet, work seems to be one long coffee break during which they talk about their problems. Nighttime fare, when the men are home, is different, but no less unreal, featuring the stoic private eye, the brave cop, the tight-lipped cowboy.

The argument about the impact of the mass media on blue-collar workers is complex, contradictory, and largely unsatisfactory. Some observers insist that the mass media represent the most powerful current by which blue-collar workers are swept into conformity with middle-class values and aspirations; others that blue-collar men especially resist exposure to middle-class manners and mores as they are presented on television—minimizing that exposure by exercising great discrimination in program choices; still others that the idealized and romanticized figures on television are so unreal to the average blue-collar viewer that they have little impact on their lives and little effect on their behavior.

Perhaps all three of these seemingly irreconcilable perspectives are true. The issue may not be *whether* television or other mass media affect people's lives and perceptions. Of course they do. The question we must ask more precisely is: In what ways are Americans of any class touched and affected by their exposure to television? For the professional middle class, it may well be an affirming experience; for the working class, a disconfirming one since there are no programs that deal with their problems, their prospects, and their values in sympathetic and respectful ways.

If their own lives in the present provide no models and the media offer little that seems relevant, what about the past? Unfortunately for young working-class couples, family backgrounds provide few examples of openness, companionship, or communication between husbands and wives:

I don't think we ever had a good concept of what marriage was about. His family was the opposite of mine. They didn't drink like mine did, and they were more stable. Yet he feels they didn't give him a good concept either. There wasn't any drinking and fighting and carrying on, but there wasn't any caring either.

Even those few who recall their parents' marriages as good ones don't remember them talking much to one another and have no sense at all that they might have shared their inner lives:

Would you describe a typical evening in the family when you were growing up?

A twenty-five-year-old manicurist, mother of two, married seven years, replies:

Let me think. I don't really know what happened; nothing much, I guess. My father came home at four-thirty, and we ate right away. Nobody talked much at the table; it was kind of a quiet affair.

What bout your parents' relationship? Do you remember how they behaved with each other; whether they talked to each other?

Gee, I don't know. It's hard to think about them as being *with* each other. I don't think they talked a lot; at least, I never saw them talking. I can't imagine them sitting down to talk over problems or something like that, if that's what you mean.

Yes, that *is* what I mean. But that was the last generation; what about this one?

Would you describe a typical evening in your own family now?

For some, less than half, it's better—a level of companionship, caring, and sharing that, while not all they dream of, is surely better than they knew in their past. Fathers attend more to children; husbands at least try to

"hear" their wives; couples struggle around . . . emotional issues . . . For most, however, nothing much has changed since the last generation. Despite the yearning for more, relations between husband and wife are benumbed, filled with silence; life seems empty and meaningless; laughter, humor, fun is not a part of the daily ration. Listen to this couple married seven years. The wife:

Frank comes home from work; now it's about five because he's been working overtime every night. We eat right away, right after he comes home. Then, I don't know. The kids play a while before bed, watch TV, you know, stuff like that. Then, I don't know; we don't do anything except maybe watch more TV or something like that. I don't know what else—nothing, I guess. We just sit, that's all.

That's it? Nothing else?

Yeah, that's right, that's all. [*A short silence, then angrily.*] Oh yeah, I forgot. Sometimes he's got one of his projects he works on. Like now, he's putting that new door in the kitchen. It's still nothing. When he finishes doing it, we just sit.

Her husband describes the same scene:

I come home at five and we eat supper right away. Then, I sit down with coffee and a beer and watch TV. After that, if I'm working on a project, I do that for a little while. If not, I just watch.

Life is very predictable. Nothing much happens; we don't do much. Everyone sits in the same place all the time and does the same thing every night. It's satisfying to me, but maybe it's not for her, I don't know. Maybe she wants to go to a show or something once in a while, I don't know. She doesn't tell me.

Don't you ask her?

No. I suppose I should, but it's really hard to think about getting out. We'd need someone to stay with the kids and all that. Besides, I'm tired. I've been out all day, seeing different people and stuff. I don't feel like going out after supper again.

Is there some time that you two have for yourselves, to talk things over and find out how you feel about things?

The wife:

There's plenty of time; we just don't do it. He doesn't ever think there's anything to talk about. I'm the one who has to nag him to talk always, and then I get disgusted.

He'd be content just living, you know, just nothing but living for the rest of his life. It don't make no difference to him where he lives or how people around him are feeling. I don't know how anybody can be like that.

A lot of times I get frustrated. I just wish I could talk to him about things and he could understand. If he had more feelings himself, maybe he'd understand more. Don't you think so?

Her husband agrees that he has problems handling

both his feelings and hers:

> I'm pretty tight-lipped about most things most of the time, especially personal things. I don't express what I think or feel. She keeps trying to get me to, but, you know, it's hard. Sometimes I'm not even sure what she wants me to be telling her. And when she gets all upset and emotional, I don't know what to say or what to do.
>
> Sometimes she gets to nagging me about what I'm thinking or feeling, and I tell her, "Nothing," and she gets mad. But I swear, it's true; I'm not thinking about anything.

Difficult for her to believe, perhaps, but it *is* true. After a lifetime of repressing his feelings, he often *is* a blank, unaware that he's thinking or feeling anything. Moreover, when emotions have been stored for that long, they tend to be feared as especially threatening or explosive. He continues:

> Maybe it sounds a little crazy, but I'm afraid once I let go, I might get past the point where I know what I'm doing. If I let myself go, I'm afraid I could be dangerous. She keeps telling me that if you keep things pent up inside you like that, something's going to bust one day.
>
> I think a lot of the problem is that our personalities are just very different. I'm the quiet type. If I have something I have to think about, I have to get by myself and do it. Elly, she just wants to talk about it, always talking about her feelings.
>
> Yakketty-yakkers, that's what girls are. Well, I don't know; guys talk, too. But, you know, there's a difference, isn't there? Guys talk about things and girls talk about feelings.

Indeed that *is* the difference, precisely the difference I have been pointing to—"Guys talk about things and girls talk about feelings"—a difference that plagues marriage partners as they struggle to find ways to live with each other.

Again, the question presents itself: Is this just a phenomenon of working-class life? Clearly, it is not, for the social and psychological processes that account for the discrepant and often incompatible development of women and men apply across class and throughout the culture. Still, there are important class differences in the way these broad socio-cultural mandates are interpreted and translated into behavior—differences that are rooted in class situation and experience. Thus, there are differences in the early childhood and family experiences of children who grow up in working-class homes and those who live in professional middle-class homes, differences in the range of experiences through their adolescence and young adulthood, and differences in the kinds of problems and preoccupations they face in their adult lives—on the job and in the family.

Whether boys or girls, children in the homes of the professional middle class have more training in exploring the socio-emotional realm and more avenues for such exploration. It's true that for the girls, this usually is the *focus* of their lives, while for the boys, it is not. Nevertheless, compared to childrearing patterns in working-class families, professional middle-class families make fewer and less rigid sex-role distinctions in early childhood. As small children, therefore, boys in such middle-class homes more often get the message that it's all right to cry, to be nurturant as well as nurtured, to be reflective and introspective, even at times to be passive—in essence, in some small measure, to relate to their expressive side.

Not once in a professional middle-class home did I see a young boy shake his father's hand in a well-taught "manly" gesture as he bid him good night. Not once did I hear a middle-class parent scornfully—or even sympathetically—call a crying a boy a sissy or in any way reprimand him for his tears. Yet, these were not uncommon observations in the working-class homes I visited. Indeed, I was impressed with the fact that, even as young as six or seven, the working-class boys seemed more emotionally controlled—more like miniature men—than those in the middle-class families.

These differences in childrearing practices are expressed as well in the different demands the parents of each class make upon the schools—differences that reflect the fact that working-class boys are expected to be even less emotional, more controlled than their middle-class counterparts. For the working-class parent, school is a place where teachers are expected to be tough disciplinarians; where children are expected to behave respectfully and to be punished if they do not; and where one mark of that respect is that they are sent to school neatly dressed in their "good" clothes and expected to stay that way through the day. None of these values is highly prized in the professional middle class. For them, schools are expected to be relatively loose, free, and fun; to encourage initiative, innovativeness, creativity, and spontaneity; and to provide a place where children—boys as well as girls—will learn social and interpersonal skills. The children of these middle-class families are sent to nursery school early—often as young as two and a half—not just because their mothers want the free time, but because the social-skill training provided there is considered a crucial part of their education.

These differences come as no surprise if we understand both the past experience and the future expectations of both sets of parents. Most highly educated parents have little fear that their children won't learn to read, write, and do their sums. Why should they? They learned them, and learned them well. Their children have every advantage that they had and plenty more: books, games, toys—all designed to excite curiosity and to stimulate imagination—and parents who are skillful in aiding in their use.

Working-class parents, however, have no such easy assurances about their children's educational prospects. Few can look back on their own school years without discomfort—discomfort born of painful reminders of all they didn't learn, of the many times they felt deficient and inadequate. Further, when they look at the schools their children attend now, they see the same pattern repeating itself. For, in truth, the socio-economic status of the children in a school is the best indicator of school-wide achievement test scores—that is, the lower the socio-economic status, the lower the scores.

Observing this phenomenon, many analysts and educators argue that these low achievement records in poor and working-class schools are a consequence of the family background—the lack of culture and educational motivation in the home—an explanation that tends to blame the victim for the failure of our social institutions. Elsewhere, I have entered the debate about *who* is to blame for these failures on the side of the victims. Here, the major point is simply that, regardless of where we think responsibility lies, working-class parents quite rightly fear that their children may not learn to read very well; that they may not be able to do even the simple arithmetic required to be an intelligent consumer. Feeling inadequate and lacking confidence that they can pass on their slim skills to their children, such parents demand that the schools enforce discipline in the belief that only then will their children learn all that they themselves did not.

This, however, is only one part of the explanation of why the sons of the professional middle class are brought up in a less rigidly stereotypic mode than are the sons of the working class—the part that is rooted in past experience. But past experience combines with present reality to create future expectations, because parents, after all, do not raise their children in a vacuum—without some idea of what the future holds for them, some sense of what they will need to survive the adult world for which they are destined. In fact, it is out of just such understandings that parental attitudes and values about child-raising are born. Thus, professional middle-class parents, assuming that their children are destined to do work like theirs—work that calls for innovation, initiative, flexibility, creativity, sensitivity to others, and a well-developed set of interpersonal skills—call for an educational system that fosters those qualities. Working-class parents also assume that their children will work at jobs roughly similar to their own. But in contrast to the requirements of professional or executive work, in most working-class jobs, creativity, innovation, initiative, flexibility are considered by superiors a hindrance. ("You're not getting paid to think!" is an oft-heard remonstrance.) Those who must work at such jobs may need nothing so much as a kind of iron-willed discipline to get them to work every day and to keep them going back year after year. No surprise, then, that such parents look suspiciously at spontaneity whether at home or at school. No surprise,

either, that early childhood training tends to focus on respect, orderliness, cleanliness—in a word, discipline—especially for the boys who will hold these jobs, and that schools are called upon to reinforce these qualities.

Finally, men in the professional middle class presently live in an environment that gives some legitimacy to their stirrings and strivings toward connection with their emotional and expressive side. The extraordinary proliferation of the "growth-movement" therapies, which thrive on their appeal to both men and women of the upper middle class, is an important manifestation of that development. Another is the nascent men's movement—a response to the women's movement—with its men's groups, its male authors who write to a male audience encouraging their search for expressiveness. While it may be true that numerically all these developments account for only a small fraction of American men, it is also true that whatever the number, they are almost wholly drawn from the professional middle class.

For working-class men, these movements might as well not exist. Most don't know of them. The few who do, look at their adherents as if they were "kooks," "queers," or otherwise deficient, claiming to see no relevance in them to their own lives. Yet if one listens carefully to what lies beneath the surface of their words, the same stirrings for more connection with other parts of themselves, for more intimate relations with their wives are heard from working-class men as well. Often inchoate and inarticulately expressed, sometimes barely acknowledged, these yearnings, nevertheless, exist. But the struggle for their realization is a much more lonely and isolated one—removed not only from the public movements of our time but from the lives of those immediately around them—a private struggle in which there is no one to talk to, no examples to learn from. They look around them and see neighbors, friends, brothers, and sisters who are no better—sometimes far worse off—than they:

> We're the only ones in the two families who have any kind of a marriage. One of my brothers ran out on his wife, the other one got divorced. Her sister and her husband are separated because he kept beating her up; her brother is still married, but he's a drunk. It makes it hard. If you never saw it in your family when you were growing up, then all the kids in both families mess up like that, it's hard to know what a good marriage is like. I guess you could say there hasn't been much of a model of one around us.

Without models, it is indeed hard—hard to know what to expect, hard to know how to act. You can't ask friends because they don't seem to have the same problems, not even the same feelings. One twenty-nine-year-old husband lamented:

> I sometimes think I'm selfish. She's the support—the moral support—in the family. But when she needs support, I just don't give it to her. Maybe it's not just selfishness, it's that I

don't know what she wants and I don't know how.

The worst thing is, I've got nobody to talk to about how a guy can be different. The guys at work, all they ever talk about is their cars or their trucks. Oh, they talk about women, but it's only to brag about how they're making it with this chick or that one. And my brother, it's no use talking to him; he don't know where anything's at. He runs around every night, comes home drunk, beats up his wife.

I know Joanie's not so happy, and I worry about what to do about it. But the guys I know, they don't worry about things like that.

Don't they? He doesn't really know because he dare not ask.

How do you know they don't worry about such things? Have you asked them?

He looks up, puzzled, as if wondering how anybody could even think of such a thing, and answers quickly:

Ask them? No! Why would I do that? They'd think I was nuts or something. People don't talk about those things; you just *know* where those guys are; you don't have to ask them.

In fact, many of those men are suffering the same conflicts and concerns—wondering, as he does, what happened to the old familiar world; fearful, as he is, that their masculine image will be impaired if they talk about the things that trouble them. But if they can't talk to brothers, friends, work mates, where do they turn?

Maybe you could talk to Joan about what you could do to make things better in your marriage?

Dejectedly, he replies:

What good would that do? She's only a girl. How would she know how a guy is supposed to act?

The women generally also suffer alone. Despite all the publicity generated by the women's movement about the dissatisfactions women experience in marriage, most working-class women continue to believe that their feelings are uniquely theirs. Few have any contact with the movement or the people in it; few feel any support for their struggle from that quarter:

They put you down if you want to be married and raise kids, like there's something the matter with you.

Nor do they want it. For the movement is still a fearsome thing among working-class wives, and their responses to it are largely ambivalent, largely dominated by the negative stereotypes of the media. "Bra-burners," "man-haters"—these labels still are often heard.

Most believe in equal pay for equal work, but even that generally is not unequivocal:

Yes, I believe women should be paid the same as men if they're doing the same job. I mean, most of the time, I

believe it. But if a man has a family to support and she doesn't, then it's different.

Few believe that women should compete equally in the job market with men:

If a man with a wife and kids needs a job, no woman ought to be able to take it away from him.

Neither response a surprise, given their history of economic deprivation and concern. Neither response to be heard among the wives of professional men. Also no surprise given their lifetime of greater financial security and the fact that they "take for granted" that their husbands will provide adequately for the family.

Beyond these two issues, one after the other the working-class women responded impatiently and with almost identical words to questions about what they know about the movement:

I don't know anything about it, and I don't care to know either.

You sound angry at the women's movement.

That's right, I am. I don't like women who want to be men. Those libbers, they want men and women to be just alike, and I don't want that to happen. I think men should be men and women should be women. They're crazy not to appreciate what men do for women. I like my husband to open the car door for me and to light my cigarettes. It makes me feel like a lady.

As if reciting a litany, several women spoke the same words over and over—"I like a man to open the car door and light my cigarettes." Perplexed at the repetition, at the assertion of value of these two particular behaviors, I finally asked:

When was the last time your husband opened a car door for you or lit your cigarette?

Startled, the open face of the woman who sat before me became suffused with color; she threw her head back and laughed. Finally recovering, she said:

I've gotta admit, I don't know why I said that. I don't even smoke.

Of course, she doesn't know why. To know would mean she'd have to face her fears and anxieties more squarely, to recognize that in some important ways the movement speaks to the issues that plague and pain her in her marriage. If, instead, she can reach for the stereotypes, she need not deal with the reality that these issues have become a part of her own life and aspirations, that their questions are also hers, that her own discontent is an example of what so many women out there are talking about.

For her, a major problem is that it remains "out there." Unlike the experience of the women in professional families, it is not *her* sisters, *her* friends, *her* neighbors who talk of these things, but women she doesn't know, has never met; women who aren't her "kind." So she hides her pain and internalizes her guilt.

Do you talk to your friends about some of the things we've been discussing—I mean about your conflicts about your life and your marriage, and about some of the things you dream about and wish for?

No, we don't talk about those kinds of things. It's kind of embarrassing, too personal, you know. Besides, the people I know don't feel like I do, so it's no point in talking to them about those things.

How do you know how they feel if you don't talk about it?

You just know, that's all. I know. It's why I worry sometimes that maybe there's something the matter with me that I'm not satisfied with what I've got. I get depressed, and then I wonder if I'm normal. I *know* none of my friends feels like that, like maybe they need a psychiatrist or something.

It's all right to complain about money, about a husband who drinks or stays out late, even about one who doesn't help around the house. But to tell someone you're unhappy because your husband doesn't talk to you—who would understand that?

You don't talk about things like that to friends like I've got. They'd think I was another one of those crazy women's libbers.

Yes, there is concern among these working-class women and men about the quality of life, about its meaning. Yes, there is a deep wish for life to be more than a constant struggle with necessity. The drinking, the violence, the withdrawn silences—these are responses of despair, giving evidence that hope is hard to hold on to. How can it be otherwise when so often life seems like such an ungiving, uncharitable affair—a struggle without end? In the early years, it's unemployment, poverty, crying babies, violent fights. That phase passes, but a whole new set of problems emerge—problems that often seem harder to handle because they have less shape, less definition; harder, too, because they are less understandable, farther outside the realm of anything before experienced. But if there is one remarkable characteristic about life among the working class, it is the ability to engage the struggle and to survive it—a quality highly valued in a world where life has been and often remains so difficult and problematic. With a certain grim satisfaction, a twenty-six-year-old housewife, mother of two, summed it up:

I guess in order to live, you have to have a very great ability to endure. And I have that—an ability to endure and survive.

QUESTIONS

1. In what ways have sex roles changed during your lifetime? What changes, if any, do you expect in the future?

2. Why does it appear that changing sex-role expectations have placed the most strain on working-class families?

3. How many members of the class are willing to grant *complete* equality to their partners in marriage? Do males and females view the matter differently?

AMITAI ETZIONI

The Family: Is It Obsolete?

The family is the most basic of all social institutions, and its health is therefore a matter of great concern in any society. This is particularly so if the family seems threatened with disintegration—which, in the view of many observers, is what is happening to the institution in the United States.

The evidence certainly supports the contention that something is seriously amiss with the traditional American family: divorce rates are soaring; the great majority of young people experience premarital sex; there is almost an epidemic of illegitimate births, particularly among teen-age mothers; homosexuality is widely accepted; new "life styles," offering alternatives to traditional marriage, abound; kinship ties seem to be weakening. Yet the significance of these and other phenomena is in doubt: Is the family system collapsing, or is it merely changing?

All institutions change with time—the economy, the political system, science, religion, the legal system, and so on. It would be remarkable indeed if the family were immune to the various influences that alter every other element in the social structure over time, especially when many of these changes have stripped the family of a number of its former functions.

In this article, Amitai Etzioni places some of the changes in the nuclear family in the context of wider social changes, and evaluates their impact on the future of the institution.

From the *Journal of Current Social Issues*, Winter 1977. Reprinted with permission of the United Church Board for Homeland Ministries.

The American middle-class family, already stripped of most non-essential duties, now faces an attack on its remaining last bastions. Sex is available premaritally, extra-maritally and non-maritally to more and more Americans. Thus, Morton Hunt reports that to the present generation of young Americans, age 18 to 25, premarital sex runs as high as 81 percent for females and 95 percent for males. Extra-marital sex is reported by about half of the males, and one out of five women. Education has long ago been taken from the family and invested in special institutions, the schools. While in the old days the members of one family often worked one farm, very few families today are also a "work" unit. The rapid rise in women who work (more than 60 percent of all married), or are on welfare, breaks economic dependence as a source of a family bond. Meals can be readily obtained at the mushrooming fast-food franchises, at the supermarket and at "Take-Homes."

Thus, as this short history of the modern family suggests, there is a continued, expanding divesture of missions from the family to other institutions. Now, even the upbringing of young children, once considered by social scientists *the* family duty (indeed, in many societies the marriage is not considered fully consummated until there are offspring), is being downgraded by an increase in the number of persons who decide not to have children at all, and those who decide that they do not need a family to bring up infants. They either delegate this duty to day care centers, as available to singles as to couples, or do the job on their own. Nine million children under the age of 18 are being raised by one parent only, mostly by women. Thirty percent are under the age of six. There are about 2.4 million one-parent families as compared to 29 million nuclear families. The growth rate of single-parent families has increased by 31.4 percent, almost three times the growth of two-parent families. According to my calculations, if the present rate of increase in divorce and single households continues to accelerate as it did for the last ten years, by mid-1990 not one American family will be left.

The historical trends which propel the decline of the family are now accelerated by an additive, a slew of arguments which justify, legitimate and, indeed, even welcome these developments. They characterize the progressive decline of the nuclear family as "progress" and provide people with additional incentive to take to the exit, to dismantle the often shaky marital bond, instead of providing for a cooling-off mechanism to cope with the occasional centrifugal forces every marriage knows. While we have not reached the stage where breaking up one's family to enjoy "all that life has to offer" has become *the* thing to do, in many and growing circles the stigma attached to divorce—even when young infants are involved—has paled, the laws' cooling mechanisms have weakened, and reasons which "justify" divorce have grown in acceptance. Indeed "no-fault" divorces, which require no grounds at all, are now available in most states.

Until quite recently these trends were viewed as pathological. In the fifties, for example, the rising divorce rate was defined as a social problem, and marriage counseling was on the rise. The attitude of marriage counselors and that of society-at-large was typified by Dr. Paul Popanoe, marriage counselor and *Ladies Home Journal* columnist, who asked "Can this Marriage be Saved?" and month after month related case histories to prove that "yes," it almost invariably could be.

During the sixties, however, an intellectual and, to a lesser extent, a public opinion turn around began to take place. The idea that spouses were morally obligated to hold their marriage together and that nine times out of ten they could succeed in doing so if they were willing to work at it moved increasingly to the right of mainstream thinking. Today's popular experts on marriage and the family seldom ask first, "Can this marriage be saved?" but instead, "should it be?" And more and more often the answer given is not only "no" but an optimistic and affirmative "no." This is due to a new popular wisdom which says that people might be better off dissolving an unsatisfactory marriage, and either live single or try again, than to go through great contortions to fix their present marriage. While the many marriage and family experts of the fifties saw their task as shoring up the family's defenses so that it could better withstand attack, a significant contingent among today's experts is ready to view the invading social forces as potential liberators.

One: Divorce Is AOK

Several related lines of argument are currently being used to identify and explain what are seen as positive aspects in the rising divorce rate. The most novel one is the idea that *second marriages are better than first marriages*. Thus, Leslie Aldridge Westoff, a Princeton demographer, writes about "blended" or "reconstituted families" rather than second marriages, in an article entitled "Second-time *Winners*." (The labels are important; blended or reconstituted sounds more approving than

"second time around.") Westoff reports that for the couples she interviewed the first marriage was a dry-run. In the second marriage they applied the lessons learned, did not repeat the same mistakes, and chose mates more wisely. "In retrospect many of the couples saw their first marriage as a kind of training school; . . . divorce was their diploma. All agreed that the second marriage was the real thing at last. With both partners older, more mature, somewhat expert at marriage, everything moves more smoothly, more meaningfully."

While Westoff may feel she is just reporting the results of some interviews with some couples, the implication to the reader, the music her writing vibrates, is that the first marriage is to the second one what premarital sex is to marital sex: evidence shows one improves the other. And indeed *if* there were sufficient data to support a view of the first marriage as a dry-run, there would be less reason for concern. But Westoff herself laments the lack of systematic research on second marriages; her insights are based on a few interviews. She also concedes that second marriages are less stable than first ones. Statistically, 59 percent of second marriages, as opposed to 37 percent of first marriages, will end in a divorce, according to Dr. Paul Glick of the U.S. Census Bureau. Nor does she show that such re-marriages, even if they do last, have no detrimental effects on the children. Do the children also consider their parents as a dry-run and their step-parents as an improvement?

Two: Disposable Marriages

The "if-at-first-you-don't succeed, try, try again" optimism about divorce is at least not down on marriage as an institution. Another increasingly common viewpoint, however, is one which interprets the rising divorce rate as a symptom that something is radically wrong with marriage and/or the family. This school of thought rejects the view that marriage can work once you know yourself well enough and choose the "right" partner; it sees it as *healthy* that individuals in great numbers want to get out of what it views as a decaying social bond. It tends to look upon the rising divorce rate with much the same hopefulness with which a Marxist approaches a new recession: as a condition which cannot be tolerated for long, and hence will force revolutionary changes in social structures. Those who subscribe to this view tend to see new family forms waiting in the wings, from contractual marriages to group-marriages.

Significantly, a common feature of most of these new marital styles is that they seek to take some of the strain off the nuclear family by de-intensifying the husband-wife relationship. One way is by limiting the duration of the relationship a priori to an agreed period of time and defining the terms of the dissolution of the relationship from its very inception. Thus, by this school's terms, divorce has become no more of a crisis than completing a stint in the army or delivering the goods as agreed to a supermarket. Another alternative is to diversify one's emotions by investing them in a large number of intimate relationships, making each one less intense and hence less all-important. Thus, it is often said that sexual fidelity puts too much of a strain on many marriages—acceptance of one or both partners' adultery may well save some relationships, since the couple can stay together while getting the sexual variety, affection or whatever from outside persons. Better yet, it is said, group-marriage secures that you'll always have a mate, even if you divorce one, two, or three. Such de-emotionalization and de-emphasis is however a two-edged sword. On the one hand, spouses who do not depend exclusively on each other and who obtain satisfactions from other persons may be able to continue living together for long periods without having to resolve their conflicts, at the risk of bringing them to a destructive head. On the other hand, such relationships may be too shallow to provide the needed emotional anchoring and security many people seek and need.

The contractual marriage or contractual cohabitation mentioned above has been widely advocated and has aroused a fair degree of popular interest. Those who favor contractual marriages tend to look upon all social life as a series of exchanges. Conflict and tension arise when one or both parties fail to live up to their parts of the bargain. Conflict is seen as more likely to arise in a relationship, such as that characterized in the traditional marriage, where the reciprocal "rights and duties" of each partner are not clearly spelled out and agreed to in advance. Thus, the male swinger who marries may do so with the implicit understanding that this change in legal status will not cramp his lifestyle while his bride may be marrying under the illusion that her husband-to-be will transform his lifestyle once they are wed. Those who propose contractual marriage suggest that a great deal of subsequent conflict between spouses (and disappointment with marriage) could be avoided by bringing such unspoken expectations into the open, to be discussed and agreed upon and then formalized in a marital contract akin to the contracts that govern relations between parties in a business transaction.

For example, the prospective marital partners might agree to write monogamy into the contract or, alternatively, include a clause permitting sexual side-trips or bisexual relations. But once each party had signed the agreement each would have to abide by the stated rules. Violation of such contractual terms could be declared in writing and signed by both parties to be grounds for immediate unilateral termination of the contractual marriage. In addition, unlike the traditional marriage bond which was supposed to be entered into as a lifelong commitment, contractual marriage typically provides for pe-riodic review and renewal (or nonrenewal) of the contract, say every three to five years.

The problem, however, is that contracts work in the business world primarily because the relationships involved are highly limited and specific, and calculative motivations are enough to sustain them. But for two people to live together, to share wealth and ill fortune and the slings and arrows of life, required a deep, encompassing, positive relationship of the kind implied in marital vows but antithetical to any contract. Contracts put people continuously on their guard: did I get my share, did he (or she) do this job? Marriage requires more altruism, less accounting, and above all a greater sense of commitment to a *shared* life.

Three: Granny—Yes, Husband—No

Another viewpoint which has become intellectually chic recently is the celebration of the extended family. Like contractual marriage it claims to reduce the pressure on the nuclear family by de-intensifying the emotional bonds between husband and wife, parent and child. The idea is that if family members had a multiplicity of sources of satisfaction for their various needs they would not become overly dependent on one single source or parent. Some of the theorists of the extended family favor a revival of older family forms in which several generations of blood relatives lived under the same roof or within close geographic proximity. Others favor the formation of "extended families of choice," e.g., communes. Thus, it is said that our typical middle-class suburban "nuclear" family is emotionally unwholesome. Segregated from grandparents and other kin, it provides the child with only two warm caring adults, both of whom are increasingly absent or harried, instead of the abundance provided by the grandparents, uncles, aunts, and nieces and nephews of the extended family.

In India, where extended families often run to hundreds of members, a baby "is never put down," there is always an uncle, cousin, or someone, to comfort a crying child. Among immigrant families extended family members provided many of the support services offered by welfare agencies, day care centers and other institutions, at great cost to the tax-payers, and often with highly impersonal if not bureaucratic paternalism. A number of Unitarian congregations, concerned with the "too many stresses which are being placed on the small nuclear family," are forming hundreds of artificially-extended families whose members vacation together or help each other with problems such as baby-sitting or care of elderly infirm relatives.

What does this have to do with the survival of the nuclear family? Ostensibly, by easing the burden on parents to be constantly responsive to one another and to their children, the extended family makes it less likely that break-up will result from spouses continually over-burdening one another. However, several of the extended family advocates take the next step and say that with family security provided by a circle of grandparents, cousins and uncles, a permanent husband's presence loses its importance. Look, they say, at how well impoverished families have managed, despite the comings and goings of common-law husbands. The mother, because she has the support of her mother and kin, is able to manage quite well.

The rub is that although it would be useful to have an extended family, most middle-class couples could not necessarily be induced to belong to or maintain one. The forces which in the past undermined the extended family pattern in the middle-class—from the need to be mobile for economic success, to the desire for individualism and privacy—are powerful ones and difficult to reverse. Thus, while a middle-class granny might be available to baby-sit here and there, if she lives nearby, and brothers and sisters may be good for a loan now and again, it is a long way from such occasional aid to surrogate parenthood. Indeed, in most societies, even those looked upon so enviously because of exotic extended family arrangements, the kernel of child raising is not the mother but a couple, the husband-wife, the nuclear family. The artificial extended families do provide a nice *supplement* to the nuclear family, but are much too thin and frail to *replace* its vital core.

Four: Broken Is Better

Perhaps the most sophisticated argument against the notion that husband-wife families are needed for the character formation and psychological well-being of young children emerges from studies of children from *broken* homes. In the public mind, and that of most officials, it is widely assumed that broken homes breed juvenile delinquents, truant or runaway kids, young drug addicts and most recently teen and pre-teen alcoholics. Statistical correlations are frequently uncovered. For instance, Dr. Gordon H. Barker found a high correlation ($r = .79$) between broken homes and delinquency. However, the commonsense interpretation of such results has been seriously challenged on the elementary ground that when broken homes are compared to non-broken ones, the fact that broken homes occur so frequently among the poor and minorities while non-broken ones are generally middle-class, is ignored. Or to put it differently, lower-class families produce more delinquent kids, whether they are children from broken homes *or not*. Indeed, if families of the same class background are compared, *most of the difference* in juvenile delinquency rates between the children from broken vs. unbroken homes *disappears*. Those familiar with these findings thus tend to conclude that having both a father and a mother is not vital to character

formation.

Looking at the same data, I suggest that proper economic conditions, housing and employment may well be more important for the proper upbringing of a child than a lasting positive relation between the parents, and between parents and child. At the same time, I am not convinced it has been shown that family stability is irrelevant; it may just be a less important factor than social class. Less important is not the same as unimportant.

Moreover, Dr. Urie Bronfenbrenner of Cornell University suggests that one way poverty damages kids is by disintegrating their families. Both suicide and lower scholastic achievement are particularly high among children whose families earn less than $4,000 a year and as many as 80 percent of such families in central cities are single-parent ones.

Finally, another finding has been widely disseminated, and even many people not familiar with the evidence cite it on their way to the marital exit: rotten marriages are worse than broken homes. In his research on adolescents in boys' training schools and high schools, Dr. F. Ivan Nye found that less delinquent behavior was evident in broken but happy homes (35 percent) than in unbroken but unhappy homes (48 percent). These data led Nye to conclude: "The *happiness* of the marriage was found to be more closely related to delinquent behavior in children than whether the marriage was an original marriage or to a remarriage or one in which the child was living with one parent only." According to Professor William J. Boode, "Psychiatric studies emphasize the difficulties experienced by people who as children lived in 'empty shell' families, in which people carry out their formal duties toward one another, but give no understanding, affection or support, and have little interest in communicating with one another. . . . It seems likely that role failure within the home has a more destructive impact on children than the withdrawal of one's spouse."

On the other hand, to the extent that families are needlessly undone by rationalizations, beliefs and arguments, probably the most widely held and destructive myth is the quest for the *perfect* relationship. The incessant search for "more" is a direct descendant of American optimism and romanticism which looks for a marriage which will be harmonious and loving, full of communication, understanding, mutual respect, joy and fulfillment through children. When all this is found out to be as close to the reality of most families as Marcus Welby is to your M.D., a million Americans a year take to the exits, not because they are anti-family but anti-*their* family. Thus, 80 percent of divorced persons will try again, and many of these will risk a third time, restlessly looking for that Hollywood made-in-heaven marriage. Even after they grow more accommodating, they still believe that they have missed out. Others, dating at 40, 50 and older, living together, breaking up, trying again, are still looking for that "happily ever after" promise that keeps eluding them.

Encouraging such utopian quests are several psychotherapists and psychiatrists, many of whom are trained to deal with individuals, not couples. Thus, sometimes deliberately, often unwittingly, by trying to help each individual client achieve a full life, they encourage their patients to break up their marriages (although many do ask people not to make major life changes while in therapy). The trouble is that if any person seeks to maximize his or her own happiness and freedom without considering the consequences to others and to a relationship, the result can be highly detrimental to all those involved and to the family as an institution. People must learn to balance the personal rewards of "doing one's own thing" against the hurt it might entail to others. No relationship, no institution, family or society can survive otherwise. In many instances, however, the effect of therapy is to encourage people to focus on their psycho-dynamics, feelings and needs, to the neglect of their spouses and even children. It does encourage divorce.

What Could Be Done?

Faced with the progressive dismemberment of the American family, there is surprisingly little public action for two reasons: first, the arguments that the current rate of family break-up may be a blessing in disguise raise doubts concerning the nature and extent of the crisis; and second, public officials feel that there is little the government could or should do in this intimate matter. To my mind, we need a thoroughgoing review of evidence concerning the consequences of family break-up to determine whether or not we have a national social problem on our hands. A Presidential or Congressional Commission could be given the task of investigating the harmful consequences of family dissolution bringing together and examining existing data and, where reliable data are not available, by carrying out studies of its own. Should the Commission find that single-parent families, contractual families and reblended families are doing as well as the declining traditional two-parent families, we can relax and enjoy the marital merry-go-round. Should it establish that the slew of "new" family rationalizations are ill-founded and we have a serious and growing problem on our hands, the very fact that a highly visible study has reached such conclusions, presenting evidence and airing pro and con arguments in public hearings, should help puncture these arguments.

Moreover, the recent fashion of "the less-the-better-Presidency" should not be allowed to obscure the great agenda-setting power the White House has in many areas outside the administrative scope of government. Hence, without at all suggesting that the federal government should take on the job of fixing a million dissolving families a year, or even one, by launching a National Institute of Marital Health or any other such agency, we do believe that a few well-presented speeches by the President or a White House Conference on the future of the family could go a long way to call public attention to the problem.

Second, as Walter Mondale keeps reiterating, the "family impact" of various government programs should be assessed and taken into account as old programs are revised and new ones formulated. Thus, day-care centers are a blessing for working women and certainly a better place for a young child than roaming the streets. But they are also costly institutional substitutes for family, and by de-emphasizing the importance of parents in children's lives, they may well further contribute to the erosion of family bonds. More opportunities for *half* time jobs, without loss of privileges (such as benefits and promotion) both for women and men, may provide some parents with an alternative preferable to day-care centers, one which is less costly to the public, less bureaucratic and more compatible with a viable family.

Also, laws which work against the family should be altered, both because the government should not encourage the dissolution of families *and* because laws symbolize public attitudes. As has often been pointed out, it is still true in about half of the states that the only way an unemployed male wage earner can get his children on welfare is to divorce his wife. There is no AFDC for unemployed fathers. Thus, to the extent that welfare laws and regulations still penalize marriage, they should be altered.

Furthermore, the regulations governing Social Security benefits for retired persons favor individuals who are single by reducing the total monetary awards to couples. An unmarried woman is eligible to receive 100 percent of her Social Security benefits, whereas this amount is significantly reduced if she is married to a man who is also receiving benefits. This is said to be a significant factor for many retired couples living together rather than marrying. It might be asked—what ill effects result from old people living together unmarried? The answer is that (a) they should be free to choose to live together or marry, but not pushed into living together by government regulations, and (b) older people set models for younger people; "If granny does not marry the guy, why should I?"

In a similar vein, Martin M. Spencer, writing in the *CPA Journal,* cites a divorced couple who reconciled but decided not to remarry, because remarriage would have jacked up their income tax bite by $5,460. Generally, income tax rates for single persons are lower than for married persons filing separate returns. (Married persons benefit from filing joint returns only if one spouse earns much more than the other.) The recent provisions allowing people to deduct the cost of child-care under certain circumstances further reward the single parent over two working partners in a marriage whose joint income tends to put them above the ceiling for allowable deductions.

Finally, it might well be advisable that a divorce cooling-off period and opportunities for counseling be reinstituted by those states that went somewhat overboard in making divorce easy and painless. While most divorce reforms are desirable, especially those that remove the necessity of declaring one party "guilty" and the other "innocent" and those which serve to avoid bitter wrangling between spouses which may be communicated to their children, divorce by mail and other reforms which have the effect of divesting divorce of its seriousness over-liberate divorce. The state should not imply that divorce is a trivial matter—something one can do on an impulse. Reinstituting—or beginning again to enforce—a 30-day minimum cooling-off period with opportunities for counseling, if the couple desires, would seem to be a reasonable compromise.

Other steps may well be devised. The main point is that preoccupied as we are with prices, jobs, shortages and energy—all related to the material aspects of our societal existence—we should not neglect what to many sociologists still seems to be the vital cell of our society. The disintegration of the family, one must reiterate these days, may do as much harm to a society as running out of its favorite source of energy.

QUESTIONS

1. In what ways is the present American family system different from that of a generation or two ago?

2. What social forces are undermining the traditional family system? Would you say that the family is in danger of disintegration, or is it merely changing to new, more viable forms?

3. Legislators have proposed a "Family Protection Act" and other legal measures aimed at preserving the traditional family system. Do you think change in the family institution can be prevented by legislation?

ROBERT N. WHITEHURST

Alternative Life Styles

Although some observers see the current plight of the American family as a matter for dismay, others regard the changes that are taking place as inevitable, perhaps even beneficial. After all, it is argued, a large part of the population is not rejecting the traditional form without reason: clearly, it is failing to meet their needs; and if alternative forms offer the potential for happier and more fulfilling relationships, so much the better.

There is no doubt that most Americans are still committed to the nuclear family, and, indeed, few sociologists see that particular form as being in any real danger of disappearing. Equally, there is no doubt that a significant minority of Americans have rejected that family pattern, and are exploring "alternative life styles," or nontraditional, alternative ways of creating and maintaining sexual bonds and, perhaps, of raising children. This tendency is very much in keeping with an overall social trend, namely, diversification. Institutional diversification is a typical characteristic of advanced industrial societies, and particularly of the United States. For example, traditional, preindustrial societies usually had only one religion; the United States has a dominant religion, Christianity, but many hundreds of alternatives. Similarly, it has a dominant public school system, but also offers a host of alternatives, many of them experimental.

In this article, Robert Whitehurst discusses several alternative life styles, whose emergence he sees as merely part of the broader social process of diversification. And he does not regard these new patterns as a cause for despair: he claims that it is not the search for alternatives that has undermined the traditional family, but, rather, it is the failure of that system for many people that has spurred the search for alternatives.

This article first appeared in *The Humanist* May/June 1975 and is reprinted by permission.

Most of the social forces that we presume made past marriages and family life solid, if not happy, seem to be evaporating in front of our eyes. At the same time, a great variety of alternatives to conventional marriage and family have suddenly loomed on the horizon. Recent changes seem to favor more divorce and family disorganization; dissatisfactions with marriage tend to create an atmosphere of distrust of this basic institution.

It may be that marriage and family forms will become even more diverse in the future; but this will probably be contingent upon economic and political conditions. In any case, it is unlikely that the nuclear family will fade out as a dominant form, unless the whole human race goes with it—a distinct possibility as human behavior is now going! In the exploration that follows, it will be suggested that marriage is not a healthy institution for many people today, but it is not about to die; further, the future of alternatives is simply not predictable, given the status of current political winds and economic uncertainties. Given certain conditions, however, some probable options might come to fruition. In the following pages, these options will be speculated upon.

Making Marriage Work

One of the first items in the discussion of the functioning of future family life is inevitably the Western institution known as marriage. Traditionally, marriage as we know it has emerged from a particular ethos. When people have experienced a strong sense of community, a strong set of principles adhered to rigidly as life guidelines, complete with strong sanctions and a tight supportive group, a customarily rigid family form has emerged. Since we have in this century weakened the basis of most of the previously effective social controllers, such as religion, the community, and the family, we should not be surprised that marriages fail more frequently. During the present period, no one knows if marriage is better, worse, or simply more of the same in qualitative terms. We only know with some degree of certainty that as a culture we are "hooked" on the notion of finding happiness in marriage but that it doesn't really seem to happen that way very often. It seems likely that the key differences between marriage in the past and contemporary marriage are attributable to our leisure, affluence, higher expectations, and mobility, coupled with an inordinately high opportunity level to meet potential mates. We are probably no more nor less neurotic as a people than those before, but we distinctly have fewer solidifying forces compelling us to obey the still-dominant conventional community norms. *Social structure, not personality, is what must be understood if we want to know why divorce is rampant and why families are not "happy."*

As a society, we have cut loose more people (the young, with their own rooms, TV sets, cars, booze, drugs, money, free time, and, most of all, freedom from responsibility), with more tragic results, than any people in history. Most of our older people are stashed in retirement villas or "nursing" homes and, as Jules Henry and others have shown, are simply the unwanted surplus of a rapidly moving technological society. The high social cost of overspecializing the family and creating children who flounder, oldsters who despair, and the rest of us who are uncertain, doubtful, or anxious can be seen not only in divorce rates but in simmering family problems that prevent real living and meaningful relating among people. The rise of alternative forms can be seen in part as a response to conventional family failure to satisfy many of the needs that have been developed recently in a freer kind of society. In contemporary life, custom, religion, and community have come to mean less. The needs for family and marriage, however, have come to mean more. We have reached a hiatus involving a large potential for those who either seek or promote alternatives to traditional marriage.

In a society changing as rapidly as ours, it is impossible to maintain stable marriage forms not aligned with people's real needs. If we free women to go into the marketplace, give people leisure, money, and opportunity to meet others, and take them away from home for long periods, solidarity in the old-fashioned sense cannot be the result. The need for intimacy is probably a constant in humans, but our sense of legitimizing multiple ways of searching for it is subject to radical changes over time. We have expected more intimacy from relationships today, and we have provided more means of searching for it than in former times. It is doubtful that people have ever been able to find much intimacy, but the fact that we *expect* it today and have *expanded means of seeking* it makes the search for alternatives an understandable imperative.

One of the salient factors in understanding the rise of alternatives may lie in comprehending the nature of the need for intimacy, both physical and emotional. Christianity has traditionally placed heavy emphasis on fidelity and monogamy. No one has yet made the case, howev-

er, that rigid insistence in such matters is mainly a reflection of a religious institution's need to control people in terms of the biases of its later apostles. The conditions that prompted these demands on humankind may have since vanished. We now have a markedly different situation. In short, as people are freed to live closer to themselves as natural, not churchly, beings, we may expect forms to emerge that reflect the true diversity of human desires and needs instead of a narrow monolithic institutional imperative. This seems to be a part of what is happening now.

It need not be feared that there is an immediate danger of masses of people dropping their marriages and joining communes, swinging clubs, or other such activities. The institutional forces still alive in the culture have enough sanctioning power to prevent total chaos from enveloping families; the institutions that prevail, however, do not have enough power to keep families and marriages on an even keel, as was more true in the past. Thus, the dilemma we now face involves having more freedom than in the past to live as many of us would wish, but not enough to live as many would see fit if we had a truly pluralistic and open society. It is in this cultural limbo, this no-man's-land of vague and shadowy family support that are more apparent than real, that we find ourselves today. Bereft of old supports to make them operate well, families limp their way along. Alternative-searching goes on in this limbo, in which we are neither enslaved to a past nor freed to a positive future, but caught in an uncomfortable place between. In such a situation, it would be difficult to conclude that family life is endangered by the existence of alternatives to marriage; marriage and family life, if they are threatened at all, are in jeopardy because the entire social structure and set of institutional underpinnings is in jeopardy. It is as rational to see alternative-seekers as trying to save the family as trying to destroy it. In some sense, however, old forms are always dying, so it is probably true that alternative-seekers may in some ways be hastening the demise of the family—at least as it is presently known. It is patently false to assume that the existence of alternatives has created the problem of the family today. The quest for alternatives is only one of many reactions to family strains and problems.

Given a situation as described above, it would be a false conclusion to claim that the family is in trouble today because people are seeking alternative routes to sexual satisfaction and family life; rather, it would be more correct to suggest that the search for alternatives grew out of conventional family failures created by a changing and unstable society that made some new forms both possible and seemingly desirable in a changing social context. Alternatives can thus be perceived less as a threat to the family than as a means of reconstituting it in different forms.

Alternatives Are Not a Threat

In the following descriptions of alternatives, it will be suggested that *none of these will replace conventional monogamous marriage as a modal form in the foreseeable future.* There is no sign of divorce rates lowering, but this does not necessarily pose a threat to family life as long as we are so enamored of marriage as the only way to live. Indeed, divorce hurts and disrupts both children and adults, but it does not appear to materially affect cultural stability. The same can probably be said for extant alternatives today. This is especially so since most of them occupy so few people in terms of statistical significance. Be this as it may, we are likely to see changing and even expanding rates of alternate life styles, dependent on future economic and political changes, especially inflation, recession, and depression. Among the rationales for the formation of alternate life styles are ecological and economic arguments, as well as stressing the needs for intimacy in groups larger than the conventional nuclear-family group. It is assumed that the forms enumerated below will predominate as alternatives, roughly in decreasing order of importance as they are described. These involve modified open marriage, post-marital singlehood, triads, a variety of cooperatives, urban collectives and urban communes, extended intimate networks, rural communes, and finally swinging, cohabitation, and part-time marriage. Rationales will be discussed of why each of these will be more or less successful and why some will persevere into the future.

Modified Open Marriage

With changing sex-role socialization, with people's liberation (including men's groups as well as women's), with increasing legal equality for children and women, and with a likely increase in women workers at all levels, it will be imperative that more marriages extend the benefits of greater freedoms to both sexes. This will eventuate in a form of marriage that will not likely be fully open in terms of free sexuality, but will be vastly different from the average marriage of today. It is probable that there will be more sexuality practiced outside of marriage because of these new freedoms for women, but the forms are not distinguishable at this time.

The basic revolution before us lies in sex roles, not in sexuality—at least the equalizing of sex roles should be the first order of business. The middle seventies have brought only the barest beginning of equality for husband and wife in work, household tasks, and child care. Whether this will in its turn bring the incidence of female sexual activity up to or beyond that of the average male is unknown. Given what we know now about female sexuality, it is likely that many females will surpass many of their brothers in this sphere; the impact of this upon mar-

riage and family forms is simply unknown.

Post-Marital Singlehood

Given the high divorce rates and the uncertainties of remarriage, larger numbers of people will probably opt for longer periods of singlehood in the future. In a world where there are more singles than ever before, we are likely to develop some norms that will put them into the "normal" range, which is not generally the case at present. Although pressures are still tremendous for people to marry and remarry, this may change so that a more benign atmosphere will enable people to tolerate singlehood more easily. Many young people today are either wary of marriage or are extremely cautious about getting into second marriages; given the continuance of this trend, social acceptance of this form as a more or less permanent adaptation to adult life will become a reality. Support for nonmarriage is developing in many avant-garde quarters. Although making predictions is risky, it is safe to suggest growing numbers in this category. Since it is likely that freer sexuality will be practiced among nonmarrieds and that our norm of valuing privacy will continue, it is probable that more people will be able to make it without marriage, supported by the apparent success of those already in the group. This will, of course, still constitute a small proportion of most of the adult population; we are still reared to think that marriage is the only right way to live. There are simply not, as yet, that many deviants in this culture, and nonmarriage is surely a form of deviancy from conventional norms. An increase in singlehood of all kinds may be predicted, but it will not become a modal form.

Triads

With present urban sex ratios favoring men in the marketplace of sex and partner selection, triads will likely become a more important form of living arrangement as an alternative to conventional marriage. Not only will more people be willing to share a spouse, but as the benefits of this form come to be known, more people are likely to be willing to try this adaptation. Among the more obvious advantages: greater flexibility in child care, more adult models in the family, better and more equitable distribution of household chores, better economic foundation for the family, less social isolation for some now living alone, and the greater ease of three people making accommodative rules and adaptations to each other than in other alternative forms.

To form a triad, there must be three people who like each other and have some tolerance for being alone at time, as well as being left out at times. There have been numerous cases of triads working for long periods of time, and they stand to become more numerous, given present conditions. If we add to this the relative ease with which the extra family member can be explained away to conventional society, we can see how this form might become more prevalent. Although the triad has its drawbacks and is definitely not a panacea, it is more likely to occur than many other forms of living arrangements now being tried.

Cooperatives, Collectives, Urban Communes, and Extended Intimates

A panoply of cooperatives, communes, and other sharing arrangements is currently being developed with varying results. Churches of moderately liberal suasion are even attempting to establish forms of community, sharing patterns, and extended intimacy networks. Although such forms at times develop into sexual sharing, this is not a dominant mode as yet and tends to be associated with problems, if not divorces and remarriages, because supports for sexuality outside marriage in the usual urban cooperative or collective have not worked smoothly. Short of large-scale renovation of marital and sexual norms, this will apparently not happen. It is also for this reason that alternatives might best be seen as an adjunct to marriage and not as a replacement for it—at least for a large number of people now participating in so-called alternate life styles. There is, however, some evidence that people unavoidably get into sexual problems outside their marital relationships once alternatives are entered. The rate of successful integration of extramarital sexuality into the average marriage is apparently low. For all this, there are many attempts to try to extend family conceptions by enlarging the number of people included in economic sharing, social rituals, and a variety of other quasi-family experiences, sometimes even including sexuality. Given economic hard times, these groupings stand to proliferate. In the less likely event of increased leisure and affluence, such arrangements still may expand on some kind of experimental basis as a way to salvage the goodness of family life and the ethic of sharing. These styles will be juxtaposed against what is perceived as the relatively isolated and encapsulated existence currently being experienced by most nuclear families.

Swinging and Group Marriage

Although the research of Larry and Joan Constantine has shown that there are some stable and lasting forms of group marriage, the complexities and problems of four or more people being married to each other loom so large that this form is impractical for large numbers. Hitherto privatized, nuclear-family cultures do not lend themselves easily to such an adaptation; our sense of possessiveness with spouses and jealousy still bulk in the way of such solutions. Perhaps another generation, reared with-

out sexism and jealousy, will adapt better to such a form, but the numbers are few who can make it work well today. Swinging, although declining as a family sport, can be said to arise basically as a variation of the older clandestine-adultery pattern. In no way does most swinging tend to alter family behavior. Most couples do not indoctrinate their young into swinging. With the exception of valuing the variety in swinging, no value changes are apparent in the lives of the swinging population. Although large numbers (but small percentages of the total populace) still continue this pattern, there is no indication that swinging will replace clandestine adultery as the model pattern of extramarital sexual practice. Among the principle ways swinging affects marriage is the creation of tension between partners with unequal commitment to the activity. Divorce, then remarriage to someone with more consonant values, often follows. Swinging does not seem to constitute a genuine alternative; rather, it involves a sorting mechanism to insure value-similar partners for the swingers' activities.

Cohabitation

Increasing interest in the living-together patterns of the unmarried over the past several years has eventuated in some good research on the topic. We still do not know if the practice, in fact, makes for better marriages; it may do so in the short run, but probably has little overall effect on marriage in the long run. Cohabitation does not appear to substantially affect marriage rates or marriage stability, at least as far as we know.

Cohabitation cannot seriously be considered as an alternative to marriage for many people; it is rather a *preliminary* for most who practice it and an occasional habit of people not yet ready to settle down into a second marriage; it is seldom an alternative to marriage. No doubt a more sensible mate-selection device than methods previously used, cohabitation does not seem to deter large numbers from the goal of formal marriage.

Part-Time Marriage

An increasing number of married partners are engaging in what might be called part-time marriages. These are usually professionals who for career reasons must separate on occasion and for varying periods of time. Some marriages survive these periods of separation and some do not. Some remain as monogamous in absence as in presence, but some do not. There seems to be a wide variation in the patterns possible in part-time marriages. Although the habit is still quite new and obviously a function of high-mobility and dual-career marriages, it may increase as people tend to find separateness an advantage for a period of time. This adaptation does not affect great numbers of people now and probably will not, unless current trends regarding women's employment and liberation proceed at a faster pace than at present.

Other Possibilities

If we engage in the mental exercise of extending current behavior patterns into the future and extrapolating from them, we may find some interesting potential for alternate life styles of the future. For example, if the clandestine-adultery pattern becomes a more ubiquitous phenomenon, it seems unlikely that nearly everyone could go on playing the hiding game forever; at some point, it is possible that a consensus will emerge that casual adultery is "okay"—given certain contexts and sets of rules by which the players must abide. Already, there is a set of informal and well-understood rules by which clandestine adultery is played. Firm consensus and more players is probably all that is necessary to create an informally institutionalized code of sexual behavior for large numbers of people. This would not necessarily constitute an alternative to marriage; rather, it would be one more addition to the already complex set of roles that spouses must play today.

For those who want something more than the "game" described above, there may be such a concept as informally sanctioned *binogamy*. Although this term bastardizes two standard terms used in family sociology (*monogamy* and *bigamy*), it seems apropos—although contemporary binogamists cannot be *married* to two wives, they very often, in fact, render loyalty and fealty to two persons, one of whom is the legal spouse. This pattern, a bit unlike triads, does not necessarily involve a common living arrangement. It is rather an extension of the long-lasting affair, which even when it becomes known is still not dropped in favor of monogamy. Caring, some sharing, and continued sexual relations may all be a part of this pattern. This pattern is already practiced by an unknown number of people and, by all signs, the number is increasing. Whether binogamy can be considered a true alternative is moot, since it is distinctly nonmonogamous and in some ways considerably alters nuclear-family interactions. It is, however, functional, in that it appears to ease social isolation, sexual frustration, and, perhaps, economic problems of some who maintain social and sexual needs and are not married.

Summary and Conclusion

A key characteristic of the times is the tendency to open up marriages and to provide more opportunities for expression of life styles at variance with older patterns. It is true that conventional marriages are floundering because of the failure of supportive institutions and groupings that once worked to keep people on track. At the same time, so-called alternatives—most of which are neither true alternatives to marriage nor threatening to it—are emerging and being practiced in a normative vacuum, which makes most of them problematic in terms of their longevity. What seems to be emerging is an era of pluralism, unlike anything ever before witnessed in the Western world. Homosexuals are "coming out," many people are less prone to keep their sex lives secret, and varieties of living forms, with some exception, are becoming at least tolerated, if not more understood. In an era of economic hardship, however, people are still careful not to jeopardize their jobs by blatantly flouting sexual mores. . . .

If the economy and the political situation both tighten up and create a repressive environment, alternatives will change form; although there will be less blatant sexuality, there will be more sharing, cooperative ventures, and perhaps a developing sense of community, as people are no longer able to use the wheeled escape. If the economic situation becomes more optimistic, there will probably be more sexual deviation surrounding marriage, more experimentation, and, perhaps, more forms yet to emerge as yet unknown. Both inflation and depression give birth to their own styles of conservation, but perhaps the days of easy affluence, which spawned much of the enhanced interest in sexuality, are gone. We have known the flower child. The earlier modes of a more constrained existence are not likely to return.

Pluralism seems to be the key word of the near future; we have not as yet learned to live easily with it. A democratic-humanistic approach can be more positive than the monolithic and repressive experience of the past. We have only made a beginning at developing enlightened cultural supports for sensuousness, pleasure, and a broader-based sexual practice that does not press all people, regardless of taste and desires, into a common behavioral mold. It is now a moral imperative to develop norms of acceptance for differences. Perhaps the rest of this century will correspond with the last one in the respect that our new laissez-faire policy will extend into our conception of other people's sexuality.

QUESTIONS

1. Can you see any reason why the traditional nuclear family should not remain the dominant form in the future?

2. Would you agree that the various alternative life styles are valid arrangements in their own right? Or are they simply a copout for people who cannot fully face their responsibilities to society and one another?

3. Identify and discuss the social forces that have stimulated the emergence of a series of alternative life styles.

CHARLES LINDHOLM
CHERRY LINDHOLM

What Price Freedom?

Human societies display a remarkable variety of norms relating to sex, marriage, and family. For example, some societies are permissive, some restrictive; some allow individual choice of marital partners, some insist on arranged marriages; some regard sex between particular kinds of relatives as incestuous, others regard such a relationship as an obligation. But whatever the practices of a society are, and however strange they may seem to outsiders, they "work" in the culture where they are found. To understand norms of sex, marriage, and family, we must see them in their own context.

The Lepcha, a traditional people living in the Himalayan mountains of north India, are a people whose family system could hardly be more different from our own. Their elaborate incest rules, for example, even forbid adult brothers and sisters to touch one another, and also make it taboo for a son to sleep with a woman his father has had sex with. The Lepcha think it normal for a grown man to force a little girl to perform sexual acts; they know little or no sexual jealousy and are largely indifferent to adultery; and they generally do not link sex and emotion. These and other cultural traits would be considered immoral or nonsensical in American culture—just as American traits might seem to the Lepcha.

In this article, Charles and Cherry Lindholm describe the family system of the Lepcha, placing it in the full context of their social and cultural life.

First published in *Science Digest*, November/December 1980. Reprinted with permission from Charles Lindholm and Cherry Lindholm.

The two-day marriage ceremony is almost over. The oxen have been sacrificed, the Buddhist priests have said their prayers, the guests have presented their gifts of cloth and money and have been given proportionate amounts of meat in return. The bride and her relatives, who have come from a far-distant village, are sitting against the left wall of her new family's house, facing the groom and his family in customary fashion. The girl, though only 14, is slightly older than her young husband and is considered quite mature to be a new bride. She covers her face with her headcloth to hide her expression as the ritual discussion of her qualities begins between the families.

"We are giving you," announces her uncle, addressing the groom's family, "the yolk of this egg that we have peeled for you."

One of the groom's party replies, "Thank you very much. It is very kind of you. But it seems to us as if this egg has been nibbled at! And we would not be surprised if her pubic hair were not as long as that of a female devil or in appearance rather like a field of fresh corn."

"We assure you," retorts the bride's uncle, "that the egg has been freshly peeled to make it easy for you to eat."

"Well, it seems to us that the shell has been off for a very considerable time!"

"And what does it matter if her pubic hair is like a tangled bush? A clever goat can find its way through any bramble!"

This sexual joking during a solemn ritual occurs among the Lepcha people of Sikkim, a small Himalayan kingdom north of India. Since 1974, it has been an "associate state" of India, and the power of the *chogyal*, or king, is purely nominal. The Lepchas live primarily on a royal preserve set aside for them by ancestors of today's *chogyal*. There, the Lepchas are relatively free to pursue their ancient culture. The preserve, Jongu, is located in the precipitous valleys of the high Himalayas. Towering over all else is snow-capped, 28,208-foot Kanchenjunga, which ironically enough is worshipped as a war god by the peace-loving Lepchas.

There is probably not a 100-foot-square piece of flatland in the whole region, and cultivation often takes place at a 60-degree angle. The Lepchas find it impossible to use even mules for porterage and are obliged to carry all baggage on their own backs. But in spite of their harsh environment, the industrious Lepchas manage to grow rice, wheat, millet and maize, as well as a variety of fruits, vegetables and spices, including the spice cardamom, their only cash crop.

The climate is extremely wet, with occasional ruinous hailstorms. Famine is greatly feared, and most of the Lepchas religious rituals are designed to ward off hunger and disease.

They were first studied in 1876 by Colonel G. G. Mainwaring, a British officer. He was so impressed by their gentleness that he thought they were the original sinless children of Eve. Halfdan Siiger, who visited them in 1949, wrote that "they are by nature extremely kind, and when they lose their immediate fear of a stranger and gain confidence in him, they meet him with a lovely smile and an open mind, and above all with friendliness." The major anthropological work—*Himalayan Village*—was written by Geoffrey Gorer, who visited them in 1937 and was struck not only by their shyness and peaceful ways but also by their humorous verbal preoccupation with sex.

Indeed, to the Lepchas sex is continually and inexhaustibly funny. During village feasts, they spend their time eating, drinking *chi* (the very formidable local millet beer), and laughing heartily at the never-ending flow of sexual jokes and innuendos. In addition to the feasts given at births, marriages, deaths, and when visiting relatives arrive from distant villages, there are the monthly Lamaist festivals and large bimonthly monastery feasts. At such a feast, 80 or 90 people may be present and the merrymaking may even continue into the next day, with people catnapping intermittently. A dozen or so lamas (Buddhist priests) will be sitting in the main prayer room of the monastery, while the smaller prayer room will be occupied by six or seven nuns and a great number of other women, old men and young children. In the monastery yard, the wives of the feast-givers and anyone else who wishes will be busy with the large cook pots, preparing the vegetables, cereal, meat and *chi*.

The younger men and women and the older boys sit about on the grass and stones outside, chatting, joking, and occasionally fetching water or firewood for the cooking. The younger boys may hang about with them and listen to the conversations, but more often they either sit quietly on the grass or else play on the hill outside the monastery grounds, chasing hens or imitating birdcalls. The girls generally tag along with their parents or an older sister and will often be carrying a younger sibling. Small groups of toddlers sit some distance from the grown-ups, clustering silently around pots of *chi*, which they drink through bamboo straws; after a time, they become quite tipsy and noticeably less quiet; they stagger around for a while and then fall asleep. No one pays them any attention.

As the night wears on, people become more and more mellow, voices become louder, gestures more expansive, and there is much laughter at the obscene remarks that fly back and forth among the guests. Full of food and drink, some guests happily doze, while others occupy themselves with braiding one another's hair. Couples may wander off into the forest or to a nearby shed from time to time. Occasionally, there will be some lighthearted sexual byplay as a young man, or sometimes a young woman, grabs at another young man's penis, to the delight of the onlookers. Or an old man, having become quite drunk, will expose himself to the laughing throng. But for the most part, the sexual joking is verbal, and the ability to talk well and tell good stories is much admired among the Lepcha people.

It is generally thought that such sexual joking is the result of sexual frustration and inhibition, but among the Lepchas this is certainly not the case. Their sex lives are notoriously active. Impotence is unheard of and sexual activity continues until quite late in life for both men and women. There is no language of seduction or foreplay employed, since the Lepchas consider that anticipation alone guarantees sufficient stimulation; one simply makes a straightforward proposition, which is usually accepted. As Gorer notes, "Sexual activity is practically divorced from emotion; it is a pleasant and amusing experience, and as much a necessity as food and drink; and like food and drink it does not matter from whom you receive it, as long as you get it, though you are naturally grateful to the people who provide you with either item regularly."

Sexual jealousy is not considered a normal emotion and there is no word for jealousy in the language. In fact, certain relatives have an absolute right to sleep with one's wife, and as Chudo, a Lepcha man, told Gorer, "If I caught my elder brother's son sleeping with my wife, I shouldn't be cross at all; on the contrary, I should be very pleased, for she would be teaching him how to do it properly, and I would know that he had a good teacher."

Aside from nephews, a man's younger brothers also have free access to his wife, and boys are usually initiated into sex by an uncle's or brother's wife. Other men are also permitted to sleep with her, providing that they are not too blatant about it and do not have sex with her in the house unless the husband is away and unlikely to come home and witness the act.

Incest Taboos

This is not to say that Lepcha society is totally promiscuous. In fact, the range of partners prohibited by incest taboos is extremely wide; sex is forbidden with a partner related back at least seven generations on the father's side and at least four on the mother's. Ideally, the prohibitions should reach back nine generations on both sides, but this would render marriage almost impossible. It is also forbidden to sleep with a woman one's father has had sex with; this is considered incestuous, and fathers instruct their young sons early as to their permitted and prohibited sexual partners. The choices are limited by the rules of exogamy (marriage outside a group of lineal relatives), the wide range of incest prohibitions, and the fact that the Lepchas are mainly patrilocal (the wife moving in with the husband's family). Hence, sex with most girls who have grown up in the village is forbidden. (A large village consists of 50 to 60 houses.) Marriage and sex partners must come from some distance away. Siiger notes that "real ingenuity has to be exercised in order to find a suitable partner for one's son or daughter," and perhaps this is the reason for allowing the sharing of women within the village. Indeed, the fact that most people at any gathering will be sexually taboo might account for the extraordinary amount of sexual joking.

Girls usually have their first sexual encounters before puberty, as it is believed that a virgin girl will not normally grow breasts or begin menstruating but must have sexual intercourse in order for these transformations to occur. There is no stigma attached to a grown man forcing a little girl of 9 or 10 to have sex with him; such an occurrence, in fact, is considered quite amusing and is a subject for joking and laughter. If a girl starts menstruating while still a virgin—as does happen occasionally—it is thought that she has been visited by a supernatural, and this is considered an extremely lucky sign. Dreams of copulating with a supernatural being are supposed to come to a woman during every menstrual period; if, one month, she fails to have this dream, it signifies that she is shortly to die. This is the only sexual dream that the Lepchas admit to having.

Since most men in the home village are prohibited, women often have their first sexual experience with a visitor, and unrelated guests can therefore be quite popular. Gorer reports that his difficulty in obtaining information about sex from the women was not due to the jealousy of the husbands, as might be the case in many societies, but to "the fact that almost every woman from eight to eighty interpreted any sort of special attention as an attempt at seduction, an attempt which—no matter what their youth or age—they had no intention of repelling."

Marriages are not arranged by the parents but by the village headman. The partners must be the correct genealogical distance and have complementary horoscopes. Girls are usually engaged around the age of 9 and boys around the age of 12. No attention is paid to the desires of the young couple, and girls especially will often resist marriage, no doubt largely because it means leaving their home village. After the pair is engaged and the bride-price given, the boy and girl are expected to copulate under the watchful eyes of their uncles; this is thought to ensure the stability of the marriage. The period of

greatest sexual adventuring for the Lepcha boy and girl occurs during the engagement, especially if the couple do not particularly like each other or if their villages are far apart.

After the engagement, the boy must perform bride-service during visits to his in-laws' house, where he is treated as a servant and subjected to a great deal of sexual teasing. He is not allowed to retaliate in kind, and if he is provoked into doing so, he will be humiliated by his fiancee's family. The relationship with in-laws is one of the utmost respect; one should not direct obscene jokes toward them nor make such jokes in their presence, though when the engagement period is over this latter proscription is often ignored. Ideally, one should also behave with similar decorum toward one's parents and siblings of the opposite sex, but in Jongu the Lepchas are rather lax on this point of etiquette. The major prohibition is one that disallows adult brothers and sisters from touching one another, except during times of illness, and the brother-sister incest taboo is the most stringent of all. (Interestingly enough, the Lepchas creation myth claims that the original mother and father of the Lepcha people were brother and sister.) The breaking of an incest taboo has extremely serious consequences: it is believed to result in a year of disaster, not only for the man and woman involved but for the entire community in which they live.

This belief illustrates the structure of Lepcha society, for the Lepcha life-style is communal. People find their identity in their *ptso* (patriline) and village membership, and the ideal of cooperation, unselfishness and sharing comes close to being a reality. The Lepchas redistribute their resources to alleviate poverty, and sharing with the poor is considered a very good custom because, as one village headman explained, "It makes everybody realize that they are part of one group and the happiness of one is the happiness of all." Both children and adults are extraordinarily unselfish and always share things. Children are taught to help others, so that others in their turn will help them, and they are told that no one will help a thief. They are instructed to receive a gift in cupped hands and always to give a small gift in return. Gift-giving, which is a continuing motif in Lepcha life, is always an exchange, never simply one-sided receiving.

Among the Lepchas, relations are based on exact reciprocity and mutual obligations, and the individual who fulfills those obligations is automatically a good person and will be well liked. People express their liking for others. "I care for my parents because they gave me food," said one man. Another explained that "When I go out to work and come back tired, my wife has a good meal ready for me and looks after me; then I think 'This is my wife, and I am pleased in my belly.'" It is interesting to note that the stomach, not the heart, is considered to be the center of the emotions, and that past events are often remembered in terms of menus.

Life takes place within the range of the extended family. A man hopes to get responsibility for his family in his mid-thirties and to give up responsibility when he reaches 60. Children are therefore greatly desired, and adoption by childless couples is common. It is expected that the child will help his parents in their old age. Boys and girls, like men and women, are considered alike in their basic natures. The same rules of behavior apply to both sexes. Male and female work roles are not greatly differentiated; both sexes work in the fields, and men will take over the cooking if necessary. Although the society is patrilineal, with women unable to inherit land, the only real difference the Lepchas see between men and women is in the genitals, which are considered to have a sort of independent life very much of their own.

No Authority Figures

The Lepchas dislike anyone who tries to show authority. They work together in gangs, but no one tells another what to do and the headman leads by suggestion and example. Deviants are those who are aggressive, domineering and violent, and people who attempt to dominate will be excluded from the communal feasting cycle. However, such individuals, and even those who commit sodomy (which is thought to be like incest), are not considered personally responsible. Their behavior is thought to be a result of malevolent action by devils of the Lepcha religion.

The picture given so far of Lepcha life is idyllic. However, there is a darker side to this picture. The suicide rate of the Lepchas is extremely high. Women commit suicide by drowning, men by taking poison, and nearly all suicides occur directly after a public reproof for such transgressions as being lazy and neglecting one's work or failing to carry out properly one's obligations toward another. The Lepchas possess an overly sensitive sense of shame, and it is very easy to shame someone. While the rules of the society are somewhat flexible, antisocial behavior leads to exclusion, and a public shaming can often result in suicide, even when a person is wrongly accused. Not having a strongly developed sense of self, such as prevails in other cultures, a Lepcha cannot withstand the disapproval of the community. His feelings of aggression in this situation find their expression in self-destruction, just as in lesser cases a Lepcha who is angry will destroy his or her own possessions.

Communal life among the Lepchas ignores individual differences and stresses obligation rather than affect, or feeling. People exist only as a part of a larger whole. They are liked and accepted according to their fulfillment of obligations, not according to their individual personalities, which are not really recognized among the Lepchas. This lack of individuality is reflected in the fact that individual names are of almost no consequence in Lepcha culture; people are called by kinship terms, and it is even possible for a man to forget the actual name of his own wife. Arranged marriages are thought to work out well since they are merely a relation of mutual obligation such as might be set up between any two people. Providing both parties fulfill these obligations, they will automatically grow to like each other.

This underdeveloped sense of individuality is accompanied by a lack of creativity. There are no local arts and crafts except storytelling, and it is forbidden to invent new stories to enlarge the traditional stock. Individual inventiveness is seen mainly in the Lepchas' sexual joking. A general sense of lack of affect is apparent in the society, since all strong emotions are suppressed as threatening to the cooperative structure of the community. Relationships tend to be cut-and-dried, without much personal content. The basic cultural stance is one of indifference, and the most commonly heard phrase is *ket manin*, "it doesn't matter." The Lepchas are easily taken advantage of by unscrupulous Hindu merchants, who place them deeply in debt. Their culture requires specific protection by the state, for it soon disappears among Lepchas who leave the preserve. The concreteness and absolute quality of all relationships make the Lepchas extremely weak at working with abstract concepts, and the stress on smooth personal relationships eliminates the tension required for creative effort.

Children are raised to be dependent, passive and conformist. They are breast-fed until the next child comes along, an average of four years, but a youngest or only child may be given the breast until puberty. Though breast-fed by the mother only, infants are handled by everyone in the extended family and given a great deal of diffuse attention, being picked up as soon as they cry. Gorer was impressed by the lack of crying and the general passivity of the children and thought that the passionless quality of adult relationships was due to the diffuseness of childhood relationships. There does not seem to be a very strong emotional tie with the parents, and children tend to relate more to their older siblings.

Though children begin participating in adult labor at a very early age, no specific tasks, such as herding cattle, are assigned them, and Gorer attributes the young men's extreme boyishness, inability to stand alone and lack of self-reliance to their general lack of individual responsibility within the family. The developmental pattern for men is slow and even, with no great life-crisis events. Women seem more mature, perhaps because they must adjust early on in life to the trauma of leaving the home village and friends when they marry.

Bedeviled Childhood

Family life is not particularly warm. Though infants are

given much attention, that attention is rather impersonal, and the older child, though desired for his labor, is treated with a sort of impersonal neglect. Despite the lack of violence in the society, children are often beaten for getting in the way or interfering with adults, though the beatings are given without anger. Children are offered violence or succor with equal impersonality. They are trained by fear, and the most common way to gain obedience is to threaten a child with the vengeance of a devil. A child who still wants the breast after a new infant has been born will be told that the infant is a devil. Children who die are thought to become devils and are considered dangerous; hence, the adults' attitude toward children is ambiguous from the start. For the child, the world is a place of pervasive anxiety, and adults remember their childhoods as times of fear, hurt and obscurity. Children are, quite simply, miniature and relatively incompetent adults who do not even have the recompense of receiving respect for their work in the household.

Anxiety does not vanish with adulthood. The world is not beautiful, it is frightening, and the Lepcha pays no attention to the mountains that rise in splendor all around him but walks instead with his eyes on the ground. The religion of the Lepchas is primarily a religion of fear. Spirits of nature and of the dead are terrifying, and the aim of ritual is to keep them at bay. It may seem contradictory that such a peaceful people should have a religion with such violent and frightening iconography, but the human emotional makeup demands a balance. What cannot be expressed within society finds its expression in ritual, and the aggression the Lepchas deny in their daily lives is encountered in the threatening gods and devils of their religion.

Unneurotic Adults

Gorer ascribed the Lepcha character to the infants' toilet training, which is out of phase with psychosexual development, combined with diffuse and impersonal attention from many adults. Such a pattern will tend to produce "a society in which the great majority of adults will be unneurotic, unaggressive, generous, with undisturbed sexual potency. . . . they will also be uninventive, with no high art and little development of the crafts; no complexity will be meaningful. There will be little intensity in adult relations, and little passion in either life or art."

This picture may be oversimplifying the factors behind the development of the Lepcha personality. It must also be remembered that the Lepchas have a long history of oppression and have been enslaved several times in the past few hundred years by their more warlike neighbors of Nepalese extraction. The word *Lepcha*, in fact, indicates the people's low status, since it is a derogatory Nepalese term meaning "nonsense speakers." The Lepchas call themselves the Rong. Furthermore, their entire rela-

tion with their ecology has totally changed from the freedom of hunting and gathering to the restrictions of intensive agriculture.

The Lepchas—there are perhaps 20,000 of them in Sikkim at this time—are a dying culture. One authority notes that the decade 1961–71 "reveals the dismal fact that the Lepchas have a negative growth rate." They have a low birthrate and a high incidence of sterlity, suicide, disease and out-migration. Struggling to protect their cultural integrity, the Lepchas have evolved a complex and inwardly turned social order in which the aggressions of the outer world are countered by cooperation and sharing within the community.

QUESTIONS

1. List some significant differences between the family pattern of the Lepcha and our own.
2. How would you respond to someone who asserts that the sex life of the Lepcha is immoral?
3. When Europeans colonized much of the undeveloped Third World, Christian missionaries immediately attempted to change whatever sexual and family patterns they found, so that they would conform to the Western, middle-class model. What effects do you think this had on the local culture and social structure?

JULES HENRY

Golden Rule-Days:
American Schoolrooms

*Education is a crucial institution in all modern socie-
ties. To function effectively in these societies, people
must be introduced to a large and complex body of
knowledge, a need that is achieved most efficiently
through the use of schools and teachers. Unhappily,
however, not everyone can agree on what should be
taught in school or how it should be taught, and there
is no guarantee that people will learn what is expected
of them.*

*As Jules Henry points out in this article, formal
schooling must cope with a series of cultural contradictions. For example, the need for education is
greatest when cultural knowledge is expanding the
fastest—but that is precisely when the schools are
most likely to lag behind, teaching yesterday's or today's knowledge to tomorrow's citizens. Similarly, the
schools are expected to teach an approved body of
knowledge, including cultural norms and values—but
the very process of education stimulates independent
thought, thus encouraging some people to question and
challenge what they have been taught (and their teachers).*

*In his article, Henry draws on extensive observa-
tions of actual classroom situations to illustrate these
and other paradoxes of schooling.*

From *Culture Against Man* by Jules Henry. Copyright © 1963 by Random House, Inc. Reprinted by permission of Random House, Inc.

Introduction

School is an institution for drilling children in cultural
orientations. Educationists have attempted to free the
school from drill, but have failed because they have gotten lost among a multitude of phantasms—always choosing the most obvious "enemy" to attack. Furthermore,
with every enemy destroyed, new ones are installed
among the old fortifications—the enduring contradictory
maze of the culture. Educators think that when they have
made arithmetic or spelling into a game; made it unnecessary for children to "sit up straight"; defined the relation between teacher and children as democratic; and introduced plants, fish, and hamsters into schoolrooms,
they have settled the problem of drill. They are mistak-
en.

Education and the Human Condition

Learning to Learn

The paradox of the human condition is expressed more in
education than elsewhere in human culture, because
learning to learn has been and continues to be *Homo sapiens* most formidable evolutionary task. Although it is
true that mammals, as compared to birds and fishes, have
to learn so much that it is difficult to say by the time we
get to chimpanzees what behavior is inborn and what is
learned, the learning task has become so enormous for
man that today learning—education—along with survival, constitutes a major preoccupation. In all the fighting
over education we are simply saying that we are not yet
satisfied—after about a million years of struggling to become human—that we have mastered the fundamental
human task, learning. It must also be clear that we will
never quite learn how to learn, for since *Homo sapiens* is
self-changing, and since the *more* culture changes the
faster it changes, man's methods and rate of learning will
never quite keep pace with his need to learn. This is the
heart of the problem of "cultural lag," for each fundamental scientific discovery presents man with an incalcul-
able number of problems which he cannot foresee. Who,
for example, would have anticipated that the discoveries
of Einstein would have presented us with the social prob-

lems of the nuclear age, or that information theory would have produced unemployment and displacement in world markets?

Fettering and Freeing

Another learning problem inherent in the human condition is the fact that we must conserve culture while changing it; that we must always be *more* sure of surviving than of adapting—*as we see it*. Whenever a new idea appears our first concern as *animals* must be that it does not kill us; then, and only then, can we look at it from other points of view. While it is true that we are often mistaken, either because we become enchanted with certain modes of thought or because we cannot anticipate their consequences, this tendency to look first at survival has resulted in fettering the capacity to learn new things. In general, primitive people solved this problem simply by walling their children off from new possibilities by educational methods that, largely through fear (including ridicule, beating, and mutilation) so narrowed the perceptual sphere that other than traditional ways of viewing the world became unthinkable. Thus throughout history the cultural pattern has been a device for binding the intellect. Today, when we think we wish to free the mind so it will soar, we are still, nevertheless, bound by the ancient paradox, for we must hold our culture together through clinging to old ideas lest, in adopting new ones, we literally cease to exist.

In searching the literature on the educational practices of other civilizations I have found nothing that better expresses the need to teach and to fetter than the following, from an account by a traveler along the Niger River in Africa in the fourteenth century:

> . . . their zeal for learning the Koran by heart [is so great that] they put their children in chains if they show any backwardness in memorizing it, and they are not set free until they have it by heart. I visited the *qadi* in his house on the day of the festival. His children were chained up, so I said to him. "Will you not let them loose?" He replied, "I shall not do so until they learn the Koran by heart."[1]

Perhaps the closest material parallel we have to this from our own cultural tradition is the stocks in which ordinary English upper-class children were forced to stand in the eighteenth century while they pored over their lessons at home. The fettering of the mind while we "set the spirit free" or the fettering of the spirit as we free the mind is an abiding paradox of "civilization" in its more refined dimensions. It is obvious that chimpanzees are incapable of this paradox. It is this capacity to pass from the jungles of the animal world into the jungle of paradox of the human condition that, more than anything else, marks off human from animal learning. It is this jungle that confronts the child in his early days at school, and that seals

his destiny—if it has not previously been determined by poverty—as an eager mind or as a faceless learner.

Since education is always against some things and for others, it bears the burden of the cultural obsessions. While the Old Testament extols without cease the glory of the One God, it speaks with equal emphasis against the gods of the Philistines; while the children of the Dakota Indians learned loyalty to their own tribe, they learned to hate the Crow; and while our children are taught to love our American democracy, they are taught contempt for totalitarian regimes. It thus comes about that most educational systems are imbued with anxiety and hostility, that they are against as many things as they are for. Because, therefore, so much anxiety inheres in any human educational system—anxiety that it may free when it should fetter; anxiety that it may fetter when it should free; anxiety that it may teach sympathy when it should teach anger; anxiety that it may disarm where it should arm—our contemporary education system is constantly under attack. When, in anxiety about the present state of our world, we turn upon the schools with even more venom than we turn on our government, we are "right" in the sense that it is in the schools that the basic binding and freeing processes that will "save" us will be established. But being "right" derives not so much from the faults of our schools but from the fact that the schools are the central conserving force of the culture. The Great Fear thus turns our hostility unerringly in the direction of the focus of survival and change, in the direction of education.

Creativity and Absurdity

The function of education has never been to free the mind and the spirit of man, but to bind them; and to the end that the mind and spirit of his children should never escape *Homo sapiens* has employed praise, ridicule, admonition, accusation, mutilation, and even torture to chain them to the culture pattern. Throughout most of his historic course *Homo sapiens* has wanted from his children acquiescence, not originality. It is natural that this should be so, for where every man is unique there is no society, and where there is no society there can be no man. Contemporary American educators think they want creative children, yet it is an open question as to what they expect these children to create. And certainly the classrooms—from kindergarten to graduate school—in which they expect it to happen are not crucibles of creative activity and thought. It stands to reason that were young people truly creative the culture would fall apart, for originality, by definition, is different from what is given, and what is given is the culture itself. From the endless, pathetic, "creative hours" of kindergarten to the most abstruse problems in sociology and anthropology, the function of education is to prevent the truly creative intellect from getting out of hand. Only in the exact and the biological sciences do we permit unlimited freedom, for we have (but only since the Renaissance, since Galileo and Bruno underwent the Inquisition) found a way—or *thought* we had found a way—to bind the explosive powers of science in the containing vessel of the social system.

American classrooms, like educational institutions anywhere, express the values, preoccupations, and fears found in the culture as a whole. School has no choice; it must train the children to fit the culture as it is. School can give training in skills; it cannot teach creativity. All the American school can conceivably do is nurture creativity when it appears. And who has the eyes to see it? Since the creativity that is conserved and encouraged will always be that which seems to do the most for culture, which seems at the moment to do the most for the obsessions and the brutal preoccupations and anxieties from which we all suffer, schools nowadays encourage the child with gifts in mathematics and the exact sciences. But the child who has the intellectual strength to see through social shams is of no consequence to the educational system.

Creative intellect is mysterious, devious, and irritating. An intellectually creative child may fail, for example, in social studies, simply because he cannot understand the stupidities he is taught to believe as "fact." He may even end up agreeing with his teachers that he is "stupid" in social studies. Learning social studies is, to no small extent, whether in elementary school or the university, learning to be stupid. Most of us accomplish this task before we enter high school. But the child with a socially creative imagination will not be encouraged to play among new social systems, values, and relationships; nor is there much likelihood of it, if for no other reason than that the social studies teachers will perceive such a child as a poor student. Furthermore, such a child will simply be unable to fathom the absurdities that seem transparent *truth* to the teacher. What idiot believes in the "law of supply and demand," for example? But the children who do tend to *become* idiots, and learning to be an idiot is part of growing up! Or, as Camus put it, learning to be *absurd*. Thus the child who finds it impossible to learn to think the absurd the truth, who finds it difficult to accept absurdity as a way of life, the intellectually creative child whose mind makes him flounder like a poor fish in the net of absurdities flung around him in school, usually comes to think himself stupid.

The schools have therefore never been places for the stimulation of young minds. If all through school the young were provoked to question the Ten Commandments, the sanctity of revealed religion, the foundations of patriotism, the profit motive, the two-party system, monogamy, the laws of incest, and so on, we would have more creativity than we could handle. In teaching our children to accept fundamentals of social relationships and religious beliefs without question we follow the ancient highways of the human race, which extend backward into the dawn of the species, and indefinitely into the future. There must therefore be more of the caveman than of the spaceman about our teachers.

Up to this point I have argued that learning to learn is man's foremost evolutionary task, that the primary aim of education has been to fetter the mind and the spirit of man rather than to free them, and that nowadays we confront this problem in our effort to stimulate thought while preventing the mind of the child from going too far. I have also urged that since education, as the central institution for the training of the young in the ways of the culture, is thus burdened with its obsessive fears and hates, contemporary attacks upon our schools are the reflection of a nervousness inherent in the school as a part of the central obsession. Finally, I argued that creativity is the last thing wanted in any culture because of its potentialities for disruptive thinking; that the primordial dilemma of all education derives from the necessity of training the mighty brain of *Homo sapiens* to be stupid; and that creativity, when it is encouraged (as in science in our culture), occurs only after the creative thrust of an idea has been tamed and directed toward socially approved ends. In this sense, then, creativity can become the most obvious conformity. In this sense we can expect scientists—our cultural maximizers—to be socially no *more* creative than the most humble elementary school teacher, and probably less creative socially than a bright second-grader.

Communication

Much of what I have to say in the following pages pivots on the inordinate capacity of a human being to learn more than one thing at a time. Although it is true that all the higher orders of animals can learn several things at a time, this capacity for polyphasic learning reaches unparalleled development in man. A child writing the word "August" on the board, for example, is not only learning the word "August" but also how to hold the chalk without making it squeak, how to write clearly, how to keep going even though the class is tittering at his slowness, how to appraise the glances of the children in order to know whether he is doing it right or wrong, et cetera. If the spelling, arithmetic, or music lesson were only what it appeared to be, the education of the American child would be much simpler; but it is all the things the child learns *along with* his subject matter that really constitute the drag on the educational process as it applies to the curriculum.

A classroom can be compared to a communications system, for certainly there is a flow of messages between teacher (transmitter) and pupils (receivers) and among the pupils; contacts are made and broken, messages can be sent at a certain rate of speed only, and so on. But there is also another interesting characteristic of communications systems that is applicable to classrooms, and that is their inherent tendency to generate *noise. Noise,* in communications theory, applies to all those random fluctuations of the system that cannot be controlled. They are the sounds that are not part of the message: the peculiar quality communicated to the voice by the composition of the telephone circuit, the static on the radio, and so forth. In a classroom lesson on arithmetic, for example, such *noise* would range all the way from the competitiveness of the students, the quality of the teacher's voice ("I remember exactly how she sounded when she told me to sit down"), to the shuffling of the children's feet. The striking thing about the child is that along with his arithmetic—his "messages about arithmetic"—he learns all the noise in the system also. It is this inability to avoid *learning the noise with the subject matter* that constitutes one of the greatest hazards for an organism so prone to polyphasic learning as man. It is this that brings it about that an objective observer cannot tell which is being learned in any lesson, the *noise* or the formal subject matter. But—and mark this well—it is *not* primarily the message (let us say, the arithmetic or the spelling) that constitutes the most important subject matter to be learned, but the noise! The most significant cultural learnings—primarily the cultural drives—are communicated as *noise.*

Let us take up these points by studying selected incidents in some of the suburban classrooms my students and I studied over a period of six years.

The Realm of Song

It is March 17 and the children are singing songs from Ireland and her neighbors. The teacher plays on the piano, while the children sing. While some children sing, a number of them hunt in the index, find a song belonging to one of Ireland's neighbors, and raise their hands in order that they may be called on to name the next song. The singing is of that pitchless quality always heard in elementary school classrooms. The teacher sometimes sings through a song first, in her off key, weakishly husky voice.

The usual reason for having this kind of a song period is that the children are broadened, while they learn something about music and singing.

It is true that the children learn something about singing, but what they learn is to sing like everybody else, in the standard, elementary school pitchlessness of the English-speaking world—a phenomenon impressive enough for D.H. Lawrence to have mentioned it in *Lady Chatterly's Lover.* The difficulty in achieving true pitch is so pervasive among us that missionaries carry it with them to distant jungles, teaching the natives to sing hymns off key. Hence on Sundays we would hear our Pilagá Indian

friends, all of them excellent musicians in the Pilagá scale, carefully copy the missionaries by singing Anglican hymns, translated into Pilagá, off key exactly as sharp or as flat as the missionaries sang. Thus one of the first things a child with a good ear learns in elementary school is to be musically stupid; he learns to doubt or to scorn his innate musical capacities.

But possibly more important than this is the use to which teacher and pupils put the lesson in ways not related at all to singing or to Ireland and her neighbors. To the teacher this was an opportunity to let the children somehow share the social aspects of the lesson with her, to democratically participate in the selection of the songs. The consequence was distraction from singing as the children hunted in the index and raised their hands to have their song chosen. The net result was to activate the competitive, achievement, and dominance drives of the children, as they strove with one another for the teacher's attention, and through her, to get the class to do what they wanted it to do. In this way the song period on Ireland and her neighbors was scarcely a lesson in singing but rather one in extorting the maximal benefit for the Self from *any* situation. The first lesson a child has to learn when he comes to school is that lessons are not what they seem. He must then forget this and act as if they were. This is the first step toward "school mental health"; it is also the first step in becoming absurd. In the first and second grades teachers constantly scold children because they do not raise their hands enough—the prime symbol of having learned what school is all about. After that, it is no longer necessary; the kids have "tumbled" to the idea.

The second lesson is to put the teachers' and students' criteria in place of his own. He must learn that the proper way to sing is tunelessly and not the way *he* hears the music; that the proper way to paint is the way the teacher says, not the way he sees it; that the proper attitude is not pleasure but competitive horror at the success of his classmates, and so on. And these lessons must be so internalized that he will fight his parents if they object. The early schooling process is not successful unless it has accomplished in the child an acquiescence in its criteria, unless the child *wants* to think the way school has taught him to think. He must have accepted alienation as a rule of life. What we see in the kindergarten and the early years of school is the pathetic surrender of babies. How could it be otherwise?

Now, if children are taught to adopt alienation as a way of life, it follows that they must have feelings of inadequacy, for nothing so saps self-confidence as alienation from the Self. It would follow that school, the chief agent in the process, must try to provide the children with "ego support," for culture tries to remedy the ills it creates.

Hence the effort to give recognition; and hence the conversion of the songfest into an exercise in Self-realization. That anything essential was nurtured in this way is an open question, for the kind of individuality that was recognized as the children picked titles out of the index was mechanical, without a creative dimension, and under the strict control of the teacher. Let us conclude this discussion by saying that *school metamorphoses the child, giving it the kind of Self the school can manage, and then proceeds to minister to the Self it has made.*

Perhaps I have put the matter grossly, appearing to credit the school with too much formative power. So let us say this: let us grant that American children, being American, come to school on the first day with certain potentialities for experiencing success and failure, for enjoying the success of their mates or taking pleasure in their failure, for competitiveness, for cooperation, for driving to achieve or for coasting along, et cetera. But school cannot handle variety, for as an institution dealing with masses of children it can manage only on the assumption of a homogeneous mass. Homogeneity is therefore accomplished by defining the children in a certain way and by handling all situations uniformly. In this way no child is directly coerced. It is simply that the child must react in terms of the institutional definitions or he fails. The first two years of school are spent not so much in learning the rudiments of the three Rs, as in learning definitions.

It would be foolish to imagine that school, as a chief molder of character, could do much more than homogenize the children, but it does do more—it sharpens to a cutting edge the drives the culture needs.

If you bind or prune an organism so it can move only in limited ways, it will move rather excessively in that way. If you lace a man into a strait jacket so he can only wiggle his toes, he will wiggle them *hard*. Since in school children are necessarily constrained to limited human expression, under the direction of the teacher, they will have a natural tendency to do with exaggerated enthusiasm what they are permitted to do. They are like the man in the strait jacket. In class children are usually not permitted to talk much, to walk around much, to put their arms around each other during lessons, to whistle or sing. But they are permitted to raise their hands and go to the pencil sharpener almost at will. Thus hand-raising, going to the pencil sharpener, or hunting in the back of a song book for a song for the class to sing are not so much activities stemming from the requirements of an immediate situation as expressions of the intensified need of the organism for relief from the five-hour-a-day pruning and confining process. This goes under the pedagogical title of "release of tension"; but in our view the issue is that what the children are at length permitted—and invited—to do, and what they therefore often throw themselves into with the enthusiasm of multiple pent-up feelings, are cultural drive-activities narrowly construed by the school. In that context the next example is not only an expression by the

children of a wish to be polite, but an inflated outpouring of contained human capacities, released enthusiastically into an available—because approved—cultural channel.

On Hanging Up a Coat

The observer is just entering her fifth-grade classroom for the observation period. The teacher says, "Which one of you nice, polite boys would like to take [the observer's] coat and hang it up?" From the waving hands, it would seem that all would like to claim the title. The teacher chooses one child, who takes the observer's coat. The teacher says, "Now, children, who will tell [the observer] what we have been doing?"

The usual forest of hands appears, and a girl is chosen to tell. . . . The teacher conducted the arithmetic lessons mostly by asking, "Who would like to tell the answer to the next problem?" This question was usually followed by the appearance of a large and agitated forest of hands, with apparently much competition to answer.

What strikes us here are the precision with which the teacher was able to mobilize the potentialities in the boys for proper social behavior, and the speed with which they responded. One is impressed also with the fact that although the teacher could have said, "Johnny, will you please hang up [the observer's] coat?" she chose rather to activate all the boys, and thus give *them* an opportunity to activate their Selves, in accordance with the alienated Selfhood objectives of the culture. The children were thus given an opportunity to exhibit a frantic willingness to perform an act of uninvolved solicitude for the visitor; in this way each was given also a chance to communicate to the teacher his eagerness to please her "in front of company."

The mere appearance of the observer in the doorway sets afoot a kind of classroom destiny of self-validation and actualization of pupil-teacher communion, and of activation of the cultural drives. In the observer's simple act of entrance the teacher perceives instantly the possibility of exhibiting her children and herself, and of proving to the visitor, and once again to herself, that the pupils are docile creatures, eager to hurl their "company" Selves into this suburban American tragicomedy of welcome. From behind this scenery of mechanical values, meanwhile, the most self-centered boy might emerge a *papier maché* Galahad, for what he does is not for the benefit of the visitor but for the gratification of the teacher and of his own culturally molded Self. The large number of waving hands proves that most of the boys have already become absurd; but they have no choice. Suppose they sat there frozen?

From this question we move to the inference that the skilled teacher sets up many situations in such a way that *a negative attitude can be construed only as treason.* The function of questions like, "Which one of you nice polite boys would like to take [the observer's] coat and hang it up?" is to bind the children into absurdity—to compel them to acknowledge that absurdity is existence, to acknowledge that it is better to exist absurd than not to exist at all.

It is only natural, then, that when the teacher next asks, "Now who will tell what we have been doing?" and "Who would like to tell the answer to the next problem?" there should appear "a large and agitated forest of hands," for failure to raise the hand could be interpreted only as an act of aggression. The "arithmetic" lesson, transformed by the teacher, had become an affirmation of her matriarchal charisma as symbol of the system.

The reader will have observed that the question is not put, "Who *has* the answer to the next problem?" but "Who *would like to tell*" it? Thus, what at one time in our culture was phrased as a challenge to skill in arithmetic, becomes here an invitation to group participation. What is sought is a sense of "groupiness" rather than a distinguishing of individuals. Thus, as in the singing lesson an attempt was made to deny that it was a group activity, in the arithmetic lesson the teacher attempts to deny that it is an individual one. The essential issue is that *nothing is but what it is made to be by the alchemy of the system.*

In a society where competition for the basic cultural goods is a pivot of action, people cannot be taught to love one another, for those who do cannot compete with one another, except in play. It thus becomes necessary for the school, without appearing to do so, to teach children how to hate, for our culture cannot tolerate the idea that babes should hate each other. How does the school accomplish this ambiguity? Obviously through competition itself, for what has greater potential for creating hostility than competition? One might say that this is one of the most "creative" features of school. Let us consider an incident from a fifth-grade arithmetic lesson.

At the Blackboard

Boris had trouble reducing "$12/16$" to the lowest terms, and could only get as far as "$6/8$". The teacher asked him quietly if that was as far as he could reduce it. She suggested he "think." Much heaving up and down and waving of hands by the other children, all frantic to correct him. Boris pretty unhappy, probably mentally paralyzed. The teacher, quiet, patient, ignores the others and concentrates with look and voice on Boris. She says, "Is there a bigger number than two you can divide into the two parts of the fraction?" After a minute or two, she becomes more urgent, but there is no response from Boris. She then turns to the class and says, "Well, who can tell Boris what the number is?" A forest of hands appears, and the teacher calls Peggy. Peggy says that four may be divided into the numerator and the denominator.

Thus Boris's failure has made it possible for Peggy to succeed; his depression is the price of her exhilaration; his misery the occasion for her rejoicing. This is the standard condition of the American elementary school, and is why so many of us feel a contraction of the heart even if someone we never knew succeeds merely at garnering plankton in the Thames: because so often somebody's success has been bought at the cost of our failure. To a Zuni, Hopi, or Dakota Indian, Peggy's performance would seem cruel beyond belief, for competition, the wringing of success from somebody's failure, is a form of torture foreign to those noncompetitive redskins. Yet Peggy's action seems natural to us; and so it is. How else would you run our world! And since all but the brightest children have the constant experience that others succeed at their expense they cannot but develop an inherent tendency to hate—to hate the success of others, to hate others who are successful, and to be determined to prevent it. Along with this, naturally, goes the hope that others will fail. This hatred masquerades under the euphemistic name of "envy."

Looked at from Boris's point of view, the nightmare at the blackboard was, perhaps, a lesson in controlling himself so that he would not fly shrieking from the room under the enormous public pressure. Such experiences imprint on the mind of every man in our culture the *Dream of Failure*, so that over and over again, night in, night out, even at the pinnacle of success, a man will dream not of success, but of failure. *The external nightmare is internalized for life.* It is this dream that, above all other things, provides the fierce human energy required by technological drivenness. It was not so much that Boris was learning arithmetic, but that he was learning the *essential nightmare*. *To be successful in our culture one must learn to dream of failure.*

From the point of view of the other children, of course, they were learning to yap at the heels of a failure. And why not? Have they not dreamed the dream of flight themselves? If the culture does not teach us to fly from failure or to rush in, hungry for success where others have failed, who will try again where others have gone broke? Nowadays, as misguided teachers try to soften the blow of classroom failure, they inadvertently sap the energies of success. The result will be a nation of chickens unwilling to take a chance.

When we say that "culture teaches drives and values" we do not state the case quite precisely. One should say, rather, that culture (and especially the school) provides the occasions in which drives and values are *experienced in events* that strike us with *overwhelming and constant force*. To say that culture "teaches" puts the matter too mildly. Actually culture invades and infests the mind as an obsession. If it does not, culture will not "work," for only an obsession has the power to withstand the impact of critical differences; to fly in the face of contradiction; to engulf the mind so that it will see the world only as the culture decrees that it shall be seen; to compel a person to be absurd. The central emotion in obsession is fear, and the central obsession in education is fear of failure. In order not to fail most students are willing to believe anything and to care not whether what they are told is true or false. Thus one becomes absurd through being afraid; but paradoxically, *only by remaining absurd can one feel free from fear.* Hence the immovableness of the absurd.

In examining education as a process of teaching the culture pattern, I have discussed a singing lesson, an arithmetic lesson, and the hanging up of a coat. Now let us consider a spelling lesson in a fourth-grade class.

"Spelling Baseball"

The children form a line along the back of the room. They are to play "spelling baseball," and they have lined up to be chosen for the two teams. There is much noise, but the teacher quiets it. She has selected a boy and a girl and sent them to the front of the room as team captains to choose their teams. As the boy and girl pick the children to form their teams, each child chosen takes a seat in orderly succession around the room. Apparently they know the game well. Now Tom, who has not yet been chosen, tries to call attention to himself in order to be chosen. Dick shifts his position to be more in the direct line of vision of the choosers, so that he may not be overlooked. He seems quite anxious. Jane, Tom, Dick, and one girl whose name the observer does not know, are the last to be chosen. The teacher even has to remind the choosers that Dick and Jane have not been chosen. . . .

The teacher now gives out words for the children to spell, and they write them on the board. Each word is a pitched ball, and each correctly spelled word is a base hit. The children move around the room from base to base as their teammates spell the words correctly. With some of the words the teacher gives a little phrase: "Tongue: watch your tongue; don't let it say things that aren't kind:" "Butcher: the butcher is a good friend to have." "Dozen: twelve of many things." "Knee: get down on your knee." "Pocket: keep your hand out of your pocket, and anybody else's." "No talking! Three out!" The children say, "Oh, oh!"

The outs seem to increase in frequency as each side gets near the children chosen last. The children have great difficulty spelling "August." As they make mistakes, those in the seats say, "No!" The teacher says, "Man on third." As a child at the board stops and thinks, the teacher says, "There's a time limit; you can't take too long, honey." At last, after many children fail on "August" one child gets it right and returns, grinning with pleasure, to her seat. . . . The motivation level in this game seems terrific. All the children seem to watch the board, to know what's right and wrong, and seem quite keyed up. There is no lagging in moving from base to base. The child who is now writing "Thursday" stops to think after the first letter, and the children snicker. He stops after another letter. More snickers. He gets the word wrong. There are frequent signs of joy from the children when their side is right.

Since English is not pronounced as it is spelled, "language skills" are a disaster for educators as well as for students. We start the problem of "spelling baseball" with the fact that the spelling of English is so mixed up and contradictory and makes such enormous demands on the capacity for being absurd that nowadays most people cannot spell. "Spelling baseball" is an effort to take the "weariness, the fever, and the fret" out of spelling by absurdly transforming it into a competitive game. Over and over again it has seemed to our psychologist designers of curriculum scenery that the best way to relieve boredom is to transmute it into competition. Since children are usually good competitors, though they may never become good spellers, and although they may never learn to *spell* "success" (which really should be written sukses), they know what it *is,* how to go after it, and how it feels not to have it. A competitive game is indicated when children are failing, because the drive to succeed in the *game* may carry them to victory over the *subject matter.* At any rate it makes spelling less boring for the teacher and the students, for it provides the former with a drama of excited children, and the latter with a motivation that transports them out of the secular dreariness of classroom routine. "Spelling baseball" is thus a major effort in the direction of making things seem not as they are. But once a spelling lesson is cast in the form of a game of baseball a great variety of *noise* enters the system, because the sounds of *baseball* (the baseball "message") cannot but be *noise* in a system intended to communicate *spelling.* Let us therefore analyze some of the baseball noise that has entered this spelling system from the sandlots and the bleachers.

We see first that a teacher has set up a choosing-rejecting system directly adopted from kid baseball. I played ball just that way in New York. The two best players took turns picking out teammates from the bunch, coldly selecting the best hitters and fielders first; as we went down the line it did not make much difference who got the chronic muffers (the kids who couldn't catch a ball) and fanners (the kids who couldn't hit a ball). I recall that the kids who were not good players danced around and called out to the captains, "How about me, Slim? How about me?" Or they called attention to themselves with gestures and intense grimaces, as they pointed to their chests. It was pretty noisy. Of course, it didn't make any difference because the captains knew whom they were going to try to get, and there was not much of an issue after the best players had been sorted out to one or the other team. It was an honest jungle and there was nothing in it that did not belong to the high tension of kid baseball. But nobody was ever left out; and even the worst were never permitted to sit on the sidelines.

"Spelling baseball" is thus sandlot baseball dragged into the schoolroom and bent to the uses of spelling. If we reflect that one could not settle a baseball game by converting it into a spelling lesson, we see that baseball is bizarrely *irrelevant* to spelling. If we reflect further that a kid who is a poor speller might yet be a magnificent ballplayer, we are even further impressed that learning spelling through baseball is learning by absurd association. In "spelling baseball" words become detached from their real significance and become assimilated to baseballs. Thus a spelling game that promotes absurd associations provides an indispensable bridge between the larger culture, where doubletalk is supreme, and the primordial meaningfulness of language. It provides also an introduction to those associations of mutually irrelevant ideas so well known to us from advertising—girls and vodka gimlets, people and billiard balls, lipstick and tree-houses, et cetera.

In making spelling into a baseball game one drags into the classroom whatever associations a child may have to the impersonal sorting process of kid baseball, and in this way some of the *noise* from the baseball system enters spelling. But there are differences between the baseball world and the "spelling baseball" world also. Having participated in competitive athletics all through my youth, I seem to remember that we sorted ourselves by skills, and we recognized that some of us were worse than others. In baseball I also seem to remember that if we struck out or muffed a ball we hated ourselves and turned flips of rage, while our teammates sympathized with our suffering. In "spelling baseball" one experiences the sickening sensation of being left out as others are picked—to such a degree that the teachers even have to remind team captains that some are unchosen. One's failure is paraded before the class minute upon minute, until, when the worst spellers are the only ones left, the conspicuousness of the failures has been enormously increased: Thus the *noise* from baseball is amplified by a *noise* factor specific to the classroom.

It should not be imagined that I "object" to all of this, for in the first place I am aware of the indispensable social functions of the spelling game, and in the second place, I can see that the rendering of failure conspicuous, the forcing of it on the mind of the unchosen child by a process of creeping extrusion from the group, cannot but intensify the quality of the essential nightmare, and thus render an important service to the culture. Without nightmares human culture has never been possible. Without hatred competition cannot take place.

One can see from the description of the game that drive is heightened in a complex competitive interlock: each child competes with every other to get the words right; each child competes with all for status and approval among his peers; each child competes with the other children for the approval of the teacher; and finally, each competes as a member of a team. Here failure will be felt doubly because although in an ordinary spelling lesson one fails alone, in "spelling baseball" one lets down the children on one's team. Thus though in the game the motivation toward spelling is heightened so that success becomes triumph, so does failure become disaster. The greater the excitement the more intense the feeling of success and failure, and the importance of spelling or failing to spell "August" becomes exaggerated. But it is in the nature of an obsession to exaggerate the significance of events.

We come now to the *noise* introduced by the teacher. In order to make the words clear she puts each one in a sentence: "Tongue: watch your tongue; don't let it say things that aren't kind." "Butcher: the butcher is a good friend to have." "Dozen: twelve of many things." "Knee: get down on your knee." "Pocket: keep your hand out of your pocket, and anybody else's." More relevant associations to the words would be, "The leg bends at the knee." "A butcher cuts up meat." "I carry something in my pocket," etc. What the teacher's sentences do is introduce a number of her idiosyncratic cultural preoccupations, without clarifying anything; for there is no *necessary* relation between butcher and friend, between floor and knee, between pocket and improperly intrusive hands, and so on. In her way, therefore, the teacher establishes the same irrelevance between words and associations as the game does between spelling and baseball. She amplifies the *noise* by introducing ruminations from her own inner communication system.

Carping Criticism

The unremitting effort by the system to bring the cultural drives to a fierce pitch must ultimately turn the children against one another; and though they cannot punch one another in the nose or pull each other's hair in class, they can vent some of their hostility in carping criticism of one another's work. Carping criticism is so destructive of the early tillerings of those creative impulses we cherish, that it will be good to give the matter further review.

Few teachers are like Miss Smith in this sixth-grade class:

The Parent-Teachers Association is sponsoring a school frolic, and the children have been asked to write jingles for publicity. For many of the children, the writing of a jingle seems painful. They are restless, bite their pencils, squirm in their seats, speak to their neighbors, and from time to time pop up with questions like, "Does it have to rhyme, Miss Smith?" At last she says, "Alright, let's read some of the jingles now." Child after child says he "couldn't get one," but some have succeeded. One girl has written a very long jingle, obviously the best in the class. However, instead of using "Friday" as the frolic day, she used "Tuesday," and several protests were heard from the children. Miss Smith defended her, saying, "Well, she made a mistake. But you are too prone to criticize. If *you* could only do so well!"

In our six years of work, in hundreds of hours of observation in elementary and high schools, Miss Smith is unique in that she scolded the children for tearing down the work of a classmate. Other teachers support such attacks, sometimes even somewhat against their will.

"For many of the children, the writing of a jingle seems painful" says the record. "They are restless, bite their pencils, squirm in their seats. . . ." What are they afraid of but failure? This is made clear by Miss Smith's angry defense of the outstanding child as she says to her critics, "If only *you* could do so well!"

In a cooperative society carping is less likely to occur. Spiro says of the *kibbutz:*

> . . . The emphasis on group criticism can potentially engender competitive, if not hostile feelings among the children. Frequently, for example, the children read their essays aloud, and the others are then asked to comment. Only infrequently could we detect any hostility in the criticisms of the students, and often the evaluations were filled with praise.[2]

But in Miss Smith's class, because the children have failed while one of their number has succeeded, they carp. And why not? However we may admire Miss Smith's defense of the successful child, we must not let our own "inner Borises" befog our thinking. A competitive culture endures by tearing people down. Why blame the children for doing it?

Let us now consider two examples of carping criticism from a fifth-grade class as the children report on their projects and read original stories.

> Bill has given a report on tarantulas. As usual the teacher waits for volunteers to comment on the child's report.
>
> Mike: The talk was well illustrated and well prepared.
> Bob: Bill had a *piece of paper* [for his notes] and teacher said he should have them on *cards*. . . .
>
> Bill says he could not get any cards, and the teacher says he should tear the paper the next time he has no cards.
>
> Bob: He held the paper behind him. If he had had to look at it, it wouldn't have been very nice.
>
> The children are taking turns reading to the class stories they have made up. Charlie's is called *The Unknown Guest.*
>
> "One dark, dreary night, on a hill a house stood. This house was forbidden territory for Bill and Joe, but they were going in anyway. The door creaked, squealed, slammed. A voice warned them to go home. They went upstairs. A stair cracked. They entered a room. A voice said they might as well stay and find out now; and their father came out. He laughed and they laughed, but they never forgot their adventure together."
>
> Teacher: Are there any words that give you the mood of the story?
> Lucy: He could have made the sentences a little better. . . .
> Teacher: Let's come back to Lucy's comment. What about his sentences?

> Gert: They were too short.
>
> Charlie and Jeanne have a discussion about the position of the word "stood" in the first sentence.
>
> Teacher: Wait a minute; some people are forgetting their manners. . . .
> Jeff: About the room: the boys went up the stairs and one "cracked," then they were in the room. Did they fall through the stairs, or what?
>
> The teacher suggests Charlie make that a little clearer. . . .
>
> Teacher: We still haven't decided about the short sentences. Perhaps they make the story more spooky and mysterious.
> Gwynne: I wish he had read with more expression instead of all at one time.
> Rachel: Not enough expression.
> Teacher: Charlie, they want a little more expression from you. I guess we've given you enough suggestions for one time. [Charlie does not raise his head, which is bent over his desk as if studying a paper.] Charlie! I guess we've given you enough suggestions for one time, Charlie, haven't we? [Charlie half raises his head, seems to assent grudgingly.]

It stands to reason that a competitive system must do this; and adults, since they are always tearing each other to pieces, should understand that children will be no different. School is indeed a training for later life not because it teaches the 3 Rs (more or less), but because it instills the essential cultural nightmare fear of failure, envy of success, and absurdity.

QUESTIONS

1. In what sense does education both "fetter" and "free" us?

2. Schools have a "hidden curriculum" consisting of norms and values that are not consciously taught or learned, but which form part of the educational process nonetheless. Give some examples, drawing if possible from your own experience.

3. Do the schools merely reflect the society that exists, or can they also change it?

Notes

1. Ibn Battuta, *Travels in Asia and Africa,* London: Broadway House, Carter Lane, 1957, p. 330. (Translated and selected by H.A.R. Gibb, from the original written in 1325–54.)

2. Melford Spiro, *Children of the Kibbutz.* Harvard University Press, 1958, p. 261.

MARY JO BANE
CHRISTOPHER JENCKS

The Schools and Equal Opportunity

One of the most cherished American beliefs is that the schools can be used effectively for social engineering. Attempts have been made, for example, to prevent drug abuse through drug education; premarital pregnancy through sex education; traffic fatalities through driver education; and so on. The failure of such programs to achieve their goals has not dampened enthusiasm for reforming society through the schools, however, and for over a decade extensive use has been made of education as a means to achieve equality of opportunity in American society.

The argument for this strategy runs as follows. The United States is a highly unequal society, which is not desirable. People with high status generally have significantly more education than those with lower status. Those with less education are therefore handicapped from the outset. If they are to enjoy equal opportunity to get ahead, the children of the poor must have improved schooling, so they can start their careers with the same educational advantages as the children of the well-to-do. By thus compensating for deficiencies in the home and neighborhood environment, the schools can give everyone equal opportunity; success or failure will then depend on individual merit, rather than family or social class background.

In his important book Inequality *(1972), Christopher Jencks challenged this argument. His analysis of the available data indicated that equal educational opportunity would have very little effect on equality of opportunity, for it would not overcome the disadvantages that the children of the poor bring to school. The schools generally reflect society rather than change it—and if Americans really want equality, they should simply redistribute wealth instead of misguidedly manipulating the schools. In this article, Mary Jo Bane and Christopher Jencks outline that position.*

From *Saturday Review of Education*, September 16, 1972, pp. 37–42. Copyright © 1972 by Saturday Review. Reprinted by permission.

Americans have a recurrent fantasy that schools can solve their problems. Thus it was perhaps inevitable that, after we rediscovered poverty and inequality in the early 1960s, we turned to the schools for solutions. Yet the schools did not provide solutions, the high hopes of the early-and-middle 1960s faded, and the war on poverty ended in ignominious surrender to the *status quo*. In part, of course, this was because the war in Southeast Asia turned out to be incompatible with the war on poverty. In part, however, it was because we all had rather muddle-headed ideas about the various causes and cures of poverty and inequality.

Today there are signs that some people are beginning to look for new solutions to these perennial problems. There is a vast amount of sociological and economic data that can, we think, help in this effort, both by explaining the failures of the 1960s and by suggesting more realistic alternatives. For the past four years we have been working with this data. Our research has led us to three general conclusions.

First, poverty is a condition of relative rather than absolute deprivation. People feel poor and are poor if they have a lot less money than their neighbors. This is true regardless of their absolute income. It follows that we cannot eliminate poverty unless we prevent people from falling too far below the national average. The problem is economic inequality rather than low incomes.

Second, the reforms of the 1960s were misdirected because they focused only on equalizing opportunity to "succeed" (or "fail") rather than on reducing the economic and social distance between those who succeeded and those who failed. The evidence we have reviewed suggests that equalizing opportunity will not do very much to equalize results, and hence that it will not do much to reduce poverty.

Third, even if we are interested solely in equalizing opportunities for economic success, making schools more equal will not help very much. Differences between schools have very little effect on what happens to students after they graduate.

The main policy implication of these findings is that although school reform is important for improving the lives of children, schools cannot contribute significantly to adult equality. If we want economic equality in our society, we will have to get it by changing our economic institutions, not by changing the schools.

Poverty and Inequality

The rhetoric of the war on poverty described the persistence of poverty in the midst of affluence as a "paradox," largely attributable to "neglect." Official publications all assumed that poverty was an absolute rather than a relative condition. Having assumed this, they all showed progress toward the elimination of poverty, since fewer and fewer people had incomes below the official "poverty line."

Yet, despite all the official announcements of progress, many Americans still seemed poor, by both their own standards and their neighbors'. The reason was that most Americans define poverty in relative rather than absolute terms. Public-opinion surveys show, for example, that when people are asked how much money an American family needs to "get by," they typically name a figure about half what the average American family actually receives. This has been true for the last three decades, despite the fact that real incomes (incomes adjusted for inflation) have doubled in the interval.

During the Depression the average American family was living on about $30 a week. A third of all families were living on less than half this amount, which made it natural for Franklin Roosevelt to speak of "one-third of a nation" as ill-housed, ill-clothed, and ill-fed. By 1964 mean family income was about $160 a week, and the Gallup poll found that the average American thought a family of four needed at least $80 a week to "get by." Even allowing for inflation, this was twice what people had thought necessary during the Depression. Playing it safe, the Johnson administration defined the poverty line at $60 a week for a family of four, but most people felt this was inadequate. By 1970 inflation had raised mean family income to about $200 a week, and the National Welfare Rights Organization was trying to rally liberal support for a guaranteed income of $100 a week.

These changes in the definition of poverty were not just a matter of "rising expectations" or of people's needing to "keep up with the Joneses." The goods and services that made it possible to live on $15 a week during the Depression were no longer available to a family with the same real income ($40 a week) in 1964. Eating habits had changed, and many cheap foods had disappeared from the stores. Housing arrangements had changed, too. During the Depression many people could not afford indoor plumbing and "got by" with a privy. By the 1960s privies were illegal in most places. Those who still could not afford an indoor toilet ended up in buildings that had broken toilets. For these they paid more than their parents had paid for privies.

Examples of this kind suggest that the "cost of living" is not the cost of buying some fixed set of goods and services. It is the cost of participating in a social system. It therefore depends in large part on how much other people habitually spend to participate in the system. Those who fall far below the norm, whatever it may be, are excluded. Accordingly, raising the incomes of the poor will not eliminate poverty if the cost of participating in "mainstream" American life rises even faster. People with incomes less than half the national average will not be able to afford what "everyone" regards as "necessities." The only way to eliminate poverty is, therefore, to make sure everyone has an income at least half the average.

Arguments of this kind suggest not only that it makes more sense to think of "poverty" as a relative rather than an absolute condition but that eliminating poverty, at least as it is usually defined in America, depends on eliminating, or at least greatly reducing, inequality.

Schooling and Opportunity

Almost none of the reform legislation of the 1960s involved direct efforts to equalize adult status, power, or income. Most Americans accepted the idea that these rewards should go to those who were most competent and diligent. Their objection to America's traditional economic system was not that it produced inequality but that the rules determining who succeeded and who failed were often unfair. The reformers wanted to create a world in which success would no longer be associated with skin color, economic background, or other "irrelevant" factors, but only with actual merit. What they wanted, in short, was what they called "equal opportunity."

Their strategy for achieving equal opportunity placed great emphasis on education. Many people imagined that if schools could equalize people's cognitive skills this would equalize their bargaining power as adults. Presumably, if every one had equal bargaining power, few people would end up very poor.

This strategy for reducing poverty rested on a series of assumptions that went roughly as follows:

1. Eliminating poverty is largely a matter of helping children born into poverty to rise out of it. Once families escape from poverty, they do not fall back into it. Middle-class children rarely end up poor.

2. The primary reason poor children cannot escape from poverty is that they do not acquire basic cognitive skills. They cannot read, write, calculate, or articulate. Lacking these skills, they cannot get or keep a well-paid job.

3. The best mechanism for breaking this "vicious circle" is educational reform. Since children born into poor homes do not acquire the skills they need from their parents, they must be taught these skills in school. This can

be done by making sure that they attend the same schools as middle-class children, by giving them extra compensatory programs in school, by giving their parents a voice in running their schools, or by some combination of all three approaches.

Our research over the last four years suggests that each of these assumptions is erroneous:

1. Poverty is not primarily hereditary. While children born into poverty have a higher than average chance of ending up poor, there is still an enormous amount of economic mobility from one generation to the next. A father whose occupational status is high passes on less than half his advantage to his sons, and a father whose status is low passes along less than half his disadvantage. A family whose income is above the norm has an even harder time passing along its privileges; its sons are typically only about a third as advantaged as the parents. Conversely, a family whose income is below average will typically have sons about a third as disadvantaged as the parents. The effects of parents' status on their daughters' economic positions appear to be even weaker. This means that many "advantaged" parents have some "disadvantaged" children and vice versa.

2. The primary reason some people end up richer than others is not that they have more adequate cognitive skills. While children who read well, get the right answers to arithmetic problems, and articulate their thoughts clearly are somewhat more likely than others to get ahead, there are many other equally important factors involved. The effects of I.Q. on economic success are about the same as the effects of family background. This means, for example, that if two men's I.Q. scores differ by 17 points—the typical difference between I.Q. scores of individuals chosen at random—their incomes will typically differ by less than $2,000. That amount is not completely trivial, of course. But the income difference between random individuals is three times as large and the difference between the best-paid fifth and the worst-paid fifth of all male workers averages $14,000. There is almost as much economic inequality among those who score high on standardized tests as in the general population.

3. There is no evidence that school reform can substantially reduce the extent of cognitive inequality, as measured by tests of verbal fluency, reading comprehension, or mathematical skill. Eliminating qualitative differences between elementary schools would reduce the range of scores on standardized tests in sixth grade by less than 3 per cent. Eliminating qualitative differences between high schools would hardly reduce the range of twelfth-grade scores at all and would reduce by only 1 per cent the disparities in the amount of education people eventually get.

Our best guess, after reviewing all the evidence we could find, is that racial desegregation raises black elementary school students' test scores by a couple of points. But most of the test-score gap between blacks and whites persists, even when they are in the same schools. So also: Tracking has very little effect on test scores. And neither the overall level of resources available to a school nor any specific, easily identifiable school policy has a significant effect on students' cognitive skills or educational attainments. Thus, even if we went beyond "equal opportunity" and allocated resources disproportionately to schools whose students now do worst on tests and are least likely to acquire credentials, this would not improve these students' prospects very much.

The evidence does not tell us why school quality has so little effect on test scores. Three possible explanations come to mind. First, children seem to be more influenced by what happens at home than by what happens in school. They may also be more influenced by what happens on the streets and by what they see on television. Second, administrators have very little control over those aspects of school life that do affect children. Reallocating resources, reassigning pupils, and rewriting the curriculum seldom change the way teachers and students actually treat each other minute by minute. Third, even when the schools exert an unusual influence on children, the resulting changes are not likely to persist into adulthood. It takes a huge change in elementary school test scores, for example, to alter adult income by a significant amount.

Equal Opportunity and Unequal Results

The evidence we have reviewed, taken all together, suggests that equalizing opportunity cannot take us very far toward eliminating inequality. The simplest way of demonstrating this is to compare the economic prospects of brothers raised in the same home. Even the most egalitarian society could not hope to make opportunities for all children appreciably more equal than the opportunities now available to brothers from the same family. Looking at society at large, if we compare random pairs of individuals, the difference between their occupational statuses averages about 28 points on the Duncan "status scale" (the scale runs from 0 to 96 points). The difference between brothers' occupational statuses averages fully 23 points on this same scale. If we compare men's incomes, the difference between random pairs averaged about $6,200 in 1968. The difference between brothers' incomes, according to our best estimate, probably averaged about $5,700. These estimates mean that people who start off equal end up almost as unequal as everyone else. Inequality is not mostly inherited: It is re-created anew in each generation.

We can take this line of argument a step further by

comparing people who not only start off in similar families but who also have the same I.Q. scores and get the same amount of schooling. Such people's occupational statuses differ by an average of 21 points, compared to 28 points for random individuals. If we compare their incomes, making the additional assumption that the men have the same occupational status, we find that they differ by an average of about $5,300, compared to $6,200 for men chosen at random.

These comparisons suggest that adult success must depend on a lot of things besides family background, schooling, and the cognitive skills measured by standardized tests. We have no idea what these factors are. To some extent, no doubt, specialized varieties of competence, such as the ability to hit a ball thrown at high speed or the ability to persuade a customer that he wants a larger car than he thought he wanted, play a major role. Income also depends on luck: the range of jobs available when you are job hunting, the amount of overtime work in your plant, good or bad weather for your strawberry crop, and a hundred other unpredictable accidents.

Equalizing opportunity will not, then, do much to reduce economic inequality in America. If poverty is relative rather than absolute, equalizing opportunity will not do much to reduce poverty, either.

Implications for Educational Policy

These findings imply that school reform is never likely to have any significant effect on the degree of inequality among adults. This suggests that the prevalent "factory" model, in which schools are seen as places that "produce" alumni, probably ought to be abandoned. It is true that schools have "inputs" and "outputs," and that one of their nominal purposes is to take human "raw material" (*i.e.*, children) and convert it into something more "useful" (*i.e.*, employable adults). Our research suggests, however, that the character of a school's output depends largely on a single input, the characteristics of the entering children. Everything else—the school budget, its policies, the characteristics of the teachers—is either secondary or completely irrelevant, at least so long as the range of variation among schools is as narrow as it seems to be in America.

These findings have convinced us that the long-term effects of schooling are relatively uniform. The day-to-day internal life of the schools, in contrast, is highly variable. It follows that *the primary basis for evaluating a school should be whether the students and teachers find it a satisfying place to be.* This does not mean we think schools should be like mediocre summer camps, in which children are kept out of trouble but not taught anything. We doubt that a school can be enjoyable for either adults or children unless the children keep learning new things. We value ideas and the life of the mind, and we think that

a school that does not value these things is a poor place for children. But a school that values ideas because they enrich the lives of children is quite different from a school that values high reading scores because reading scores are important for adult success.

Our concern with making schools satisfying places for teachers and children has led us to a concern for diversity and choice. People have widely different notions of what a "satisfying" place is, and we believe they ought to be able to put these values into practice. As we have noted, our research suggests that none of the programs or structural arrangements in common use today has consistently different long-term effects from any other. Since the character of a child's schooling has few long-term effects, and since these effects are quite unpredictable, society has little reason to constrain the choices available to parents and children. If a "good school" is one the students and staff find satisfying, no one school will be best for everyone.

Since there is no evidence that professional educators know appreciably more than parents about what is good for children, it seems reasonable to let parents decide what kind of education their children should have while they are young and to let the children decide as they get older.

Short-term considerations also seem decisive in determining whether to spend more money on schooling or to spend it on busing children to schools outside their neighborhoods. If extra resources make school life pleasanter and more interesting, they are worthwhile. But we should not try to justify school expenditures on the grounds that they boost adult earnings. Likewise, busing ought to be justified in political and moral terms rather than in terms of presumed long-term effects on the children who are bused. If we want an integrated society, we ought to have integrated schools, which make people feel they have a stake in the well-being of other races. If we want a society in which people are free to segregate themselves, then we should apply that principle to our schools. There is, however, no compelling reason to treat schools differently from other social arrangements, including neighborhoods. Personally, we believe in both open housing and open schools. If parents or students want to take buses to schools in other neighborhoods, school boards ought to provide the buses, expand the relevant schools, and ensure that the students are welcome in the schools they want to attend. This is the least we can do to offset the effects of residential segregation. But we do not believe that forced busing can be justified on the grounds of its long-term benefits for students.

This leads to our last conclusion about educational reform. Reformers are always getting trapped into claiming too much for what they propose. They may want a particular reform—like open classrooms, or desegregation, or vouchers—because they think these reforms will make schools more satisfying places to work. Yet they feel obliged to claim that these reforms will also reduce the number of nonreaders, increase racial understanding, or strengthen family life. A wise reformer ought to be more modest, claiming only that a particular reform will not harm adult society and that it will make life pleasanter for parents, teachers, and students in the short run.

This plea for modesty in school reform will, we fear, fall on deaf ears. Ivan Illich is right in seeing schools as secular churches, through which we seek to improve not ourselves but our descendants. That this process should be disagreeable seems inevitable; one cannot abolish original sin through self-indulgence. That it should be immodest seems equally inevitable; a religion that promises anything less than salvation wins few converts. In school, as in church, we present the world as we wish it were. We try to inspire children with the ideals we ourselves have failed to live up to. We assume, for example, that we cannot make adults live in desegregated neighborhoods, so we devise schemes for busing children from one neighborhood to another in order to desegregate the schools. We all prefer conducting our moral experiments on other people. Nonetheless, so long as we confine our experiments to children, we will not have much effect on adult life.

Implications for Social Reform

Then how *are* we to affect adult life? Our findings tell us that different kinds of inequality are only loosely related to one another. This can be either encouraging or discouraging, depending on how you look at it. On the discouraging side, it means that eliminating inequality in one area will not eliminate it in other areas. On the encouraging side, it means that inequality in one area does not dictate inequality in other areas.

To begin with, genetic inequality is not a major obstacle to economic equality. It is true that genetic diversity almost inevitably means considerable variation in people's scores on standardized tests. But this kind of cognitive inequality need not imply anything like the present degree of economic inequality. We estimate, for example, that if the only sources of income inequality in America were differences in people's genes, the top fifth of the population would earn only about 1.4 times as much as the bottom fifth. In actuality, the top fifth earns seven times as much as the bottom fifth.

Second, our findings suggest that psychological and cultural differences between families are not an irrevocable barrier to adult equality. Family background has more influence than genes on an individual's educational attainment, occupational status, and income. Nonetheless, if family background were the only source of economic inequality in America, the top fifth would earn only about twice as much as the bottom fifth.

Our findings show, then, that inequality is not determined at birth. But they also suggest that economic equality cannot be achieved by indirect efforts to manipulate the environments in which people grow up. We have already discussed the minuscule effects of equalizing school quality. Equalizing the amount of schooling people get would not work much better. Income inequality among men with similar amounts of schooling is only 5–10 per cent less than among men in general. The effect is even less if we include women.

If we want to eliminate economic inequality, we must make this an explicit objective of public policy rather than deluding ourselves into thinking that we can do it by giving everyone equal opportunity to succeed or fail. If we want an occupational structure which is less hierarchical and in which the social distance between the top and the bottom is reduced, we will have to make deliberate efforts to reorganize work and redistribute power within organizations. We will probably also have to rotate jobs, so that no individual held power very long.

If we want an income distribution that is more equal, we can constrain employers, either by tax incentives or direct legislation, to reduce wage disparities between their best- and worst-paid workers. We can make taxes more progressive, and we can provide income supplements to those who do not make an adequate living from wages alone. We can also provide free public services for those who cannot afford to buy adequate services in the private sector. Pursued with vigor, such a strategy can make "poverty" (*i.e.*, having a living standard less than half the national average) virtually impossible. Such a strategy would also make economic "success," in the sense of having, say, a living standard more than twice the national average, far less common than it now is. The net effect would be to make those with the most competence and luck subsidize those with the least competence and luck to a far greater extent than they do today. Unless we are prepared to do this, poverty and inequality will remain with us indefinitely.

This strategy was rejected during the 1960s for the simple reason that it commanded relatively little popular support. The required legislation could not have passed Congress, nor could it pass today. That does not mean that it is the wrong strategy. It simply means that, until we change the political and moral premises on which most Americans now operate, poverty and inequality will persist at pretty much their present level. Intervention in market processes, for example, means restricting the "right" of individuals to use their natural advantages for private gain. Economic equality requires social and legal sanctions—analogous to those that now exist against capricious firing of employees—against inequality within work settings. It also requires that wage rates, which Americans have traditionally viewed as a "private" question to be adjudicated by negotiation between (unequal) individuals or groups, must become a "public" question subject to political control and solution.

In America, as elsewhere, the long-term drift over the past 200 years has been toward equality. In America, however, the contribution of public policy to this drift has been slight. As long as egalitarians assume that public policy cannot contribute to equality directly but must proceed by ingenious manipulations of marginal institutions like the schools, this pattern will continue. If we want to move beyond this tradition, we must establish political control over the economic institutions that shape our society. What we will need, in short, is what other countries call socialism. Anything less will end in the same disappointments as the reforms of the 1960s.

QUESTIONS

1. Why do you think programs of driver education, drug education, and sex education have had little or no impact on the problems they were intended to solve?

2. What factors account for the generally depressed educational achievement of children from the working and lower classes?

3. Assess the argument that equality could be best achieved through political and economic rather than educational reform. Are such reforms likely?

THOMAS ROBBINS
DICK ANTHONY

New Religions, Families, and Brainwashing

Unlike many societies, the United States has no "official" religion, and Americans are generally tolerant of one another's religious beliefs. But tolerance of religious diversity has its limits, and there is considerable distrust of, and antagonism toward, some of the newer and smaller sects, such as the Hare Krishna movement, the Children of God, and the Unification Church (or "Moonies").

The objection to these sects seems to be twofold. First, their beliefs appear, from the viewpoint of the dominant Judeo-Christian tradition, to be somewhat bizarre. Second, their converts, typically living in closed communities, are widely regarded as the victims of "brainwashing"—in other words, as persons whose thought processes and freedom of choice have been crippled by intense, systematic psychological pressure. An anticult movement has now arisen, composed largely of parents and other family members who use various techniques, sometimes including kidnapping and forcible "deprogramming" by self-styled experts, to win the converts back from the sects.

In this article Thomas Robbins and Dick Anthony question whether the concept of "brainwashing" is a valid one, and argue that families have no intrinsic right to interfere in their members' religious choices. A more important issue, they contend, is why young people are tempted to relinquish their critical faculties and join these authoritarian sects in the first place.

The religious wars of the seventies have involved accusations that new religious movements brainwash their converts. They are alleged to be using mind control in seducing young persons from conventional familial processes and career plans so as to psychologically imprison them in communes and monasteries. Increasingly the state is sanctioning the forcible abduction of adult converts for purposes of counterindoctrination or deprogramming. The involvement of the state in facilitating such reeducation programs has been both active and passive: passive through refusal of local courts to prosecute the perpetrators of extralegal abductions; active because of a more recent tendency of lower-court judges to issue thirty-day conservatorships to parents of allegedly incompetent religious converts. Parents who obtain conservatorships are then empowered to receive the assistance of police in forcibly seizing the converts and turning them over to deprogrammers.

Such conservatorships are frequently granted in ex parte "hearings" in the judge's chambers from which the potential conservatee and his legal representative are excluded. In such a closed hearing the proposed target of the conservatorship has no opportunity to challenge information which parents, deprogrammers, and apostate devotees may impart to a judge. Nor may the religious converts present counter-testimony regarding the impugned cult or their own mental state.

In addition to existing state laws facilitating these practices, several state legislatures have been asked to consider new legislation supporting the forcible removal of adults from cults. The Vermont senate, moreover, has recently passed a bill empowering judges to issue conservatorships in such cases without adversary hearings.

These procedures have raised serious questions with respect to the issues of due process of law and freedom of religion. Are there *any* circumstances under which the administrative processes of the state can properly be used to change a person's religious beliefs without jeopardizing the traditional separation of church and state? Should even incompetent persons be forcibly subjected to religious counterindoctrination?

Defenders of deprogramming argue that the true issue is not freedom of religion but freedom of thought. Such freedom is—given this interpretation—impossible while a convert is in the grips of the malevolent mind control which cults and pseudoreligions are accused of practicing on helpless young persons. As attorney Michael Trauscht stated at a well-publicized San Francisco hearing involving conservatorships over five followers of Reverend Sun Myung Moon: "Certainly the First Amendment guarantees freedom of religion, but necessary to each guaranteed freedom is freedom of thought." Since cultists allegedly do not possess this freedom of thought, their forcible seizure and physical restraint for purposes of deprogramming does not violate civil liberties. Such liberties are to pertain exclusively to rational and responsible persons who are not brainwashed.

Critics have noted an element of mystification in the controversy over alleged cultic brainwashing. Thomas Szasz argues: "Brainwashing is a metaphor. A person can no more wash another's brain with coercion or conversion than he can make him bleed with a cutting remark." Other psychiatrists might quarrel with the absolutist dictum that the concepts of brainwashing and coercive persuasion are inherently subjective and obscurantist. Nevertheless, most psychiatrists would probably be hesitant about transferring a concept developed in the study of P.O.W. camps to the context of formally voluntary spiritual movements. It seems far-fetched to equate movements such as Hare Krishna or the Unification church, which exhibit a rapid turnover and a high dropout rate (even without deprogramming), with P.O.W. camps.

As voluntary associations go, these movements *are* relatively authoritarian and totalistic. To the degree that they are, however, they are not really cults at all. The authoritarian movements to which this concept has been popularly applied by the anticult movement—the Children of God, the Unification church, or Hare Krishna—really correspond more to the sociological concept of sect than to the concept of cult, which generally denotes a relatively unstructured, loosely organized, and tolerant collectivity. (However, *sect* has a vaguely respectable connotation, while *cult* evokes occultism and the image of men wearing hoods and performing secret rituals in cellars. These unsavory associations to the term *cult* have been exploited at the expense of linguistic precision by the anticult movement.)

Nevertheless, even authoritarian sects such as the Unification church and Hare Krishna are not in the final analysis true total institutions in which the management has total control over movement to and from the premises. The psychological and peer group pressures which are mobilized to inhibit leaving cults should probably not be equated with armed guards and fences in their capacity to influence attitudes. Such nonphysical pressures are indeed frequently unavailing, since many converts do leave voluntarily. Moreover, a high percentage of those who attend initial meetings or workshops do not subsequently return for further indoctrination.

The metaphor of brainwashing can probably best be understood as a social weapon which provides a libertarian rationale for persecuting unpopular social movements and ideologies. There are three aspects of the current use of the metaphor which allow it to serve this purpose: its subjective status, a concealed concern with the content of others' beliefs, and an authoritarian denial that unpopular beliefs could be voluntarily chosen.

Subjectivity of Brainwashing Notions

The subjectivity of *brainwashing, psychological kidnapping,* and *mind control* notions—as they are being used in the present controversy—suggests that these terms are being used as weapons of repression. It is easy to maintain that this or that monastery or commune interweaves dogma and ritual in such a way as to lock converts into rigid thought patterns. Why has it been mainly foreign Communists and domestic religious minorities who have been popularly believed to use mind control techniques (i.e, not parents, parochial schools, or marine boot camp)?

Edgar Schein has commented on this matter in *Coercive Persuasion,* a report on his research on Americans "brainwashed" by Chinese Communists. He argues that if the notion of coercive persuasion is to achieve objective status, it must be acknowledged as occurring in a variety of culturally valued contexts, e.g., religious orders, the army, fraternities, and mental hospitals. In his view the nature of the influence process is essentially the same in the Chinese and traditional American contexts. The Chinese case is distinguished from the others not by the techniques involved but rather by our general disapproval of the goal of the former process, namely the conversion of American citizens into Chinese patriots.

In his work Schein dealt with this issue with some subtlety. However, the present antagonists of cults have neglected to distinguish—as he did—between factual and evaluative claims about influence processes. They have capitalized upon the popular dislike of Chinese influence over American citizens by pointing out vague similarities in the influence process between the thought reform context and cultic conversion. Because the goal of the influence process, i.e., conversion to Chinese citizenship, was widely disapproved of in the Chinese case, they have argued that the goal of vaguely similar processes of influence, i.e., religious conversion, should be legitimately suppressed in the present instance. They have failed to acknowledge, as Schein did, that such influence processes are very common in traditional social institutions. The logic of their argument, then, would lead either to legal suppression of monasteries, fraternities, the Boy Scouts, and Alcoholics Anonymous, or to granting courts a discretionary authority in suppressing membership in voluntary associations, which is inconsistent with our legal traditions. While the former is not likely to occur, the granting of inherently subjective discretionary power to the courts in suppressing unpopular cults via the conservator laws has been noted above.

In spite of his own impeccable ideological neutrality, Schein has probably contributed somewhat to this subjective use of the brainwashing notion by downplaying the role of physical restraints (e.g., Chinese internment of American citizens) in coercive persuasion. In the absence of tangible physical restraint, what is the criterion for inferring a washed brain or an imprisoned will? Unless one focuses on explicit physical force—restraint over protest—it is impossible to prove or disprove the allegation that this or that program of heavy-handed sectarian indoctrination constitutes mind control which is inappropriate to a degree which justifies legal intervention. Brainwashing divorced from physical restraint is generally in the eye of the beholder.

Concealed Concern with Beliefs

The subjective use of the brainwashing metaphor in the manner noted above allows its proponents to argue that they are not really concerned with the content of beliefs and opinions but rather with the way in which these opinions are held or the manner in which they have been developed (i.e., through mind control). Parents and deprogrammers claim to be responding not so much to the specific insupportable beliefs, but to a general "brainwashed state of mind" manifested by young devotees. If this were so it might be anticipated that deprogramming would not necessarily alter beliefs but would enable devotees to hold their beliefs in a more flexible manner, i.e., a rigid Moonie might become a thinking Moonie. But the assault on specific beliefs is relentless. A frequent technique of deprogrammers in the Northeast is to guide their charges through hours of bible study to expose the allegedly false scriptural interpretations of Reverend Moon and other gurus. Byong-suh Kim, a sociologist who studied deprogramming in New Hampshire, characterizes the process as an "attempt to remove that belief system which was perceived as a function of the 'mind-controlling.' " Joe Alexander, senior deprogrammer at the Freedom of Thought Foundation at Tucson, Arizona, has acknowledged that he aims at convincing his charges that their involvement with Reverend Moon or Hare Krishna is not "of God."

Thus, candidates for deprogramming are actually viewed as brainwashed mainly by virtue of their affiliation with a certain religious group and their adherence to certain beliefs. More importantly, a deprogrammee is viewed as having been liberated from mind control and having regained mental competence only when he actually recants his beliefs. Pressure can thus be applied to reli-

gious or political movements and their members can be subjected to forcible confinement for purposes of counter-indoctrination without the acknowledgment of any intention to suppress a point of view. In this connection it is noteworthy that deprogrammers are frequently foiled by dissimulation on the part of their captives.

According to the Los Angeles *Herald Examiner,* one deprogrammer has warned that "the therapist has to be astute because a cultee can try to fool him into thinking the deprogramming has been successful when it hasn't." Indeed there have been instances where persons earned release from captivity (or a lightening of physical restraint facilitating escape) by dissimulating, and subsequently returned to their cult. Obviously such therapists are highly vulnerable to dissimulation because they are using religious belief as an essential criterion of mental health. Additional criteria of mental health would render the therapist less dependent upon the deprogrammee's overt profession of belief or nonbelief. Deprogramming can thus be seen as an inquisition against heresy formulated in terms of mental health and freedom from brainwashing.

"Involuntary" Nature of Unpopular Beliefs

The application of brainwashing and mind control metaphors to members of a social movement implies that they are not acting or thinking voluntarily and are not therefore entitled to the freedom of religion and freedom from physical restraint which applies to rational individuals. . . . But are converts to authoritarian sects merely passive victims of conditioning? The latent assumption of those who support coercive deprogramming seems to be that no one would ever voluntarily surrender intellectual freedom and flexibility; hence those who submit to regimentation must have been coercively persuaded to do so. But people have been voluntarily joining totalistic movements for centuries, and much of the literature on Christianity in its first century of existence depicts the early Christians in totalistic and authoritarian terms.

Sectarian commitment might be alternatively conceptualized as an exchange relationship. This point has been made effectively by Mark Rasmussen, who observed a Unification church indoctrination workshop. Although personally hostile to Moonism, Rasmussen concluded that "the desire to abandon reason for emotion had to be present before the person came to the workshop. No one was drugged or hypnotized or strapped to a chair. And the new identity which emerged from the workshop was an assertion of self that came from *submission:* submission to emotion, to the group, to a commitment to a new set of ideals. It was a willful submission." Rasmussen further comments: "I think the Moonies gave up a lot in their regimented devotion—they gave up the chance to think, to read, to confront—and the struggle for me was to recognize and respect the fact that they found in Moon something that was more important to them than certain things I value."

The Brainwashing Metaphor and the Decline of Familism

If the current use of the brainwashing metaphor is indeed best understood as a social weapon being used against forms of heresy, we might well ask, Heresy against what? What is the nature of the social reality being threatened by nontraditional religions, and who has a stake in protecting it? Members of the anticult movement have argued that the social reality which they are protecting is the integrity of the American family.

Part of the motivation for conversion to currently popular religious movements *is* the decline of American familism. However, the anticult movement not only fails to protect the family but may in some ways hasten its decline. (At best the movement may enable some of its members to conceal from themselves the reality and the causes of that decline.) The brainwashing metaphor and the style of argumentation within which it operates is a form of false consciousness which is itself a symptom of the social forces which it purports to explain.

The present use of the brainwashing concept involves an application of the medical model to religion. Certain religious beliefs are consigned to the realm of involuntary pathological symptoms. Despite growing criticism of the medical model by labeling theorists and antipsychiatrists, the importance of the model is likely to be enhanced in a society in moral flux in which authorities are hesitant to acknowledge a punitive intent and thus increasingly rely on social scientists to provide therapeutic legitimations for social control. . . .

The present revival of brainwashing mystiques is taking place in the context of a general backlash against forms of dissent and nonconformity which flourished in the late sixties and early seventies. Feminists, gay militants, and new religions are all experiencing retaliation for their stridency in the past decade (ironically, some guru groups and Jesus sects are antifeminist and socially conservative). . . .

"Cults" like gay militants apparently are being used as scapegoats for the decline of American familism. "Brainwashing" is a convenient stick with which to beat totalistic sects which "break up families" and remove converts from conventional social processes. Countercult groups which are mushrooming across the nation thus generally dedicate themselves to "reuniting families" as well as "freeing minds." It is of course quite true that some of the more authoritarian sects such as The Children of God, Hare Krishna, or the Unification church of Reverend Sun Myung Moon have discouraged the main-

tenance of close family ties outside the movement. It is worth noting, however, that there has been a recurrent tendency in the history of American sectarianism for new movements to exalt the spiritual "brethren" at the expense of the "fleshly" kindred. This is hardly a new development or a consequence of a new technology of mind control. What is new is the availability of a technodeterministic vocabulary (e.g., *programming, mind control*) with which frustrated relatives may express their anger and bewilderment.

Kenneth Keniston in *All Our Children: The American Family under Pressure* has shown that the integrity of the family has declined at least partly because other social institutions, e.g., schools, the medical profession, social welfare agencies, and psychotherapy, have taken over many of its functions. Such agencies have stripped the family of its legitimacy but have not been able to replace it as a context for supplying interpersonal warmth and commitment. Such trends seem relevant to the current controversy. Young people are at a stage in life when they are neither locked into the impersonal bureaucratic institutional structure nor the discredited traditional family structure. Therefore they are more likely than their parents to attempt to resolve the tension between the two realms by choosing a radical alternative to both.

It is not surprising that young people have turned to novel religions in seeking alternative social forms within which such tensions may be lessened. Traditional religion has normally served to legitimize the family's status as the arbiter of expressivity. Religion has in theory been the ultimate authority on affective issues but it has ceded practical authority to the family. . . . Psychiatrists and social welfare agencies have increasingly usurped these functions from the family—and from traditional religion as well. Understandably, young people have turned to nontraditional religions as a way of returning ultimate control over affective legitimacy to groups, i.e., cults, which resemble extended families.

An increasing consensus of informed commentators—most recently Harvey Cox in his book *Turning East*—have viewed the growing popularity of exotic sects and cults in these terms. Many such groups provide a reintegration of affective and instrumental functions into a coherent social unit in a way which the discredited family no longer can. The groups which attempt the most radical sectarian solution to this problem, e.g., Reverend Moon's Unification church and the Hare Krishna movement, tend to encourage withdrawal from normal worldly involvements—most explicitly from bureaucratic institutions which have compromised the integrity of the family.

As Keniston has argued, larger institutions have usurped the authority of the family but not its culpability. Parents continue to think of themselves as responsible for the way their children turn out because schools and psychotherapists blame them when things go wrong. It is not surprising that they react defensively when their children repudiate the social institutions with which they are identified. Nor is it surprising—although it is ironic—that they have chosen a metaphor, i.e., brainwashing, to account for such repudiation which originates from within social scientific rhetoric.

. . .

. . . By their acceptance of this metaphor, parents tend to mask the nature of the value conflict between themselves and their children. No one could disagree with the logic of bureaucratic social processes and be in his right mind, goes this line of reasoning. Our children only *appear* to be repudiating our values because they have been driven crazy by evil men. In this way parents are able to absolve themselves of responsibility for their children's defection. Moreover, by using the social scientific style of explanation of deviant behavior, they hope to enlist the aid of those institutions to which they have ceded their authority, e.g., courts and psychiatrists, in subduing their children's desertion from themselves and their world.

There is a nice irony here. Many cults such as Scientology, *est*, Hare Krishna, or Nicheren Shoshu eagerly exploit the pervasive sense of powerlessness which afflicts many Americans. These groups offer techniques which will enable the individual to "take power in his life" or "make his life work." . . . Mastery and self-management are emphasized, but the latent premise is that in today's milieu no one is spontaneously masterful; only the person who meditates, chants, or is "trained" really has free will. Everyone outside of the movement is enmeshed in Karma or ensnared by Satan, etc. Deprogrammers merely reverse the scenario and view only those in cults as incapable of rational mastery. Only cultists are brainwashed, the rest of us are free—bureaucratic domination, media manipulation, and monopoly capitalism notwithstanding. . . .

In our view, the upsurge of cults is indeed associated with trends undermining familial solidarity in America, but cultism is more a consequence than a cause of such trends. A study of J. Stillson Judah indicates that West Coast Moonies frequently become alienated from both parents and conventional routines *prior* to conversion to the Unification church. . . . Research conducted by James T. Richardson suggests that conversion to a communal Jesus sect is not an isolated discrete event but is generally part of a broader sequence of spiritual seeking and experimentation with new lifestyles which Richardson terms a conversion "career." Available research is thus not consistent with a model of psychological kidnapping in which an otherwise dutiful and conformist young citizen is hypnotically overwhelmed and imprisoned in a deviant lifestyle which would otherwise be anathema.

. . .

As Rasmussen and others have noted, there is a strong likelihood that such devotees have really *chosen* to enter an ordered utopian environment and partake of the available rewards in terms of identity creation, interpersonal warmth, and a sense of service to mankind. In our view persons have a right to enter totalistic subcultures and have done so voluntarily for centuries, although more in certain periods than in others. What should be asked is why such people are choosing to eliminate ambiguity from their lives by committing themselves to dogmatic totalism. The hysterical overreaction of some parents, rationalized by their utilization of the brainwashing metaphor, seems to embody an attempt to resolve their own ambivalence about the contemporary technocratic situation. By denying that religious alternatives to contemporary social institutions could conceivably be voluntarily chosen, they betray their fear of examining their own involvement.

The Solution That Becomes the Problem

There is thus considerable mystification in the notion that deviant cults are breaking up families. The efforts of countercult groups often have the consequence of widening rather than healing the gulf between devotees and their parents. It is possible that parents might tolerate and try to relate to their children's commitments if the anticult movement did not encourage them to take drastic measures to rescue their child from brainwashing. . . . Within this perspective, the use of the brainwashing metaphor is a symptom rather than an explanation of the conflict between the converts and their families. The use of such imagery tends to be seen by converts as an example of the denial of personal authenticity which they are seeking to escape in the first place. It is not surprising that the use of the brainwashing metaphor has amplified hostility between cults and their antagonists—and thus often between parents and children—and has further polarized the situation. It has encouraged parents to define their children's protests as the actions of dehumanized robots.

While deprogrammers generally induce their charges to read Robert Lifton's *Chinese Thought Reform and the Psychology of Totalism* to help them realize how they have been manipulated by mind control, Moon devotees on the West Coast are now being required by their leaders to study the same volume to prepare themselves against brainwashing at the hands of the deprogrammers. Each side is convinced that their opponents are using insidious mind control techniques and mobilizing a legion of zombies against them.

Young persons who enter communal religious sects sometimes marry and raise children within the religious community. Parents who endeavor to remove their children from these sects are acting to break up their families . . . Thus the actual situation with regard to the allegation that cults are breaking up families is rather complex and it is by no means certain that prodeprogramming countercult groups such as Citizens Engaged in Reuniting Families (CERF) have reintegrated more families than they have further sundered apart.

. . .

QUESTIONS

1. Is "deprogramming" justified?
2. A profusion of new sects and cults has emerged in the United States since the 1960s, with most of them appealing primarily to young people. Why do you think this is?
3. Should all sects and cults be tolerated, or should the activities of some be restricted?

PETER M. WORSLEY

Cargo Cults

*Human religions present an astonishing array of be-
liefs and practices, but certain themes recur fairly frequently. One form of organized religious expression
that has occurred in many parts of the world is the
millenarian movement—one that prophesies the end of
the world or some similar upheaval in the immediate
future.*

*Millenarian movements have been most often re-
corded among the indigenous peoples in countries that
have been conquered and colonized by outsiders, but
even in modern industrial societies there are many
groups—such as the Jehovah's Witnesses—that es-
pouse these beliefs. A general feature of millenarian
prophecies is that those who join the movement will in
some way benefit after the cataclysm, while those who
do not (and are therefore defined as the wicked, the
oppressors, or the like) will suffer. Naturally, the
movements appeal primarily to poor, oppressed, or
otherwise disadvantaged people, for the prophecies offer their only hope of a better future.*

*In this article, Peter Worsley discusses the "cargo
cults" that still exist among some peoples of Melanesia. Impressed by the variety of manufactured goods
that arrive by sea and air for the consumption of the
whites who live in their territories, these peoples have
come to accept prophecies claiming that if certain rituals are performed (such as building airstrips and
piers), the cargo will finally be diverted to its rightful
owners, the indigenous peoples themselves.*

Patrols of the Australian Government venturing into the
"uncontrolled" central highlands of New Guinea in 1946
found the primitive people there swept up in a wave of
religious excitement. Prophecy was being fulfilled: The
arrival of the Whites was the sign that the end of the
world was at hand. The natives proceeded to butcher all
of their pigs—animals that were not only a principal
source of subsistence but also symbols of social status and
ritual preeminence in their culture. They killed these valued animals in expression of the belief that after three
days of darkness "Great Pigs" would appear from the
sky. Food, firewood and other necessities had to be stock-
piled to see the people through to the arrival of the Great
Pigs. Mock wireless antennae of bamboo and rope had
been erected to receive in advance the news of the millennium. Many believed that with the great event they
would exchange their black skins for white ones.

This bizarre episode is by no means the single event of
its kind in the murky history of the collision of European
civilization with the indigenous cultures of the southwest
Pacific. For more than 100 years traders and missionaries
have been reporting similar disturbances among the
peoples of Melanesia, the group of Negro-inhabited islands (including New Guinea, Fiji, the Solomons and the
New Hebrides) lying between Australia and the open Pacific Ocean. Though their technologies were based largely upon stone and wood, these peoples had highly developed cultures, as measured by the standards of maritime
and agricultural ingenuity, the complexity of their varied
social organizations and the elaboration of religious belief
and ritual. They were nonetheless ill prepared for the
shock of the encounter with the Whites, a people so radically different from themselves and so infinitely more
powerful. The sudden transition from the society of the
ceremonial stone ax to the society of sailing ships and now
of airplanes has not been easy to make.

After four centuries of Western expansion, the densely
populated central highlands of New Guinea remain one
of the few regions where the people still carry on their
primitive existence in complete independence of the
world outside. Yet as the agents of the Australian Government penetrate into ever more remote mountain valleys, they find these backwaters of antiquity already

deeply disturbed by contact with the ideas and artifacts of European civilization. For "cargo"—Pidgin English for trade goods—has long flowed along the indigenous channels of communication from the seacoast into the wilderness. With it has traveled the frightening knowledge of the white man's magical power. No small element in the white man's magic is the hopeful message sent abroad by his missionaries: the news that a Messiah will come and that the present order of Creation will end.

The people of the central highlands of New Guinea are only the latest to be gripped in the recurrent religious frenzy of the "cargo cults." However variously embellished with details from native myth and Christian belief, these cults all advance the same central theme: the world is about to end in a terrible cataclysm. Thereafter God, the ancestors or some local culture hero will appear and inaugurate a blissful paradise on earth. Death, old age, illness and evil will be unknown. The riches of the white man will accrue to the Melanesians.

Although the news of such a movement in one area has doubtless often inspired similar movements in other areas, the evidence indicates that these cults have arisen independently in many places as parallel responses to the same enormous social stress and strain. Among the movements best known to students of Melanesia are the "Taro Cult" of New Guinea, the "Vailala Madness" of Papua, the "Naked Cult" of Espiritu Santo, the "John Frum Movement" of the New Hebrides and the "Tuka Cult" of the Fiji Islands.

At times the cults have been so well organized and fanatically persistent that they have brought the work of government to a standstill. The outbreaks have often taken the authorities completely by surprise and have confronted them with mass opposition of an alarming kind. In the 1930s, for example, villagers in the vicinity of Wewak, New Guinea, were stirred by a succession of "Black King" movements. The prophets announced that the Europeans would soon leave the island, abandoning their property to the natives, and urged their followers to cease paying taxes, since the government station was about to disappear into the sea in a great earthquake. To the tiny community of Whites in charge of the region, such talk was dangerous. The authorities jailed four of the prophets and exiled three others. In yet another movement, that sprang up in declared opposition to the local Christian mission, the cult leader took Satan as his god.

Troops on both sides in World War II found their arrival in Melanesia heralded as a sign of the Apocalypse. The G.I.'s who landed in the New Hebrides, moving up for the bloody fighting on Guadalcanal, found the natives furiously at work preparing airfields, roads and docks for the magic ships and planes that they believed were coming from "Rusefel" (Roosevelt), the friendly king of

America. The Japanese also encountered millenarian visionaries during their southward march to Guadalcanal. Indeed, one of the strangest minor military actions of World War II occurred in Dutch New Guinea, when Japanese forces had to be turned against the local Papuan inhabitants of the Geelvink Bay region. The Japanese had at first been received with great joy, not because their "Greater East Asia Co-Prosperity Sphere" propaganda had made any great impact upon the Papuans, but because the natives regarded them as harbingers of the new world that was dawning, the flight of the Dutch having already given the first sign. Mansren, creator of the islands and their peoples, would now return, bringing with him the ancestral dead. All this had been known, the cult leaders declared, to the crafty Dutch, who had torn out the first page of the Bible where these truths were inscribed. When Mansren returned, the existing world order would be entirely overturned. White men would turn black like Papuans, Papuans would become Whites; root crops would grow in trees, and coconuts and fruits would grow like tubers. Some of the islanders now began to draw together into large "towns"; others took Biblical names such as "Jericho" and "Galilee" for their villages. Soon they adopted military uniforms and began drilling. The Japanese, by now highly unpopular, tried to disarm and disperse the Papuans; resistance inevitably developed. The climax of this tragedy came when several canoeloads of fanatics sailed out to attack Japanese warships, believing themselves to be invulnerable by virtue of the holy water with which they had sprinkled themselves. But the bullets of the Japanese did not turn to water, and the attackers were mowed down by machine-gun fire.

Behind this incident lay a long history. As long ago as 1857 missionaries in the Geelvink Bay region had made note of the story of Mansren. It is typical of many Melanesian myths that became confounded with Christian doctrine to form the ideological basis of the movements. The legend tells how long ago there lived an old man named Manamakeri ("he who itches"), whose body was covered with sores. Manamakeri was extremely fond of palm wine, and used to climb a huge tree every day to tap the liquid from the flowers. He soon found that someone was getting there before him and removing the liquid. Eventually he trapped the thief, who turned out to be none other than the Morning Star. In return for his freedom, the Star gave the old man a wand that would produce as much fish as he liked, a magic tree and a magic staff. If he drew in the sand and stamped his foot, the drawing would become real. Manamakeri, aged as he was, now magically impregnated a young maiden; the child of this union was a miracle-child who spoke as soon as he was born. But the maiden's parents were horrified, and banished her, the child and the old man. The trio sailed off in a canoe created by Mansren ("The Lord"), as the old man now became known. On this journey Mansren rejuvenated himself by stepping into a fire and flaking off his scaly skin, which changed into valuables. He then sailed around Geelvink Bay, creating islands where he stopped, and peopling them with the ancestors of the present-day Papuans.

The Mansren myth is plainly a creation myth full of symbolic ideas relating to fertility and rebirth. Comparative evidence—especially the shedding of his scaly skin—confirms the suspicion that the old man is, in fact, the Snake in another guise. Psychoanalytic writers argue that the snake occupies such a prominent part in mythology the world over because it stands for the penis, another fertility symbol. This may be so, but its symbolic significance is surely more complex than this. It is the "rebirth" of the hero, whether Mansren or the Snake, that exercises such universal fascination over men's minds.

The 19th-century missionaries thought that the Mansren story would make the introduction of Christianity easier, since the concept of "resurrection," not to mention that of the "virgin birth" and the "second coming," was already there. By 1867, however, the first cult organized around the Mansren legend was reported.

Though such myths were widespread in Melanesia, and may have sparked occasional movements even in the pre-White era, they took on a new significance in the late 19th century, once the European powers had finished parceling out the Melanesian region among themselves. In many coastal areas the long history of "blackbirding"—the seizure of islanders for work on the plantations of Australia and Fiji—had built up a reservoir of hostility to Europeans. In other areas, however, the arrival of the Whites was accepted, even welcomed, for it meant access to bully beef and cigarettes, shirts and paraffin lamps, whisky and bicycles. It also meant access to the knowledge behind these material goods, for the Europeans brought missions and schools as well as cargo.

Practically the only teaching the natives received about European life came from the missions, which emphasized the central significance of religion in European society. The Melanesians already believed that man's activities—whether gardening, sailing canoes or bearing children—needed magical assistance. Ritual without human effort was not enough. But neither was human effort on its own. This outlook was reinforced by mission teaching.

The initial enthusiasm for European rule, however, was speedily dispelled. The rapid growth of the plantation economy removed the bulk of the able-bodied men from the villages, leaving women, children and old men to carry on as best they could. The splendid vision of the equality of all Christians began to seem a pious deception in face of the realities of the color bar, the multiplicity of rival Christian mission and the open irreligion of many whites.

For a long time the natives accepted the European mission as the means by which the "cargo" would eventually be made available to them. But they found that acceptance of Christianity did not bring the cargo any nearer. They grew disillusioned. The story now began to be put about that it was not the Whites who made the cargo, but the dead ancestors. To people completely ignorant of factory production, this made good sense. White men did not work; they merely wrote secret signs on scraps of paper, for which they were given shiploads of goods. On the other hand, the Melanesians labored week after week for pitiful wages. Plainly the goods must be made for Melanesians somewhere, perhaps in the Land of the Dead. The Whites, who possessed the secret of the cargo, were intercepting it and keeping it from the hands of the islanders, to whom it was really consigned. In the Madang district of New Guinea, after some 40 years' experience of the missions, the natives went in a body one day with a petition demanding that the cargo secret should now be revealed to them, for they had been very patient.

So strong is this belief in the existence of a "secret" that the cargo cults generally contain some ritual in imitation of the mysterious European customs which are held to be the clue to the white man's extraordinary power over goods and men. The believers sit around tables with bottles of flowers in front of them, dressed in European clothes, waiting for the cargo ship or airplane to materialize; other cultists feature magic pieces of paper and cabalistic writing. Many of them deliberately turn their backs on the past by destroying secret ritual objects or exposing them to the gaze of uninitiated youths and women, for whom formerly even a glimpse of the sacred objects would have meant the severest penalties, even death. The belief that they were the chosen people is further reinforced by their reading of the Bible, for the lives and customs of the people in the Old Testament resemble their own lives rather than those of the Europeans. In the New Testament they find the Apocalypse, with its prophecies of destruction and resurrection, particularly attractive.

Missions that stress the imminence of the Second Coming, like those of the Seventh Day Adventists, are often accused of stimulating millenarian cults among the islanders. In reality, however, the Melanesians themselves rework the doctrines the missionaries teach them, selecting from the Bible what they themselves find particularly congenial in it. Such movements have occurred in areas where missions of quite different types have been dominant, from Roman Catholic to Seventh Day Adventist. The reasons for the emergence of these cults, of course, lie far deeper in the life-experience of the people.

The economy of most of the island is very backward.

Native agriculture produces little for the world market, and even the European plantations and mines export only a few primary products and raw materials: copra, rubber, gold. Melanesians are quite unable to understand why copra, for example, fetches 30 pounds sterling per ton one month and but 5 pounds a few months later. With no notion of the workings of world-commodity markets, the natives see only the sudden closing of plantations, reduced wages and unemployment, and are inclined to attribute their insecurity to the whim or evil in the nature of individual planters.

· · ·

Europeans who have witnessed outbreaks inspired by the cargo cults are usually at a loss to understand what they behold. The islanders throw away their money, break their most sacred taboos, abandon their gardens and destroy their precious livestock; they indulge in sexual license or, alternatively, rigidly separate men from women in huge communal establishments. Sometimes they spend days sitting gazing at the horizon for a glimpse of the long-awaited ship or airplane; sometimes they dance, pray and sing in mass congregations, becoming possessed and "speaking with tongues."

Observers have not hesitated to use such words as "madness," "mania," and "irrationality" to characterize the cults. But the cults reflect quite logical and rational attempts to make sense out of a social order that appears senseless and chaotic. Given the ignorance of the Melanesians about the wider European society, its economic organization and its highly developed technology, their reactions form a consistent and understandable pattern. They wrap up all their yearning and hope in an amalgam that combines the best counsel they can find in Christianity and their native belief. If the world is soon to end, gardening or fishing is unnecessary; everything will be provided. If the Melanesians are to be part of a much wider order, the taboos that prescribe their social conduct must now be lifted or broken in a newly prescribed way.

Of course the cargo never comes. The cults nonetheless live on. If the millennium does not arrive on schedule, then perhaps there is some failure in the magic, some error in the ritual. New breakaway groups organize around "purer" faith and ritual. The cult rarely disappears, so long as the social situation which brings it into being persists.

At this point it should be observed that cults of this general kind are not peculiar to Melanesia. Men who feel themselves oppressed and deceived have always been ready to pour their hopes and fears, their aspirations and frustrations, into dreams of a millennium to come or of a golden age to return. All parts of the world have had their counterparts of the cargo cults, from the American Indian ghost dance to the communist-millenarist "reign of

the saints" in Münster during the Reformation, from medieval European apocalyptic cults to African "witch-finding" movements and Chinese Buddhist heresies. In some situations men have been content to wait and pray; in others they have sought to hasten the day by using their strong right arms to do the Lord's work. And always the cults serve to bring together scattered groups, notably the peasants and urban plebeians of agrarian societies and the peoples of "stateless" societies where the cult unites separate (and often hostile) villages, clans and tribes into a wider religio-political unity.

Once the people begin to develop secular political organizations, however, the sects tend to lose their importance as vehicles of protest. They begin to relegate the Second Coming to the distant future or to the next world. In Melanesia ordinary political bodies, trade unions and native councils are becoming the normal media through which the islanders express their aspirations. In recent years continued economic prosperity and political stability have taken some of the edge off their despair. It now seems unlikely that any major movement along cargo-cult lines will recur in areas where the transition to secular politics has been made, even if the insecurity of prewar times returned. I would predict that the embryonic nationalism represented by cargo cults is likely in the future to take forms familiar in the history of other countries that have moved from subsistence agriculture to participation in the world economy.

QUESTIONS

1. What social factors account for the popularity of millenarian movements in Melanesia?

2. What are the similarities, if any, between millenarian movements such as the cargo cults and American religious movements that prophesy that the end of the world is at hand?

3. Sociological research in industrial societies has shown that the social status of members of fundamentalist sects is, on average, significantly lower than that of members of the other denominations. Why is this so?

GEORGE J. GMELCH

Baseball Magic

Earlier in this century, the anthropologist Bronislaw Malinowski studied the native inhabitants of islands in the southwestern Pacific. He was intrigued by one aspect of the people's behavior when they went fishing. If they were in the calm waters of a lagoon, they treated the event as a routine occurrence of no religious significance. But if they were to fish in the dangerous shark-infested waters beyond the coral reef, they performed various rituals designed to harness magical powers for their safety and protection. What caused the difference? Malinowski concluded that, as a general rule, humans are most likely to appeal to magical or other occult powers whenever they face situations whose outcome is uncertain and beyond their own control.

Magic is related to, but slightly different from, religion. Religion is a set of beliefs and practices oriented toward some supernatural realm; magic is the attempt to utilize supernatural forces for human ends. The supernatural forces in religion tend to be worshiped or at least appeased; those in magic are merely put to use. Belief in magic is quite common even in a modern industrial society such as the United States: witness people's reliance on rabbits' feet, St. Christopher medals, lucky numbers, and other items supposed to bring good luck.

In this article, George Gmelch discusses some of the magical rituals found in baseball, and uses the evidence to test Malinowski's hypothesis that magic is most likely to be used in unpredictable situations.

We find magic wherever the elements of chance and accident, and the emotional play between hope and fear, have a wide and extensive range. We do not find magic wherever the pursuit is certain, reliable, and well under the control of rational methods. [*Bronislaw Malinowski*]

Professional baseball is a nearly perfect arena in which to test Malinowski's hypothesis about magic. The great anthropologist was not, of course, talking about sleight of hand but of rituals, taboos and fetishes that men resort to when they want to ensure that things go their own way. Baseball is rife with this sort of magic, but, as we shall see, the players use it in some aspects of the game far more than in others.

Everyone knows that there are three essentials of baseball—hitting, pitching and fielding. The point is, however, that the first two, hitting and pitching, involve a high degree of chance. The pitcher is the player least able to control the outcome of his own efforts. His best pitch may be hit for a bloop single while his worst pitch may be hit directly to one of his fielders for an out. He may limit the opposition to a single hit and lose, or he may give up a dozen hits and win. It is not uncommon for pitchers to perform well and lose, and vice versa; one has only to look at the frequency with which pitchers end a season with poor won-lost percentages but low earned run averages (number of runs given up per game). The opposite is equally true: some pitchers play poorly, giving up many runs, yet win many games. In brief, the pitcher, regardless of how well he performs, is dependent upon the proficiency of his teammates, the inefficiency of the opposition and the supernatural (luck).

But luck, as we all know, comes in two forms, and many fans assume that the pitcher's tough losses (close games in which he gave up very few runs) are eventually balanced out by his "lucky" wins. This is untrue, as a comparison of pitchers' lifetime earned run averages to their overall won-lost records shows. If the player could apply a law of averages to individual performance, there would be much less concern about chance and uncertainty in baseball. Unfortunately, he cannot and does not.

Hitting, too, is a chancy affair. Obviously, skill is required in hitting the ball hard and on a line. Once the ball is hit, however, chance plays a large role in determining where it will go, into a waiting glove or whistling past a falling stab.

With respect to fielding, the player has almost complete control over the outcome. The average fielding percentage or success rate of .975, compared to a .245 success rate for hitters (the average batting average), reflects the degree of certainty in fielding. Next to the pitcher or hitter, the fielder has little to worry about when he knows that better than 9.7 times in ten he will execute his task flawlessly.

If Malinowski's hypothesis is correct, we should find magic associated with hitting and pitching, but none with fielding. Let us take the evidence by category—ritual, taboo and fetish.

Ritual

After each pitch, ex-major leaguer Lou Skeins used to reach into his back pocket to touch a crucifix, straighten his cap and clutch his genitals. Detroit Tiger infielder Tim Maring wore the same clothes and put them on exactly in the same order each day during a batting streak. Baseball rituals are almost infinitely various. After all, the ballplayer can ritualize any activity he considers necessary for a successful performance, from the type of cereal he eats in the morning to the streets he drives home on.

Usually, rituals grow out of exceptionally good performances. When the player does well he cannot really attribute his success to skill alone. He plays with the same amount of skill one night when he gets four hits as the next night when he goes hitless. Through magic, such as ritual, the player seeks greater control over his performance, actually control over the elements of chance. The player, knowing that his ability is fairly constant, attributes the inconsistencies in his performance to some form of behavior or a particular food that he ate. When a player gets four hits in a game, especially "cheap" hits, he often believes that there must have been something he did, in addition to his ability, that shifted luck to his side. If he can attribute his good fortune to the glass of iced tea he drank before the game or the new shirt he wore to the ballpark, then by repeating the same behavior the following day he can hope to achieve similar results. (One expression of this belief is the myth that eating certain foods will give the ball "eyes," that is, a ball that seeks the gaps between fielders.) In hopes of maintaining a batting streak, I once ate fried chicken every day at 4:00 P.M., kept my eyes closed during the national anthem and changed sweat shirts at the end of the fourth inning each night for seven consecutive nights until the streak ended.

Fred Caviglia, Kansas City minor league pitcher, explained why he eats certain foods before each game: "Everything you do is important to winning. I never for-

get what I eat the day of a game or what I wear. If I pitch well and win I'll do it all exactly the same the next day I pitch. You'd be crazy not to. You just can't ever tell what's going to make the difference between winning and losing."

Rituals associated with hitting vary considerably in complexity from one player to the next, but they have several components in common. One of the most popular is tagging a particular base when leaving and returning to the dugout each inning. Tagging second base on the way to the outfield is habitual with some players. One informant reported that during a successful month of the season he stepped on third base on his way to the dugout after the third, sixth and ninth innings of each game. Asked if he ever purposely failed to step on the bag he replied, "Never! I wouldn't dare, it would destroy my confidence to hit." It is not uncommon for a hitter who is playing poorly to try different combinations of tagging and not tagging particular bases in an attempt to find a successful combination. Other components of a hitter's ritual may include tapping the plate with his bat a precise number of times or taking a precise number of warm-up swings with the leaded bat.

One informant described a variation of this in which he gambled for a certain hit by tapping the plate a fixed number of times. He touched the plate once with his bat for each base desired: one tap for a single, two for a double and so on. He even built in odds that prevented him from asking for a home run each time. The odds of hitting a single with one tap were one in three, while the chances of hitting a home run with four taps were one in 12.

Clothing is often considered crucial to both hitters and pitchers. They may have several athletic supporters and a number of sweat shirts with ritual significance. Nearly all players wear the same uniform and undergarments each day when playing well, and some even wear the same street clothes. In 1954, the New York Giants, during a 16-game winning streak, wore the same clothes in each game and refused to let them be cleaned for fear that their good fortune might be washed away with the dirt. The route taken to and from the stadium can also have significance; some players drive the same streets to the ballpark during a hitting streak and try different routes during slumps.

Because pitchers only play once every four days, the rituals they practice are often more complex than the hitters', and most of it, such as tugging the cap between pitches, touching the rosin bag after each bad pitch or smoothing the dirt on the mound before each new batter, takes place on the field. Many baseball fans have observed this behavior never realizing that it may be as important to the pitcher as throwing the ball.

Dennis Grossini, former Detroit farmhand, practiced the following ritual on each pitching day for the first three months of a winning season. First, he arose from bed at exactly 10:00 A.M. and not a minute earlier or later. At 1:00 P.M. he went to the nearest restaurant for two glasses of iced tea and a tuna fish sandwich. Although the afternoon was free, he observed a number of taboos such as no movies, no reading, and no candy. In the clubhouse he changed into the sweat shirt and jock he wore during his last winning game, and one hour before the game he chewed a wad of Beechnut chewing tobacco. During the game he touched his letters (the team name on his uniform) after each pitch and straightened his cap after each ball. Before the start of each inning he replaced the pitcher's rosin bag next to the spot where it was the inning before. And after every inning in which he gave up a run he went to the clubhouse to wash his hands. I asked him which part of the ritual was most important. He responded: "You can't really tell what's most important so it all becomes important. I'd be afraid to change anything. As long as I'm winning I do everything the same. Even when I can't wash my hands [this would occur when he must bat] it scares me going back to the mound. . . . I don't feel quite right."

One ritual, unlike those already mentioned, is practiced to improve the power of the baseball bat. It involves sanding the bat until all the varnish is removed, a process requiring several hours of labor, then rubbing rosin into the grain of the bat before finally heating it over a flame. This ritual treatment supposedly increases the distance the ball travels after being struck. Although some North Americans prepare their bats in this fashion it is more popular among Latin Americans. One informant admitted that he was not certain of the effectiveness of the treatment. But, he added, "There may not be a God, but I go to church just the same."

Despite the wide assortment of rituals associated with pitching and hitting, I never observed any ritual related to fielding. In all my 20 interviews only one player, a shortstop with acute fielding problems, reported any ritual even remotely connected to fielding.

Taboo

Mentioning that a no-hitter is in progress and crossing baseball bats are the two most widely observed taboos. It is believed that if the pitcher hears the words "no-hitter" his spell will be broken and the no-hitter lost. As for the crossing of bats, that is sure to bring bad luck; batters are therefore extremely careful not to drop their bats on top of another. Some players elaborate this taboo even further. On one occasion a teammate became quite upset when another player tossed a bat from the batting cage and it came to rest on top of his. Later he explained that the top bat would steal hits from the lower one. For him, then, bats contain a finite number of hits, a kind of baseball "image of limited good." Honus Wagner, a member of baseball's Hall of Fame, believed that each bat was

good for only 100 hits and no more. Regardless of the quality of the bat he would discard it after its 100th hit.

Besides observing the traditional taboos just mentioned, players also observe certain personal prohibitions. Personal taboos grow out of exceptionally poor performances, which a player often attributes to some particular behavior or food. During my first season of professional baseball I once ate pancakes before a game in which I struck out four times. Several weeks later I had a repeat performance, again after eating pancakes. The result was a pancake taboo in which from that day on I never ate pancakes during the season. Another personal taboo, born out of similar circumstances, was against holding a baseball during the national anthem.

Taboos are also of many kinds. One athlete was careful never to step on the chalk foul lines or the chalk lines of the batter's box. Another would never put on his cap until the game started and would not wear it at all on the days he did not pitch. Another had a movie taboo in which he refused to watch a movie the day of a game. Often certain uniform numbers became taboo. If a player has a poor spring training or a bad year, he may refuse to wear the same uniform number again. I would not wear double numbers, especially 44 and 22. On several occasions, teammates who were playing poorly requested a change of uniform during the middle of the season. Some players consider it so important that they will wear the wrong size uniform just to avoid a certain number or to obtain a good number.

Again, with respect to fielding, I never saw or heard of any taboos being observed, though of course there were some taboos, like the uniform numbers, that were concerned with overall performance and so included fielding.

Fetishes

These are standard equipment for many baseball players. They include a wide assortment of objects: horsehide covers of old baseballs, coins, bobby pins, protective cups, crucifixes and old bats. Ordinary objects are given this power in a fashion similar to the formation of taboos and rituals. The player during an exceptionally hot batting or pitching streak, especially one in which he has "gotten all the breaks," credits some unusual object, often a new possession, for his good fortune. For example, a player in a slump might find a coin or an odd stone just before he begins a hitting streak. Attributing the improvement in his performance to the new object, it becomes a fetish, embodied with supernatural power. While playing for Spokane, Dodger pitcher Alan Foster forgot his baseball shoes on a road trip and borrowed a pair from a teammate to pitch. That night he pitched a no-hitter and later, needless to say, bought the shoes from his teammate.

They became his most prized possession.

Fetishes are taken so seriously by some players that their teammates will not touch them out of fear of offending the owner. I once saw a fight caused by the desecration of a fetish. Before the game, one player stole the fetish, a horsehide baseball cover, out of a teammate's back pocket. The prankster did not return the fetish until after the game, in which the owner of the fetish went hitless, breaking a batting streak. The owner, blaming his inability to hit on the loss of the fetish, lashed out at the thief when the latter tried to return it.

Rube Waddel, an old-time Philadelphia Athletic pitching great, had a hairpin fetish. However, the hairpin he possessed was only powerful as long as he won. Once he lost a game he would look for another hairpin, which had to be found on the street, and he would not pitch until he found another.

The use of fetishes follows the same pattern as ritual and taboo in that they are connected only with hitting or pitching. In nearly all cases the player expressed a specific purpose for carrying a fetish, but never did a player perceive his fetish as having any effect on his fielding.

I have said enough, I think, to show that many of the beliefs and practices of professional baseball players are magical. Any empirical connection between the ritual, taboo and fetishes and the desired event is quite absent. Indeed, in several instances the relationship between the cause and effect, such as eating tuna fish sandwiches to win a ball game, is even more remote than is characteristic of primitive magic. Note, however, that unlike many forms of primitive magic, baseball magic is usually performed to achieve one's own end and not to block someone else's. Hitters do not tap their bats on the plate to hex the pitcher, but to improve their own performance.

Finally, it should be plain that nearly all the magical practices that I participated in, observed or elicited, support Malinowski's hypothesis that magic appears in situations of chance and uncertainty. The large amount of uncertainty in pitching and hitting best explains the elaborate magical practices used for these activities. Conversely, the high success rate in fielding, .975, involving much less uncertainty, offers the best explanation for the absence of magic in this realm.

QUESTIONS

1. List some "magical" objects and rituals that are in use in American society. Do the conditions of their use tend to confirm Malinowski's theory?

2. Is the use by Americans of St. Christopher medals, rabbits' feet, numerology, and so forth, any different from the bone-throwing, potion-brewing, and pin-sticking rituals of people in simple, preindustrial societies?

3. How widespread in the class is belief in such quasi-religious phenomena as astrology, good luck, ghosts, superstition, fortune-telling, tarot-card reading, seances, palmistry, and the like? Can any of these beliefs be reconciled with a commitment to the Judeo-Christian religious tradition?

MARTIN E. MARTY

Fundamentalism Reborn

*One of the most remarkable sociological features of
the United States is the strength of fundamentalist
sects and denominations in the society. This situation
has few parallels elsewhere in the modern world. The
other major industrial nations, such as Britain and
France, are far less "religious" in terms of such measures as belief in God or attendance at church. Moreover, fundamentalist interpretations of the Scriptures
have little appeal in these societies, where the overwhelming majority of church members adhere to the
more mainstream, liberal denominations.*

*Yet fundamentalism is currently undergoing a revi-
val in the United States; the fastest-growing denominations and sects are such organizations as the Seventh-
Day Adventists, the Southern Baptist Convention, and
the Mormons. This revival is linked to a growing political activism by groups, such as the "Moral Majority," that base their views on a fundamentalist interpretation of the Bible.*

*The historical and cross-cultural record shows two
recurrent features of fundamentalist revivals: first,
they tend to occur in times of uncertainty or rapid social change; second, they tend to appeal primarily to
people from the lower rather than the higher classes in
society. In his article, Martin Marty analyzes the
meaning of the current fundamentalist revival and
places it in a broader social context.*

Americans know that in the modern world religion is of
no account—and yet there was the television picture, relayed from Teheran, telling a different story altogether.
United by fanatic loyalty to fierce Shi'ite Islam, millions
of Iranians, led by a scowling Ayatollah, toppled the
hated Shah, thereby embarrassing the United States. Ten
months later embarrassment turned to terror as Iranian
students and militants stormed the American embassy
and took more than 50 members of the staff hostage.

Many of the images that reached screens here were, of
course, familiar. Burnings in effigy, snipers, and street
demonstrations have been nightly news fare for years.
But other signs of the revolution evoked only incompre-
hension. Why would Teheran women leave behind the
modish dress they wore in their offices and take to the
streets in black garb and the *chador*, the veil from prelib-
eration days? How could people today wage war in the
name of the *Qu'ran*, an ancient scripture? And why
would anyone want to turn war, which is always evil
enough, into a *jihad*, a "struggle," or holy war? To get
the phenomenon into focus, the media and the nation settled on a term: fundamentalism—Shi'ite Islam was so
remote from experience as to seem useless—with the
word "militant" often preceding it.

Soon fundamentalism became a buzz word, just as a
year earlier, after Jonestown, every intense religious
group was tagged as a "cult." Everyone from the *hare
krishna* chanters to the amiable Amish came to be cults,
and none of them liked it. Similarly, American Protestant
fundamentalists resent being pushed into the same camp
with the Moslems, whom they regard as infidels. For
their part, Islamic scholars protest that to borrow a term
from the American experience—"fundamentalism"
comes from *The Fundamentals*, a group of mild-man-
nered tracts published in the U.S. after 1910—and apply
it to Moslems half a world away is a sign of imperialism,
as if America had to provide a model for every movement, even those in other nations.

Now such disclaimers have some justification. Not
everyone labeled a fundamentalist is one, nor does only
one kind of fundamentalism exist. Nevertheless, there is
no denying that in the 1980s religion is back with a vengeance—and not just in Iran. Most of the burgeoning

movements around the world are militantly antimodern, fanatical, and hold in contempt the separation of church and state. Every day, it seems, brings forth new evidence of the growing power and determination of the religious recalcitrants. While millions of individuals, thousands of congregations, and hundreds of movements may be moderate in outlook, I know of no place where wide-scale and aggressive liberalism is holding its own against the spiritual opponents of the modern impulse.

In the Islamic world, besides Iran, there is the example of Saudi Arabia, where around 200 Moslem fanatics (said to call themselves the New Kharajites) invaded the Grand Mosque at Mecca because they considered the Saudi regime unworthy of representing the true faith. According to reports, about 300 people were killed before Saudi troops retook the mosque. Ayatollah Ruholla Khomeini's charge that the incident was backed by the U.S. and "Zionists" incited an attack on the U.S. embassy in Pakistan, where General Zia-ul-Haq is trying to forge an Islamic republic.

In Japan, the most literate and technologically advanced society on earth, people are not behaving as had been predicted. Instead of becoming completely private about religion, the way moderns normally are, or dropping faith entirely, many of them are joining new religions like Soka-gakkai and Rissho-koseikai. Members of these Buddhist sects do not completely fit the Khomeini mold, and would resent being tarred with the same brush. They have been more supple than the Iranians in adapting to urban styles, and the salvation they offer, unlike that of Islam, is this-worldly. But as uprooted moderns they seek authority, discipline, a kind of earnest religious experience. As at home with the media as the Iranians are, the Soka-gakkai people have chosen to go political and work through the highly nationalistic Komeito, or Clean Government party. With its less political but ideologically more conservative partner, this religion has to be reckoned with.

Militancy reappeared on Indian soil, where some once-gentle Hindus have been roused to battle over—and please pardon what sounds like a cliché but is literal—sacred cows. In West Bengal and Kerala, where Western modernism is powerful, thanks to Communist dominance, the Moslem and Christian minorities fear Hindu fanatics who object, sometimes violently, to the eating of beef. The cows are only one of many symbols of tension between religious communities in that nation.

In Israel, the Bloc of the Faithful, or Gush Emunim party, cherishes the reputation but not the name of militant fundamentalism. Operating on the West Bank as an annexationist no-compromise group, its followers take literally the ancient scriptural covenant between God and Abraham, and are ready to go to war for their beliefs.

In the USSR, while moderate religion complies with the state, fundamentalist Baptists and Pentecostals re-

main belligerent in their dissidence. Even Aleksandr Solzhenitsyn, whose criticisms of the West have cheered many masochists here, is fired by a rigid Eastern Orthodox outlook and Slavophilia. It is his fundamentalist style that gives the novelist such power and eloquence. The last thing he wants to understand is Western pluralism and its tolerance.

Meanwhile, over in the Catholic Church, militants are rallying around leaders like French Archbishop Marcel Lefèbvre, who insists on clinging to Latin liturgy and rejecting most of the policies adopted by the Second Vatican Council. Even Pope John Paul II, because he is cracking the whip on progressive theologians like Hans Küng, is sometimes lumped with religious right-wingers. What spares him is his sometimes radical view of world politics, an expansive personal mien, and his embrace of Vatican Council reforms.

Finally, there are those American Protestant militants whose distinguishing characteristic is meanness; they are mean and want to be seen as mean. The scowl is as much a part of their image as it is that of Khomeini or the Pittsburgh Steelers' defensive line. Their view has been propounded by George W. Dollar in his *A History of Fundamentalism in America*. True believers, he writes, must "both expound and expose . . . because of new forms of middle-of-the-roadism, worldliness, and friendliness to apostate church activities." Translate: Billy Graham and his kind. Doubt never crosses the minds of people like Dollar. His book breathes the spirit that Finley Peter Dunne put into the mouth of his Mr. Dooley: "A fanatic is a man that does what he thinks th' Lord wud do if he knew th' facts in th' case."

People who do not turn their TV dials to the right channels may still think of fundamentalists as apolitical. With good reason. Only a dozen years or so ago, the rightists attacked moderate and liberal religious leaders in the mainline denominations and in the National Council of the Churches of Christ and the World Council of Churches and the Vatican for "speaking out" on such issues as the war on poverty, civil rights, and peace. Fundamentalists said this violated the law of God in the scriptures.

But who says fundamentalists cannot change? Today it is hard to picture a candidate for office trembling because the ecumenical councils or the boards of social concern of the United Methodist Church or the United Church of Christ or the United anything else have advocated policies contrary to his own. But . . . not a few candidates have ducked for cover to escape the fundamentalist barrage.

Militant fundamentalists control a large percentage of the 1,400 radio and 35 television stations that make up the Protestant media network; it currently claims 47 million devoted hearers who turn to religious TV for entertainment, conversion, healing, positive thinking, and political signal calling. Moreover, fundamentalist leaders like the Reverends Jerry Falwell and Pat Robertson—who take in more money than the Republican and Democratic parties—are mastering the mails. Along with direct-mail wiz Richard Viguerie, they work through fronts with names like Religious Round Table, the Moral Majority, and Christian Voice to spread their views. They have helped unseat former Senators Thomas J. McIntyre and Dick Clark, and they have the power to send other legislators whom they have targeted to political oblivion.

But their larger enemies are humanism, liberalism, and immorality. "Fifteen years ago," says Falwell, "I opposed what I'm doing today, but now I'm convinced this country is morally sick and will not correct itself unless we get involved." Involvement means, for him, "fighting a holy war. . . . What's happened to America is that the wicked are bearing rule. We have to lead the nation back to the moral stance that made America great." The echoes of the Iranian militants are loud and clear.

Why fundamentalism now? After all, on no calendars but their own were militant fundamentalists supposed to have power in the 1980s. Already in the 1780s people of the Enlightenment foresaw the end of irrational religion in the face of the rise of reason. But the 1880s religious liberals seemed to be adapting to modernity so suavely that the obscurantists seemed to be heading for obscurity. And although militant fundamentalism has a long history in the U.S., America seemed to be on a thoroughly modern course after 1964. The mainline and moderate churches had prospered during the Protestant-Catholic-Jewish suburban boom in the Eisenhower era. John Kennedy, Pope John XXIII, Martin Luther King, Jr., Paul Tillich, and the remembered Pierre Teilhard de Chardin were heroes to the upbeat religionists. In his best-seller of 1965 Harvey Cox wrote that *The Secular City* was no less than a transcription for our times of "the Biblical image of the Kingdom of God." It would be "the commonwealth of maturity and interdependence."

What went wrong? The curious but correct answer is "modernity and modernization." In his *The Ordeal of Civility*, John Murray Cuddihy argues that victims of modernization experience life as being all chopped up, too full of choice. Modernity, they know, separates church from state, ethnicity and region from religion, fact from value. It cruelly sunders and rarely supports. People in its wake experience "hunger for wholeness." On this scene the Ayatollah is almost a pure demodernizer. He would counteract the differentiations and diffusions that make religion so flexible, that cause it to be such a thin spread in the life of dispersed moderns. Fortunately for him, there was a villain of modernization: the Shah, who imported but hoarded the best features of technology and left the oppressed of Iran with nothing except trampled customs and a disintegrating culture. Like all funda-

mentalism, then, the Shi'ite version is reactive; it repeals trends and wants to recover what has been lost.

This brings us to the crucial point: fundamentalism and traditionalism are far from the same thing. Tradition comes from *traditio*, "handing over," and refers to what God hands over to the Church in Jesus Christ and the succession of believers. But such tradition, as the great scholar Yves Congar reminded fellow-Catholics, is a flowing stream, not a still and stagnant pond. Motion, development, flow—these are precisely what the fundamentalist world-view cannot tolerate.

So with conservatism. It can be supple, absorptive, and empathic. Western, chiefly biblical, faith is grounded in history. . . . This faith celebrates remembered events such as exodus and exile, or for Christians, the words and ways of Jesus. Conservatives do not freeze everything back in biblical times. They conserve or save what they find of value in the inherited intuitive wisdom of subsequent people, whether saints or martyrs or sinners. The fundamentalist codifies everything.

The sociopsychological underpinnings of fundamentalism and other such phenomena were eloquently described by the late Talcott Parsons. In one of his few eloquent passages, the sociologist wrote that moderns, like their ancestors, must still endow their good fortune and their suffering alike with meaning. They cannot let these occur as something that "just happens." But modernity calls forth ever more human initiative in the search for meaning. Greater demands call for greater daring. So the human "takes greater risks. Hence the possibility of failure and of the failure being his fault is at least as great as, if not greater than, it ever was." The firm ground is gone. If the venturer is on the high-wire, he asks for a secure net.

During such tense periods, fundamentalists seek high-intensity religious experiences in order to find meaning. Then, to channel and rein these experiences, they need strong authority. The "kids" found it in "the cults," where a master stated all Truth and a surrogate family provided all support. As long as people are unsure of their identities, mistrustful of strangers, threatened by erosive creeds, and wary of conspiracies, some of them will huddle into fundamentalism. Through such movements around the world they seek to ward off the devils, the shahs abroad, or the humanists at home. They will find company with other true believers and remake or unsettle their part of the world before the End. As long as there are potential followers for such movements, there will be no lack of leaders to exploit their impulses.

In America, fortunately, pluralist democracy and an affluent society provide counterforces and many benefits to pass around, thus keeping fundamentalists from forming armies. Still, militants will attract people to the notion that if Russia has its atheistic creed and Iran its Moslem ideology, both of which work because they allow for no doubt or ambiguity, then "we" need equally fierce dogmas to match theirs. Religious counterparts to the SALT treaties falter, and interfaith or ecumenical strivings seem to be nothing but foolish memories.

Will the fundamentalists win? Some who answer yes to that question foresee the end of the age of Enlightenment, the decline of liberalism, the demise of dialogue. Certainly the fundamentalist and tribalist outbreaks have checked empathic or responsive instincts in many cultures. Moderate church people are envious of the growth among authoritarian groups. No one today writes about massive outpourings of understanding between people. The new prophets envision an age in which religiosity fuses with weaponry to produce upheavals in Iran, unsettlements in America, and statist creeds and faiths.

Yet prophets have been wrong before. As surprising as the survivals and reappearances of militant fundamentalisms have been, so also has the presence of people who combine faith with openness. Even if it is not their half of the inning, there are still those who believe that one can combine deep commitment with urgent civility. They refuse to accept the argument that all would be well if only religion would go away. Whatever one wishes, most people are going to continue their search for meaning, whether in benign or malign company and spirit. When they desert religious symbols, they often transfer their fanaticism to nationalist or totalitarian ideologies. The civil, committed believers, meanwhile, urge an end to distinctions between kinds of religious faith.

They need but are not finding alliance with the other intended victim of holy wars, currently named humanist. Mr. Falwell has found his scapegoat: "255,000 secular humanists," he said in January, "have taken 214 million of us out to left field." He wanted to lead the crowd back to right field. The Moral Majority wants "the vast majority of Americans" to ally against what they call, along with Falwell, "humanism."

Previously, academic humanists were of little help. Historically uninformed as some of them were; reacting against their childhood faith as were others; unwilling to recognize the varieties of historic religious experience, writers like Joseph Wood Krutch, Harry Elmer Barnes, and Walter Lippmann decided that all religious certainty had to be murderous, all religious tolerance heretical, and fundamentalist faith alone had integrity. Such twitting of liberals was a luxury in 1925. It helped humanists keep their distance from open-minded theists who stood in developmental traditions of faith.

Today when Ayatollah fundamentalism violates the rules of diplomatic games or adopts the weapons of terror, such luxuries are less attractive. If "the fundamentalists are coming," it is important, this time, to understand both their grievances and their impulses. Some reconnaissance, to determine who is in their camp and who is not, is strategically wise. Most of all, after the appearance in our century of people like Pope John XXIII, Mohandas Gandhi, Abraham Joshua Heschel, and Martin Luther King, Jr., it no longer seems necessary to equate faith with certainty and both of them with murder. There are happier alternatives, even if they are less visible than ever, less favored than fanaticism in today's world of conflict.

QUESTIONS

1. Are there any parallels between the fundamentalist revivals currently occurring in the United States and those in much of the Islamic world?

2. Religion has always held a dominant place in traditional, preindustrial societies. Why should fundamentalism have so much appeal in a highly industrialized, rational-scientific society like the United States?

3. To what extent are a person's religious beliefs influenced by the social environment?

STEPHEN JAY GOULD

The Finagle Factor

Ideally, the accumulated body of scientific knowledge should consist of facts and theories that have been checked and tested as rigorously as possible. And, in fact, the public image of science—which is carefully promoted by scientists themselves—is of a scrupulously objective enterprise in which dedicated men and women pursue the truth without regard for their personal biases or ambitions.

Most scientific investigation probably does follow the ideal, but sociological research has shown that scientists do sometimes allow conscious or unconscious personal considerations to affect their work, even to the point of seriously distorting their findings. Scientists, after all, are human; like anyone else, they may have their own pet theories and prejudices, may be blind to facts they do not wish to see, or may attach undue significance to some evidence that seems favorable and too little importance to evidence that challenges their assumptions.

In this article, Stephen Jay Gould shows how one scientist, in trying to make the facts about cranial size fit his theories about racial intelligence, successfully deluded himself and—at least for a while—his public.

The myths of science are so powerful that they sometimes intoxicate great artists as much as they delude scientists themselves. In 1917 the Russian writer Maxim Gorki expressed a hope that science would guide his newly awakened land:

"Art is emotional; all too easily it succumbs to the subjective peculiarities of the creator's psyche; it is too dependent on what is conventionally called mood, and, for these reasons, it is rarely truly free, it rarely transcends the barriers imposed by the powerful influences of individualism, class, and national and racial prejudices.

"The experimental sciences, which have developed mightily in the grateful soil of exact observation, are guided by the iron logic of mathematics, completely free from these influences. The spirit of the experimental sciences is truly international and for all humanity."

If it operated in such a manner, I suspect that science would have to be the work of unfeeling robots, not of human beings with passions and egos. The joy of science, for this practitioner at least, lies in its affinity with creative activity in the arts. Scientists play hunches, nurture hopes, and pursue their private battles with all the zeal of literary critics attacking their *bêtes noires*. Scientific debates may be resolved—often, to state a conventional faith, because an intelligible external reality exists—but this does not diminish the intensely personal and subjective character of creativity.

On the bright side of subjective intrusion into the affairs of science, we have numerous stories of fruitful hunches and stubborn resistance to ancient prejudice—Galileo and Urban VIII, Darwin reading Malthus. On the dark side, we have equally numerous (but largely suppressed) stories of fudging, finagling, and even outright fraud. Their exposure has become a small but thriving cottage industry among historians of science. The great are caught as often as the insignificant. Newton fudged outrageously to attain a pseudoprecision that his instruments could not have provided. Mendel's ratios, reported from his pea gardens, are far too close to predicted values.

True fraud—the manufacturing of data to conceal opposite conclusions—seems to be rare. It is also not very interesting except as gossip. When scientists uncover a

From *Human Nature*, July 1978. Copyright © 1978 by Human Nature, Inc. Reprinted by permission of the publisher.

case, they excommunicate its perpetrator, smugly proclaim that science polices itself, and get back to work. But finagling—the manipulation of data, often unconsciously, to support an evident "truth"—is probably rampant in science. Newton and Mendel fall into this category. They believed in the theories that their cooked data supported so well—and they were right. As a historical phenomenon, finagling is highly instructive. It is more often the soft underbelly of genius than the refuge of a scoundrel. If we wish to understand the role of human nature in science, we will have to study finagling as the flip side of insight's record.

Although I regard finagling as rampant and probably unavoidable, I do not wish to convey the impression that I condone it. Finagled data are the bane of science. They enter textbooks and persist there for generations. They occupy the precious time of scientists who must try to distill answers from conflicting testimony. Most important, and most simply, they spread falsehood.

Finagling is especially prevalent when data are few, hard to obtain, ambiguous in meaning, and when passions ride high on the outcome. No subject, therefore, has been more congenial to finagling than scientific ideas about human races and their status.

The story that I want to tell, of a forgotten man expounding a forgotten doctrine during the 1840s, may strike some readers as an antiquarian exercise, however interesting. I regard it as an example of a most revealing phenomenon that may teach us a great deal about human motivation and the social context of our actions. Finagling exposes much about all of us, not just the sins of errant individuals.

Craniometry was for the 19th Century what intelligence testing has been for the 20th. Millions of people submitted their heads to measurement during its halcyon days in the late 19th Century. Craniometricians established elaborate classifications of race, usually in order of perceived merit and always with their own group on top and the inhabitants of enslaved or captured nations on the bottom. External measurements of the cranial index (width/length) and degree of jaw jutting were obtained most easily, but brain weight or cranial capacity was valued more highly as a criterion for ranking. Few scientists doubted that brain size served as a rough but statistically reliable index of intelligence (a premise now recognized as false).

We often hear of the great European craniometricians, of Sir Francis Galton in England and Paul Broca in France. Many imagine that the rise of evolutionary theory provided an impetus for gathering such data. But the first extensive compilation of the cranial capacities of different races was made by an American before the Civil War, and in the midst of a debate on whether races were diversified products of a single creation or truly separate species.

The name Samuel George Morton does not roll easily off the tongue these days, but in his own time (he died in 1851) he was known throughout the scientific world as the finest of American researchers. Morton was raised in a prominent Quaker household in Philadelphia and became a physician and general scientific savant. Morton began collecting skulls in 1830. He did no field work and obtained his treasures by a combination of correspondence, importuning, and purchase. He amassed the world's largest collection; when he died it contained more than 1,000 skulls. His friends and admirers called it the "American Golgotha." Morton's collection was admired by scientists throughout the world. During his first American visit Louis Agassiz, the Swiss zoologist, was overwhelmed: "Imagine a series of 600 skulls, mostly Indian from all tribes who now inhabit or formerly inhabited America. Nothing else like it exists elsewhere. This collection alone is worth a journey to America."

At first Morton focused on the crania of American Indians. In 1839 he published the first of his three major works, *Crania Americana*—a report on 147 Indian skulls complete with cranial capacities and a phrenological appendix rating native Americans on such traits as "amativity" and "submissiveness." Morton then turned his attention to the skulls in ancient Egyptian catacombs, publishing a companion volume, *Crania Aegyptiaca,* in 1844. Five years later he printed his final catalogue, an account of more than 600 skulls, encompassing all major racial groups.

Morton did not pursue his consuming hobby out of disembodied interest in the pure facts of human ethnography. He was an active participant in one of the great scientific debates of his day: What are human races? One school, the monogenists, hewed to the Biblical tale of Adam and Eve as the progenitors of all human beings. They attributed racial diversity to the direct action of climate; inferior races had degenerated further from the primal perfection of the divine original. The polygenists, on the other hand, argued that the differences were too great to pass off on climate. They must have been present from the start. Races are separate species. (Evolution did not exist as a serious alternative in these pre-Darwinian days.) Morton was a prominent polygenist.

Of course, regarding races as separate species did not guarantee a ranking of superior and inferior. But separate, as the Supreme Court once said in another context, is inherently unequal. As Louis Agassiz, now settled in America as the chief theoretician of polygeny, wrote in 1850, "There are upon earth different races of men, inhabiting different parts of its surface . . . and this fact presses upon us the obligation to settle the relative rank among these races." Agassiz kept no one in suspense about his suspicions; he wrote of the "submissive, obsequious, imitative negro" and the "tricky, cunning, and cowardly Mongolian" two pages later.

The polygenists needed "evidence" to back Agassiz's theory and rhetoric, and Morton supplied it. Morton floated some ethnological and historical arguments to back the conventional ranking. He noted, for example, that blacks were depicted as slaves and servants in Egyptian hieroglyphs (how else, since they were conquered people in Egypt; how did they depict themselves in Zimbabwe?).

But Morton's reputation rested on his "hard" data—his seemingly irrefutable tables showing the cranial capacities of the races. Morton filled each skull with white mustard seed, poured the seed into a graduated cylinder, and measured the volume. His results fulfilled the expectation of every well-bred and right-thinking American WASP—whites on top, Indians in the middle, and blacks on the bottom; and among whites, English and Germanic stocks first, Jews in the middle, and Hindus on the bottom. The social and the natural order are the same; economic privilege and political power follow the dictates of biology.

It cannot be irrelevant that a nation torn apart by the issue of slavery served as a stage for the monogenist-polygenist debate. (The argument proceeded in European scientific circles as well, but with much less intensity. In a rare reversal of early 19th Century roles, America, the developing nation, led cultured Europe. European scientists even referred to Morton and his polygenist colleagues as the "American school" of anthropology.) Polygeny might have served as a major argument for slavery; "separate and inferior" forms a better rationale for subjugation than "wayward brother." Indeed, the South's leading medical journal stated in its eulogy for Morton: "We of the South should consider him as our benefactor, for aiding most materially in giving to the negro [sic] his true position as an inferior race." Nonetheless, most slaveholders did not wish to pay the price that polygeny demanded for its excellent argument—a denial of scriptural authority in the tale of Adam and Eve. The planters stuck to their Bibles and justified their livelihood with more conventional arguments for black subjugation—degeneration and eternal servitude under the curse of Ham, for example. Still, Morton's influence extended far beyond his ephemeral doctrine of polygeny. Racial ranking was a theme common to all schools of 19th Century anthropology. Morton's tables maintained their influence until intelligence testing replaced head measurement as the favored tool of scientific racism.

Taken together, the summary tables of Morton's three major works seem to form an overwhelming case for the hierarchy he had expected from the start. The first work, *Crania Americana,* focused on Indians and placed the average of the large sample (147 skulls) squarely between Caucasians above and African blacks below.

After he completed this lengthy volume, Morton became dissatisfied with his method. The white mustard seed was too variable in size and did not pack well. Repeated measurements of the same skull might vary by as much as 4 cubic inches. So Morton switched to lead shot, remeasured all his skulls, and reported only the measurements made with 1/8-inch shot, "of the size called BB," in his last two treatises. Morton claimed that repeated measurements of the same skull now never varied by more than a cubic inch. I have no reason to doubt his contention that lead shot provided accurate, objective, and repeatable data.

In his second work, the *Crania Aegyptiaca,* Morton tried to show that cranial capacity declined as the proportion of black ancestry rose. Morton felt that he could assign the mummified remains from the ancient tombs to precise racial groupings. He divided Caucasians into Pelasgics (ancient Greeks by his mistaken identification), Semites, and Egyptians. Morton then designated as Negroid a series of skulls that he regarded as half-breeds between Caucasians and pure blacks. In his tables, the Caucasian subgroups were ranked in anticipated WASPish order, probably by circular reasoning since I suspect that a large head was Morton's primary criterion for calling a skull Pelasgic. Negroids fell below the lowest Caucasian group and above pure blacks.

In 1849 Morton published his final table, a report on 623 skulls from all major racial groups. Again, the "objective" data could not have been more welcome, both in its general ranking of major races (Caucasian, Malay, Mongolian, American Indian, and Negro) and in its finer subdivisions within them (Germans, English, and Anglo-Americans atop the Caucasian heap).

When Morton died in 1851, the *New York Daily Tribune* rightly proclaimed in its eulogy: "Probably no scientific man in America enjoyed a higher reputation among scholars throughout the world than Dr. Morton." Morton did not achieve this reputation by trenchant argument or brilliant theorizing. He won it because he had followed the advice that Thomas Edison codified later in the century—99 percent perspiration and 1 percent inspiration. Morton had labored where others had only speculated. He had collected and measured assiduously. The most important subject of his age had finally been grounded in objective fact. Baron Alexander von Humboldt, Europe's greatest scientific celebrity, wrote to Morton: "Your work is equally remarkable for the profundity of its anatomical views, the numerical detail of the relations of organic conformation, and the absence of those poetical reveries which are the myths of modern physiology."

Morton viewed himself as an empiricist who would resolve an outstanding issue with the brute force of copious facts. For this I am profoundly grateful since it led Morton to publish all his raw data—a very rare procedure among scientists. We can trace exactly how he got from raw measurements to the summary tables. To put it succinctly: I spent several months tracking down Morton's data and reworking his analyses. They are, first of all, a patchwork of finagling. Second, when properly reconstituted, they yield no differences at all in cranial capacity among races. Finally, I find not a hint of conscious fraud in Morton's work. He deluded himself grandly, but honestly. (Or, if he falsified consciously, he did nothing to cover his tracks; his errors are either stated patently or are easily reconstructed from his published raw data.)

The giveaway comes right at the beginning of his first treatise, the *Crania Americana* of 1839. He prefaces the account of Indian crania with a disquisition on the "essential" character of human groups. These short descriptions immediately discredit his later claims to unbiased, dispassionate inquiry about the meaning of racial differences. Morton's colleagues must have read these comments as evident truth, not as Caucasian prejudice. The notion of objectivity is as culturally bound as any specific claim made under its aegis. Of the "Greenland esquimaux" he wrote: "They are crafty, sensual, ungrateful, obstinate and unfeeling, and much of their affection for their children may be traced to purely selfish motives. They devour the most disgusting aliments uncooked and uncleaned . . . . Their mental faculties from infancy to old age, present a continued childhood . . . . In gluttony, selfishness and ingratitude, they are perhaps unequalled by any other nation of people." Of the Hottentots: They are "the nearest approximation to the lower animals. . . . Their complexion is a yellowish brown, compared by travellers to the peculiar hue of Europeans in the last stages of jaundice . . . . The women are represented as even more repulsive than the men." Yet, when compelled to characterize a Caucasian tribe as "a mere horde of rapacious banditti," Morton quickly added: "Their moral perceptions, under the influence of an equitable government, would no doubt assume a much more favorable aspect."

To Morton, the difference of 5 cubic inches between Indians and Caucasians was a matter of no small importance: "The benevolent mind," he wrote, "may regret the inaptitude of the Indian for civilization . . . . The structure of his mind appears to be different from that of the white man, nor can the two harmonize in their social relations except on the most limited scale." Morton's 147 Indian skulls spanned the hemisphere from Canada to Peru. But Inca Peruvians were particularly well represented, forming about 25 percent of the sample. Incas have the smallest mean capacity among Morton's Indian subgroups. Their overrepresentation in the total sample is fortuitous. (With different collectors, Morton's sample might have been 25 percent Iroquois, a subgroup with a mean capacity greater than white Englishmen.) The large number of Inca skulls pulls down the Indian average unfairly. All subgroups should be weighted equally, and when this is done, the Indian mean rises to 83.8 cubic inches.

But why do Incas have such small brains? That bothered Morton conspicuously, given their achievements—though he consoled himself with the ease of their subsequent defeat by the conquistadors. Now we come to the crux of Morton's difficulty, and his blindness to explanations other than his favored claim of innate mental differences. We now know that body size is the primary determinant of differences in brain size within human groups. Big people, on the average, have larger brains than small people; men have larger brains than women (though women come out slightly ahead when we make the appropriate correction for body size). Stature and sex differences were staring Morton in the face in all his sets of data. Yet he never recognized or acknowledged them. All variation among his Indian subgroups can be explained by differences in stature—differences that Morton cites in other contexts. Inca Peruvians are among the smallest people he considered.

Still, we cannot blame Morton for failing to weight his subsamples equally. Statisticians do this instinctively today, but statistics scarcely existed as a discipline in Morton's time. Yet we find that Morton was aware of problems engendered by unequal sizes of subsamples. In computing the Caucasian mean of 87 cubic inches, he threw out a large subsample of Hindus for the following reason, openly stated: "It is proper, however, to mention that but 3 Hindoos are admitted in the whole number, because the skulls of these people are probably smaller than those of any other existing nation. For example, 17 Hindoo heads give a mean of but 75 cubic inches; and the three received into the table are taken at that average." In other words, Morton included a large subsample (25 percent) of small-brained Incas to pull down the Indian average, but tossed out a large subsample (also 25 percent) of Hindus to raise the Caucasian mean. When we recompute the Caucasian mean with equally weighted subsamples, we get 84.5, or no difference worth mentioning from the corrected 83.8 of Indians.

But what of the lower black average? The next work, *Crania Aegyptiaca*, gives us a clue. In a footnote, Morton now cites 85 cubic inches for the mean of 58 adult black skulls. Morton had switched from the highly subjective and poorly controlled method of white mustard seed to the presumably objective procedure of lead shot in the interim—and he had remeasured all his skulls. I compared the before and after figures with the following remarkable result. All average values were higher with shot, not surprising since the heavy and uniform shot packs so much better and fills all spaces. For Caucasian skulls, the average difference between seed and shot measures for the same skull is 1.8 cubic inches. For Indians, it is 2.2 cubic inches. For blacks, it is a whopping 5.4 cubic inches. I have no reason to doubt that shot measures are objective and unaffected by unconscious finagling. (Morton could always repeat a measure to the nearest cubic inch.) The seed measures could easily be affected by prior expectation. It is not hard to construct a reasonable scenario. Morton picks up a distressingly small white skull, pours in the seed, shakes vigorously, pushes as hard as he can on the foramen magnum (the hole at the base of the skull), and pours in more seed. Next he takes an equally distressing large black skull, pours in the seed, and shakes gingerly. So easy to do without the slightest awareness of impropriety. And the result: The difference between an objective high measure and a subjective and easily finagled low measure is greatest for blacks, intermediate for Indians, and lowest for whites.

As for the summary chart in *Crania Aegyptiaca,* it too falls victim to noncorrection for sex and stature. The sex of a clean skull can rarely be specified with certainty, but Morton knew and recorded the sex for many of his mummified Egyptian remains—though he never recognized the influence of sex upon average cranial capacities. With some uncertainty produced by a few undesignated skulls, I believe that the difference between Caucasians and Negroids in Morton's Egyptian chart arises only because the Caucasian sample is half male and the Negroid sample only one third male. My best estimate of means by sex is, for males, Caucasians 86.5, Negroids 87.5; for females, Caucasians 77.2, Negroids, 75.5. Male Negroids are a bit bigger than Caucasians, females a bit smaller. Again, no difference worth mentioning. The single Negro skull is, as you may have guessed, a female.

The final table of 1849 is a potpourri of finagling. First of all, I found two errors in calculation, both in Morton's favor. The German mean, reported at 90, is 88.4. The Anglo-American average, also reported at 90, is 89.1. The high English mean of 96 is correct, but the sample is all male (mostly hanged felons). An equal weighting of the corrected Caucasian subsamples yields 85.3 cubic inches (even leaving the high English mean as it is).

The Mongolian mean of 82 is a selective fabrication. Morton excluded a large Chinese skull (98 cubic inches) that he had recently acquired. Yet I know that he had the skull when he made his table, because several skulls with higher catalogue numbers are included. Moreover, Morton never mentions three Eskimo skulls, with an embarrasingly high mustard-seed mean of 86.8, recorded 10 years before in *Crania Americana.* True, they were not part of his collection; he had borrowed them from a friend and never had the opportunity to remeasure them with shot. Still, he might have mentioned them (especially since he bewails the absence of Eskimo skulls in his collection) and admitted that the shot mean would probably be higher. In any case, if I put back the excluded Chinese skull and give Morton an advantage by using the seed mean for Eskimos, I obtain a conservative Mongolian average of 85 cubic inches, exactly the same as for Caucasians.

Morton's Indian mean has plummeted to 79, but this only reflects a growing inequality of subsample sizes. Small-brained and small-statured Incas had formed 25 percent of the sample in 1839; now they have risen to nearly half (155 of 338 skulls). A recalculation with equal weighting of subsamples yields 86.0 cubic inches. (The seed value had been 83.8 and the average correction from seed to shot was 2.2.)

As for the Negro mean, we must drop the Australoid subgroup. Morton wished to assess the status of African blacks and we no longer accept a close relationship between the two groups; dark skin evolved more than once in human evolution. I also drop the Hottentot sample of three; it is a small all-female sample from a group of small-statured people. I then amalgamate native and American-born blacks to produce a single sample with an average between 82 and 83 cubic inches, but closer to 83.

Finally, I present the corrected [measurements]. All races lie between 83 and 86 cubic inches. There are no statistically significant differences among them, and whites are not on top.

Corrected values

Race	Mean capacities (cubic inches)
Native American	86
Mongolian	85
Modern Caucasian	85
Malay	85
Ancient Caucasian	84
Africans (Negro)	83

The history of scientific ideas on race, and on the heritability of intelligence in general, has been plagued by finagling in the unconscious (or conscious) service of prior expectations. Sir Cyril Burt's flagrant, clearly conscious finagling of data on IQ in twins is merely the latest and most spectacular example—though I have not the slightest doubt that Sir Cyril fudged to proclaim a "truth" that he deeply believed. But truth, in science as in art, is culturally bound. Science operates under empirical constraint; when data press strongly, even the most stubborn must eventually submit. The Inquisition showed Galileo the instruments of torture, but his ideas prevailed within a century. But data do not press at all for the vexatious subject of racial differences in character and intelligence. Nonetheless, scientists have rarely hesitated to proclaim an opinion, and they have often invested a prejudice with apparent documentation. The history of scientific views on race is a mirror of social beliefs among the privileged. Individuals have been courageous and iconoclastic, but majorities have followed the hand that feeds—wealthy patrons in the past, government agencies these days. All this would be more transparent if scientists could not hide behind the myth of objectivity and freedom from cultural constraint. The prevalence of finagling exposes that myth, for it demonstrates the imposition of hope and prejudice upon evidence.

In a fit of pique, Louis Agassiz wrote in 1850: "Naturalists have a right to consider the questions growing out of men's physical relations as merely scientific questions, and to investigate them without reference to either politics or religion." Yet Agassiz, much as I respect him for his brilliance as a naturalist, was a virulent racist who accepted the doctrine of polygeny in an episode more akin to instant religious conversion than to scientific persuasion—when he saw black people for the first time at age 39 in a Philadelphia hotel and experienced surprise and repulsion at the physical differences. I cannot analyze Agassiz's neurosis, but I can assert that both religion and politics pervaded his racial views. His statement is a smoke screen, not a ringing affirmation of scientific freedom. It also displays science for what it is—something far more interesting that the pap presented about objectivity and the scientific method in high schools. It is a gutsy human activity, pursued with passion, infested (as all creative activity must be) with influences of culture, class, and politics, but stumbling somehow toward a better understanding of our world.

QUESTIONS

1. Why is it so important that scientists (unlike, say, politicians or business executives) try to exclude personal biases from their work?

2. What factors could cause a scientist to lose objectivity in research?

3. What safeguards are available to the scientific community to prevent gross distortions of research findings?

JEREMY RIFKIN
TED HOWARD

Who Should Play God?

One of the most distinctive features of Western civilization has been an ability to develop scientific knowledge and to apply that knowledge to technology. Upon that cultural trait has been built the entire edifice of the modern industrial society and the array of material conveniences it offers. But scientific and technological innovations have not been without their critics, for many have charged that science and technology create as many problems as they solve.

This argument has new relevance now that scientists have cracked the genetic code and are beginning to apply that knowledge to the technology of genetic engineering. This technology is still very much in its infancy, but its potential uses in the decades ahead are awesome. Scientists can already alter the genetic make-up of laboratory specimens, breeding new generations with characteristics their species never had before; and it seems only a matter of time before this technology is available for humans. Scientists have succeeded in making clones—genetic replicas—of some lower animals. Other scientists are studying cellular processes to find some way of slowing down, or even halting, the aging process. And these are only some of the achievements of the new biology. In other, related fields new technologies are being perfected—for example, to allow the sex of a child to be preselected, or to permit one woman to give birth to a child conceived by another.

In this article, Jeremy Rifkin and Ted Howard consider some of the ethical and practical problems posed to society by such innovations.

On a few momentous occasions in mankind's history, the body of accumulated human knowledge has spawned dramatic new inventions and discoveries which people, in turn, have used to regulate, control, and moderate the external world—the discovery of fire, the invention of the wheel, the formulation of written language, the discovery of the principles of gravity, and the development of the internal combustion engine. The splitting of the atom and the dawn of the nuclear age is the latest development in this long pursuit of means by which to harness nature.

Now a dramatic new scientific discovery has given some of us the power, for the first time, to shift attention from shaping and controlling the external world of matter and energy to shaping and controlling the internal world of life itself. With the discovery of DNA and its workings, scientists have unlocked the very secrets of life. It is only a matter of a handful of years before biologists will be able to change the evolutionary wisdom of billions of years by creating new plants, new animals, and new forms of human and post-human beings.

Today, only a tiny handful of people are privy to the secrets of life and how to manipulate and change it. Most of us are totally unaware of this new-found power. The concept of designing and engineering life, especially human life, is so utterly fantastic that it is difficult even to comprehend its meaning and implications. Yet, even as the public is kept virtually ignorant of this unparalleled new scientific discovery, microbiologists are busy in hundreds of laboratories across the country spending tens of millions of dollars in pursuit of the "mastery of life."

Breakthroughs in genetics research are making genetic engineering feasible for the first time, an in-house memorandum prepared by Cetus, a West Coast corporation, proudly announced in 1975. "This concept is so truly revolutionary," the memo asserted, "that by the year 2000 virtually all the major human diseases will regularly succumb to treatment" by genetic procedures.

The most significant genetic breakthrough of recent years has been recombinant DNA—a laboratory technique for splicing together genetic material from unrelated organisms to manufacture novel forms of life. While the scientific community has become deeply divided over the health and safety problems presented by recombinant DNA, lay observers are increasingly questioning how this new technology will be used to modify human life as we know it.

The goals of today's genetic engineers range from the sublime to the ridiculous. The most modest among them advocate using genetic engineering to cure some 2,000 "monogenic" diseases—disorders caused by the malfunctioning of a single gene. Others are turning their attention to the artificial production of new strains of plants and "super" grains, while still others focus on redesigning various animal species to equip them to do society's unpopular jobs.

More ominous, however, are the well-credentialed and well-financed researchers who propose the complete restructuring of human life. Name your wildest fantasy (or nightmare) and some authority somewhere is seriously proposing it—from redesigning the human stomach so that people, like cows, will be able to consume cheap hay and grass to hybridizing a cross between man and lower primates. There are even genetic engineers who eagerly await the day when their work will produce the "final solution": the construction of a genetic superrace that will move far beyond *homo sapiens* on the evolutionary ladder.

There was a time when all of this could be dismissed as science fiction. No more. No matter how wild or fantastic the scenarios today's prestigious scientists envision, it is clear that they themselves are in earnest. As a tool of human genetic engineering, recombinant DNA literally offers us the opportunity to move beyond ourselves on the evolutionary scale. Man, the engineer, may soon become man, the engineered.

Until recently, population control programs focused on decreasing the numbers of births. Now, with geneticists and social planners worrying aloud about the deterioration of the human gene pool, there is interest in limiting the types and quality of births as well. Bentley Glass, former president of the American Academy for the Advancement of Science, warns, "In an overpopulated world, it can no longer be affirmed that the right of the woman and man to reproduce as they see fit is inviolate. . . ." Glass contends that the right of parents to procreate must become a secondary consideration to the "right of every child to be born with a sound physical and mental constitution, based on a sound genotype."

Thanks to new processes for manufacturing life, scientists can offer at least eight possible ways of controlling reproduction: artificial insemination of a woman with sperm from her mate; artificial insemination of a woman with sperm from an anonymous donor; transplantation of an ovum (egg) from one woman to another and subsequent artificial insemination with sperm from either a mate or a donor; fertilization of an egg in vitro (glass) followed by implantation into a woman; extra-corporeal gestation ("test-tube" life); parthenogenesis (the devel-

opment of an unfertilized egg); nuclear transplantation or cloning (the reproduction of a cell which has been given a "foreign" nucleus), and embryo fusion (the joining of two individual embryos to form a human with four biological parents instead of two).

The combination of microbiological manipulation with the new reproductive techniques opens the way to full-scale genetic engineering. Bio-engineering is on the verge of moving from promise to performance. Artificial insemination is already marketable, and its popularity is growing. One million living Americans have been born by this process, and the number is increasing by more than 20,000 each year. The ability to deep-freeze human sperm for virtually any length of time has fueled a budding national industry—the commercial sperm bank. Banks are located in twelve cities, and business has never been better. John Olsen, president of Cryogenic Laboratories in St. Paul, notes, "In the last two years, the number of physicians requesting and using frozen donor sperm has doubled. We're having a difficult time keeping up with the requests coming in." Cryogenic supplies doctors in forty-five cities around the country.

Other methods of controlling reproduction represent a greater degree of sophistication. They are not yet perfected, but extensive experimentation has proceeded on each. The process of removing impregnated eggs from one herd animal and implanting them in the uterus of another animal of the same species is a widely used practice among animal breeders who combine artificial insemination with this embryo "flushing" and implantation to create super-herds of prize cattle.

At the next level of sophistication is the use of deep-frozen embryo banks that permit long-term storage of "superembryos." The first success in this area occurred in 1972, when scientists at the Atomic Energy Commission's Oak Ridge Laboratory thawed and implanted frozen mouse embryos. At about the same time, scientists in England announced the birth of Frosty, a bull calf born from a deep-frozen embryo.

Researchers point out that there are considerable similarities in embryo implantation and development between such lower mammals as mice and rabbits, and humans. So far, a human egg transplant has not been attempted, but several egg depositories exist at universities across the country. Commercial human ova banks are right around the corner.

A related area of experimentation is the fertilization of an egg in the laboratory and its subsequent implantation into a woman, a technique which some scientists feel is likely to be general medical practice within ten to twenty years. This research is making significant contributions in the quest to produce test-tube life.

The ability to keep tissue alive in glass has been recognized since 1907, when frog cells were first grown in petri dishes. A few years later, a scientist removed a piece of tissue from a chicken heart and placed it in a glass container filled with fluid, where it lived for thirty-three years (outliving the scientist by two years). As far back as the 1940s, a scientist succeeded in fertilizing a human egg with sperm in a test tube.

Joseph Fletcher, professor of medical ethics at the University of Virginia School of Medicine, regards test-tube life as finishing the work begun by the contraceptive pill. Because laboratory-created life is "willed, chosen, purposed, and controlled," rather than emotionally or accidentally produced, Fletcher believes "laboratory reproduction is radically human compared to conception by ordinary heterosexual intercourse."

Researchers have succeeded in growing a mouse embryo in vitro through approximately half of its gestation period, and E.S.E. Hafez, chairman of the department of animal sciences at Washington State University, is certain that the day of complete test-tube life is nearer than most of us suspect. To drive home his point, Hafez once posed for a photo which appeared in a national news magazine. There, in full color, was the scientist, a set of test tubes labeled "man," "sheep," and "swine" held in his outstretched hands; the caption read, "the barnyard of the future—complete with farmer."

With our present technology, incubators can keep alive a baby born as many as three months prematurely. The key now is to gain control of the first twenty-four weeks of life. Robert Goodlin of Stanford has been a leader in the search for an artificial womb for more than a decade, and has developed a pressurized steel-and-glass world in which an oxygen-rich saline solution constantly bathes a fetus. Intense pressure—roughly the equivalent of pressure felt under water at a depth of 450 feet—drives oxygen through the skin so that the baby's lungs do not have to work. No fetus has survived in the chamber for more than forty-eight hours, but Goodlin is working on a system to draw off carbon dioxide and waste materials that become deadly unless removed.

No genetic engineering possibility provokes more "sci fi" thinking than cloning. But cloning, the production of genetically duplicate individuals from the biological information contained in a single body cell, is clearly not science fiction. Within our lifetimes, carbon-copy human beings will walk among us.

Recombinant DNA has become an especially useful tool in cloning experiments. A scientist at Oxford has taken an unfertilized egg cell from an African clawed frog, destroyed the egg nucleus with ultraviolet radiation, and then successfully implanted cells taken from the frog's intestinal wall into the empty egg. The egg cell, equipped with the full chromosomal make-up necessary to become an African clawed frog, was then tricked into "thinking" it had been fertilized. The cell began to divide. A clone was born.

Researchers have yet to clone a mammal in this way, but experts agree that human cloning is on the horizon. The switch to control the reproductive power of the human cell is almost known.

Joshua Lederberg, a Nobel Prize winning biologist, is a leading proponent of human cloning. "If a superior individual—and presumably, genotype—is identified," he argues, "why not copy it directly, rather than suffer all the risks, including those of sex determination, involved in the disruptions of recombination [sexual procreation]? Leave sexual reproduction for experimental purposes."

Most scientists agree that, given enough research money, all these reproduction technologies can be operational within the next ten to thirty years. And many argue that selective breeding, using these technologies, is our only option if we are to survive as a society. Joseph Fletcher maintains that not to initiate such policies would be immoral and irresponsible, since we have a sacred duty to control our heredity, just as we accept the responsibility of controlling our social life and behavior. James Bonner of the California Institute of Technology assures us that selective breeding of children is really just an extension of our age-old practice of domesticating animals and plants, and should, therefore, not be viewed with alarm.

Proponents of genetic engineering assert that decisions to procreate cannot be trusted to the individual. Nobel Prize winner Linus Pauling proposes that a symbol showing one's genotype be tattooed on the forehead of every young person. "If this were done," says Pauling, "two young people carrying the same seriously defective gene . . . would recognize the situation at first sight and would refrain from falling in love with one another." Pauling favors legislation along these lines.

In an article published by the National Aeronautics and Space Administration, James Bonner discussed a plan in which genetic material from each individual would be removed immediately after birth, and the individual would promptly be sterilized: "During the individual's lifetime, records will be kept of accomplishments and characteristics. After the individual's death, a committee decides if the accomplishments are worthy of procreation into other individuals. If so, genetic material would be removed from the depository and stimulated to clone a new individual. If the committee decides the genetic material is unworthy of procreation it is destroyed." Bonner contends, "The question is indeed not a moral one but a temporal one—when do we start?"

As selective breeding begins to eliminate certain genotypes that are deemed undesirable, gene surgery will soon be used to "upgrade" existing individuals. This year scientists in California were successful in turning bacteria into a cellular "factory" that manufactures the genes necessary to produce insulin, a substance required by diabetics. The next step is to "switch on" these genes to begin insulin production. Researchers hope there will soon be cures, not only for diabetes, but also for hemophilia, PKU, and Tay-Sachs disease.

Genetic engineers also talk of using genetic surgery to "adapt" people to existing environments. If certain workers are more susceptible than others to the harmful effects of particular pollutants and carcinogens, for example, adapting workers will be less expensive than eliminating dangerous chemicals.

Gene surgery could not only provide a hedge against disease, proponents of genetic engineering believe, but also improve worker satisfaction by adapting brain functions. As justification for extending genetic surgery to the redirection of human emotion and intellect, many molecular biologists maintain that schizophrenia and other "abnormal" psychological states result from genetic disorders. "There can be no twisted thought without a twisted molecule," a prominent neurophysiologist has stated. Reports supposedly demonstrating that crime, social protest, poverty, and intelligence are also the result of people's genetic make-up—not of institutional injustice—are being published in large numbers.

Gene surgery has a high priority within Government-funded medical research. The National Institute of General Medical Sciences yearly awards more than $117 million for its development. With advances in recombinant DNA, the possibilities of gene surgery are almost limitless, suggests one scientist: "If one considers the purpose of a drug to be to restore the normal function of some particular process in the body, then DNA should be considered to be the ultimate drug."

The goal of perfecting the human race (or portions of it) through biological redesign is, of course, not new. It has spawned some of the most brutal social and political movements of the Twentieth Century. Whenever dramatic new discoveries in genetics have been made, they have soon been translated into political and social programs. And whenever societies have wanted to alter the social, economic, or political life of specific classes, they have encouraged geneticists to experiment with new ways to accomplish such ends.

This symbiotic relationship between genetic engineering and social policy reached its most conspicuously abhorrent level in the genetic policies of Hitler's Third Reich. Long before Hitler's rise to power, however, American geneticists and social ideologues had begun working together to fashion similar policies designed both to eliminate the so-called inferior stock from the human species and, at the same time, to create a master race.

The early genetic engineering movement in this country was called "eugenics." It arose in the wake of the first massive immigration wave, militant union organizing drives, and the mushrooming growth of city slums in the late 1890s. It promised an easy cure for economic inequalities and social ills at a time when social reformers were increasingly disheartened and when science was being heralded as the linchpin of American greatness. Eugenics offered both a scientific explanation for social problems and a scientific approach to their solution.

Eugenics appealed to the country's "best people"—powerful old-line ruling families, and upper-middle-class academics and professionals who turned the ideology into a form of secular evangelism. They preached eugenics in university lecture halls, before professional conventions, and on political platforms from one end of the country to the other. The message was always the same: America's salvation hinged on its resolve to eliminate the biologically inferior types and breed the perfect human race.

The acceptance of eugenics by much of the general public was due, in large part, to the early and enthusiastic support of some of the most prominent scientists of the time. Almost half of the nation's geneticists became involved in the movement, believing they could help reverse what they saw as a decline in society's hereditary quality.

Eugenicists looked to sterilization as a major tool in their campaign to weed out biologically inferior stock from the American population. As a result of their relentless drive, tens of thousands of American citizens were involuntarily sterilized under various laws enacted by thirty states to cure everything from crime to feeblemindedness. The extent to which sterilization mania was carried is perhaps best reflected in a bill introduced in the Missouri legislature calling for sterilization of those "convicted of murder, rape, highway robbery, chicken stealing, bombing, or theft of automobiles."

One of the most bizarre twists in the eugenics movement was the Fitter Family Contests run by the American Eugenics Society. Blue ribbons were presented at county and state fairs throughout the Midwest to those families who could produce the best family pedigrees. Families were judged on their physical and mental qualities right alongside the breeding contests for pigs and cows.

From its peak in 1924, the eugenics movement steadily declined, eventually collapsing with the stock market crash in 1929. With America's financial elite jumping out of windows and middle-class professionals and academics standing in unemployment lines alongside Italian, Polish, and Jewish immigrants, and blacks, and with responsible scientists exposing the racism of their colleagues, the myth that certain groups were biologically superior was no longer tenable.

The American eugenics movement lay dormant through World War II. But the bomb on Hiroshima sparked a new interest in genetics, as scientists and government officials began to worry about the effects of radiation on the gene pool. And the bomb also triggered a renewed interest in eugenics. Prominent scientists claimed that increased radiation was causing massive mutations in the human gene pool, and that these were spreading with each generation. In addition, they argued, breakthroughs in medical treatment of "gentically defective" individuals were keeping alive biologically unfit people who, in turn, were passing on their "defects" to their offspring.

The new eugenics—today called "sociobiology"—has caught on. And as the tools of genetic modification have acquired new sophistication, so has the genetic engineering rhetoric. Today's arguments are couched in less openly racist terms: Many modern-day eugenicists agree with Bernard Davis, professor of bacterial physiology at Harvard, that we need a eugenics program "aimed primarily at reducing the production of individuals whose genetic endowment would limit their ability to cope with a technologically complex environment."

Such pronouncements become of even greater concern when prominent scientists attempt to convince the public that institutional environmental reforms are useless.

The genetic engineers argue that man, the machine, is not keeping pace with the advances that have been made in a larger environment that is becoming increasingly technologized. "Human culture has grown so rapidly," says Joshua Lederberg, "that the biological evolution of the species during the last hundred generations has only begun to adjust to it." Man is still imperfect, often unpredictable, and prone to subjective miscalculations. These imperfections have a dysfunctional effect on the rest of the techno-system. If we are to prevent the entire system that we have synthesized from collapsing on itself, as it is showing signs of doing, then the only hope, says the biological engineer, is to bring the last major component of the system into line with technical design. That means humanity itself.

Our schools are preparing us for the age of genetic engineering. More than one million school children are being given special drugs to control behavior attributed to "minimal brain dysfunction." Genetic injections are being discussed by scientists and educators alike as a means of improving the general intelligence of the population. Proponents of gene therapy contend that it is merely an internal aid to education—designed to achieve the same ends as calculators, computers, and videotapes.

The consumer market for mood altering genetic surgery is already so firmly established that even critics doubt it will be possible to forestall its widespread use as soon as it becomes available. Their pessimism is based on the fact that psycho-active drugs have, in just a few years, become the most heavily prescribed medications in the country, and are now used by more than 40 per cent of all women and 22 per cent of all men.

Ciba Geigy advertises that its anti-depressant, Tofranil, will help the individual readjust when "losing a job to the computer may mean frustration, guilt, and loss of esteem." Merck Company's Triavil is for people who are "sad or unhappy about the future. . . . easily tired and who have difficulty in making decisions." The Sandoz Company claims its product Serentil is "for the anxiety that comes from not fitting in. The newcomer in town who can't make friends. The organization man who can't adjust to altered status within his company. The woman who can't get along with her daughter-in-law. The executive who can't accept retirement."

In a society in which millions of people feel increasingly alienated at the hands of the giant bureaucracies that regulate their lives, and powerless to cope with pollution, urban decay, unemployment, inflation, and a host of other problems, psycho-drugs offer the ideal solution. And any consumer who has become habitually addicted to the purchase of psycho-drugs is a ready market for a "genetic fix."

The Cetus Corporation knows this and is prepared. The significance of the power of genetic engineering cannot be exaggerated, Cetus contends in its in-house memo: "A new industry with untold potential is about to appear."

Recognizing this untold potential, Standard Oil of Indiana is spending $5 million to capture controlling interest in Cetus. Cetus shareholders with convertible preferred stock are being offered $330 a share for stock that cost only $100 a share less than five years ago. The giant corporation sees Cetus as a hedge against the world's dwindling oil reserves.

Cetus is only the tip of the iceberg of corporate involvement in genetic engineering. Seven major pharmaceutical companies are also engaged in the race to exploit this new industry, and a dozen more drug, chemical, and agricultural companies are poised to enter the field, which *Fortune* magazine predicts will soon become a "multibillion dollar industry."

Many scientists advocating genetic engineering have a financial stake in these corporations. On the board of directors and advisers at Cetus are such world renowned scientists as Joshua Lederberg; Stanley Cohen, associate professor of medicine at Stanford University Medical School and the acknowledged leader in the new technology of gene manipulation; Arnold Demain, professor of applied microbiology at MIT; and Donald Glaser, Nobel laureate and professor of physics and molecular biology at the University of California.

Broad-scale genetic engineering will probably be introduced to Americans gradually, almost imperceptibly. As each new genetic advance becomes commercially practical, corporations, aided by scientific expertise and Government approval, will attempt to exploit a new consumer need, either real or manufactured. Whether the genetic revolution or the social revolution prevails depends, ultimately, on how we respond. Restructuring the institutions of society means rejecting the technological imperative and making an active commitment. Genetic engineering, to succeed, will require only our passive acceptance.

QUESTIONS

1. Ought there to be a system of formal control over the application of some kinds of scientific knowledge? If so, who should exercise control—scientists, voters, courts, government, industry, or some other authority?

2. Some scientists believe they will be able to arrest the aging process and thus indefinitely postpone death. What impact might such an innovation have on society?

3. How do you respond to the idea that scientists might be able to intervene genetically to perfect the human species?

PETER BARRY CHOWKA   *Hamburger's Last Stand*

Modern economic life centers around impersonal corporations rather than the individual entrepreneurs of a century ago. Virtually every significant aspect of economic life in the United States, from manufacturing to retailing to banking, is now controlled by large corporations. But although they provide the goods, the services, and many of the jobs on which we all depend, opinion polls have consistently shown public suspicion and antipathy toward large corporations.

The objections are many: that corporations abuse their power by influencing the political process; that they create monopolies or oligopolies that force out smaller businesses and thus reduce product diversity; that they engage in misleading advertising; that they manipulate consumer tastes, creating "needs" where none existed; that they sometimes produce shoddy or even dangerous products; that they try to evade social responsibility for their behavior: in short, that they care only for profits, not people.

This article by Peter Chowka deals with a corporate enterprise that has almost become an American institution: McDonald's, the fast-food chain. This corporation and its many imitators have had an extraordinary effect on the American diet, and, therefore, on the health of the millions of people who consume their fare. The impact of the corporation does not stop there; its influence ranges from such issues as local zoning laws to the level of the national minimum wage. The comments in this article are directed specifically at McDonald's, but many of them might be applied to the corporate economy as a whole.

McDonald's is a name ringed with a certain nursery rhyme magic, reinforced by the persuasive power of billions of dollars' worth of the best media advertising. During the past decade McDonald's has become a household word—its fast-food menu representing a universal language—to hundreds of millions of people throughout the United States, Central America, Europe, the Middle East, Japan, and Australia.

Its relatively brief history as a corporation to date has been written mostly in superlatives and statistics that always are bigger than life: McDonald's is the single largest purveyor of food in the U.S., accounting for 6 percent of the total restaurant market; a majority of Americans over age 12 eat at a McDonald's at least once a month; its servings are self-consciously tallied in tens of billions. (If all the hamburgers McDonald's has sold over the years were piled up in one place, the entire state of Illinois—56,400 square miles—would be covered in a layer of burgers knee deep.)

Equally impressive-looking is McDonald's economic picture, especially for a company limited to selling cheap hamburgers, French fried potatoes, and soft drinks—a company, it has been said repeatedly by those who keep track of such things, that ranks in wealth, power, and influence with the giants in steel, automobiles, petrochemicals, and communications. In the U.S. in 1977, Dunn's Review ranked McDonald's stock sixtieth in overall market value; *Forbes* in 1978 listed the firm 128th in the top 500 corporations; its profits have increased 1,300 percent since 1968. On the surface, omnipresent in cities and suburbs and expanding worldwide now, McDonald's seems invincible, with nowhere to go but up.

Appearances, however, are deceiving. Undeniably McDonald's has enjoyed a heyday. Approaching the 1980s, though, a variety of factors are combining to presage serious trouble ahead for the burger behemoth.

McDonald's, foremost, is an industrial organization based on centralization, standardization, volume, and profit; but conditions today are beginning to threaten such wasteful, unadaptable systems. It appears that during the past year McDonald's momentum has been checked; for the first time its growth in profits has been unable to keep pace with inflation. The likelihood of fuel

From *East West Journal*, June, 1979. Reprinted with permission.

shortages, recession, high meat costs, and revised consuming patterns have the corporation's investors worried; leading Wall Street analysts are advising their clients not to buy McDonald's stock. Incredibly, according to Don Trott, research chief for the brokerage house A. C. Becker (quoted in the *Washington Post*, February 28, 1979), for McDonald's, soon, "the game will be over."

Paralleling the present unmistakable stagnation, and fantastic-sounding but probable vulnerability, of McDonald's—perhaps partially causing these conditions—is an increasing public awareness of the frivolity and ultimately tragic toll on our health of participating in the McDonald's "experience." It is clear to millions of people now that McDonald's—in fact, all fast-food chain restaurants—present serious dangers to the economic, social, and physical health of local communities and their inhabitants.

Franchise Fever: The American Way

Gradually the humble hamburger has wormed its way deeply into the fabric of American life, overtaking the hot dog and all other prepared and processed foods in popularity; today the beef-patty-between-a-bun provides the basis for financial empires. The hamburger's first appearance is disputed, attributed to both the 1904 St. Louis World's Fair (which also introduced iced tea and ice cream cones) and Louis Lunch, a small New Haven, Connecticut, diner of the same period.

In the late 1800s the pace of life, reflecting the introduction of trains and other mass transit systems, was beginning to accelerate; in response, Americans started to consume more meals on the run. The hamburger, and the then-more-popular hot dog, were adapted perfectly to this trend. Hamburgers and hot dogs, especially the take-out varieties purchased at lunch counters, sporting events, and diners, were popular as occasional foods through the Depression. The widespread rationing, in-plant feeding, and C-rations that accompanied World War Two further dulled the American palate and intensified the acceptance of fast, homogenized, industrially-produced food as standard fare.

Mac and Dick McDonald were two enterprising brothers from New Hampshire who migrated to California in the 1930s. In Pasadena in 1940 they opened their first hamburger stand. Eight years later, at another stand in San Bernardino, they perfected the McDonald's formula that would make them and scores of other people millionaires—a system that dictated location near a well-traveled highway; incredibly fast service; a cheap, standardized menu; no plates, dishes, or choice of condiments and eye-catching golden arches.

An aging traveling salesman of restaurant equipment (paper cups, milk shake mixers, and the like) named Ray Kroc was fascinated by the McDonald brothers' San Bernardino stand, especially its annual gross income of $250,000 (by the early 1950s) from selling fifteen-cent hamburgers. He convinced the brothers to sell him all rights to future distribution of the promising business right down to the last details including the name and the arches.

Kroc is the kind of single-minded entrepreneur who gives credence to the overworked Horatio Alger myth of success. One of Kroc's favorite slogans, borrowed from Calvin Coolidge, is "Nothing in this world can take the place of persistence . . . Persistence and determination alone are omnipotent." In a 1972 interview with *Institutions*, a food service magazine, Kroc said, "Look, it is ridiculous to call this an industry. This is not. This is rat eat rat, dog eat dog. I'll kill 'em, and I'm going to kill 'em before they kill me. You're talking about the American way of survival of the fittest." (Kroc reportedly has accumulated $500 million in personal profit—making him one of the dozen wealthiest people in the country—by directing McDonald's.)

As a traveling salesman for a quarter century, Kroc had the experience, and the motivation, to foresee McDonald's potential for becoming a focal point—a cheap, clean, reassuring, familiar, pit-stop home-away-from-home—amidst the rootless, mobile, suburban culture that North America was becoming. In more ways than one McDonald's and fast foods are linked symbiotically with the automobile—the revolutionary technological advance that altered not only the landscape of the country but its entire economy and the mindset of its people. By correctly identifying the automobile-created suburbs as the most likely targets for profitable hamburger stands, Kroc ensured McDonald's enormous growth; in turn the proven economic model for achieving this insinuation was the franchise system, first used by General Motors in 1898 to market steamers.

GM decided to sell its steamers, forerunners of the successful internal combustion engine vehicles, through a chain of licensed, independent dealers; GM became the franchisor, and the local dealer was the franchisee. Franchising allows rapid growth of an industry because most of the capital for such expansion is provided by the franchisee, freeing the franchisor for more profitable endeavors, such as research, development, production, and advertising. By 1968, 95 percent of all U.S. passenger cars were sold by franchisees. Many other industries followed the same principle; over one thousand in all, they included soft drinks, processed supermarket foods like white bread, cosmetics, hotels/motels, and fast foods. White Castle was the first franchise hamburger chain in the 1920s, but its stands were located mostly in central cities. Other early familiar food franchises were Howard Johnsons and A&W Root Beer.

In the 1950s, giant corporations began usurping greater shares of certain markets, leading to oligopolies—shared monopolies. Many small entrepreneurs, especially traditional "mom and pop" business owners, unable to compete, in effect were forced either to become franchisees for large corporations or to get out of business. By 1967 franchised industries enjoyed sales worth $90 billion annually, representing ten percent of the Gross National Product and 24 percent of the retail trade industry.

Fast-food operations like McDonald's lent themselves especially well to franchising: For a certain investment and an annual payment based on a percentage of sales, a budding entrepreneur could buy into an established, high-profit, national business that sold few items, had a relatively simple operation, experienced few inventory problems, relied exclusively on cash sales, and could flourish by using unskilled labor. In 1945 the U.S. had 3,500 fast-food outlets; in 1975 there were 440,000, a majority of them franchised. The system was not without peril for the franchisee, however. Harold Brown, in *Franchising: Trap for the Trusting*, writes that the franchisor "inculcates the franchisee with the necessity of being taught, guided, and controlled not only during the initial training period but throughout the existence of the franchise."

The economic tentacles that link franchisor and franchisee are never-ending. Federal antitrust laws prevent franchisors like McDonald's from directly selling supplies to their franchises. Most franchisors, however, have secret "sweetheart" arrangements with so-called approved purveyors (a dozen or so supporting industries in the case of McDonald's). By contract with the franchisor, the franchisees are required to purchase all of their food, equipment, and other necessities from these specified suppliers. Brown's book notes court hearings revealing that some fast-food chain franchisees have had to pay 600 percent over normal prices for food and other items from their approved suppliers.

Building the Burger Empire

McDonald's took the franchising system one more profitable step further: After 1960, in order to add to the fees it received from its franchisees, the corporation asserted more control over the entire operation—selecting potential local McDonald's sites, buying the land, building the restaurant, installing the equipment, and renting it as a package to an operator who, thus, would be both licensee/franchisee and tenant. The McDonald's franchisee pays a rental fee of at least 8.5 percent based on annual revenues, along with the yearly service charge (3.5 percent), a fee to support national advertising (3 to 5 percent), and a one-time payment that permits the licensee to operate for twenty years ($250,000). A McDonald's financial officer is quoted in *Time*'s September, 1973, cover story, "The Burger that Conquered the Country,"

as saying, "We're just like the Mafia, we skim it right off the top."

Through the 1960s and early 1970s McDonald's growth was phenomenal. Part of it was based on the company's increasing application of assembly line industrialization techniques to the procurement, preparation, sale, and delivery of food, always toward the ends of lowering costs and increasing volume for greater profits. Everything became calculated and rigidly enforced—size of hamburger patties (to one one-hundredth of an inch), cooking times (controlled by a computer), design and layout of the restaurants, degree of cleanliness of the public washroom toilets, and behavior and appearance of the employees.

Another vital element in the McDonald's success story was cheap labor. Ninety percent of McDonald's 150,000 employees are part-time teenage workers and students who are paid the bare minimum wage; in the U.S. only farm laborers and domestic servants earn less money. Working conditions at McDonald's are poor, and include arbitrary shift assignments, boring work, pressure from managers and customers, no paid holidays, and no hospital insurance. The employee turn-over rate in an average McDonald's is 300 percent a year.

An article in *In These Times*, November 8 to 14, 1978, presents observations from several McDonald's employees. One of them, Bryant Cunningham, a twenty-one-year-old black, says, "You don't have a name. They [management] yell, 'Backroom, we need a Coke change.' I'd say, 'Hey, I'm back here, but my name ain't Backroom.'" Another worker, Mike Sorriano, comments, "All they see is hamburger. They don't see you. You're just there to turn hamburger."

As long ago as 1972 McDonald's was maneuvering cynically and secretly to insure a continued supply of plentiful, cheap labor. In that year Ray Kroc donated $250,000 to President Nixon's re-election campaign in exchange for Nixon's commitment to support the "youth differential" clause in the revised minimum wage bill that was about to be debated in Congress. This "McDonald's bill," as it came to be known, advocated a paltry subminimum wage for workers aged sixteen to seventeen, who provide the backbone for McDonald's operation. Ultimately, the youth differential section of the legislation was defeated. With the latest federally-guaranteed minimum wage that went into effect in January, 1979—$3 per hour—McDonald's requirement for cheap labor is being threatened.

Contributing to McDonald's quick ascendancy was the climate for industrial growth that reigned during the corporation's formative years. The 1960s, especially, were a time of quasi-pathological expansion in many sectors of the economy. As in the fabled years of the 1920s which preceded The Great Depression, waves of speculation sent certain "glamor" stocks zooming upward;

McDonald's, using skillful public relations and other tactics, was among them. One of McDonald's strategies, not unusual in other quick-growth industries, was to anticipate the next three months' profit and obligate it in the way of debt for immediate expansion, which in turn guaranteed additional eventual profit; the process was repeated indefinitely.

When its shares were introduced on the New York Stock Exchange in 1965, McDonald's handed out free hamburgers on the trading floor; the stunt gained the corporation national publicity. By that time its growth—from nowhere in 1955 to 710 stands in 44 states, with plans to expand internationally—already was very impressive. Through the mid-1970s McDonald's sustained its growth, in sales and profits, of 30 to 40 percent a year. It was common for McDonald's stock to be part of prestigious institutional portfolios. Some observers, however, noted serious problems. In a 1973 article in *Barron's*, Professor Abraham Briloff accused McDonald's of misrepresenting its financial statements to show higher profits than actually were earned. Sen. Lloyd Bentsen (D-Tex.), speaking in 1974, cited McDonald's as having a 1972 book value of $200 million, while its stock value was $2.1 billion. In contrast, Sen. Bentsen observed, U.S. Steel's book value was $3.6 billion, while its total stock was worth $2.2 billion. "Something is wrong," Sen. Bentsen commented, "when the stock market is long on hamburgers and short on steel."

The Newest Shell Game: The Selling of the Burger

Despite the apparent simplicity of its early operation, McDonald's has never been just a place that sells hamburgers. The real roots of its unprecedented success lie in a considerably more complex interweaving of modern American philosophy and motivational advertising.

In the early 1970s Ray Kroc told the authors of *Big Mac* [Boas and Chain, 1976], "Our theme is kind of synonymous with Sunday school, the Girl Scouts, and the YMCA. McDonald's is clean and wholesome." He spoke of the corporation's image without mentioning its food; the omission is not an isolated one. The four-hundred-page manual that governs each restaurant's operation specifies things like "Your windowmen and outside order takers must impress customers as being 'All American' boys"; it insists that a certain percentage of sales be given to specified charities, with accompanying promotional fanfare; and it dictates that a U.S. flag, floodlit at night, fly prominently outside the building.

In 1967 McDonald's undertook its first national advertising campaign, budgeted at $5 million, to make the chain (which by then had 1,000 units) a household word. Within two years $15 million was being spent on advertising; in 1973 the figure was $50 million annually, and today it approaches $150 million. McDonald's is now

among the thirty largest advertisers in the country. Its sophisticated media messages are targeted to saturate prime time network TV; one of every ten television commercials for food (that means one in every thirty TV commercials) is for McDonald's. In the significant Los Angeles market, McDonald's is the single largest advertiser. The inundation of commercials evidently has paid off: A recent survey, published in the *Washington Post*, in October, 1978, noted that 54 percent of all Americans over the age of twelve eat at a McDonald's at least once a month. Significantly, though, an internal McDonald's study, cited in *Big Mac*, revealed that the typical customer patronized a McDonald's only twice a month (a figure that apparently worried the company's executives), and only 10 percent of the residents who lived *near* a McDonald's came in more than one time a month.

Needham, Harper, and Steers, one of the country's most prominent advertising agencies, has handled the McDonald's account since 1970. The campaign it designed to distinguish McDonald's from the other proliferating chains—"you deserve a break today"—stresses the "experience" of patronizing a McDonald's, not the food. An account executive, in *Big Mac*, explains, "The message we're trying to get across is that going to a McDonald's can be a fun experience for an American family. For a housewife, it's a minibreak in the day's routine. For dad it's an opportunity to be a hero to the kids, but in a way which won't cost much money. For the children, it's plain fun."

Since another internal study revealed that in three-quarters of the cases where a family decides to eat out the children choose the restaurant, McDonald's advertising often appeals directly to young TV viewers. McDonald's television commercials have created a whole array of cartoon fantasy characters: Ronald McDonald, Captain Crook, the Hamburglar, Mayor McCheese, and Evil Grimace. Ronald, especially, is heavily promoted: actors are hired to dress up as Ronald and appear prominently in holiday parades, at shopping mall openings, in charity telethons, and wherever else the "McDonald's experience" message can be conveyed without a too-blatant taint of commercialism. Recent polls show that 96 percent of American children can identify Ronald McDonald; he is second in public recognition only to Santa Claus.

Questionable Nutrition

Perhaps McDonald's avoids mentioning nutrition in its advertising, because the food it sells is not primarily responsible for the corporation's success; moreover, calling attention to its food could increase McDonald's vulnerability to charges that its menu is deficient and harmful. Twice recently, in 1973 and again in 1977, McDonald's attempted to generate evidence to the contrary by spending $500,000 for analyses of its food by the WARF Institute in Madison, Wisconsin (a supposedly-independent laboratory, actually owned by Ralston-Purina, which operates the Jack-in-the-Box fast-food chain). WARF examined each menu item elaborately in terms of selected vitamins, minerals, and other nutrients. The *ingredients* of the foods, however, were not revealed. McDonald's jealously guards its recipes (which are as secret as the formula for Coca-Cola) supposedly to protect itself from competitors. WARF's published findings, which are copyrighted by McDonald's System, Inc. (the corporation's legal name), contain no general conclusions but rather extensive tables showing what percentage of one's Recommended Daily Allowance of popular vitamins and minerals one gets from eating McDonald's foods. Conspicuously absent in the report is any mention of the glucose (refined sugar) content of the foods, the percentage of calories derived from fat, and the type of fat (saturated vs. unsaturated) present. Many nutritionists believe that these three neglected areas are of greater importance in assessing the health-sustaining value of foods than any mere listing of RDAs for certain known vitamins.

Writing in the *New York Times Magazine* in July, 1974, Jean Mayer, Ph.D., then a professor of nutrition at Harvard University's School of Public Health, notes, "The typical McDonald's meal—hamburgers, French fries, and a malted—doesn't give you much nutrition. It's very low in vitamins B and C, but very high in saturated fats. It's typical of the diet that raises the cholesterol count and leads to heart disease." (Since then, in interviews elsewhere, however, Dr. Mayer has appeared to defend McDonald's.) Dr. George Christakais, of New York's Mt. Sinai Medical School, in a speech to the American Public Health Association in 1974, said that the food that was fueling the "McDonald's generation . . . can set the stage for chronic disease later in life."

Surprisingly, considering the vast quantities that are consumed, fast-foods and their substantial effects on health rarely have been subjected to comprehensive, independent scientific scrutiny. The situation is somewhat similar to that which prevails in the pharmaceutical industry; aspirin, Darvon, Percadon and other over-the-counter and prescription drugs consumed by the billions, seldom are studied in terms of their overall impact.

The advent of fast-food restaurants has had an enormous impact on the American diet. Today, according to *Dietary Goals*, most Americans derive 66 percent of their calories from fat and sugar, and only 22 percent from vegetables, whole grains, and fruits. This diet is virtually identical to the fast-food diet. Letitia Brewster and Michael Jacobson, Ph.D., in *The Changing American Diet* (published by Center for Science in the Public Interest in 1978) assert that the following dietary changes are attributable almost exclusively to the fast-food invasion:

frozen potato use climbed from 6.6 pounds per person in 1960 to 36.8 pounds per person in 1976; beef consumption increased from 64.3 pounds per person in 1960 to 95.4 pounds per person in 1976; during the same period use of tomato catsup, sauce, and paste, and chili sauce rose from 7.6 to 13.3 pounds per person; soft drink consumption rose from 192 8-ounce servings per year in 1960 to 493 8-ounce servings per person in 1976.

One independent study of fast foods, conducted by the Institute Bureau, published in *Good Housekeeping*, November, 1975, found McDonald's Big Mac to have the highest percentage of calories from fat—53 percent—of any fast-food tested. (McDonald's French fries are 50 percent fat, and its chocolate shake, 22 percent.) *Dietary Goals*, published by the U.S. Senate's Select Committee on Nutrition and Human Needs, recommends that people reduce the current high levels of fat consumed in the modern day diet. Too much fat in the diet is linked to the modern epidemics of heart disease, cancer, hypertension, obesity, and other chronic, degenerative diseases.

Another independent analysis, conducted by the Nutrition Institute of America (NIA) for WABC-TV, New York, published in *Caveat Emptor*, April, 1977, discloses that the high moisture content of fast foods (in excess of 50 percent in some cases) tends to mask their actual high concentrations of fat and sugar. (McDonald's WARF study claims the fat content of its hamburgers is between 11 and 18 percent, although this figure was determined before the moisture, which adds no calories, was subtracted.) The NIA report adds, "The (hamburger) buns are made of processed carbohydrates stripped of most of their nutrition, which provide only empty calories. Refined sugar has been liberally added as a preservative, filler, and tooth sweetener. The glucose content in McDonald's French fries is concentrated to two and three-fourths times what is normal blood sugar in humans."

In 1978 Barry Commoner, Ph.D., director of the Center for the Biology of Natural Systems at Washington University in St. Louis, released the results of a study that pointed to additional health hazards of hamburgers. It was found that cooking chopped meat on metal surfaces above 300 degrees Fahrenheit (which is how McDonald's cooks its hamburgers) produces mutagens, substances that cause genetic change. Although it has not yet been shown that these mutagens lead to human cancer, 90 percent of all mutagens ever tested cause cancer in laboratory animals. Dr. Commoner's research team said that hamburger mutagens in fact "may represent a risk of cancer in people." Dr. Gio B. Gori, then director of the Diet, Nutrition, and Cancer program at the National Cancer Institute, described Dr. Commoner's hamburger research as "first class science."

Of fast-food drinks, the study in *Good Housekeeping* notes that the shakes "are frozen from a liquid mix of nonfat dry milk powder, vegetable fat, flavoring, and sweetener." *Consumer Reports'* study (May, 1975) observes that both the shakes and cola drinks provide "empty calories . . . devoid of other nutrients." NIA's report adds that "The colas served at these establishments have appalling glucose contents . . . McDonald's is more than twenty-four times the normal blood sugar level. Such a concentration of refined carbohydrates is almost frightening, considering how much we've learned lately about refined carbohydrates' contribution to dental problems, mouth and gum diseases, high cholesterol levels, heart disease, diabetes, hypoglycemia, and other maladies that plague modern Americans."

Fast foods are very high in refined, commercial salt (primarily sodium chloride) to which have been added a variety of chemicals, including dextrose (sugar), sodium aluminum silicate, chalk, and iodine. The minerals that are present in sun-dried sea salt, meanwhile, including potassium, calcium, magnesium, iron, and copper have been removed. *Dietary Goals* notes that excessive consumption of commercial salt (about 40 percent pure sodium) has been linked to a variety of serious diseases, especially hypertension (high blood pressure), the most widespread degenerative disease in Western societies. Too much sodium also has been implicated in helping to cause stomach cancer, cerebrovascular disease (stroke), cardiovascular disease, edema, high blood pressure in children, and other frequently fatal conditions. Large quantities of sodium also disrupt the important, delicate balance between sodium and potassium which, according to *Dietary Goals*, "is required for the proper flow of fluids among and through cells."

The Food and Nutrition Board of the National Academy of Sciences has recommended that a healthy person ingest no more than 3 grams of salt per day (1.2 grams pure sodium). Present per capita daily salt consumption is between 6 and 18 grams. Many foods naturally contain sodium, but always in correct proportion to other elements and minerals. Fast foods are especially high in sodium, not only because beef, processed cheese, and fish contain sodium but because salt is added liberally to most fast foods during cooking. (Interestingly, the Senate report cites an NAS study that found that freezing foods increases their sodium content and depletes the supply of potassium; most fast foods, of course, are frozen and thawed for quick cooking.)

According to McDonald's WARF study, one meal of a Quarter Pounder burger with cheese, French fries, chocolate shake, and cherry pie provides 2.107 grams of sodium (or 5.2675 grams commercial salt), almost twice the recommended daily maximum suggested by the NAS and the first edition of *Dietary Goals*. This figure, necessarily, does not take into account the quantity of salt that many people add to fast foods as a seasoning after purchase.

Consumer Reports found that iodine is present in surprisingly high concentrations in fast-food meals; on the average, one such meal contains thirty times the daily recommended intake of iodine. It is known that excessive iodine affects the proper functioning of the thyroid gland. *CR* suggests that the source of the iodine may be the refined, iodized salt that is used liberally to season fast foods; iodates added to bread, rolls, and buns during processing; or residues from iodine compounds that are employed to clean and sterilize food processing equipment.

Another health hazard of fast foods, among many, deserves mention. Robert E. Cornette, D.Sc., director of Maple Knoll Laboratories in Columbus, Ohio, in an unpublished study dated December 11, 1978, notes that cooked fast-food hamburgers normally contain unusually large amounts of bacterial contamination (live bacterial, presumptive coliform, and staphlococcus). "The very act of producing hamburger," Dr. Cornette writes, "predisposes it to a multitude of contaminants, not the least of which is live bacteria in the classification of pathogenic, or capable of causing a disease state in the individual who consumes it."

The conclusions of NIA's study merit a review: "The fast-food diet, with the exception of the protein from hamburgers, is not of a high standard nutritionally; protein is only a small part of the human body's requirements. Fast foods fail to provide roughage and fiber needed to keep our digestive tracts clear and in good order. And the accoutrements of the meal—the buns, French fries, syrupy colas, chemical shakes, and sugary turnovers—provide little but concentrated, high caloried carbohydrates that often overload the body's digestive system."

More Adverse Impacts

Because of the tremendous volume of trade that they generate, their effective monopolistic control of a significant sector of the restaurant industry, and their ability to advertise and offer food at prices that seem inexpensive, the fast-food chains have driven much of the competition out of business. McDonald's (with over 4,500 U.S. outlets) and the other prominent chains now dominate the North American landscape. In many instances the only actual choice offered the traveler is a Big Mac, a Whopper, or a box of greasy Kentucky Fried Chicken.

When an area is first targeted for a fast-food franchise, the people who live there are softened up with a preliminary barrage of claims that they will benefit directly. In 1976 the Institute for Local Self Reliance, a public interest research group in Washington, D.C., investigated the flow of money through a local McDonald's outlet in order to measure what the surrounding community actually gained. The findings, published in the Institute's journal, *Self Reliance*, November, 1976, show that, in a typical McDonald's restaurant, only 17 percent of the store's expenditures clearly remains in the community where it is based: 15 percent for local labor (always hired at minimum wage) and 2 percent for local taxes. Generally 73 percent of the gross receipts, according to the study, leaves the area: 42 percent for food and paper purchased by contract from one of the distant, approved purveyors; 20 percent for rent, national advertising, headquarters accountants and lawyers, and corporate debt service (all paid to McDonald's corporation in Illinois); about 6 percent for taxes to state and federal governments; and roughly 5 percent for corporate management salaries. The McDonald's restaurant in Washington, D.C., that was studied enjoyed sales of $750,000 a year, and earned $50,000 in profit before taxes. *Self Reliance* reports, "Over $500,000 of this money leaves the community; as much as $67,500 more may also be 'exported.' Were the buildings owned locally, management hired from local residents, and supplies purchased locally, some of this leakage could be effectively plugged."

Fast-food chains exert different sorts of deleterious effects on the ecology of individual communities and the country as a whole. A major complaint of people who live within several miles of fast-food restaurants concerns the trash which tends to collect on their property and neighboring streets. Don Newgren, Ph.D., of York University in Toronto, determined that an average purchase at McDonald's entails a minimum of ten pieces of trash, much of it nonbiodegradable—plastic straws, plastic covers for the paper cups, styrofoam burger containers, and plastic condiment containers. Dr. Newgren figured that on Martha's Vineyard, where McDonald's proposed to open the first fast-food restaurant in late 1978, the minimum business the outlet planned to conduct would have generated over five million pieces of trash annually—an enormous amount for a small community, yet typical of the national pattern.

In 1972, when McDonald's was less than one-half its present size, Bruce Hannon, an engineer at the University of Illinois, studied the chain. His report was published in the *San Francisco Examiner*, November 12, 1972. Hannon determined that the sustained yield of 315 square miles of forest was required to keep McDonald's supplied with paper packaging for one year. The electric power consumed annually by its restaurants equaled the energy output of 12.7 million tons of coal, enough to keep Boston, Washington, D.C., and San Francisco supplied with electricity for an entire year.

Saying No to Big Mac

During the past five years, from the Champs-Elysée in Paris, to the Mission District in San Francisco, to Lane Cove in Sydney, people have organized themselves to oppose McDonald's. Their motivations have ranged all the way from vague feelings of discontent or alienation when they first see a McDonald's being constructed nearby up to a mounting horror when they arrive at a fuller understanding of the corporation's philosophy, economic underpinnings, intentions, and effects on health.

During the winter of 1977-1978 national attention focused on one such battle between the McDonald's System and the citizens of Martha's Vineyard; a UPI news account dubbed the controversy "the great hamburger war." One of the first things the Vineyard's anti-McDonald's organizers determined was that their effort was not unique and that opposition to junk food establishments is not limited to out-of-the-way places. Citizen's groups—most recently in Newton, Massachusetts; Washington, D.C.; Prince Georges County, Maryland; and Manchester Center, Vermont—have mounted successful campaigns to keep fast-food restaurants out of their neighborhoods.

Until McDonald's came along, Martha's Vineyard had managed to resist many of the leveling trends that have beset the rest of the country; its residents enjoyed a rare tranquility that was not marred by shopping centers, parking meters, superhighways, or a single traffic light or neon sign. In such a context then, a McDonald's outlet (which the company planned to install in a building that houses a natural foods market) and its effects would have stood out in garish detail.

The No Mac Committee canvassed the community by distributing anti-McDonald's petitions. Within a month one-quarter of the island's year-round residents had signed them in an effort to repel the "Big Mac Attack." Attempts were made to involve the entire community at every level: by talking up the issue wherever people met (in homes and workplaces; at political, professional, and social gatherings); by encouraging debates in schools; and by enlisting local artists to design and sell No Mac bumper stickers, T-shirts, and posters. This spring, local officials overwhelmingly rejected McDonald's proposed site for the hamburger stand.

Opponents to fast-foods chains tend to be drawn from a wide variety of socio-economic backgrounds. In San Francisco in 1972, scores of disparate organized ad hoc groups joined together actively to block McDonald's efforts at locating restaurants within that city. Joe Belardi of the AFL-CIO culinary workers union described "The basic issue (as) whether the people of San Francisco can decide what types of business are harmful to our community standards." Peter Boudoures, the vice-president of San Francisco's Permit Appeals Board, in voting against McDonald's coming to his own community, said, "McDonald's is after the almighty dollar, and they don't care about neighborhoods and how many small businesses they ruin." An anonymous official of the Marriott Corporation (which operates the similar Roy Rogers fast-food franchises) confirmed the red bottom line of the business when he boasted, in *Politics* (April 11, 1978), "When we move into a neighborhood, local independents lose business."

In 1972 Joe Belardi criticized McDonald's for being "an unfair competitor engaged in exploitation of young people for profit and personal gain." Belardi's union held McDonald's responsible for depressing wage levels throughout the entire industry. In fact, McDonald's always has been vehemently anti-union; to this day, none of its 150,000 employees is allowed to join a union. A sophisticated, secret, internal anti-labor apparatus effectively roots out pro-union sympathizers from within employee ranks. According to *In These Times,* November 8 to 14, 1979, McDonald's assembles dossiers on certain employees, forces its workers to submit to lie detector tests, and compels attendance at sessions called "the rap."

In *Big Mac*, Boas and Chain describe "the rap," which brings workers and management together in informal sessions, as "a combination bull session, psychodrama, and interrogation. The 'rap' substituted talk for action and served to monitor the young hamburger workers . . . It swung into action before the rumbles in the kitchen reached a boiling point. In effect, it was little more than a sophisticated interrogation technique."

By now McDonald's has penetrated over twenty foreign countries. In each one the corporation retains its successful formula virtually intact, including printing menus in English. In Japan, however, McDonald's has made minor attempts to adapt to local customs: Ronald's name was changed to the more easily pronounced "Donald" McDonald; also, because of *taghigui* (the reluctance to eat while standing or walking), McDonald's restaurants in Japan contain larger seating areas. Opposition to McDonald's in foreign countries comes from many of the same sources as in the U.S.: poor nutrition, exploitation of workers, harm to local businesses, excessive trash, and exporting capital. Yvonne Malykke, editor of *Cosmos* magazine in Sydney, Australia, wrote in a letter to me recently, "The local Lane Cove Council here has refused McDonald's permission to set up one of their operations in this area, and it even went so far as going to court. The Council's reason was that as the site was a key position on a main highway it would cause traffic congestion." The spectre of an international rip-off has not gone unnoticed: foreign-based McDonald's outlets import almost all of their equipment and technology, and much of their food, from the United States.

As effective as grassroots anti-McDonald's citizens' efforts occasionally have been, they usually depend on challenges made in narrow areas and take advantage of technicalities in zoning and other community by-laws. A reawakening of people's innate awareness of what truly constitutes wholesome food and the spread of personal decisions to reject fast foods will signal a more broadly-based and decisive end to the domination by McDonald's and similar chains.

Bottom Lines

Pyramid schemes, whether fast-food chains or chain letters, are organized along hierarchical lines and on quick, exponential growth, involving many participants/investors. The first people to invest reap the greatest profits; the ones who join later, providing the essential, ever-expanding breadth of the pyramid base, increasingly find themselves with little or nothing (except the cumbersome weight of the pyramid above them) as the growth spiral runs its course.

Because of their continued high visibility through slick media advertising and their physical presence in most communities, the fast-food chains appear to be strong and viable. In fact, they are weak and their managements are seriously worried. Any continuation of their success is predicated on many tenuous factors: an obligation to maintain growth rates of 30 to 40 percent a year; the continued availability of cheap meat, cheap transportation, cheap energy, cheap labor, and a never-ending supply of new restaurant locations. A sudden, unfavorable change in any one of these elements could be disastrous to the chains' very existence.

Although the nutritional aspects of fast foods have received scant attention, their economics are now being subjected to close scrutiny. Three recent articles (two of them appearing within one week of each other) in two of the most influential newspapers in the country confirm the bleak outlook for McDonald's. Financial writer Robert Metz, in the *New York Times,* March 5, 1979, describes McDonald's stock as "mediocre," its shares "way ahead of themselves" when they peaked in 1973 (since then the stock has dropped 37 points to its present level of 40). Metz notes that "soaring beef prices" now pose another particular problem for the chain; he quotes Carl F. De Biase, who recently completed what Metz describes as "a negative study of (McDonald's) prospects for the brokerage firm Sanford C. Bernstein & Company." Metz writes, "Mr. De Biase contends that McDonald's has been able to achieve earnings' gains only through expansion, inflation, and new products, particularly breakfast food and breakfast sales are already topping out as a percentage of total store sales. Meanwhile, fierce competition with two other chains, Burger King and Wendy's, is limiting the number of good potential store sites for all three." Early in this decade, the glut of fast-food franchises caused the smaller, weaker ones to go bankrupt; the field was left to the giants—McDonald's, Burger King, Kentucky Fried Chicken, Wendy's, Burger Chef, Pizza Hut—that are now fighting each other for survival. The stakes are high: The next crop of losers, like the earlier ones, may fade away entirely.

Unique among contemporary get-rich-quick schemes, McDonald's System, Inc., represents the ultimate extension of the industrial paradigm to eating; but something so basic, alive, life-giving, and essential as food resists being manipulated quite so easily. Cognizant of this basic fact from the beginning, McDonald's does not sell food so much as a state of mind; it does not advertise hamburgers but a fantasyland. Because its actual product is so ephemeral and its economic base is so tenuous, McDonald's, in order to prosper, has been compelled to compete in the dog-eat-dog arena of modern manipulation. Besides entailing the many abuses that have been listed here, it is a self-defeating game.

America without McDonald's may seem difficult to imagine, but this is exactly what the leading financial seers, and what our own still voice of common sense, are now predicting.

QUESTIONS

1. The article is critical of McDonald's and, by implication, of the corporate economy. What defense can be made against these criticisms?

2. Despite the vast sums that corporations spend on advertising and public relations, opinion polls consistently show public suspicion of large corporations. Why do you think this is? Is this antipathy justified? Would we be better off without large corporations?

3. Identify some other large corporations and their specific impact on some areas of American life.

References

Boas, Max, and Chain, Steve, *Big Mac—The Unauthorized Story of McDonald's*. New York: E.P. Dutton, 1976.

RICHARD J. BARNET
RONALD E. MÜLLER

Multinational Corporations

*How might Americans react if the commanding
heights of the American economy—in agriculture, mining, manufacturing, banking, and the like—were controlled by citizens of, say, Uganda, Hong Kong, or
Mexico? The reaction would probably be one of bitter
resentment. It should come as little surprise, then, that
the penetration of the global economy by multinational
corporations based in the United States and a handful
of other of nations has become a source of international controversy.*

*Multinational corporations are huge commercial or-
ganizations which, though headquartered in one country, own or control other corporations and subsidiaries
in countries around the world. Linked by interlocking
membership of their boards of directors and by a common goal of ever increasing growth and profit, a few
hundred multinational corporations have become major actors on the international political and economic
scene. Many of these corporations have larger budgets
than some of the countries in which they operate, and
they are able to use their immense influence to shape
the foreign policies of their own governments and the
domestic policies of the host countries.*

*Although the corporations have unquestionably
spurred economic development in the less developed
nations, it seems that this has been, at best, a mixed
blessing: typically, an economy once organized to meet
local needs is transformed into one that meets the demands of a foreign multinational; profits tend to be
expatriated rather than reinvested locally; and such
wealth as remains in the host country does not reach
the masses, but rather, is enjoyed by a small local
elite that collaborates with the foreigners. In this article, Richard Barnet and Ronald Müller explore some
of the problems posed by the concentration of so much
economic power into the hands of a few corporate officials.*

From the article in *The New Yorker*, Dec 2, 1974, pp. 54–82, excerpted
from their book, *Global Reach.* Copyright © 1974 by Richard J. Barnet
and Ronald E. Müller. Reprinted by permission of Simon & Schuster, a
Division of Gulf & Western Corporation.

The men who run modern international corporations are
the first in history with the organization, the technology,
the money, and the ideology to make a credible try at
managing the world as an integrated unit. The global visionary of earlier days was either a self-deceiver or a mys-
tic. When Alexander the Great wept because there were
no more worlds to conquer, his global claims rested on
nothing more substantial than the ignorance of his map-
maker. As the boundaries of the known world have expanded, kings and generals have tried to establish empires of ever more colossal scale, but none of them has
succeeded in turning his dreams into lasting reality. The
Napoleonic system, Hitler's Thousand-Year Reich, the
British Empire, and the Pax Americana of our day have
all left their traces, but none has managed to create anything approaching a global organization for administering the planet which could last even a generation.

The managers of the world corporate giants proclaim
that where conquest has failed business can succeed.
George Ball, a former Under-Secretary of State in the
Kennedy and Johnson administrations and now a partner
in the international investment-banking firm of Lehman
Brothers, has said, "Working through great corporations
that straddle the earth men are able for the first time to
utilize world resources with an efficiency dictated by the
objective logic of profit." The global corporation is usher-
ing in a genuine world economy, or what the business
consultant and writer Peter Drucker calls a "global shopping center," and it is accomplishing this, according to
Jacques Maisonrouge, a senior vice-president of IBM.
"by doing what came naturally in the pursuit of its legitimate business objectives."

The rise of the global enterprise is producing an organizational revolution as profound in its implications for
modern man as the Industrial Revolution and the rise of
the nation-state. Within the last ten years, global corporations have grown so fast that their combined total sales
exceed the gross national product of every country except
the United States and the Soviet Union. With more than
200 billion dollars in physical assets under their control,
the international corporations' average growth rate since
1950 has been two to three times greater than the growth
rate of the most advanced industrial countries, including

the United States. . . . By making ordinary business decisions, the managers of firms like GM, IBM, General Electric, and Exxon now have more power than most sovereign governments to determine where people will live; what work they will do, if any; what they will eat, drink, and wear; what sorts of knowledge schools and universities will encourage; and what kind of society their children will inherit. Indeed, the most revolutionary aspect of the giant international corporations is not their size but their world view. Their managers are seeking to put into practice a theory of human organization that will profoundly alter the nation-state system around which society has been organized for more than 400 years. What they are demanding, in essence, is the right to transcend the nation-state, and, in the process, to transform it. "I have long dreamed of buying an island owned by no nation and of establishing the World Headquarters of the Dow Company on the truly neutral ground of such an island, beholden to no nation or society," Carl Gerstacker, the chairman of the Dow Chemical Company, said in 1972, at the White House Conference on the Industrial World Ahead. And Charles Kindleberger, a professor of economics at the Massachusetts Institute of Technology and one of the leading American authorities on international economics, comments. "The international corporation has no country to which it owes more loyalty than any other, nor any country where it feels completely at home."

It is not hard to understand why American corporate giants feel that they have outgrown national boundaries. . . . In the last ten years, it has been substantially easier to make profits abroad than in the United States. The result has been that American corporations have been shifting more and more of their total assets out of the United States. In 1971, about a quarter of the assets of the chemical industry, about a third of the assets of the consumer-goods industry, about 40 percent of the assets of the electrical industry, and about a quarter of the assets of the pharmaceutical industry were outside the country. Of the 40 billion dollars invested worldwide by the American petroleum industry, roughly half is invested beyond American shores. In recent years, more than 60 percent of American exports and more than a third of American imports were bought and sold by United States multinational corporations.

The global corporation is revolutionizing the world economy through its increasing control over four fundamental elements of economic life—technology, finance capital, labor markets, and marketplace ideology. The internationalization of production means simply that more and more of the world's goods and services are being produced in more and more countries, and that the production process increasingly ignores national frontiers. A watch or a car, or even a shirt, may include various components produced in widely scattered places. . . . Judd

Polk, formerly chief economist with the United States Council of the International Chamber of Commerce, calculates that by the turn of the century a few hundred companies will, if they maintain their present growth rates, produce goods and services amounting to 4200 billion dollars, or about 54 percent of the value of all goods and services.

The rise of these corporations represents far more than the overseas expansion of American business, of course, for the global corporation is neither an American invention nor an American phenomenon. Among the earliest of the multinationals were Royal Dutch Shell and Unilever, which are British and Dutch corporations. Non-American global corporations already own more than 700 major manufacturing enterprises in the United States. World production figures compiled by the United Nations show a sharp decline in the American domination of the global market. . . . While American companies still hold a commanding lead in the internationalization of production and the development of the global market, the world corporation is far more than an American challenge. Japanese and West European companies have expanded aggressively in such traditional United States economic preserves as Brazil.

The internationalization of finance capital is as crucial to this process as the internationalization of production. Global corporations can borrow money almost anywhere. Dollars, despite the patriotic slogans on the bills, have no nationality. In the 1960s, the Eurodollar market, now estimated at more than 100 billion dollars, was developed. This first transnational money market, which consists of dollars deposited in banks outside the United States and is one of the most important innovations of modern capitalism, was the creation of a Soviet bank. During the same period, the international loan syndicate and the international bank consortium appeared. . . . Through the use of centralized, computerized cash-management systems, global corporations are in a unique position to play the world capital markets, arranging where possible to have their accounts payable in weak currencies and receivable in strong currencies. Because of their advantages, they are able to attract local finance capital, particularly from poor countries. For an Argentine or Uruguayan businessman (to take examples of countries where the flight of capital is creating economic and social crisis), it is much more attractive to invest in the Eurodollar market than to take the risks of inflation and revolution by investing at home.

The introduction of the global payroll has produced dramatic changes in world labor markets. The essential strategy of the global corporation is based on a division of labor. Top management continues to be recruited from rich countries; workers increasingly come from low-wage areas. For a world corporation, this combination is ideal. While automation continues to reduce the total labor costs in the manufacturing process, wage differentials are becoming more critical in maintaining competitive profit margins for the global corporations themselves. A few years ago, only the industries most reliant on labor would go abroad looking for cheap help. In recent years, Fairchild Camera and Texas Instruments have settled in Hong Kong to take advantage of a labor pool in which 60 percent of the adults work a seven-day week and which includes 34,000 children aged 14 or younger, half of whom work ten or more hours a day. Timex and Bulova make an increasing number of their watches in Taiwan, where they share a union-free labor pool with R.C.A., Admiral, and Zenith, among many others. European companies are also moving to Southeast Asia. Rollei, having figured out that wages make up 60 percent of the cost of the modern complex camera and that wages are six times higher in Germany than Singapore, has built a huge factory in Singapore. . . . The ability of global companies to shift production from one facility to another perhaps thousands of miles away is already having a crucial impact on organized labor around the world.

. . .

The challenge of the global shopping center, as the corporate managers see it, is at once to retail old needs to new customers and to create new needs for old customers. For instance, the rising middle class in Latin America is a key target for established products such as automobiles. With population growth slowing in much of the industrial world, and with highways already choked, market expansion in the developed nations is slackening, but in countries like Brazil and Mexico thousands of people in the middle class are beginning to have sufficient income to discover that they cannot exist without a car. In the developed world, the problem is different. There, established companies compete for greater shares of a relatively stable market through innovation and advertising. Companies such as the Big Three automakers, the big television manufacturers, and the big computer makers compete with one another, contrary to standard economic theory, not by seeking to undercut one another in price but by means of what economists call oligopolistic competition. In any industry, a few companies compete for ever-larger shares of the market according to certain well-established but unstated rules. The principal rule is that price competition, except on very limited occasions, is an antisocial practice, and one to be strictly avoided, since it threatens to destroy the whole club. Similarly, the products offered by members are more or less identical; introducing radically new technology is considered unsporting. Instead, these companies compete in the less volatile arenas of cost-cutting (through automation and the removal of factories to low-wage areas) and product differentiation (beating out the competition by means of more attractive and convenient packaging and more arresting advertising). Since a dollar in advertising is likely to have a quicker payoff than a dollar invested in the product itself—how much better than a Camel can you make a Chesterfield?—the "breakthroughs" in consumer products tend to be trivial changes tailored to advertising campaigns.

Advances in the techniques of centralization have made the world corporation possible, and sophisticated coordination at the world-headquarters level remains its chief distinguishing characteristic. The early-nineteenth-century British economist David Ricardo, in his famous example, pointed out that it was to the advantage of pastoral Britain to exchange wool with wine-producing Portugal rather than to try to produce both wool and wine itself. The multinational corporation owns the modern equivalent of both wineries and wool factories, and in effect derives a double "comparative advantage" by arranging to trade with itself. Put most simply, each part of the enterprise does what it does best and cheapest. It makes sense for General Electric to ship components to Singapore, where they can be assembled at about 30 cents an hour, rather than to produce them in the Ashland, Massachusetts, plant for three dollars and 40 cents an hour, so it is not surprising that between 1959 and 1969 GE built 61 plants overseas. Where you locate a plant depends, of course, upon many factors, including not only comparative wages, tariffs, and transportation costs but the political and labor-relations climate as well. (Singapore and Hong Kong, for example, can arrange for their corporate guests to avoid strikes and other labor difficulties.) Because the corporate managers can weigh all these factors and coordinate decisions on pricing, financial flows, marketing, tax avoidance, research and development, and political intelligence on a global level, the world corporation has extraordinary power.

The science of centralization is based largely on the sophisticated control of communications. As the late economist Stephen Hymer, of the New School, noted in a 1972 paper, "At the bottom of the pyramid, communications are broken horizontally so there is no direct interaction between operations centers—what communication there is must pass through the higher power centers." To accomplish such a strategy, IBM has demonstrated a computer system that makes it possible for corporations to monitor, 24 hours a day, various aspects of their global activities—sales, purchases, cash flow, credit lines, inventories. Information from around the world moves to headquarters and then is relayed on what IBM calls a "controlled access" basis to executives around the world. The higher the manager's rank, the more he is allowed to see. IBM officials explain, in demonstrating the system, that managers of subsidiaries get upset if they see the global tote board. They do better if they get only what they need for their own operation.

. . .

The ultimate test of the corporate managers' vision of

global peace and abundance will be the underdeveloped world. This vast expanse of Asia, Africa, and Latin America, where three-quarters of the earth's population lives, makes up the world's least exclusive club. The only membership requirement is mass poverty. "By any quantitative measure the post-World War II era has been the most successful in international economic history," President Nixon's 1973 "International Economic Report" proclaimed. But not for the poor, who, as Robert McNamara, president of the World Bank, put it, "remain entrapped in conditions of deprivation which fall below any rational definition of human decency." Two hundred million people in India attempt to survive on incomes that average less than 40 dollars a year. Two-thirds of the people of the underdeveloped world—a billion three million of them—are members of farm families, but 900 million of them earn less than a hundred dollars a year. "We are talking about hundreds of millions of desperately poor people throughout the whole of the developing world," McNamara concluded in his 1972 address to the World Bank's board of governors. "We are talking about 40 percent of entire populations. Development is simply not reaching them in any decisive degree."

For the modern corporate managers, the underdeveloped world is the supreme management problem. To market a vision that bypasses those parts of the planet where most of the population lives, where the problems of survival are the starkest, and where political explosions are everyday occurrences is beyond the capacity of even the most accomplished masters of oversell. A global shipping center in which 40 to 50 percent of the potential customers are living at the edge of starvation and are without electricity, plumbing, drinkable water, medical care, schools, and jobs is not a marketable vision. In their bid for managerial power on a worldwide scale, the men who run the global corporations must demonstrate that they have answers to the problems of world poverty. As the development crisis outlined by McNamara and others becomes more obvious, the corporate managers' claims that they have the answers to such problems are increasingly being questioned. A by-product of the development crisis is a crisis of confidence in the capacity of the global corporation to manage the world economy in the interests of those who are neither its stockholders nor its employees. . . .

How is it that the nations of the underdeveloped world, so fortunately endowed with raw materials, a huge labor force, and great potential markets, are in fact so poor? It is often said that poor countries are poor because they are deficient in what economists call capital stock; that is, they lack the tangible (and expensive) social structure that enables modern developed societies to function and to create more wealth—roads, communications systems, machines, and factories. But capital stock does not grow wild. Its appearance at a particular time and place is the result of specific investment decisions made in the past. When a primitive society begins to produce more than it consumes, it ceases to be what economists call a static society and begins the process of growth. The essential ingredient in this process is knowledge. The introduction of new ways of organizing work—a hoe instead of one's bare hands, a tractor instead of a hoe—increases human productivity and generates savings that can be used to promote further productivity. When these savings are invested for the purpose of maintaining and creating more wealth, economists call them "finance capital." Whether finance capital will in fact produce further wealth for a country or, more important, whether it will create wealth-producing structures depends upon what those who control that capital decide to do with it. If a country is poor in wealth-producing structures (capital stock), it is because those who control its wealth decided to invest their finance capital in something else.

The finance capital generated by the natural wealth of many underdeveloped countries has not been used to develop local factories, schools, and other structures for generating more wealth but has been siphoned off to the developed world, first as plunder and then in the more respectable form of dividends, royalties, and technical fees; it has been used to finance the amenities of London and Paris and the industrial expansion of affluent societies. Most of the remaining capital is in the control of a small local elite, which knows how to consume it in lavish living and where to invest it abroad for a good return. Because power over the national wealth is largely in the hands of foreigners, the finance capital generated by past wealth-producing activities is not even used to maintain, much less expand, the local economy. This depletion has inevitably resulted in lower consumption for the local population.

. . .

The industrialized nations, as the studies of Raul Prebisch, the former director of the United Nations Latin American Institute for Economic and Social Planning, and others have shown, have used their technological superiority to set terms of trade that, not surprisingly, favor them at the expense of their weaker partners. Over the past 25 years, because of the falling prices of certain essential raw materials, underdeveloped countries have had to exchange more and more of their resources to get the finished goods and the technological expertise they need. This steady worsening of the terms of trade between the rich countries and the poor is an important reason that the gap between them continues to grow. . . .

The lack of bargaining power of underdeveloped countries results from three major institutional weaknesses. The first is a system of antiquated governmental structures. The laws for collecting taxes, controlling foreign business, or preventing the drain of finance capital are inadequate. Typically, these laws were drafted in an earlier and simpler day, before accountants and tax lawyers had arrived on the scene. Many were written by the colonial civil service or by foreign corporations that were only too happy to provide technical assistance to the governmental agency in charge of regulating their activities. The laws on foreign investment in Liberia, to give just one example of such international legal aid, were drafted by the United States government. The second source of institutional weakness in these countries is the lack of a strong labor movement. With the possible exceptions of Argentina and, until recently, Chile, there is no labor movement in all Latin America that can effectively bargain with global corporations. The third source of institutional weakness is lack of competition from local business. It would seem that native entrepreneurs, who must compete with the global giants under disadvantageous terms for supplies, capital, and customers, would like to see them effectively controlled. And many countries do exercise some degree of control. The Guatemala Chamber of Commerce has so far waged a successful campaign to keep Sears, Roebuck out of Guatemala, claiming that a Sears invasion would put 3–4 thousand Guatemalan shopkeepers out of business. In Colombia, the president of the national banking association has publicly denounced the large international banks and called for laws prohibiting their near-monopoly of Colombian banking. As the possibility of keeping more profits in the country improves, such nationalistic businessmen will surely become more vocal.

But, as a recent study of the attitudes of Argentine businessmen suggests, many local entrepreneurs up to now have been tolerant, even enthusiastic, about the penetration of their economy by global corporations. The reason, of course, is that they have decided to join them rather than fight them. Some local businessmen find that by cooperating with global firms they can do very well. (Many global corporations, for varying reasons, are trying to make maximum use of local suppliers.) But, equally important for local businessmen, the arrival of a global company may mean an early opportunity to sell the family business at a good price. (Once foreign giants become established in the local market, the alternative may well be a forced sale at an adverse price, or bankruptcy.) In an earlier age in the United States, family enterprises went public in order to raise sufficient finance capital to maintain their competitiveness against larger national corporations, or sold out to them, or were finally put out of business by them; now many local capitalists owning national businesses in the underdeveloped countries are faced with identical alternatives. Available statistics indicate that the usual outcome is that the family business is sold off. Of the 717 "new" manufacturing subsidiaries established in Latin America by the top 187 global corporations based in the United States during the years 1958 through 1967, 331, or 46 percent, were established

by buying out an existing local company. Because of their superior power, global corporations are able to use local finance capital and their technological advantage to absorb local industry. It is a process that some local businessmen may deplore but one that they have yet to find a way to stop. . . .

Most underdeveloped countries have already made the decision to emulate the economies of the developed countries through industrialization; therefore, a dependency on outside technology, finance capital, and market-manipulation techniques is built into their model of progress. Once American and European consumption values become the primary goals of economic growth for a nation, it has no choice but to sacrifice the development of its own technological capacity—a long and difficult process—for the possibility of the quick boom that foreign investment can bring. But there is an obvious price: The nation's technology becomes subject to foreign control. . . .

The same cumulative rhythm is felt in the case of finance capital, the second basic element of corporate power. Subsidiaries of global companies are able to borrow from local banks and financial institutions on better terms than are local businesses, because their credit is backed by the worldwide financial resources of the parent company. When savings are in short supply, as is typical in underdeveloped countries, it is simply good business to lend to Ford or Pfizer rather than to the local laundry or sugar mill. . . . Clearly given the worldwide backing of a global subsidiary, any bank will prefer lending to it rather than to local grocers and farmers.

But there are other reasons, too. . . . Because of interlocking interests in ownership and management of the financial groups that control both global corporations and global banks, they do not deal with one another as strangers. Even if a branch bank were tempted to lend scarce local capital to a local firm in preference to a subsidiary of a global company, it would think twice before doing so, since it must protect its long-term relationship with the parent company. . . .

. . .

The third source of power for the global corporations in underdeveloped countries is their control over communications—their extraordinary competitive edge in using the technology of market manipulation to shape the tastes, goals and values of the workers, suppliers, government officials, and, of course, customers on whom their own economic success in that society depends. Marketplace technology is concentrated in the advertising agencies. The rise of the global corporation and the global bank has been accompanied by the globalization of the Madison Avenue agency. In 1954, the top 30 American advertising agencies derived a little over 5 percent of their total billings from overseas campaigns. In 1972, the total billings of these agencies had increased more than fivefold, and a third of these billings came from outside the United States. (In 1971, the two largest American advertising agencies, J. Walter Thompson and Interpublic, of which McCann-Erickson is a subsidiary, earned, respectively 52 percent and 55 percent of their profits outside the United States.) The big American agencies enjoy a decisive competitive advantage over local agencies, because, like manufacturers, they can extend techniques developed for the United States market to the foreign market at little extra cost. The local agencies must start from scratch, and in poor countries capital for the high investment needed to make presentations to potential clients is not easy to find. For this reason, J. Walter Thompson and McCann-Erickson have increased their share of the Latin American market, which they have dominated for many years. In the four countries of Latin America where most of the investment of American-based global corporations is concentrated (Mexico, Brazil, Argentina, and Venezuela), 54 percent of the major advertising agencies in 1970 were American-owned or American-affiliated—up from 43 percent in 1968. Because local companies usually lack the modern technology for overcoming customer resistance and customer indifference, they are dependent upon the United States giants.

The most effective media for spreading an advertising message are TV and radio, especially in countries with high rates of illiteracy. In 1970, CBS, for example, distributed its programs to a hundred countries. Its newsfilm service, according to its 1968 annual report, "using satellite delivery for major stories," was received in "95 percent of the free world's television homes." CBS shows, such as "I Love Lucy," "Gomer Pyle," "Hogan's Heroes," "Mary Tyler Moore," and "Perry Mason," are distributed in as many as a hundred countries. "Hawaii Five-O" is dubbed into six languages and sold in 47 countries. In the TV field, American-based global corporations dominate underdeveloped countries because they can offer old programs at a fraction of the cost a local producer would have to pay to create new programs. As a writer in the magazine *Television* pointed out in October of 1966, "ABC can sell 'Batman' to an advertiser and then place 'Batman' along with designated commercials in any . . . country where the advertiser wants it to appear." Thus, the competitive advantage of the foreign networks is based not only on superior knowledge—programming and marketing techniques—but also on superior contracts.

The three essential power structures in underdeveloped societies are typically in the hands of global corporations: the control of technology, the control of finance capital, and the control of marketing and the dissemination of ideas. The process of emulation, which was the response of Western Europe and Japan to foreign expansion by American global companies, does not ordinarily occur in underdeveloped countries, because their basic institutions, including domestic business enterprises, are too weak to make such a challenge. The result in most underdeveloped countries is the pervasive penetration of the global corporation into every key sector of the economy. . . . The colossal power of the global corporation to shape the societies of the underdeveloped world is not a matter for debate. The evidence comes largely from the corporations' own annual reports. But the major political issue concerns the use of that power. Is the global corporation in the business of exploitation or that of development?

By the end of the 1960s, despite dramatic economic growth in a few poor countries during what the United Nations hailed as the Decade of Development, it had become clear that the gap between rich and poor throughout the world was widening. A succession of studies by the United Nations and other international agencies established the statistics of global poverty: for 40 to 60 percent of the world's population, the Decade of Development brought rising unemployment, decreases in purchasing power, and lower consumption. . . . Particularly in those countries that have experienced "economic miracles," the pattern is one of increasing affluence for a slowly expanding but small minority and increasing misery for a rapidly swelling majority. The concentration of income in Mexico, for example, has increased significantly during the "Mexican miracle." In the early 1950s, the richest 20 percent of the population had ten times the income of the poorest 20 percent. By the mid-sixties, the rich had increased their share to 17 times what the poor received. A 1969 United Nations study reported that in the Mexico City area the richest 20 percent of the population lived on 62.5 percent of the area's income, while the poorest 20 percent attempted survival on just over 1 percent of the income. During the 1960s, according to United States government estimates, the share in the "Brazilian miracle" for the 40 million people at the bottom dropped from 10.6 percent to 8.1. By 1970, a United Nations report indicated, the richest 5 percent in Brazil had increased their share of the national income from 44 percent to 50. In September of 1972, McNamara reported to the World Bank's board of governors on what the continuation of prevailing development policies, with their modest annual growth rates and their income concentration, would mean by the year 2000: "Projected to the end of the century—only a generation away—that means the people of the developed countries will be enjoying per-capita incomes, in 1972 prices, of over $8,000 a year, while these masses of the poor (who by that time will total over 2.25 billion) will on average receive less than $200 per capita, and some 800 million of these will receive less than $100."

When the global corporations proclaim themselves engines of development, we can judge their claims only if we know what policies they are pursuing. If a development model is to have any real meaning in a world in which most people are struggling just to stay alive, it must, as the British development theorist Dudley Seers, former director of the Institute of Development Studies at the University of Sussex, has pointed out, provide solutions to the three great social problems of the late twentieth century: Poverty, employment, and inequality. A strategy that does not cope with these problems must assume either increasing mass misery on an unimaginable scale or the mysterious disappearance of the world's poor. . . . [Yet] after all, global corporations do spread goods, capital, and technology around the world. They do contribute to a rise in overall economic activity. They do employ hundreds of thousands of workers, often paying more than the prevailing wage. Most poor countries appear to be eager to lure these corporations—so eager, in fact, to create a tempting "investment climate" that they are generous with tax concessions and other advantages. If corporations were really spreading poverty, unemployment, and inequality, why would they be welcomed?

The negative impact of global corporations on living standards, employment rates, and economic justice has occurred despite the fact that many corporate officials would like it to be otherwise and believe that it can be. The unfortunate role of the multinational business in maintaining and increasing worldwide poverty results primarily from the dismal reality that global corporations and poor countries have different—indeed, conflicting—interests, priorities, and needs. The primary interest of the corporation is profit maximization, and this means that it is often advantageous for the balance sheet if income is diverted from poor countries. Eager as they are to be good corporate citizens, the managers owe their primary allegiance to company shareholders. Their businesses, they like to say, are neither charities nor welfare organizations, although some do devote modest resources to good works. The claims of the global corporations rest instead on a theory of the marketplace which says, in effect, that by enriching themselves they enrich the whole world. This, unfortunately, has not been the reality.

. . .

QUESTIONS

1. Suggest advantages and some disadvantages of the penetration of the world economy by multinational corporations.

2. In what ways are multinational corporations altering international political and economic relations?

3. Although the United States endorses the values of liberty and equality, it is not particularly popular in the less developed Third World. Why do you think this is so?

Newsweek

Single-Issue Politics

The "official" picture of the American political process—as envisioned in the Constitution and as still taught in high school civics classes—is one of representative democracy. According to this model, the people elect representatives whose votes in Congress reflect the will of their public. But the actual political process is, of course, far more complex—and probably far less representative of the will of the ordinary voter.

In practice, legislative votes are strongly influenced by the lobbying and other activities of a variety of special-interest groups. These groups range immensely in their size, power, and objectives. Some, like labor unions, industrial organizations, or even specific large corporations, are primarily interested in protecting or enhancing their economic interests. Others, like the women's movement or the National Rifle Association, campaign for what they regard as their members' rights. Still others, like the "Moral Majority" or the right-to-life movement, are concerned with public morality.

The interest groups may have different resources and may use varied tactics, but all have one purpose in common—to short-cut the process of representative democracy by applying direct pressure on the legislative process to make it serve their own ends. This article examines some of the special-interest groups and the ways in which they shape the laws behind the scenes.

Four years ago, Manuel Maloof, a political gadfly and community leader in Atlanta, won election to the De Kalb County Commission. Environmental groups supported him because he favored preserving Soapstone Ridge, a wild corner of the country. Once in office, Maloof became convinced that the county desperately needed to expand its industrial base. When he said he was willing to consider a plan for an industrial park that touched one corner of Soapstone Ridge, environmentalists denounced him for a solid year. This year, he is not running for re-election. "Today it is not just the big boys but the little groups that are a threat to our system," he says. "They look out for their interests, they have numbers on their side—and they are terrorizing us."

"I hate to get on the plane for Denver," says Sen. Gary Hart of Colorado. "For three hours, the lobbyists just line up in the aisle to get a word with me." Most of them are special pleaders for business, says Hart, and they generally have two messages. "The first is that there is too much government, too much taxation and spending—and that they want government off their backs. The second is that they want something specific from the Federal government."

Sen. Dick Clark of Iowa, a longtime friend of labor, is up for re-election next week. When he decided to vote for the natural-gas deregulation bill, he received a call from an official of the Machinists and Aerospace Workers union, which opposes the bill. He urged Clark to change his mind about how he would vote. As Clark tells it: "He said to me, 'OK, if that's the case, we won't support you.' I responded, 'Look at my voting record as a whole. Don't make a decision like this based on a single vote." His reply was: 'We don't give a damn about your overall voting record. We're interested in this bill—period.'"

From the grass roots on Capitol Hill, the nation is caught up in a rugged new game of single-issue politics. Every conceivable issue seems to have competing pressure groups—from gun control and import quotas to abortion and nuclear power. Thirty years ago, there were fewer than 2,000 lobbyists in Washington; last year, 15,000 of them spent $2 billion pushing their pet issues. The result is a new era of Me-First factionalism that threatens to fragment the nation's political system. "Representative government . . . is in the worst shape I have seen it in my sixteen years in the Senate," says Teddy Kennedy. "The heart of the problem is that the Senate and the House are awash in a sea of special-interest campaign contributions and special-interest lobbying."

The special-issue groups, old and new alike, have developed a potent array of weapons. They have formed political-action committees that now raise more money than either the Democratic or Republican parties. They are using computerized mailing lists to identify supporters and enlist their money and muscle to cajole, influence and even threaten legislators. And they have learned well the extra-parliamentary tactics practiced in the civil-rights and antiwar movements of the 1960s.

Goats and Roses

During the just-concluded 95th Congress, ERA backers, American Indians, and postal workers, the aging, traveling salesmen and chiropractors all marched on Washington. The anti-abortion forces came into town bearing red roses. Militant farmers rode in on tractors and cluttered the Capitol steps with goats.

Such fragmentation has made it increasingly difficult to legislate on major issues. Traditionally, the principal political parties have acted as the glue of representative government—building broad coalitions that sought compromise among competing factions and trying to reach consensus on major issues. By contrast, the single-issue groups breach party lines and make uncompromising, all-or-nothing demands on legislators. They see every roll-call vote as a litmus test of a legislator's commitment to their cause, caring little for overall voting records or party loyalties. "The net result," says Mayor George Moscone of San Francisco, "is that it is very hard to lead the country, the state, the county, the city, the neighborhood—or even a city block."

The single-issue groups have proliferated partly because of the increasing weakness of the Republican and Democratic parties. Each year, fewer and fewer voters identify themselves as Republicans or Democrats; ticket splitters abound; the pool of independent voters grows deeper. The proliferation of direct primaries (17 in 1968, 30 in 1976) has taken the selection of Presidents out of the hands of party leaders—as George McGovern and Jimmy Carter have demonstrated. TV image builders and direct-mail fund raisers are replacing ward heelers and party elders alike. "Get out any ninth-grade civics book and see what political parties are supposed to do," says GOP pollster Robert Teeter. "The ad hoc interest groups have become the political parties of today."

Pressure groups, of course, have been around since the founding of the Republic, and in many cases, their efforts have brought about important changes—from those of the abolitionists who fought slavery to those of the suffragettes who won the vote for women. The Constitution guarantees the right to petition the government to redress grievances, and in recent years, the growth of Big Government has practically demanded an increase in lobbying. But even the Founding Fathers recognized that there was such a thing as too much democracy; James Madison bluntly warned against the "violence of faction." Today, many political scientists worry that single interests are tearing at the fabric of government. "We are moving to an increase of direct democracy," says Prof. Norman Ornstein of Catholic University in Washington. "We don't give our representatives the leeway they need in a representative system."

Troubled Times

The drift has come about partly out of disillusionment with the political parties—and with the performance of government itself. The grass roots now rustle with the spin-offs of Proposition 13 and a run of recall elections, referendums and local initiatives. The *angst* of the single interests seems to be a function of troubled times, their hardnosed tactics a matter of self-defense. Unchecked inflation has frightened the electorate, soured its temper and shaken its faith in the President and Congress. The remoteness of Big Government, Big Labor and Big Business seems to create an intolerable sense of powerlessness—and an understandable urge to fight back.

The fight is frequently staged in Congress, and the single-issue groups are finding that Congress itself is badly fragmented, a near-perfect arena for their efforts. Well-meant reforms have made a shambles of the old seniority system without replacing it with something that works better. A maverick crew of freshmen and sophomore representatives—nearly half the House—regularly bucks its own leaders. Hypersensitive to pressure groups, particularly around election time, Democrats and Republicans alike try to become all things to all people, making sound legislation more and more elusive. "There's no cohesion in Congress," says Rep. Robert Bauman, a Maryland Republican. "Party discipline is a thing of the past."

The single-issue groups often overwhelm Congress with their sheer numbers. During the debate over the energy bill, 117 separate lobbying groups were in action just on natural-gas pricing—and the complexity of the bill that emerged reflects the cross fire and satisfied practically no one. Labor now fields 109 different lobbies, running from the AFL-CIO's huge 58-member office to the leaner one-man operation of the Jockey's Guild.

The Crowd in the Lobby

There are 500 corporate lobbies, 53 lobbies for minority groups, 34 for social-welfare agencies, 33 for women, 31 for environmental issues, 21 for religions, 15 for the aging and 6 for population control. A dozen gun lobbies compete for votes (five for weapons manufacturers, four pro-guns, three for gun control). Japan's interests are pushed by 61 lobbies, Israel's by ten.

In theory, this sturdy representation of interests is healthy for the system; in practice, the results often aren't. For one thing, many groups represent refractory issues that don't lend themselves easily to the traditional processes of political compromise ("How can you compromise and say, 'I'm going to allow 30,000 publicly funded abortions, but no more'?" asks one close student of the new groups). For another, their strategies and tactics often tend to accentuate the negative. "It's much easier to wage a campaign *against* something than for it," says Mike Thompson of the Florida Conservative Union, a right-wing and anti-gay rights group. Finally, these groups frequently put personal values above regard for all-too-vulnerable public institutions. "I'd say we are being common-caused to death by well-intentioned people," Congressman Michael Harrington of Massachusetts told *Newsweek's* Phyllis Malamud.

Making No Apologies

In many ways, Common Cause, the "citizens' lobby," has been the prototype for the newer lobbies. "Everybody's organized but the people," was its rallying cry in 1970, when former HEW Secretary John Gardner founded it. Since then it has raised 44 million; it has more individual contributors than the Democratic Party and it can mobilize its forces through chain telephone calls, telegrams and mail to bring pressure on city councils, state legislators, representatives, senators and Presidents. It has won significant battles in the field of campaign-finance reform and helped gain passage of numerous bills. And it makes no apologies. "We have had a system in which a Richard Nixon could flourish, where a Tongsun Park or a Gulf Oil could operate with impunity and where the political parties had been weakening for decades," says Common Cause senior vice president Fred Wertheimer. "Our argument has been that you have to correct the problems that exist in the system if it's going to function."

Most other lobbying groups justify their activities similarly, and they have learned some tricks of the trade from Common Cause. One of the most effective is grass-roots lobbying. "You win or lose a bill not in Washington on the merits but in the districts on the politics," says Mark Green, director of Congress Watch, a Ralph Nader operation. Last week, responding to the defeat of the consumer protection agency in the 95th Congress, Green sent profiles of twelve congressmen to their home districts; the profiles included voting records on consumer issues and a breakdown of campaign gifts. Five profiles were positive and seven were blasts. One profile reported

that Rep. E. Thomas Coleman of Missouri, a Republican, had initiated only four bills, one of which authorized the printing of memorial pamphlets to his deceased predecessor. Stung, Coleman angrily demanded that Green supply written proof that he had not collaborated on a hatchet job with his opponent in next week's election.

More and more traditional and corporate lobbies are also adopting the tactics of grass-roots lobbying. "It's the Utah plant-manager school of lobbying," says business lobbyist Tom Korologos. "You use local guys to lobby their own senators. That's how business beat the consumer protection agency and labor-law reform." During the debates over the energy and tax packages, the National Federation of Independent Business used an elaborate system of letter alerts, Mailgram messages and a telephone bank to energize its 545,000 local members, who in turn bombarded congressmen and senators with pro-business positions. Even the venerable United States Chamber of Commerce now has six regional offices and 50 staffers to press its issues through 1,500 local Congressional Action committees. Last year, the chamber batted .630 in its legislative battles on the Hill. This year, it hopes to do even better. "When the government can tell you how much cream to put in ice cream, you have no choice but to influence government," says Korologos.

Most new single-issue groups are primed to spring into action quickly. This year, the U.S. Treasury proposed a plan to require standard serial numbers on guns. (As things stand now, guns made by different manufacturers may carry the same serial number.) The T-men said they were simply trying to make it easier to trace weapons used in crimes. But the gun lobby decided the idea was a plot leading to universal gun registration, which it opposes, and brought fierce pressure on the House Appropriations Committee. Rep. John Ashbrook of Ohio, an ally of gun lobbyists, got Treasury officials to estimate that it would require $4.2 million a year in future budgets to administer the plan. Ashbrook then succeeded in driving the proposal back for more study. He also managed to delete $4.2 million from the Treasury's appropriation for next year. "The turkeys in the Treasury slit their own throats on that one," says John M. Snyder, chief lobbyist for the Citizens Committee for the Right to Keep and Bear Arms.

Reprisals and "Litmus Tests"

In their for-us-or-against-us zealotry, the single-issue groups leave little room for statesmanship. When Sen. Abraham Ribicoff of Connecticut, a staunch friend of Israel, supported President Carter's plan to sell F-15 jets to Saudi Arabia, the American Israeli Public Affairs Committee struck back. Among other reprisals, it circulated to its Connecticut members a memo saying that Ribicoff had once attended a luncheon for a Palestine

Liberation Organization representative at the United Nations. Holding his ground, Ribicoff voted for the plane sale. Now, most experts believe that the Camp David accord—and its tacit acceptance by the Saudis—wouldn't have been possible without the arms sale. "If Abe Ribicoff hadn't stood very damned tall and hard in place on that one," says a colleague, "a lot of us would have had to take a second look at our vote."

Many single-interest groups use the stick of "litmus tests" as their favorite weapons. The basic approach was used by Common Cause during the fight for public financing of Congressional elections. Common Cause sent questionnaires to congressmen asking where they stood on the issue. Those who answered negatively or dubiously were the first to feel pressure from their constituents. Others have stepped up such pressure. Not long ago, a representative of the Boilermakers union told a group of congressmen in Washington that his union would base its campaign gifts for next week's election on five key votes: anyone who refused to vote "right" on all five would be cut off. "No one here is a 100 per cent," exploded Rep. Edward Beard, a house painter from Rhode Island—and a card-carrying union man. "If you vote that way, something is wrong."

Son of Frankenstein

This kind of pressure cooker can boil legislation to a pulp—and sometimes explode in the face of single-interest groups themselves. On the day before the Senate voted on the natural-gas-pricing bill, six lobbyists gathered in the office of Sen. Gary Hart. They represented Big Oil, Big Labor and several consumer groups. The lobbying of all six had contributed to the final shape of the compromise, but for six different and conflicting reasons, all six wanted Hart to vote the bill down. "Each had prodded Congress from a different direction, and when Congress produced its own Frankenstein monster, they came running to the bürgermeisters for help," Hart says. "They wanted me to strangle the monster we had created in response to their individual demands." Hart voted for the bill.

When politicians go home from Washington, single-interest groups can make life hellish for them. "Once when you traveled around in my state you'd come into town squares where men would be whittling," says Senate Minority Leader Howard Baker of Tennessee, a target of opponents of the Panama Canal treaties. "Now, you get the feeling they are whittling guillotines." In South Dakota, a group of 25 young college kids turned up at the state fair and stridently demanded that Sen. George McGovern vote for the Hyde anti-abortion amendment. He declined. "They left without a good word for anything I had ever done in twenty years in public life," he said. One day at an energy fair in New Hamp-

shire, a small contingent from the Clamshell Alliance denounced Sen. Thomas McIntyre for supporting the Seabrook nuclear-power plant. "There are no ifs, ands or buts on this issue," says a weary state party man. "Either you go with them over the barricades or you are off their list forever."

The Day of the Naysayers

By definition, single-interest groups remain small, permanent minorities; but they have become more and more powerful at the polls. Democratic pollster Peter Hart estimates that one in four voters is now willing to drum a politician out of office for his position on a single issue. Pollster Richard Wirthlin puts single-interest strength at 10 to 15 per cent of the general electorate. "There is danger in destabilizing our political system too much if the politics of fragmentation goes too far," he says. Because single-interest groups are so highly motivated and deftly organized—and because so many ordinary voters don't turn out on Election Day—single interests grow stronger each year. "We are supposed to be a democracy guided by a majority," says Hart. "Now a majority could be 17 per cent. There is no consensus issue today, so all the 1 percents count—and it's the nay-sayers who carry the day."

A classic case of naysaying is shaping up in Minnesota, where friends and opponents of abortion, the environment and tuition tax credits seem to be pulling apart the Democratic-Farmer-Labor Party, a coalition once held together by the compromise politics of Hubert H. Humphrey. In a DFL primary for Humphrey's Senate seat, Robert Short, a conservative businessman, defeated Rep. Donald Fraser. Short was supported by anti-abortionists and local residents of the Boundary Waters Canoe Area, who want to open the vast wilderness in northeast Minnesota to motorboats and snowmobiles. In a second Senate race, Sen. Wendell Anderson has run into similar problems with educational groups, who oppose his support for tuition tax credits and BWCA residents, outraged by his plan to open only part of the area to general use. "The DFL has been split apart by single issues," one Republican leader told *Newsweek's* Richard Manning. The GOP now has its best opportunity in 30 years to make a comeback.

In tight elections, the impact of any single-interest group can be devastating. In Cook County, Ill., Rep. Abner Mikva, a Democrat, won re-election in the heavily Republican Tenth Congressional District two years ago by 201 votes. This year, the single-interest groups could easily tip the result the other way. A supporter of gun control, Mikva has become a prime target of the National Rifle Association. "It could be that there are people out there who are Democrats on every other issue, but when they see this, they become instant Republicans," he says.

"When you get a single-issue voter, if the Democratic Party comes out for something he's against, then he simply says: 'I'm not a Democrat anymore.' "

The disturbing truth seems to be that neither political party reflects the enormous changes that have taken place in the economy, mood and expectations of the country in the last decade. "The rise of special interests is directly related to the loss of trust that people have had in the traditional political institutions, parties specifically," says pollster Wirthlin. "They don't have confidence that the parties will deliver things in their own best interest, so they seek groups where they *know* their money will be spent for things they feel strongly about—ERA, gay rights, tax questions, guns."

Sociologists and psychologists, reports *Newsweek's* Michael Reese, believe that many people tend to feel more comfortable with smaller issues, while larger matters of domestic and foreign policy often seem as remote, unmanageable and frustrating as big government itself. The danger is that when too much energy flows into small issues, fragmentation takes place. "Washington has become a special-interest state," says Patrick Caddell, the President's polltaker. "It's like medieval Italy—everyone has his own duchy or kingdom."

The Woe of the Parties

The decline of the Republican and Democratic parties has contributed to this hodgepodge. The lines of Franklin D. Roosevelt's coalition of liberal Democrats, labor, minority groups and the Solid South have blurred or broken; the GOP has become a permanent minority, controlling only 38 of 100 seats in the Senate, 146 of 435 House seats, 12 of 50 governorships and both houses of the legislature in only five states. Vietnam divided the Democrats and undermined faith in their leadership; Watergate spoiled the GOP's reputation for good government and integrity. Internal left-right ideological splits afflict both parties, and the damage has not yet been repaired.

The accelerating pace of the '70s and the effects of technology have also combined to hurt the parties and help the single interests. "Part of the problem is just impatience," says Catholic University's Ornstein. "Things change too quickly, and people expect as rapid a change from the political system as they do from fashions, television and music." Computers and polling techniques now enable politicians to X-ray the mood of the voters, leading to the temptation to pander to the whims of the electorate rather than to lead it.

TV has invaded the national conventions of the two parties, discrediting the smoky, sometimes corrupt, but stabilizing processes of horsetrading in the back room. The tube also offers politicians plenty of channels to reach voters directly without going through the parties. "TV plus the tendency of politicians to build and rely on

their own organizations has pulverized the party system," says political scientist James MacGregor Burns of Williams College. "Now we have a bunch of Chinese war tongs."

The Damage of Reform

Ironically, reforms designed to open the parties and put them back in touch with the times have also done a good deal to advance the strength of single-interest groups. The problem has been particularly acute within the Democratic Party. After the disastrous 1968 convention, the McGovern-Fraser reform commission set rules for recruiting more women, youth, old people and minorities as convention delegates. To comply, states began to hold open delegate primaries: anyone identifying himself or herself as a Democrat could qualify—and the rewards for years of party service vanished almost overnight.

Public financing of Presidential elections—another important reform—has diverted money to the extra-party campaign organizations of Presidential candidates. "What we did with that law was kill grass-roots party politics," says Anne Wexler, an experienced party organizer from Connecticut and Jimmy Carter's adviser on special interests. As party activity shrank, the field was left open to single-issue organizations—and the PAC's.

There is a painful irony in all this for Jimmy Carter. After gaining the Presidential nomination without the backing of the Democratic Party, he now finds that the lack of party discipline in Congress has hurt his own legislation. Despite a huge Democratic majority, Congress passed energy and tax bills that bore little resemblance to what Carter originally proposed. With only weak party ties to their President, many Democratic congressmen simply bowed to the stronger pressure of lobbyists. Carter has learned the hard way that he, too, must play the special-interest game, and aides now regularly run briefings for key groups to drum up legislative support. "In this era of special interests, you have to go after these constituencies literally one by one," says Wexler. "You can't assume anyone's support anymore."

That is especially true in Congress, where an extraordinary changing of the guard is taking place. When the 96th Congress convenes next January, half of the senators will have served one six-year term or less and at least 230 representatives will have four years or less of experience. Two dozen single-interest caucuses now Balkanize the House. Alarmed by cheap steel imports, Reps. Joseph Gaydos of Pennsylvania and Charles Carney of Ohio ignored the Democratic leadership and formed their own "steel caucus." Within weeks, it had 123 members, an invitation from Jimmy Carter to the White House and an Administration promise to look into the problem. The caucus now has 170 members and a small staff that is a good deal more loyal on this particular issue to steel than to party or President.

Party leadership in Congress, once iron-strong, now seems regularly to turn to putty. In the House, the freshman and sophomore classes of the 94th and 95th Congresses have organized bipartisan caucuses full of unbiddable new representatives. "Our class is issue-oriented, not party-oriented," says sophomore Rep. Butler Derrick, 42, of South Carolina. "We are merely reflecting the situation back home." House Speaker Thomas P. O'Neill calls them "bomb throwers," and even his best Boston Irish wiles can't always keep them in line. Last year, the House failed to index the minumum wage against inflation. But a few months later, it adopted a GOP proposal that indexed capital-gains taxes to go down as the cost of living goes up. "Can you imagine?" says O'Neill in disbelief. "A Congress of 285 Democrats fails to index the minimum wage—then indexes capital gains!"

"The Filter to the Big Guy"

The attempt at reform in Congress has also played inadvertently into the hands of interest groups. Dismantling the old seniority system corrected many abuses of power, but it also undermined the authority of new committee chairmen. "If I as Agriculture Committee chairman say to a member, 'I don't like your bill and I'm not going to schedule it,' I'll walk into the committee room and find a meeting going on without me," says Rep. Thomas Foley, a Democrat from Washington. More and more bills are now produced at the subcommittee level by relatively junior members and their staff. "One advantage we have is that staffers tend to be younger and more idealistic," says one environmental lobbyist. "Sometimes we can get their ear and things then go through the filter to the big guy." Another consequence is that many bills don't get good screenings from full committees—and a good deal of shoddy legislation reaches the floor.

Congressmen who rejoice in their new freedom from party discipline quickly learn to regret their loss of party protection, which has left them more exposed than ever to the whims of moody voters and the machinations of single-interest groups. This forces them into a mad scramble of trips home and constituent services that leaves less and less time for thoughtful legislating. Some congressmen demand frequent votes simply to drive up their attendance records, which single-interest groups follow like baseball box scores. Others prefer to simply duck hard votes, to protect their ratings with groups like the AFL-CIO's Committee on Political Education or the American Conservative Union. "Congress deserves to have its hide peeled off," says Republican National Committee Chairman William Brock. "It makes you sick to go into the cloakroom and hear guys saying, 'Gee, I know this is the right approach—I wish I could vote that way.'"

Legislators must win elections to serve, of course, and in an era when a pet peeve or hobbyhorse back home can destroy years of hard work, considerable anxiety is understandable. Where the pressures will lead, however, is a question that troubles many thoughtful politicians. "Everyone who wants to get re-elected has to take 21 single-issue groups worth 2.5 per cent each to build a majority," says Rep. David Obey of Wisconsin, only half in jest. Even that kind of bloc politics may be impossible, given the contrary nature of so many of the blocs. The real solution seems to lie elsewhere. "The principal failing of Congress is not that it isn't bright or hardworking or honest," says Rep. Otis Pike, an outspoken New York Democrat who is retiring. "There is not sufficient courage in facing the voter."

A Call for Compromise

Whether elected representatives should lead their constituents or simply follow their wishes is a question as old as the Republic. It is largely moot today: no legislator can satisfy all the demands single-interest groups make. To a degree, it is healthy that there is so much political activity rather than apathy. And representatives need to respond to their constituents. But it is also true that no nation can govern itself without a way of moderating its differences and achieving compromise. "Machines, deals, bargains . . . They're all nasty words, but they have to exist to some extent for policy to be made effectively," says political scientist Seymour Martin Lipset of Stanford University.

Somehow, politicians and their parties must harness these new energies without further hobbling themselves. So far, the parties don't show much sign of accomplishing the job. If they can't, some new political coalition may well arise to take the task out of their hands.

QUESTIONS

1. In theory, power in a democracy is ultimately located in the electorate. Is this true of the United States?

2. What are the advantages of interest-group activities? What are the disadvantages?

3. Consider the view that special-interest groups stimulate democracy (a) by providing group members with access to power that they would not otherwise have, and (b) by providing an organized system of checks and balances that presents legislators with different views on each issue.

ROBERT SHERRILL

Jousting on the Hill

"Government regulation" has become a major issue in American politics: almost everyone agrees that there is too much of it, and, indeed, the present administration was elected in part on its pledge to reduce unnecessary and burdensome regulation wherever possible. But the general consensus on the need for reform quickly breaks down on specifics, for the regulations that one interest group deems unnecessary are often considered essential by another.

On closer examination, very few interest groups are opposed in principle to government regulation: they merely resent those rules that they consider inconvenient. The auto industry decries the safety regulations that add hundreds of dollars to the cost of a new car—yet it demands that the government introduce new regulations to restrict the import of competitive automobiles from Japan. Farmers complain about the burden of Agriculture Department regulations—except the ones that ensure price supports for their products. Many conservatives who vehemently oppose federal regulation in general want the government to regulate other people's access to abortions or pornography.

Government regulations are not simply the product of capricious, busybody bureaucrats. They emerge, or disappear, primarily because some interest group wanted them or some more powerful interest group did not. Nowhere, perhaps, is this political process more obvious than in controversy surrounding the Federal Trade Commission, a body that issues regulations designed to protect consumers—and that therefore, as Robert Sherrill's article shows, arouses the ire of the producers.

From *Saturday Review*, March 1980. Copyright 1980 by Saturday Review. All rights reserved. Reprinted with permission.

Congress seems determined to cripple further the Federal Trade Commission, Washington's best-known "consumer protection" agency. Many consumers won't care if this happens because they don't have even a vague notion of what the FTC is or does. Recent polls revealed that eight out of 10 Americans are in that benighted condition.

With a budget of about $60 million—enough to run the Pentagon for about 15 minutes—and, until recently, a history of timidity and inaction, the FTC is one of Washington's smallest regulatory agencies. Lately, though, the FTC has been doing that for which it was created: fighting the concentration of economic power and investigating "unfair or deceptive" business practices. Under a string of dynamic leaders and armed with a revision of its own power, the new commission has taken on such giants as the funeral and the "kid vid" industries.

Unfortunately Congress, which is, after all, responsible for the existence of the FTC, doesn't like the new commission. Some members claim that federal agencies should assume the role of arbitrator, not advocate; others contend that the FTC has been overzealous in its pursuit of deceptive business practices. Congressman Bill Frenzel, a Minnesota Republican, calls the FTC "a king-sized cancer on our economy." Senator John C. Danforth, a Missouri Republican with strong pro-business sentiments, says the FTC is "out of control."

In fact, many congressmen appear to be most concerned with their campaign coffers, which are largely taken care of by business "political action committees." The feeling on Capitol Hill runs so strong that the FTC's present chairman, Michael Pertschuk, sometimes arouses vicious personal attacks. An official of Formica Corporation described him as "a complete socialist" and "one of the most dangerous men in America."

Such responses might be almost funny if they were not merely the latest notation in a long history of abuse.

In 1912–1913 Congress, investigating the Money Trust, decided there was a dangerous concentration of economic power in America that should be broken up. In the spirit of reform it passed the Federal Reserve Act of 1913, the Clayton Antitrust Act of 1914, and the Federal Trade Commission Act of 1914.

None of these acts has reduced even slightly the concentration of economic power in America. Indeed, it has grown more intense. The largest 500 firms today account for more than 80 percent of all the manufacturing and mining assets in the country, an increase of more than 20 percent in the last two decades. The reforms of 1913–1914 were long ago mummified. The Federal Reserve Board became practically a tool of the major banks. The Clayton Antitrust Act has been treated by succeeding administrations as a quaint relic of an almost forgotten populist era. And, for most of its life, the Federal Trade Commission has been only a bad joke.

On paper, of course, Congress intended to give the FTC great authority. The legislation empowered the commission to take legal action against monopolies and cartels (a power it shared with the Justice Department) and to stamp out unfair and deceptive business practices. In short, it was supposed to police the commercial world in such a way that honest businesses would not be placed at a disadvantage with unscrupulous competitors and that consumers would not be cheated.

But having given these pious marching orders, Washington's politicians promptly abandoned the FTC. Not only did it receive little encouragement, but it was not allowed to show any independent inclination to fulfill its congressional mandate. When the FTC tried to break up interlocking corporate directorates, when it issued a comprehensive study of the international oil cartel and pushed for antitrust action, when it tried to force conglomerates to issue line-of-business reports on their income (a tremendous aid in the FTC's antitrust efforts), the FTC was smothered by political opposition. For most of its 66 years the FTC has gotten no moral support from Congress; it has gotten virtually none from the executive branch. And, until recently, the agency was sodden internally with despair, lack of talent, and conflict of interest. It was what journalist David Burnham called "a patronage dumping ground for friends of powerful Southern Democrats."

So passed its first half century. Frustrated in all major efforts, reduced to the listless pursuit of trivia, it was generally considered to be the most useless regulatory agency in Washington: timid, lazy, inept, indifferent, and totally intimidated by big business.

Year after year, the FTC churned out hundreds of inconsequential rulings relating to such matters as the price of fruit pies in Salt Lake City, the operation of gift shops in the Virgin Islands, the mislabeling of weasel coats in New York City, and the attempt of a bubblegum manufacturer to monopolize baseball picture cards. Commonly, prosecution of cases of mislabeling, false advertising, and deceitful practices would be dragged out by the FTC for so many years that they just fell apart and died—the witnesses scattered, the evidence misplaced, and often the accused company itself gone into bankruptcy. It took the

old FTC, as Jean Carper, columnist and co-author of *Eating May Be Hazardous to Your Health*, once pointed out, "13 years to make Geritol stop claiming it cured 'tired blood' and 30 years to make Holland Furnace Company salesmen stop faking explosions in people's basements."

Then one of Washington's rare miracles occurred: A bureaucratic corpse, electrified by criticism, began to stir.

The first criticism came from Ralph Nader's investigators who, in 1969, issued a ferocious exposé showing that the FTC was staffed by political hacks who strenuously avoided fighting the frauds of big business. Though the Nader report was taken seriously, the Washington establishment accepted it with reservations because most of the investigators were recent law-school graduates suspected of being hyped on the then-new consumer movement. President Nixon asked for a second opinion from the American Bar Association. Instead of discrediting Nader, the ABA concluded that the FTC was so worthless that "if change does not occur, there will be no substantial purpose" in keeping the agency alive.

Thus forced into a put-up or shut-up position, Nixon for once put up. He first appointed Casper Weinberger, California's director of finance, to take over the FTC and begin a "complete reorganization." Weinberger had hardly begun the job, however, when Nixon pulled him out and transferred him elsewhere in the bureaucracy. Next, Nixon appointed as chairman Miles Kirkpatrick, the Philadelphia lawyer who had headed the ABA investigation of the FTC. Kirkpatrick also took his assignment seriously. Suddenly the FTC was leveling charges of deceptive promotion against such sanctified outposts of capitalism as the Coca-Cola Company, McDonald's Hamburgers, Reader's Digest, and Procter & Gamble. The FTC was even so bold as to suggest that Wonder Bread really wasn't doing anything wonderful enough to build strong bodies 12 ways. In its fresh heretical frenzy, the FTC insisted that manufacturers of electric razors, air conditioners, and automobiles send evidence of the accuracy of their advertisements.

Even more startling, the FTC began to show imagination. It thought up a new system for balancing false advertisements: Instead of merely ordering manufacturers to quit lying about their products, the FTC demanded that they place *corrective* ads in which they acknowledged that their previous claims had been false.

Many of Nixon's big money supporters were furious. Herbert Klein, Nixon's director of communications, announced that the White House felt the FTC was going "too far" in its zeal to protect consumers, and shortly thereafter Kirkpatrick was persuaded to step down. He had lasted three years. His successor, Lewis A. Engman, who had recently served as assistant director of the White House Domestic Council, was greeted by consumer groups with deep suspicion. They thought he would probably represent Nixon's interests in protecting big business from regulation. Instead, Engman proved to be an independent, fairly gutsy fellow who carried on the reforms begun by Kirkpatrick and started some of his own.

The most important new power given Engman was the Magnuson-Moss Act of 1974. Previously, the FTC had been restricted to policing the conduct of individual companies. If Company X was caught in deceptive practices, the FTC could move against it—but all the other companies in the industry, even if they were equally guilty, might escape until a later day of judgment. Such a time-consuming company-by-company process left the FTC incapable of achieving sweeping reforms. The Magnuson-Moss Act, among other things, enabled the FTC to make industry-wide rules.

Armed with that authority, Engman launched 11 rule-making investigations into questionable activities involving vocational schools, mobile-home dealers, food advertisers, prescription-drug marketers, over-the-counter drug marketers, hearing-aid companies, health spas, and the funeral industry.

The next FTC head, Calvin Collier, followed Engman's lead. In a single year he initiated four other industry-wide rule-making investigations into such things as the practices of used-car dealers and eyeglass hucksters. By the end of 1976, the FTC had more than 750 investigations underway. It was also breaking up some illegally interlocking directorates, and it was slowly nursing along an antitrust suit filed in 1973 against eight major oil companies.

At 35, Collier was the youngest chairman in FTC history. Critics of the agency—noting that by January 1977 the FTC had replaced one out of every 10 lawyers on its staff with recruits from that year's class and that 20 percent of the young newcomers were Phi Beta Kappas—began to complain that business was being victimized by smart-alecky kids. The criticisms were especially ominous because they came from executives of such giants as Kellogg, General Foods, General Motors, Exxon, and Sears—all of whom had recently been hit by FTC action.

This was the situation that prevailed when, in April 1977, Michael Pertschuk, then 44 years old, was sworn in as the new chairman. The future was murky. The FTC was again under intense fire from *Fortune*'s 500 on down. It was again being accused of going too far, of carrying out vendettas against business. Some influential conservatives were again urging the ultimate reform—abolition of the agency.

Pertschuk's appointment did little to soothe them. Son of a wealthy furrier, educated at private prep schools and at Yale, Pertschuk had flourished on Capitol Hill during its most pro-consumer era. For more than a dozen years he had served as chief counsel of the Senate Commerce Committee, and for many of those years he was thought by some to be as influential as the committee's chairman, Senator Warren Magnuson. Pertschuk was known to be one of the few persons in Washington with Ralph Nader's private phone number, and it was not difficult to see the results of that friendship in the legislation Pertschuk helped write: on health warnings for cigarette labeling, no-fault insurance, auto safety, truth-in-packaging—a list that is, in the words of Senator Magnuson, "as long as your arm."

Still, despite his do-gooder credentials, many business lobbyists knew Pertschuk to be "a reasonable, practical, sensible problem solver," as one of Washington's corporate lawyers described him to the *New York Times*. Fanatics don't get to be chief counsel of the Senate Commerce Committee. He was a consummate wheeler-dealer when it came to bringing opposing parties together in the drafting of legislation. One of the oft-told stories around Washington was how he got Ralph Nader and Lloyd N. Cutler, lawyer for the auto industry, to cooperate on a Commerce Committee report. He put Nader in one room and Cutler in another, eventually persuading these vigorous opponents to redraft the report in such a way that Congress would pass the National Traffic and Motor Vehicle Safety Act.

At the time Pertschuk was sworn in, his friends and enemies did agree on one thing: Under his leadership the FTC would surely have an easier time with Congress than it had had under its recent Republican management. The logic of the prediction was simple enough: With the White House once again occupied by a Democrat, the President's nominee would be more kindly treated by a Democratic Congress, especially when he was Congress's own protégé.

Ironically, the results were just the opposite. The partisanship on which Pertschuk might have depended for his strength in earlier eras was fast disappearing from Washington. Party leaders—which is to say, party fund raisers—no longer had the influence they once held. The public treasury (for presidential candidates) and business "political action committees" (for congressmen) had replaced the old-style party fund raisers. With most politicians getting their money independently, their loyalty to the party machine declined sharply. The appointee of a Democratic President could no longer automatically expect friendship from a nominally Democratic Congress. The once-reliable Pennsylvania Avenue marriage was being broken up by money from special-interest groups.

In 1974, when many of the pro-consumer laws were being rushed through Congress, there were only 89 corporate political action committees spreading money around. But four years later, just as Pertschuk was taking on his new job, the Federal Election Commission reported the existence of 784 corporate political action committees and 451 trade and professional action organizations.

These groups—each of which is permitted to spend up to a total of $10,000 in primary and general elections—were becoming the big source of campaign funds for congressional candidates. Political committees linked with the American Medical Association, for example, gave more than $4.9 million to House and Senate candidates between 1974 and 1978.

Pertschuk, for all his political sophistication, apparently did not realize the profound change these moneyed groups were making. He seemed oblivious to the massive army that was already arrayed against further FTC regulations. He walked into his new job spouting the most quixotic plans for turning the FTC into what he boldly called "the best public-interest law firm in the country." In an interview with *U.S. News & World Report*, he implied that he might even get the FTC to make advertisers toe the line according to some politically ordained "national policy." If the "national policy" was to save energy, he said, the FTC might outlaw "an automobile ad that touted a car for its large size, quick starts, and power—while obscuring its poor fuel efficiency. . . ." He hinted that, to boost competition, the FTC might impose a ceiling on how much some giant corporations could spend for advertising.

Even before he was sworn in, he was vowing to crack down on the $600 million "kid vid" industry, the portion of the television advertising industry specializing in appeals to children—a group that too often, said Pertschuk, "manipulates sounds and symbols to exploit the vulnerability of a child's mind." He said it was unfair to go on television and fast-talk a six-year-old into eating sugar-laden foods that might ruin his teeth and health. Kellogg and colleagues accepted these comments as a declaration of war.

Between rhetorical outbursts, Pertschuk plunged into the varied rule-making activities he inherited from his Republican predecessors. But he did so with such enthusiasm that the Republican origins of the proposed rules were forgotten. Pertschuk alone got the blame for the trouble the FTC was causing business. He became the target—the symbolic, preeminent villain in a town where it had become quite faddish, even among liberals, to be against government regulation. At a White House Christmas party in 1979, one of the Senate's tougher members sidled up to Congressman Bob Eckhardt, chairman of a consumer protection subcommittee and very much a supporter of Pertschuk, to say cheerily: "We're going to get your boy next year."

The irony of the current get-Pertschuk movement—or to be more exact, the latest get-the-FTC movement, for there are four other members of the commission who must be considered, as they have generally given Pertschuk strong support—is that he could be classified as a white knight only by comparison with Washington's usual run of flaccid bureaucrats. By the standards of any real reformer, Pertschuk's knightly color would have to be gray.

The changes Pertschuk's FTC has ordered various industries to make in their conduct—or that it has said it *may* order them to make—are quite ordinary. They are such casual reforms, in fact, that one reads through the list with amazement that such changes hadn't been imposed long ago.

One is also dumbfounded to discover that of the 18 rule-making proceedings begun as a result of the Magnuson-Moss Act, only four have been completed. The commission has proceeded with excruciating caution. For example, it spent seven years of the most painstaking investigation and heard 327 witnesses before handing down its rules for reforming the funeral industry.

Here, in brief, are the four industry-wide rulings passed by the FTC:

1. Funeral directors were ordered to itemize price information rather than give "package" prices, and quote prices over the phone so that bereaved customers can shop around for the cheapest funeral. Directors were also ordered not to deceive people into thinking they had to get their dead embalmed if in fact they didn't have to, or buy a coffin for a cremation if that wasn't necessary. In short, funeral merchants were told they shouldn't take advantage of grieving people to sell a $2,500 funeral—the average price these days for the package—when they really would have preferred to buy one for $600.

2. Vocational schools were ordered to provide students with an escape clause and a rebate plan. No longer would some unsuspecting ghetto kid be locked into paying for a "guaranteed employment" computer course that he couldn't possibly complete.

3. State laws that prohibited advertising by optometrists were struck down. Also, doctors were ordered to give prescriptions to their customers so that they could do comparison buying. (That one rule has reportedly saved consumers $500 million since 1978.)

4. Manufacturers of home insulation were ordered to stop making unsubstantiated claims of energy-saving performances and to start telling consumers exactly what they could expect from their product in the way of R-value—the measure of insulating power.

Obviously, those four rules fall far short of being revolutionary. Pertschuk says the four rules show "judiciousness and restraint." Indeed, they are so restrained as to hardly qualify as reform. They are no more than housekeeping regulations that would, in the long haul, help the affected industries as much as they helped the public.

But the response of industry was predictably excessive. Even *proposed* investigations by the FTC prompted hysteria. When the commission announced that it was going to look into charges that Sunkist Growers Incorporated was suppressing competition, Sunkist wailed that it was being picked on, that federal law specifically exempted government regulation of cooperatives. (Sunkist is quite correct in that, but the law was aimed at assisting the *little* co-ops; it was decidedly not written for a giant that controls 60–80 percent of the western lemon and orange market.)

Used-car dealers said that the FTC had no right even to consider forcing them to inspect and list the defects of the 20 million used cars Americans buy each year; insurance companies were outraged when the FTC began investigating charges that consumers were being cheated of billions of dollars in the interest paid on their policies.

Big business did more than complain. Either by lawsuits or by legislation, it succeeded in getting all four rules to be put on hold. The FTC was stopped dead in its tracks—at least momentarily.

Legislation, as everyone knows, is written with money. A team of reporters from the *Philadelphia Inquirer* discovered that industries under investigation by the FTC had pumped more than $5 million into congressional races in 1978; the tally for 1980 is, of course, still far from over but it is expected to be at least as generous.

The money seems to have been profitably invested. Congress passed legislation to significantly stunt the agency's independence—the House favoring a draconian one-house veto power over FTC rules, the Senate choosing a more gentlemanly two-house overriding process. Both House and Senate also singled out specific rule-making proceedings—children's TV ads, funeral pricing, etc.—that they insist the agency back away from. (To be sure, the FTC could have done worse. Before the Senate vote a top agency official had said, "We can't count on more than 10 percent of their members." In fact the FTC got the support of 13 percent.)

As of this writing the conference committee has not put the prohibitions into a compromise package. But the general congressional message is already plain, and it has had its desired effect. The bounce has gone out of the commission once again.

Pertschuk no longer sounds much like a militant reformer. Compromise is in the air. Now he soothes congressional critics by conceding that some of his staff may have been a little too zealous and he claims that these zealots "are no longer with" the FTC. He tells conservatives that he is "not unsympathetic with the motivation for a legislative veto," though he does not think it would work. He insists that both he and his commission are, at bottom, full of "institutional humility."

Such a shift in attitude on his part, though perhaps politically smart, makes consumer advocates very uneasy. Nancy Drabble, a staff attorney at Nader's Congress Watch, says, "Our concern is that the FTC may become scared, that it may go back to being the little old lady of

Pennsylvania Avenue."

That would be a tragedy. For the FTC is finally beginning to be useful. Recently Arthur F. Burns, the former chairman of the Federal Reserve Board, asked Pertschuk: "The Federal Trade Commission has been around for a good many years. What major contributions has it made to creating or maintaining a healthy competitive environment in this country? Or, to put the same question another way, if the commission were abolished today, would we have a very different world?"

Pertschuk replied accurately, "I would have to say that the commission cannot claim any great credit for reshaping the structure of this economy."

If Congress and its business buddies have their way, the FTC's valiant battle to change that situation will have been for nothing.

QUESTIONS

1. What are the advantages of government regulation? What are the disadvantages?

2. In conflicts among interest groups, what factors determine which group wins?

3. Should government issue extensive regulations to protect consumers from false advertising, faulty products, dangerous ingredients, and so on, or should these matters be left to the individual in the free marketplace?

UNIT 5 *Social Change in the Modern World*

PAUL R. EHRLICH
ANNE H. EHRLICH

What Happened to the Population Bomb?

*There is a general public awareness that population
growth poses a threat of severe social and economic inconvenience within the United States, and of a mass
calamity in the less developed nations of the world,
where resources of land, food, education, health care,
and other essentials simply cannot keep pace with population increase.*

*Much of this awareness dates from the publication
of Paul Ehrlich's best-selling* The Population Bomb
*(1968), which interpreted demographic projections for
the ordinary reader and sounded a warning of the dire
consequences that would follow if population growth
continued on its predicted course. But demography is
an inexact science, and its projections are always subject to correction in the light of subsequent unanticipated events. As Paul and Anne Ehrlich point out in
this article, population growth in the United States
and in the world as a whole has since proved to be
somewhat lower than demographers had predicted.
The Ehrlichs discuss the reasons for this trend, and
suggest why some less developed countries have had
far more success in limiting population growth than
others.*

*It should be noted that, despite the slight slowing of
the population growth rate, the problems of overpopulation still haunt us. Some are already with us, and
the others have not disappeared; they have merely been
briefly postponed.*

When *The Population Bomb* [1968] was written, the
United States population explosion was alive and well—
and projected to get even healthier. Virtually all demographers thought that the early 1970s would be a time
of rising birth rates in the United States and that it would
take decades, at the very least, for fertility to decline to
replacement reproduction (an average family size at
which each generation just replaces itself). We agreed
with them; their reasoning made sense.

But we were all dead wrong. In the early 1970s the
women who had been born in the postwar baby boom
were in their early 20s, their prime reproductive years.
Because a high proportion of the population were young
people at an age when they would be having families,
demographers had predicted a surge in the birth rate
(conventionally expressed as the number of babies born
per 1,000 people in the population per year). But contrary
to all expectations, the birth rate plunged dramatically
from 18.4 in 1970 to around 15 by 1973, and it has
remained there ever since.

Correspondingly, the net reproductive rate in the
United States has fallen to just below one and has stayed
there. The net reproductive rate is a measure of the relative reproduction of generations. A rate of one is replacement reproduction—technically, each female baby born
alive in one generation is replaced by exactly one female
baby born alive in the next. A rate of two theoretically
indicates a population that roughly doubles each generation; a rate of .5, a population that halves each generation. In the mid 1970s the net reproductive rate in the
United States was about .9, a little below replacement. If
this level of fertility continued and if there were no immigration, population would decline.

Why were the experts confounded by the people? How
could there have been a lowering of desired family size so
drastic that it overwhelmed the effect of the increased
number of women of childbearing age? In retrospect
there may have been several factors involved. One was a
tight job market for young people as the expansive 1960s
gave way to the economically troubled 1970s. Another
was the women's liberation movement, which made it increasingly acceptable for women to seek fulfillment in
ways other than by producing numerous offspring. A

third was increased public awareness of the problems of further population growth—an awareness generated in part by citizen action groups like Zero Population Growth (ZPG) and by books like *The Population Bomb*. Finally, as reasons for having smaller families became widely discussed, effective means for preventing birth became more accessible. The pill and IUDs became available during the 1960s, family planning services were provided for low-income groups, and between 1967 and 1973 abortion was progressively legalized.

Above all, the demographic surprise of the early 1970s showed that, when conditions are right, social change can occur with astounding rapidity. In our view this is the most cheering event since the end of World War II, because it raises the hope that other social transformations necessary to assure the survival of civilization could occur with equal speed.

Unfortunately, the drop of fertility to below replacement level has been widely misinterpreted as meaning the end of population growth in the United States. Newspaper and television commentators proclaimed that the United States had "reached ZPG," membership in population organizations plummeted, and people in general relaxed because "the population explosion is over." But when a previously growing human population reaches a net reproductive rate of one, its growth does not halt immediately. It continues to expand because human beings of several generations live simultaneously (a generation spans about 25 years). A growing population has disproportionately more people in the high birth-rate, low death-rate younger generation than in the low birth-rate, high death-rate older generations. This means that for a while, even at a net reproductive rate of one or less, the more numerous young adults who are just replacing themselves will generate more births than the relatively few older people will contribute deaths. And as long as births exceed deaths, a population will increase.

This tendency for a population to grow even after replacement reproduction is reached is often referred to as "the momentum of population growth." In the United States that momentum means that, *if completed family sizes remain about where they are now*—which is slightly below replacement—the population will stop its natural increase in about 50 years with a peak population of about 250 million, about 30 million more than today. After that a slow decline will set in. (These estimates include continued legal immigration at current rates, but do not include illegal immigration, for which no solid information exists.)

The slowing of population growth in the United States over the past decade no doubt has already had significant social and economic effects, some of which have gone largely unrecognized. It has, of course, been blamed in part for the sluggishness of economic growth in the 1970s that has plagued most overdeveloped countries. Some

problems, such as higher unemployment rates due to the sudden increase of women in the work force, clearly are traceable to the rapid social change of which lower birth rates are a part.

But if our population had continued to expand at rates like those prevailing in the early 1960s, the increased demand for food, energy, and housing, to name a few important examples, would probably have severely strained the social order. All three have been subject to supply shortages and spiraling prices during the 1970s. Even though political factors have played a part, especially for energy, pressures generated by a large, growing, affluent population must bear a large measure of responsibility. A good case can be made for the proposition that the economic troubles of the 1970s (and those we can expect in the 1980s and beyond) would be considerably worse if the birth rate had not been reduced. Conversely, a further reduction in population growth would result in less pressure by affluent Americans on the world's threatened resource base.

What about the population explosion in the rest of the world? Many other overdeveloped countries have also experienced birth-rate declines in the past decade. Several countries in western Europe that have had relatively low birth rates for one or two generations now have passed their population peaks and begun to decline, notably the two Germanies, Luxembourg, and the United Kingdom. (In the latter, emigration has been an important factor in hastening ZPG.) In these comparatively densely populated countries, already heavily dependent on imports of food, energy, and raw materials to maintain high living standards, the ending of population growth can hardly be considered anything but beneficial. The sooner it can be accomplished for overdeveloped countries that are still growing, the better.

According to the latest projections by the U.S. Census Bureau, population momentum ensures that, if present fertility rates persist, the industrialized world as a whole (including the United States) will expand from 1.13 billion people to about 1.33 billion by the year 2000, and slackening growth will continue into the next century. Population projections for the overdeveloped world may seem less alarming than they did a decade ago, but nonetheless the population explosion of the rich countries is far from over. In view of these countries' greatly disproportionate impact on resources and global ecological systems, *any* growth in their populations must be seen as a future threat.

Turning to the less developed countries, we find even less cause for complacency. There the projected effects of population momentum are far more spectacular than in the overdeveloped countries. In 1970 Harvard demographer Nathan Keyfitz predicted that if a typical less developed country reduced fertility to replacement level by the year 2000 (which is unlikely for most), its population nevertheless would continue to grow for a century, soaring to two and a half times its 1970 size. If India, with a 1970 population of about 600 million, were to achieve a birth-control miracle and reach a net reproductive rate of one in the year 2000, its peak population size would be about 1.5 billion people (assuming no rise in death rates). That is more than the present population of Africa, South America, North America, Oceania, and Europe combined.

The most recent demographic estimates anticipate that the world's population will grow from its current size of slightly over four billion to about 6.2 billion at the end of the century. Momentum is expected to carry the population to an ultimate peak of somewhere between nine and 12 billion in the 22nd Century. Such projections make ecologists wish the population-control movement had caught on 50 years ago. With any humane method of stopping population growth, the "braking distance" is long indeed.

Family planning programs have been established in the majority of less developed countries in the last 15 years. But, except for a handful of small, relatively prosperous, and "advanced" countries (such as Hong Kong, Singapore, Taiwan, South Korea, Costa Rica, and Trinidad and Tobago), hardly a dent has been made in their birth rates. Many of their populations are still growing at 2.5 to 3.5 percent per year (doubling in roughly 20 to 30 years). It was something of a mystery that some countries by 1975 had succeeded in reducing their birth rates to around 25 to 30 per 1,000 (almost approaching the levels that had prevailed in overdeveloped countries a decade or two ago), while other countries, apparently equally well "developed," experienced no significant change, their birth rates remaining at approximately 35 to 45 per 1,000.

Then, in 1972, some light was shed on the mystery. The People's Republic of China joined the United Nations and began to disclose previously secret information about its population and its own activities in "birth planning." While externally blasting Malthusian ideas and the family planning efforts of other nations, China had been carrying on what is probably the world's most vigorous population control program—and possibly the most successful. The U.S. Census Bureau estimates that China's 1975 population was about 935 million and that its growth rate is about 1.5 percent and declining. The available demographic information on China is, however, by no means solid. Some demographers estimate that both total size and growth rates are somewhat lower; others believe they are higher.

The secret of success in reducing birth rates now appears not to be a high level of industrial development, as was previously thought. An essential factor seems simply to be equity. When people are given access to the basics of life—adequate food, shelter, clothing, health care,

education (particularly for women), and an opportunity to improve their well-being—they seem to be more willing to limit the size of their families. Viewed in this light, it becomes clear why the family planning efforts of many "relatively advanced" less developed countries seem to get nowhere; often only the highest income groups (perhaps a quarter or less of the population) are benefiting from "development." The poor usually are excluded, and in many countries their condition is even deteriorating. This situation unfortunately prevails in numerous less developed countries, including several of the largest and fastest growing, for instance, Brazil, Mexico, and to some extent India.

Because of population momentum, all less developed countries must look forward to vastly increased populations over the next century and to the array of horrendous problems that such growth entails. Doubling a population in a generation implies that all resources (food, energy, raw materials), services, and facilities must also be doubled in that time. Those less developed countries whose growth has begun to slow may have somewhat brighter prospects (depending in part on their resources and political leadership) than countries where birth rates remain high.

All of the standard demographic projections contain that assumption that death rates can only remain constant or decline; they cannot rise. That this assumption is absurd is made clear by the rises in death rates due to famines that in the 1970s afflicted the Sahel and parts of southern Asia. It is made more absurd by even the briefest consideration of the state of Earth's ecosystems and of our social-political-economic systems.

Most people who try to monitor the functioning of these systems agree that the likeliest source of an unpleasant demographic surprise in the next decade or so is a massive famine. The global agricultural system, in combination with the world's fisheries, must provide almost 2 percent more food each year in order to keep up with population growth. In this decade, on the average, agricultural productivity has barely managed to do that and there have been several rather severe setbacks. This would be serious enough if the world's food were reasonably well distributed. But it is not; the rich, especially in overdeveloped countries, are if anything overfed, while the poor, especially in less developed countries, are chronically underfed. There has been no serious attempt at redistribution. The proportion of humanity that is hungry is usually estimated to be about 15 to 25 percent, and this probably has remained roughly constant over the years.

Considering the constant *proportion* of hungry people, however, tends to conceal a vast tragedy that is exposed by a look at the increasing *numbers* of the undernourished. One sometimes hears statements of the following sort: "The poor are always with us—the proportion of hungry people is no greater today than in 1850." Perhaps that is true (frankly we doubt it). But if so, it means the absolute number of those who go to bed each night inadequately fed has increased from perhaps 250 million to one billion. And a billion people is just about what the *total* population of the earth was in 1850.

Unfortunately, world fisheries production shows every sign of running up against biological limits. In decades to come it may be necessary for agricultural production not only to hold its place in the race with population growth, but also to take up the slack left by faltering fisheries production. There is good reason to believe that it will not be able to do so. The hoped-for transformations in the economics and sociology of agriculture, so widely discussed at the time of the World Food Conference in 1974, are not materializing. The weather has been generally favorable for the past few years, and famines have largely dropped from the headlines. Partly as a result, pressure to create an institution to hold world grain reserves, to institute other distribution reforms, and to improve agricultural productivity on a long-term basis in less developed countries has died away.

In the absence of a large-scale famine, such urgent tasks as land and tenancy reform in the poor nations continue to be neglected, and in the rich ones ecologically unsound agro-ecosystems and dietary habits are perpetuated. Meanwhile those in power can easily ignore the inequities and hazards of the present world food supply system. Widespread famine could, however, be just around the corner. An extended period of bad weather (which is thought to be quite possible by the most knowledgeable meteorologists), combined with environmental deterioration resulting from inadequate land management and ecologically unsound agricultural practices, could precipitate massive famines. This would provide a tragic "solution" to the population problem through a rapid rise in death rates.

There are other routes to such a "solution," routes we travel in part because of population pressures. One might be a pandemic, leading to a breakdown in the world health system. Crowding and malnutrition—common in poor countries—would be major contributors to such a disaster.

Nuclear war could bring about an even more efficient "solution." This route is made more likely by the spread of nuclear power, which we are told (erroneously) is necessary to keep up with a demand for more energy resources and raw materials. Or a war could be precipitated simply by some nation's perceived need for *Lebensraum.* Some of the stickiest international wickets are made even stickier by unequal rates of population growth between adversaries: The Arabs and Israelis and the Chinese and Russians are outstanding examples.

We must emphasize that the rapidly increasing level of overpopulation on our planet is only one element in the human predicament—albeit a major one. Achieving a

birth-rate solution to the population explosion—one that would, we hope, lead to a gradual population decline—will not solve all our problems. We must also have profound transformations in our systems of economics and social justice, transformations that above all will permit Earth's ecosystems to continue to supply their indispensable, but little recognized, services to civilization. Hope that such transformations are possible can be taken from the dramatic and unexpected declines of birth rates in the United States and a number of other overdeveloped countries. However, this hope must be balanced by overall trends that remain gloomy. The staggering projected increase in the number of human beings overhangs all of our other problems, threatening not just the functioning of essential ecological systems but of human institutions as well. The old saying remains truer today than ever before: "Whatever your cause, it's a lost cause without population control."

QUESTIONS

1. The rich nations are growing richer and their populations are stabilizing; the poor nations are growing poorer and their populations are growing. Can and should the rich nations do anything about it?
2. What factors cause population growth in a society to level off or decline?
3. How would (a) population increase, (b) zero population growth, or (c) population decline affect American society?

MICHAEL H. BROWN

Love's New Model City

Industrial societies offer their inhabitants many advantages, including a general standard of living that is the envy of people in less developed nations. But industrialism has its costs, and one of them is pollution. Fortunately, the nation has become ecologically aware since the 1960s, and choked rivers, filthy air, and ravaged landscapes are now widely recognized as assaults on the natural environment and as threats to human health. But these are visible forms of pollution. There is another, lurking beneath the surface, that may be far more damaging to us in the long run, and far more difficult to counteract.

For over a century, American industry has been dumping its toxic chemical wastes at thousands of sites across the nation. The total number of these dumps, their contents, and their condition are all unknown, for in many cases, records have long since been lost. Some dumps contain chemicals that were considered safe years ago but are now known to cause cancer or other ailments; some were created perilously close to human communities. The result is that seepage has gradually contaminated a significant part of the nation's ground water, on which more than half the population depends for domestic use. Since it can take years for ground water to travel even a few miles, and longer still for the effects of poison to show up in humans, the full scale of the problem may not be apparent for decades.

In this article, Michael Brown describes the impact of toxic chemicals on the community in Love Canal, New York, whose residents had to abandon their homes in 1980.

From *Laying Waste: Love Canal and the Poisoning of America*, by Michael Brown. Copyright © 1979, 1980 by Michael Brown. Reprinted by permission of Pantheon Books, a Division of Random House, Inc.

At each turn, the schizophrenia of Niagara Falls, New York, is starkly evident. A city of unmatched natural beauty, it is also a tired industrial workhorse, beaten often and with a hard hand. In summertime the tourist limousines, heading toward the spectacular falls, move alongside soiled factory tank trucks. All the vehicles traverse a pavement film-coated with oils and soot, past large T-shaped steel constructions that string electrical lines above the densely wooded ravines to the horizon. In the southwest, a rising mist of spray from the downward force of the cataracts contends for prominence in the skyline with the dark plumes of towering smokestacks.

These contradictions stem from the magnificent river—a strait of water, really—that connects Lake Erie to Lake Ontario. Flowing north at a pace of half a million tons a minute, the watercourse widens into a smooth expanse near the city before it breaks into whitecaps and takes its famous 186-foot plunge. Then it cascades through a gorge of overhanging shale and limestone to haystack rapids higher and swifter than anywhere else on the continent. From there, it turns mellow again.

Newlyweds and other tourists have long treated the falls as an obligatory pilgrimage, and they once had come in long lines during the warmer months. At the same time, the plunging river provides cheap electricity for industry, particularly chemical producers, so that a good stretch of its beautiful shoreline is now filled with the spiraled pipes of distilleries. The odors of chlorine and sulfides hang in the air.

A major proportion of those who live in the city of Niagara Falls work in chemical plants, the largest owned by the Hooker Chemical Company. Timothy Schroeder did not. He was a cement technician by trade, dealing with the factories only if they needed a pathway poured or a small foundation set. Tim and his wife, Karen, lived on 99th Street in a ranch-style home with a brick and wood exterior. They had saved all they could to redecorate the inside and to make additions, such as a cement patio covered with an extended roof. One of the Schroeders' most cherished possessions was a fiberglass pool, built into the ground and enclosed by a redwood fence. Though it had taxed their resources, the yard complemented a house that was among the most elegant in a residential zone where most of the homes were small frame buildings, prefabricated and slapped together *en masse*. It was a quiet area, once almost rural in character, and located in the city's extreme southeast corner. The Schroeders had lived in the house only since 1970, but Karen was a lifelong resident of the general neighborhood. Her parents lived three doors down from them, six miles from the row of factories that stood shoulder to shoulder along the Upper Niagara.

Karen Schroeder looked out from a back window one October morning in 1974 and noted with distress that the pool had suddenly risen two feet above the ground. She called Tim to tell him about it. Karen then had no way of knowing that the problem far exceeded a simple property loss—that in fact it was the first sign of a great tragedy.

Accurately enough, Mrs. Schroeder figured that the cause of the uplift was the unusual groundwater flow of the area. Twenty-one years before, an abandoned hydroelectric canal directly behind their house had been backfilled with industrial rubble. The underground breaches created by this disturbance, aided by the marshy nature of the region's surficial layer, had collected large volumes of rainfall, and this water had undermined the backyard. The Schroeders allowed the pool to remain in its precarious position until the next summer and then pulled it from the ground, intending to replace it with a cement one. Immediately, the gaping hole filled with what Karen called "chemical water," rancid liquids of yellow and orchid and blue. These same chemicals, mixed with the groundwater, had flooded the entire yard; they attacked the redwood posts with such a caustic bite that one day the fence simply collapsed. When the groundwater receded in dry weather, it left the gardens and shrubs withered and scorched, as if by a brush fire.

How the chemicals had got there was no mystery: they came from the former canal. Beginning in the late 1930s or the early 1940s, the Hooker Company, whose many processes included the manufacture of pesticides, plasticizers, and caustic soda, had used the canal as a dump for at least 20,000 tons of waste residues—"still-bottoms" in the language of the trade. The chemical garbage was brought to the excavation in 55-gallon metal barrels stacked on a small dump truck and was unloaded into what, up to that time, had been a fishing and swimming hole in the summer and an ice-skating rink during the city's long, hard winter months.

When the hazardous dumping first began, much of the surrounding terrain was meadowlands and orchards, but there was also a small cluster of homes on the immediate periphery, only thirty feet from the ditch. Those who lived there remembered the deep holes being filled with what appeared to be oil and gray mud by laborers who rushed to borrow their garden hoses for a dousing of water if they came in contact with the scalding sludge

they were dumping. Children enjoyed playing among the intriguing, unguarded debris. They would pick up chunks of phosphorus and heave them against cement. Upon impact the "fire rocks," as they were called, would brilliantly explode, sending off a trail of white sparks. Fires and explosions erupted spontaneously when the weather was especially hot. Odors similar to those of the industrial districts wafted into the adjacent windows, accompanied by gusts of fly ash. On a humid moonlit night, residents would look toward the canal and see, in the haze above the soil, a greenish luminescence.

Karen's parents had been the first to experience problems with seepage from the canal. In 1959, her mother, Aileen Voorhees, noticed a strange black sludge bleeding through the basement walls. For the next twenty years, she and her husband, Edwin, tried various methods of halting the irritating intrusion, coating the cinder-block walls with sealants and even constructing a gutter along them to intercept the inflow. Nothing could stop a smell like that of a chemical plant from permeating the entire household, and neighborhood calls to the city for help were unavailing. One day, when Edwin punched a hole in the wall to see what was happening, quantities of black liquid poured out. The cinder blocks were full of the stuff.

Although later it was to be determined that they were in imminent danger, the Voorhees treated the problem at first as a mere nuisance. That it involved chemicals, industrial chemicals, was not particularly significant to them. All their life, all of everyone's life in the city, malodorous fumes had been a normal ingredient of the surrounding air.

More ominous than the Voorhees' basement seepage was an event that occurred in the Schroeder family at 11:12 P.M. on November 21, 1968. Karen gave birth to her third child, a seven-pound girl named Sheri. But no sense of elation filled the delivery room, for the baby was born with a heart that beat irregularly and had a hole in it, bone blockages of the nose and partial deafness, deformed external ears, and a cleft palate. By the age of two, it became obvious that the child was mentally retarded. When her teeth came in, there was a double row of them at the bottom. She also developed an enlarged liver.

The Schroeders looked upon these health problems, as well as certain illnesses among their other children, as acts of capricious genes, a vicious quirk of nature. Like Aileen and Edwin Voorhees, they were mainly aware that the chemicals were devaluing their property. The crabapple tree and evergreens in the back were dead, and even the oak in the front of the house was sick; one year, the leaves fell off on Father's Day.

The canal was dug with much fanfare in the late nineteenth century by a flamboyant entrepreneur named William T. Love. Love arrived in town with a grandiose dream: to construct a carefully planned industrial city with ready access to water power and major markets. The setting for Love's dream was to be a navigable power channel that would extend seven miles from the Upper Niagara near what is now 99th Street to a terrace known as the Niagara Escarpment, where the water would fall 280 feet, circumventing the treacherous falls and at the same time providing cheap power. A city would be constructed near the point where the canal fed back into the river, and it would accommodate 200,000 to 1 million people, he promised. Love's sales speeches were accompanied by advertisements, circulars, and brass bands, with a chorus singing a special ditty to the tune of "Yankee Doodle": "Everybody's come to town,/Those left we all do pity,/For we'll have a jolly time/At Love's new Model City."

So fired by Love's imagination were the state's leaders that they allowed him the rare opportunity of addressing a joint session of the senate and assembly. He was given a free hand to condemn as much property as he liked and to divert whatever amounts of water. But Love's dream quickly became Love's folly, and, financially depleted, he abandoned the project after a mile-long trench, 10 to 40 feet deep and generally 15 yards wide, had been scoured perpendicular to the Niagara River. Eventually the site was acquired by Hooker.

Except for the frivolous history of Mr. Love, and some general information on the chemicals, little was known publicly about the dump in 1977. Few of those who lived in the numerous houses that had sprung up by the site were aware that the large barren field behind them was a burial ground for toxic wastes. That year, while working as a reporter for a local newspaper, the *Niagara Gazette*, I began to inquire regularly about the strange conditions on 99th Street. The Niagara County Health Department and the city both said it was a nuisance condition but no serious danger to the people. The Hooker Company refused to comment on their chemicals, claiming only that they had no records of the burials and that the problem was not their responsibility. In fact, Hooker had deeded the land to the Niagara Falls Board of Education in 1953 for a token $1. At that time the company issued no detailed warnings about the chemicals; a brief paragraph in the quitclaim document disclaimed company liability for any injuries or deaths that might occur at the site. Ralph Boniello, the board's attorney, said he had never received any phone calls or letters specifically describing the exact nature of the refuse and its potential effects, nor was there, as the company was later to claim, any threat of property condemnation by the board in order to secure the land. "We had no idea what was in there," Boniello said.

Though surely Hooker must have been relieved to rid itself of the contaminated land, when I read its deed I was left with the impression that the wastes there would be a hazard only if physically touched or swallowed. Otherwise, they did not seem to be an overwhelming concern. In reality, the dangers of these wastes far exceeded those of acids or alkalines or inert salts. We now know that the drums dumped in the canal contained a veritable witch's brew of chemistry, compounds of truly remarkable toxicity. There were solvents that attacked the heart and liver, and residues from pesticides so dangerous that their commercial sale had subsequently been restricted or banned outright by the government; some of them are strongly suspected of causing cancer.

Yet Hooker gave no more than a hint of that. When approached by the educational board for the parcel of property it wanted for a new school, B. Klaussen, then Hooker's executive vice-president, replied in a letter to the board:

> Our officers have carefully considered your request. We are very conscious of the need for new elementary schools and realize that the sites must be carefully selected so that they will best serve the area involved. We feel that the board of education has done a fine job in meeting the expanding demand for additional facilities and we are anxious to cooperate in any proper way. We have, therefore, come to the conclusion that since this location is the most desirable one for this purpose, we will be willing to donate the entire strip between Colvin Boulevard and Frontier Avenue to be used for the erection of a school at a location to be determined. . . .

The school board, apparently unaware of the exact nature of the substances underneath this generously donated property, and woefully incurious, began to build the new school and playground at the canal's midsection. Construction progressed even after the workers struck a drainage trench that gave off a strong chemical odor and then discovered a waste pit nearby. Instead of halting the work, the board simply had the school site moved 80 feet away. Young families began to settle in increasing numbers alongside the dump; many of them had been told that the field was to be a park and recreation area for their children.

If the children found the "playground" interesting, there were times they found it painful as well. When they played on this land that Hooker implied was so well suited for a school, they sneezed and their eyes teared. In the days when dumping was still in progress, they swam at the opposite end of the canal, at times arriving home with hard pimples on their bodies. And Hooker knew that children were playing on its spoils. In 1958, the company was made aware that three children had been burned by exposed residues on the surface of the canal, much of which, according to the residents, had been covered over with nothing more than fly ash and loose dirt. Because it wished to avoid legal repercussions, the company chose not to issue a public warning of the dangers only it could have known were there, nor to have its chemists explain to the people that their homes would have been better placed elsewhere.

The Love Canal was simply unfit to be a container for hazardous substances, even by the standards of the day, and now, in 1977, the local authorities were belatedly finding that out. Several years of heavy snowfall and rain had filled the sparsely covered channel like a sponge. The contents were overflowing at a frightening rate, seeping readily into the clay, silt, and sandy loam and finding their way through old creekbeds and swales into the neighborhood.

The city of Niagara Falls, I was assured, was planning a remedial drainage program to reduce chemical migration off the site. But it was apparent that no sense of urgency had been attached to the plan, and it was stalled in a ball of red tape. There was hopeless disagreement over who should pay the bill—the city, Hooker, or the board of education—and the engineers seemed confused as to what exactly needed to be done for a problem that had never been confronted elsewhere.

At a meeting in Buffalo during the summer of 1977, I cornered an independent consultant for the city and requested more information on the dump and the proposed remedial action.

"We're not really sure what the final solution should be," he said. "You can't be sure until you know what you're dealing with."

Was there a chance of harm to the people?

He shrugged his shoulders.

How were the potential dangers to be searched out?

"Someone's going to have to dig there and take a good look," he answered. "If they don't, your child or your children's children are going to run into problems."

The same questions were repeated for months, with no answers. Despite the uncertainty of the city's own consultant, the city manager, Donald O'Hara, persisted in his view that the Love Canal, however displeasing to the eyes and nasal passages, was not a crisis but mainly a matter of aesthetics. O'Hara was pleased to remind me that Dr. Francis Clifford, the county health commissioner, supported his opinion. Besides making light of the seepage, O'Hara created an aura of secrecy around information regarding the canal. His concerns appeared to be financial and legal in nature. As manager, O'Hara had pulled the city out from under a staggering debt, and suddenly, with hardly a moment to enjoy a widely publicized budget surplus, his city hall was faced with the prospect of spending an unplanned $400,000 for a remedial program at the dumpsite. And it was feared there would be more expensive work to do later on—and lawsuits.

With the city, the school board, and Hooker unwilling to commit themselves to a remedy, conditions between 97th and 99th streets continued to degenerate until, by early 1978, the land was a quagmire of sludge. Melting snow drained a layer of soot onto the private yards, while the ground on the dump itself had softened to the point of collapse, exposing the crushed tops of barrels. When a city truck attempted to cross the field and dump clay on one especially large hole, it sank up to its axles. Masses of sludge beneath the surface were finding their way out at a quickening rate, forming constant springs of contaminated liquid. So miserable had the Schroeder backyard become that the family gave up trying to fight the inundation. They had brought in an old bulldozer to attempt to cover pools of chemicals that welled up here and there, but now the machine sat still. Their yard, once featured in a local newspaper for its beauty, now had degenerated to the point where it was unfit even to walk upon. Of course, the Schroeders could not leave. No one would think of buying the property. They had a mortgage to pay, and on Tim's salary, could not afford to maintain the house while they moved to a safer setting. They and their four children were stuck.

. . .

Industry had begun its grip on the river as early as the mid-1700s, when Daniel Joncaire constructed a lumber mill just above the American falls, employing a system of overshoot wheels and pulleys to make practical use of the river's swift flow. Ventures like Joncaire's proliferated for the next hundred years, and included the excavation of another canal from the upper river to the lower to create additional power for flour-mill operations. There was concern at the time that sucking in water from above the falls and diverting it around the cataracts would lessen the flow to the point where it would detract from the beauty of the falls, but the Niagara Falls Hydraulic Company dispelled the notion: "Its attractiveness as a watering place will continue undiminished; for the proposed situation of the factories is such as to preclude the possibility of their detracting in the least from the grandeur of the cataract." Electricity was first produced from river power in 1881. Industries quickly filtered into the city, supplied by what was called the Niagara Falls Power Company at the turn of the century. Within a short span, aluminum, calcium chloride, ferroalloys, and other products were being manufactured quite economically because of the availability of cheap hydroelectricity.

The city had made the decision to accommodate industry at the expense of its great natural attractions. Tourists who ventured into town had to pass a two-mile row of unsightly factories before arriving at the key vantage points near the falls, and when they did, they could see streams of brownish suds in the turbulent waters at the base of the cataracts. Fishing had been largely destroyed in both the river and Lake Ontario, and parks and beaches, once of scenic value, had deteriorated so greatly that it was only on the hottest days they drew large gatherings. The smell of dead fish and garbage often permeated the winds, and the rapids of the river were now at lower levels than ever before—the electrical generators were sucking in too much water. Mink and deer that had once foraged in the brush were unable to reproduce as they formerly had, and the populations of muskrat and ringneck pheasant were dwindling at a rapid rate. The fertility of mallard duck eggs was less than half what it had been in previous decades, and other birds laid eggs with shells so brittle that they cracked from the slightest impact. The wildlife problems coincided strikingly with the increased volumes of chlorinated compounds being produced on the Niagara Frontier.

Despite the frightening environmental indications, O'Hara and the mayor, Michael O'Laughlin, continued to cater to industrial whims and to ignore those who might cause trouble for the plants. When residents appeared at city council meetings, O'Laughlin cut them short in their complaints during the public sessions. Karen Schroeder, for one, had great difficulty reaching the mayor or O'Hara on the phone to tell them of her distress. At one meeting, she said, Tim was told by a councilman, Pierre Tangent, that it was difficult for the city to attack the Hooker Chemical Company while negotiations for its new building were in progress. Obviously, a city-initiated lawsuit against the firm would have been quite untimely.

At the very time City Manager O'Hara was explaining to me that the Love Canal was not threatening human lives, both he and other authorities were aware of the nature of Hooker's chemicals. In the privacy of his office O'Hara, after receiving a report on the chemical tests at the canal, had discussed with Hooker the fact that it was an extremely serious problem. Even earlier, in 1976, the New York State Department of Environmental Conservation had been made aware that dangerous compounds were present in the basement sump pump of at least one 97th Street home, and soon after, its own testing had revealed that highly injurious halogenated hydrocarbons were flowing from the canal into adjoining sewers. Among these were the notorious PCBs—polychlorinated biphenyls. The Hudson River had become so badly polluted with these compounds that a $200 million project was initiated to dredge contaminated river sediments. PCBs, which are known to kill even microscopic plants and animals, also poisoned animal feed in at least seventeen states during 1979, leading to the destruction of millions of chickens and eggs from Oregon to New Jersey. Quantities as low as 1 part of PCBs to a million parts of normal water are enough to create serious environmental concern; in the sewers of Niagara Falls, the quantities of halogenated compounds were thousands of times higher. The other materials tracked in sump pumps or sewers were just as toxic as PCBs, or more so. Prime among the more hazardous ones was residue from hexachlorocyclopentadiene, C-56 for short. Few industrial products approach the toxicity of C-56, which was deployed as an

intermediate in the manufacture of several pesticides whose use had created well-known environmental crises across the nation. The chemical is capable of causing damage to every organ in the body.

While the mere presence of C-56, however small the quantities, should have been cause for alarm, government remained inactive. It was not until early 1978—a full eighteen months after C-56 was first detected—that air testing was conducted in basements along 97th and 99th streets to see if the chemicals had vaporized off the sump pumps and walls and were present in the household air. The United States Environmental Protection Agency conducted these tests at the urging of the local congressman, John La Falce, the only politician willing to approach the problem with the seriousness it deserved.

While the basement tests were in progress, the spring rains arrived, further worsening the situation at the canal. Heavier fumes rose above the barrels. More than before, the residents were suffering from headaches, respiratory discomforts, and skin ailments. Many of them felt constantly fatigued and irritable, and the children had reddened eyes. Tim Schroeder developed a rash along the back of his legs and often found it difficult to stay awake. Another Schroeder daughter, Laurie, seemed to be losing some of her hair. Karen could not rid herself of throbbing pains in her head. Yet the Schroeders stayed on.

Three months passed before I was able to learn what the EPA testing had shown. When I did, the gravity of the situation immediately became clear: benzene, a known cancer-causing agent in humans, had been readily detected in the household air up and down the streets. A widely used solvent, benzene in chronic-exposure cases is known to cause headaches, fatigue, loss of weight, and dizziness at the onset, and later, pallor, nosebleeds, and damage to the bone marrow.

There was no public announcement of the benzene hazard. Instead, it seemed that some officials were trying to conceal the finding until they could agree among themselves on how to present it. Indeed, as early as October 18, 1977, Lawrence R. Moriarty, an EPA regional official in Rochester, had sent to the agency's toxic substances coordinator a lengthy memorandum stating that "serious thought should be given to the purchases of some or all of the homes affected. . . . This would minimize complaints and prevent further exposure to people." There was concern, he said, "for the safety of some 40 or 50 homeowners and their families." In an unsuccessful effort to learn the test results, I had regularly called the EPA and other sources, including the private laboratory contracted to conduct the tests; nervousness frequently crept into these discussions. No one wanted to talk.

Up until the second week of May 1978, I was still being told that the results were not ready, so I was surprised that same week to read a memorandum that had been sent from the EPA's regional office to Congressman La Falce. Buried in the letter was a sentence that referred to the analyses, saying that they suggested "a serious threat to health and welfare."

Immediately, local officials grew upset that the results had been publicly released. After an article of mine on the benzene hazard appeared in the *Niagara Gazette*, I received a telephone call from Lloyd Paterson, a state senator representing the Niagara area at the time.

"That Love Canal story," he began. "You know, you can panic people with things like that."

I explained to the senator that the finding was newsworthy and therefore it was my duty to print it. He responded that he did not want to see "people screaming in the streets." Irritation filled his voice as he continued: "We had a meeting last week, and there was no specific agreement on when this would be released."

The county health commissioner, Dr. Clifford, seemed unconcerned that benzene had been detected in the air many people were constantly breathing. There was no reason to believe their health was imperiled, he said. "For all we know, the federal limits could be six times too high," he stated with striking nonchalance. "I look at EPA's track record and notice they have to err on the right side." City Manager O'Hara, when I spoke to him in his office about the situation, told me I was overreacting to the various findings. He claimed the chemicals in the air posed no more risk than smoking a couple of cigarettes a day.

Dr. Clifford's health department refused to conduct a formal study of the people's health, despite the air-monitoring results. His department made a perfunctory call at the 99th Street Elementary School, and when it learned that classroom attendance was normal, it ceased to worry about the situation. For this reason, and because of growing resistance among the local authorities, I went to the southern end of 99th Street to make an informal health survey of my own. A meeting was arranged with six neighbors, all of them instructed beforehand to list the illnesses they knew of on their block, with names and ages specified, for presentation at the session.

The residents' list was startling. Either they were exaggerating the illnesses, or the chemicals had already taken an impressive and disheartening toll. Many people, unafflicted before they moved there, were now plagued with ear infections, nervous disorders, rashes, and headaches. One young man, James Gizzarelli, said he had missed four months of work because he had breathing troubles. His wife had experienced epilepsy-like seizures that she said her doctor was unable to explain. Meanwhile, freshly applied paint was inexplicably peeling from the exterior of their house. Pets too were suffering, most seriously if they had been penned in the backyards nearest the canal; they lost their fur, exhibited skin lesions, and, at quite early ages, developed internal tumors. There

seemed also to be many cases of cancer among the women. Deafness was prevalent: on both 97th and 99th streets, traffic signs warned the passing motorists to watch out for deaf children playing near the road.

One 97th Street resident, a woman named Rosalee Janese, displayed a number of especially suspicious symptoms. She lived at the canal's southern end, where the chemicals were leaking fastest and surface deterioration was most pronounced. Pimples and sores on her feet, arms, and hands caused her constant pain, and she suffered from daily bouts of nausea, faintness, internal pains, and a thick and oddly colored perspiration. The symptoms had begun suddenly, within weeks after a routine cleaning of her family's in-ground pool. During that chore, Mrs. Janese had been forced to hurriedly grab a rag and stuff it in the bottom drain: a black sludge was oozing through it into the pool.

Evidence continued to mount that a large group of people, all of the hundred families immediately by the canal and perhaps many more, were in imminent danger. While they watched television, gardened, or did the wash, even while they slept, they were inhaling a mixture of damaging chemicals. Their hours of exposure were far longer than those of a chemical factory worker, and they wore no respirators or goggles. Nor could they simply walk out of the door and escape. Helplessness and despair were the main responses to the blackened craters and scattered cinders behind their backyards. But public officials often characterized the residents as hypochondriacs, as if to imply it was they who were at fault.

Timothy Schroeder looked out over his back land and shook his head. "They're not going to help us one damn bit," he said, throwing a rock into a puddle coated with a film of oily blue. "No way." His calls to the city remained unanswered while his shrubs continued to die. Sheri needed expensive medical care, and he was afraid there would be a point where he could no longer afford to provide it. A heavy man with a round stomach and a gentle voice, he had always struck me as easy-going and calm, ever ready with a joke and a smile. That was changing now. His face—the staring eyes, the tightness of lips and cheeks—candidly revealed his utter disgust. Every government agency had been called on the phone or sent pleas for help, but none of them offered aid.

For his part, Commissioner Clifford expressed irritation at my printed reports of illness, and there was disagreement in the newsroom on how the stories should be printed. "There's a high rate of cancer among my friends," he argued. "It doesn't mean anything." While it was true that the accounts of illness which I printed regularly were anecdotal, Dr. Clifford had even fewer grounds for an evaluation: Mrs. Schroeder said he had not visited her home, and neither could she remember his seeing the black liquids collecting in the basements. Nor had Dr. Clifford even properly followed an order from the state commissioner to cover exposed chemicals, erect a fence around the site, and ventilate the contaminated basements. Instead, he had arranged to have two $15 window fans installed in the two most polluted basements and a thin wood snow fence erected that was broken within days and did not cover the entire canal. When I wrote an article on a man who had contracted Hodgkin's disease at thirty-three, after a childhood spent swimming in the canal, Dr. Clifford telephoned me. He was brief: "When," he asked, "are you going to go back to being a reporter?"

Partly as a result of the county's inadequate response and pressure from La Falce, the state finally announced in May 1978 that it intended to conduct a health study at the southern end. Blood samples would be taken to see if there were any unusual enzyme levels indicating liver destruction, and extensive medical questionnaires were to be answered by each of the families. Hearing this, the many residents who had maintained silence, who had scoffed at the idea that buried chemicals could hurt them, began to ask questions among themselves. Would their wives have trouble bearing babies? Would their developing children be prone to abnormalities? Twenty years from now, would the chemicals trigger cancer in their own bodies?

As interest in the small community increased, further revelations shook the neighborhood. In addition to the benzene, as many as eighty other compounds had been discovered in the makeshift dump, at least ten of them potential carcinogens. The possible physiological effects were profound and diverse. Fourteen of the compounds could affect the brain and central nervous system. Two of them, carbon tetrachloride and chlorobenzene, could readily cause narcosis or anesthesia. Many others were known to cause headaches, seizures, loss of hair, anemia, and skin rashes. When combined, the compounds were capable of inflicting innumerable illnesses, and no one knew what different concoctions were being mixed underground. But even then no one realized, since only Hooker could know, that beyond the pesticides and solvents, far beyond the fly ash, one hundred additional chemicals would be identified during the next year, including one recognized by the state health laboratories as the most toxic substance ever synthesized by man.

. . .

On July 14 I received a call from the state health department with some rather shocking news. The preliminary review of the health questionnaires was complete, and it showed that women living at the southern end of the canal had suffered a high rate of miscarriage and given birth to an abnormally large number of children with birth defects. In one female age group, 35.3 percent had records of spontaneous abortion. That was far in excess of the norm: the odds against its happening by chance are 250 to 1. Four children in one small section of

the neighborhood had documentable birth defects, clubfeet, retardation, and deafness. These tallies, it was stressed, were "conservative" figures. The people who had lived there longest suffered the highest rates.

. . .

The data on miscarriages and birth defects, coupled with the other accounts of illness, finally pushed the state's hierarchy into motion. A meeting was scheduled for August 2, at which time the state health commissioner, Dr. Robert Whalen, would formally address the issue. The day before the meeting, Dr. Nicholas Vianna, a state epidemiologist, told me that it also appeared that residents were incurring some degree of liver damage: blood analyses had shown hepatitis-like symptoms among the enzyme levels. Dozens if not hundreds of people had been adversely affected. . . .

. . .

When I arrived at the government complex in Albany . . . I rode to the fourteenth-floor health offices with Dr. Clifford, who made joking references to the local newspaper's story on possible evacuations at the dump. He found that quite absurd. I entered the department's public relations office and picked up a copy of the *New York Times*. There on the front page, in the lower left corner, was the story: "Upstate Waste Site May Endanger Lives."

Dr. Whalen had begun his meeting just before I arrived. As I entered the auditorium where he was speaking, I spotted the Schroeders and Aileen Voorhees in the small audience, watching intently. But not Tim; he was bent over in his chair, staring at the floor. None of them expected anything to happen, but they had traveled the five hours to Albany anyway, to make their presence felt.

Minutes later, to their surprise, Dr. Whalen read a lengthy statement in which he urged that pregnant women and children under two years of age leave the southern end of the dumpsite immediately. He declared the Love Canal an official emergency, citing it as a "great and imminent peril to the health of the general public."

QUESTIONS

1. Is industrial development really progress? Is pollution simply part of the price we must pay for our way of life?

2. In situations where resource development and environmental conservation seem incompatible (such as the destruction of landscapes to provide coal for energy), which do you think should have priority?

3. How does the case study reveal the different perspectives and involvements of the various interest groups concerned? To what extent is national environmental policy similarly subject to interest-group politics?

THOMAS McKEOWN

Determinants of Health

*Opinion polls about the relative prestige of various oc-
cupations have consistently shown that physicians rank
higher than the holders of any other job. This fact is
indicative of the immense respect that the general population has for modern medicine and its many achievements, which are supposed to include returning us to
health when we are ill, and dramatically extending
our life expectancies by combating the diseases that
once sent so large a part of humanity to an early
grave.*

*In this article, Thomas McKeown questions wheth-
er modern medicine can really take all the credit for
these achievements. While he does not downplay the
remarkable and effective advances that have taken
place in medical science during this century, he argues
that other factors have been more important in extending life expectancy, and can have a greater influence
on keeping us well.*

*The high infant mortality rates of the past, he
points out, began a sharp decline before, not after,
such innovations as vaccinations, and they did so for
reasons that were primarily social. Similarly, he argues that our health depends less on the ability of
physicians to make us well when we are ill than on the
social and environmental factors that make us ill when
we should be well.*

Modern medicine is not nearly as effective as most people
believe. It has not been effective because medical science
and service are misdirected and society's investment in
health is misused. At the base of this misdirection is a
false assumption about human health. Physicians, bio-
chemists, and the general public assume that the body is
a machine that can be protected from disease primarily
by physical and chemical intervention. This approach,
rooted in 17th Century science, has led to widespread
indifference to the influence of the primary determinants
of human health—environment and personal behavior—
and emphasizes the role of medical treatment, which is
actually less important than either of the others. It has
also resulted in the neglect of sick people whose ailments
are not within the scope of the sort of therapy that interests the medical professions.

An appraisal of influences on health in the past suggests that the contribution of modern medicine to the increase of life expectancy has been much smaller than
most people believe. Health improved, not because of
steps taken when we are ill, but because we become ill
less often. We remain well, less because of specific measures such as vaccination and immunization than because
we enjoy a higher standard of nutrition, we live in a
healthier environment, and we have fewer children.

For some 300 years an engineering approach has been
dominant in biology and medicine and has provided the
basis for the treatment of the sick. A mechanistic concept
of nature developed in the 17th Century led to the idea
that a living organism, like a machine, might be taken
apart and reassembled if its structure and function were
sufficiently understood. Applied to medicine, this concept
meant that understanding the body's response to disease
would allow physicians to intervene in the course of disease. The consequences of the engineering approach to
medicine are more conspicuous today than they were in
the 17th Century, largely because the resources of the
physical and chemical sciences are so much greater.
Medical education begins with the study of the structure
and function of the body, continues with examination of
disease processes, and ends with clinical instruction on
selected sick people. Medical service is dominated by the
image of the hospital for the acutely ill, where technolog-

ical resources are concentrated. Medical research also reflects the mechanistic approach, concerning itself with problems such as the chemical basis of inheritance and the immunological response to transplanted tissues.

No one disputes the predominance of the engineering approach in medicine, but we must now ask whether it is seriously deficient as a conceptualization of the problems of human health. To answer this question, we must examine the determinants of human health. We must first discover why health improved in the past and then go on to ascertain the important influences on health today, in the light of the change in health problems that has resulted from the decline of infectious diseases.

It is no exaggeration to say that health, especially the health of infants and young children, has been transformed since the 18th Century. For the first time in history, a mother knows it is likely that all her children will live to maturity. Before the 19th Century, only about three out of every 10 newborn infants lived beyond the age of 25. Of the seven who died, two or three never reached their first birthday, and five or six died before they were six. Today, in developed countries fewer than one in 20 children die before they reach adulthood.

The increased life expectancy, most evident for young children, is due predominantly to a reduction of deaths from infectious diseases. Records from England and Wales (the earliest national statistics available) show that this reduction was the reason for the improvement in health before 1900 and it remains the main influence to the present day.

But when we try to account for the decline of infections, significant differences of opinion appear. The conventional view attributes the change to an increased understanding of the nature of infectious disease and to the application of that knowledge through better hygiene, immunization, and treatment. This interpretation places particular emphasis on immunization against diseases like smallpox and polio, and on the use of drugs for the treatment of other diseases, such as tuberculosis, meningitis, and pneumonia. These measures, in fact, contributed relatively little to the total reduction of mortality; the main explanation for the dramatic fall in the number of deaths lies not in medical intervention, but elsewhere.

Deaths from the common infections were declining long before effective medical intervention was possible. By 1900, the total death rate had dropped substantially, and over 90 percent of the reduction was due to a decrease of deaths from infectious diseases. The relative importance of the major influences can be illustrated by reference to tuberculosis. Although respiratory tuberculosis was the single largest cause of death in the mid-19th Century, mortality from the disease declined continuously after 1838, when it was first registered in England and Wales as a cause of death.

Robert Koch identified the tubercle bacillus in 1882,

but none of the treatments used in the 19th or early 20th Centuries significantly influenced the course of the disease. The many drugs that were tried were worthless; so, too, was the practice of surgically collapsing an infected lung, a treatment introduced about 1920. Streptomycin, developed in 1947, was the first effective treatment, but by this time mortality from the disease had fallen to a small fraction of its level during 1848 to 1854. Streptomycin lowered the death rate from tuberculosis in England and Wales by about 50 percent, but its contribution to the decrease in the death rate since the early 19th Century was only about 3 percent.

Deaths from bronchitis, pneumonia, and influenza also began to decline before medical science provided an effective treatment for these illnesses. Although the death rate in England and Wales increased in the second half of the 19th Century, it has fallen continuously since the beginning of the 20th. There is still no effective immunization against bronchitis or pneumonia, and influenza vaccines have had no effect on deaths. The first successful treatment for these respiratory diseases was a sulfa drug introduced in 1938, but mortality attributed to the lung infections was declining from the beginning of the 20th Century. There is no reason to doubt that the decline would have continued without effective therapeutic measures, if at a slower rate.

In the United States, the story was similar; Thomas Magill noted that "the rapid decline of pneumonia death rates began in New York State before the turn of the century and many years before the 'miracle drugs' were known." Obviously, drug therapy was not responsible for the total decrease in deaths that occurred since 1938, and it could have had no influence on the substantial reduction that occurred before then.

The histories of most other common infections, such as whooping cough, measles, and scarlet fever, are similar. In each of these diseases, mortality had fallen to a low level before effective immunization or therapy became available.

In some infections, medical intervention *was* valuable before sulfa drugs and antibiotics became available. Immunization protected people against smallpox and tetanus; antitoxin treatment limited deaths from diptheria; appendicitis, peritonitis, and ear infections responded to surgery; Salvarsan was a long-sought "magic bullet" against syphilis; intravenous therapy saved people with severe diarrheas; and improved obstetric care prevented childbed fever.

But even if such medical measures had been responsible for the whole decline of mortality from these particular conditions after 1900 (and clearly they were not), they would account for only a small part of the decrease in deaths attributed to all infectious diseases before 1935. From that time, powerful drugs came into use and they were supplemented by improved vaccines. But mortality would have continued to fall even without the presence of these agents; and over the whole period since cause of death was first recorded, immunization and treatment have contributed much less than other influences.

The substantial fall in mortality was due in part to reduced contact with microorganisms. In developed countries an individual no longer encounters the cholera bacillus, he is rarely exposed to the typhoid organism, and his contact with the tubercle baccillus is infrequent. The death rate from these infections fell continuously from the second half of the 19th Century when basic hygienic measures were introduced: purification of water; efficient sewage disposal; and improved food hygiene, particularly the pasteurization of milk, the item in the diet most likely to spread disease.

Pasteurization was probably the main reason for the decrease in deaths from gastroenteritis and for the decline in infant mortality from about 1900. In the 20th Century, these essential hygienic measures were supported by improved conditions in the home, the work place, and the general environment. Over the entire period for which records exist, better hygiene accounts for approximately a fifth of the total reduction of mortality.

But the decline of mortality caused by infections began long before the introduction of sanitary measures. It had already begun in England and Wales by 1838, and statistics from Scandinavia suggest that the death rate had been decreasing there since the first half of the 18th Century.

. . .

A further explanation for the falling death rate is that an improvement in nutrition led to an increase in resistance to infectious diseases. This is, I believe, the most credible reason for the decline of the infections, at least until the late 19th Century, and also explains why deaths from airborne diseases like scarlet fever and measles have decreased even when exposure to the organisms that cause them remains almost unchanged. The evidence demonstrating the impact of improved nutrition is indirect, but it is still impressive.

. . .

Experience in developing countries today leaves no doubt that nutritional state is a critical factor in a person's response to infectious disease, particularly in young children. Malnourished people contract infections more often than those who are well fed and they suffer more when they become infected. According to a recent World Health Organization report on nutrition in developing countries, the best vaccine against common infectious diseases is an adequate diet.

. . .

In summary: The death rate from infectious diseases fell because an increase in food supplies led to better nutrition. From the second half of the 19th Century this advance was strongly supported by improved hygiene and safer food and water, which reduced exposure to infection. With the exception of smallpox vaccination, which played a small part in the total decline of mortality, medical procedures such as immunization and therapy had little impact on human health until the 20th Century.

One other influence needs to be considered: a change in reproductive behavior, which caused the birth rate to decline. The significance of this change can hardly be exaggerated, for without it the other advances would soon have been overtaken by the increasing population. We can attribute the modern improvement in health to food, hygiene, and medical intervention—in that order of time and importance—but we must recognize that it is to a modification of behavior that we owe the permanence of this improvement.

But it does not follow that these influences have the same relative importance today as in the past. In technologically advanced countries, the decline of infectious diseases was followed by a vast change in health problems, and even in developing countries advances in medical science and technology may have modified the effects of nutrition, sanitation, and contraception. In order to predict the factors likely to affect our health in the future, we need to examine the nature of the problems in health that exist today.

Because today's problems are mainly with noncommunicable diseases, physicians have shifted their approach. In the case of infections, interest centers on the organisms that cause them and on the conditions under which they spread. In noninfective conditions, the engineering approach established in the 17th Century remains predominant and attention is focused on how a disease develops rather than on why it begins. Perhaps the most important question now confronting medicine is whether the commonest health problems—heart disease, cancer, rheumatoid arthritis, cerebrovascular disease— are essentially different from health problems of the past or whether, like infections, they can be prevented by modifying the conditions that lead to them.

To answer this question, we must distinguish between genetic and chromosomal diseases determined at the moment of fertilization and all other diseases, which are attributable in greater or lesser degree to the influence of the environment. Most diseases, including the common noninfectious ones, appear to fall into the second category. Whether these diseases can be prevented is likely to be determined by the practicability of controlling the environmental influences that lead to them.

The change in the character of health problems that followed the decline of infections in developed countries has not invalidated the conclusion that most diseases, both physical and mental, are associated with influences that might be controlled. Among such influences, those which the individual determines by his own behavior (smoking, eating, exercise, and the like) are now more important for his health than those that depend mainly on society's actions (provision of essential food and protection from hazards). And both behavioral and environmental influences are more significant than medical care.

The role of individual medical care in preventing sickness and premature death is secondary to that of other influences; yet society's investment in health care is based on the premise that it is the major determinant. It is assumed that we are ill and are made well, but it is nearer the truth to say that we are well and are made ill. Few people think of themselves as having the major responsibility for their own health, and the enormous resources that advanced countries assign to the health field are used mainly to treat disease or, to a lesser extent, to prevent it by personal measures such as immunization.

. . .

The most immediate requirement in the health services is to give sufficient attention to behavioral influences that are now the main determinants of health. The public believes that health depends primarily on intervention by the doctor and that the essential requirement for health is the early discovery of disease. This concept should be replaced by recognition that disease often cannot be treated effectively, and that health is determined predominantly by the way of life individuals choose to follow. Among the important influences on health are the use of tobacco, the misuse of alcohol and drugs, excessive or unbalanced diets, and lack of exercise. With research, the list of significant behavioral influences will undoubtedly increase, particularly in relation to the prevention of mental illness.

Although the influences of personal behavior are the main determinants of health in developed countries, public action can still accomplish a great deal in the environmental field. Internationally, malnutrition probably remains the most important cause of ill health, and even in affluent societies sections of the population are inadequately, as distinct from unwisely, fed. The malnourished vary in proportion and composition from one country to another, but in the developed world they are mainly the younger children of large families and elderly people who live alone. In light of the importance of food for good health, governments might use supplements and subsidies to put essential foods within the reach of everyone, and provide inducements for people to select beneficial in place of harmful foods. Of course these aims cannot exclude other considerations such as international agreements and the solvency of farmers who have been encouraged to produce meat and dairy products rather than grains. Nevertheless, in future evaluations of agricultural and related economic policies, health implications deserve a primary place.

Perhaps the most sensitive area for consideration is the funding of the health services. Although the contribution of medical intervention to prevention of sickness and premature death can be expected to remain small in relation to behavioral and environmental influences, surgery and drugs are widely regarded as the basis of health and the essence of medical care, and society invests the money it sets aside for health mainly in treatment for acute diseases and particularly in hospitals for the acutely ill. Does it follow from our appraisal that resources should be transferred from acute care to chronic care and to preventive measures?

Restricting the discussion to personal medical care, I believe that neglected areas, such as mental illness, mental retardation, and geriatric care need greatly increased attention. But to suggest that this can be achieved merely by direct transfer of resources is an oversimplification. The designation "acute care" comprises a wide range of activities that differ profoundly in their effectiveness and efficiency. Some, like surgery for accidents and the treatment of acute emergencies, are among the most important services that medicine can offer and any reduction of their support would be disastrous. Others, however, like coronary care units and iron treatment of some anemias are not shown to be effective, while still others—most tonsillectomies and routine check-ups—are quite useless and should be abandoned. A critical appraisal of medical services for acute illnesses would result in more efficient use of available resources and would free some of them for preventive measures.

What health services need in general is an adjustment in the distribution of interest and resources between prevention of disease, care of the sick who require investigation and treatment, and care of the sick who do not need active intervention. Such an adjustment must pay considerable attention to the major determinants of health: to food and the environment, which will be mainly in the hands of specialists, and to personal behavior, which should be the concern of every practicing doctor.

QUESTIONS

1. What social factors have contributed toward the generally improved conditions of health in the modern industrial societies?

2. Is the high prestige of physicians really justified?

3. What social and environmental factors contribute to illness in modern America?

KIRKPATRICK SALE

Trend

The general tendency in human history over the last few thousand years has been for communities to become steadily larger, and even for the bulk of buildings within those communities to increase. Humans once lived exclusively in small roving bands of a few dozen people, but they are now more likely to occupy vast, towering metropolises containing many millions of inhabitants.

Sociologists have long been aware that the size of a community has far-reaching effects on its social life. In the small, traditional community, primary relationships predominate: people are apt to know one another personally, to be oriented toward the community, to share the same values. In the large, urban community, on the other hand, secondary relationships predominate: most people are strangers to one another; values are diverse and often conflicting; and in an impersonal, anonymous environment, people are oriented toward their own interests rather than those of the entire group.

Although the history of world urbanization is almost uniformly one of increasing growth and population density, an exception to this pattern has recently appeared: in the United States, there is a small but significant drift away from large cities and toward small towns and rural areas that offer more sense of community and the amenities that this implies. In this article, Kirkpatrick Sale speculates about some of the factors that may impel a new trend toward life on a "human scale."

Until 1972, Bob Light, then 30, and his wife Lee, 28, lived a rather ordinary suburban life in Upper Saddle River, New Jersey, one of those plush redwood-deck-and-blacktop-driveway places outside of New York City. He worked for his father in a successful textile machinery plant, she did freelance work, together they raised two children, and much of their free time they spent in the chic nightspots of New York—all the stuff of statistical tables and Hollywood movies. Then, that year, they sold their split-level house and moved to a 25-acre farm just outside the tiny village of Plainfield, Vermont.

The Lights put most of their life savings into restoring the 150-year-old farmhouse and broken-down barn, with the help of neighbors with whom they would swap work-shifts. Around the wood stove in winter they would plan for the summer, calculate what lands to clear, what crops to grow, what repairs to make, and then, with the first thaw of spring, working from dawn to sunset, they would set about making those winter dreams a reality—or nearly. They sought out the locals for help on how to make a go of the place, carefully amassed some cattle, a few hogs, some chickens, turned several acres over to corn for the livestock, established a vegetable garden in back of the house, and planted a field of strawberries and some fruit trees. Within a few years they were able to raise 80 percent of the food they needed to live on, and with a neat sign on their lawn reading, "Milk, Butter, Eggs" they were able to sell some of their dairy products for an extra $3,000 a year. Bob Light figures that with another few thousand dollars, maybe $7,000 or so from the milk-butter-eggs trade, he and Lee will be fully separated from most of the market economy and be able to live within a network of their friends and neighbors.

"What we want," Bob Light says, "is self-sufficiency—to make and produce as much as we can so we have to have as few dollars as possible. We don't want to support the system. We don't want to support the factories belching out the smoke. It's not our goal to make money."

The Lights, of course, are not "typical" of anything; among other things, they started with some savings and some money from the sale of their New Jersey house and have been able to put $60,000 or so into buying and fixing up their property. Nor is there any suggestion of one-swallowism; the Lights are part of a notable new development in America, but they are as yet only a tiny minority in the American landscape compared to all those at workaday jobs and familiar professions.

Still, there is no gainsaying the importance of what they represent. The *New York Times* has described their transformation as one part of "a full-scale back-to-the-land movement" that "has attracted tens of thousands of people across the United States," people who aim "to find ways to live simply but well on the land, outside the economic institutions that dominate the United States . . . rely on their own personal resources and labor, especially for their food and shelter," using "more wind and solar power" and "less machinery, less technology, less everything that comes from and depends on big business." They are a movement "deeply antagonistic to the American economic system, whose adherents it sees as controlled by unbridled corporate power, corrupted with surfeit and crazed by an impulse to consume and throw away more and more faster and faster."

To have "tens of thousands" of Americans in such a sweeping movement is consequential enough, but the back-to-the-landers are in turn part of a major new population shift that has taken the demographers by surprise and may signal something of a transformation in America's basic living styles. In the last decade there has been an abrupt reversal in the pattern of urbanization that has characterized the United States since the 1820s, and now more Americans are moving *out* of the big cities than *into* them—in fact, for every 100 that moved into metropolitan areas in the 1970–75 period, according to a Rand Corporation study, 131 moved out. For the first time in decades, small towns under 2,500 people are growing at a faster rate than any others, and rural areas all over the country, from Vermont to Arkansas, Oregon to Texas, are experiencing unprecedented population influxes.

And *that*, in turn, is part of a still larger demographic movement that has taken place over the last thirty years, the migrations out of the big cities into the suburban and exurban areas and, in a parallel move, out of the older cities into the warmer and younger regions of the Sunbelt.

All of these demographic changes reflect what I suspect is that innate desire for a little clean air, some green grass, a home one could call one's own, a town where a family could sink its roots, and a bit of room to move around in. They add up to an extraordinary phenomenon of people "voting with their feet" for a more natural world and a more communitarian setting than they could find in the choking and overgrown cities, a phenomenon of which Bob and Lee Light are only the most recent and most dramatic examples.

There is an unmistakable trend in American society—indeed in much of the Western world—that has been gaining momentum at least since World War II but most particularly in the last few years, the trend, one may call it broadly, toward human-scale values. I don't for one minute suggest that this trend will necessarily prevail. The forces arrayed against it are obviously considerable, and it runs smack against the entrenched messages of our culture that say big is better. But I do suggest that this is something quite undeniable, something that seems to be growing year after year pretty much on its own, something that anyone concerned with our future must reckon with. Indeed, one would not have any substantive reason to believe in the possibility of a human-scale future of any kind if there was not already a very real, very significant trend in that direction.

Examine just these few items:

1. At least 18 million adults now are allied to the alternate religions and spiritual movements of the last fifteen years that Theodore Roszak—who has managed to enumerate no fewer than 140 of them—says make up "the biggest introspective binge any society has undergone." A *New York Times* survey in 1977 indicated these movements "are gaining a foothold for an enduring future" and "appear to represent serious challenges to Western thought that have caused many people to turn away from material gain, competition and the success ethic."

2. The consumer movement that began with a few cranky protesters in the 1960s has blossomed into a full-scale political force of, according to pollster Louis Harris, "staggeringly" large proportions. Interestingly, his polls have found, Americans do not believe that business can police itself or that government can regulate it, and in overwhelming numbers they opt for some kind of grass-roots regulatory powers.

3. Patrick Caddell, the professional pollster and one of Jimmy Carter's closest advisors, explained the President's "moral-equivalent-of-war" campaign against energy waste in 1977 by saying, "The idea that big is bad and that there is something good to smallness is something that the country has come to accept much more today than it did ten years ago. This has been one of the biggest changes in America over the past decade."

4. The back-to-nature spirit in America has become so intense that it has outpaced the leisure boom of which it is a part: visits to national parks have grown from 80 million in 1960 to 283 million in 1978, an increase three times greater than that in general sports attendance in those years. There are estimated to be 8.6 million backpackers and 7.7 million wilderness campers in the U.S. today.

5. Individuals operating on their own outside of the standard market economy, doing business by barter and cold cash and keeping free of the IRS, have created an

"underground economy" that by the late 1970s was thought to amount to hundreds of *billions* of dollars. According to *U.S. News*, as many as 4.5 million Americans get all their income from this hidden, non-corporate economy and 15 million more get some of their support from it.

6. New York City, which drove itself to near bankruptcy through reckless giantism, gave itself a new decentralized City Charter in 1977 designed (according to the *New York Times)* to provide "a sharply increased role for local communities in the conduct of city government and the gradual assumption of responsibility for the delivery of most services." (The performance may not live up to this promise—that would be par for New York—but the direction of the reform is important in itself.)

7. At least 71 million Americans belong to one kind of cooperative or another, obtaining credit, health care, food, housing, car repairs, electric power, agricultural supplies, and other goods and services outside the profit-centered business system; credit unions have grown from 17 million members in 1965 to 32 million in 1977, health co-ops from 3.4 million to 6.1 million, electricity co-ops from 4.9 million to 6.6 million. The food co-op movement has burgeoned so much in so many places that there is no way to be sure just how many various outlets there are in existence at any given moment, but the latest figure contrived by a food co-op newspaper (yes, they have their own newspaper) is 10,000, which works out to more than two in every city or town over 5,000 across the land.

8. Some 32 million American households are estimated to do backyard and city-lot gardening nowadays, perhaps twice as many as ever before, producing goods reckoned to be worth more than $13 billion on the market. "There has been nothing like it since the patriotic Victory Gardens of World War II," says the *New York Times*.

9. It is impossible to measure the total number of people who have turned their backs on traditional American society over the last decade or so, but the Stanford Research Institute in 1977 reported that 4 to 5 million adults have actively "dropped out" into a life of—as they so quaintly put it—"voluntary simplicity."

10. "Do-it-yourself," according to the Bureau of Building Marketing Research, had become a $16.5-billion-a-year business by 1977, a 200 percent increase from 1974.

Very disparate, all these nuggets, but I don't have to emphasize that they are all pointing in a single general direction, toward individual self-worth, community cooperation, harmony with nature, decentralization of power, self-sufficiency—the human-scale values.

Indeed, I think we can find this same direction in the progress of every significant movement for social and political change of the past two decades. The civil-rights and black-power movements were searching for self-identity and pride, community power, equality of opportunity, and meaningful participation; so too the later "ethnic revivals" among descendants of European immigrants. The women's movement was—and is—a movement for individual self-worth, for communality among women, dignity and equality in the workplace, and full participation in political and economic matters; similarly for the homosexual-rights movements. The New Left was an expression of a whole generation's demand that the individual "share in those social decisions determining the quality and direction of his life" (as SDS's *Port Huron Statement* put it) and that power be redistributed from centralized systems to the grass roots; it grew—or at least the healthier parts of it grew—into a movement in the 1970s that rooted itself in communities, worked on community organizing and development, became concerned with local rather than national issues, and is found today working in alternative local organizations and institutions of all kinds. The counterculture that began in that same era was a movement in the main for individual expression, sexual freedom, and communal living, and proclaimed a denial of old standards like the work ethic, Puritanism, success, materialism, the profit motive, and authority. The consumer movement, though begun as a simple protest against high prices and shoddy goods, developed into a broad demand for consumer participation, individual rights, an end to corporate exploitation, and in recent years has set itself explicitly against the large monopolistic corporations and the government agencies that perform as their handmaidens. And, finally, the environmental and alternate-technology movements have been impelled by a concern for the natural world and its despoliation, for the proper role of humans within the ecosystem, and for the preservation of animal and plant species, which has broadened out in recent years to include alternative sources of energy, simple living, intentional ecological communities, natural foods, self-sufficiency, community health and communications services, and the like.

But I think it is possible to locate even broader manifestations of the inchoate trend toward a human-scale future, profounder currents so large and slow as to be almost imperceptible in our daily lives, yet of the sort that future historians may well mark as the dominant characteristics of our time. Which citizens of fifth-century Athens actually realized they were living in the Golden Age of Greece? How many Europeans of the twelfth century thought they were in the Dark Ages? Did the people of the nineteenth century know they were going through something that would be the Industrial Revolution? Just so, how many of us ever think to stop and measure the subcutaneous pulses that will be read as the heartbeat of this era by ages still to come? Yet at the risk of presumption, and certainly of oversimplification, let me try to isolate a few of these pulses that seem most particularly to define this period.

Feminism

In the broad view of history, at no time since the Romantic Age at the turn of the nineteenth century have the values associated with feminism in the largest sense been so triumphant. I don't mean simply the rise of the women's movement and its quick political and economic consequences all across this country, important though those have been; nor just the changing ideas in many sectors about women's roles, child-rearing, the patriarchal family, sexual stereotypes, and all that we now mean by sexism, radical though those have been. I mean the ascendance of what have been regarded, in our culture, as the womanly virtues: spontaneity, permissiveness, sexuality, emotion, softness, cooperation, lovingness, participation, as against, say, analysis, authoritarianism, denial, reason, hardness, competition, sternness, elitism, what might be called the manly virtues. Obviously both of these sets of elements play a part in our current society, as in all societies, but who could look at the current revolt against and distrust of authority, the free expression of sex in all ages and quarters of the population, the rise of communal and communitarian arrangements, the growing permissiveness in homes, schools, offices, even boot camps, the upsurge in the nurturing skills of gardening and husbandry, the relative status of the scholar as against the soldier, the growing acceptance of homosexuality, the rise of pacifist, anti-war, and anti-nuclear sentiments, the revival of fundamentalist and transcendental religions—who could look at these alone and deny the ascendance of the feminine virtues over the last decades? Indeed, if masculine cultures are associated with sky-gods (as in ancient Egypt, Judaism, Christianity) and feminine cultures with earth-gods (Phoenicia, Greece, Phrygia), the present widespread interest in ecological and environmental matters suggests that we may be experiencing a profound feminist alteration in our culture.

Naturalism

This new concern for the natural world, the unprecedented concern for everything from renewable resources to endangered species, may be a very deep biological reaction to the damage we are inflicting on our environment, a primordial human impulse toward self-preservation. But it is an extraordinary phenomenon, whatever the roots, and it finds expression just now in every Western nation, among all segments of society. In the U.S. the most dramatic manifestation has been the emergence, and the clout, of the environmental movement, which, as former *New York Times* columnist William Shannon has noted, "is one of the few big popular movements that continues to enlist volunteers, excite idealism, and evoke steadfast and unselfish commitment . . . in every region and virtually every community." Along with it has come the swift development of the alternate-technology crusade, with British economist E. F. Schumacher at its head and literally thousands of solar and compost-toilet entrepreneurs in his wake, and the closely allied drive against nuclear-power plants in almost every state of the union. Today the spirit of naturalism is seen in everything from the boom in health foods (one New England company in 1977 reported selling, it's hard to believe, twelve *tons* of granola a month), through the development of a $200-million-a-year houseplant business, never before known in our economy (it is now so big that it has inspired a plant-napping profession in the Sunbelt states where most of the greenery is grown), to the mania for backyard gardening, now carried to rooftops and corner lots (born no doubt of the desire to taste, before it is too late, a real, non-square, non-gassed, non-mealy tomato).

Localism

Part of the disintegration of national loyalties in the West—witness the sharp decline in patriotism in the United States—and the rise of separatist and regional movements—among American Indians, blacks, Inuits, Quebecois, Scots, Welsh, Basques—has to do with a resurgence of local interests and local allegiances that has probably not been so intense for more than a century. René Dubos, the eminent biologist who has been studying the human animal for some fifty years now, believes that "the most interesting and powerful force in our time is that people are getting more and more interested in regional and local affairs," and he has noted another remarkable fact: the American people's great mobility has produced an "extraordinary social trend—for the first time in human history a large and increasing number of people can *select* their place of residence" rather than simply take it as a matter of birth. This undoubtedly accounts for the sweeping population migrations noted above, and for the fierce passions that people tend to exhibit over the places they have selected to live. Hence the spontaneous growth of block associations and neighborhood associations over the last few years, of community organizations and communes and intentional communities; hence also, in a darker vein, the growth of neighborhood vigilante groups and "voluntary civilian patrols" in the 1970s as local responses to the increase in crime, a development favored, according to one survey, by at least 62 percent of urban dwellers. Dubos, again, makes the point that localism can only increase in the future: first, because of increased mobility; second, because of the drying up of shippable fuel sources (such as oil and gas) and the turn to unshippable local ones (solar, wind, wave);

third, because of the need for societies, buildings, and technology to adapt to local conditions to harness local energy and preserve local ecosystems; and fourth, because of the need for greater regional self-sufficiency to avoid overdependence on foreign resources and to supply food for growing populations. All of this, he predicts, "will have enormous effects on the evolution of this country."

Populism

It is safe to say that not since the late nineteenth century have the goals and ideas broadly associated with populism been so pervasive as they are today. The current mood of disillusionment with big government, big business, and big labor to which the polls continually attest is reminiscent of nothing so much as that period when, as historian Mark Sullivan put it, "the average American had the feeling he was being 'put upon' by something he couldn't quite see or get his fingers on . . . he felt his freedom of action was being frustrated . . . his economic freedom and his capacity to direct his political liberty . . . was being circumscribed in a tightening ring." The classical populist response is the one we are witnessing now: the rise of alternative institutions, the growth of consumer and citizen protest, and the emergence of mainstream political activity aimed at reducing government interference rather than applying government remedies. The list of alternative organizations and networks that have grown up over the past fifteen years is almost unlimited, but for a start there are free schools, free clinics, storefront law offices, food co-ops and suppliers, community newspapers, counterculture magazines, alternative publishing houses, "underground" churches, independent credit unions, community day-care centers, communal houses, garage and tag sales, and health-food restaurants, and they are common now in every large city and most college towns, coast to coast. A similar people-oriented opposition to the established systems has produced the remarkable number of citizen-action groups on all fronts just in the last decade or so: Common Cause, the Sierra Club, Friends of the Earth, the National Organization for Women, Ralph Nader's Public Citizen and local Public Interest Research Groups, the National Association of Neighborhoods, the Peoples Business Commission, California's Campaign for Economic Democracy, the Congress of Racial Equality, and literally dozens more, plus another hundred or so statewide action groups organized around consumer protection, utility regulation, taxation, the environment, and other political issues. Taken altogether, these alternative groups have at least twice as many contributors as the two major political parties (about 1.4 million to 520,000), and they get even more money in donations and dues ($16.6 million to $13.6 million in 1976, a presidential election year), which gives a

good nut-cutting idea of their relative importance in the eyes of the populace. . . .

Individualism

Probably as a result of the proven inadequacy of so many governmental, corporate, and academic remedies, and possibly in biological response to the increasing pressures of depersonalization and homogenization in our society, Americans are asserting a new kind of individualism, a claim for self-identity and self-worth. It can be seen in the fashions of our times, the physical-fitness boom, personalized gifts and clothing, "self-assertiveness" training for women, do-it-yourselfers, individualistic styles of dancing and dress, at-home "gourmet" cooking, the search for "roots" and family trees, the demands of women to control their own bodies, even the demands of cancer victims for laetrile. It is there in the new religious movements, which, in the words of San Francisco State sociologist Jacob Needleman, "can no longer be taken as a transitory cultural aberration but rather as a central feature of the profound change through which the American civilization is now passing." And it is the wellspring of the contemporary currents toward "flextime," workplace democracy, self-management, worker participation in decision-making, employee-ownership plans, and the like, currents that are gradually changing the nature of many offices and factories in the industrialized world. In a larger sense, this spirit of individualism is what people like Daniel Bell have been denouncing for the last decade or so, a spirit in which "the self is taken as the touchstone of cultural judgments," the individual asserts claims above those of society, and large segments of the populace ask for equality, not simply of opportunity, but of results, with the redistribution of wealth and power from a few individuals to many. This "sociologizing mode," in Bell's phrase, replacing traditional economic values with a new set of social ones—not how much you make but how well you live—is today the dominant mode in all Western societies.

These five pulses of our era—feminism, naturalism, localism, populism, and individualism—must be reckoned, if not as the only defining characteristics of the present period, at least as among the most important. They are all durable, indeed all have existed in one form or another through most of history, now waxing, now on the wane, but never really extinguished, as if they described at least one set of priorities and passions basic to the human psyche. They are all connected, all part of some complicated reticular pattern—so the nurturing of feminism relates directly to the rootedness of localism, and both to the ecological harmony of naturalism—that expresses similar concerns in different but reinforcing ways. And they have all become resurgent in a fairly short span of time, roughly in the years since 1960, despite the obvious array of static and traditional styles that oppose them. That suggests to me that the trend they reflect is a real and powerful one and that it is in their direction that the entire societal pendulum may perhaps be swinging.

It is that which can give one some hard-nosed optimism about the potential, though hardly inevitable, emergence of a new period of human history in the not-too-distant future in which small communities and self-sustaining cities, locally rooted and ecologically sound, cooperatively managed and democratically based, developing new resources and technologies according to their new philosophies, might evolve a society built to the human scale.

It is said that his contemporaries laughed with scorn when Sophocles, as a young man, told them that Athens—just then engaged in a costly and protracted war with the Persian Empire—was about to enter into a Golden Age.

QUESTIONS

1. What are the advantages and disadvantages of life in large cities?

2. Do you agree that there is a trend toward a more "human scale"—or does the article simply represent nostalgic wishful thinking?

3. How many members of the class hope to live in small towns or rural areas? Do you think there is any relation between their home origins and their future residential intentions?

MURRAY MELBIN

Night as Frontier

Sociologists often take an ecological approach to the study of urban development. In other words, they see patterns of city growth as the outcome of a variety of environmental pressures and opportunities. For example, natural features, such as rivers and mountains, affect the shape of cities; economic factors, such as the demand for prime residential or industrial property, influence the location of specific activities; social factors, such as population decline or racial prejudice, affect the distribution of various social groups.

In essence, this approach sees human beings as colonizing, adapting to, and changing particular ecological niches in space, whether the space is a densely populated city or a sparsely inhabited frontier. But in his thoughtful article, Murray Melbin suggests that people also colonize a different kind of ecological niche—one that exists in a different dimension, time.

Just as population pressure may encourage some urban residents to colonize frontier areas, so it may also encourage urbanites to colonize the night. Melbin shows that nighttime activity is very much on the increase in large cities, and draws a number of fascinating parallels between social conditions in the historic frontier and the contemporary urban night.

From *American Sociological Review*, 43: 3–22, February 1978. Reprinted with permission.

Humans are showing a trend toward more and more wakeful activity at all hours of day and night. The activities are extremely varied. Large numbers of people are involved. And the trend is worldwide. A unifying hypothesis to account for it is that night is a frontier, that expansion into the dark hours is a continuation of the geographic migration across the face of the earth. To support this view, I will document the trend and then offer a premise about the nature of time and its relation to space. Third, I will show that social life in the nighttime has many important characteristics that resemble social life on land frontiers.

The Course of Expansion

We were once a diurnal species bounded by dawn and dusk in our wakeful activity. Upon mastering fire, early humans used it for cooking and also for sociable assemblies that lasted for a few hours after darkness fell. Some bustle throughout the 24-hour cycle occurred too. Over the centuries there have been fires tended in military encampments, prayer vigils in temples, midnight betrothal ceremonies, sentinels on guard duty at city gates, officer watches on ships, the curing ceremonies of Venezuelan Indians that begin at sundown and end at sunrise, innkeepers serving travelers at all hours. In the first century A.D., Rome was obliged to relieve its congestion by restricting chariot traffic to the night hours (Mumford, 1961: 217).

Yet around-the-clock activity used to be a small part of the whole until the nineteenth century. Then the pace and scope of wakefulness at all hours increased smartly. William Murdock developed a feasible method of coal-gas illumination and, in 1803, arranged for the interior of the Soho works in Birmingham, England, to be lighted that way. Other mills nearby began to use gas lighting. Methods of distributing coal-gas to all buildings and street lamps in a town were introduced soon after. In 1820 Pall Mall in London became the first street to be lit by coal-gas. Artificial lighting gave great stimulus to the nighttime entertainment industry (Schlesinger, 1933: 105). It also permitted multiple-shift factory operations on a broad scale. Indeed by 1867 Karl Marx (1867: chap.

10, sec. 4) was to declare that night work was a new mode of exploiting human labor.

In the closing decades of the nineteenth century two developments marked the changeover from space to time as the realm of human migration in the United States. In 1890 the Bureau of the Census announced that the land frontier in America had come to an end, for it was no longer possible to draw a continuous line across the map of the West to define the edge of farthest advance settlement. Meanwhile, the search for an optimum material for lantern lights, capable of being repeatedly brought to a white heat, culminated in 1885 in the invention of the Welsbach mantle—a chemically impregnated cotton mesh. The use of the dark hours increased thereafter, and grew further with the introduction of electric lighting.

Here and there one may find documentation of the trend. During the First World War there was selective concern, expressed by Brandeis and Goldmark (1918) in *The Case Against Night Work for Women*, about the impact of off-hours work. A decade later the National Industrial Conference Board (1927) published a comprehensive survey with an account of the characteristics of the off-hours workers.

The most systematic evidence of steadily increasing 24-hour activity in the U.S. is the growth of radio and television broadcasting. Broadcasters authorize surveys to learn about the market that can be reached in order to plan programs and to set advertising rates. The number of stations active at given hours and the spread of those hours around the clock reflects these research estimates of the size of the wakeful population—the potential listeners. Television hours in Boston ended at 11:30 in 1949, and then widened to include the Late Show and then the Late Late Show in the intervening years until 1974. Each medium has moved increasingly to 24-hour programming and mirrors the growth in nighttime activity.

In the present decade, for the first time, the U.S. Bureau of Labor Statistics (1976: Table 1) asked about the times of day that people worked. In 1976, of 75 million in the work force, 12 million reported they were on the job mainly after dark and 2.5 million of those persons worked a full shift beginning about midnight. Since these figures do not include *the clientele* that used such establishments as restaurants, hospital emergency wards, gambling rooms, and public transportation, these numbers are conservative estimates of how many people are up and about at night.

Today more people than ever are active outside their homes at all hours engaged in all sorts of activities. There are all-night supermarkets, bowling alleys, department stores, restaurants, cinemas, auto repair shops, taxi services, bus and airline terminals, radio and television broadcasting, rent-a-car agencies, gasoline stations. There are continuous-process refining plants, and three-shift factories, post offices, newspaper offices, hotels, and hospitals.

There is unremitting provision of some utilities—electric supply, staffed turnpike toll booths, police patrolling, and telephone service. There are many emergency and repair services on-call: fire fighters, auto towing, locksmiths, suppliers of clean diapers, ambulances, bail bondsmen, insect exterminators, television repairers, plate glass installers, and funeral homes.

. . .

Space and Time Frontiers and Settlements

Time, like space, is part of the ecological niche occupied by a species. Although every type exists throughout the 24-hour cycle, to reflect the way a species uses its niche we label it by *the timing of its wakeful life*. The terms diurnal and nocturnal refer to the periods the creatures are active. We improve our grasp of the ecology of a region by recognizing the nighttime activity of raccoons, owls and rats, as well as by knowing the spatial dispersion of these and other animals. The same area of a forest or meadow or coral reef is used incessantly, with diurnal and nocturnal creatures taking their active turns. We make geographic references to humans in a similar way. We refer to an island people or a desert people, or the people of arctic lands as a means of pointing out salient features of their habitats.

This similar treatment of time and space rests on the assumption that both of them are containers for living. Consider the dictionary definition of the word *occupy*: "2. To fill up (take time or space): *a lecture that occupied three hours*" (*American Heritage Dictionary*, 1970:908). Geographers study activities rather than physical structures to decide whether and how people occupy space (Buttimer, 1976:286). The mere presence of buildings and related physical structures in places like Machu-Pichu, Petra, and Zimbabwe do not make us believe they are habitations now. The once-boisterous mining centers in the American West that have become ghost towns are settlements no longer. Conversely, we say a farming region in which people are active is inhabited even though buildings are few. The presence of human-built structures is not the criterion for occupying a region, it is people and their activities.

Like rural settlements, the occupation of time need not be dense. For example, London Transport lists 21 all-night bus routes. On many of these routes "all-night" service means no more than once an hour. Yet, even though the bus does not pass during the intervening 59 minutes, the schedule is said to be continuous. If an active moment interacts with quiet moments around it, the entire period is taken as occupied.

Of course, no time has ever been used without also using it in some place. No space has ever been used without also using it some hours of the days. Space and time together form the container of life activity. We forget this in the case of former frontiers because expansion then occurred so dramatically across the land. Less notice was paid to the 16 hours of wakefulness because the daily use of time was rather constant as the surge of geographic expansion kept on over the face of the earth. As time use remained unchanged, it was disregarded in human ecological theory. In different eras, however, expansion may proceed more rapidly in either space or time. Recently expansion is taking place in time. Since people may exploit a niche by distributing themselves and their activities over more hours of the day just as they do by dispersing in space, a frontier could occur in the time dimension too.

A *settlement* is a stable occupation of space and time by people and their activities. A *frontier* is a pattern of sparse settlement in space or time, located between a more densely settled and a practically empty region. Below a certain density of active people, a given space-time region is a wilderness. Above that point and continuing to a higher level of density, the presence of people in activities will make that area a frontier. Above that second cutoff point the further denseness of active people turns the area into a fully inhabited region. In a given historical period the frontier's boundaries may be stable or expanding. When expanding the frontier takes on the aspect of venturing into the unknown and is often accompanied by novelty and change.

Similarities Between Land Frontiers and Time Frontiers

Two kinds of evidence would support the hypothesis of night as frontier. One is that the forces for expansion into the dark hours are the same as those resulting in expansion across the land. That is, a single causal explanation should account for the spread of people and their activities, whether in space or in time. I offered such an outline in another essay: it includes enabling factors, demand push, supply pull, and stabilizing feedback (Melbin, 1977). The other line of evidence is that the same important features of social life should be found both in time and in space frontiers. The rapid expansion in after-dark activity has been taking place mostly in urban areas. Therefore the culture of the contemporary urban nighttime should reveal the same patterns and moods found in former land frontiers.

I have chosen to review life in the U.S. West in the middle of the nineteenth century along with the present-day nighttime. Of course there were other land frontiers and the hypothesis should apply to all of them. However there are good reasons to begin by demonstrating it for the U.S. West. One is that the archives holding information about this westward flow are thorough, well organized, and readily available. Another reason is that the U.S. West has continuity with expansion into the night. The movement westward reached the California coast. California's main cities have since become areas of great activity in the dark hours, as if the flow across the continent swerved into the nighttime rather than spilling into the sea.

Specifically, the land frontier to be discussed is the area west of the Mississippi River during the middle decades of the nineteenth century, about 1830–1880. The urban nighttime will be any major urban area during the stretch from about midnight to 7:30 a.m. during the decades of the 1960s and 1970s. Most of my examples will be findings from a recent study of Boston. There are many aspects in which social life at night is like the social life of other frontiers.

1. Advance Is in Stages

There is a succession of steps in colonizing any new region. People ventured into the western outskirts "in a series of waves . . . the hunter and the fur trader who pushed into the Indian country were followed by the cattle raiser and he by the pioneer farmer" (Turner, 1965:59; 1893:12, 19–20). Life styles were distinctive in each stage as well. The hunters and trappers did not dwell like the miners who followed, and they in turn lived differently from the pioneer farmers who came later (Billington, 1949:4–5). Although living conditions were generally crude then, there was a decided increase in comfort for the farmers settled in one place compared with the earlier-day trappers who were usually on the move.

There is also a succession of phases in settling the nighttime. Each stage fills the night more densely than before and uses those hours in a different way. First came isolated wanderers on the streets; then groups involved in production activities, the graveyard-shift workers. Still later those involved in consumption activities arrived, the patrons of all-night restaurants and bars, and the gamblers who now cluster regularly by midnight at the gambling table in resorts.

The rates of advance are unequal in both cases. Population gains and development are not unbroken. In the West economic growth was erratic. Periods of depression, dry seasons and other hardships drove many people to abandon their homesteads and move back east. Similarly, during the oil embargo of 1973–1974 there was some retreat from nighttime activity, as restaurants and auto service stations and other businesses cut back hours of serving the public.

2. Population Is Sparse and Also More Homogenous

At first only a few people venture into the new region. The frontier line in the U.S. West was drawn by the Census Bureau through an area of density of two to six inhabitants per square mile. The other side of the line was tabbed the "wilderness." The demographic composition of the western frontier was mostly vigorous young males with proportionately fewer females and aged persons than found in the populations of the eastern states (Riegel, 1947:624; Godkin, 1896:13: Dick, 1937:7, 232). This demographic picture fits the night as well. There are fewer people up and about and most of them are young males.

. . .

Estimates of the ages of passersby were also made during field observations. Whereas people of all ages were on the streets during the day, no one over 59 was seen between midnight and 5 a.m.; and from 2 to 5 a.m. no one over 41 was seen.

3. There Is Welcome Solitude, Fewer Social Constraints, and Less Persecution

The land frontier offered tranquillity, a place for relief from feelings of being hemmed in. "Fur traders . . . were psychological types who found forest solitudes more acceptable than the company of their fellow men" (Billington, 1949:4). It was appealing to escape into the wilderness, to leave deceit and disturbance, and vexing duties and impositions of the government behind (Robbins, 1960:148). " 'Oh, how sweet,' wrote William Penn from his forest refuge, 'is the quiet of these parts, freed from the troubles and perplexities of woeful Europe' " (Turner, 1893:262). Even later the West was "a refuge . . . from the subordination of youth to age" (Turner, 1932:25). The outer fringes offered escape from persecution too. Mormons and Hutterites both made their ways westward to avoid harassment from others.

In a parallel way, many have enjoyed the experience of walking at night along a street that is ordinarily jammed during the day. Individuals who are up and about then report a feeling of relief from the crush and anonymity of daytime city life. The calm of those hours is especially appealing to young people, who come to feel that they possess the streets. (A test of this proposition must of course control for the fear of criminal assault in the dark; I will discuss this further in items 7 and 8 below.) Also, a portion of the people out at night are those avoiding social constraints and perhaps persecution. Street people and homosexuals, for example, find more peace in the dark because surveillance declines. Some night owls are urban hermits. Some individuals who are troubled or stigmatized—such as the very ugly or obese—retreat from the daytime to avoid humiliation and challenge. They stay up later, come out when most others are gone, and are more secure as they hobnob with nighttime newsdealers and porters and elevator men. In this way the night affords an outlet. Like the West it serves an insulating function that averts possible tensions from unwanted encounters.

4. Settlements Are Isolated

Initially migration beyond the society's active perimeter is scattered. The land frontier settlements were small and apart from one another. There was little communication across districts and much went on in each in a self-sufficient way. People in the East did not think of the relevance of borderland activities for their own existence and the pioneers were indifferent to outside society (Billington, 1949:96, 746).

As the city moves through phases of the day it switches from coordinated actions to unconnected ones. Pockets of wakeful activity are separated from one another, are small scale compared to daytime events, and there is less communication between the pockets. The people of the daytime give little thought to those active in the dark and do not view them as part of the main community.

5. Government Is Initially Decentralized

Whatever high-level group may decide the laws and policies for a nation or a community, outside the purview of superiors there are subordinates who make decisions that would otherwise be the domain of the higher-ups or subject to their approval. As the land frontier moved farther from the national center of policy making, the interpretation of the law and judicial decisions were carried out by individuals who were rarely checked on and who rarely consulted with their superiors. Hollon (1973:96) notes that events took place "remote from the courts of authorities . . . [and] the frontiersmen not only enforced their own law, they chose which laws should be enforced and which should be ignored."

Today, although many organizations and cities are continually active, their primary administrations—directors, heads of departments, mayors—are generally on duty only during the daytime. At night they go to sleep and a similar decentralization of power follows. To some extent this is an explicit delegation of authority. But discretion is stretched for other reasons too. Night nurses decide not to wake up the doctor on duty because he gets annoyed at being disturbed for minor problems (Kozak, 1974:59). Shift supervisors choose not to bother the plant manager for similar reasons. Lesser officials make decisions that in the daytime are left for higher-ranking administrators. The style and content of the way the organization or the city is run at night changes accordingly. For example, for the same types of cases, decisions by police officers at night will be based less on professional role criteria and more on personal styles. This results in more extreme instances of being strict and lenient, arbitrary and humane.

6. New Behavioral Styles Emerge

Both land and time frontiers show more individualism because they are remote, the environment is unusual (compared with the centers of society), and others subjected to the same conditions are tolerant. Those who traveled to the western borders broke from ordinary society. The casual observance by others, the constituted authority, and the familiar settings and the norms they implied were gone. This left room for unconventional behavior. Easterners thought westerners were unsavory. The president of Yale College said, "The class of pioneers cannot live in regular society. They are too idle, too talkative, too passionate, too prodigal, and too shiftless to acquire either property or character" (cited in Turner, 1893:251). Another traveler in the same period wrote, "It is true there are worthless people here [in settlements hundreds of miles from any court of justice] and the most so, it must be confessed, are from New England" (Flint, 1826:402). He did go on to say that there were also many who were worthy.

Deviance was also *created* out west. Many pioneer wives lived on the plains for extended periods without ordinary social contacts, especially when their husbands left on journeys for days or weeks. These women often became withdrawn and untalkative, so shy and uneasy with strangers that they would run away when one approached (Humphrey, 1931:128). From the evidence at hand, these were normal, happy women in the cities when they were growing up, but they were affected by the frontier environment. On the western boundary people were used to this behavior on the part of lonely, isolated women and accepted it. In the eastern cities the same conduct would have been taken as odd.

There is also a popular image of the night as the haunt of weirdos and strange characters, as revealed in comments like "I don't know where they hide during the day but they sure come out after dark." Moreover, at night one can find people who, having lived normal lives are exposed to unusual circumstances that draw them into unconventional behavior. Becker (1963:79, 97, 98) gives such an account of jazz musicians. They work late in the evening and then associate with very few daytime types in their recreation after midnight. The milieu harbors a deviant subculture that is tolerated and even expected.

7. There Is More Lawlessness and Violence

Both land frontier and the nighttime have reputations as regions of danger and outlawry. Interestingly, both do not live up to the myths about them, for the patterns of aggression are selective and localized.

On the one hand there is clear evidence of lawlessness and violence. Walter P. Webb observed that the West was lawless "because the law that was applied there was not made for the conditions that existed. . . . It did not fit the needs of the country, and could not be obeyed" (cited by Frantz and Choate, 1955:83). There was also a lack of policemen and law enforcement agencies were few (Riegel, 1947:627; Billington, 1949:480). There was violence in the gold fields (Hollon, 1974:211). In the cow towns, mining camps and boom towns in the early days, practically everyone carried guns. Fighting words, the ring of revolvers, and groans of pain were common sounds

out there. Some western settlements were renowned for concentrations of gamblers and gougers and bandits, dance-hall girls and honky-tonks and bawdy houses. Horse thieving was widespread. The stage coach was held up many times. There was habitual fear of attack from either Indians or renegades. In the face of this, the people practiced constant watchfulness and banded together for self-protection (Billington, 1954:8; Doddridge, 1912: 103). Towns had vigilante groups. The covered wagons that crossed the plains were accompanied by armed convoys.

Yet the violence was concentrated in certain places; otherwise killings and mob law were remarkably infrequent. Such infamous towns as Tombstone and Deadwood, and the states of Texas and California had more than their share of gunfights (Frantz and Choate, 1955:83; Billington, 1949:63; Hollon, 1973:96). But the tumult in the cow towns was seasonal, and took place when the cowboys finally reached Abilene, Ellsworth, and Dodge City after the long drive. And the mayhem was selective. Flint (1826:401) wrote, "Instances of murder, numerous and horrible in their circumstances, have occurred in my vicinity . . . in which the drunkenness, brutality, and violence were mutual. . . . [Yet] quiet and sober men would be in no danger of being involved." W.T. Jackson (1973:79) adds, "Homicides and murders occurred so infrequently that when they did the community was shocked and outraged." Concerning violence, Hollon (1973:97–8) concludes that there was

a natural tendency to exaggerate the truth and emphasize the exception . . . not a single shoot-out took place on main street at Dodge City or any of the other Kansas cow towns in the manner of the face-to-face encounter presented thousands of times on television.

Why, then, did the land frontier have the reputation of a "Wild West?" One reason may be that outlaw killers were drifters, so the same person may have contributed exploits over large areas. Another reason was boredom. The stories of violence persisted and spread because there was little to do or to read about in pioneer homes. The tedium of daily life was countered by exciting stories told and retold around the stove in the general store.

It is plausible that western desperados and nighttime muggers would have similar outlooks. Both believe there is less exposure, which improves their chances for succeeding at the risks they take. One relied on dry-gulching; the other uses the dark to set an ambush. Escape is easy because both could move from the scene of the crime into unpopulated areas and elude pursuers.

The nighttime has been noted also as a place of evil. It is thought of as crime-ridden and outside of ordinary social control. Medieval and Renaissance cities had no public illumination. Assaults by ruffians and thieves were so common after dark that wayfarers took to paying others to precede them through the streets carrying lighted torches. In the seventeenth century this escort-for-hire was called a "link boy" in London, and a "falot" (lantern companion) in Paris. Delivery of black market goods to stores, such as fuel oil to gasoline stations during the oil embargo of 1973–1974, was accomplished under cover of darkness. Lawlessness is possible then because police coverage is sparse (Boston *Globe*, 1977:1). In addition, the officers on duty make themselves unavailable by sleeping in their cars, an old custom in New York City where the practice is called "cooping" (*New York Times*, 1968). The same was informally reported to me about Boston police as well; they are found snoozing in their police cars in the Arboretum by the early morning joggers.

In Boston today, carrying arms is more common at night. For fear of mugging or rape, escort services are provided on many college campuses for women returning to their dorms at night, or for women on the evening shift going from their places of work to the parking lot or subway station. An escort is provided for nurses at Boston City Hospital because of an increase in robberies in that area. And some apartment houses, with their sentries at the door, become vertical stockades to which people in the city retreat at night.

However, like the former West, lawlessness and violence at night are concentrated in certain hours in certain places and are otherwise uncommon. Fights reach their peak about midnight, but are least frequent from 2:30 to 11:00 a.m. The area of Boston in which many brawls and muggings take place, where prostitution is rampant and bars and lounges feature nude go-go dancers, is called the "combat zone." A large transient population of relatively young males come into the area to patronize the moviehouses featuring X-rated films and become drunk and aggressive in bars and on the streets. Although this description may approximate what was once reported of mining towns in the West, these combat zones do not function so after 2:30 a.m. or during the daytime. In the daytime the areas are parts of business districts. Many people shop at department stores nearby, or otherwise pass through and patronize eating places and businesses there. So the combat zone designation refers to these places only at certain hours and is not true for all the city all night.

8. There Is More Helpfulness and Friendliness

Hollon (1974:211–2) remarks that "For every act of violence during the frontier period, there were thousands of examples of kindness, generosity, and sacrifice . . ." He quotes an English traveler who said, " 'Even the rough western men, the hardy sons of the Indian frontier, accustomed from boyhood to fighting for existence, were hospitable and generous to a degree hard to find in more civilized life.' "

Reports of life on the land frontier are replete with accounts of warmth toward strangers, of community house building and barn raisings, and of help for those in need (Darby, 1818:400; Frantz and Choate, 1955:64; Billington, 1949:96, 167; Riegel, 1947:81). "Neighbors were ready to lend anything they possessed. No man driving along with an empty wagon on a good road would pass another on foot without inviting him to ride" (Dick, 1937:512). Travelers returning from the outskirts said they were treated more kindly than they had been in the cities (Flint, 1826:402–03; Hollon, 1974:212).

At first these stories of openhanded western hospitality may seem inconsistent in the face of the high risks of thievery and violence. But the circumstances are actually related to one another. Dick (1937:510) observed that "As the isolated settlers battled against savage men, . . . and loneliness, they were drawn together in a fellowship." Billington (1972:166) added,

Cooperation is normal within every in-group, but accentuates when the in-group is in conflict with an out-group and group solidarity is strengthened. This was the situation in frontier communities where conflicts with Indians, with raw nature, and with dominating Easterners heightened the spirit of interdependence.

That people want to affiliate under such conditions with others like themselves was demonstrated experimentally by Schachter (1959). He showed that the greater the risk people thought they were facing, the more anxious they were; and the more anxious they were, the more they wanted to be with others—even strangers—facing the same risk. Schachter (1959) concluded that being with others in the same boat served to reduce anxiety, and also provided an opportunity to appraise one's own feelings and adjust them appropriately to the risk. With less emotional uncertainty and with the knowledge that others share the circumstances, individuals feel better about confronting a stressful situation.

Because the night is a time of more violence and people feel more vulnerable then, those up and about have a similar outlook and behave toward others as pioneers did in the West. At night people are more alert to strangers when they pass on the street. Each tries to judge whether the other is potentially dangerous. Upon deciding that the other is to be trusted, one's mood shifts from vigilance to expansiveness. If not foe, then friend. Aware that they are out together in a dangerous environment, people identify with each other and become more outgoing. The sense of safety that spreads over those together at night in a diner or in a coffee shop promotes camaraderie there.

Also, on both frontiers people may be more hospitable because they have time to devote to strangers. Pioneers had plenty to do; yet often they had nothing to do. They were not closely synchronized in daily tasks as people were in the eastern cities, and the norm of punctuality was not emphasized. One man who grew up in the West

> . . . recalled the boredom he could never escape. . . . [T]he worst time of all was Sunday afternoon, when he had nothing to do. There were no newspapers to read and no books other than the family Bible, there was no one his age to talk with and the nearest store was miles away. (Hollon, 1974: 196)

In the city during the day, the mood of pressured schedules takes hold of folk and makes their encounters specific and short. The tempo slows markedly after midnight. The few who are out then hurry less because there are fewer places to rush to. Whereas lack of time inhibits sociability and helpfulness available time clears the way for them.

. . .

9. Exploitation of the Basic Resource Finally Becomes National Policy

Westward expansion began long before anyone officially recognized the land frontier's possibilities for our society. It took years to realize even that the U.S. West was habitable. At one time the land west of the Missouri River was labeled on maps as the Great American Desert. Almost no one thought that some day many people would want to migrate and settle there (Hicks, 1948:508). Nor was the catch phrase "Manifest Destiny" applied to colonizing the West until 1845, centuries after the effort had been under way. In 1837 Horace Greeley introduced the slogan "Go West, Young Man, go forth into the Country." He looked upon such migrations as a means of relief from the poverty and unemployment caused by the Panic of 1837. By 1854 Greeley was urging, "Make the Public Lands free in quarter-sections to Actual Settlers . . . and the earth's landless millions will no longer be orphans and mendicants" (cited in Smith, 1950:234–5). In 1862, with the passage of the Homestead Act, it became a deliberate policy of the U.S. government to use the western territory to help relieve the conditions of tenant farmers and hard-pressed city laborers. A member of Congress declared, in support of the Homestead Act, "I sustain this measure . . . because its benign operation will postpone for centuries, if it will not forever, all serious conflict between capital and labor in the older free states" (Smith, 1950:239). The policy makers finally saw the exploitation of western space as a means of solving social problems.

Similarly, in the first 150 years after Murdock's coal-gas illumination was introduced, there was no national consciousness in England or the United States about colonizing the nighttime. People went ahead, expanding their activities into the dark hours without declaring that a 24-hour community was being forged. Now in the 1970s policy makers have begun talking about cheap time at night the way they once spoke of cheap western land. V.D. Patrushev (1972:429) of the Soviet Union writes that "Time . . . is a particular form of national wealth. Therefore it is imperative to plan the most efficient use of it for all members of a society." Daniel Schydlowsky (1976:5), an economist who specializes in development in Latin America and who recently ended a three-year study there, has concluded that multiple-shift work would produce remarkable gains in reducing unemployment and improve the economies of overpopulated developing cities. His claim for the use of time echoes the attitudes of nineteenth century proponents of the use of western lands as a solution for those who were out of work.

The advocates of westward expansion also saw it as a way to draw off great numbers of people from the cities and forestall crowding there (Smith, 1950:8, 238). Today Dantzig and Saaty (1973:190–3) recommended dispersing activities around the clock as a means of reducing congestion. And Meier (1976:965) writes, "Scarce land and expensive human time can also be conserved by encouraging round-the-clock operation. . . . By such means people can live densely without stepping on each other's toes."

10. Interest Groups Emerge

As the U.S. frontier matured, the population became more aware of its own circumstances and organized to promote its own concerns. Turner (1893:207; 1965:54) remarked that the West felt a keen sense of difference from the East. He wrote:

> . . . [F]rom the beginning East and West have shown a sectional attitude. The interior of the colonies was disrespectful of the coast, and the coast looked down upon the upland folk. . . . [The westerners finally] became self-conscious and even rebellious against the rule of the East. . . . [I]t resented the conception that it was merely an emanation from a rival North and South; that it was the dependency of one or another of the Eastern sections. . . . It took the attitude of a section itself. (1932:25–30)

Sections are geographically-based interest groups. One hundred years ago the West gave rise to such pressure groups and farm bloc organizations as the Greenback Party, the National Grange, and the Populists. The Granger movement, for example, grew with the westerners' problems with transportation in their region. There were no significant river or canal systems out west and so the settlers were at the mercy of railroads. But the rates in the newer regions of the West were far higher than those in the East, and it was protest against the disparity that aided the movement in the 1870s (Robbins, 1960:271).

The night also isolates a group from the main society. Antagonism may develop as daytimers deprecate the nighttimers and the latter resent the neglect shown by the others. People active after dark find their life style differing from that of daytime society, become aware of having a separate identity, and evolve into interest groups. New alignments in the tradition of sectionalism begin to emerge. This has already happened for two groups usually linked with the nighttime: homosexuals and prostitutes. The Gay Liberation Front is one nationwide organization devoted to the rights of homosexuals. Prostitutes also have a union. Appropriately they adopted the name of a creature renowned in the U.S. West for howling at night—the coyote. COYOTES (Call Off Your Old Tired Ethics) seek legislation to decriminalize their activities and protest courtroom discrimination against women who earn their living by prostitution (Boston *Globe*, 1976a).

An actual day vs. night contest has already been fought in Boston. The city's airport is flanked by residential neighborhoods and its afterdark activity became a nuisance to people wanting an undisturbed night's sleep. In 1976 dwellers in those neighborhoods, as private citizens and through two organized groups—Fair Share, and the Massachusetts Air Pollution and Noise Abatement Committee—made a concerted effort to stop airplane flights between 11 p.m. and 7 a.m. It led to counterarguments by the business community stressing the economic benefit of continuing the flights. The pro-nighttime group was a coalition among commercial interests, airline companies, unions, and airport employees holding jobs at night (some of whom lived in those very neighborhoods). This group argued that the curfew would result in the loss of thousands of jobs, millions of dollars in sales, and further would discourage business investment in the New England area. Joined by the governor, the mayor and many legislators, the coalition successfully won a decision from the Massachusetts Port Authority that the nighttime flights should be kept going. (Some proposals for noise reduction during the night accompanied the decision.) A month later, Eastern Airlines announced it was adding an airbus and expanding its staff at the airport "as a direct result of the recent decision . . . not to impose a night curfew at Logan [airport]." As one businessman put it, "The curfew decision was regarded as the shootout at the OK Corral" (Boston *Globe*, 1976b; 1976c).

. . .

Conclusion

What is the gain in thinking of night as a frontier? A single theoretical idea gives coherence to a wide range of events: the kind of people up and about at those hours, why they differ from daytimers in their behavior, the beginnings of political efforts by night people, the slow realization among leaders that public policy might be applied to the time resource. Even the variety of endeavors becomes understandable—from metal smelting plants to miniature golf courses, to mayor's complaint offices, to eating places, to computerized banking terminals that dispense cash. The niche is being expanded. Bit by bit, all of society migrates there. To treat this as a sequel to the geographic spread of past centuries is to summarize the move within familiar ecological concepts of migration, settlement, and frontier.

Though I have reviewed materials for one period in U.S. history, these conditions are features of all frontiers. They should apply to the Russians crossing the Urals, to the Chinese entering Manchuria during the Ch'ing dynasty, to the Boers settling South Africa, to Australians venturing into the Outback, to present-day Brazilians colonizing the Amazon interior, as well as to Americans migrating into the night. The patterns are confirmed by essays in Wyman and Kroeber's anthology on frontiers.

We should also consider the uniqueness of this new frontier. Each settlement beyond established boundaries has its own qualities. Here are some differences between the West and the night: (1) On the land frontier settlers lived rudely with few services at hand. At night a large portion of the total range of activities is services. (2) Utilities cost more on the western fringes; at night the fees for telephone calls, electricity, and airplane travel are lower. (3) While western settlements were in remote contact with the East, day and night are joined so that either can be affected quickly by events in the other. Twenty-four hour society is more constantly adjusting, more unstable. (4) Looking westward, pioneers saw no end to the possibilities for growth, but we know that expansion into the night can only go as far as the dawn. (5) The land frontier held promise of unlimited opportunity for individuals who ventured there. Miners and pioneers endured hardships because they lived for the future. They hoped to make their fortunes, or at least a better life. At night there are large numbers of unskilled, menial, and dirty tasks; but charwoman and watchman and hospital aide and porter are dead-end jobs. Many people so employed are immigrants or members of minority groups and this expanding margin of society is a *time ghetto*. The ghetto encloses more than minorities and immigrants, for ultimate control in 24-hour organizations remains with top management in the daytime. Policy making, important decisions, employee hiring, and planning are curtailed during off-hours. Since evening and night staffs are prevented from taking many actions that would lead to the recognition of executive ability, and since their performance is not readily observable by the bosses, all have poorer chance for advancement. (6) The western frontier's natural resources were so extensive that we became wasteful and squandered them. At night there is nothing new to exploit but time itself, so we maximize the use of fixed assets and become more frugal. (7) Migrating westward called for rather significant capital investment—outlays for a covered wagon, mining equipment, cattle, the railroad.

There is little extra capital required for a move to the night. Instead, the incessant organization's need for more personnel reflects a swing toward more labor intensive operations. So the night frontier may appeal to developing countries with meager treasuries and teeming populations of unemployed.

This expansion is also unusual because it happens in time rather than in space. We change from a diurnal into an incessant species. We move beyond the environmental cycle—alternating day and night—in which our biological and social life evolved, and thus force novelty on these areas. (8) In the past a single set of minds shut down an enterprise one day and started it up the next. It permitted easy continuity and orderly administration. For coverage around the clock, we introduce shifts of personnel. Several times a day another set of minds takes over the same activity and facilities. (9) A physiological upset is imposed on people who work at night and maintain ordinary recreation and social life on their days off. Each time they switch their active hours they undergo phase shifts in body rhythms such as heartbeat, temperature, and hormonal production. The several days' malaise that results was known to such workers long before air travel across time zones popularized the phrase "jet fatigue."

Ibsen's (1890: Act II) character, Eilert Löuvborg, describes the two sections of the book he has written, "The first deals with the . . . forces of the future. And here is the second forecasting the probable line of development." We may believe we understand the forces, the conditions under which humans enlarge their niche, but what is the probable line of development? Forecasting is called for despite the difficulties of social prediction. We should consider the possibilities of an era in which unremitting activity is even more commonplace. What is the carrying capacity of the 24-hour day? What will happen when saturation occurs? Time will have extraordinary leverage as it gets used up, for time is a resource without direct substitute. It is unstretchable; we cannot do with it as we did with land by building up toward the sky and digging into the ground. Time is unstorable; we cannot save the unused hours every night for future need.

In his essay "The Frontier in American History," Frederick Jackson Turner (1893:38) reviewed the impact of the advance into western lands upon our society and remarked, "And now, four centuries from the discovery of America, at the end of a hundred years of life under the constitution, the frontier has gone." But it has not gone. During the era that the settlement of our land frontier was being completed, there began—into the night—a large-scale migration of wakeful activity that continues to spread over the world.

QUESTIONS

1. What are the "frontier" characteristics of the urban night?

2. Are there any practical obstacles to fully colonizing the night, in such a way that the various activities of the day could be duplicated during those hours?

3. What are the ecological factors (social, economic, demographic, environmental, etc.) that might induce people to colonize a frontier (or the night)?

References

American Heritage Dictionary of the English Language
1970 Boston: Houghton Mifflin.

Becker, Howard
1963 Outsiders: Studies in the Sociology of Deviance. New York: Free Press.

Billington, Ray Allen
1949 Westward Expansion. New York: Macmillan.
1954 The American Frontiersman. London: Oxford University Press.
1972 "Frontier democracy: social aspects." pp. 160–84 in G.R. Taylor (ed.), The Turner Thesis: Concerning the Role of the Frontier in American History. 3rd ed. Lexington, Ma.: Heath.

Boston Globe
1976a "Prostitutes speak of pride, but they are still victims." June 15:1, 10.
1976b "Dukakis decides to go against Logan curfew." August 12:1, 20.
1976c "Logan anti-noise plan offered." August 13:35.
1977 "Boston police today." April 4:1, 3.

Brandeis, Louis D. and Josephine Goldmark
1918 The Case Against Night Work for Women. Rev. ed. New York: National Consumers League.

Buttimer, Anne
1976 "Grasping the dynamism of lifeworld." Annals of the Association of American Geographers 66:277–92.

Dantzig, George B. and Thomas L. Saaty
1973 Compact city. San Francisco: Freeman.

Darby, William
[1818] 1969 "Primitivism in the lower Mississippi valley." Pp. 399–401 in M. Ridge and R.A. Billington (eds.), America's Frontier Story. New York: Holt.

Dick, Everett
[1937] 1954 The Sod-House Frontier, 1854–1890. New York: Appleton-Century.

Doddridge, Joseph
[1912] 1969 "Life in the old west." Pp. 101–6 in M. Ridge and R.A. Billington (eds.), America's Frontier Story. New York: Holt.

Flint, Timothy
[1826] 1969 "Frontier society in the Mississippi valley." Pp. 401–3 in M. Ridge and R.A. Billington (eds.), America's Frontier Story. New York: Holt.

Frantz, J.B. and J.E. Choate
1955 The American Cowboy: The Myth and Reality. Norman: Uni-

versity of Oklahoma Press.

Godkin, Edwin L.
[1896] 1969 "The frontier and the national character." Pp. 13–6 in M. Ridge and R.A. Billington (eds.), America's Frontier Story. New York: Holt.

Hicks, John D.
1948 The Federal Union. Boston: Houghton Mifflin.

Hollon, W. Eugene
1973 "Frontier violence: another look." Pp. 86–100 in R.A. Billington (ed.), People of the Plains and Mountains. Westport, Ct.: Greenwood Press.

1974 Frontier Violence. New York: Oxford University Press.

Humphrey, Seth K.
1931 Following the Prairie Frontier. Minneapolis: University of Minnesota Press.

Ibsen, Henrik
[1890] 1950 Hedda Gabler. Tr. E. Gosse and W. Archer. Pp. 42–74 in J. Gassner (ed.), A Treasury of the Theatre. New York: Simon and Schuster.

Jackson, W. Turrentine
1973 "Pioneer life on the plains and in the mines." Pp. 63–85 in R.A. Billington (ed.), People of the Plains and Mountains. Westport, Ct.: Greenwood Press.

Kozak, Lola Jean
1974 "Night people: a study of the social experiences of night workers." Michigan State University, Summation 4:40–61.

Marx, Karl
[1867] 1906 Capital. New York: Modern Library.

Meier, Richard L.
1976 "A stable urban ecosystem." Science 192:962-8.

Melbin, Murray
1977 "The colonization of time." In T. Carlstein, D. Parkes, and N. Thrift (eds.), Timing Space and Spacing Time in Social Organization. London: Arnold.

Mumford, Lewis
1961 The City in History. New York: Harcourt Brace.

National Industrial Conference Board
1927 Night Work in Industry. New York: National Industrial Conference Board.

New York Times
1968 " 'Cooping': an old custom under fire." December 15: Sec. 4, 6E.

Patrushev, V.D.
1972 "Aggregate time-balances and their meaning for socio-economic planning." Pp. 429–40 in A. Szalai (ed.), The Use of Time. The Hague: Mouton.

Riegel, Robert E.
1947 America Moves West. New York: Holt.

Robbins, Roy M.
1960 Our Landed Heritage. Princeton: Princeton University Press.

Schachter, Stanley
1959 The Psychology of Affiliation. Stanford: Stanford University Press.

Schlesinger, Arthur
1933 The Rise of the City: 1878–1895. New York: Macmillan.

Schydlowsky, Daniel
1976 "Multiple shifts would produce 'revolutionary results' for Latin American economy." Boston University, Spectrum 4 (September 9):5.

Smith, Henry Nash
[1950] 1957 Virgin Land. New York: Vintage.

Turner, Frederick Jackson
[1893] 1920 The Frontier in American History. New York: Holt.

1932 The Significance of Sections in American History. New York: Holt.

[1965] America's Great Frontiers and Sections.

1969 Unpublished essays edited by W.R. Jacobs. Lincoln: Nebraska University Press.

U.S. Bureau of the Census
1975 Historical Statistics of the United States, Vol. 1: ser. A195–209. Washington, D.C.: U.S. Government Printing Office.

U.S. Bureau of Labor Statistics
1976 Current Population Survey. Unpublished paper. May 12: Table 1. Washington, D.C.

Wyman, Walker D. and Clifton B. Kroeber (eds.)
1957 The Frontier in Perspective. Madison: University of Wisconsin Press.

KAREN JANSZEN

Meat of Life

One common form of collective behavior is the fad, a temporary form of conduct that attracts a body of enthusiastic adherents. Notable fads of recent years have included fascinations with the hula hoop, roller disco, CB radio, streaking, so-called organic foods, and video games.

Fads have certain characteristics in common. First, their appeal is short-lived, for it relies largely on novelty. Once "everybody is doing it," the appeal wears off. Second, fads are usually regarded a little scornfully by most of the population, who see the actual participants as blindly following a trend simply because it has "caught on." Third, fads appeal primarily to adolescents and young adults, for they seem to provide a means of asserting personal identity; older people, with more stable and secure personalities, are less inclined to indulge themselves in sudden and novel enthusiasms. But fads are not necessarily of little or no significance, for behavior that starts out as a fad can sometimes have an enduring effect if, directly or indirectly, it becomes permanently incorporated into the culture.

In this article, Karen Janszen examines a new fad, found primarily on the West Coast: the practice by parents of eating the afterbirth when their child is born.

"It was a conceptually mind-blowing and radical thing to do. I approached it in a reverent way because it felt spiritual, like something I wouldn't do lightly."

What this American from Seattle found astounding, not just to witness but to experience, was placentophagia. Like some residents of Los Angeles and Boston, he did not journey far to take part in this unusual practice. In fact, he traveled no farther than his own backyard. "It was a natural cadence to the birth—the whole birth was a wonder."

Placentophagia, the act of eating a newborn baby's placenta, has probably been practiced in the United States for as long as the American home-birth movement has been important—about a decade—and may be growing more commonplace as home births continue to increase in popularity.

By having babies at home, parents wind up holding the placenta. What some hospitals sell for about 50 cents to drug and cosmetic companies, some Americans are planting, dumping in the garbage, flushing down the toilet—or eating.

Americans who eat placenta are individualists who do what they believe is natural and take it seriously. Like most parents who prefer home over hospital as their baby's place of birth, placenta eaters tend to be young, white, middle class and college educated. Some are bookkeepers, college teachers, land surveyors, community counselors, furniture designers and chiropractors. But placenta eaters have more often experimented with alternatives such as food cooperatives and macrobiotic vegetarianism.

Midwives from different regions of the United States, the people most knowledgeable about home-birth practices, estimate that placenta eating now occurs following roughly 1 to 2 percent of home births in East Coast states and after about 5 percent in West Coast states.

While there is no consensus among placenta eaters on what "natural" is—solar heating, meatless spaghetti sauce or giving birth without painkillers—all agree there is nothing more "natural" than eating placenta, and that is why they do it. To them, "natural" is what is assumed to be healthful and fitting to the human species. In short, since they believe many other mammals and members of some human societies eat placenta, they assume it must make good sense nutritionally and medically and that the reason Americans do not normally do so is because we are overcivilized.

Birth Ritual

If placenta eating is natural in concept, it may be more than natural in practice—it may be a new American birth ritual. The occasion is the celebration of a successful home birth.

A human placenta is a small, soft, beefy disk; it is about eight inches long, one and a half inches thick and weighs approximately a pound. It is expelled during the third stage of labor, 15 to 30 minutes after the birth of a baby. For this reason, it is commonly called the afterbirth. Both the placenta and the embryo are made by the fertilized ovum, though the placenta contains maternal as well as fetal blood.

The spongy, blood-filled organ acts as a fetal lung, intestine and kidney and is almost solely responsible for the intra-uterine welfare of the developing fetus. Substances such as salts, amino acids, simple fats and vitamins are exchanged between maternal and fetal bloodstreams via the placenta and umbilical cord. The placenta itself produces progesterone, estrogen and other steroids as well as protein hormones, all necessary to the maintenance of a pregnancy.

While most hospitals incinerate placentas along with other biological waste, some hospitals sell them to pharmaceutical or cosmetic companies that extract the hormones and proteins for use in manufacturing drugs or beauty products. Hospitals associated with medical schools or research institutions often collect them for use in experimental research. Scientists are still working out the details of what the placenta does and how it does it. They say knowledge of placental actions and functions may assist cancer, organ-aging and birth-control research. A few placenta-based beauty products, such as TiaZolin Placenta, an instant hair-repair treatment, list human placenta extract as an ingredient, but most are made from less expensive bovine placenta bought from slaughterhouses.

Placenta is eaten raw or cooked, depending on the sensitivity of diners' palates and stomachs. When cooking it smells like liver frying and even tastes like liver or kidney but is sweeter and milder. It is a tender meat. Cooking preparations range from simple to gourmet, limited only by the imaginations of the chefs—usually the new fathers. Placenta can be boiled in salted water, pan fried in butter and garlic, stir fried in soy sauce with vegetables, sautéed in wine and spices, or sun dried in strips for jerky. Placenta stew is an old favorite; a recipe can be found in the *Birth Book*, a popular collection of first-person accounts of home birth.

Many American placenta eaters admit they found the thought of placenta eating shocking and unimaginable at first. But in time the skeptical and squeamish not only got used to the idea but began to feel it was a good one. "I used to make jokes about placenta burgers, but it began to sound very natural to me in a primitive way," says a father who ate part of his newborn son's placenta.

Placenta eaters believe that some native American tribeswomen ate their placentas by custom and that other mammals eat their placentas by instinct. Placenta eating is viewed as the natural conclusion to the birth process—nature's way of restoring needed hormones, iron and nutrients to contract the uterus, heal tissues and enrich a mother's blood.

"Unkilled Meat"

Surprisingly, vegetarians are enthusiastic about eating placenta. Some vegetarians simply do not classify placenta as meat. Others do but feel placenta is not taboo for reasons that depend on why they follow a meatless regime. Vegetarians who avoid meat so as not to be party to the killing of another living being for food believe placenta is the only "unkilled" meat available. They reason, "Nobody had to die to get this meat; it is meat of life, not death."

Vegetarians who do not eat meat because they believe most meat sold for public consumption to be contaminated with chemicals and additives say placenta is of known composition and origin if the mother has eaten unadulterated foods. "The whole idea struck us as so perfect that after the birth you eat that concentrated food—meat is the most concentrated form of food—especially if it's your own body and you know what it is. What has come out, you put back in," says one.

Unlike many other vegetarians, placenta-eating vegetarians do not deny that meat contains essential amino acids and vitamins.

Most terrestrial placental mammals eat the afterbirth. This is true of domesticated animals such as cats and dogs, as well as of wild animals such as antelopes and monkeys. Primatologists claim that all monkey mothers lick the afterbirth and usually eat it, too, if other aspects of the delivery have gone normally.

The placenta is either grasped in the mouth by mammalian females and consumed as it emerges from the vaginal opening, or it is picked up off the ground and eaten along with fetal membranes, amniotic fluid, blood and mucus. The placenta is eaten regardless of normal diet. Even such exclusively herbivorous, or vegetarian, mammals as guinea pigs, deer and giraffes eat the afterbirth.

Why mammals eat the placenta is a matter of conjecture among ethologists. Since the placenta contains lactogenic, or milk-stimulating, hormones, its consumption by the female may help establish lactation. Some herbivores, such as the deerlike impala, may consume the afterbirth to clean up the birth site. By eating the odorous birth products, mothers may prevent their relatively helpless newborn from being detected by predators.

The placenta is a more obvious source of nutrition for carnivorous mammals. Placenta, as animal tissue, may provide enough nourishment to make it unnecessary for a female to leave her young to hunt for food for herself during their first day of life. While childbirth customs and the fate of the placenta have interested few travelers, historians or even ethnographers until recently, human placentophagia is referred to in the Bible and has been reported in several areas of the world.

The concluding verses of chapter 28 of Deuteronomy in the King James Version warn the Israelites of punishments they will incur if their Lord's wishes are not heeded. A man shall be forced to "eat the fruit of thine own body, the flesh of thy sons and of thy daughters," while a woman will look toward "her young one that cometh out from between her feet, and toward her children which she shall bear: for she shall eat them. . . . " According to Dr. William Ober, an obstetrical and gynecological pathologist interested in placentophagia, the phrase "that cometh out from between her feet," written in the Greek text as *chorion* and as *secundinae partes* in the Vulgate, clearly refers to the placenta. Ober believes the passage may refer to "a remote tribal memory, now suppressed, of a period when placentas were eaten, at least in times of famine."

Secret Eaters

In an obscure book on tribal obstetrics published in 1883, Dr. G. J. Englemann, an American professor of obstetrics from Missouri Medical College, wrote of human placentophagia that some of the women of Brazil, "if it can be done secretly, eat the organ which has been recently expelled in a solitary labor. If observed, they bury or burn it."

Anthropologists have found that placenta is consumed in small portions in cultures that have faith in its medicinal powers. Dr. Donn Hart of Northern Illinois University reports that in the Philippines a new mother will occasionally be fed a porridge by a midwife, containing, without her knowledge, a minute amount of charred placenta or a few drops of placental blood. This secret addition is thought to help the mother regain her strength and guard against relapse. According to Southeast Asia specialist Dr. Richard Coughlin, there are numerous medical prescriptions in traditional Sino-Vietnamese medicine that call for powdered placenta as an ingredient. Such drugs are thought to cure disorders ranging from sterility to senility.

What some mammalian species seem to do instinctively and what some human societies have learned is that the afterbirth is indeed good food for a new mother who has just lost blood during a delivery. While not advocating human-placenta eating, Dr. Judith Wurtman, a member of the Department of Nutrition and Food Science at Massachusetts Institute of Technology, admits that placenta, like any organ rich in blood, contains a wealth of iron, vitamins and proteins. Because of the iron alone, the Harvard biologist John Kirsch believes eating placenta is a "very good idea" for a mother and not eating it is "truly a waste."

Great Source of Iron

Several medical doctors agree. "Why waste a solid beefsteak containing a pint of blood," asks endocrinologist Ann Forbes of Massachusetts General Hospital. "It is nutritionally equivalent to a pound of liver or any other raw, bloody meat." Dr. Sanford Rosenberg, a reproductive endocrinologist who teaches at the Medical College of Virginia, says, "Placenta seems to be an extraordinary source of iron because it is a very vascular, rapidly growing tissue with a tremendous amount of blood in it."

Placenta may also contain some unknown beneficial substance, according to some physicians. "There must be something unique in it, since most other mammals eat it," says Dr. Forbes. "Predator concealment is an unlikely reason, because the smell of the afterbirth will probably remain no matter how well it is cleaned up." Other doctors suggest that the placenta's hormones, specifically the prostaglandins, may assist muscle contraction; other hormones such as estrogens and placental lactogen may promote blood clotting and lactation respectively. Dr. Forbes points out that human mothers are unusual among mammalian females in having a two-to-three-day delay in milk production—a delay conceivably related to a failure to eat placenta. There are also those who argue that placentophagia among humans may be neither appropriate, natural nor healthful.

For starters, most mammals eat the placenta immediately after the birth; the mother alone and unaided chews the umbilical cord and licks the newborn clean. Eating the placenta is the final step in a sequence of birth actions taken by the female. Females tend to seclude themselves from males for birthing, and so males rarely if ever assist females with cleaning the newborn or eating the placenta.

Some American placenta eaters are aware of the novelty of male placenta consumption. Says one man, "Eating the placenta was nothing for my wife, but it was from her body. When I watched her eat it, it seemed to me like the appropriate thing for her to do, as it is for a mother cat. Male cats certainly wouldn't. I was eating it just to do it—for the experience. I certainly didn't need the nourishment. It's like the difference between biting your own fingernails and biting someone else's. It's just not appropriate."

In fact, placenta may not be all that welcome in the male body, particularly because of its estrogen content. Estrogen has a feminizing effect on males, promoting breast growth, for example, when consumed in large quantities over extended periods. And cooking, while destroying much of what is physiologically active in placenta, does not inactivate estrogen. "Since there is estrogen in the placenta at the time of birth, a male would consume a certain amount of it when eating placenta," says Dr. Rosenberg. But, he adds, "this estrogen is not likely to be orally effective since it cannot be absorbed by the body from the digestive tract." Most doctors concur that "one dose" of placenta is not dangerous to males but that chronic ingestion may be less safe.

Apes, the animals most closely related to humans and the most similar to the animals from which we evolved, frequently leave the placenta unconsumed. While members of other groups of primates, such as prosimians and monkeys, normally eat the placenta, chimpanzees may consume it only in a third to a half of all births. Dr. Jane Goodall reports that a wild chimpanzee, like a captive one in the London Zoo, did not eat the placenta but carried it around together with her infant until it was fly-blown and stinking. Gorillas and orangs, at least in captivity, usually do not eat placenta, but they may nibble and suck on it.

Human placentophagia seems to have been relatively uncommon. According to the Human Relations Area File, which documents past and current customs of hundreds of societies throughout the world, the eating of fresh, whole placenta by humans is rare. Even some reported instances of human placentophagia may be suspect.

However, anthropologists have observed the placenta being burned or buried. In most non-Western human cultures, the placenta is an object treated with great respect and is often the subject of a variety of superstitions as well. Some cultures regard it as the baby's brother, others as a twin, as a blood relative of the same sex or as a guardian spirit. Proper disposal is deemed necessary, for what becomes of the placenta might affect the newborn's health or intelligence or his mother's or father's fertility.

Superstitions

Hopi Indians traditionally bury the placenta at the village's edge so that no one can walk on it. Stepping on a placenta is thought to cause sore and chapped feet, yellowing of the eyes, and thick urine. The Arikara Indians wrap the afterbirth in a bundle along with tobacco and a wisp of sage and hang it in the branches of a thorny tree. Smoke offerings are made and prayers said to encourage

disease to attack the bundle, not the newborn. Among the Caticugans of the Philippines, the father buries the placenta to increase the bonds of affection between himself and his new child.

Among Americans who have home births, many buy berry bushes or young fruit trees and place the placenta in the hole dug for planting. The child grows up along with a special tree. Ravin Lang, co-author of the *Birth Book* and a California midwife, claims many parents will not throw placenta away. She is told, "It's too sacred an organ to put in the garbage and take to the dump." We bury our dead, so why not bury our placentas?

Friends, even doctors, attending home births where the family does not want the placenta sometimes claim it for their gardens and compost pits. But beware, warns Dr. Kirsch: The placenta's iron content may make it a poor fertilizer.

The relative absence of placenta eating among humans has not gone unnoticed. Although the human species is usually distinguished from other animals, including primates, by the presence of unique features such as upright walking and symbolic language, the animal ecologist G. E. Hutchinson has suggested that the human species be defined by the unique absence of a feature: humans can be defined as the primate that does not normally eat placenta.

Harvard's Erik Trinkaus, an expert on human evolution, speculates that humans may not be placenta eaters by nature because our apelike ancestors probably stopped routinely eating placenta when they began cleaning newborns by washing and wiping rather than by the usual mammalian licking. An anthropologist with the San Diego Zoo, Dr. Donald Lindburg, agrees that the loss of placenta eating occurred during the gradual shift from performing tasks with the mouth to performing them with the hands that characterized human evolution. Cleaning by licking may be the link in the chain of behaviors between birthing and placenta eating, broken sometime during the last million years or more of our past.

Some researchers argue that if placenta eating were adaptive to humans in any way, such as predator avoidance, nutrition or lactation, it would have survived as a universal human behavior.

Dr. Gary Mitchell, a psychologist at the University of California, suggests that the absence of placenta eating in humans may reflect the diminishing reliance on hormones to trigger behaviors such as maternal care in the more advanced primates. Decreasing reliance on placenta eating is already evident in the great apes. The zoologist R. F. Ewer suggests that the chimpanzee habit of carrying the placenta around until it rots is a transitional behavior. "It seems as though the usual habit of eating the placenta is being abandoned, but no satisfactory alternative method of disposing of it has been evolved."

Ewer posits two ways in which placenta eating may

actually be maladaptive to apes. Simian mothers may have tended to eat the placenta too enthusiastically, injuring the newborn in the process. Or possibly, in eating the placenta too quickly, mothers deprived newborns of the placenta blood that could have given them a useful reserve of iron.

Organic-Food Craze?

Clearly, in America, placenta eating is not strictly "natural" in practice even if it is "natural" in rationale. Americans are taking metaphors from nature and elaborating on them. And for the most part they know this. But, if American placentophagia is more than just functional "natural" behavior, what is it? Is it an unusual organic-food craze rooted in back-to-natural ideas? Or is it perhaps a deeply personal and expressive act that satisfies some psychological need?

Those Americans who eat placenta do not agree on its cultural origins or its personal or social importance. To some, placenta eating is "just a thing," "a neat idea," "a fad," "an immediate experience only," which is not mentioned to one's conservative parents.

Many of these Americans feel that placenta eating is part of the ultimate natural childbirth. Says one, "We share a very strong desire to return to basics, a back-to-nature collection of ideas. We think of placenta eating as a symbol of that."

These placenta eaters, very self-conscious about what is natural, approach placentophagia nonchalantly, for the most part, as a practice totally acceptable in their social circles. "I have never been to a party where the idea is to have a feast with a baby's placenta, but I know plenty of people who have," says one.

At the same time, even at the same party, there may be people who say the act of consuming placenta has more meaning, meaning related to both the novelty of the situation and the presence of friends. The words *ritual, ceremony, spiritual, sacred* and *reverence* are frequently used by such placenta eaters when describing their feelings and actions.

But placenta eaters, if they feel moved, feel moved to different degrees. "I felt that if I ate the stew, I would be acknowledging some kind of special relationship to the baby," one said.

An anthropology graduate student likens her presence at a home-birth party and her consumption of placenta to "one of those field experiences like going into the bush and eating grubs."

If the placenta eaters cannot agree on what placenta eating is all about, neither can the social scientists. Most are surprised to hear of American placentophagia, knowing its rarity among the world's cultures, but they will obligingly speculate about what they think is going on.

The Harvard anthropologist Nur Yalman notes that

hospital procedure and paperwork usually authenticate the birth and paternity of a child in our society. "In taking births out of hospitals, you take away the bureaucracy as well. The less the bureaucracy, the more the need for some form of hocus-pocus."

Dr. Irven DeVore, an anthropologist, views placenta eating in the United States as "one of various symbolic ways for bringing about stronger social and psychological investment by fathers and by a community in a child."

DeVore and Yalman both think that the social act of eating together, rather than the food itself, is what is crucial. In contrast, other researchers believe the act of eating placenta is especially significant because placenta is human flesh.

Cooked placenta is human flesh. And eating human flesh is usually considered cannibalism. Yet a placenta eater may feel "no more like a cannibal than a Martian." To them, cannibals are "savages" or starving wagon-train pioneers or airplane-crash survivors.

But placenta eating does count as cannibalism, and its practitioners know this subconsciously if not consciously, according to biologists and social scientists alike. Dr. Kirsch says, "Anyone who doesn't see placenta eating as cannibalism must be performing some sort of mental acrobatics. While the placenta is genetically related to both parents and physically grows in the mother, it is created from embryonic tissues. Thus, eating placenta is eating a piece of the child. No matter how you cut it, it's eating human flesh."

Pros and Cons

Experts on the subject of cannibalism agree with Kirsch. In his recent book, *The Man-Eating Myth*, anthropologist William Arens argues that socially sanctioned cannibalism has never existed anywhere. He believes placenta eating is not cannibalism in the classic sense of eating someone's flesh but that it falls under the general heading of a term such as blood drinking. "It's a very strange case," he says. "The problem is that it doesn't seem to be part of anyone." The author of *Cannibalism* and self-taught psychoanalytic sociologist, Eli Sagan, declares, "Psychologically, if in no other way, it is cannibalism. Placenta is eaten for the same kinds of reasons."

Cannibalism has been reported in many parts of the world, including Fiji, New Guinea, northwestern America, Nigeria, Zaire and Australia, and evidence of it has been found in a Neanderthal archeological site near Rome. It is a behavior that humans share with gorillas, chimpanzees and several other types of primates, as well as other kinds of animals. In some human societies, people eat, during mourning ceremonies, part of a relative who has died of accidental or natural causes. In other societies, only people outside the group, killed during warfare or head-hunting expeditions, are eaten. Different societies are said to favor different parts of the body. The more meaty arms and legs are usually preferred, but skin, liver, brain, genitalia and bone marrow are also eaten.

Many anthropologists think human flesh is consumed for psychological reasons. The wish to acquire the deceased's courage or other personal qualities may motivate cannibalistic acts. Cannibalism is also viewed as a way of dealing with something that is threatening by consuming it. Eli Sagan believes "affectionate" cannibalism, the eating of dead relatives, satisfies the anger of survivors toward the deceased for abandoning them. "Aggressive" cannibalism, the eating of slain enemies, is thought by Sagan to be the ultimate revenge.

To Sagan, American placenta eating combines the affectionate and aggressive motives. "It is aggressive because it is a way of symbolically killing and eating the infant and affectionate because it is a way of identifying with the child. It is an ambivalent situation, but the net result is affectionate: the child lives."

Social scientists agree that American placentophagia is a "very odd business," a practice that is probably even more repugnant to a majority of Americans than black magic, witchcraft and other unconventional activities. People react to it much as they do to another forbidden act, incest. And placenta eaters know this—it's part of why it is such a mind-boggling experience for them.

Most Americans who have eaten placenta felt fine about it when it happened, but some are slightly embarrassed and a little defensive in retrospect. One mother says, "It seemed like a fine thing to do at the time. The first person I thought I wouldn't tell was my mother. Now I am more embarrassed than I was then."

One placenta eater, though unusual in considering herself a cannibal, recalls that she didn't think of it as a violation of her value system. "I'm not ashamed of it now, and I don't think I did anything morally reprehensible."

The anthropologist Bradd Shore of Sarah Lawrence College observes that "We live in a permissive and narcissistic society, one based on individual freedom and self-indulgence, one that gives people incentive to break what are seen as artificial social rules by glorifying what is natural."

Shore believes that people's curiosity about placenta eating is connected to the attention currently being paid to the once forbidden subjects of incest and cannibalism. "These are behaviors that represent the last frontiers of what supposedly makes us human," says Shore. "The conquering of frontiers has always been a part of the American consciousness. The same license to conquer nature that Americans attribute to humans is often presumed in the popular mind as a license to conquer our own nature. If incest and cannibalism are held up as limits, it is perfectly consistent for these limits also to fall." Shore thinks that placenta eating allows people to "play" with the idea of cannibalism.

"Some Mothers Crave It"

Whatever is behind it, consumption of the afterbirth will only take hold as a new American birth custom if home births continue to rise in popularity. According to Dr. David Stewart, of the National Association of Parents and Professionals for Safe Alternatives in Childbirth, the number of out-of-hospital births has tripled nationwide since 1973 and now accounts for over 2 percent of all registered American births. In California, Oregon and Washington, the number of out-of-hospital births has been doubling every year and may be as high as 15–20 percent of 1980 California births. At the same time, placenta eating is "slowly catching on," says Ravin Lang. "There is something very powerful about that meat. Some mothers crave it."

Just the same, placentophagia is not for everyone. It may not be natural to human beings in an evolutionary sense, but it is probably at worst harmless to one's health and is even perhaps beneficial to one's social and psychological well-being. All the evidence isn't in yet—and it might be years before a combination of biomedical, social and psychological research gives us the whole story.

QUESTIONS

1. What is your reaction to the idea of eating the afterbirth? Explain your response.

2. Do you think that eating the afterbirth will prove to have been a fad practiced by the few, or do you think it might become a widely accepted practice in American culture? Justify your answer.

3. It may come as little surprise that this fad is practiced primarily in California. Why do you think California has its reputation as the origin of so many fads and social trends?

JOHN GLIEDMAN

The Wheelchair Rebellion

*History does not "just happen." Within the context of
the time and place in which human events occur,
people shape their own destinies, whether they do it
consciously or not. And a deliberate attempt to change
society need not arise only from the political leadership: often, broad masses of people join together to resist or bring about social change—sometimes on a
small scale, sometimes with sweeping effects. Social
movements are of particular interest to sociologists
precisely because they represent a collective attempt to
actively intervene in the process of social change.*

*Particularly since the 1960s, the United States has
seen campaigns by a number of social movements,
usually for the protection or enhancement of certain
rights. Prominent among these have been the movements for civil rights, for women's liberation, for gay
liberation, for the rights of the aged, for the protection
of the environment, for consumer rights, against nuclear power, and against abortion. More recently, another social movement has begun to promote the interests of a neglected group of Americans—the nearly 20
million people who suffer social and economic discrimination because of their handicapped status.*

*In this article, John Gliedman outlines some of the
problems faced by the handicapped and describes the
goals that their social movement hopes to achieve.*

By the early 1970s, many of the nation's black leaders,
political activists, and liberal reformers had been exhausted by a decade of confrontation and violence. Un-
daunted, or perhaps too desperate to care, people with
various kinds of handicaps nevertheless began to organize
a civil rights movement of their own. A new generation of
groups for the disabled was born, such as the American
Coalition of Citizens with Disabilities and Mainstream,
Inc. Like older and more established groups, they lobbied
for better social services and protested the endless Catch-
22 provisions in the welfare laws that hurt the severely
disabled. But they also demanded something more: they
called for significant structural changes in housing, public buildings, and transportation that have long posed
barriers to their mobility; and they began working for an
end to the prejudice and job discrimination that had
proved far more obstructive to an active life than such
handicaps as blindness, deafness, or paraplegia.

For all its achievements in the rehabilitation and education laws of the 1970s, what many have called the
"Quiet Revolution" in disability was an incomplete and
one-sided revolution. It was one-sided because the new
image of the handicapped as an oppressed minority group
was held only by some of the disabled themselves, their
relatives, and many professionals who cared for them.
The legislative reforms that the organizers succeeded in
winning in the 70s were not the result of massive grass-
roots pressure from millions of handicapped people and
their able-bodied allies. Moreover, key provisions in the
laws are in jeopardy because of the recent Supreme Court
ruling that held that a college is not required to admit a
deaf person who cannot benefit from the program without substantial modification of its standards.

Even today, the civil rights movement for the disabled
is relatively small. The impetus for change comes from
the top. A sympathetic Congress (many of whose members themselves have disabled relatives), the efforts of
diligent lobbyists, the initiative of legal advocates, and a
federal bureaucracy receptive, at least in principle, to the
idea of treating the disabled as another disadvantaged
minority group—all contributed to the relatively unpub-
licized passage of land-mark legislation in the 1970s.
Nevertheless, Frank Bowe, director of the American Co-

alition, sized up the status of the movement this way: "It is possible to legislate rights, and this has been done. But rights become reality only after political struggle."

Bowe says more than half of all working-age disabled adults who could work are jobless. There is systematic discrimination against those who do work, according to Bowe and others, which keeps them in menial or futureless jobs; across the United States, a network of "sheltered workshops" employs 200,000 handicapped people whose wages average under $1 an hour—far less than the minimum wage. Little energy goes to inventing, producing, or marketing products specially designed for the disabled, and what is marketed generally goes through the medical or social-service system as mediator. Thus are the handicapped barred from behaving as independent producers, consumers, and citizens in the economy.

Along with those tangible disadvantages, the disabled must also cope with a kind of paternalism from their able-bodied allies that has long been discredited in race relations. Even today, many unprejudiced Americans accept traditional stereotypes about different kinds of handicaps. However, instead of reacting cruelly because of the fears and anxieties aroused by those disabilities, we take a more humane approach. We extend to handicapped people what seems to be an enlightened model of medical tolerance. Rather than blame them for their pitiful condition, we say that their social and mental incompetence is produced by a disease or a diseaselike condition beyond their control to alter. We believe that, in a social sense, they are chronic patients; and that we owe them the same struggle with our fears and prejudices, the same understanding and tolerance, that we owe victims of any serious disease or injury.

The problem with this analysis, from the disabled person's point of view, is that it allows him or her no scope whatsoever for leading an adult social life. As Talcott Parsons first noted, the role of a patient in middle-class society is functionally very similar to that of a child. We expect the patient to be cheerful and accepting, to obey doctors' orders, and, in general, to devote all his energies to getting well. When an able-bodied person falls sick, he ceases to be judged as an adult; in return, he is expected to work actively to get well. The area defined as his to control shifts to the sickbed. But in America a person labeled handicapped is assigned a specially destructive variant of the sick role. Not merely powerless because he is sick, he is defined as doubly powerless because he cannot master the job of "getting well." Unable to fill that role obligation, he is seen as socially powerless, deprived of a political identity—until he chooses to assert one.

Many members of the civil rights movement for the disabled have told me that the annual cerebral palsy telethon symbolizes for them the deeply humiliating paternalism of society's medical tolerance toward handicapped people. Michael Poachovis, a political organizer on the West Coast, said, "It's absolutely degrading. Watching those telethons you might think that all palsied adults are mentally retarded, pathetically trusting, asexual children." Others find little comfort in the usual image of disabled people presented in the media. Ron Whyte, a writer in New York City, summed up his feelings this way: "You don't learn about Harlem by listening to 'Amos 'n' Andy'." Only rarely are we forced to confront the paternalism that lurks behind our attempts to deal fairly with the handicapped. Witness the discomfort of audiences watching Jon Voight as a demanding, rebellious, and unabashedly erotic crippled veteran in the recent film *Coming Home*.

Over the past five years, I have studied the problems of disability while on the research staff of the Carnegie Council on Children. Handicapped children were the point of departure for my work. But, along with my colleague William Roth, I eventually devoted as much time to adults as to children, since the problems of the different age groups tend to be closely related.

In the 1960s and 1970s, about 20 million people of working age described themselves as disabled. Those estimates might easily be 50 percent too high or too low. They might be too low because they do not include most people whom a psychologist would classify as mildly retarded; most people who have experienced a major mental illness; or those with speech or learning disabilities. The figures might be too high because they are based upon answers to the question, "Do you have any medical condition or other impairment lasting three months or longer that limits the kind or amount of work that you can do?" Answers given to this kind of question are highly unreliable. On the other hand, it is perfectly possible that these contradictory factors cancel out, and that the figure of 20 million is not too far off after all.

Accepting this estimate provisionally, it seems reasonable to assume that disabled people comprise between 5 and 10 percent of the total working-age population. This is a huge number, at least as large as the number of able-bodied hispanics in this age range and quite possibly as large as the number of able-bodied blacks.

Disabilities are, of course, much more common among the elderly. The best guess is that between one-third and one-fourth of all people 65 years or older are currently disabled. But the sociological relationships between disability and old age require further study; it is quite possible that the social experiences of most elderly people in possession of their mental faculties can also be described by the minority-group model of disability, which views the social stigma as attached to the condition of being aged rather than a result of any actual disability.

It is even more difficult to assess the number of children with real disabilities. Many kinds of handicaps that pass unnoticed among adults may be blown up out of proportion by parents, teachers, and a child's peers. A host of clinical findings also suggests that perceptions of the severity of a handicap are exquisitely sensitive to social milieu. What some people in one social stratum treat as a mild or negligible disability may be considered severely disabling in another. For the present, one can only guess that the total number of disabled children and youths lies somewhere between five and 10 million.

Members of an oppressed social group have little in common apart from the fact that society singles them out for systematic oppression. Examples abound: European Jews in the 1920s and 1930s, many of whom did not consider themselves primarily Jewish; and, closer to home, women, homosexuals, the elderly. Similarly, handicapped people are beginning to see themselves as an oppressed minority because society exposes most of them to a common set of pressures that violate their civil rights. Long ago, the social psychologist Kurt Lewin called the defining characteristic of a minority group an "interdependence of fate." Discrimination—much of it in the economic marketplace—constitutes the sociological fate of the disabled. This discrimination imposes a minority-group identity upon a collection of adults and children, each of whom has, in most other respects, as much in common with able-bodied people as with one another.

Two or three decades ago, sociologists often studied the phenomenon of "passing"—the attempt of light-skinned blacks to pass as whites, of Jews to pass as gentiles. That phenomenon helps to clarify the relevance of a minority-group analysis to disabled people. The first group of disabled people who fit the minority-group model are those who can rarely pass as able-bodied. They include the deaf, the blind, the physically disabled, the cosmetically disfigured, the very short, and individuals with chronic diseases whose symptoms are unpleasant and obtrusive. Another group of disabled people encounters many of the same problems as the black who passed as white in the 1930s or 1940s. They can usually come off as able-bodied, but they often pay a high psychological price for their successful strategies of concealment. The passers include many people once institutionalized in mental hospitals or custodial institutions for the mildly retarded; many epileptics; many people with severe reading disabilities; many with concealable but socially stigmatizing medical conditions or chronic diseases.

For most people with cancer, heart disease, diabetes, and back ailments, the minority-group analysis is probably of secondary importance. Still, even those with such disabilities would benefit greatly from an end to job discrimination against disabled persons, improvement in the quality of the nation's social and health services, and, in many instances, elimination of architectural and transportation barriers to mobility. One other group of disabled adults requires mention—those who are so incapacitated by their mental or emotional limitations that they could not lead normal lives even if society's considerable

prejudice against them were to melt away. That group includes the severely (and intractably) psychotic, and somewhere between one-tenth and one-fourth of all mentally retarded people.

Measured against two centuries of neglect, stigma, and degradation, the gains registered by disabled people in the 1970s were impressive indeed. Even as the Equal Rights Amendment for women was stalled, Congress overrode two Nixon vetoes of the first legislation that specifically prohibited discrimination against disabled workers. The legislation, the Rehabilitation Act of 1973, required affirmative-action or nondiscriminatory hiring programs to be instituted in all federal agencies for all federal contractors doing more than $2,500-a-year worth of work for the government, as well as in any public or private organization that receives federal funds.

The section of the Rehabilitation Act dealing with discrimination against the disabled has been regularly challenged and regularly reaffirmed in the courts. But in June, the Supreme Court established limits on its scope when it ruled that Southeastern Community College in North Carolina was within its rights in refusing admission of Frances B. Davis, a hearing-impaired woman, to its nursing program. Mrs. Davis, who relies largely on lip-reading to understand others, is a practical nurse who sought admission to the clinical part of the registered-nurse curriculum that would have brought her into contact with patients. Reversing an appeals court ruling, the justices held that the law does not require a college to compromise its admission standards or make "extensive modifications" of its program to accommodate all handicapped persons; it prohibits only discrimination against those who are "otherwise qualified" in spite of their handicaps.

Leaders of handicapped people's organizations believe that while the decision establishes a potentially harmful precedent, it may apply to only a small number of cases. "It's the kind of case I call a 'blind busdriver' claim," said Leslie Milk, executive director of Mainstream, Inc., implying that it is not unreasonable for an employer to refuse to let a blind man drive a bus. "The court ruled very narrowly, apparently to limit the implications of the decision, and left it to HEW to go on clarifying the situation as it makes regulations. It's a limitation on the law, but one we can live with."

Frank Bowe of the American Coalition also thinks the court's decision makes some sense. Bowe, who is himself deaf, said that most people would agree that hearing impairment could prevent a nurse from responding effectively to a patient in all critical situations. "But most disabled people are like me," Bowe said. "They want to enter fields where their disability doesn't interfere with the job." But both Milk and Bowe fear that the ruling will have a deterrent effect: that it may discourage some handicapped people from applying to professional schools, or encourage some schools to believe that they can avoid compliance with the law in the future.

The ruling does not curtail the great progress made in primary and secondary education. While public interest in the desperate plight of the inner-city school ebbed, a series of class-action suits on behalf of mentally retarded children established the right of every handicapped child to a free and appropriately designed public education. Responding to these legal decisions, Congress passed a law that attempts to end the traditional pattern of segregated public education for handicapped children: it stipulates that every child should be educated in the least-segregated educational setting that does justice to his academic and emotional needs. The law's insistence upon the school's accountability to the child's parents and its requirement that the school provide an individualized program of education to every child represent an even more far-reaching departure from traditional practice in public education.

In making its case to the able-bodied mainstream, the central obstacle confronted by the movement is the widespread acceptance of the medical model. Even when it is invoked out of a genuine desire to help the disadvantaged—for instance, as when homosexuality is defined as a disease—this set of assumptions can be damaging. Regardless of whether the economy is growing or contracting, the disabled have a right to their fair share of jobs, goods, and services. But the moment any group is defined as a collection of ill or defective people, social priorities insensibly change. Questions of stigma and systemic discrimination fade into the background: the first priority goes to *treating* the putative inferiority.

As in the case of other disadvantaged groups, the professionals who work with the disabled are often among the worst offenders. Most workers in the human services still acquire in their training a basically medical view of social problems, what the historian Christopher Lasch has recently called the social-pathology model. The disease metaphor is far more pervasive in care of the disabled than in most other areas. It influences not only the policymakers and the care-givers, but also the social scientists who are doing the very research that could bring about changes in attitudes.

Most often, such researchers will postulate the presence of a single diseaselike entity that colors the attitudes of the majority of able-bodied people—a maladjustment in relating to disabled people—and then proceed to measure the prevalence of the disease among the groups studied. Even the best of this work suffers from the failing of so much social science: the discovery of striking facts whose exact significant is unclear because the underlying social phenomenon is far more complex than the experimenters' theories admit. Studies of the attitudes of able-bodied people toward the handicapped usually report what they say about the disabled, not how they act to-

ward them. Virtually none of the research sorts out the relative roles of fear, ignorance, inexperience, or prejudice.

Jerome Siller, professor of educational psychology at New York University, has done extensive studies on able-bodied people's expressed attitudes toward different disability groups. Siller asked his subjects what characteristics they attribute to different sorts of disability (for instance, amputees may be seen as more intelligent, aggressive, or kind than people with other handicaps).

He uncovered a hierarchy of acceptability. The most acceptable disabilities were the relatively minor ones, like partial vision or hearing loss, a speech impediment or a heart condition. Amputees were a rung lower on the acceptability hierarchy. The deaf and the blind ranked somewhere in the middle, then came the mentally ill; below them stood people with epilepsy, cerebral palsy, or total paralysis.

When ranking included blacks, they usually ended up in the middle of the hierarchy, near the deaf and the blind. In some studies, such as one of employer attitudes made in the early 1970s by clinical psychologist James A. Colbert and his associates, blacks were preferred above all disability groups. Here, too, the sociological implications of these results are unclear. For instance, many investigators have found that the most negative attitudes of all expressed are about obese people. Yet it is hard to believe that we actually equate the stigma attached to being fat, crushing as it may be, with the kinds of stigma experienced by inner-city blacks, epileptics, or people with cerebral palsy. Some important distinctions among those stigmata are being missed by the research design.

Similar ambiguities cloud the interpretation of what is still the most important finding in the field: Stephen A. Richardson of Albert Einstein College of Medicine discovered that as children age, there are significant changes in their expressed attitude toward physical disabilities. Richardson found that a stable preference-ladder first appeared around age six. Asked their feelings about six pictures of children—all but one of them disabled—six-year-olds tended to rank slight facial disfigurement as most acceptable, second only to normalcy. Eight- to 10-year-olds ranked those with crutches and leg braces as most acceptable after the able-bodied child, followed by a child in a wheelchair, one with an amputated forearm, one with facial disfigurement, and finally, an obese child. By senior year, girls set facial disfigurement as least acceptable while boys ranked it fourth out of six in acceptability. (Male and female adults tend to follow the same pattern.) Again, there was the paradoxical finding that race was less stigmatizing than disability, and obesity often more stigmatizing.

. . .

...Medical biases compromise the value of much present-day theory and research in education for the handicapped. A generation ago, educators assessed the academic needs of black children and handicapped children in the same way, by measuring the disadvantaged child's academic behavior against what was assumed to be normal for a white, middle-class, able-bodied child. After determining the ways in which the child deviated from these presumably universal norms, the educator devised special compensatory programs to cure or to lessen the child's academic deviance.

Increasingly, this conception of minority education has come under sharp attack. As Frank Riessman, professor of education at Queens College, notes, "If one analyzes the approaches that have been successful in improving the educational performance of inner-city children, one realizes that they are rooted in the strengths and the cognitive styles of the children rather than in a compensatory emphasis on deficiencies." Sadly, the deviance approach so common in minority education in the 1960s continues to go unchallenged in special education.

By far the greatest abuses of the medical model of disability occur in the technical literature that discusses the economic needs of disabled people. Most of this literature simply assumes that the employment problems of disabled people are caused by their physical limitations, rather than by the interaction of their limitation with job discrimination, environmental obstacles to mobility, and other forms of discrimination. The assumption has the unhappy ring of arguments that the economic problems of black Americans are caused by inherited genes that make them biologically inferior.

For society at large, the "therapeutic state" (to recall Nicholas N. Kittrie's term) is a threat, not a reality. But millions of disabled Americans already live within the invisible walls of a therapeutic society. In this society of the "sick," there is no place for the ordinary hallmarks of a present or future adult identity, no place for choice between competing moralities, no place for politics, no place for work, and no place for sexuality. All political, legal, and ethical issues are transformed into questions of disease and health, deviance and normal adjustment, proper and improper "management" of the disability. To recall political scientist Sheldon S. Wolin's fine phrase, the "sublimation of politics" has proceeded furthest of all with handicapped people. Of all America's oppressed groups, only the handicapped have been so fully disenfranchised in the name of health.

QUESTIONS

1. Characterize the general social attitude toward the handicapped. How do you think this attitude appears from the viewpoint of a handicapped person?

2. How do you react when passing a handicapped person in the street? How do you react when introduced to a handicapped person in a small group? Analyze your responses.

3. What are the similarities between the situation of the handicapped and that of other minorities that suffer stigma, prejudice, and discrimination? Are there any differences?

ARTHUR C. CLARKE

Hazards of Prophecy

What will society be like a hundred or a thousand or ten thousand years from now? We cannot know; we can only make informed speculations and inspired guesses. And if the past is any guide, the chances are good that our prophecies will be hopelessly wrong.

History is littered with failed prophecies, ranging from the religious to the social and the scientific. Religious zealots have prophesied the end of the world time and again over the centuries, using the same biblical texts but interpreting them to fit the events and concerns of their own time. Theorists of various kinds have anticipated an endless variety of social scenarios, ranging from placid utopias to the Thousand Year Reich. Scientists have anticipated many innovations that now seem absurd—and, all too often, have declared impossible many advances that subsequently did occur.

In this article, Arthur C. Clarke examines the latter phenomenon—the recurrent failures of nerve and imagination that have so often made scientists blind to potential advances in their own fields.

The Failure of Nerve

Before one attempts to set up in business as a prophet, it is instructive to see what success others have made of this dangerous occupation—and it is even more instructive to see where they have failed.

With monotonous regularity, apparently competent men have laid down the law about what is technically possible or impossible—and have been proved utterly wrong, sometimes while the ink was scarcely dry from their pens. On careful analysis, it appears that these debacles fall into two classes, which I will call "failures of nerve" and "failures of imagination."

The failure of nerve seems to be the more common; it occurs when *even given all the relevant facts* the would-be prophet cannot see that they point to an inescapable conclusion. Some of these failures are so ludicrous as to be almost unbelievable, and would form an interesting subject for psychological analysis. "They said it couldn't be done" is a phrase that occurs throughout the history of invention; I do not know if anyone has ever looked into the reasons *why* "they" said so, often with quite unnecessary vehemence.

It is now impossible for us to recall the mental climate which existed when the first locomotives were being built, and critics gravely asserted that suffocation lay in wait for anyone who reached the awful speed of thirty miles an hour. It is equally difficult to believe that, only eighty years ago, the idea of the domestic electric light was pooh-poohed by all the "experts"—with the exception of a thirty-one-year-old American inventor named Thomas Alva Edison. When gas securities nose-dived in 1878 because Edison (already a formidable figure, with the phonograph and the carbon microphone to his credit) announced that he was working on the incandescent lamp, the British Parliament set up a committee to look into the matter. (Westminster can beat Washington hands down at this game.)

The distinguished witnesses reported, to the relief of the gas companies, that Edison's ideas were "good enough for our transatlantic friends . . . but unworthy of the attention of practical or scientific men." And Sir William Preece, engineer-in-chief of the British Post Office, roundly declared that "Subdivision of the electric light is an absolute *ignis fatuus.*" One feels that the fatuousness was not in the *ignis.*

The scientific absurdity being pilloried, be it noted, is not some wild-and-woolly dream like perpetual motion, but the humble little electric light bulb, which three generations of men have taken for granted, except when it burns out and leaves them in the dark. Yet although in this matter Edison saw far beyond his contemporaries, he too in later life was guilty of the same shortsightedness that afflicted Preece, for he opposed the introduction of alternating current.

The most famous, and perhaps the most instructive, failures of nerve have occurred in the fields of aero- and astronautics. At the beginning of the twentieth century, scientists were almost unanimous in declaring that heavier-than-air flight was impossible, and that anyone who attempted to build airplanes was a fool. The great American astronomer, Simon Newcomb, wrote a celebrated essay which concluded:

> The demonstration that no possible combination of known substances, known forms of machinery and known forms of force, can be united in a practical machine by which man shall fly long distances through the air, seems to the writer as complete as it is possible for the demonstration of any physical fact to be.

Oddly enough, Newcomb was sufficiently broad-minded to admit that some wholly new discovery—he mentioned the neutralization of gravity—might make flight practical. One cannot, therefore, accuse him of lacking imagination; his error was in attempting to marshal the facts of aerodynamics when he did not understand that science. His failure of nerve lay in not realizing that the means of flight were already at hand.

For Newcomb's article received wide publicity at just about the time that the Wright brothers, not having a suitable antigravity device in their bicycle shop, were mounting a gasoline engine on wings. When news of their success reached the astronomer, he was only momentarily taken back. Flying machines *might* be a marginal possibility, he conceded—but they were certainly of no practical importance, for it was quite out of the question that they could carry the extra weight of a passenger as well as that of a pilot.

Such refusal to face facts which now seem obvious has continued throughout the history of aviation. Let me quote another astronomer, William H. Pickering, straightening out the uninformed public a few years *after* the first airplanes had started to fly.

> The popular mind often pictures gigantic flying machines speeding across the Atlantic and carrying innumerable passengers in a way analogous to our modern steamships. . . . It seems safe to say that such ideas must be wholly visionary, and even if a machine could get across with one or two passengers the expense would be prohibitive to any but the capitalist who could own his own yacht.
>
> Another popular fallacy is to expect enormous speed to be obtained. It must be remembered that the resistance of the air increases as the square of the speed and the work as the cube. . . . If with 30 h.p. we can now attain a speed of 40 m.p.h., then in order to reach a speed of 100 m.p.h. we must use a motor capable of 470 h.p. . . . it is clear that with our present devices there is no hope of competing for racing speed with either our locomotives or our automobiles.

It so happens that most of his fellow astronomers considered Pickering far *too imaginative;* he was prone to see vegetation—and even evidence for insect life—on the Moon. I am glad to say that by the time he died in 1938 at the ripe age of eighty, Professor Pickering had seen airplanes traveling at 400 m.p.h. and carrying considerably more than "one or two" passengers.

Closer to the present, the opening of the space age has produced a mass vindication (and refutation) of prophecies on a scale and at a speed never before witnessed. Having taken some part in this myself, and being no more immune than the next man to the pleasures of saying, "I told you so," I would like to recall a few of the statements about space flight that have been made by prominent scientists in the past. It is necessary for *someone* to do this, and to jog the remarkably selective memories of the pessimists. The speed with which those who once declaimed "It's impossible" can switch to "I said it could be done all the time" is really astounding.

As far as the general public is concerned, the idea of space flight as a serious possibility first appeared on the horizon in the 1920's, largely as a result of newspaper reports of the work of the American Robert Goddard and the Rumanian Hermann Oberth. (The much earlier studies of Tsiolkovsky in Russia then being almost unknown outside his own country.) When the ideas of Goddard and Oberth, usually distorted by the press, filtered through to the scientific world, they were received with hoots of derision. For a sample of the kind of criticism the pioneers of astronautics had to face, I present this masterpiece from a paper published by one Professor A. W. Bickerton, in 1926. It should be read carefully, for as an example of the cocksure thinking of the time it would be very hard to beat.

> This foolish idea of shooting at the moon is an example of the absurd length to which vicious specialisation will carry scientists working in thought-tight compartments. Let us critically examine the proposal. For a projectile entirely to escape the gravitation of the earth, it needs a velocity of 7 miles a second. The thermal energy of a gramme at this speed is 15,180 calories. . . . The energy of our most violent explosive— nitro-glycerine—is less than 1,500 calories per gramme. Consequently, even had the explosive nothing to carry, it has only one-tenth of the energy necessary to escape the earth. . . . Hence the proposition appears to be basically impossible. . . .

Indignant readers in the Colombo public library pointed angrily to the "Silence" notices when I discovered this little gem. It is worth examining it in some detail to see just where "vicious specialisation," if one may coin a phrase, led the professor so badly astray.

His first error lies in the sentence: "The energy of our most violent explosive—nitro-glycerine . . ." One would have thought it obvious that *energy*, not violence, is what we want from a rocket fuel; and as a matter of fact nitroglycerin and similar explosives contain much less energy, weight for weight, than such mixtures as kerosene and liquid oxygen. This had been carefully pointed out by Tsiolkovsky and Goddard years before.

Bickerton's second error is much more culpable. What of it, if nitroglycerin has only a tenth of the energy necessary to escape from the Earth? That merely means that you have to use at least ten pounds of nitroglycerin to launch a single pound of payload.

For the fuel itself has not got to escape from Earth; it can all be burned quite close to our planet, and as long as it imparts its energy to the payload, this is all that matters. When Lunik II lifted thirty-three years after Professor Bickerton said it was impossible, most of its several hundred tons of kerosene and liquid oxygen never got very far from Russia—but the half-ton payload reached the Mare Imbrium.

As a comment on the above, I might add that Professor Bickerton, who was an active popularizer of science, numbered among his published books one with the title *Perils of a Pioneer*. Of the perils that all pioneers must face, few are more disheartening than the Bickertons.

Right through the 1930's and 1940's, eminent scientists continued to deride the rocket pioneers—when they bothered to notice them at all. Anyone who has access to a good college library can find, preserved for posterity in the dignified pages of the January 1941 *Philosophical Magazine*, an example that makes a worthy mate to the one I have just quoted.

It is a paper by the distinguished Canadian astronomer Professor J.W. Campbell, of the University of Alberta, entitled "Rocket Flight to the Moon." Opening with a quotation from a 1938 Edmonton paper to the effect that "rocket flight to the Moon now seems less remote than television appeared a hundred years ago," the professor then looks into the subject mathematically. After several pages of analysis, he arrives at the conclusion that it would require *a million tons* of take-off weight to carry *one pound* of payload on the round trip.

The correct figure, for today's primitive fuels and technologies, is very roughly one ton per pound—a depressing ratio, but hardly as bad as that calculated by the professor. Yet his mathematics was impeccable; so what went wrong?

Merely his initial assumptions, which were hopelessly unrealistic. He chose a path for the rocket which was fantastically extravagant in energy, and he assumed the use of an acceleration so low that most of the fuel would be wasted at low altitudes, fighting the Earth's gravitational field. It was as if he had calculated the performance of an automobile—when the brakes were on. No wonder that he concluded: "While it is always dangerous to make a negative prediction, it would appear that the statement that rocket flight to the moon does not seem so remote as television did less than one hundred years ago is over-optimistic." I am sure that when the *Philosophical Magazine* subscribers read those words, back in 1941, many of them thought, "Well, *that* should put those crazy rocket men in their place!"

Yet the correct results had been published by Tsiolkovsky, Oberth and Goddard years before; though the work of the first two would have been very hard to consult at the time, Goddard's paper "A Method of Reaching Extreme Altitudes" was already a classic and had been issued by that scarcely obscure body, the Smithsonian Institution. If Professor Campbell had only consulted it (or indeed *any* competent writer on the subject—there were some, even in 1941) he would not have misled his readers and himself.

The lesson to be learned from these examples is one that can never be repeated too often, and is one that is seldom understood by laymen—who have an almost superstitious awe of mathematics. But mathematics is only a tool, though an immensely powerful one. No equations, however impressive and complex, can arrive at the truth if the initial assumptions are incorrect. It is really quite amazing by what margins competent but conservative scientists and engineers can miss the mark, when they start with the preconceived idea that what they are investigating is impossible. When this happens, the most well-informed men become blinded by their prejudices and are unable to see what lies directly ahead of them. What is even more incredible, they refuse to learn from experience and will continue to make the same mistake over and over again.

Some of my best friends are astronomers, and I am sorry to keep throwing stones at them—but they do seem to have an appalling record as prophets. If you still doubt this, let me tell a story so ironic that you might well accuse me of making it up. But I am not that much of a cynic; the facts are on file for anyone to check.

Back in the dark ages of 1935, the founder of the British Interplanetary Society, P. E. Cleator, was rash enough to write the first book on astronautics published in England. His *Rockets through Space* gave an (incidentally highly entertaining) account of the experiments that had been carried out by the German and American rocket pioneers, and their plans for such commonplaces of today as giant multi-stage boosters and satellites. Rather surprisingly, the staid scientific journal *Nature* reviewed the book in its issue for March 14, 1936, and summed up as follows:

> It must be said at once that the whole procedure sketched in the present volume presents difficulties of so fundamental a nature that we are forced to dismiss the notion as essentially impracticable, in spite of the author's insistent appeal to put aside prejudice and to recollect the supposed impossibility of heavier-than-air flight before it was actually accomplished. An analogy such as this may be misleading, and we believe it to be so in this case. . . .

Well, the whole world now knows just how misleading this analogy was, though the reviewer, identified only by the unusual initials R.v.d.R.W. was of course fully entitled to his opinion.

Just twenty years later—*after* President Eisenhower had announced the United States satellite program—a new Astronomer Royal arrived in England to take up his appointment. The press asked him to give his views on space flight, and after two decades Dr. Richard van der Riet Woolley had seen no reason to change his mind. "Space travel," he snorted, "is utter bilge."

The newspapers did not allow him to forget this, when Sputnik I went up the very next year. And now—irony piled upon irony—Dr. Woolley is, by virtue of his position as Astronomer Royal, a leading member of the committee advising the British government on space research. The feelings of those who have been trying, for a generation, to get the United Kingdom interested in space can well be imagined.

Even those who suggested that rockets might be used for more modest, though much more reprehensible, purposes were overruled by the scientific authorities—except in Germany and Russia.

When the existence of the 200-mile-range V-2 was disclosed to an astonished world, there was considerable speculation about intercontinental missiles. This was firmly squashed by Dr. Vannevar Bush, the civilian general of the United States scientific war effort, in evidence before a Senate committee on December 3, 1945. Listen:

> There has been a great deal said about a 3,000 miles high-angle rocket. In my opinion such a thing is impossible for many years. The people who have been writing these things that annoy me, have been talking about a 3,000 mile high-angle rocket shot from one continent to another, carrying an atomic bomb and so directed as to be a precise weapon which would land exactly on a certain target, such as a city.
>
> I say, technically, I don't think anyone in the world knows how to do such a thing, and I feel confident that it will not be done for a very long period of time to come. . . . I think we can leave that out of our thinking. I wish the American public would leave that out of their thinking.

A few months earlier (in May 1945) Prime Minister Churchill's scientific advisor Lord Cherwell had expressed similar views in a House of Lords debate. This was only to be expected, for Cherwell was an extremely conservative and opinionated scientist who had advised the government that the V-2 itself was only a propaganda rumor.

In the May 1945 debate on defense, Lord Cherwell impressed his peers by a dazzling display of mental arithmetic from which he correctly concluded that a very long-range rocket must consist of more than 90 per cent fuel, and thus would have a negligible payload. The conclusion he let his listeners draw from this was that such a device would be wholly impracticable.

That was true enough in the spring of 1945, but it was no longer true in the summer. One astonishing feature of the House of Lords debate is the casual way in which much-too-well-informed peers used the words "atomic bomb," at a time when this was the best-kept secret of the war. (The Alamogordo test was still two months in the future!) Security must have been horrified, and Lord Cherwell—who of course knew all about the Manhattan Project—was quite justified in telling his inquisitive colleagues not to believe everything they heard, even though in this case it happened to be perfectly true.

When Dr. Bush spoke to the Senate committee in December of the same year, the only important secret about the atomic bomb was that it weighed five tons. Anyone could then work out in his head, as Lord Cherwell had done, that a rocket to deliver it across intercontinental ranges would have to weigh about 200 tons—as against the mere 14 tons of the then awe-inspiring V-2.

The outcome was the greatest failure of nerve in all history, which changed the future of the world—indeed, of many worlds. Faced with the same facts and the same calculations, American and Russian technology took two separate roads. The Pentagon—accountable to the taxpayer—virtually abandoned long-range rockets for almost half a decade, until the development of thermonuclear bombs made it possible to build warheads five times lighter yet several hundred times more powerful than the low-powered and now obsolete device that was dropped on Hiroshima.

The Russians had no such inhibitions. Faced with the need for a 200-ton rocket, they went right ahead and built it. By the time it was perfected, it was no longer required for military purposes, for Soviet physicists had bypassed the United States' billion-dollar tritium bomb cul-de-sac and gone straight to the far cheaper lithium bomb. Having backed the wrong horse in rocketry, the Russians then entered it for a much more important event—and won the race into space.

Of the many lessons to be drawn from this slice of recent history, the one that I wish to emphasize is this. Anything that is theoretically possible will be achieved in practice, no matter what the technical difficulties, if it is desired greatly enough. It is no argument against any project to say: "The idea's fantastic!" Most of the things that have happened in the last fifty years have been fantastic, and it is only by assuming that they will continue to be so that we have any hope of anticipating the future.

To do this—to avoid that failure of nerve for which history exacts so merciless a penalty—we must have the courage to follow all technical extrapolations to their logical conclusion. Yet even this is not enough, as I shall now demonstrate. To predict the future we need logic; but we also need faith and imagination which can sometimes defy logic itself.

The Failure of Imagination

[Until now I have] suggested that many of the negative statements about scientific possibilities, and the gross failures of past prophets to predict what lay immediately ahead of them, could be described as failures of nerve. All the basic facts of aeronautics were available—in the writings of Cayley, Stringfellow, Chanute, and others—when Simon Newcomb "proved" that flight was impossible. He simply lacked the courage to face those facts. All the fundamental equations and principles of space travel had been worked out by Tsiolkovsky, Goddard, and Oberth for years—often decades—when distinguished scientists were making fun of would-be astronauts. Here again, the failure to appreciate the facts was not so much intellectual as moral. The critics did not have the courage that their scientific convictions should have given them; they could not believe the truth even when it had been spelled out before their eyes, in their own language of mathematics. We all know this type of cowardice, because at some time or other we all exhibit it.

The second kind of prophetic failure is less blameworthy, and more interesting. It arises when all the available facts are appreciated *and* marshaled correctly—but when the really vital facts are still undiscovered, and the possibility of their existence is not admitted.

A famous example of this is provided by the philosopher Auguste Comte, who in his *Cours de Philosophie Positive* (1835) attempted to define the limits within which scientific knowledge must lie. In his chapter on astronomy (Book 2, Chapter 1) he wrote these words concerning the heavenly bodies:

> We see how we may determine their forms, their distances, their bulk, their motions, but we can never know anything of their chemical or mineralogical structure; and much less, that of organised beings living on their surface. . . . We must keep carefully apart the idea of the solar system and that of the universe, and be always assured that our only true interest is in the former. Within this boundary alone is astronomy the supreme and positive science that we have determined it to be . . . the stars serve us scientifically only as providing positions with which we may compare the interior movements of our system.

In other words, Comte decided that the stars could never be more than celestial reference points, of no intrinsic concern to the astronomer. Only in the case of the planets could we hope for any definite knowledge, and even that knowledge would be limited to geometry and dynamics. Comte would probably have decided that such a science as "astrophysics" was *a priori* impossible.

Yet within half a century of his death, almost the whole of astronomy *was* astrophysics, and very few professional astronomers had much interest in the planets. Comte's assertion had been utterly refuted by the invention of the spectroscope, which not only revealed the "chemical structure" of the heavenly bodies but has now told us far more about the distant stars than we know of our planetary neighbors.

Comte cannot be blamed for not imagining the spectroscope; *no one* could have imagined it, or the still more sophisticated instruments that have now joined it in the astronomer's armory. But he provides a warning that should always be borne in mind; even things that are undoubtedly impossible with existing or foreseeable techniques may prove to be easy as a result of new scientific breakthroughs. From their very nature, these breakthroughs can never be anticipated; but they have enabled us to bypass so many insuperable obstacles in the past that no picture of the future can hope to be valid if it ignores them.

Another celebrated failure of imagination was that persisted in by Lord Rutherford, who more than any other man laid bare the internal structure of the atom. Rutherford frequently made fun of those sensation mongers who predicted that we would one day be able to harness the energy locked up in matter. Yet only five years after his death in 1937, the first chain reaction was started in Chicago. What Rutherford, for all his wonderful insight, had failed to take into account was that a nuclear reaction might be discovered that would release more energy than that required to start it. To liberate the energy of matter, what was wanted was a nuclear "fire" analogous to chemical combustion, and the fission of uranium provided this. Once that was discovered, the harnessing of atomic energy was inevitable, though without the pressures of war it might well have taken the better part of a century.

. . .

Too much imagination is much rarer than too little; when it occurs, it usually involves its unfortunate possessor in frustration and failure—unless he is sensible enough merely to write about his ideas, and not to attempt their realization. In the first category we find all the science-fiction authors, historians of the future, creators of utopias—and the two Bacons, Roger and Francis.

Friar Roger (c. 1214–1292) imagined optical instruments and mechanically propelled boats and flying machines—devices far beyond the existing or even foreseeable technology of his time. It is hard to believe that these words were written in the thirteenth century:

Instruments may be made by which the largest ships, with only one man guiding them, will be carried with greater velocity than if they were full of sailors. Chariots may be constructed that will move with incredible rapidity without the help of animals. Instruments of flying may be formed in which a man, sitting at his ease and meditating in any subject, may beat the air with his artificial wings after the manner of birds . . . as also machines which will enable men to walk at the bottom of the seas. . . .

This passage is a triumph of imagination over hard fact. Everything in it has come true, yet at the time it was written it was more an act of faith than of logic. It is probable that all long-range prediction, if it is to be accurate, must be of this nature. The real future is not *logically* foreseeable.

A splendid example of a man whose imagination ran ahead of his age was the English mathematician Charles Babbage (1792–1871). As long ago as 1819, Babbage had worked out the principles underlying automatic computing machines. He realized that all mathematical calculations could be broken down into a series of step-by-step operations that could, in theory, be carried out by a machine. With the aid of a government grant which eventually totaled £17,000—a very substantial sum of money in the 1820's—he started to build his "analytical engine."

Though he devoted the rest of his life, and much of his private fortune, to the project, Babbage was unable to complete the machine. What defeated him was the fact that precision engineering of the standard he needed to build his cogs and gears simply did not exist at the time. By his efforts he helped to create the machine-tool industry—so that in the long run the government got back very much more than its £17,000—and today it would be a perfectly straightforward matter to complete Babbage's computer, which now stands as one of the most fascinating exhibits in the London Science Museum. In his own lifetime, however, Babbage was only able to demonstrate the operation of a relatively small portion of the complete machine. A dozen years after his death, his biographer wrote: "This extraordinary monument of theoretical genius accordingly remains, and doubtless will forever remain, a theoretical possibility."

There is not much left of that "doubtless" today. At this moment there are thousands of computers working on the principles that Babbage clearly outlined more than a century ago—but with a range and a speed of which he could never have dreamed. For what makes the case of Charles Babbage so interesting, and so pathetic, is that he was not one but *two* technological revolutions ahead of his time. Had the precision-tool industry existed in 1820, he could have built his "analytical engine" and it would

have worked, much faster than a human computer, but very slowly by the standards of today. For it would have been geared—literally—to the speed with which cogs and shafts and cams and ratchets can operate.

Automatic calculating machines could not come into their own until electronics made possible speeds of operation thousands and millions of times swifter than could be achieved with purely mechanical devices. This level of technology was reached in the 1940's, and Babbage was then promptly vindicated. His failure was not one of imagination: it lay in being born a hundred years too soon.

One can only prepare for the unpredictable by trying to keep an open and unprejudiced mind—a feat which is extremely difficult to achieve, even with the best will in the world. Indeed, a completely open mind would be an empty one, and freedom from all prejudices and preconceptions is an unattainable ideal. Yet there is one form of mental exercise that can provide good basic training for would-be prophets: Anyone who wishes to cope with the future should travel back in imagination a single lifetime—say to 1900—and ask himself just how much of today's technology would be, not merely incredible, but *incomprehensible* to the keenest scientific brains of that time.

1900 is a good round date to choose because it was just about then that all hell started to break loose in science. As James B. Conant has put it:

Somewhere about 1900 science took a *totally* unexpected turn. There had previously been several revolutionary theories and more than one epoch making discovery in the history of science, but what occurred between 1900 and, say, 1930 was something different; it was a failure of a general prediction about what might be confidently expected from experimentation.

P.W. Bridgman has put it even more strongly:

The physicist has passed through an intellectual crisis forced by the discovery of experimental facts of a sort which he had not previously envisaged, and which he would not even have thought possible.

The collapse of "classical" science actually began with Roentgen's discovery of X-rays in 1895; here was the first clear indication, in a form that everyone could appreciate, that the common-sense picture of the universe was not sensible after all. X-rays—the very name reflects the battlement of scientists and laymen alike—could travel through solid matter, like light through a sheet of glass. No one had ever imagined or predicted such a thing; that one would be able to peer into the interior of the human body—and thereby revolutionize medicine and surgery—was something that the most daring prophet had never suggested.

The discovery of X-rays was the first great breakthrough into the realms where no human mind had ever ventured before. Yet it gave scarcely a hint of still more astonishing developments to come—radioactivity, the internal structure of the atom, relativity, the quantum theory, the uncertainty principle. . . .

As a result of this, the inventions and technical devices of our modern world can be divided into two sharply defined classes. On the one hand there are those machines whose working would have been fully understood by any of the great thinkers of the past; on the other, there are those that would be utterly baffling to the finest minds of antiquity. And not merely of antiquity; there are devices now coming into use that might well have driven Edison or Marconi insane had they tried to fathom their operation.

Let me give some examples to emphasize this point. If you showed a modern diesel engine, an automobile, a steam turbine, or a helicopter to Benjamin Franklin, Galileo, Leonardo da Vinci, and Archimedes—a list spanning two thousand years of time—not one of them would have any difficulty in understanding how these machines worked. Leonardo, in fact, would recognize several from his notebooks. All four men would be astonished at the materials and the workmanship, which would have seemed magical in its precision, but once they had got over that surprise they would feel quite at home—as long as they did not delve too deeply into the auxiliary control and electrical systems.

But now suppose that they were confronted by a television set, an electronic computer, a nuclear reactor, a radar installation. Quite apart from the complexity of these devices, the individual elements of which they are composed would be incomprehensible to any man born before this century. Whatever his degree of education or intelligence, he would not possess the mental framework that could accommodate electron beams, transistors, atomic fission, wave guides and cathode-ray tubes.

The difficulty, let me repeat, is not one of complexity; some of the simplest modern devices would be the most difficult to explain. A particularly good example is given by the atomic bomb (at least, the early models). What could be simpler than banging two lumps of metal together? Yet how could one explain to Archimedes that the result could be more devastation than that produced by all the wars between the Trojans and the Greeks?

Suppose you went to any scientist up to the late nineteenth century and told him: "Here are two pieces of a substance called uranium 235. If you hold them apart, nothing will happen. But if you bring them together suddenly, you will liberate as much energy as you could obtain from burning ten thousand tons of coal." No matter how farsighted and imaginative he might be, your pre-twentieth century scientist would have said: "What utter nonsense! That's magic, not science. Such things can't happen in the real world." Around 1890, when the foundations of physics and thermodynamics had (it seemed)

been securely laid, he could have told you exactly why it was nonsense.

"Energy cannot be created out of nowhere," he might have said. "It has to come from chemical reactions, electrical batteries, coiled springs, compressed gas, spinning flywheels, or some other clearly defined source. All such sources are ruled out in this case—and even if they were not, the energy output you mention is absurd. Why, it is more than a *million* times that available from the most powerful chemical reaction!"

The fascinating thing about this particular example is that, even when the existence of atomic energy was fully appreciated—say right up to 1940—almost all scientists would still have laughed at the idea of liberating it by bringing pieces of metal together. Those who believed that the energy of the nucleus ever could be released almost certainly pictured complicated electrical devices—"atom smashers" and so forth—doing the job. (In the long run, this will probably be the case; it seems that we will need such machines to fuse hydrogen nuclei on the industrial scale. But once again, who knows?)

The wholly unexpected discovery of uranium fission in 1939 made possible such absurdly simple (in principle, if not in practice) devices as the atomic bomb and the nuclear chain reactor. No scientist could ever have predicted them; if he had, all his colleagues would have laughed at him.

It is highly instructive, and stimulating to the imagination, to make a list of the inventions and discoveries that have been anticipated—and those that have not. Here is my attempt to do so.

The Unexpected	The Expected
X-rays	automobiles
nuclear energy	flying machines
radio, TV	steam engines
electronics	submarines
photography	spaceships
sound recording	telephones
quantum mechanics	robots
relativity	death rays
transistors	transmutation
masers; lasers	artificial life
superconductors; superfluids	immortality
atomic clocks; Mössbauer effect	invisibility
determining composition of celestial bodies	levitation
dating the past (Carbon 14, etc.)	teleportation
detecting invisible planets	communication with dead
the ionosphere; Van Allen Belts	observing the past, the future telepathy

All the items on the left have already been achieved or discovered, and all have an element of the unexpected or the downright astonishing about them. To the best of my knowledge, not one was foreseen very much in advance of the moment of revelation.

On the right, however, are concepts that have been around for hundreds or thousands of years. Some have been achieved; others will be achieved; others may be impossible. But which?

The right-hand list is deliberately provocative; it includes sheer fantasy as well as serious scientific speculation. But the only way of discovering the limits of the possible is to venture a little way past them into the impossible. . . . This is exactly what I hope to do; yet I am very much afraid that from time to time I too will exhibit failure of imagination if not failure of nerve. For as I glance down the left-hand column I am aware of a few items which, only ten years ago, I would have thought were impossible. . . .

QUESTIONS

1. Why have scientists so often been wrong in their prophecies about the future? Given the limitations imposed on them by their social environments, could "nerve" and "imagination" really have helped them be more accurate?

2. Which, if any, of the expected but unachieved concepts on Clark's list do you think will always be impossible? Can you be sure?

3. What will your grandchildren's world be like?

JAMES TRAUB

Futurology: The Rise of
the Predicting Profession

Although there are still many hazards in social prophecy, attempts to predict the future have, in recent years, taken a more organized and systematic form. Indeed, a burgeoning new science, futurology, focuses on this very task.

Futurology relies heavily on the insights of sociology, and many futurologists are sociologists by training. This should come as no surprise, for sociology, since its foundation, has always been concerned with two fundamental problems—social order (why and how societies hold together) and social change (why and how societies alter over time). Thus far, sociologists understand a good deal more about social order than about social change, and it seems that a full understanding of the latter requires a complete grasp of the former. As James Traub's article shows, futurology remains a highly inexact science, based largely on the uncertain projection of current trends into the future.

Futurologists frequently offer widely divergent views of the future, but all share a common assumption: if the future is to offer humanity a better life than the past, we must know where we are headed so that we can, if necessary, shape the world that is to come.

Speculation over the future has always been a popular pastime; most everyone, after all, hazards an occasional prediction over his own destiny. But until recently, forecasting on a grander scale was left to poets and prophets, who were supposed to enjoy special powers of insight. No longer. Today, when businessmen and bureaucrats and public organizations feel in need of some image of the time to come, they turn to a whole new species of intellectual: the professional futurologist. Unlike the old-fashioned seer, this new breed of thinker considers himself a rigorous analyst, studying the laws that govern social, political, and economic trends and their effect upon one another. And unlike many pioneers in a new profession, futurologists have enjoyed instant success: Twenty-five years ago futures studies had no organized existence; today more than 200 research institutes turn out futures studies, with a number of them pulling in $2 million or more from government and corporate contracts.

Despite this remarkable surge of popularity, futurology has come in for some withering criticism, especially within the intellectual community. Economist Lester Thurow calls the study "the intellectual's version of going to the palm reader," pointing out that anxiety over the present naturally leads to a preoccupation with the future. Robert Heilbroner, a social thinker as well as an economist, says, "There's an awful lot of chic in this thing," and adds that "people take long-range forecasting much too seriously." Indeed, a close inspection of forecasts prepared more than five years ago shows a pretty dismal record of accuracy; further, the predictions now being churned out by a myriad of think tanks together produce, not a coherent view of the future, but a bewildering and contradictory cluster of images.

Still, futurology has come a long way from the Book of Revelation or even from H. G. Wells. In the prescientific era, no distinction was made between "the future" and "the ultimate state." The future announced by biblical prophets provided an image of God's final purpose for the world, and not some evolutionary process. Even the more concrete futures of Aldous Huxley and Jules Verne represented visions of an inevitable tide of history, rational rather than theological.

The advent of professional futurology coincided with

the acceptance of the idea that history has no ironclad laws and no ruling deity, that the future belongs to man. It also coincided with a new source of anxiety about the future—the Cold War. The nation's first major think tank, the Rand Corporation, was established in 1946 in Santa Monica, California, by the Air Force and Douglas Aircraft. Its mission was to do a better job dreaming up military technology than the Russians. But its engineers and physicists started getting restless, partially owing to Rand's narrow scope; and in 1961 one of the analysts, Herman Kahn, left to form the Hudson Institute in New York. Two more Rand analysts, Olaf Helmer and Theodore Gordon, left in 1966 to form the Institute of the Future. Gordon then left to set up the Futures Group, in Connecticut, in 1971. By that time, futurist think tanks had sprung up across the country, catering to a growing legion of large corporations and government agencies.

Nothing that is human is alien to the futurologist; he will study the future of anything. Energy studies have been the think-tank meal ticket of the last half-decade and promise to keep futurists in business a long time. Such studies aren't cheap: The Social Policy Research Center, a branch of SRI International, the gigantic West Coast think tank, charged the Department of Energy (DOE) $275,000 for a study of the feasibility of solar power. Many think tanks issue 10-year forecasts on the world economy and the geopolitical situation. Other subjects abound: Hudson recently finished a study of the future of Arizona for a number of business firms. Forecasting International, in Washington, is hard at work on a study of the vulnerability of off-shore installations (for example, drilling operations) to terrorist attack. A copy of *World Nitrogen Supply and Demand* is available from Predicasts, of Cleveland, for $625. Nothing is too minute for the futurologist's inspection; included in a 10-year forecast produced by the Institute of the Future were the assertions that "an increasing proportion of males may not wear underpants because trousers can be washed easily and often," and "the use of dental floss may increase from 15 percent to 25 percent for even low-income adults."

Such studies would never have been written without the sponsorship of corporate and governmental clients. For businesses such as utilities that must formulate long-range plans, futurologists provide immediately applicable information—i.e., the likely level of electrical demand in 20 or 30 or 50 years—to be compared to figures compiled within the company. But most corporations have something less concrete in mind when they hire a futurist think tank. Most of the executives who deal with futurologists admit that their firms have never based a specific decision on a long-range prediction. They go to think tanks, instead, for broad contexts and a sense of larger trends— to find out, for example, where their industry will fit into a changing economy. "We use long-term forecasting as a starting point for all strategic planning," says Ian Wilson of General Electric, describing the company's new "interactive multilevel planning system." Wilson concedes the inaccuracy of much long-range forecasting but feels that even inaccurate predictions "force everyone to spell out their assumptions about the future." And if you're GE or Exxon, you can afford to spend $20,000 a year to have your assumptions spelled out.

Since most futurologists are willing to churn out a report on anything a client wants to know, the mechanics of one research group tends to resemble those of another. There are, however, discernible differences of character. Some groups prefer to deal with specific problems and readily quantifiable subjects, grinding out the sort of unspectacular analysis generally associated with the social sciences. Others try to provide the Big Picture: the shape of world history, shifts in social order and values, the rise of new consciousness. And finally, others, in the most distant precincts of futurology, are downright metaphysical. They have trouble getting clients.

In this latter category comes the New York Center for World Games Studies, a three-man group now hard at work on the Star Tube, a 200-foot tunnel that would lean against the New Mexican mesa. The group plans to equip the tunnel with maps showing the position of the earth and stars during the last 25,000 years; politicians and plain folk could walk through and experience "the earth as an eco-system," according to founder and president Mico Delianove. As soon as benefactors pony up $300,000 to $1.5 million, says Delianove, the Star Tube will go from the drawing board to the desert. The center's checkered past makes this philanthropy look unlikely. Their previous project, a solar refrigerator that would solve the world food problem, also looked great on paper, but Delianove notes that "we're still working out some bugs that we can't quite put our finger on."

In contrast, the Futures Group, despite its heady name and $2 million annual revenues, is a fairly modest bunch as futurologists go. Its tidy headquarters and the well-groomed suburb of Hartford in which it is located make for a highly unfuturific setting. Most of its researchers have rather scanty academic backgrounds—Jan Cohen, the director of one of the major research projects, began as a secretary. And on every tongue is the watchword of caution: "Most forecasting fails to take a reasonable level of uncertainty into account," says resident population expert John Stover.

Much of the Futures Group's revenue comes from studies of specific problems for individual clients: energy consumption for DOE and a number of utilities; female participation in the labor force for the U.S. Labor Department; and an ongoing project on Third World population and its economic consequences for the Agency for International Development. Some of these studies don't even involve predictions. A "strategic backdrop analysis" on energy consumption for DOE offers no conjectures about future events—"Please don't say we're making forecasts, we're just setting planning targets," says vice-president Lillian Deitch. Instead, it examines the foreseeable consequences of certain energy choices—the effect of an acceleration in coal production, for example, on mining capacity and rolling stock. The study sets no goals; that's DOE's job.

The Futures Group also performs a series of so-called Prospects studies, which monitor markets and offer 10-year predictions about their behavior for groups of regular subscribers. These programs now cover the pharmaceutical, hospital-goods, and consumer-products markets. Clients are connected to a vast body of information—more than 100 variables are monitored in each case—by a computer system called Futurscan. Although all markets tend to be volatile, and thus difficult to predict, the projects involve painstaking information-gathering; and many clients, especially the smaller ones, use the service as much for the raw data as for the projections of 1990 coronary-vasodilator sales.

While the Futures Group is considered relatively circumspect and narrow in focus, the Hudson Institute, and its founder and demiurge, Herman Kahn, are nothing of the sort. Cloistered in Croton-on-Hudson, a bucolic, upper-class suburb north of New York, the home office of the institute sits on a 22-acre compound cleared from the surrounding woods and is housed in seven quaint Tudor buildings, one of which formerly served as a home for the insane. It is not a place to entertain gloomy meditations; and Herman-on-Hudson, as it is also called, is famed for its optimism as well as for the vast scope of its ruminations.

Despite its 30 full-time researchers and four offices on three continents, the Hudson Institute is dominated by the brilliant, audacious, and thoroughly imposing Herman Kahn. Kahn first gained notoriety from the morbid gusto with which he addressed such subjects as "The Utility of Protecting Gold From Nuclear Attack" and "Chess as a Model for Thermonuclear War," and from his coinage of such terms as "mega-deaths." With Armageddon falling out of fashion, Kahn shifted his sights in the mid-Sixties to the world political and economic order, abandoning his fascination with doom for an equally iconoclastic credo of global optimism. Now critics attack him for opportunism. Kahn's many opponents note that he seems to have glowing news to report to anyone willing to hire him. A well-known economist claims that Kahn will "sell or say anything for a dollar."

Such charges are probably unfair; Kahn will say anything for an *argument*. A fierce controversialist, the immense, bearded polymath is fond of launching an outrageous proposition with a pudgy forearm sawing the air and then defending it to the hilt. "The biggest single problem in our society is basically maintenance," he asserts, referring to mechanical incompetence. Or, "OPEC has no control over market prices; it's not even a cartel." Kahn still enjoys thinking the unthinkable and defends his juggling of thermonuclear strategies in his usual tones: "To be in this business without any thought at all [about tactics] is so obscene that you shouldn't be a member of the human race anymore."

Even Kahn's critics grant that he is overwhelming. Equally at home in the minutiae of mineral stocks and the vast sweep of history, he leaps across great intellectual territories, pausing only long enough to remark, "You first and foremost have got to have a certain amount of modesty." As he grows excited, his already rapid speech accelerates to a supersonic velocity, and he begins warming up one sentence in the middle of its predecessor. There's no arguing with Herman Kahn.

Most of Kahn's books begin with a set piece on "The Multifold Trend in World History," a set of 14 evolving characteristics of the last half-millennium. This concern with metahistory also permeates Hudson's projects. The Corporate Environment Program, which Kahn built up through personal visits to corporate grandees, provides long-range and short-range monitoring of world trends for 40 multinational companies. The goal of the program, in the words of director George Whitman, is to "present a world view for corporations with emphasis on certain contemporary issues." Among the subjects discussed in the program have been, "The New Atlantic Trade Context," "The End of the Single-Family Housing Boom (for Now)," and—presented by Kahn himself—"A New Kind of Class Struggle in the United States?"

Hudson also conducts a wide range of individual studies for government agencies and groups of companies. Kahn's influence is apparent here, too, especially in the institute's series of reports on the future of countries and regions—Japan, Korea, Brazil, South Africa, Arizona, Westchester County in New York—that have dedicated themselves to the sort of rapid economic growth that Kahn cherishes. In addition, the institute turns out a staggering load of articles and books—52 of the latter so far—that gain it a far wider audience than most other think tanks enjoy.

Despite revenues about equal to those of the Futures Group and an enthusiastic following of corporate moguls, Hudson's and Kahn's star has been falling of late. Leading futurologists admit to being embarrassed by Kahn's extravagant claims; Norman Nisenoff, an analyst for Forecasting International, describes Kahn as "grossly out of synchrony with everything that is real." Although the Corporate Environment Program's membership is fairly stable and most of the subscribers remain fascinated with the provocative ideas that it provides, some members are unimpressed. "Hudson's scenarios seem plausible enough, but what are we supposed to do with them?" asks

Neil Holden, chief economist at Union Carbide. Holden admits that he would just as soon see his company leave the program for less speculative shores.

Like any claimants of new intellectual territory, futurologists have devoted a great deal of attention to the question of methodology. How is one to think about something that does not yet exist? Unlike clairvoyants, futurists claim no special powers of insight into human destiny; all they know, like the rest of us, is the present and the past. All they can do, then, is to study the way trends progress and interact, and speculate about events that may change the course of those trends. This is not essentially different from the way meteorologists think about the weather or the way any of us might think about making an investment.

Futurologists have managed to give new names to this standard form of deduction. The Futures Group, for example, has coined the term "Trend Impact Analysis" to refer to their own methodology. In their report on the labor-force participation rate of women, commissioned by the U.S. Labor Department, the group listed nine events that could affect the present growth rate of participation. These include a birth-rate increase, a divorce-rate decrease, a recession, the passage and enforcement of a federal full-employment law. Each event was assigned a probability of occurrence by 1982 and by 1990, and a "maximum impact" (how much the possible event would change the trend), as well as a figure for the number of years needed before that impact would be reached. How does the Futures Group decide that day-care centers have a 35 percent chance of becoming widely available by 1990, and that such a change could add 2 percent to the female work force? "It ultimately has to come down to a question of judgment," says Lillian Deitch.

Because the accuracy of such judgments, no matter how well informed by research and cogitation, is a highly debatable matter, futurologists have generally moved away from predictions in favor of "alternative futures." This method avoids the embarrassment of being proved wrong, since the analyst does not offer conjectures about outcomes but rather draws up a group of "scenarios," or possible images of the future, no one of them necessarily more probable than another. Although no policy-maker would base a decision on 10 evenly weighted scenarios, he would get a sense of the variety of possibilities, as well as of the interconnectedness of apparently disparate events.

The man most responsible for the popularity of the scenario—almost every futurist think tank now uses it liberally—is Herman Kahn. In his nuclear-disaster days, Kahn had speculated over the likely train of consequences of one hostile action or another; he imported this method of thinking into his political and economic thinking. In On Alternative Futures, a book-length study of world political and military order written for aerospace contractor Martin Marietta in 1965, Kahn and collaborators Edmund Stillman and William Pfaff explored 15 scenarios—visions of a world dominated by, variously, Russian aggressiveness, a new European confederation, or an unexpected new power.

But the scenario has its problems. It may completely miss the target with its intellectual grapeshot. None of the 15 scenarios in On Alternative Futures considers the eventuality of a new power center in the Middle East, and none deals with the possibility of a conflict over dwindling resources, perhaps the most plausible inducement to great-power warfare today. Nevertheless, with its high entertainment value and low risk, the scenario is almost sure to remain in general circulation.

Virtually the only subject that a futurologist will not talk about readily is his batting average. Nobody pays a think tank to tote up its past performance, and trepidation has prevented almost all the groups from doing so on their own. Most of them have done a competent job of discussing the consequences of basic modern trends: the advent of post-industrial society, the continuing alienation from large institutions, accelerated growth in the Third World, and the like. But ask them to recall a specific long-range forecast that correctly foresaw a change in trend, and futurologists get evasive. They not only have forecast all sorts of things that have yet to come to pass, but have missed, pretty much to a man, the major upheavals that have largely shaped the past decade. Economist Lester Thurow sums up the failure of forecasting: "These people would only be useful if they could tell us about change. But did any of them predict the war in Vietnam, the sudden drop in the growth rate of the population, the advent of structural inflation, or the intensity of the entrance of women into the labor force?"

Nor did the most important event of the 1970s, the quadrupling of oil prices in 1973, come in for much more than feeble adumbration. In their 1972 book on the Seventies and Eighties, Things to Come, Kahn and B. Bruce-Briggs never even mention resource shortages, or energy, and pause only briefly in their discussion of "The Chronic Confrontations" to observe that "the Third World has little economic strength" and "can contribute little to a world struggle." A study produced by the Institute of the Future in September 1973 did expect an energy crisis "early rather than late," but also had China flatly refusing to deal with multinational corporations, to secure long-term foreign loans, or to open significant trade relations with the United States; Iran representing "an island of stability in a Third World sea of change"; Egypt remaining unflinchingly hostile to the West; and so on.

Though demographic trends are widely considered the surest bets in the forecasting trade, neither experts nor futurists expected the sudden exhaustion of the baby boom in the mid-Sixties. American population in the year

2000 was generally projected at more than 300 million; now, even assuming a far greater number of immigrants than used to be expected, the figure is put at roughly 260 million. Nor was anyone prepared for the sudden entry of women into the labor force and its radical impact on American employment patterns. Herman Kahn hazarded a typical guess, in 1965, that the female labor participation rate would reach 42 percent by the year 2000; it is already over 50 percent.

Futurology's shoddy record on the economy should come as no surprise, since even short-term forecasting hasn't proved much more accurate than throwing dice. Futures studies in the 1960s had inflation tip-toeing up to 4.5 percent if things got really grim, but otherwise remaining at more moderate levels. General Electric's 1967 report on "Our Changing Business Environment," drawn up by widely respected futurist Ian Wilson, constitutes something of a text of such errors: Explosive world economic growth, it says, will become permanent; markets and economies generally will be far more stable; American unemployment rates will oscillate between 3 and 4.5 percent; black youths will experience "better than 50 percent gains" in employment.

The fact that futurologists swing at thin air so often should not generally be blamed on poor research or personal blindness so much as the intractability of the subject matter. We simply do not know the rules that govern the occurrence of accidents in economic, political, or social life; we do not know if there *are* rules. This failure would have been unimportant several centuries ago, when technology and social order could be trusted to stay moored in place over long periods of time. But now, when we live in a time of unparalleled dynamism, we realize how superficially we understand the laws of change. "The more important the study of the future becomes, the harder it becomes," says Roy Amara, head of the Institute of the Future.

But futurologists have not been daunted by this regrettable state of ignorance; instead, they have conducted a search for some sort of intellectual Holy Grail. Jay Forester, the computer wizard who designed the world model used in the Club of Rome's momentous *Limits of Growth* study, has seized on the Kondratieff Cycle, a supposed 50-year pattern of expansion and depression, to explain the world economy. The cycle, says Forester, predicts a depression for the mid-1980s. W. W. Rostow, on the other hand, argues that the cycle predicts *good* times for the 1980s. Dr. Gary Fromm, a taciturn, even-keeled economist at SRI International, rejects the Kondratieff Cycle entirely, but has begun work on the catastrophe theory, a mathematical theory that, when imported into the social sciences, is supposed to predict discontinuities in any system. Roy Amara is searching for a "unified field theory," an all-encompassing explanation for human events equivalent to the laws that Einstein hoped would explain physical events. Amara reports no luck so far.

The future of futurology looks just about as confusing as its past. It would be unreasonable to expect all scholars to agree on a single subject, of course, but the wild disparity in the futurologists' expectations gives the impression that any point of view can be justified. Some scribes, for example, have seen world population ultimately rising to 20 billion; Hudson guesses 10 billion; and Lester Brown, head of the environmentalist Worldwatch Institute, expects growth to stop before 6 billion. Predictions about oil prices are equally disparate: An official at the Department of Energy concerned about the price of oil 10 years hence could, depending on what result he wanted to hear, consult Norman Nisenoff at Forecasting International to find that the price of oil will triple in that period; consult the experts adverted to in a recent *Business Week* foray into futurology and discover that the price will rise "2 to 4 percent a year," or roughly 40 percent during the next decade; or hire Herman Kahn to learn that the real price of oil will decline. Futurologists do agree that the next 10 to 20 years will be even more volatile than the preceding decades: Kahn calls the upcoming period "L'Epoque de Malaise"; Willis Harman, head of the Social Policy Research Center, refers to it as "the slough of despond," taking a leaf from *Pilgrim's Progress*. Futurists don't agree, however, on our outlook for the more distant future; some expect things to start looking really bad at the turn of the century, while others believe that at that time we'll pull out of our funk.

The partisans of doom have been in the ascendant in the 1970s, a highly un-American state of affairs that speaks eloquently of the death of the idea of progress, still looked upon as the American civic religion. The publication of *The Limits of Growth*, with its shocking conclusion that the industrial dream would suffer "overshoot and collapse" before the end of the next century, and probably a good deal earlier, made cataclysm fashionable. Lester Brown, who calls his Worldwatch Institute an "early warning system" for potential environmental crises, sees that "our major problems will get much worse before they get better." Edward Cornish, a journalist who has been bitten by the futurology bug and now edits *The Futurist* magazine, offers "a 50-50 chance that our civilization in its present high industrial form will no longer be around in 50 years." One could go on—but catastrophe becomes numbing after a while.

Facing down these nattering nabobs of negativism is the dauntless Herman Kahn. Kahn believes that "all of our technological problems can be solved in 25 years" by a commitment to growth and to the capacities of technology not yet perfected or invented. Such apparently severe problems as food shortages have been grossly exaggerated, he claims, and can be expected to evaporate before the advance of technology. After the confusion and divisiveness of the "Epoque de Malaise," Kahn expects things to get better and better until the year 2175 sees a world in which 10 billion people produce $20,000 (in present currency values) per capita. The dynamism of the industrial period will be behind us, and we will float on a sea of affluence.

Kahn has several unlikely comrades-in-utopia. Willis Harman, a fierce enemy of Kahn's high-tech world and an apparently profound pessimist who has written that "the industrialized world may be approaching its own rock-bottom phase," foresees a soft-technology, naturalistic version of Kahn's El Dorado. Harman sees the crisis of the next 25 years leading to an equally grave crisis of values. Out of this crucible will emerge "the perennial philosophy" of self-realization through the community and the cosmos; the new spirit will be participatory, ecological, frugal, and spiritual—what Kahn sneers at as "Consciousness III," the transcendent state described in Charles Reich's *The Greening of America*. Harman feels that the change is already upon us, citing a survey indicating that "roughly half the people in the United States have had their lives changed by a mystical experience."

Despite its dismal track record on the past, and the disorder with which it confronts the future, futurology cannot simply be dismissed. No one would argue that planning is bad in and of itself; and one can no more plan an economy or a city without adopting some view of the future than one can organize a trip without considering what the weather is likely to be. Bertrand de Jouvenel, the philosophical patriarch of futurology, has written that the only way out of the trap of crisis-management, to which governments are so prone, "lies in acquainting ourselves with emerging situations while they can still be molded. . . . In other words, without forecasting there is effectively no freedom of decision."

Perhaps what is needed, rather than the admittedly attractive option of throwing out the baby with the bathwater, is a more humble form of futurology, one that would approach predictions with greater trepidation and make a more concerted effort to understand the rules that govern individual areas before venturing out onto the tortured web of interdisciplinary study. A futurology of this sort might be short on dental-floss use; but it might help get us through the megacrisis waiting right around the corner.

Of course, if we agreed with the Greeks that "fate is too strong for thee and for the gods," then futurology would be a moot point; yet we recognize that the decisions we make today—decisions about the deployment of technology or of capital resources—will shape the future, though whether in the image of Herman Kahn or Willis Harman or Lester Brown remains to be seen. Futurologists cannot provide answers to the ultimate question of what the future *ought* to look like; this decision society itself must make. Until that moral consensus is reached, however, futurology will remain as divided and contentious as it is today.

QUESTIONS

1. Is futurology worthless?

2. Discuss the following assertion: If we knew exactly what the future was to be, we would know how to change it; and if it could be changed, we would not know exactly what it would be.

3. List some current trends in American society that seem important to you. Then see to what extent you and others can agree on what the outcome of these trends will be by the end of the century.

LLOYD J. DUMAS

Human Fallibility and Weapons

Ever since the first atomic bomb was used at Hiroshima in 1945, the world has lived in the shadow of a potential holocaust of almost unimaginable proportions. Today, the United States and the Soviet Union each have thousands of missiles equipped with nuclear warheads aimed at each other's strategic centers, which in many cases include densely populated areas. If nuclear war broke out, at least 30 million Americans would be killed within the first hour or so of the preliminary exchange of missiles, and many millions more would be blinded, burned, horribly maimed, or left to suffer the effects of exposure to high levels of radiation.

In such a war there would be no victors; the societies involved would face a complete breakdown of their social and economic structures, and recovery, if it came at all, might take decades. Indeed, the assumption behind the nuclear arms race is that no rational leadership in any country would deliberately embark on the self-destructive course of launching such a war and that, therefore, the nuclear threat provides some guarantee of peace.

Even if this assumption is correct, however, the possibility remains that a nuclear war could be started accidentally. As Lloyd Dumas points out in this article, the machines of war and the human beings who control them are fallible; any malfunction, such as computer error or human psychosis, could send the world tottering toward nuclear destruction. And as nuclear weapons proliferate over the next two decades to other nations—including some that are deeply hostile to one another, such as India and Pakistan—the situation can grow only more perilous.

Everything will work the way it is supposed to work.

Nothing will happen until it is supposed to happen.

Virtually all of the public—and much of the private—discussion of the nuclear arms race proceeds under these implicit assumptions. Yet they have no basis in fact: No systems designed, produced, deployed or activated by human beings can ever achieve perfection.

The fallibility inherent in human activity is generally no more than a nuisance. But where weapons of mass destruction are involved, the consequences can be catastrophic. As the military systems in which these weapons are imbedded have become more complex, geographically dispersed and technologically sophisticated, there is increased probability that they will eventually fail.

Given this simple technological fact, two things are clear: First, even small failures involving weapons of mass destruction are an extremely serious matter. Second, the problem of preventing disaster is greatly complicated by the number and variety of these weapons dispersed throughout the world.

> Seemingly inexplicable, inconsistent and unpredictable human 'goofs' account for 50 to 70 percent of all failures of major weapons and space vehicles. That puts human errors . . . ahead of mechanical, electrical and structural failures . . . as a source of system troubles.
>
> The consequences range from minor delays to major disasters. . . . [For example,] the loss of the submarine Thresher with its entire crew [was due to] improper installation of a relief valve . . . of the propulsion subsystem.

The problem of malfunction in military systems is, of course, multifaceted. But, as the quotation points up, human reliability is a significant factor. Rather than attempting to deal with this one factor as a whole, which would include design and manufacture, I shall focus on the human component in the control and operation of military systems.

Alcoholism, drug addiction, mental illness and other related problems are pervasive in our society. It is not possible to avoid them in the military.

A 1972 study on drug use in the military, commissioned by the Department of Defense, divided drugs into marijuana, other psychedelics, stimulants, depressants, and narcotics. The study then projected that *daily* drug use for each of the armed services was not less than 0.4 percent for any category, and in some was as high as 8 percent.[2] According to an article in the *Air Force Magazine*, however, there may be reason for some skepticism:

> The stories that get into the public prints represent only the top of the iceberg . . . neither the Air Force nor the other services, nor, for that matter, the civilian authorities, are in any position to produce definitive figures on drug abuse in their jurisdiction. What is known is that the use of drugs of all kinds has for the past several years been dramatically on the upswing.[3]

On July 10, 1978, ABC-TV aired a documentary concerning drug use in the "elite Berlin Brigade" of the U.S. Army in Europe, the "backbone" of roughly 6,000 troops stationed in this politically sensitive military outpost. When asked about the drug problem in the Brigade, General Walter Adams, the commanding officer, replied: "Well, I recognize there is a drug problem in the Berlin Brigade. I do not believe that it is a very serious one . . . in the month of April we tested 751 soldiers. . . . 2.3 percent . . . came up using hard drugs. In May we had about 587 and I believe that came up with about 2.0 percent."[4] But Mike D'Arcy, a drug counsellor for the Berlin Brigade with three years' experience and hence personal knowledge of the problem, came up with different conclusions when interviewed by reporter Geraldo Rivera:

> *Rivera:* The official statistics on the urinalysis test conducted by the command of the Berlin Brigade indicates that only 2 percent of the brigade is abusing heroin. Do you think that statistic is accurate?
> *D'Arcy:* No. I do not.
> *Rivera:* What would you estimate the true statistic to be?
> *D'Arcy:* I would estimate the true statistic to be roughly 65 percent recreational abuse of heroin, hard drugs: 85 percent soft drugs, considered [to be] hashish, mad dog, soft drugs that are not addictive. Hard core heroin abuse I would estimate between 7–10 percent.[5]

Rivera further reports that General George Blanchard, senior field commander in Europe, "now estimates that 8 percent of all GIs stationed in Europe are using hard drugs." When applied overall to active U.S. armed forces, even the low numbers imply not fewer than 8,400—and perhaps as many as 167,000—U.S. military personnel are daily users of one or more of the drugs specified in the 1972 report. And between 42,000 and 167,000 are hard drug abusers, although not necessarily on a daily basis.[6]

To focus the issue more sharply, we must move from armed forces personnel as a whole to those individuals having direct access to nuclear weapons, direct responsibilities in the nuclear release process, or both. The Department of Defense operates a Personnel Reliability Program that, in the words of Assistant Secretary of Defense for Atomic Energy D.R. Cotter, "is designed to prevent assignment of unreliable or potentially unreliable persons to nuclear duties through a screening process, *and then to remove from nuclear duties*, those persons whose reliability, trustworthiness, and dependability become inconsistent with the standards" (emphasis added). He further points out, quite correctly, that "No initial screening process can guarantee future behavior. . . ."[7]

Data provided by Cotter indicate that a total of 119,541 service personnel were subject to the program in 1975 and 115,767 in 1976, implying that 5 or 6 percent of all U.S. armed forces personnel have such critical nuclear access or control positions. In response to Congressional inquiry, the Department of Defense has reported that under the Personnel Reliability Program, roughly 5,000 military personnel were removed from the nuclear weapons program annually from 1975 to 1977. That is, they were disqualified subsequent to their certification, not before entering the program.

Periodically, specific stories emerge about cases of military personnel with mental or drug-abuse problems who are involved with nuclear weapons. For example, in August 1969, an Air Force major was suspended after having allowed three men, described as having "dangerous psychiatric problems," to continue to guard nuclear weapons at a base near San Francisco. One of the guards was accused of going berserk with a loaded carbine while at the base. His lawyer said that the man had pleaded not to be assigned to a job in which he would handle explosives or weapons. Yet he was frequently on duty as senior officer of a two-man team guarding nuclear missiles. The major testified that although he had received unfavorable psychiatric reports on the three guards, he had not removed them because he was short of staff and without them, "people from Haight-Ashbury" would try to get the weapons.[8]

Later that same year, ten army personnel manning nuclear-capable missile batteries near Miami were arrested for possession or sale of LSD.[9] In March 1971, three men working with U.S. nuclear war plans, all with top security clearance, were arrested for possession of marijuana and LSD. The three airmen had been assigned to the computer section in which the war plans for all U.S. nuclear armed forces are maintained, at the top secret underground Strategic Air Command base near Omaha, Nebraska.[10]

In late 1974, the *Milwaukee Journal* published an interview with an Army code specialist, Donald Meyer, who stated that he had smoked hashish "two or three times every four hours nearly every day for 29 months" while stationed at a U.S. Army nuclear missile base in Germany in the early 1970s. According to the report:

> Meyer said he was under the influence of the drug sometimes when he worked with secret material and that *missile soldiers sometimes were high when they attached nuclear warheads to the missiles. So were soldiers, 'who connected the two pieces up' to make the missile operational* [emphasis added].[11]

Drug abuse, mental illness and aberrant behavior are thus observed, year after year, in thousands of U.S. military personnel with access to or control over weapons of mass destruction. One can only speculate on the extent of such problems in the Soviet military, but there is no reason to believe that it is significantly less.

Stress, boredom and isolation are inherent in the modern military scene, particularly in the nuclear forces. Spending endless hours interacting with electronic control consoles, repeating essentially the same lengthy and detailed routines—this is the stuff of life in the strategic forces.

The deleterious effects of monotony on performance are by now well established. During World War II, N.H. Mackworth of England was commissioned by the Royal Air Force to find out why radar operators on anti-submarine patrol sometimes let U-boats escape detection. He set up laboratory experiments in which detection efficiency was shown to decay considerably in less than an hour of screen watching. In 1957, Woodburn Heron, in a *Scientific American* article aptly titled "The Pathology of Boredom," described laboratory research funded by the Canadian Defense Research Board. For several days, subjects were deprived, not of sensory stimulation, but of patterned stimuli. For example, they saw light and heard sounds, but it was diffuse light and constant, droning sound. It was found that some subjects had great difficulty concentrating; many experienced emotional oscillations and loss of perspective; and many had both aural and visual hallucinations. The subjects appeared eager for stimulation during the experiments, and would whistle, sing or talk to themselves.

These were rather extreme, highly artificial laboratory situations. Yet given the wide variability in human sensitivities, and the interaction of boring work situations with the whole complex of other physical and emotional factors that impinge differentially on individuals, it is difficult to predict the thresholds of monotony that will trigger some of these experiences in "real life."

Most military activity, of course, is not performed in situations of individual isolation, but in groups. Particularly in the strategic nuclear forces, however, these groups are often isolated from society for varying periods of time. It is therefore relevant to ask how individuals in socially isolated groups are affected in terms of job performance, stress and interpersonal relationships within the group.

Beginning in the mid-1960s, social psychologist Irwin Altman of the Naval Medical Research Institute and the University of Utah has published a series of papers reporting on laboratory research into these questions, conducted mainly on Navy personnel. Some of his basic conclusions are:

1. While mild degrees of stress are associated with enhanced performance, increased stress produces leveling off or reduced effectiveness.[12]
2. Group social isolation is stress inducing.[13]
3. Being on long missions with access to separate compartments for privacy and without outside contact tends to be highly stressful.[14]
4. Men in socially isolated groups show more "territorial behavior" and increased social withdrawal.[15]

Taken as a whole, these findings indicate a tendency to reduced human reliability in job performance and in increased potential for psychologically dangerous "brooding" or personal withdrawal.

Moving from the carefully controlled milieu of the laboratory into the reality of operating nuclear strategic forces, some insight into these problems can be gained from the 1971 report of a former Air Force deputy missile combat crew commander, Ted Wye, on life in the hardened silos of the U.S. land based missile force.

> There is no entertainment to pass the time and relieve monotony. Except for an occasional alarm, a capsule tour consists of hours of quietude . . . Under near maddening conditions of isolation, boredom and frustration missile crews develop a different perspective than superiors. . . . The idle time on a missile officer's hands must be similar to a prisoner's life in solitary confinement . . . only . . . there are two of you. A crew member tries not to think about his ultimate responsibility, which could lead to the killing of millions of people. . . . He is not supposed to have a conscience. . . . He learns to contrast his personal feelings and the role he is expected to play unquestioningly and automatically. The hypocrisy of this game he's playing creates a feeling of disinvolvement. He tends to see his personal life and official life as totally separate; the launch officer becomes schizoid.[16]

Even healthy human beings who are not subjected to extraordinary stress or grinding boredom and isolation may contribute to the human reliability problem in the military because of the control difficulties inherent in all bureaucracies of size. In particular, there is a serious problem of transmission of valid information to the upper echelons, especially where such information points out errors, made either by subordinates or by top-level decision-makers.

Subordinates may report only information supporting their own view. They tend to avoid senior officers who might report facts they might want suppressed, even to the point of not reporting potential dangers.[17] Personal beliefs, rigid world views and concepts of loyalty also have been shown to inhibit the generation and communication of factual information to superiors.[18]

The result may be an accumulation of misinformation at the top that can lead, at best, to a false concept of reality and at worst to a loss of control—an extraordinarily dangerous situation where weapons of mass destruction are concerned. These issues are given additional reality by former missileman Ted Wye's report that in a silo-based strategic nuclear missile force, "Crew members dare not tell higher command that the regulations are flouted. Noncommunication with higher command is endemic in the missile field, with the result a gap between regulations and what is really done in the capsule."[19]

Not only do these informational difficulties exist, but they tend to get worse, not better, as the decisions involved become more important.[20] And the organizational barriers to communication create problems in the downward as well as the upward flow of directives.

There are various ways in which the human reliability problem interacts with the enormous stockpile of weapons of mass destruction in order to produce potentially dangerous or disastrous situations. There have been a number of serious accidents involving both nuclear weapons and major nuclear weapons carriers. More than 60 have been made public since 1950.

Clearly, human failure in the transport or handling of weapons or in the operation of a nuclear weapons carrier could, and most likely has, produced such an accident. And while there have been no publicly reported accidents involving the explosion of a nuclear weapon, there have been incidents in which the conventional material that surrounds the nuclear material has been detonated resulting in the scattering of some of the plutonium in the weapon.

Human failure could also play a major role in precipitating an accidental nuclear exchange. Aside from the Strangelovian scenario of a war triggered by a mentally unbalanced, high-ranking military officer, which certainly cannot be dismissed, there are other possibilities. False warnings of a major nuclear attack, false alerts, or even improperly authorized (but properly coded) messages ordering the launching of nuclear weapons could accidentally generate a holocaust, or at least provide the preconditions. Would all the safeguards so painstakingly designed into the military system prevent any such communications?

"A hoax message was transmitted on an intradistrict teletype net to 22 units of the Eighth Coast Guard District on the morning of February 27, 1972 [during President Nixon's trip to China]. The gist of the message was that the President had been assassinated and that World

War III had been declared by the Vice President [Spiro Agnew]."[21]

"A [Minuteman nuclear missile launch] crew I knew played a practical joke by recording a launch message and playing it when their friends came to relieve them. Their friends were . . . overwhelmed on hearing what appeared to be a valid launch message. . . ."

"Four officers in a Minuteman squadron of 50 missiles can without any authorization begin World War III. If four men in two capsules turn their keys, no one could stop the launch."

"A crew [could] open the launch codes and transmit a valid launch message via all the various radios and teletype communications at their disposal. . . ."[22]

On October 5, 1960, the central war room of NORAD (North American Air Defense Command) received a top priority warning from the Thule, Greenland, Ballistic Missile Early Warning System station indicating a massive missile attack had been launched against North America from the direction of the Soviet Union. A radar malfunction was apparently responsible.[23]

On February 20, 1971 an operator at the National Emergency Warning Center at NORAD headquarters accidentally transmitted an emergency message, authorized by the proper code for that date, directing all radio and TV stations to leave the air by order of the President. For 40 minutes the operator was unable to cancel the message, even though he realized his mistake immediately, because he could not find the proper cancel code.[24]

On November 9, 1979 a false warning of a limited missile attack against the United States by a Soviet submarine was sent from the NORAD complex to a chain of defense command centers across the United States. Jet interceptors were scrambled and missile bases put on alert.[25] Roughly six months later, on June 3, 1980, ". . . about 100 B-52 bombers armed with nuclear weapons were prepared to take off after a duty officer at the Strategic Air Command received computer data indicating that a Soviet missile attack was underway." Three days later, on June 6, 1980, the latter false warning incident was repeated.[26]

On September 18, 1980, an explosion rocked a Titan II missile silo in Arkansas. The rocket's fuel exploded "with sufficient force to lift and pulverize the 750-ton door" and leave a 250-foot diameter crater in its place. Twenty-one people were injured and one died.

The huge multi-megaton nuclear warhead atop the missile was, by early reports, hurled several hundred feet from the silo. At this time the extent of damage to the warhead is unclear. The apparent cause of the accident: human error. A technician dropped a wrench socket that fell 70 feet and ruptured the missile's fuel tank.[27]

While nuclear extermination by accident is demonstrably possible, there is a far more likely prospect that a renegade government, criminal organization or terrorist group could buy or seize one or more weapons of mass destruction.

The certain prevention of such an occurrence requires *perfect* systems for both the detection of any unauthorized "quiet" removals from the weapons inventories and for the protection of these stockpiles against purposeful attack. One weapon, successfully seized, could spell disaster. But even theoretically, 100 percent perfect detection and protection systems are impossible, and 99.9 percent effective systems, applied to our huge weapons stockpile, leave some 30 nuclear warheads in the "uncontrolled" area.[28] Beyond this, the whole range of human reliability considerations guarantees that in practice, we are very far from even the inadequate theoretical limits.

Over the past five years Congress has concerned itself with these problems, including increased appropriations to the military for enhanced security. Yet despite these efforts the horror stories continue.

Some of the most spectacular are contained in a set of 1979 Congressional hearings in which Joseph Albright, a national correspondent for the Cox newspapers, testified:

> "Posing as a fencing contractor [no one asked him for proof], I talked my way past the security guards at *two* SAC nuclear weapons depots and was given a tour of the weak links in their defenses against terrorist attack. Without doing anything illegal, I also purchased blueprints [by *mail*] showing the *exact* layout of two weapons compounds and the nearby alert areas where [nuclear bomb laden] B52s are ready to take off in case of war . . . *a method of knocking out the alarm circuits* . . . [and] two *unguarded* gates through the *innermost security* fence [emphasis added].
>
> "As an imposter at that SAC base [December 5, 1977], I came within a stone's throw of four metal tubes that . . . Air Force officials now acknowledge . . . were actual nuclear weapons. . . . At that moment I was riding about 5 MPH in an Air Force pickup truck that was being driven by my only armed escort [with one pistol and both hands on the wheel]. . . . [No one] had searched me or inspected my bulky briefcase, which was on my lap."

And, as a nearly perfect illustration of bureaucratic inertia,

> "After my articles appeared . . . a set of revised blueprints, disclosing . . . the wiring diagram for the solenoid locking system for the B52 alert area, was mailed to me by the Corps of Engineers several days after Brig. Gen. William E. Brown, chief of Air Force security policy, issued a worldwide directive to all Air Force major commands reemphasizing vigilance against intruders. . . ."[29]

We have created a world in which perfection is required if a disaster beyond history is to be permanently avoided. But in the world of human beings perfection is unachievable. The more weapons we deploy, and the greater their geographic dispersion, the more people will be interacting with them. And the greater will be the likelihood of disaster resulting from human error.

Nor can we circumvent this dilemma by turning control over to machines, by somehow automating the human element out of the nuclear forces. For who designs the machines and who will build them? If machines had been in control, a counterattack would almost certainly have been launched when the Ballistic Missile Early Warning System station at Thule, Greenland, sent its false warning of attack in 1960. The judgment of human beings intervened and saved the day on that and countless other occasions.

We cannot escape our fallibility, so we must exercise the wisdom and the instinct for survival that are also fundamental parts of our humanity. We must find a way to coexist permanently with our innate imperfection.

Not until we have sharply reduced the vast arsenals of weapons of mass destruction will we have even a serious chance of keeping human reliability problems from eventually triggering a catastrophe. Reversal of the arms race must be our highest priority international goal.

Is it not possible, for example, that a perfectly safe and conservative initiative, like the public dismantling of 15 percent of our land-based missiles, would bring so much international political pressure to bear on the Soviet Union that it might dismantle some of its own nuclear arsenal? Is it not even possible that the USSR might choose to reciprocate out of its own self-interest, to relieve its overburdened economy or to step farther away from the nuclear precipice?

By a series of such initiatives, waiting for reciprocation at each step, perhaps we could achieve through our actions what we have not been able to achieve with all our words and diplomacy—moving back to a more rational force structure.

If our treaty or action initiatives fail, what will we have lost by trying? Our deterrent would still be unstoppable, so we would certainly not be jeopardizing our national security. Any action initiatives would, in fact, increase our security by reducing the possibilities of accidents, including accidental war, and nuclear terrorism.

QUESTIONS

1. Try, from a sociological viewpoint, to imagine what would happen to American society, or what was left of it, after an all-out nuclear war between the superpowers.

2. Poll the class about whether the members believe a nuclear war is likely in (a) their lifetimes or (b) their children's lifetimes. Analyze the results and discuss

the implications for the way members live and plan their lives.

3. Do you think that the possession of nuclear weapons by the superpowers helps maintain world security, or do you think it undermines that security?

Notes

1. Charles E. Cornell, "Minimizing Human Errors," *Space/Aeronautics* (March 1968), p. 72.

2. Allan E. Fisher, *Preliminary Findings from the 1971 Department of Defense Survey of Drug Use*, Technical Report 72–8, Human Resources Research Organization (March 1972), sponsored by Advanced Research Projects Agency, Department of Defense.

3. William Leavitt, "Meeting the Drug Challenge," *Air Force Magazine* (Jan. 1971), p. 29.

4. American Broadcasting Company-TV, "20/20" (July 10, 1978).

5. Ibid.

6. U.S. armed forces personnel data derived from Secretary of Defense Donald H. Rumsfeld, *Annual Defense Department Report FY 1978*, p. 285.

7. D. R. Cotter, Assistant Secretary of Defense (Atomic Energy), to Lloyd J. Dumas (Sept. 9, 1977).

8. "3 Atom Guards Called Unstable: Major Suspended," *New York Times* (Aug. 18, 1969).

9. "Ten Missile Men Arrested in U.S. for Having LSD," *International Herald Tribune* (Oct. 5, 1969).

10. "Three at Key SAC Post are Arrested on Drug Charges," *International Herald Tribune* (March 29, 1971).

11. Alex P. Dobish, "U.S. Missile Unit Used Drugs Regularly, G.I. Says Eased Boredom of Missile Base," *Milwaukee Journal* (Dec. 16, 1974).

12. Irwin Altman and William Haythorn, "Effects of Social Isolation and Group Composition on Performance," *Human Relations*. Vol. 20, No. 4 (1967), p. 337.

13. W. Haythorn, I. Altman and T. Myers. "Emotional Symptomatology and Subjective Stress in Isolated Pairs of Men," *Journal of Experimental Research on Personality,* 1 (1966), pp. 290–305.

14. D.A. Taylor, L. Wheeler and I. Altman. "Stress Relations in Socially Isolated Groups," *Journal of Personality and Social Psychology*, Vol. 9, No. 4 (1968), p. 375.

15. I. Altman and W. Haythorn, "The Ecology of Isolated Groups," *Behavioral Science*, Vol. 12, No. 3 (May 1967), pp. 169–82.

16. Ted Wye (pseudonym), "Will They Fire in the Hole?," *Family*, supplement of *Air Force Magazine* (Nov. 17, 1971).

17. Morton H. Halperin, *Bureaucratic Politics and Foreign Policy* (Washington, D.C.: The Brookings Institution, 1974), pp. 235–79.

18. James Thompson, "How Could Vietnam Happen?," *The Atlantic* (1968), pp. 47–53; David Halberstam, *The Best and the Brightest* (New York: Random House, 1972).

19. Ted Wye, "Will They Fire?"

20. Chris Argyris, "Single Loop and Double Loop Models in Research in Decision Making," *Administrative Science Quarterly* (Sept, 1976), p. 366.

21. "On the Alert on a Hoax," *Newsday* (March 8, 1972).

22. Ted Wye, "Will They Fire?"

23. *Boston Traveler*, Dec. 12, 1960.

24. "War Alert a Comedy of U.S. Errors," *London Times* (Feb, 22, 1971); "Why America Ignored This Message of Doom," *London Times* (Feb. 28, 1971).

25. A. O. Sulzberger, Jr., "Error Alerts U.S. Forces to a False Missile Attack," *New York Times* (Nov. 11, 1979).

26. Richard Burt, "False Nuclear Alarms Spur Urgent Effort to Find Flaws," *New York Times* (June 13, 1980).

27. Wendell Rawls, Jr., "Explosion Rocks a Silo for Nuclear Missile in Arkansas," *New York Times* (Sept. 20, 1980), p. 1.

28. Lloyd J. Dumas, "National Insecurity in the Nuclear Age." *Bulletin of the Atomic Scientists* (May 1976), pp. 29–32.

29. Subcommittee on Military Construction Appropriations, Committee on Appropriations. U.S. House of Representatives, 95th Congress, Second Session. *Hearings on Military Construction Appropriations for 1979*, pp. 137–337.